Roman Tombs and the Art of Commemoration

The history of funerary customs in Rome contains many unanswered questions and controversial debates, especially concerning the significant developments of the second century CE. In this book, distinguished historian Barbara E. Borg employs the full range of material and written evidence to explore four key questions that change our view of Roman society and its values. For the first time, senatorial burial practices can be reconstructed and contrasted with those of other classes. Borg then explains the change from incineration to inhumation as a revival of old Roman mores that accelerated after the example set by Hadrian. In the third chapter, she argues that tombs became prime locations for promoting and displaying long family lines among the elite, which then inspired freedmen to undertake similar commemorative practices. Finally she explores the association of deceased persons with the divine and apotheosis through portraits on divine body shapes and temple tombs.

BARBARA E. BORG is Professor of Classical Archaeology at the University of Exeter. She has published widely on Greek and Roman art, archaeology and history, and her monographs include *Crisis and Ambition: Tombs and Burial Customs in Third-Century CE Rome* (2013). She is editor of *Paideia: The World of the Second Sophistic* (2004) and *The Blackwell Companion to Roman Art* (2015).

Roman Tombs and the Art of Commemoration

Contextual Approaches to Funerary Customs in the Second Century CE

BARBARA E. BORG

University of Exeter

CAMBRIDGE
UNIVERSITY PRESS

University Printing House, Cambridge CB2 8BS, United Kingdom

One Liberty Plaza, 20th Floor, New York, NY 10006, USA

477 Williamstown Road, Port Melbourne, VIC 3207, Australia

314-321, 3rd Floor, Plot 3, Splendor Forum, Jasola District Centre, New Delhi - 110025, India

103 Penang Road, #05-06/07, Visioncrest Commercial, Singapore 238467

Cambridge University Press is part of the University of Cambridge.

It furthers the University's mission by disseminating knowledge in the pursuit of education, learning and research at the highest international levels of excellence.

www.cambridge.org
Information on this title: www.cambridge.org/9781108460354
DOI: 10.1017/9781108690904

First published 2019
First paperback edition 2022

A catalogue record for this publication is available from the British Library

Library of Congress Cataloging in Publication data
Names: Borg, Barbara, author.
Title: Roman Tombs and the Art of Commemoration : Contextual Approaches to Funerary Customs in the Second Century CE / Barbara E. Borg, University of Exeter.
Description: Cambridge; New York, NY: Cambridge University Press, 2019. | Includes bibliographical references and index.
Identifiers: LCCN 2018048990 | ISBN 9781108472838 (hardback) | ISBN 9781108460354 (pbk.)
Subjects: LCSH: Funeral rites and ceremonies – Rome. | Burial – Rome. | Tombs – Rome. | Sepulchral monuments – Rome. | Rome – History – Antonines, 96–192.
Classification: LCC DG103.B677 2019 | DDC 393/.930937–dc23
LC record available at https://lccn.loc.gov/2018048990

ISBN 978-1-108-47283-8 Hardback
ISBN 978-1-108-46035-4 Paperback

Contents

Figures and Illustrations

Figures

Illustrations

Preface

Tombs are among the best-studied remains of the Roman world. Not only are many of them very well preserved, as they are normally at least partly underground and less often overbuilt in later centuries than the cities to which they belonged, they are also an excellent source for the historian. With forensic sciences becoming more available in the study of human remains, we are gaining amazing insights into ancient diets, living and working conditions, diseases and the origins of the deceased. Nevertheless, the much larger number of tombs for which such data are not available still yield a wealth of information, especially where these tombs were deliberately designed as locations for commemoration. At Rome, this intention is often explicitly stated, for instance by calling a tomb *memoria*. Yet already the term most commonly used to describe a tomb, *monumentum*, essentially means 'that which brings to mind', which, in this context, is obviously the deceased and whatever they or those left behind wanted to communicate about the dead. Some epitaphs explain the idea in more detail. Edmund Thomas quotes a tomb stone that states:

> A rich man builds a house [*aedes*], a wise man a monument [*monumentum*]. The first is the lodging of the body, the second is his home. At the former we linger for a little while, at the latter we live.[1]

The addressees of these *monumenta* varied depending on both the patron's intention and means, but a monument really only makes sense when there is an audience to appreciate it and there was often even a competitive aspect involved in designing and building one. One testator specified in his will that his heirs should be fined if they did not erect for him a monument 'like that of P. Septimius Demetrius which stands on the via Salaria'. Ironically, the case came before the court because the heirs were unable to identify this model for the testator's tomb and wanted to know what to do to avoid the fine.[2] That the case even found its way into Justinian's *Digest*

---

[1] Thomas, *Monumentality*, 183–4, on an epitaph in Castle Howard; Borg et al., *Castle Howard*, 144 no. 91 pl. 77.1 (H. v. Hesberg) Cf. Lattimore, *Themes*, 245–6 with n. 244; Carroll, *Spirits*, 30–2; Ricci, 'Sepulcrum'.
[2] *Digest* 35.1.27 (Alfenus Varus); cf. Hope, *Death*, no. 2.33, for the full text.

suggests that such prescriptions were neither rare nor confined to the first century BCE, when the original case was brought. Location and shape, external and internal decoration, the containers for ashes or bones, sculpture and inscriptions all worked together to communicate those aspects of the deceased's lives that they and their families felt worth commemorating. They were, therefore, carefully chosen and designed. While the majority opted for formulae and designs that were standardised and unoriginal, this should not lead us to think that they were necessarily meaningless. Rather, they demonstrate the degree to which the diverse members of Roman society shared a common *habitus*. Moreover, this tendency to fit in with the rest of society makes the changes in funerary customs all the more significant. For all these reasons, tombs and burial customs are an excellent source that helps us gain a better understanding of ideologies and value systems, social relationships and eschatological beliefs (or the lack of these). It is in such questions that I am interested in the following chapters.

While this book's chronological focus is on the second century, it is not a sequel to my 2013 volume *Crisis and Ambition: Tombs and Burial Customs in Third-Century CE Rome*.[3] The research presented here originates in what was once planned as an introduction to that book, yet I do not intend a comprehensive survey of second-century funerary practices. Especially for this period, excellent surveys have been published,[4] as well as more specialist studies on many key aspects such as mortuary practices and the legal framework,[5] tomb types,[6] cinerary urns and altars,[7] sarcophagi[8] and the tombs' interior decoration.[9] There is no need to repeat these observations and conclusions here. Rather, I focus on aspects or questions that are highly controversial, hardly researched at all, or to which I hope to make a substantial contribution by disagreeing with prevailing views.

The format of this book was ultimately suggested by an invitation to deliver the 2015 Carl Newell Jackson Lectures at the Department of Classics

---

[3] Borg, *Crisis and Ambition*.

[4] Toynbee, *Death and Burial*; Carroll, *Spirits*; Hope *Death*; Hope, *Roman Death*; Hope and Huskinson (eds.), *Memory*.

[5] On mortuary practices: e.g. Heinzelmann (ed.), *Bestattungsbrauch*; Scheid, *Faire*, 161–209; Graham, *Urban Poor*; Graham, 'Corporeal concerns'. On legal and practical aspects: de Visscher, *Droit*; Kaser, 'Grabrecht'; Schrumpf, *Bestattung*.

[6] Hesberg, *Grabbauten*, but also many studies of individual necropoleis.

[7] Boschung, *Grabaltäre*; Sinn, *Marmorurnen*.

[8] The bibliography is vast, but among recent publications with further references see Elsner and Huskinson (eds.), *Life*; Zanker and Ewald, *Myths*; Birk, *Depicting the Dead*; Meinecke, *Sarcophagum posuit*; Borg, 'Leben und Tod'; Newby, *Greek Myths*, 273–319; Borg, 'No one is immortal'.

[9] Feraudi-Gruénais, *Innendekoration*; Feraudi-Gruénais, 'Decoration'.

at Harvard University. I am extremely grateful to Mark Schiefsky, Richard J. Tarrant and Kathleen Coleman, as well as the department as a whole, for the honour of their kind invitation, and for the challenging questions from and inspiring conversations with students and colleagues there. The present four essays are based on the four lectures I delivered, although the original audience will notice that my thoughts have developed since then, not least thanks to their feedback.

Each essay stands on its own, but the chapters are connected in several ways. One is a focus on the city of Rome and its harbour towns, Ostia and Portus. This restriction is not just borne out of necessity, in terms of the impossibility of including a multitude of types of evidence while also covering a wide range of areas around the Mediterranean. Local funerary customs with their artistic and material remains were highly diverse across the empire. Rome was special in that it was home to the emperor and his family, as well as to the central administration and the majority of the senatorial elite. Since commemorative practices could convey powerful statements about social hierarchy and status, they were a factor to reckon with when it came to maintaining or renegotiating the fragile relationship between the emperor and the rest of the Roman elite. And it was also in Rome that certain practices of the imperial family could have the easiest and most direct impact on the habits and material culture of private individuals, not least through the activities of their super-rich and powerful freedmen. Gaining a better understanding of the specifics of metropolitan Roman funerary practices will therefore help us to appreciate more fully both the commonalities and the diversity around the empire, which are sometimes obscured by studies that draw on empire-wide evidence.

A second feature that all the essays have in common is that they aim to make a more general methodological point as well as a more specific, historical claim. As the title of this book suggests, the most fundamental methodological premise is a contextual approach to the evidence. Not least for practical reasons, funerary culture has often been studied with a focus on just one type of evidence, be it tomb types, epitaphs, sarcophagi, interior decoration, consolatory literature and so forth.[10] This has resulted in a rather fragmented and sometimes even contradictory picture. I cannot claim to have integrated every type of evidence that may be relevant to a specific question, nor have I tried to do so. Nevertheless, previous specialist research has allowed me to take account of a wide range of sources that appeared to me to be the most relevant to my enquiry. As I hope will become clear in

---

[10] See nn. 5–9 above.

the following chapters, a contextual approach does not only result in a more comprehensive coverage of commemorative practices. It can open our eyes to data and phenomena that would be virtually invisible in the fragmented world of disciplinary specialisms; it sometimes even changes the picture entirely with regard to key questions; and it helps to reconstruct a more holistic and coherent, but at the same time more differentiated, picture of Roman commemorative practices.

Such differentiation – and this is the third aspect that joins the four essays together – in particular concerns distinctions between different social strata in society. As Franziska Feraudi-Gruénais observed with regard to senatorial tombs, scholarship has frequently resorted to the methodologically problematic resolve of filling the gaps in our evidence by reference to more lavish sub-elite tombs,[11] implicitly suggesting that there were no substantial differences between elite and sub-elite ideologies and practices. Yet is this really the case? I argue in this book that a contextual approach *does* allow us to differentiate between the choices made by members of different social classes, and that attention to class-specific interests and intents also helps better explain certain key phenomena in Roman funerary practices and their origin.

The first essay, 'In search of deceased senators', is devoted to senatorial tombs and burial customs. Given the attention that mortuary practices have received in general, and the fact that this class is normally thought to be better known than any other thanks to the biases of our literary sources, this focus may come as a surprise. And yet, literature does not tell us much about the funerary realm, especially not after the Julio-Claudian period. There is a wealth of evidence for the burial customs of the sub-elite, especially for the milieu of well-off freedmen and their descendants.[12] More recently, evidence has also increased considerably for 'poor' burials in simple shaft graves with no or very few grave goods and no grave marker that would have left any traces.[13] Ironically, what is conspicuously lacking is research on the tombs of the first two orders, and especially of the senatorial class.[14] It is the same few examples, mostly from the late first century

---

[11] Feraudi-Gruénais, 'Ewigkeit', 137, 140–1.
[12] E.g. Calza, *Isola Sacra*; Baldassarre et al., *Necropoli di Porto*; Heinzelmann, *Nekropolen*; Mielsch and Hesberg, *Mausoleen A–D*; Mielsch and Hesberg, *Mausoleen E–I*; Steinby, *Via Triumphalis*; Liverani and Spinola, *Necropoli Vaticana*; Liverani et al., *Necropoli Vaticane*. For interpretations see e.g. Hope, 'Roof'; Petersen, *Freedman*, 184–226; Borbonus, *Columbarium Tombs*. For further bibliography see Chapter 3.
[13] For an overview and analysis, see Griesbach, *Villen und Gräber*, 83–141 (for potential patrons, see 137–8); Graham, *Urban Poor*.
[14] For notable exceptions, see Eck, 'Rome and the outside world', 79–93, and Feraudi-Gruénais, 'Ewigkeit', on senatorial tombs, and Spalthoff, *Repräsentationsformen*, on equestrians.

BCE, that are cited over and over again, such as the enormous tumuli of Caecilia Metella or the Plautii (Figure 3.4), or the pyramid of C. Cestius.[15] However, while some epigraphists have drawn attention to the fact that – rather unsurprisingly – there are inscriptions for senators testifying to the *existence* of post-Julio-Claudian senatorial tombs in suburban Rome, the few more recent attempts at understanding later senatorial burial practices have concluded somewhat frustratingly that we do not, and cannot, know much about them beyond what their epitaphs tell us.[16] Moreover, the lack of senatorial tombs that are anywhere near as well preserved as those of the sub-elite and, perhaps more importantly, as the conspicuous elite tombs of the first century BCE, has left scholars wondering whether the former had ever been very conspicuous in the first place, and whether the elite retreated into the private sphere. Yet how does this suggestion fit with the extensive evidence for elite competition that we find in the literary sources? Other writers have turned to the above-mentioned solution of filling the gaps with examples from wealthy sub-elite tombs. However, what evidence is there to support this approach? Against these views, and based on a new collection of available evidence of various kinds, I argue that the picture of senatorial commemorative practices we gain from that evidence is much richer than it is normally considered to be, that it is remarkably consistent and differs in key aspects from sub-elite preferences. Senatorial tombs were neither modest nor removed from sight, they are merely poorly preserved. Temple tombs erected entirely of marble (thus prone to looting and destruction), which resembled the temples of the gods and imperial *divi*, were the preferred tomb type. In the decoration of tomb interiors and the containers of ashes and bones, the elite opted for monumentality and simplicity rather than busy ornamentation and emotionally charged mythological images, which were largely confined to the sub-elite. The messages conveyed through inscriptions and image decoration predominantly revolved around public offices, virtues and values that are known from, and were inspired by, imperial precedent and that demonstrated the family's superiority in the public and semi-public realms. Rather than being places of retreat, after private individuals were largely banned from promoting themselves through public buildings and honorific monuments in the public space of the city, elite mausolea became prime locations for advertising all the elements that added prestige and status to the family concerned.

---

[15] Ditto Feraudi-Gruénais, 'Ewigkeit', 139.

[16] Ibid., esp. 137, 141, 149. Meinecke, *Sarcophagum posuit*, 105–8 discusses some archaeological evidence for senatorial tombs, but makes no attempt to draw any general conclusions.

The second essay, 'Reviving tradition in Hadrianic Rome: From inciner-ation to inhumation', offers a fresh look at, and a new interpretation of, the change from one way of disposing of the corpse to another in the second century CE. This change has long mystified scholars and has sparked much controversy, not least because our written sources are remarkably uninter-ested in it. Earlier scholarship had suggested as explanations religious change or influence from the Greek East, either through freedmen or else via new senatorial families from the eastern provinces. Often, the Second Sophistic is allocated a major role, the trend that made Greek culture (*pai-deia*) a hallmark of education, and both a marker of status for the elite and an opportunity for social advancement for the sub-elite when they had mastered the required skills and knowledge. Both these explanations have failed to convince. While there is no indication of any change in religious beliefs or practices, neither the bottom-up nor the top-down model of influ-ence from the Greek East coincides chronologically with the phenomenon at issue, and they mistakenly connect the introduction of inhumation with that of mythological sarcophagi. Recent scholarship has either given up on the issue, or sided with Arthur Darby Nock[17] and reduced it to a change of fashion. Yet fashions are meaningful in themselves.[18] Why did it become a 'fashion' to inhume the dead? What was the attraction of doing so? And why did it happen when it did? In order to gain a better understanding of this change, I first look in more detail at evidence for inhumation over the course of the first centuries BCE and CE. I argue that inhumation never went out of use entirely in elite circles, and that it had already become increasingly popular during the later first and early second centuries CE. This confirms that the change was independent of any image decoration (and especially unrelated to mythological images). Moreover, I argue that inhumation was considered to be an old *Roman* practice linked to the kings, especially Numa Pompilius, whose sarcophagus was supposedly found at the foot of the Ianiculan Hill in 181 BCE (Livy 40.29.3–5; Pliny, *NH* 13.84 (27); Valerius Maximus 1.1.12), and some of the most respected Roman *gentes* such as the Cornelii. What we observe in the second century is therefore not radical innovation, but rather a relatively sudden acceler-ation of change from about 140–150 CE onwards. In a second step, I revisit a suggestion that has occasionally been made before, namely that Hadrian had an instrumental role in changing the emperors' form of burial, thus also promoting inhumation in Roman society more widely. Discussing literary

---

[17] Nock, 'Cremation and burial', 357.
[18] Davies, 'Before sarcophagi', 24.

and material evidence for imperial burial and deification ceremonies, I provide a fuller and more up-to-date argument than previous studies for Hadrian's and his successors' choice of inhumation. In contrast to other scholars who formerly allocated Hadrian a key role in the change, I argue that it was not Hadrian's philhellenism that instigated it, but his desire to link himself to Roman tradition. As in so many other areas of activity, he was not quite the radical innovator he is often made out to be, but rather someone who jumped on a bandwagon that had already gained considerable momentum and whose leap markedly accelerated its speed.

Chapter 3, 'Family matters: The long life of Roman tombs', takes issue with generally accepted views of the role of the family in commemorative practice. Following eminent scholars such as Fernand De Visscher, Max Kaser or Richard Saller and Brent Shaw,[19] it is widely believed that across all social classes the family unit that was relevant in funerary contexts was the nuclear family; that each new generation preferably established its own new tomb; and even that this focus on the nuclear family reflects a decline in the relevance of the family clan in Roman society more generally, and a growing individualism within the lower classes. Yet how does this fit with our literary sources, which attest to the elite's continued use of ancestry and family lineages in their competition for honour and status? How does it relate to the astonishing phenomenon of polynomic naming practices? And, in the case of the sub-elite, what should have been the advantage of this individualism? I argue that the widespread views are a misconception based on two fundamental flaws in the methodology applied. As a detailed study of the epigraphic evidence from individual tombs and funerary precincts reveals, tomb *tituli* are not a comprehensive record of a tomb's intended use, but first and foremost a kind of foundation deed. Statistical, non-contextual approaches to the relationship between commemorator and commemorated in epitaphs equally fail to account for both the intended and the de facto use of a tomb. While they identify relationships of close emotional or obligational links between family members, they represent only a snapshot of a moment in time, a single event in the long history of a tomb. Based on general observations and on the close examination of a range of case studies, I argue that tombs were most frequently founded as multigenerational mausolea that gained in significance with every new generation using them. In elite families, the idea of the gentilicial family clan lived on into late antiquity and, after the *atria* with their *imagines maiorum*

---

[19] De Visscher, *Droit*; Kaser, 'Grabrecht'; Saller and Shaw, 'Tombstones'.

may have gone out of use, mausolea constituted the main location at which the longevity and dignity of a family were celebrated and commemorated.

This general idea was shared by many freedmen, even though they had to adapt it to their means and circumstances. More often than in the first order, in the mausolea of freedmen we find affection and *pietas* towards kin taking precedence over concerns for the family name. Yet even here, more was frequently at stake. A legal, and legally protected, family was not just a one-time achievement obtained with manumission, as is usually stressed. The aim was to create a family line, for which the persistence of the name was essential. Especially in the second century, freedmen emulated, as much as and as best they could, ideas embodied by the gentilicial tombs of the elite. Lacking legal ancestry and often also (surviving) off-spring, they secured the survival of their name through freedmen heirs to whom, in turn, the tomb's founder and other previous generations became 'ancestry'. While the vast majority of these freedpeople seem to have failed to establish a lasting agnatic family, they made the most of the concept of *familia*, which did not distinguish between kin and non-kin, and was still a powerful institution of which to be proud. This concept was sometimes remarkably successful, with tombs and burial plots remaining in the family name for up to a hundred years or more.

The final and longest essay, 'Straddling borderlines: Divine associations in funerary commemoration', reviews this somewhat notorious phenomenon, in particular the meaning of portraits that assimilate their subjects to gods and goddesses, and of the temple tombs mentioned above. The impulse to revisit this question comes from recent research that aims, after decades of rationalist and ritualist approaches, to bring back the gods, 'belief' and even faith to Roman (and Greek) religion, and has changed views on the Hellenistic ruler cult, *consecratio*, the cult of the *divi* and questions of ancient belief in divinities more generally. These debates have been largely confined to the literature-based realm of historians (of religion and of Roman culture) and classicists.[20] In contrast, the interpretation of Roman funerary art and architecture, especially of the early and high empire, has so far taken little notice of this research. It has continued either in the rationalistic vein (although emotions have become a focus of interest in recent years)[21] or else along the lines of Franz Cumont's highly speculative eschatological interpretations of funerary symbolisms, which have recently seen some explicit attempts at rehabilitation. In his review of Janine and Jean-Charles Balty's

---

[20] See for instance Versnel, *Coping with the Gods*; Erskine, 'Ruler cult'; Morgan, *Faith*.

[21] E.g. Zanker, 'Gefühlskult'; Ewald, 'Rollenbilder'; Ewald, 'Paradigms'; Borg, 'Leben und Tod'.

reprint of, and extended commentary on, Cumont's seminal *Recherches sur le symbolisme funéraire des Romains*, Jaś Elsner concluded that 'any attempt to reinvigorate Cumont's own interpretations' is bound to fail due to the fundamental methodological flaws on which they are based, 'but there is no doubt … that too much of the baby that Cumont so deeply cherished has been thrown out with the bathwater of his (in my view understandable and politically laudable) methodological excess'.[22] I agree with both claims, and Elsner is also right in observing that the 'substantial point of how to write the history of religious art', and especially how texts can be used (rather than mis- or overused) for the interpretation of art, needs to be addressed by more explicit methodological reflection. My chapter cannot claim to deliver on that request, as a fuller discussion of methodological issues from a theoretical point of view would have greatly exceeded its scope, and I do not propose either that the implicit methodology applied solves the general problem. What I hope to have achieved, though, is a reintegration of some specific and conspicuous artistic peculiarities with their ancient discourses as they can be reconstructed primarily through written sources, which include discourses around divinity, apotheosis and the afterlife in particular.

I argue that there is evidence for a range of different readings of both rhetorical and visual divine associations including, significantly, belief in the genuine divinity of humans, which was possible since divinity was ultimately in the eye of the beholder and – except in philosophical thought – not an ontological category. Portraits in divine costume could express such divinity, and it was precisely their potential to sit on the borderline between a range of readings that ensured their attraction and suitability for a number of different contexts and audiences. I argue further that temple tombs were inspired by and modelled on temples for the imperial *divi* and *divae*, and on the Templum Gentis Flaviae in particular, the only imperial tomb that was simultaneously a temple. The first to adopt this type of monument were powerful, exceedingly rich freedmen with particularly close connections to the imperial court, and the most decorated of senators. I review evidence for notions (rather than concepts) of potential life after death and posthumous apotheosis, concluding that – again outside of philosophical debates – they are extremely rare and mostly restricted to the idea of an immortal soul, although claims to divinity are sometimes made. They are

---

[22] http://bmcr.brynmawr.edu/2016/2016-06-38.html (last accessed 22/02/2017). Elsner is particularly good at recontextualising Cumont's approach in the desperate years of the Second World War.

also, however, an indication of status, since the world beyond was envisaged as a mirror image of social relationships and hierarchies on earth. To this extent, images of apotheosis such as the deceased on an eagle, or tombs in the shape of proper podium temples, express claims to status that are meant to persist and be recognised in eternity.

I would like to add a health warning here. This book is intended for an audience from a range of different backgrounds, who will approach it with an equal variety of expectations. Some, especially those who are not classical archaeologists and the few who already know the evidence very well, may find parts of the book rather descriptive. However, as my argument is mainly developed from a re-evaluation of primary sources that are rarely discussed in context, partly poorly known and often published in such a way that some readers will find them hard to access, it was important to present the supporting evidence in a degree of detail. For instance, in order to demonstrate, against prevailing views, that we *can* tell which mausolea, sarcophagi and so on the senatorial elite preferred, I need to present the data on which we can draw. The same goes for my claim that tombs were used over multiple generations. I hope that the intermittent and final sections of conclusions will help those who want the broader picture and results, rather than the detailed argument, to find what they are interested in without the need to wade through too much specialist detail.

Acknowledgements

The research presented here has been conducted over almost ten years, mostly alongside other projects that were more or less closely connected with the present evidence and questions. Over these years, I have been very generously supported with funding and research leave by a number of institutions, including the Leverhulme Foundation, the British School at Rome, the J. Paul Getty Foundation, the Onassis Foundation and the University of Exeter. A fellowship from the Loeb Classical Library Foundation made it possible to present the book in the present form, especially with its multiple illustrations. The British School at Rome, its former director Christopher Smith and all its staff have hugely facilitated my research by providing me with a home in Rome, access to their fantastic library and the arrangement of permits to visit otherwise inaccessible archaeological sites. I am further grateful to the Archaeological Institute of the University of Heidelberg (Diamantis Panagiotopoulos and Reinhard Stupperich), the Winckelmann Institute at Berlin's Humboldt University (Susanne Muth) and the German Archaeological Institutes at Rome and Berlin for their hospitality and permission to access their library resources, without which I could not have conducted my work. I have been able to present earlier versions of the present chapters at numerous institutions that cannot be listed here in full. These occasions were instrumental in helping me focus, shape, adjust and occasionally revise my ideas, and I am thankful for my colleagues' invitations and the audiences' helpful comments and questions. I am particularly grateful to Kathleen Coleman and the Classics department at Harvard for their invitation to give the 2015 Carl Newell Jackson Lectures, and for a great week at this distinguished institution. This experience inspired me to write this book. I struggled most with the final essay on divine associations, and therefore feel particularly indebted also to Ineke Sluiter and Markus Asper for their invitation to present some of this material as a lecture in the 2016 'Forum Antiquum' series at Leiden University's Classics department, and as the 2017 August Boeckh Lecture and Seminar of the August-Boeckh-Antikezentrum at Berlin's Humboldt University. I benefited hugely from the audiences' comments and questions. Of the many individuals to whom I owe thanks I would like to mention specifically Jane Fejfer (who, with her husband Palle Soerensen, has also accommodated me in Rome over many years), John Bodel, Janet DeLaine, Marco Maiuro, Consuelo Manetta, Eric Moorman, Coen van Galen (who drew my attention to his PhD work on the importance of cognate family relationships), Marianne Bergmann, Rolf Michael Schneider and an anonymous reader for Cambridge University Press, as well as my departmental colleagues at Exeter. I am also most indebted to those colleagues and other individuals who have granted me permission without charge to use their drawings and photographs to illustrate this volume, most notably Gregor Borg, Rita Amedick, Filippo Coarelli, Alessio de Cristofaro, Hans R. Goette, Roberto Libera, Roberta Loreti and Lucia D. Simeone, Daniela Rossi, Paolo Viti, Rita Volpe, and those named and unnamed individuals and institutions who generously made available under the Creative Commons License excellent photographs of their own. The book could also not have been presented in the way it is without the careful editing of my English expression by Sally Osborn, Marcelina Gilka's meticulous editing of my Endnote library and Brigitte Parsche's skilful work on several illustrations in this volume. Last but not least, I would like to gratefully acknowledge the support and contribution by the editorial and production teams working for Cambridge University Press, and especially from Michael Sharpe.

Abbreviations

Abbreviations of titles of ancient authors follow the Oxford Classical Dictionary. In addition, the following abbreviations have been used:

AE	*L'année épigraphique*
ANRW	H. Temporini (ed.), *Aufstieg und Niedergang der römischen Welt* (Berlin: de Gruyter, 1972–)
ArchLaz	*Archeologia Laziale (Quaderni dell'Istituto di Studi Etruschi e Italici)*
ASR	C. Robert et al., *Die antiken Sarkophagreliefs* (Berlin: Gebr. Mann Verlag, 1890–)
BdI	*Bullettino dell'Istituto di corrispondenza archeologica*
BCom	*Bullettino della Commissione archeologica Comunale di Roma*
CIG	*Corpus inscriptionum graecarum* (Berlin: Reimer; de Gruyter, 1828–)
CIL	*Corpus inscriptionum latinarum* (1863–)
CLE	F. Bücheler and E. Lommatzsch (eds.), *Carmina Latina Epigraphica* (Leipzig: Teubner 1895–1926)
EpGr	G. Kaibel (ed.), *Epigrammata graeca: ex lapidibus conlecta* (Berlin: Reimer, 1878)
GG	W. Peek (ed.), *Griechische Grabgedichte: griechisch und deutsch* (Schriften und Quellen der alten Welt 7) (Berlin: Akademie-Verl., 1960)
GVI	W. Peek, *Griechische Vers-Inschriften Vol. I: Grab-Epigramme* (Berlin: Akademie-Verl., 1955)
IG	*Inscriptiones graecae* (1873–)
IGUR	*Inscriptiones Graecae Urbis Romae* (Rome, 1968–)
ILS	H. Dessau (ed.), *Inscriptiones Latinae Selectae* (Berlin: Weidmann, 1892–1916)
LTUR	E. M. Steinby (ed.), *Lexicon topographicum urbis romae* (Rome: Quasar, 1993–2006)
LTURS	A. La Regina (ed.), *Lexicon topographicum urbis romae: Suburbium* (Rome: Quasar, 2001–08)
MNR	A. Giuliano (ed.), *Museo Nazionale Romano* (Rome: De Luca, 1979–95)

Monumenti inediti	*Monumenti inediti pubblicati dell'Instituto di Corrispondenza Archeologica*
NSc	*Notizie degli scavi di antichità*
PIR	*Prosopographia Imperii Romani Saeculi I, II, III*, 1st edn E. Klebs and H. Dessau (1897–98); 2nd edn E. Groag, A. Stein, et al. (1933–)
RAC	E. Dassmann, *Reallexikon für Antike und Christentum* (Stuttgart: Hiersemann, 1941–)
RM	*Mitteilungen des Deutschen Archäologischen Instituts, Römische Abteilung*
SEG	*Supplementum Epigraphicum Graecum* (Leiden: Brill, 1923–)
ThesCRA	*Thesaurus Cultus et Rituum Antiquorum, I–V + index vol.* (Los Angeles: J. Paul Getty Museum 2004–14)
ZPE	*Zeitschrift für Papyrologie und Epigraphik*

1 | In Search of Deceased Senators

The extent to which senators' ambition and competition were manifest in their tomb monuments during the final decades of the Republic is all too obvious, and is well researched. The social and financial elite competed for the largest, most extravagant buildings and the best locations to attract maximum attention.[1] Cicero's search for the best location for his deceased daughter's tomb is a good case in point: in thirty of his letters to his friend Atticus, who also acted as his agent, he considers various places that he assesses for their general beauty, their suitability for including a garden but also their visibility:[2]

> sed nescio quo pacto celeberritatem requiro; itaque hortos mihi conficias necesse est. maxima est in Scapulae celebritas, propinquitas praeterrea urbis, ne totum diem in villam.

> But somehow I want it to be in the public way; so you *must* get me a place in the suburbs. Scapula's is very much in the public way and furthermore has the advantage of being close to town so that one would not have to spend a whole day in a country house. (*ad Att.* 12.37; transl. D.R. Shackleton Bailey)

Of the numerous tomb types available, the tumuli, round monuments topped with an earthen mound, are arguably the most conspicuous, and it therefore comes as no surprise that it was not only Augustus and Hadrian (see later Figure 2.10) who chose this shape for their family mausolea.[3] Among the senatorial tumuli and cylindrical tombs, the huge mausolea of Caecilia Metella on the via Appia and of the Plautii near Tivoli (see

---

[1] On tomb types see: Eisner, *Typologie*; Hesberg, *Grabbauten*, 19–37, 55–181, 202–30. On tumuli: Schwarz, *Tumulat Italia tellus*. On *arae*: Kleiner, *Altars*. On the 'streets of tombs': Hesberg and Zanker (eds.), *Gräberstraßen*; Koortbojian, 'Streets of tombs'; Griesbach, *Villen und Gräber*, 20–8, 143. On their role in elite competition see also Hesberg and Zanker, 'Einleitung', 9–12; Purcell, 'Tomb and suburb', esp. 32–3; Heinzelmann, 'Einleitung', 12–13.

[2] Hesberg, *Grabbauten*, 6; Schrumpf, *Bestattung*, 209–10, with references in n. 526; Griesbach, *Villen und Gräber*, 28–30.

[3] On the Mausoleum of Augustus, see Hesberg and Panciera (eds.), *Mausoleum*; *LTUR* III (1996), 234–9 s.v. Mausoleum Augusti (H. v. Hesberg, M. Macciocca). On Hadrian's mausoleum, see most recently Abbondanza et al. (eds.), *Apoteosi* and Chapter 2 below.

Figure 3.4 in Chapter 3) are the best known and largest examples.[4] Other shapes included pyramids – that of C. Cestius is best preserved[5] – but also cubic and tower-like monuments and a few unique shapes.[6]

Most of the extravagant first-century BCE tomb types became rare after Augustus, typically featured smaller dimensions and disappeared altogether from about the middle of the first century CE,[7] and initially they seem not to have been replaced by other types of mausolea that were similarly ambitious. It has been suggested that this was a reaction to political and social developments. In the late Republic, during the civil wars, self-representation in the funerary realm was part of the general fierce competition for acknowledgement and offices. After the establishment of the empire, offices, privileges and status no longer depended on the Roman people but largely on the emperor, so that advertising oneself to the public no longer made sense. The funerary sphere, so it is suggested, increasingly became a private affair where family, affection and personal relationships were more important than self-representation targeted at strangers. The decline of monumental senatorial tombs has often been explained by the

---

[4] On Caecilia Metella: Schwarz, *Tumulat Italia tellus*, 183–5 cat. M 51; *LTURS* II (2004), 9–14 s.v. Caeciliae Metellae sepulcrum (R. Paris). On the Plautii: Schwarz, *Tumulat Italia tellus*, 217–21 cat. M 95; Impeciati, *Mausoleo dei Plauzi*. Of the seven known owners of non-imperial tumulus tombs from the environs of Rome, three belonged to the senatorial class and two to equestrians, among them the *praefectus fabrum* L. Cornelius, personal architect of the consul Q. Catulus by whom he was promoted to this office. Two owners were rich *liberti*. See Schwarz, *Tumulat Italia tellus*, 90–5 with table 12. The *liberti* tumuli (ibid., 251–2 cat. F30 and F31) are only preserved through their inscriptions. If it is strictly true that only *humiliores* mention the size of their burial plots or tombs in their inscriptions (Eck, 'Grabinschriften', 63 n. 12), the small tumulus on the via Collatia (5.9 x 5.9 m) must be added to this list. See Collini, 'Via Collatina'; Schwarz, *Tumulat Italia tellus*, 204–5 cat. M 78. This view would be confirmed if a small altar with a dedication to a M. Pomponius Valens belonged to the tomb, which also differs from the majority of tumuli in having a large, round inner chamber with cinerary niches.
[5] Eisner, *Typologie*, 138–41 cat. O1; *LTUR* IV (1999), 278–9 s.v. Sepulcrum: C. Cestius (C. Krause).
[6] Of the 111 more conspicuous tombs from the first century BCE to the Hadrianic period collected by Eisner, at least eight and possibly eleven belonged to the senatorial and equestrian classes (Eisner, *Typologie*). In three cases, it is not entirely clear whether or not the respective inscriptions belong to the tomb: ibid., cat. Lt/Lb2; Lb3. Apart from the two possible cases in n. 4, only one monument can be attributed to an *ingenuus*, the well-known tomb of M. Vergilius Eurysaces. Its owner was a wealthy baker and official supplier of bread to the state. Whether he was a *libertus* because of his *cognomen*, as has been suggested, or was just alluding to his erudition with a mythologising name remains an open question. See ibid., cat. Lb1; *LTUR* IV (1999) 301–2 s.v. Sepulcrum: M. Vergilius Eurysaces (P. Ciancio Rossetto); Petersen, *Freedman*, 84–120.
[7] Eisner's *Typologie* is still the most comprehensive survey. On tumuli, see Schwarz, *Tumulat Italia tellus*, esp. 94–5; Stanco, *Acilii Glabriones*, with table 5.

assumption that the *ordo* now deliberately opted for less ostentatious burials situated in their private villas.[8]

More recently this view has been qualified to some extent, and it is now generally acknowledged that certain sectors of society continued to use their tombs for self-display at prominent locations.[9] It also did not escape notice that the epitaphs themselves, boasting as they do of offices held and honours received, demonstrate the elite's eagerness to commemorate their achievements, and also require some visibility to make any sense at all.[10] The so-called *vita romana* sarcophagi that depict their patrons in public and military roles have equally been recognised as images of the pride these patrons took in their offices. Yet they have typically been studied in isolation, with no attempt at reconciling them with the claim of the elite's retreat. So far, no study exists that would unite the different types of evidence we have for senatorial funerary monuments, exploring in a more comprehensive way the messages they were meant to convey and the audiences they addressed.[11] This is the purpose of the present chapter, which aims to demonstrate that, through a contextual approach, senatorial tomb types and image decorations, and the ideology on which they are based, emerge very clearly and in a remarkably rich and consistent picture.

---

[8] The idea was first proposed by Hesberg and Zanker ('Einleitung', 12–16), albeit not just for the first order but as a general trend. Cf. Hesberg, 'Planung', esp. 60; Hesberg, *Grabbauten*, 37–45; Hesberg, 'Profumo', esp. 47. It has found almost general approval despite minor qualifications: e.g. Heinzelmann, 'Grabarchitektur', esp. 189, although he excludes the first order (p. 185 n. 24). Feraudi-Gruénais (*Innendekoration*, passim, esp. 209–16) rejects, however, the concept of 'internalisation' promoted by von Hesberg and Zanker (e.g. Zanker, *Macht*: 273–9; Hesberg, *Grabbauten*, 42–5, and implicitly 214–21, 229–30; Zanker and Ewald, *Myths*, 21, 27, 175–82, 189 and elsewhere); Petersen, *Freedman*, 196–7, 215 and elsewhere (with minor qualifications). De Cristofaro ('Monumento funerario', 280) regards the tomb of M. Nonius Macrinus, to be discussed below, as a rare exception.

[9] E.g. Griesbach (*Villen und Gräber*, 146–9), although he eventually agrees with the idea of retreat into the private sphere For his version of this trend cf. also n. 73 below; Heinzelmann, 'Grabarchitektur', 185 n. 24; Borg, 'What's in a tomb?'

[10] Esp. Eck ('Senator', 3), who explicitly acknowledges the first *ordo*'s continued competitiveness.

[11] Mayer (*Middle Classes*, 137–42) considers a range of different types of features and comes to similar general conclusions as I do here. However, his results are largely based on evidence that has never been disputed (such as the tomb of the Scipios, Herodes Atticus' commemorative practices or the *vita romana* sarcophagi) and ranges too widely in time and space to answer our more specific questions around senatorial tombs after the Augustan period. I have discussed some of the following arguments in Borg, 'What's in a tomb?' and 'Roman cemeteries'.

Senatorial Tombs After the Late Republic: Augustus and a New Decorum

As already stated, there can be no doubt that the most conspicuous tomb types that senators used during the first century BCE experienced a steep decline after the Augustan era, and were largely abandoned after about the middle of the first century CE. Not only did the more eccentric shapes such as the pyramids disappear, but also the large, often tower-like tumuli. The few post-Augustan, first-century senatorial tombs we can identify are small in comparison, even though their outer appearance was not necessarily unassuming. Henner von Hesberg in particular has drawn attention to the remains of some highly luxurious mausolea that now employed the precious material of marble for sometimes very elaborate monuments.[12] Among such mausolea, only three can be attributed to the senatorial class, all relatively austere in design compared with Hesberg's other examples. The late Augustan or early Tiberian so-called 'tomb of the Platorini' (Figure 1.1 below), erected by M. Artorius Geminus, the son of Augustus' physician and himself *praefectus aerarii militaris* in 10–14 CE, still measured 7.44 x 7.12 m and probably had the shape of a monumental altar. It was entirely covered in marble and travertine.[13] The slightly later tomb of L. Considius Gallus, located close to the via Tiburtina and inside the Aurelianic Wall, was considerably smaller (5.3 x 4.1 m), but featured a marble front with an impressive 4.8 m-long *titulus* and travertine on its other sides.[14] The original tomb of the Licinii from the Tiberian period measured just 1.5 x 3.6 m, but featured at least five statues and at least some of the above altars at its front (see Figures 3.5–3.7 in Chapter 3).[15]

---

[12] Hesberg, 'Profumo'. Yet Hesberg himself downplays the impact the outer appearance of these monuments would have made on their viewers, insisting that their more miniaturist shapes and lavishly decorated interiors would attest to a changed attitude, which focuses on seclusion and the family rather than the public. As will also become clear, I am not convinced by this conclusion, but rather see these precious interiors as an additional feature.

[13] Ibid., 36. Hesberg rightly notes that the tomb did not look entirely like an altar but also comprised elements of a temple. Cf. Silvestrini, *Sepulcrum*; *LTUR* IV (1999) 275–6 s.v. Sepulcrum: M. Artorius Geminus (F. Silvestrini); Alföldy in *CIL* 6.41057 and p. 4783 on *CIL* 6.31761, on the inscriptions and patronage.

[14] *CIL* 6.31705 with pp. 4776–7 (G. Alföldy); Feraudi-Gruénais, 'Ewigkeit', 142 with no. 25; *LTUR* IV (1999) 280 fig. 128 s.v. Sepulcrum: L. Considius L. f. Gallus (C. Lega), with bibliography. Gallus' identity, and thus the date of the tomb, are not entirely clear, but he is most likely the *praetor* of 31 CE mentioned by Tacitus (*Ann.* 5.8; *PIR* C 1280).

[15] See below pp. 33, 41, 58–66, and Chapter 3. *CIL* 6.41086 is a remarkable fragment with *litterae aureae*, which was found in foundations of Ponte Umberto on the right bank of the Tiber. If Alföldy's date in the first century CE, based on the letter shape, is accepted (ad loc.; cf. Feraudi-Gruénais, *Ewigkeit*, no. 45), this tomb must be added to the list. Eisner also dates two small

Figure 1.1 Tomb of the Platorini (of Artorius Geminus), originally on the right bank of the Tiber near the pons Agrippae, turn of first century BCE/CE. Rome, Museo Nazionale delle Terme

anonymous tumuli to the late Tiberian/early Claudian and the Claudian period, respectively, and a slightly larger one to the late Claudian/early Neronian period: Eisner, *Typologie*, 206–7, on P/T1 (5.9 x 5.9 m; cf. above n. 4), F4 (5.35 x 5.35 m) and T6 (9.3 x 9.3 m). Similar dates are proposed in Schwarz, *Tumulat Italia tellus*, cat. M 78, F 33. New excavations on the via Flaminia have brought to light a further anonymous tumulus tomb with a rectangular base measuring 9.2 x 9.2 m, which can be dated to the Claudian or Neronian period: Chiocci and Zaccagnini, 'Mausoleo B', with p. 183 on the date; Gasseau, 'Mausoleo B'.

The contrast in size to the first-century BCE monuments is striking, but whether this change was due to a lack of interest in competition and self-representation in favour of inward-looking concern for private matters is less clear. In that case, would we not expect a longer process of gradual decline? Instead, as Werner Eck has observed, the speed of this decline is strongly reminiscent of the equally abrupt cessation of public portrait monuments.[16] During the Republic, huge numbers of statues were erected to honour and promote both major and minor dignitaries. About the same time as the tombs in question disappeared, honorific statues ceased to be erected in public spaces, except for a few endorsed by the emperor in special cases for their *pietas immobilis erga principem*, and often only after the honourand's death. The emperor had claimed these public spaces for himself.[17] The same applies to most types of public buildings, which used to double up as even more noticeable monuments to their patrons.[18]

Restrictions concerning the amount of display in funerary contexts are well known from various periods, including the Augustan.[19] Burial in prominent places in the Campus Martius needed permission from the emperor,[20] and the same may have been true for other conspicuous locations, and possibly for tomb types as well. Cicero, in 45 BCE, mentions a surcharge for tombs that exceeded certain limits of size, and a *columnarium*, a special tax on columns, which apparently only applied in particular prominent locations.[21] The last public *pompa funebris* of a private individual is attested

---

[16] Eck, 'Self-representation' and elsewhere in his later publications.

[17] Lahusen, 'Ehrenstatuen' and *Untersuchungen*, 97–107; Eck, 'Self-representation', 143–8; Alföldy, 'Pietas immobilis'; Eck, 'Emperor', 94–9.

[18] Eck, 'Self-representation', 138–42, 'Emperor', 92–3 and 'Senatorische Häuser', 208–9. However, in a recent paper Robert Coates-Stevens has drawn attention to the fact that private individuals still could and did attach their names to buildings, either, to a limited extent, when they held offices connected with public building or, more importantly, when erecting baths and commercial buildings.

[19] An inscription on the Pyramid of Cestius records that the *aediles* prohibited the deposition of expensive carpets in the tomb with reference to a sumptuary law: *CIL* 6.1375 (= Dessau 917a); cf. Cicero, *Leg.* 2.23.58–2.27.69. At 2.25.62, Cicero complains that in his time there were no restrictions on the lavishness of tomb buildings; he was wrong, though, as he soon found out when he intended to build the *fanum* for his daughter (*Att.* 12.35). See also Hesberg, *Grabbauten*, 10–13; Verzár-Bass, 'Mausolei', 403. On sumptuary laws, see Engels, *Grabluxusgesetze*, 155–87, with bibl., and the contributions to *Mélanges de l'École française de Rome – Antiquité* 128.1, 2016 (eds. J. Andreau and M. Coudry), none of which, nevertheless, focuses on funerary activities.

[20] Wesch-Klein, *Funus publicum*, 108–9.

[21] Cicero, *Att.* 12.35, 12.36; 13.6.1. The territory of his villa seems to exempt him from fines while leaving him anxious about a change of ownership. Cf. Engels, *Grabluxusgesetze*, 172; Hesberg, *Grabbauten*, 10–13; Verzár-Bass, 'Mausolei', 403.

for 22 CE.[22] While it is unlikely that Augustus formally introduced a specific sumptuary law on them,[23] tombs were another major means of bestowing honour upon a deceased and his or her family, and one had to strike the right balance in order to avoid appearing to rival the emperor in this respect. According to Tacitus, the 'tomb erected for Otho was modest, and therefore likely to endure', and prior to his death the short-lived emperor had warned his nephew: 'never forget or too constantly remember that Otho was your uncle'.[24] It is therefore probably safe to assume that the social and financial elite steered away from the most ostentatious traditional tomb types and locations, not entirely under their own impetus.[25]

This view is supported by the exceptions to the rule, among which the most powerful imperial freedmen feature prominently. In one of his letters, Pliny complains about the pretence of M. Antonius Pallas, one of Claudius' particularly powerful freedmen, who boasted in his tomb inscription about *ornamenta praetoria* and other honours granted him by the senate *ob fidem pietatemque erga patronus* ('for the loyalty and piety towards his patron', i.e. the emperor) in a language that is strongly reminiscent of honorific inscriptions for the most deserving members of the aristocracy.[26] His tomb at the beginning of the via Tiburtina was close enough to the road for Pliny to be able to read the text. Only one inscribed block survives from the tomb of Nero's notorious freedman Epaphroditus, which was situated in his *horti* north of the via Praenestina on the later course of the Aurelianic Wall, but it is impressive enough. The full length of this inscription, which detailed Epaphroditus' various extraordinary achievements, was 5 m and the largest letter size – used for his name – was 23 cm, matching that of imperial

---

22 Tacitus, *Ann.* 3.76.1–2. Cf. Wesch-Klein, *Funus publicum*, 19–38; Bodel, 'Death on display', 271.

23 For the informal nature of restrictions imposed on senatorial self-display, see esp. Eck, 'Emperor'.

24 Tacitus, *Hist.* 2.49.4 (*Othoni sepulchrum extructum est modicum et mansurum*) and 2.48.2 (*neu patruum sibi Othonem fuisse aut obliviceretur umquam aut nimium meminisset*). Both passages also cited by Kragelund, 'Emperors', 202–3 with nn. 65 and 68.

25 Similarly, Eck ('Self-representation', 148 with nn. 158–9 and 'Emperor', 105–10), Engels (*Grabluxusgesetze*, 173) and Verzár-Bass ('Mausolei', 412–15) even suggested for the highly competitive first century BCE that some chose locations on their *praedia* in the wider environs of Rome when they wanted to build particularly pretentious tombs and avoid sanctions (ditto Griesbach, *Villen und Gräber*, 28–30). On the need for emperors to exceed the rest of the Roman elite in honour, and their attempts to monopolise appreciation by the common people, cf. Lendon, *Empire of Honour*, 107–75. Weisweiler ('Honorific statues', 321–4) explains why a ban on public monuments in Rome became the almost inevitable consequence of the emperor's self-fashioning as first among *equals* and the need to be *princeps*.

26 Eck, 'Grabinschriften', 76–7 on Pliny, *Ep.* 7.29, 8.6.

inscriptions on public monuments.[27] The tomb that Domitian's freedman Abascantus dedicated to his wife Priscilla at the second mile of the via Appia must equally have been an outstanding monument in a particularly prominent location, and is again explained by its owner's special relationship with the emperor.[28] Of the monuments discussed by von Hesberg,[29] at least two were also erected by non-elite persons with excellent connections to the imperial court. A marble aedicula tomb with the statues of its patron and his wife at the fourth milestone of the Appia commemorated M. Servilius Quartus. Servilius was probably the freedman who is also known from his ambitious dedication of the interior decoration of a room in Diana's sanctuary at Nemi amid the earlier senatorial dedications.[30] T. Claudius Secundus Philippianus, another of Nero's freedmen and his *coactor argentarius* (money receiver), whose son had already been made an *eques* before he reached the age of ten, erected his monument a little further down the road.[31] The details of this rectangular structure are not entirely clear, but it was *c.* 6.5 m wide and at least its front was built of marble.[32]

The image that emerges is therefore very similar to that for the use of portrait monuments and public buildings. Only under certain conditions could individuals be honoured in public spaces, in or near Rome, by ostentatious monuments of a traditional kind, with special permission from the senate and approval by the emperor.

Is it still correct to say, then, that the elite retreated into the private sphere and had modest tombs, even if not entirely deliberately? This may indeed be

---

[27] The block was found reused in the so-called 'Temple of Minerva Medica': *NSc* (1913), 466–7 (G. Mancini). Cf. Eck, *Grabinschriften*, 77–8 pl. 8b and 'Grabmonumente', 171–3 fig. 4.

[28] For references and detail, see Chapter 4, pp. 251–3.

[29] See above p. 4 with n. 12.

[30] For an Augustan date of the Nemi dedication, see Green, *Roman Religion*, 34. Vincenzi ('Il mosaico') notes that the interior decoration and mosaic could be dated to any time between the late first century BCE and the end of the Julio-Claudian era, and is not contemporary with the room itself, which dates most likely to the mid-first century BCE. On the tomb, see Hesberg ('Profumo', 41 figs. 7–8), who dates it to the Tiberian age on account of its decorative details. His reconstruction has been corrected following new excavations by Fancelli and Tomaro ('Antonio Canova'). Cf. Spera and Mineo, *Bovillae*, 123–4 figs. 110–11; *LTURS* 5 (2008), 67–8 s.v. M. Servilii Quarti sepulcrum (A. Bianchi); *CIL* 6.26426. That Servilius stresses in his epitaph that he paid for the tomb from his own funds rules out his being a member of the elite.

[31] Hesberg, 'Profumo', 37 fig. 3. *LTURS* 2 (2004), 111–13 s.v. Ti. Claudii Aug. lib. Secundi Philippiani sepulcrum (A. Bianchi), also for further links of this patron to prominent individuals and potential family members.

[32] Hesberg (*Profumo*, 37) suggests that it featured statues of the deceased on inscribed bases, but Bianchi (*LTURS* 2 (2004), 111–13 s.v. Ti. Claudii Aug. lib. Secundi Philippiani sepulcrum) identifies the 'bases' as altars and notes that, in any case, the statues attributed to the monument by Canina, who excavated the monument and put together the pasticcio we now see, do not belong.

true to some extent for much of the first century CE. However, we should not forget that many senators were born not in Rome but elsewhere in Italy and, increasingly, in the provinces. From Trajan onwards, senators were obliged to invest a certain percentage of their capital in Rome, but even then many of them never lost touch with their home town. They appreciated the opportunity to stand out as local benefactors and 'celebrities' in these places, which provided them with greater opportunities for self-display than did the metropolis. Accordingly, many senators chose to be buried in their home town.[33]

Secondly, we must keep in mind that a typical senatorial tomb would normally serve not only an individual or the generation who built it, but generations to come, so that there was no need to build new tombs for the old Roman families. In fact, the continued use of family mausolea over generations is an important aspect of senatorial funerary practice, which deserves fuller coverage and will be discussed in Chapter 3.

Senatorial Tombs of the Second Century

From around the turn of the second century, we have evidence again for newly built senatorial tombs of more impressive size and design. Some of them revived and enhanced building types known from the previous century. The designated consul M. Antonius Antius Lupus, for instance, was honoured in 193/94 by a free-standing altar on a tall podium that displayed the insignia of the deceased's offices as well as his *cursus*.[34] He had been put to death by Commodus, but two years later his *memoriae* and *honores* were restored to him in a *senatus consultum* under Pertinax.[35] A few late first- to second-century tumuli also exist, although only one can be attributed with certainty to a member of the *ordo amplissimus*. It was recently excavated on the via Flaminia, and consisted of a tall tambour decorated with *fasces*

---

[33] Eck, 'Rome and the outside world'; Eck, 'Emperor', 106–10. Heinzelmann (*Nekropolen*, 57 with n. 213) equally points to the continuation of ostentatious tombs in the rest of Italy.

[34] Schäfer, *Imperii insignia*, 272–80 cat. 19 pls. 40–3. The tomb was destroyed by Pope Sixtus V and the marble used for S. Maria Maggiore (ibid., 273 n. 242).

[35] *CIL* 6.1343 (tomb inscription); Scriptores Historiae Augustae, *Commodus* 19.2; Scriptores Historiae Augustae, *Pertinax* 6.8; Cassius Dio 73.5.2; Schäfer, *Imperii insignia*, 277 with n. 280. Four similarly impressive altar monuments dated to the Hadrianic to early Antonine period had been erected on the via Tiburtina close to Ponte Lucano, but they remain anonymous: Eisner, *Typologie*, 108–10 nos. T3 and T4 pls. 42.1–5 and 43.1–3; Mari, *Tibur IV*, 211–19 no. 233 figs. 332–46; Mari, 'Tivoli', 193–6 figs. 29–35.

and axes that sat on a rectangular base of *c.* 12 x 12 m.[36] The majority of patrons, however, opted for new types of monuments, free-standing brick and marble tombs, of which the temple tombs with their imitation of full-fledged podium temples are the most ambitious variety.[37]

One of the earliest preserved newly established senatorial tombs after the Julio-Claudian period is the likely mausoleum of C. Valerius Paullinus, consul in 107, whose father, like himself, originated from Forum Iulii (Fréjus) and was promoted to senatorial rank by Vespasian. The family most likely purchased their estate on the via Latina not much later. They considerably enlarged, modified and redecorated the villa and built a family mausoleum right next to its entrance, conventionally called the 'Tomba dei Pancratii' after an association that used the tomb in the later third century (Figure 1.2).[38] The tomb chambers are exceptionally well preserved and particularly impressive (Figures 1.3 and 1.4). They consist of a vestibule and a large, richly decorated burial chamber. In its centre still stands an enormous marble sarcophagus with a roof-like lid, which was divided into two

[36] Chiocci and Zaccagnini, 'Mausoleo A', with 210 on the date; Gasseau, 'Mausoleo A'. Another large, round monument in a very prominent position on the Flaminia, marble fragments of which were found built into the ancient Porta Flaminia, belonged to the Gallonii of the mid-second century. However, it is unclear whether the inscription was added to a pre-existing tumulus, which must then have been inherited over generations, or whether it was newly erected (*CIL* 6.31714, cf. p. 4778; *LTUR* IV (1999), 289 s.v. sepulcrum: Gallonii (E. Papi); cf. Chapter 3, pp. 147–8 for a fuller bibliography and discussion). Note also the curved inscribed blocks from a monument of the equestrian P. Valerius Priscus that bordered on the via Casilina, which dates to the first half of the second century (*CIL* 6.3654; Quilici, *Collatia*, 704–6 n. 625; *LTURS* V (2008) 228 s.v. P. Valerii Prisci sepulcrum (S. Evangelisti)). It is generally assumed that the inscription belongs to a tumulus, the remains of which have been found in the same location. Yet as Hesberg (*Grabbauten*, 109) observes, the tumulus is probably much earlier than the epitaph. Since Valerius was from Hispania and his family is unlikely to have possessed a family mausoleum in Rome, and since elements from other round monuments have been found nearby (Quilici, *Collatia*, 706), it is most likely that his epitaph belonged to one of those.

[37] Scholars have used the term 'temple tomb' for a range of different tomb types that feature elements of temple architecture. For clarity, I am restricting the term to only those monuments that have a free-standing front porch and podium, thus resembling the most prominent types of temples to the gods.

[38] Coarelli, 'L'urbs', 47–9; Vorster, *Römische Skulpturen*, 161–77; *LTURS* II (2004) 198–9 s.v. Demetriae praedium (D. De Francesco). The lead pipe attesting the family's ownership of the villa mentions the daughter of Paullinus, but extensive building activities and the tomb's interior decoration of the later Flavian period suggest that she inherited the estate from her father and only continued the building. On the tomb, cf. esp. Petersen, 'Secondo sepolcro'; Feraudi-Gruénais, *Innendekoration*, 108–14 no. K48; Filippi (ed.), *Archeologia e giubileo*, 290–2; *LTURS* III (2005) 165–7 figs. 133–4, 139–43 s.v. Latina via (F. Montella). See also below pp. 35–9 on its interior decoration and date.

Ann. d. Inst. 1861.   *Tav. d'agg. I.*

Figure 1.2 Tomb of the Valerii from the Flavian period at the third mile of the via Latina, plan and section by Fornari

compartments internally and contained several bodies.[39] The superstructure is mostly lost and the remains have not attracted much attention in scholarship. It seems that the area above the hypogeum consisted of a rectangular space with a white mosaic floor in which a large skylight occupied

---

[39] *BdI* 1858, 86 (H. Brunn).

Figure 1.3 Tomb of the Valerii, burial chamber with sarcophagus

an almost central position. It is likely that the space was open to the sky.[40] Between this structure and the street were further rooms, and Fortunati's plan seems to suggest that these may have belonged to a larger building complex. However, only new excavations could clarify the situation. While we do not know what exactly a passer-by would have been able to see from the road – one would expect an impressive *titulus* at the very least – the size of the tomb and its position right next to the via Latina suggest that Paullinus was interested in making an impact on his new home city, as the large estate would have offered many less conspicuous locations.[41]

Some time after Paullinus' death, probably around the middle of the century, the villa must have changed proprietorship, as is indicated by another lead pipe attesting ownership by M. Servilius Silanus, *consul suffectus* of 152 and *consul ordinarius* of 188. Most likely, the Servilii purchased the

---

[40] Fortunati, *Relazione*, 61. This is suggested by the sloping floor of the tomb and a lead pipe leading the water to the outside, as well as the floor of the hypogeum vestibule beneath the skylight, which sloped slightly towards a well to channel rain water.

[41] F. Montella (in *LTURS* III (2005) 165) seems to suggest that the upper parts of the tomb were visible from the road, but there is no indication of the evidence for this. Moreover, the chronology of the surrounding structures is not clear.

Figure 1.4 Tomb of the Valerii, stucco relief showing an apotheosis in the centre of the burial chamber's vault

estate from Paullinus' daughter when they moved to Rome from their native Hippo Regius in North Africa.[42] It is obvious from the archaeological evidence of Paullinus' tomb that the new owner did not continue to use the Valerii mausoleum. Most likely, the family built their own tomb right opposite the entrance to the villa, conventionally but erroneously known as the 'Tomba dei Valeri' (Figure 1.5).[43]

This tomb has been completely rebuilt in modern times. Originally it comprised two levels. Underground burial chambers were accessed via

[42] On their origin, cf. a letter by Fronto written between 157 and 161: Coarelli, 'L'urbs', 48; Solin, 'Analecta', 94–6. On the family, cf. also Alföldy, *Konsulat*; Leunissen, *Konsuln*.

[43] The fullest description and drawings, made shortly after the excavation by Fortunati in 1857, are given in Fortunati, *Relazione*, 41–3, and esp. Petersen, 'Sepolcro'. Cf. Filippi (ed.), *Archeologia e giubileo*, 289–90; *LTURS* III (2005) 168 s.v. Latina via (F. Montella). On its interior decoration, see below pp. 39–40. I shall discuss and justify the attribution in more detail elsewhere, but for now see Coarelli, 'L'urbs', 47–9, and Borg, *Crisis and Ambition*, 146–50.

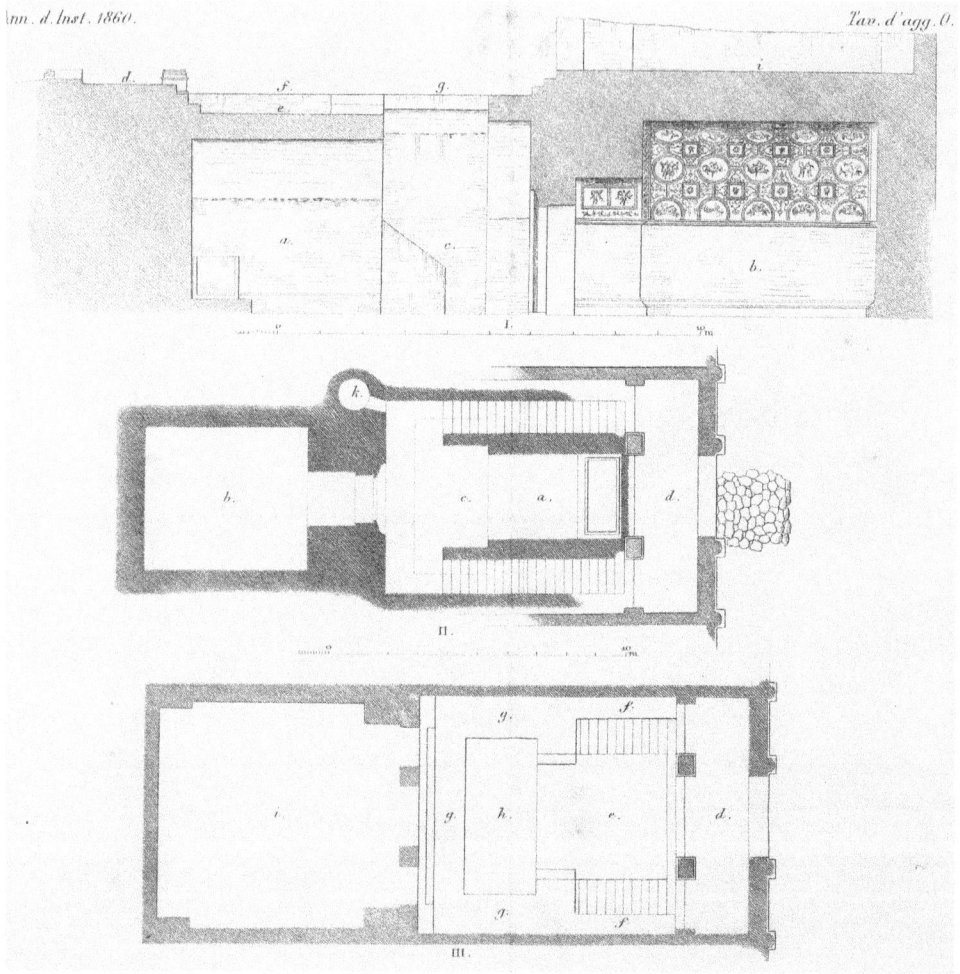

Figure 1.5 Tomb of the Servilii from around 160 CE at the third mile of the via Latina, plan and section by Fornari

two symmetrically placed lateral stairs, which led into a kind of vestibule that was open to the sky. On one side this extended into a wide *ala* with a platform for a sarcophagus, on the other it gave access, through a short corridor, into the larger main burial chamber. These particularly elegant spaces featured an all-white design, with walls and floors covered in white marble and vaults in plaster or, in the main chamber, in the most exquisite white stucco (Figure 1.6 and 1.7). Above ground, the tomb was surrounded by pre-existing structures, the exact date and purpose of which are still unclear. A probably only one-storey, temple-like building with Ionic columns *in antis*, of which a marble capital and base were still seen

Figure 1.6 Tomb of the Servilii, main burial chamber

and drawn by Petersen, was situated above the main burial chamber.[44] The lowest parts of the building's walls are original and partly preserve a thick layer of white plaster containing marble dust. A stamped tile from 159 CE was found in situ in the vault, which is consistent with the approximate date of the fragments of four large sarcophagi found within.[45] Across an open space that extended to both sides beyond the limits of the tomb, the building faced a porticus that rested on pilasters and marble columns. Its back wall closed off the street front and contained the entrance door. On the street side, the wall featured a moulded wall foot, Corinthian half-columns and a cranked, ornamented epistyle, all of marble.

Interestingly in our context, we know of another villa of a Servilius Silanus, most probably Marcus' brother Quintus, situated north of the via Tiburtina between its eleventh and twelfth milestones, through the inscription from a tomb for his wife.[46] As this inscription sits on an architrave

---

[44] The Corinthian capital that was reused for the somewhat dull modern reconstruction must have belonged to the portico.

[45] *BdI* 1858, 36–9 (G. Henzen); Herdejürgen, 'Via Latina', 213–20. On these, see further below 67–8.

[46] On the inscription, see *AE* 1983, 0144; Mari, *Tibur III*, 78 figs. 96–7; Andermahr, *Totus in praediis*, no. 486. For important correction and comment see Solin, 'Analecta', 94–6. Whether

Figure 1.7 Tomb of the Servilii, main burial chamber, stucco relief showing an apotheosis in the centre of the ceiling

with faces on both sides, Quintus also opted for a temple tomb with a free-standing marble porch.[47]

a statue group of the Capitoline Triad found on the Tiburtina estate a few years ago necessarily implies imperial ownership, as is sometimes suggested, is not clear (Calci and Mari, 'Via Tiburtina', 204–6). If it does, this is further confirmation that both brothers fell victim to Commodus.

[47] Calci and Mari ('Via Tiburtina', 204–6) attribute the architrave to a large tumulus tomb (Torraccia dell'Inviolata) in the same area, which they date to the turn of the second century

Figure 1.8 Tomb of M. Nonius Macrinus at the fifth mile of the via Flaminia; heavily ornamented architectural elements and inscription uncovered during the excavation

The most spectacular temple tomb discovered so far, however, is slightly later than these buildings and was only discovered in the autumn of 2008 (Figures 1.8 and 1.9).[48] It was situated between the fifth and sixth milestones of the via Flaminia, right next to the road, and was buried by a landslide, which preserved a large number of marble blocks. It can be reconstructed as a richly ornamented temple tomb, erected entirely of marble within a precinct surrounded by a wall with travertine half-columns.[49] Sitting on the rear part of the particularly long podium measuring 19.6 x 8.55 m was a temple-like building with a splendid tetrastyle Corinthian front porch, and pilasters around its other sides.[50] The architrave was covered by an inscription detailing the *cursus honorum* of M. Nonius Macrinus, consul suffect in 154, *comes* and *amicus* of the Emperor Marcus Aurelius, whose last office

based on its *opus latericium*. However, not only is the technique already attested in the first century BCE (Eisner, *Typologie*, esp. 210, with 116–17 no. T/N2 on the tomb), they would have to assume a front porch for the tumulus (as in Mari, *Tibur III*, 75–83 no. 28 figs. 84–94, esp. fig. 84), for which there is no archaeological support. More importantly, the Servilii appear to have moved to Rome only around the middle of the second century, and it is unthinkable that they usurped an earlier tomb at that point.

[48] Rossi and Arizza (eds.), *Via Flaminia*.

[49] Chiocci and Zaccagnini, 'Mausoleo C', 228 figs. 18–19.

[50] Ibid.; Gasseau, 'Mausoleo C'; De Cristofaro, 'Monumento funerario'. The actual tomb, including its porch, measured 8.36 x 10.64 m.

Figure 1.9 Tomb of M. Nonius Macrinus, reconstruction of its façade

was proconsul of Asia in 170/71.[51] The monument was dedicated to him
and his wife by his son, M. Nonius Arrius Mucianus Manlius Carbo, who
was consul suffect under Commodus.[52]

---

[51] On Macrinus, see Gregori, 'Vita e gesta', with bibl.
[52] A temple tomb, unfortunately anonymous, found near the via Casilina about 6 miles from
Rome, featured a similar Corinthian marble front, while the rest of the tomb was built in
opus latericium. Its front is now reassembled and displayed in the Museo Nazionale delle
Terme: *MNR* I,8 (1985) 170–7 no. iv,3 inv. 121509 (P. Pensabene); Griesbach, *Villen und*

While the temple tombs discussed so far were of the more familiar rectangular type, the extravagant Herodes Atticus, Greek sophist, teacher of the imperial princes and Roman consul (in 143), opted for a circular monument when he dedicated his famous Triopion and a cenotaph to his wife Regilla on their estate at the third milestone of the via Appia. Established shortly after 160, according to a number of inscriptions, two of them long poems composed by Marcellus of Side (?), the Triopion was a kind of rural or garden sanctuary with vines, olive trees and meadows, and surrounded by a wall.[53] It featured a temple of Demeter and the deified empress Faustina Maior, worshipped as the 'new Demeter', to whom a seated statue of Regilla was dedicated (*IG* 14.1389 A ll. 1–2. 5–8),[54] and a heroön-cenotaph for

---

Gräber, 52–3, 171 no. 28 pls. 9.3–4; De Cristofaro, 'Monumento funerario', 266–7 fig. 17, for a colour photograph but with erroneous location; Quilici, *Collatia*, 577–88 no. 479, for a description of the site and other finds, including a *togatus* and fragments of at least two marble sarcophagi. For the largest piece, a large Dionysiac sarcophagus from around 220–30 CE, see Matz, *ASR 4.2*, 244 no. 104b pl. 93; *MNR* I,3 (1982) 68–9 no. iii,3 inv. 121514 (L. Musso). Griesbach (*Villen und Gräber*, 48 n. 439) lists an additional thirteen tombs with substantial amounts of marble, and connects one of them at Colle Nocella, some 2.6 km north-west of Tivoli, with an anonymous senator and governor of Cilicia, whose altar was found somewhere in the vicinity (*CIL* 14.3617). However, the inscription on the marble architrave (*CIL* 14.3735) commemorates an A. Caelius Euphrosynus, who was free born but clearly of libertine descent, and certainly not the same person as the one commemorated by the altar. Cf. Mari, *Tibur IV*, 89–95 no. 39 figs. 82–9 (tomb) and 40 (villa); Griesbach, *Villen und Gräber*, 51 (for the date), 139, 169 cat. 19 pl. 7.4.

53 *IG* 14.1389 A l. 49–50, *IG* 14.1389 B ll. 69–72, with Skenteri, *Herodes Atticus*, 29–65; cf. also Gleason, 'Herodes Atticus'. From the vast bibliography on the Triopion, see esp. Galli, *Lebenswelt*, 110–44; Griesbach, *Villen und Gräber*, 32–8; *LTURS* V (2008) 189–201 (G. Pisani Sartorio, M. Maiuro, F. Rausa); and most recently Paris et al., 'Via Appia Antica', with bibl. From the details recorded, we may assume that the Triopion was not too small, but it is nowhere stated that it would have been coextensive with the villa estate, as assumed by Galli (explicitly at p. 127), or nearly so, as most scholars believe. Rather, it follows the tradition of *cepotaphia*, which were always limited in size. Cf. Gregori ('Horti sepulchrales') for epigraphic evidence, where a size of 546 x 524.5 ft (163.80 x 157.35 m) is the largest given. Cf. also Hesberg, *Grabbauten*, 6; Dräger, *Religionem significare*, 147–51; Griesbach, *Villen und Gräber*, 55–6, with further examples of temple tombs possibly situated in gardens. The relatively small area from which the inscriptions were retrieved, and the fact that the Triopion was surrounded by a wall, equally suggest a more limited size. On the symbolic relevance of pastoral idylls as evoked by the poem (*IG* 14.1389 A l. 48) as well as by reality, see Skenteri, *Herodes Atticus*, 42. For a detailed discussion of the Triopion see Borg, 'Herodes Atticus'. On Herodes in general, cf. also Ameling, *Herodes Atticus*.

54 Griesbach ('Villa e mausoleo', 4 n. 28 and *Villen und Gräber*, 33–5) suggests that the inscription actually does not refer to a temple for the two goddesses, but is alluding metaphorically to two aspects or personifications of Regilla: the wife raped by death (Persephone) and the fertile mother (Demeter). In this way, he ends up with only one building, which is a temple-cenotaph for Regilla, in which only her statue was placed. However, this ignores the different nature of the two poems (cf Skenteri, *Herodes Atticus*, 29–65, for the most detailed discussion), one of which (A) is about Regilla and her statue, while the other (B) is on the protection of the Triopion as a whole and evokes various protective deities. Moreover, Regilla's statue was

Regilla, said not to be a tomb but a *mnemeion* (memorial) in a now-lost inscription that must have featured somewhere on this building:

> Herodes erected this also to be a memorial of his misfortune and of his wife's virtue. But it is not her tomb. Her body is in Greece and now with her husband. Her son was proposed to the Senate by the Emperor Antoninus, called Pius by his fatherland and by all, and by decree of the Senate was enrolled in Rome among the patricians. (*IG* 14.1392)[55]

The cenotaph is thus a monument not only to Regilla, but to Herodes and his now patrician son as well, and illustrates the way in which funerary monuments were used to advertise the status of an entire family, not just the individual to whom the monument was first dedicated. As the panegyric by Marcellus tells us, Regilla's actual tomb was in Greece and also had the shape of a temple (*IG* 14.1389 A l. 46).

A substantial number of archaeological remains from the left side of the Appia have been identified as belonging to the Triopion. And yet it is highly unlikely that the *cepotaphion* extended to that side of the road, as all evidence that can be securely attributed was found on its right side.[56] Most important among these, and the only remains actually found in situ, were a round, Pantheon-like building of approximately 8.5 m diameter with an entrance hall, of which two inscribed columns have survived (Figure 1.10). Pirro Ligorio was present at its discovery, measured and drew the remains, and reported the location of the structure to the west of the Appia, between the southern perimeter wall of the Castrum Caetani and the modern via di Cecilia Metella, roughly at the location of the present-day restaurant at via Appia Antica 198.[57] If his reconstruction is essentially correct, the building could hardly have been anything else but Regilla's heroön.[58]

---

dedicated *to* the Demeters, who in turn honour Regilla (*IG* 14.1389 A, ll. 6–9). *IG* 14.1389, A l. 48 explicitly states that it is pleasing to Faustina (τοῦτο δὲ Φαυστείνηι κεχαρισμένον ἦσται ἄγαλμα) and the text goes on to explain Regilla's veneration of the deified empress. Gleason ('Herodes Atticus', 143–4 with n. 72) rightly notes that the temple for the Demeters must have existed prior to the dedication of Regilla's statue, but she erroneously identifies it with the Caryatid building illustrated by Piranesi, *Antichità III*, 144–5 fig. 7.5.

[55] *IG* 14.1392; translation Lewis and Reynold, *Roman Civilization*, 264. Cf. Ameling, *Herodes Atticus*, 151–2.

[56] For the most recent summary of the find spots and important corrections of earlier accounts, see Paris et al., 'Via Appia Antica' and Borg, 'Herodes Atticus'.

[57] *LTURS* V (2008) fig. 139.1. Rausa (*Pirro Ligorio*, 57–8 no. 5) and Galli (*Lebenswelt*, 127 with fig. 53) offer a transcript of Pirro Ligorio's text. For the location, see Paris et al., 'Via Appia Antica', 280–1.

[58] As suggested by Galli, *Lebenswelt*, 127–32. The columns (now in Naples, Museo Nazionale Archeologico) are inscribed with a dedication to Demeter, Kore and the *dii manes*, and some

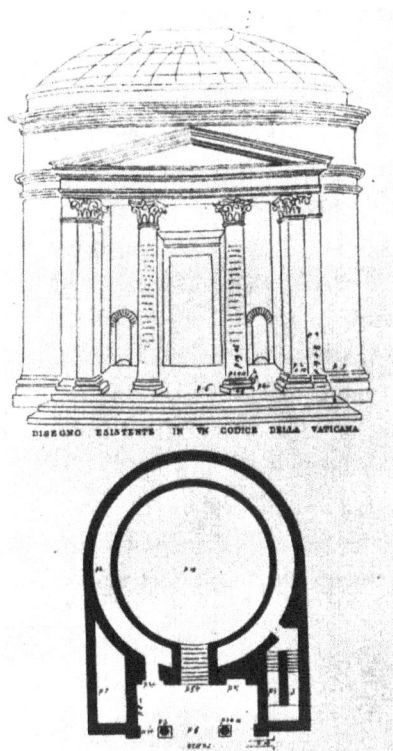

DISEGNO ESISTENTE IN UN CODICE DELLA VATICANA

Figure 1.10 Cenotaph of Annia Regilla, found at the third mile of the via Appia as drawn by Luigi Canina after Pirro Ligorio

Round tombs whose interior space was covered with a cupola have been built in Rome and elsewhere since the Augustan period.[59] Of these, a semi-interred *opus latericium* building of about 8 m diameter, surrounded by a drainage channel apparently similar to the Triopion building, is particularly interesting in our context. It was erected in the early second century, immediately to the east of the so-called 'Villa di Casal Bruciato' between the

---

scholars want to place them at the entrance to the Triopion (e.g. Ameling, *Herodes Atticus*, 149–50). I do not see a need to do so, but even if they did not belong to the round building, this would not affect my argument. On the columns, see also Pomeroy (*Regilla*, 167) with an English translation of the inscription (*IG* 14.1390).

[59] Cf. Stanco, *Acilii Glabriones*, esp. 36–45 with tables 8–11, for an overview. For details, see Schwarz, *Tumulat Italia tellus*, cat. M 3, 8, 12, 30, 32, 41, 42, 85, of which only the last is situated in Rome (cf. ibid., 209–10: second half of the first century); *ArchLaz* 4, 1981, 153 (C. Mocchegiani Carpano). Some of them sit on a rectangular podium, but others either have a circular podium or lack one, as in our case.

third and fourth milestones of the via Tiburtina.[60] It is accessible via stairs built in *opus mixtum* that descend into a small *vestibulum* whose walls are painted blue. The main chamber featured a black-and-white mosaic floor on which tendrils growing from a crater are still identifiable, four niches set into the walls below the cupola and four windows. Pedestals along the walls may have supported cinerary urns. The funerary character of the building is confirmed by fragments of sarcophagi found inside.[61] Its outer face is only poorly preserved, so that it is impossible to reconstruct its appearance with any certainty. It probably lacked a porch like that of Regilla's cenotaph, so that, typologically, it may be located somewhere between the earlier tumuli and round temple tombs.[62] The villa, built in the later first century CE at some distance from the consular road on an elevation above the Fosso Bocca di Leone, has been attributed tentatively to M. Aquilius Regulus, *consul suffectus* about 80–85, based on its date and location.[63]

We are beginning to see a pattern here that is confirmed by more fragmentary evidence. Two *antae* decorated with *fasces* from Ostia could have been part of a temple tomb, which thus would have belonged to another curule magistrate of consular or praetorian rank.[64] A senatorial temple

---

[60] See Calci and Messineo, 'Casal Bruciato'; Calci and Mari, 'Via Tiburtina', 181–2; DeFranceschini (ed.), *Ville*, 139–43 no. 51 figs. 51.1–5. The date is suggested by the use of *opus mixtum* for the drainage channel and connected wall. The building and mosaic were repaired in later periods, suggesting its use well into late antiquity.

[61] Calci and Messineo ('Monumento circolare', 164, and 'Casal Bruciato', 447) consider the possibility that the building may initially have served as a summer *triclinium*. However, given the travertine pedestals, which they also think could have supported cinerary urns (they cite another tomb on the Tiburtina for comparison), the sarcophagi (see *MNR* I.10.1 (1995), 133–5 no. 85 (L. Musso), for one of them), the size of the building and the status of the entire complex, I find it hard to imagine that the building ever served any other purpose than that of a tomb. Accordingly, Calci and Mari ('Via Tiburtina', 181–2) accept the building as a mausoleum outright.

[62] For later circular temple tombs, see Borg, *Crisis and Ambition*, 38–9, 56–7.

[63] The location of Regulus' villa is indicated by his close friend Martial in epigrams 1.12.82 and 7.31. The authors in n. 60 above accept the attribution as plausible. Cf. also Andermahr, *Totus in praediis*, 157–8 no. 48. On literary sources on Regulus, see Iodice Di Martino, 'Villa di Aquilio Regolo'. Calci and Mari ('Via Tiburtina', 181–2) also note that the villa has building phases in the third and fourth centuries, and that also the mausoleum was used over a very long time. The latter fact suggests that the villa remained in the same family for over two centuries. While it is unclear whether Aquilius' line continued after his death, the continuation may point to a family of status. A similar round building of approximately the same size has been found just a few metres from the margins of the ancient via Campana, where it branches off from the via Portuensis. However, it is not entirely clear whether it was planned to be used as a mausoleum, and it may never have been used as such. Cf. Cianfriglia and Giacopini, 'Via Portuense', 407–10.

[64] Schäfer, *Imperii insignia*, 375 no. B4 pls. 86, 87.1. The axes in the *fasces* indicate that the owner of the tomb was a curule rather than a municipal magistrate.

tomb is also suggested by an architrave from the turn of the second century found near the Theatre of Marcellus, a particularly honourable location probably assigned by the senate, and belonging to an anonymous proconsul of Sicily.[65] The fragments of a mausoleum with marble façade at the eighth milestone of the via Latina are likely also to have belonged to a temple tomb, and if the wreath of a relief portrait from this tomb refers to the *ornamenta triumphalia*, we are looking here at another highly decorated member of the first order, this time from the early second century.[66] Another architrave is likely to have belonged to a temple tomb somewhere near the Tiber. It was dedicated to a certain *[---]lius Rugianus, vir clarissimus* and legate of *legio XIII Gemina*, who died in the first third of the third century.[67] Still later is a probable epistyle block commemorating the *hominus novus* D. Simonius Proculus Iulianus, consul in 238 or 239, and *praefectus urbi* between 244/45 and 254.[68]

Obviously, temple tombs are by no means restricted to social climbers and freedmen, as is often suggested,[69] and they were used for senatorial burials at least until the mid-third century. Moreover, these tombs can easily compete in splendour – albeit not necessarily in size – with their first-century BCE predecessors.[70] It is therefore striking that they have attracted so little attention in scholarship.[71] One reason surely is their usually very poor state of preservation, which is due exactly to their former splendour. Stripped of their marble decoration for the adornment of palazzi and churches, or even just for burning lime, they had become extremely vulnerable to weathering and decay,[72] quite unlike the late Republican to early imperial monuments

---

[65] *CIL* 6.41090; Feraudi-Gruénais, 'Ewigkeit', 157 no. 53.

[66] *NSc* (1912), 34–8 (G. Mancini); *MNR* I8,1 (1985) 214–16 no. iv,15, Inv. 58200 = 124708
      (L. Musso); cf. Chapter 4 p. 257.

[67] *CIL* 6.41207; Feraudi-Gruénais, 'Ewigkeit', 159 no. 87; *BCom* 92, 1987–88, 375–6 fig. 76
      (M. C. De Spagnolis); Eck, 'Rugianus'.

[68] *CIL* 6.41232; Feraudi-Gruénais, 'Ewigkeit', 159 no. 94. On this and the previous example, see
      also Borg, *Crisis and Ambition*, 33.

[69] E.g. Wrede, *Consecratio*, 93–105, 161–3 and 'Claudia Semne'; Hesberg and Zanker,
      'Einleitung', 12–13. Strictly speaking, Wrede refers primarily to portraits in the guise of
      divinities (*in formam deorum*), but the close connection he makes between these and what
      he calls a *Grabtempel* has suggested to others that temple tombs – whatever the specific
      scholar understands by this term – belonged primarily to the freedmen class as well. Contra
      Griesbach, *Villen und Gräber*, 139–40. Cf. also *infra* Chapter 4.

[70] For the range of sizes of temple tombs and related mausolea, see Griesbach, *Villen und Gräber*,
      70–1 table 1.

[71] A notable exception is ibid., 165–92, with a catalogue of 123 temple tombs and related tomb
      types. There is no systematic study yet of this type of mausoleum.

[72] Ditto Feraudi-Gruénais, 'Ewigkeit', 151–2. For close observation of spoliation and reuse of
      Macrinus' tomb, see Chiocci et al., 'Attività'.

with their massive concrete cores, or the dense clusters of tombs in sub-elite necropoleis, which were preserved by being buried under their own debris, by the sand of the sea or by landslides, or sealed by St Peter's Basilica. The occasional good condition of some isolated brick and temple tombs is therefore usually due to their later conversion into churches, mills or parts of farmhouses.

Location

The view that – as is alleged for tombs in general – senatorial tombs were now situated further away from the roadside and more closely attached to their patrons' villas also needs some qualification, especially when this argument is used to support the hypothesis of a lack of interest in competitive display, a retreat into the private sphere, an 'internalisation' of attitudes to death and commemoration or an 'introverted representation'.[73] Of the senatorial tombs just discussed, all except for the one potentially belonging to Aquilius Regulus were erected immediately next to the road, and the same is true for many anonymous temple tombs. Prints and drawings by Piranesi, Canina and others of the section of the Appia between the fourth and fifth milestones can further demonstrate this point.[74] They were meant to, and did, make as much of an impression on the passer-by as their Republican predecessors did. Griesbach observes that more extravagant tombs with marble fronts tended to be located at a greater distance from Rome,[75] and the tomb of P. Cluvius Maximus Paullinus (Figure 1.13) as well as the rock tomb of Palazzolo could be taken to support this view.[76] On the one hand, if this reflects a real trend and is not a side-effect of better preservation at more remote locations, it only demonstrates the continued desire of senators to erect such daring structures, even if at the cost of distance from Rome. On the other, the Servilii at the third mile of the Latina, Herodes

---

[73] Especially Griesbach, 'Villa e mausoleo'; Griesbach, *Villen und Gräber*, 146–9. Following the authors in n. 8 above to some extent, he links changes in location to an alleged trend towards an increasing focus on emotional attachment and the importance of the family for the apotheosis and commemoration of the deceased.

[74] E.g. Piranesi, *Antichità III*, pl. 8; Canina, *Prima parte*, pl. 31. While Piranesi's drawings exaggerate the size of tombs and Canina offers some rather fanciful reconstructions, the structures they record have normally been confirmed by archaeology. One may even argue that Piranesi's images, while not strictly proportional, reflect the impression these buildings made on their viewers.

[75] Griesbach, *Villen und Gräber*, 21, 48.

[76] Cf. below at nn. 96 and 98.

Atticus at the third mile of the Appia and two of the architraves listed above attest to marble-fronted temple tombs close to the city.[77]

Other mausolea were indeed located away from the road, but by no means necessarily removed from sight.[78] They tended to be erected on slopes and elevations of the landscape so that they were still very visible.[79] Today this fact is often obscured by modern buildings, but paintings and drawings from the seventeenth to the nineteenth centuries occasionally help our imagination.[80] Moreover, through their removal from the road-side and closer connection to *horti* or villas, these tombs were ideologically more closely associated with these markers of status. By being kept at a distance from the ordinary people on the street, they hinted at their patrons' social distinction.

Only a relatively small number were erected in locations that were not aiming at visibility from a major road. One example is the temple tomb built around 200, probably by a new owner of the Villa *ad duas lauros* off the via Labicana.[81] At some 450 m away from the road it was probably hardly visible from there, if at all. Yet it was situated directly next to the entrance to the splendid villa, impossible for any visitor to miss (Figure 1.11). Around 100 years after its foundation, it was redecorated and surrounded by a

---

[77] See above at nn. 43, 56, 65 and 67.

[78] This is conceded for some instances by Hesberg, *Grabbauten*, 43, and Griesbach, *Villen und Gräber*, 37. Yet there is also no indication that the walls sometimes surrounding these tombs would have obscured the view to the extent that the tomb would have been virtually invisible, as Hesberg ('Planung', 58–9) suggests (somewhat ambiguous is Griesbach, *Villen und Gräber*, 47). In the special case of the so-called 'Tomba dei Valerii' (mislabelled by Hesberg ('Planung', pl. 2c and *Grabbauten*, 43 with fig. 144) as the Tomb of the Pancratii; cf. here Figure 1.5), the *murus* was decorated on the outside with half-columns and other marble decorative elements. Moreover, the height of this wall is unknown and the columns of the temple tomb were both situated on higher ground and on pedestals (Petersen, 'Sepolcro', pls. O and P), suggesting that at least the upper part of the building was visible. This was definitely the case elsewhere: see e.g. the tombs under St Peter's. Cf. Hesberg, 'Planung', figs. 3–4. That such walls were used for representation in their own right is also confirmed by the large griffon marble slabs of another tomb on the Via Appia: *LTURS* I (2001) 131 fig. 127 s.v. Appia via (S. Mineo); Spera and Mineo, *Bovillae*, 166 no. 169 figs. 166–7; Griesbach, *Villen und Gräber*, 183 cat. 80.

[79] See the discussion of tomb locations in Griesbach, *Villen und Gräber*, 50–6.

[80] See, for instance, illustrations of the so-called 'Sedia del Diavolo', a two-storey temple tomb off via Nomentana: *LTURS* IV (2006), 111 fig. 105 s.v. Nomentana via (U. Fusco). For eighteenth-century illustrations, see e.g. Edward Lear (1881) in De Rosa and Trastulli (eds.), *Campagna*, 223 cat. 87 pl. 87.

[81] Volpe, 'Via Labicana', 225–7; DeFranceschini (ed.), *Ville*, 176–9 no. 62; Griesbach, *Villen und Gräber*, 176–7 cat. 53 pls. 11.1–3; Armellin, *Sepolcro a tempietto*, esp. 85–98; Borg, *Crisis and Ambition*, 36, 130–1 fig. 20. For further examples in a similar location, see Griesbach (*Villen und Gräber*, 52, 188 cat. 106 pl. 19; 52, 178 cat. 59 pl. 12; 53, 175 cat. 45; 55, 177 cat. 55 pl. 11.4), but note that distances between tombs and villas can vary widely (pp. 50–6).

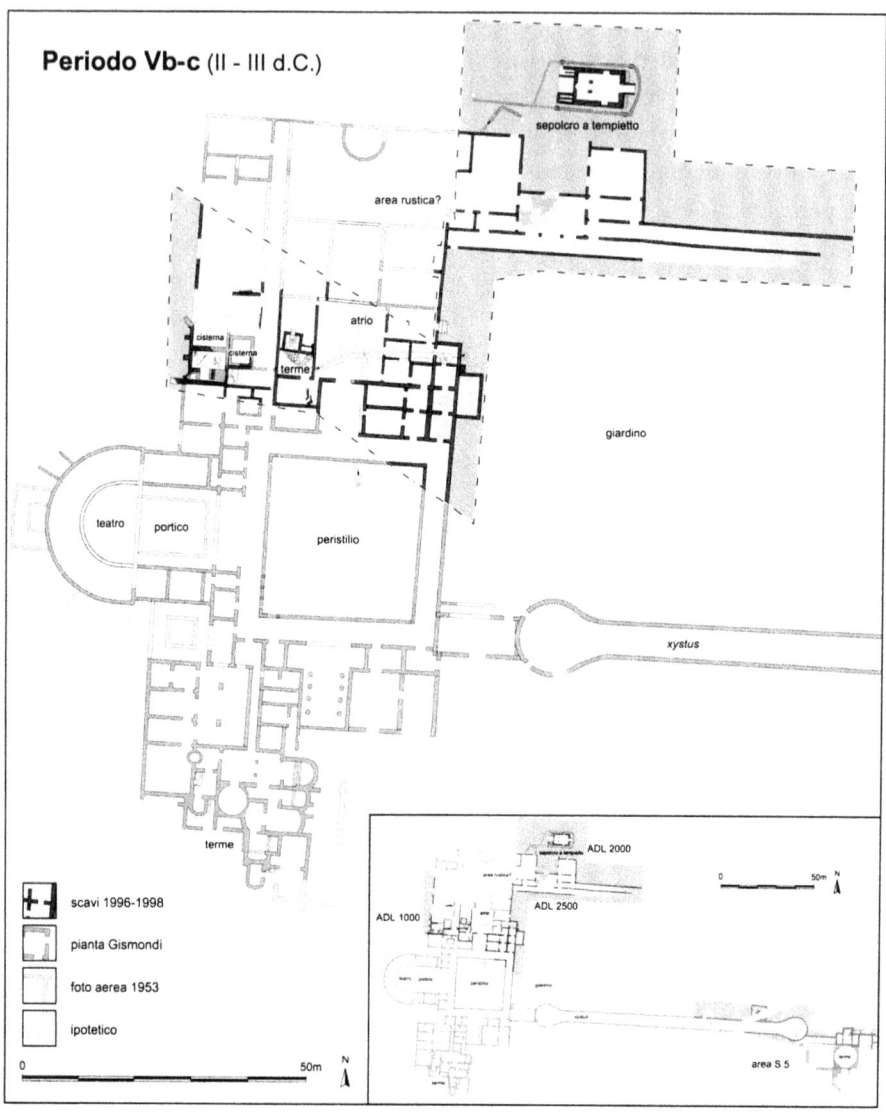

Figure 1.11 Villa *ad duas lauros*, plan of the villa at the beginning of the third century

colonnaded courtyard similar to the one around the mausoleum of Romulus in Maxentius' villa on the Appia.[82] It thus featured as the central element in a monumentalised vestibule to one of the most luxurious villas at the time, and its message, the distinction and long family tradition of the villa's owner,

---

[82] Rasch, *Maxentius-Mausoleum*.

will not have escaped anyone invited to the estate.[83] The temple tomb that belonged to the similarly extraordinary villa of Sette Bassi, built some fifty years earlier, was situated not within the entrance peristyle, but opposite the entrance and directed towards it.[84] Both are highly likely to have belonged to the senatorial class.[85] Such locations probably suggest a shift in the elite's primary target audience, which had become focused on the patron's peers and clients, but not a waning interest in self-display. One even wonders whether such habits were harking back to Republican practices, when the most prominent families had their tombs next to their houses even within the city.[86]

Messages

So far, we have established that the senatorial elite were keen to continue to use their mausolea for self-display. However, what exactly did they want to communicate? Some answers can be found in the exterior and interior decoration of their tombs, which I shall address in turn.

Exterior Decoration

The exterior of temple tombs is in itself a highly ornate and ambitious feature. Those temple tombs we can identify as senatorial all had marble fronts, which assimilated them with the temples of the gods and especially the imperial *divi* and *divae*. The significance of the temple type as such deserves a more detailed discussion, which will be part of Chapter 4. Here, I would just like to point out that we should not necessarily assume that all senatorial temple tombs had full marble fronts or were even entirely built

---

[83] On tombs demonstrating a long line of ancestors, see Chapter 3.

[84] Griesbach, *Villen und Gräber*, 56, 172 cat. 35 pls. 10.1–2; DeFranceschini (ed.), *Ville*, 209–14 no. 75; *LTURS* IV (2005) 186–90 s.v. Latina via (F. Diamanti), all with bibl., esp. Lupu, 'Sette Bassi', 179–84 figs. 59–61, 63. The latest brick stamp observed is from 145–55 (ibid., 179–80 n. 3). The exact relationship between the consular rock tomb at Palazzolo (Griesbach, *Villen und Gräber*, 59 with bibl. in n. 533; see also at n. 120 below) and the remains of a villa on the other side of the road on which it borders is not entirely clear, but should the two features be contemporary, they would equally strongly link monumental tomb and villa entrance at the cost of roadside visibility.

[85] For both villas, this is suggested by their extraordinary size and splendour. For the Villa *ad duas lauros*, the very long time during which the villa seems to have belonged to the same family equally points to a noble family (cf. Borg, *Crisis and Ambition*, 130–1, for further speculation about a potential owner).

[86] Verzár-Bass, 'Mausolei', 404–6.

Figure 1.12 Architectural ornaments from a temple tomb on the via Flaminia at
Grottarossa (not to scale)

from marble. As we rely for their identification mostly on inscriptions and
imperii insignia carved from stone, we may in fact be missing some other
tombs that are less well preserved. To be sure, marble is the costliest material,
but one feature of second-century tombs is an appreciation of different
materials and colours on one and the same building. For instance, a poorly
preserved temple tomb at Grottarossa at the sixth mile of the Flaminia (note
that it was situated just 5.5 m from the road) featured windows, an entablature and a pediment decorated with the most richly adorned moulded
brick ornaments, while delicate open-work marble ornaments consisting of
double spirals and palmettes sat atop the *sima* (Figure 1.12).[87]

Other tombs may dispense completely with marble, but are not necessarily less impressive for this fact as they take the technique of brick building
to the utmost perfection. The so-called Tomba Barberini, for instance, a
three-storey building at the third mile of the via Latina, not only features
the contrasting red and yellow bricks that offset decorative elements such as
pilasters and epistyles from the rest of the walls, as is typical for tombs of the
second half of the second and the first half of the third centuries; it boasts the
richest brick ornaments on window and tabula frames, cornices, pediments
and Corinthian capitals. These ornaments were also painted in various
colours and partly gilded, and the frieze at the front was set in marble.[88]

---

[87] Bruto and Vannicola, 'Grottarossa'; Messineo, *Via Flaminia*, 130–4 figs. 154–8.

[88] *LTURS* 3 (2005) 162, 164–5 s.v. Latina via (F. Montella), with bibl. According to Pirro Ligorio's
drawing of a fragmentary inscription in the *titulus* frame, the patron of this tomb was one

Some façades were further decorated with ornamented relief plaques of multicoloured brick and dark tuff inlays.[89] The visible bricks of the façades were typically specially crafted with concave upper and bottom sides to allow for them to be laid with the finest possible mortar joints at the front, which, in turn, were sometimes accentuated by painted white or yellow lines,[90] and the bricks themselves had a fine, polished finish that enhanced their colour. In some of these tombs, the art of brick building has reached a degree of perfection previously unknown and never reached afterwards, and its appreciation can be seen in imitation of such *opus latericium* with fine white 'mortar joints' painted on red plaster, which covered the walls and façades of less preciously built tombs.[91] Even acknowledging a general hierarchy of materials in which marble ranked highest, there is certainly no reason to dismiss these brick buildings as inferior to, or less ostentatious than, earlier elite tombs.

In addition to – and sometimes instead of – such ornamental exuberance, the first order continued the display of their status symbols on the outside of their tombs, especially the *sella curulis* and *fasces* with axes attesting to their curule magistracies; arguably, the most obvious and easily readable senatorial status display.[92] Thomas Schäfer attributes twenty (or just under 30 per cent) of his sixty-six representations of *imperii insignia* to second-century curule magistrates; that is roughly the same number as he found in the first centuries BCE and CE.[93]

Cornelius of consular rank (Rausa, 'Disegni', 526–8 no. 11 pls. 12–14; *CIL* 6.1712*). There is no obvious fault in this inscription, and recent Italian publications as well as Griesbach (*Villen und Gräber*, 139) consider that it may be genuine. What probably counts against this is the large number of anonymous arcosolium burials in the underground chambers, which suggest a hierarchy typical of the sub-elite, where kin were buried in sarcophagi in the space above and dependants in simple graves underneath, while the first order buried their *familia* elsewhere.

[89] E.g. the temple tomb opposite the Villa dei Quintili on the via Appia Nuova. See De Rossi, *Tellenae*, 16 no. 2 figs. 2–9; Kammerer-Grothaus, 'Deus Rediculus', 211–13 pl. 26; Griesbach, *Villen und Gräber*, 181–2 no. 70, with full bibl. This mix of colours and materials is not new to the second century, but features already on some early tombs such as the *Monumentum Liviae* (Kammerer-Grothaus, 'Camere sepolcrali'), or the particularly beautiful 'Tomba degli archetti' at Ostia from the Tiberian or Claudian period (Heinzelmann, *Nekropolen*, 167–72 no. PR B6 figs. 76–82).

[90] This feature is hardly ever mentioned, but for published examples cf. the (non-senatorial) Mausolea F, L, V and Chi underneath St Peter's: Zander, 'Necropoli Vaticana', 21–2, 49, 53 fig. 19; Feraudi-Gruénais, 'Ewigkeit', 152 fig. 5.3; Zander, *Necropoli di San Pietro*, 118 fig. 176.

[91] E.g. the façade facing the street of Isola Sacra tomb 86, which belongs to a courtyard added later (around 150) to a tomb with a beautiful real brick façade of around 120. Cf. Angelucci et al., 'Sepolture e riti', 70 fig. 19.

[92] Schäfer, *Imperii insignia*; Feraudi-Gruénais, 'Ewigkeit', 145–6, for a summary. The few late tumuli radiate a distinct air of austerity in comparison with the temple tombs.

[93] Schäfer, *Imperii insignia*.

The tombs' façade inscriptions equally sing of honours received and deeds done, as they typically detail the *cursus honorum* of their patrons in much the same way as honorific inscriptions do.[94] I am aware of only three, or potentially four, instances of second-century senatorial tombs where the entire outward appearance with its location of *tituli* is known, but there is every reason to assume that they are typical examples of their peers' habits. One is the temple tomb of M. Nonius Macrinus discussed above, which had its entire architrave covered with the cursus (Figure 1.8 and 1.9).[95] The second example is the mausoleum of M. Servilius Silanus' colleague as consul suffect in 152 and proconsul (designate?) of Asia, P. Cluvius Maximus Paullinus (Figure 1.13). His huge tomb was dedicated to him by his homonymous son after 158/59 CE on the via Praenestina on the slope of the hill of S. Teresa near Monteporzio Catone, about 18 km from Rome.[96] It did not have a free-standing porch but pediments and pilasters, and was built entirely of marble. A *titulus* of 2.06 x 1.10 m at the front over the door stated in beautifully carved, 18 cm-high letters his name and his two most important offices, consul and *VIIvir epulonum*. In addition, two reliefs on both long sides detailed his full *cursus honorum* and displayed the symbols of his administrative and priestly offices. The third example is the altar tomb of M. Antonius Antius Lupus mentioned above.[97] The epitaph explicitly states that the tomb was designed to preserve his name in the memory of the Roman people for eternity.

The date of the final example is not entirely clear, but the spectacular rock tomb of an unknown consul at Palazzolo may also be of second- or early third-century date.[98] The tomb façade is 10 m tall. It uses an artificial rock face above Lago di Albano on the west slope of the Alban Mountains, with a road at its bottom. The tomb's podium of about 4.80 m in height, above which the relief with the *imperii insignia* (2.35 x 5.80 m) is cut into the native rock, must have displayed a lost inscription. Above the relief,

---

[94] For the difficulties resulting from this similarity in distinguishing between sepulchral and honorific inscriptions, see Eck, 'Rome and the outside world', 81–2, 84–5; Andermahr, *Totus in praediis*, 10–14; Salomies, 'Inscriptions', 150–1. For typical features of such inscriptions, see Alföldy, 'Individualität und Kollektivnorm'. For a list of senatorial inscriptions from Rome, cf. Feraudi-Gruénais, 'Ewigkeit', and Faßbender, *Untersuchungen*.

[95] P. 17 with n. 48 above.

[96] Schäfer, *Imperii insignia*, 364–5 no. A2 pl. 78; Caraffa, *Monumento sepolcrale*; Degrassi, 'Paullinus'; *AE* 1940, 99 (= *AE* 1946, 168); Alföldy, *Konsulat*, 342; Rüpke and Glock, *Fasti sacerdotum*, 899 no. 1275, on his date; Granino Cecere, 'Homo novus'.

[97] P. 9 with n. 34.

[98] Schäfer, *Imperii insignia*, 265–72 no. 18 pls. 38–9, second century.

Figure 1.13 Tomb of P. Cluvius Maximus Paullinus on the via Praenestina on the slope of a hill near Monteporzio Catone, mid- to late Antonine

a stepped pyramid crowns the façade, topped by a platform that possibly supported an altar or the statues of the deceased.[99]

Other tombs featuring *imperii insignia* may be anonymous, but they were clearly ambitious buildings and erected closer to Rome than the last three examples. I have already mentioned the second-century tumulus tomb excavated opposite the temple tomb of Nonius Macrinus.[100] Of a marble tomb erected somewhere on the Appia, only one block with *fasces* and another with a weapon frieze survive.[101] Yet the marble monument must have been of considerable size, since the *fasces* block, measuring 1.67 x 0.44 m,

[99] Salomonson ('Relief', 11–12 and *Chair*, 27–8) has argued for a date around 200 based on formal similarities with the relief for Antius Lupus. This is getting very close to the earliest possible date for two strigilated sarcophagi that may have belonged to the tomb though, admittedly, their provenance is not beyond doubt and it cannot be excluded either that they were placed in the tomb at a later date. Schäfer's argument for a pre-166 CE date, however, is based on an alleged ruling by M. Aurelius prohibiting the erection of tombs within a villa (*Imperii insignia*, 271 with n. 235), which, if it ever existed (it is only attested in the notorious *Historia Augusta* (Scriptores Historiae Augustae, *Marcus* 13.4)), clearly was not applied; ditto Griesbach, *Villen und Gräber*, 13 with n. 108.

[100] Cf. above at n. 36.

[101] Schäfer, *Imperii insignia*, no. A9 pl. 83.5.

displays only the middle part of four *fasces*. It requires a continuation of the relief on at least five more blocks of similar dimensions, and a building fitting the relief's size.

The extent to which death and a tomb were connected with honour and praise even in the case of senatorial women is demonstrated by the inscription from Annia Regilla's cenotaph quoted above,[102] which devoted half of the available space to the recording of an official honour awarded to her son Bradua, his admission among the patricians. As the poem by Marcellus insists (*IG* 14.1389 A ll. 23–6), the emperor's intention was to console Herodes' grief. Yet that Herodes advertised the honour in at least two inscriptions from the Triopion indicates the importance of communicating it also to a wider public.[103]

Normally, during the second century senatorial women were not commemorated on the façades of their tombs. However, wherever they were commemorated with an epitaph, they were typically praised by association with their husbands' and fathers' achievements. The same applies to children and those who died before they could hold any notable offices for themselves: the honour gained by one family member rubs off on his or her relatives, and all family members' achievements accumulate and contribute to the esteem of the family as a whole.[104]

Not exactly a feature of the tomb proper but closely attached to it are the statues that were often erected in front of a mausoleum. This habit had already started in the late Republic. The famous Mausoleum of the Scipiones on the Appia received a new façade during the second half of the second century BCE that was decorated with the statues of P. Scipio Africanus Maior, L. Scipio Asiaticus and the poet Ennius, two prominent ancestors and the poet who had sung the family's praises (see Figure 3.3).[105] At the beginning of the first century BCE, a travertine statue of Servius Sulpicius Galba, most likely showing the consul of 108 BCE sitting on a *sella curulis*, was set up either in front or on top of his tomb.[106] Two bronze statues stood in front of

---

102 Cf. n. 55 above with the full text.
103 See also the conclusion to Chapter 4. That his honour may also have helped to convince the public that any rumour of Herodes' involvement in his wife's death was just slander was surely welcome, but not the only aim.
104 Adembri (ed.), *Suggestioni egizie*, 45–7.
105 Coarelli, *Scipioni* and *Revixit ars*; Lauter-Bufe, 'Fassade'; Giuliani, *Bildniskunst*, 172–5; *LTUR* IV (1999) 281–5 figs. 136–8 s.v. Sepulcrum (Corneliorum) Scipionum (F. Zevi); Volpe et al., 'Scipioni', esp. 182–5 (R. Volpe). For further details see Chapter 3 pp. 127–32.
106 The statue must have been part of the outside display, since the monument was inaccessible. The *sella* is not preserved, but as Galba is dressed in the *toga exigua* it must have been the curule seat, and the *fasces* were displayed on the tomb's walls. See Ferrea, 'Sulpicius Galba'; *CIL* 6.31617.

C. Cestius' pyramid.[107] In the first century CE, M. Artorius Geminus (?) and a later prominent female family member, probably Antonia Furnilla, were honoured by statues in front of their tomb's entrance, the so-called 'Platorini tomb' (Figure 1.1).[108] The mausoleum of the Licinii on the via Salaria also featured statues at its front: those of M. Licinius Crassus Frugi and his wife Scribonia, who were killed in 47 CE, as well as at least two female relatives and possibly Pompey the Great and an unidentified boy (see Figure 3.7).[109]

For the second century, we have the first poem by Marcellus mentioned above, which refers to a seated (?) statue of Regilla although, while being located in the *cepotaphium*, it was dedicated to the two Demeters (*IG* 14.1389 A ll. 1–2. 5–8).[110] The text of the inscription is not entirely clear about its location and it is usually assumed that it stood inside their temple. However, the way in which the text refers to the statue indicates that one was actually able to see the image while reading.[111] The form and size of the stone slab on which the text is inscribed suggest its attachment somewhere outside the temple.[112] Moreover, the inscription is a long panegyric to the deceased (and to her and Herodes' families), in praise of Regilla, not of the two goddesses, who in turn are said to honour Regilla.[113] Accordingly, it seems likely that not just the inscription but the statue too was erected in the open air. Possibly, the inscription was even mounted on the statue base.[114]

---

[107] For bibl. see n. 5 above.

[108] Silvestrini, *Sepulcrum*, 73–9 figs. 40–1, 43–4. The statues were found within the tomb, that of Artorius in several pieces. However, this is likely due to later changes to the area, especially the building of the Aurelianic Wall in the immediate vicinity. On the tomb in general see n. 13 above.

[109] For details and bibliography, see Chapter 3 pp. 140–43.

[110] Since we do not know how far the temple was from Regilla's cenotaph, there remains the possibility that all three features could be viewed together. On Griesbach's doubts regarding the existence of the Demeters' temple (*Villen und Gräber*, 33–4 with n. 310), see the discussion above pp. 19–20 with n. 54. There is no evidence that the statue had any attributes of Persephone, and the epithet *euzonos*, 'well-girdled' (*IG* 14.1389 A l. 8), cannot be used to reconstruct the statue's iconography. It is a Homeric metaphor for beauty (Skenteri, *Herodes Atticus*, 60) and more specifically is used for Briseis while Achilles mourns her loss (Hom. *Il.* 1.429), as noted by Gleason, 'Herodes Atticus', 148.

[111] Skenteri (*Herodes Atticus*, 39, 40, 45–6) suggests that the poem was written for the occasion of the erection of Regilla's statue. Galli (*Lebenswelt*, 116) misunderstands the passage as referring to a statue of Faustina.

[112] *IG* 14.1389 A: 122 x 54 cm. The original depth of the stones can no longer be determined due to modern alterations. See Peek, 'Marcellus', 77. Cf. the drawing in Galli, *Lebenswelt*, 114–15 fig. 47. Peek ('Marcellus', 79) and Ameling (*Herodes Atticus*, 156) locate stele A at the entrance to the *temenos*, but this would only be convincing if temple and statue were located there as well.

[113] Skenteri, *Herodes Atticus*, 39.

[114] I owe this suggestion to Jane Fejfer.

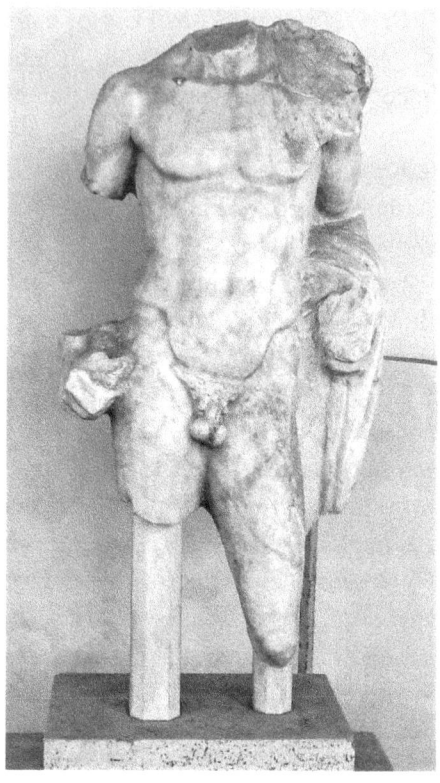

Figure 1.14 Seated female statue from the Tomb of M. Nonius Macrinus on the via Flaminia

Figure 1.15 Male statue in 'heroic' costume from the Tomb of M. Nonius Macrinus on the via Flaminia

A few second-century statues have been found in front of tombs, although only one instance can be attributed to the senatorial class with some confidence. A headless statue of a seated woman in the *pudicitia* scheme, the fragment of another seated female and a headless nude male statue with a Hellenistic cuirass beside his feet were found in the debris of Nonius Macrinus' tomb (Figures 1.14 and 1.15). They must have belonged to his mausoleum and probably stood on the platform in front of its façade, just as statues used to do in the case of proper temples.[115] While the female statues

---

[115] Chiocci and Zaccagnini ('Mausoleo C', 224–7, 230 figs. 15–17) and De Cristofaro ('Monumento funerario', 252, 269–70 figs. 2–3) consider that the statues could also have stood elsewhere within the precinct. However, as Thomas (*Monumentality*, 188) notes, also in the case of the Tempe of Faustina and Antoninus Pius on the Forum Romanum, the statues of the two stood at the corners of the stairs in front of the façade. Cf. *LTUR* I (1993), 46–7 s.v. Antoninus, divus, templum (A. Cassatella), with fig. 28 for a coin attesting the fact.

present Arria Flavia (?) as Macrinus' modest wife, the commander himself is depicted in a Greek heroic iconography. The statues of a seated magistrate on his *sella curulis* and that of what was possibly his wife, both of Trajanic age, were found between the first and second milestones of the via Casilina. However, the magistrate's statue is mutilated and it is not entirely clear what level of magistrate we are looking at.[116] A toga statue also belonged to the spectacular but anonymous marble temple tomb of Torraccio di Torrenova.[117] A few statue bases with epitaphs for senators further attest to the habit of setting up portrait statues for the deceased, although their exact location and relation to a tomb can no longer be determined.[118] These statues and their inscribed bases thus transfer another aspect of honorific monuments into the funerary sphere.

Interior Decoration

One might expect the tone to become more personal once we enter the mausolea, but the same interest in status display also informs much of the interior decoration and the design of altars and sarcophagi. Due to the relatively poor state of preservation of most senatorial tombs, we know relatively little about their wall and floor decoration, but some general trends clearly emerge. First, narrative mythological images seem to be even scarcer than they are among the sub-elite.[119]

The tomb of C. Valerius Paullinus is an early and rare exception, in that the underground chamber is lavishly decorated, and this decoration is executed in painting and stucco rather than marble incrustation

---

[116] *NSc* (1948), 143–8 (B. M. Felletti Maj). Generally: *MNR* I,2 (1981) 20–3 no. 16 (= Inv. 124540 (L. de Lachenal)); 26–7 no. 18 (= Inv. 124539 (L. Nista)). On the dates see Goette, *Togadarstellungen*, 77–8 no. M 56. I am grateful to Jane Fejfer for this reference (cf. Fejfer, *Roman Portraits*, 110 pls. 10–11). Whether the seated statue of a patrician magistrate from Velletri comes from a tomb, as Goette (*Togadarstellungen*, 78 at no. M 72) assumes (following Leunissen, 'Statuen', 68–9), and, if so, whether it stood in front of the tomb, can no longer be established due to the lack of any report on the circumstances of its discovery.

[117] *MNR* I,8 (1985) 170–7 no. iv,3 inv. 121509 (P. Pensabene); cf. n. 52 above.

[118] E.g. *CIL* 6.1387, p. 4690, for L. Stertinius Quintilianus Acilius Strabo (Feraudi-Gruénais, 'Ewigkeit', no. 66: shortly after 161/62). From the third century: *CIL* 6.1368, p. 3141; *CIL* 6.1345 for Antonius Fronto Salvianus; *CIL* 6.1368 for Servius Calpurnius Dexter (cf. Camodeca, 'Curatores', 225–8). And possibly from the second or third century: Faßbender, *Untersuchungen*, nos. 12, 268 and 845. The habit of displaying statues outside of a tomb or in its façade was, of course, not limited to the elite.

[119] For a general overview of known interior decorations, see Feraudi-Gruénais (*Innendekoration*, passim), who plausibly suspects that the elite may have preferred marble incrustation instead (ibid., 215).

(Figures 1.2–1.4). The vestibule was redecorated in the third century and thus should not concern us here. In the main chamber, the floor around the sarcophagus was laid out with a relatively simple black-and-white geometric mosaic, but the walls and vault were all the more vibrant for that. The walls were covered in a rich yellow and, above a protruding cornice with dentils and a plain white frieze, the cross vault and lunettes were decorated in colourful stucco and painting.[120] Four mythological narratives feature on the vault and depict the Judgement of Paris; a unique image of Admetus with his lion and boar-driven chariot winning the hand of Alcestis from Pelias, with Diana and Apollo watching; Priam before Achilles; and another unique image: Artemis, Athena and Dionysus listening to Hercules playing a large lyre while another, smaller seated figure is playing the double *aulos*. Although the meaning of the fourth panel is not entirely clear,[121] the three other narratives are chosen from a well-known heroic repertoire. They have no obvious connection to death or a vision of the afterlife, but heighten the tone by their reference to epic poetry and revolve around the deeds of great heroes of old.[122] Other figures include centaurs fighting wild beasts and various images with religious or Dionysiac connotations: male and female dancers, a wide range of Dionysiac personnel, as well as swans, griffons, sphinxes, Jupiter Ammon heads and so on. Eight sacro-idyllic landscape paintings oscillate between notions of *pietas* and *locus amoenus*. Stucco

[120] On the interior decoration, see Petersen, 'Secondo sepolcro'; *Monumenti inediti* 6, 1861, pls. 49–53; Wadsworth, 'Stucco reliefs', 73–8 pls. 25–35; Mielsch, *Stuckreliefs*, 171–2 K 115 pl. 82; and *Wandmalerei*, 189, 202–3 figs. 226, 243; Feraudi-Gruénais, *Innendekoration*, 108–14 no. K 48 figs. 109–19, and references to the tomb throughout; Newby, Greek Myths, 255–8. Following Mielsch, the latter two authors date the tomb and its decoration to the middle or second half of the second century. Yet the mosaics in the upper structures are clearly secondary; the style of the decoration has close parallels in much earlier examples, including the Domus Aurea, where the same colour scheme also appears in several ceilings, while the second-century tombs underneath St Peter's differ both in colour scheme and overall design patterns. For a Flavian date cf. Filippi (ed.), *Archeologia e giubileo*, 290, 292. For the Domus Aurea, see Meyboom and Moormann, *Decorazioni*. For the tombs under St Peter's, see Mielsch and Hesberg, *Mausoleen A–D* and *Mausoleen E–I*.

[121] Petersen ('Secondo sepolcro', 231) thinks that the scene must show an otherwise unattested contest between Hercules and the second figure, at which the divinities serve as judges. However, as he observes himself, the two perform at the same time. He notes the Bacchic features of all male figures and the fact that Hercules frequently appears in Dionysiac company, but also that this makes it even harder to explain the presence of the goddesses (pp. 231–3). Most scholars now identify the seated figure as a satyr, so that the three figures on the right make a Dionysiac group, but the presence of Diana and Athena remains unexplained.

[122] Significantly, the scene of Priam's ransom does not show Hector's body and really looks like a supplication. Petersen ('Secondo sepolcro', 233–7) ponders the possibility of some eschatological meanings of the scenes, none of which is convincing.

female figures representing the four seasons support the cross-vault at its corners. They hint at the abundance of nature and add a cosmic dimension, but also allude to the eternity of life with its perpetual seasonal cycle, of which the tomb's patrons are also part.[123]

The lunettes feature three filigree *aediculae* reminiscent of the fourth Pompeian style, each with a single figure at its centre, except for the entrance side, where only two *aediculae* are framing a window above the door. Opposite the entrance, and the first image to face the viewer, is a winged archaistic Victory with shield and shouldering a huge palm branch. She is flanked by a bearded Dionysus on the left, representing a life of abundance and joy,[124] and on the right with his cithara Apollo, the multifaceted deity who was intricately connected with war and victory.[125] Two tritons with *aplusta* (ornaments from ships' sterns taken as war spoils) above the panels equally originate in Augustan victory imagery.[126] Tritons appear again above the entrance, where the side panels show Mercury and a young nude Dionysus with a *thyrsos*. One could read both gods as symbolising the comfortable and prosperous life resulting from victory, and even wonder how widespread was the appreciation of Mercury by Horace who, in his *Odes*, makes Mercury, and not Apollo, Rome's (and his own) saviour; who claims that he disguised himself as Augustus; and who also presents Mercury as

---

[123] For the symbolism, see Hanfmann, *Season Sarcophagus*. Müller (*Peleus and Thetis Sarcophagus*, 51–64) is too pessimistic when he thinks that the message comes down to saying 'You are part of the cosmos, and therefore mortal' (p. 56). Cf. Borg, *Crisis and Ambition*, 200.

[124] Feraudi-Gruénais (*Innendekoration*, 109) refers to him as a potential Dionysus-Sardanapal. The depiction is no replica of the statue type named after the copy in the Vatican with its enigmatic inscription from the so-called 'Villa of Cato Uticensis' near Monte Porzio (*LIMC* III (1986) 545 no. 37*), but clearly evokes a Dionysus of similar character.

[125] See Zanker, *Power*, 49–53, 63–70, 85–90, and elsewhere, focusing on art and architecture; Miller, 'Apollo's bow and lyre', and *Apollo*, focusing on poetry; Bergmann et al., 'Exciting provocation'. On Apollo's role in Nero's imitation of Augustus' triumphs and his self-fashioning as citharode and actor, see Miller, 'Triumphus'; Champlin, 'Nero, Apollo, and the poets'; Champlin, *Nero*, 112–44; Power, *Kitharôidia*. For Domitian, see Newlands, 'Statius'; Bergmann et al., 'Exciting provocation', 17–19.

[126] Originally, this was the victory at the naval battle at Actium (Zanker, *Power*, 83; cf. Vergil, *Aeneid* 10.207–12, for Aulestes' ship with triton decoration), but the imagery was later employed more generally. Tritons are often found presenting a *clipeus* with portrait; cf. e.g. an architrave fragment in the Capitoline, on which two tritons present the *clipeus* of Faustina Maior. Cf. Fittschen and Zanker, *Kinderbildnisse*, 99–100 cat. 99 pl. 108. Tritons also accompanied the famous Commodus-as-Hercules bust in the Capitoline: Fittschen and Zanker, *Kaiser- und Prinzenbildnisse*, esp. 87–8, where Fittschen proposes that the tritons may have held a *parapetasma* or similar. In this case, Commodus' assimilation to Hercules, and the two Amazons kneeling at the foot of the bust, radiate an air of *virtus* and triumphalism. On sarcophagi, they often oscillate between triumphalism and the carefree joy of a marine *thiasos*. See Brandenburg, 'Meerwesensarkophage', esp. 236–7, on tritons representing the *felicitas* resulting from a general's victories.

another lover of poetry.[127] The stucco reliefs of the left-hand lunette feature the epic heroes Odysseus, Diomedes with the *palladion* and the wounded Philoctetes. Their weapons are visibly displayed or even brandished, so that they become epitomes of heroic warriors. The space equivalent to that of the tritons is filled by two putti with weapons, who reappear in the right-hand lunette, which also shows three male figures. Here, two armed men are flanking a nude figure with a spear, leaning on his raised right leg and resting his other hand on his back. It is not entirely clear who they are, but the cuirassed figures appear to be subordinate to the central one. Petersen suggested that the latter is Achilles, who is flanked by similar warriors in the supplication scene, which would complete the list of four key Homeric heroes on whose participation in and contribution to the Trojan War the Greeks' eventual victory depended.[128] The relief in the centre of the vault was damaged when the excavators tried to remove an iron device from which one of the nine lamps that illuminated the chamber could be suspended. It showed an eagle with Jupiter's thunderbolt carrying to heaven a draped male figure wearing sandals (Figure 1.4). The latter is usually thought to be Jupiter himself, or potentially the consul,[129] but the image is also strikingly similar to the apotheosis of Homer on the Herculaneum silver calathus, and of a similar poet on the terra sigillata mould in Schloss Fasanerie.[130] Given the Homeric themes in the surrounding panels, the apotheosis of Homer cannot be excluded as a subject either.

There is no stringent programme of images according to which the decoration may have been chosen and should be read, but core ideas emerge. There are the heroic figures and their deeds, mostly – albeit not exclusively – linked to the most famous of wars, the Trojan, and the most venerated of poets, Homer. They link into the victory theme that is encapsulated in the figure of Victoria in a key location, symbolised by the Tritons on the lunettes and implied by the Achilles panel on the vault that so much resembles contemporary

---

[127] On Horace, see Miller, *Apollo*, 44–53. For an early imperial prince depicted as Mercury, probably in an imperial residence, see Hallett, *Roman Nude*, 175–6 fig. 99. Mercury can also act as *psychopompos* (leader of the souls into the underworld), but there is no hint at this role in the images from the tomb.

[128] Petersen, 'Secondo sepolcro', 241–2.

[129] Consul: ibid., 202–4, and F. Montella in *LTURS* III (2005), 166. Jupiter: Wadsworth, 'Stucco reliefs', 73 with pl. 25; Mielsch, *Stuckreliefs*, 171; Feraudi-Gruénais, *Innendekoration*, 109. If the image did depict Paulinus, he would have been fully assimilated to Jupiter, since the figure is clearly wearing sandals, not Roman shoes. For further discussion of the image, see Chapter 4.

[130] Calathus: Naples, Mus. Nat. Arch. 25301; Pannuti, 'Apoteosi', with bibl.; Lang, *Wissen*, 113, 189 pl. 43 fig. 261. Terra sigillata: Möbius, *Alexandria und Rom*, 25–6 pls. 7.3–4; Pannuti, 'Apoteosi', 47.

supplication scenes. Feraudi-Gruénais noted the similarity of themes between the stuccos and the two Hoby cups, which are likely to have belonged originally to C. Silius A. Caecina Largus, governor of Germania Superior 14–21 CE, and depict Philoctetes and Priam's supplication before Achilles.[131] While more recent scholarship has dismissed the idea that Achilles has been given the features of Augustus or Tiberius, his head looks quite unlike most other representations of the hero and is very Julio-Claudian indeed. An intended comparison between the emperor and the hero is generally acknowledged. We may therefore assume that Paullinus was thinking along similar lines.[132] The rest of the decoration relates to *pietas* and the veneration of the gods, as well as to a lifestyle marked by joy and abundance.

The only other likely senatorial tomb with preserved figure decoration is the Servilii tomb on the other side of the road, although it lacks any narrative images. Here, the lunettes and ceiling vault of the main burial chamber were decorated with delicate stucco, this time kept in a pristine monochrome white (Figure 1.6).[133] The lunette at the back is covered with elegant tendrils inhabited by leisurely seated nymphs. A central rectangular field shows three female dancers connected by a garland. Whether they are the Horai or the Graces,[134] they radiate an air of playful innocence and festive occasion. On the top frame, an almost heraldic image sets a different tone. In the centre, an archaistic, veiled deity flanked by griffons holds unidentifiable objects in her outstretched hands.[135] The vault is covered by a system of framed, rectangular and round fields that are mostly filled with further tendrils and stylised flowers as well as putti. The half-circles along the long walls depict swans, the birds of Apollo, while six of the round fields feature satyrs and maenads, the entourage of Dionysus. The other *tondi* depict nereids riding on various sea monsters and carrying musical instruments or *thyrsoi*, thus linking their world to that of Dionysus. The figure in the

---

[131] Feraudi-Gruénais, *Innendekoration*, 200. Ownership is suggested by inscriptions on the cups and their date. For the cups, see Gabelmann (*Tribunalszenen*, 142–7), who equally makes the connection between the stucco and the cup and cites further comparisons. See also Müller, 'Bildprogramm'; Marvin, *Language of the Muses*, 183–6 with n. 67 figs. 8.16–18.

[132] Again, as Feraudi-Gruénais (*Innendekoration*, 184, 200) has observed, none of these images is typically funerary, and they are normally found in domestic contexts.

[133] Petersen, 'Sepolcro'; Wadsworth, 'Stucco reliefs', 69–72 pls. 22–4; Filippi (ed.), *Archeologia e giubileo*, 289; Feraudi-Gruénais, *Innendekoration*, 105 no. K 47; *LTURS* 3 (2005) 168 s.v. Latina via (F. Montella).

[134] Petersen ('Sepolcro', 413) thinks they are Horai; Feraudi-Gruénais (*Innendekoration*, 105) thinks they are Graces.

[135] Petersen ('Sepolcro', 413–14) thinks of Diana or Hecate; Feraudi-Gruénais (*Innendekoration*, 105) prefers Diana.

central *tondo* (Figure 1.7) much resembles the nereid entourage around her, but on closer inspection turns out to be heavily veiled and riding on a griffon. Hairstyle and dress make it clear that we are looking here at a woman, and she can only be a female member of the patron family.[136] Her presence also explains the choice of image decoration of the tomb, where the themes of heroism and victory that dominated Paullinus' tomb, and that we will encounter on senatorial altars and sarcophagi as well, are absent except for a pair of putti on the vault above the entrance corridor, who are presenting a shield. This is also consistent with the fact that the six *tondi* with satyrs and maenads are relegated to the margins of the vault, substantially outnumbered by the nineteen nereids. Sarcophagi with marine *thiasoi* were predominantly, though not exclusively, dedicated to women, showing that the subject was considered particularly suitable to them.[137] We may therefore conclude that a female death has instigated the building of the tomb and determined its decoration, even though there was nothing out of place for her male relatives, who extended the repertoire through their sarcophagus decoration.[138]

We also need to keep in mind that all the walls and floors were riveted with white marble slabs set off by moulded marble cornices, so that the interior decoration as a whole toned down even further the playful elements of the ceiling imagery. It must have appeared as an expensive but neutral background against which the sarcophagi, most likely with some features enhanced in colour, stood out. Such marble revetment on walls and floors appears to have been typical of temple tombs, as demonstrated by small fragments, clamp holes or the imprints that the slabs left in their plaster. The tomb chamber of L. Plotius Sabinus perhaps equally featured an all-white decoration, although only the white mosaic floor and the white marble covering of the platform for his sarcophagus are mentioned in the excavation reports.[139] The single-storey temple tomb in the Villa of Sette Bassi was covered in marble up to the vault, which in turn was decorated in

---

[136] On this image, see Chapter 4. On the marine *thiasos*, see Zanker and Ewald, *Myths*, 112–29.

[137] If we take not just inscriptions but also portraits as an indication of the primary receiver(s) of the caskets, twenty-seven out of forty (or 67.5 per cent) were set up for women, seven for men and six for couples. This is the clearest gender imbalance of any decorative subject. Cf. Borg, *Crisis and Ambition*, 208.

[138] On which see *infra* 67–8. It is not unusual that the decoration of a tomb takes special account of the first family member to be buried within it. An extreme example is the tomb of the Octavii, who decorated their entire hypogeum with imagery chosen to commemorate their six-year-old daughter's death. See Borg, *Crisis and Ambition*, 65–8, 214–15, with bibl.

[139] Gatti, 'Epigrafe sepolcrale'; Meinecke, *Sarcophagum posuit*, 347–8, with further bibl.

stucco,[140] and the same was probably true for the equally large temple tomb at the entrance to the Villa *ad duas lauros*.[141]

Altars and Sarcophagi

There is a distinct taste for austere monumentality rather than busy orna-mentation in the design of many altars and sarcophagi too, although more exuberant decoration does exist. Most altars only carry an inscrip-tion with a name and, where applicable, the *honores* of the deceased, and the collection of the Licinii altars are representative of the class' tastes as a whole (see Figure 3.6).[142] When they do have additional decoration, it usually consists of garlands carried by *bucrania*, eagles or Victories; that is, elements that radiate an air of religious festiveness as well as power and status. Mythological subjects, sometimes found on sub-elite altars, are entirely absent.[143]

Inscribed Sarcophagi

Similar tastes inform the earliest senatorial sarcophagi. Many of them are characterised by simplicity and monumentality, as is Paullinus' casket (see Figure 1.3),[144] or they feature motifs taken over from public monuments and linked to victory and *pietas*. As I shall discuss further in Chapter 2, the senatorial elite never entirely stopped using marble (and other) sar-cophagi, which mostly featured very simple decoration, if any at all (see Figure 2.4). Plain sarcophagi continued to be used by the elite throughout the second century, as a double sarcophagus from the Licinii-Calpurnii tomb[145] and L. Plotius Sabinus' casket demonstrate. The latter's plain marble sarcophagus, covered with an equally plain lid, stood on top of a 65 cm-high platform that was riveted with white marble and built against the rear wall of the semi-interred lower chamber of his tomb. An inscribed marble slab of 2.18 x 1.15 m was leant against the front of the platform, detailing the *cursus honorum* of the deceased *praetor*.[146]

---

[140] See n. 106 above.
[141] Armellin, *Sepolcro a tempietto*, esp. 94–5 with figs. 2–5 (A. Camilli); cf. at n. 81 above.
[142] Boschung, *Grabaltäre*, 58–9 nos. I 10–18; Østergaard, 'Licinian altars', 46–54; Østergaard and Moltesen, 'Catalogue', 109–11 figs. 35–45; Van Keuren, 'Unpublished documents'.
[143] Cf. Boschung, *Grabaltäre*, 55 with nn. 796 and 797, for a list of senatorial altars.
[144] See n. 38 above.
[145] See Chapter 2 below at n. 56.
[146] Cf. n. 139 above. Cf. *CIL* 6.41111; *PIR²* P517. Sabinus probably died shortly after his praetorship under Antoninus Pius.

Figure 1.16 Sarcophagus of C. Bellicus Natalis Tebonianus, around 100 CE; Pisa, Campo Santo B4 est

The earliest example of an inscribed decorated senatorial coffin from our period is the garland sarcophagus of C. Bellicus Natalis Trebonianus, consul in 87 (Figure 1.16).[147] In the left garland swag, Dionysus is reclining on a rock, an epiphany taking Pan by surprise; in the right one, a Satyr is dancing in front of a *tropaion*. As Herdejürgen has pointed out, these images refer to the Indian Triumph of Dionysus. The story was first modelled on Alexander's return from his Indian campaign and then imitated by Hellenistic rulers, Roman commanders and the Roman triumph. Henning Wrede argued that this idea was indeed the primary association of the theme on sarcophagi too, where it proves to be particularly popular with the elite.[148] It was the only possibility for depicting a triumph in narrative rather than symbols after the real Roman triumph had been monopolised by the emperor.[149]

Ti. Iulius Celsus Polemaeanus, *consul suffectus* in 92 CE, *proconsul Asiae* in 105 or 106, (or his son) opted for a more toned-down version around the same time. His garland sarcophagus has a gabled lid and volutes at the corners like an altar, and victories support the garlands at the casket's corners.[150] Some fifty years later, 28-year-old *tribunus plebis* L. Iulius

---

[147] Herdejürgen, *Stadtrömische und italische Girlandensarkophage*, 79–81 cat. 6 pls. 10.2–3, 11.1, 12; 38 cat. 13 pl. 6.5.

[148] Wrede, *Senatorische Sarkophage*, 39, with reference to Künzl, *Triumph*, 102–5.

[149] On this process, see Eck, 'Emperor', 91–4.

[150] Hueber and Strocka, 'Bibliothek', 483 with fig. 12. On the dates, cf. Strocka, 'Celsusbibliothek'. Cf. *PIR*² J 260; Eck, *Prosopographische Untersuchungen*, 66–8 with n. 75, 99 n. 22.

Figure 1.17 Sarcophagus of L. Iulius Larcius Sabinus, 150–60 CE; Pisa, Camposanto C5 est

Larcius Sabinus boasts in the inscription on a *clipeus* in the centre of his huge double sarcophagus that he was the grandson of the famous Prifernius Paetus consul (Figure 1.17).[151] The *clipeus* is presented by two Victories with *vexilla* (military standards) and supported by a palm tree, against which two captured barbarians are seated. The rest of the front is occupied by a triumphant Dionysus and two centaur-drawn chariots, while the short sides are decorated with a raving *thiasos*. The decoration thus mixes elements of contemporary victory iconographies, as we know them from state monuments, and Dionysus' mythical triumph. In the early Severan period, the *praetor* M. Vibius Liberalis, son of the homonymous consul of 166, was honoured by a sarcophagus decorated all over the front with the god's victorious procession.[152]

In some instances, even women and girls were drawn into this general theme. In the last quarter of the second century, a senatorial girl, Metilia Torquata, received a monumental Attic sarcophagus with Achilles on Skyros on the front and short sides (Figure 1.18).[153] The casket alone is

[151] Turcan, *Représentations dionysiaques*, 36–8 pl. 20a; Matz, *ASR 4.4*, 455–6 no. 260; Arias et al., *Camposanto*, 128–30 no. C 5 est figs. 140–6; Wrede, *Senatorische Sarkophage*, 38; *CIL* 11.1431; *Inscriptiones Italiae* 7.1 72–3 no. 122. Priferinus is either the *consul suffectus* of 146 (*PIR*² P 939) or T. Prifernius T. f. Quir. Paetus Rosianus Geminus, *Proconsul Asiae* in the early years of Antoninus Pius (*PIR*² P 937). Cf. Raepsaet-Charlier, *Prosopographie*, 259–60 no. 290 stemma 49. The casket measures an impressive 2.38 x 1.16 x 1.12 m.

[152] Comstock and Vermeule, *Sculpture in Stone*, 153 no. 244; Wrede, *Senatorische Sarkophage*, 39; Rogge, *ASR 9.1*, 133 cat. 19 pls. 26.2, 30.2, 31, 37.1, 38.3.

[153] Sichtermann and Koch, *Griechische Mythen*, 5–6 no. 1 pls. 1–3; Rogge, *ASR 9.1*, 133 cat. 19 pls. 26.2, 30.2, 31, 37.1, 38.3; Müller, *Peleus and Thetis Sarcophagus*, 106; Wrede, *Senatorische*

Figure 1.18 Sarcophagus of Metilia Torquata, early Antonine, front; Museo Archeologico Nazionale di Napoli inv. 124325

gigantic and the lost roof-like lid added another 60–65 cm of height. It must have been one of the largest sarcophagi ever set up in Rome, not just among those for a girl. Her name is written in carefully carved letters in the upper part of the background of the front relief, similar to Bellicus' inscription. As I explain in greater detail elsewhere,[154] the discovery of Achilles among the daughters of Lycomedes and the hero's playing of music among the girls on the short sides imply that the deceased girl stood out among her peers in terms of both character and education, as Achilles did among the daughters of Lycomedes. The imagery links in with a discourse around *virtus* of women and girls, which in our example is dominating the well-executed back of the chest (Figure 1.19). There, two opulent garlands are supported in the centre by a large eagle, and lion griffons feature in the garland swags. These images, with overtones both of sacrifice, cult and *pietas*, and of power and ambition, would be befitting of any male member of the elite as well.

The total number of inscribed senatorial sarcophagi from the second century is not overwhelming, but the consistency of subjects chosen for their decoration can hardly be coincidental, especially since they only express in

---

Sarkophage, 15 with n. 14. On Metilia Torquata, who was related to, and possibly the daughter of, M. Metilius Aquillius Regulus Nepos Volusius Torquatus Fronto, *cos. ord.* 157, cf. *CIL* 9.658; *PIR²* M 556; Raepsaet-Charlier, *Prosopographie*, 454 no. 549 stemma 27.

[154] Borg, 'No one is immortal', 190–2.

Figure 1.19 Sarcophagus of Metilia Torquata, back; Museo Archeologico Nazionale di Napoli inv. 124325

a symbolic way ideas well known from the imagery of the so-called '*vita romana* sarcophagi',[155] which have long been identified as senatorial, based on their image repertoire and status insignia such as *calcei senatorii* (senatorial shoes).[156]

[155] The term '*vita romana* sarcophagus' has been suggested for those *vita humana* sarcophagi that refer mostly or entirely to the public roles of their subjects: see Reinsberg, *Vita-Romana-Sarkophage*, 15–17.

[156] It is sometimes questioned whether the attribution of these sarcophagi can be based on such indicators (e.g. Zanker and Ewald, *Myths*, 226–7). To be sure, there is both more lenience in the sepulchral sphere than there is in civic public space, and also less control. However, to the extent that these caskets were monuments to the deceased and his family – and this was obviously the whole point of them – their patrons must have considered at least the embarrassment, if not worse, if a resentful neighbour or competitor had noticed the usurpation. As Reinsberg (*Vita-Romana-Sarkophage*, 155 and 172 n. 1517) points out, there is no example in Schäfer's *Imperii insignia* or in Sinn's *Marmorurnen* (on marble urns), in which the *insignia* and actions depicted do not coincide with the offices of their patrons. A sarcophagus lid in Tunis depicting a *lictor* in the magistrate's procession of the equestrian *scriba* is the only exception (Reinsberg, *Vita-Romana-Sarkophage*, 154–6, 234 no. 141 pls. 101.3, 121.3). Yet in North Africa, Rome was far away, and the *lictor* on the lid is rather small. Usurpation of status symbols can never be ruled out completely, but their numbers seem to be negligible and do not render our conclusions on the sarcophagi invalid. Ditto ibid., 154–5 and elsewhere, esp. 172–3 with nn. 1517–18. That patrons did indeed pay attention to the appropriateness of the roles in which they depicted themselves is further demonstrated by a sarcophagus in Florence, where the military scenes were reworked into their civic equivalents (ibid., 22–4, 192–5 no. 12 pls. 1.4, 9.3–4, 10, 11, 12.3–5, 124.3), and by the magistrates' sarcophagi of the third century that equally eliminate military imagery after the senatorial *legati Augusti pro praetore* were replaced by equestrian procurators (Wrede, *Senatorische Sarkophage*, 59–62, 69–76; Reinsberg, *Vita-Romana-Sarkophage*, 162, 177 and 129–69, on the relevant sarcophagi generally; Borg, *Crisis and Ambition*, 182–92).

Vita Romana *Sarcophagi*

Produced from around 160 CE, these sarcophagi depict scenes from the public life of senatorial, often consular, magistrates.[157] On a core group of caskets, the centre is occupied by a general in military gear pouring a libation onto a burning altar and supervising the sacrifice of a bull in front of a temple (e.g. Figure 1.20). On the right-hand side, the same man (at least in many examples), now dressed in the toga and senatorial shoes, shakes hands with his wife in the presence of other figures including Concordia, the personification of concord, in a wedding scene. On the left, the general is depicted again in military costume, standing on a *suggestus* (platform) with the personification of Virtus carrying a *vexillum* behind him, while soldiers present to him supplicating barbarians. The victorious battle is indicated either by Victory herself or by an abbreviated battle scene at the far left of the relief.

Since Gerhard Rodenwaldt's groundbreaking article of 1935, these scenes have been read as representations of the Roman 'cardinal virtues', also inscribed on Augustus' *clupeus virtutis* – *virtus, clementia, pietas* and *concordia* – since their iconographic schemes were taken over from state monuments and coins advertising these very virtues.[158] Henning Wrede was the first to demonstrate in detail that such a reading is too reductionist, and that the reliefs also refer to paradigmatic roles that senators adopted over the course of their lives. More specifically, they characterise senators as *viri militares* and provincial governors.[159] While this is now generally accepted, it is important to note that the episodes 'reflect the life of the metropolitan political elite … not as individual biographies but in normative and prestigious sequences that express social status and moral values', as Carola Reinsberg rightly insists.[160] Susanne Muth has added further clarification by pointing out that the reliefs illustrate the governor's accomplishments in the three key areas of elite life and responsibility: the family, the state

---

[157] Key publications include Rodenwaldt, *Stilwandel*; Reinsberg, 'Senatorensarkophage'; Wrede, *Senatorische Sarkophage*, 21–43, 53–60; Muth, 'Drei statt vier'; Muth, 'Wertediskurs', 268–72; Reinsberg, *Vita-Romana-Sarkophage*, 61–109.

[158] Rodenwaldt, *Stilwandel*.

[159] Wrede, *Senatorische Sarkophage*, 21–43, 53–60.

[160] Reinsberg, *Vita-Romana-Sarkophage*, 170–3, quotation on p. 170. There is no chronological sequence of events, and where a scene of childcare is depicted on a short side or lid, it does not refer to the childhood of the governor but to a key role of his wife. Reinsberg further notes that it is not even certain that each governor actually fought a victorious war, or performed a sacrifice before his *profectio*. The point is that these are activities typically associated with the *office* the governor held. To this extent, the term 'biographical sarcophagi' is misleading. Alföldy ('Individualität und Kollektivnorm') stresses the equally general, paradigmatic character of the *cursus honorum* in inscriptions.

and the gods.[161] Wrede had already suggested that the left part of the reliefs shows not two separate scenes that could represent *virtus* and *clementia*, but only one that focuses on *clementia*. However, as Muth argues, *clementia* is an important virtue for an emperor, but is not central to senatorial self-representation. The *submissio* scene on the caskets is also not as straight-forwardly a representation of *clementia* as is often insinuated, since its iconography oscillates between *clementia* and *iustitia*. Its primary interest is not the way the barbarians are treated, but the governor's superior position of power, and his exercising of *imperium*. The fact that the battle scene or figure of Victory was added at all confirms the importance of also including references to the governor's *virtus* and *victoria*, virtues that we have seen to be key messages elsewhere.[162] Muth therefore rightly concludes that the sarcophagi are visualisations of the same achievements that are celebrated by the *imperii insignia* on senatorial tomb façades, and the *cursus honorum* in their *tituli*.[163]

In contrast to the senator's *imperium*, however, the two other main realms where a member of the elite had to excel, the relationship with the gods and with his family, are not achievements as such; rather, the achievement consists in the way the individuals conduct these relationships. True, the capacity of leading a state sacrifice as indicated by the *servi publici* is a career achievement and an honour. Yet the central position and width of the sacrificial scene suggest that *pietas* is indeed a primary message. This becomes particularly obvious where the personification of Pietas or the governor's wife, mimicking Pietas in her *orans* (prayer) pose, also appears in the scene.[164] As Reinsberg has shown, the message is *pietas erga deos* and *erga patriam* in imitation of the emperor on the male part, and *pietas erga familiares* on the female one.[165] In the wedding scene on the right, the personification of Concordia equally speaks for herself,[166] although Muth is surely right to insist that the image is shorthand for 'exemplary marriage' in general.[167] The sarcophagi thus proudly present a whole range

---

[161] Muth, 'Drei statt vier', 266–70; Muth, 'Wertediskurs', 268–72.

[162] Cf. Wrede, *Senatorische Sarkophage*, esp. 24–7, 31–5. Strocka ('Manchinger Silberbecher', 340–8) also stresses that, in both sarcophagus and state reliefs, genuine scenes of *clementia* are rather rare.

[163] Muth, 'Drei statt vier', 269–70 and 'Wertediskurs', 270.

[164] Wrede, *Senatorische Sarkophage*, 29–30; Reinsberg, *Vita-Romana-Sarkophage*, 70–5 on nos. 6 (Pietas), 15, 20 and possibly 76 (wife in the iconography of Pietas).

[165] Reinsberg, *Vita-Romana-Sarkophage*, 70–3. On *pietas* on Roman sarcophagi, see also Borg, 'Ikonographie', 163–6.

[166] Wrede, *Senatorische Sarkophage*, 30–1; Reinsberg, *Vita-Romana-Sarkophage*, 75–85.

[167] Muth, 'Wertediskurs', 272. For the further significance of the wedding scene, see below pp. 56–7.

Figure 1.20 General's sarcophagus, around 170 CE; Mantova, Palazzo Ducale 186

of achievements, related to both offices and *honores* and personal qualities, which increasingly constituted an element in honorific inscriptions
as well.[168] The latter characterise not only the general but also his wife, with
whom he is connected in concord.[169]

The relevance of family is further demonstrated by the childrearing and
teaching scenes on the short sides of some of the sarcophagi,[170] and by an observation that is usually interpreted differently. It has long been noted that on the
Mantova sarcophagus (Figure 1.20), the male protagonist in the sacrifice is a
youth rather than an adult man. Wrede and Reinsberg have interpreted this as
a deliberate hint at the biographical character of the scenes.[171] Yet this is hard
to maintain, not least because such a visual strategy would be without parallel,
and reference to a life course could be made in much easier and more obvious
ways, for instance by showing the protagonists of these caskets consistently at
different stages of their life and in the proper sequence, as a *cursus honorum*
does. On several senatorial sarcophagi of the third century, the inclusion of
different generations and even other adult relatives is beyond any doubt,[172] so

---

[168] Wrede (*Senatorische Sarkophage*, 57) rightly makes this connection, although the focus during
the second century seems to be on some provinces, while the habit becomes more widespread
only in the third century. Cf. Alföldy, 'Individualität und Kollektivnorm', 47–9.

[169] Reinsberg (*Vita-Romana-Sarkophage*) was the first to point out the prominence of messages
related to the female realm on *vita romana* sarcophagi. For the importance of marital concord,
see also the many sub-elite epitaphs claiming that a couple had lived together *sine querella*,
and Treggiari, *Roman Marriage*, 251–3.

[170] Wrede, *Senatorische Sarkophage*, 51 with pls. 3.3, 6.1, 14.1. Cf. Reinsberg, *Vita-Romana-
Sarkophage*, 99–104 with nos. 12, 29, 61, 85.

[171] Wrede (*Senatorische Sarkophage*, 57–9) rightly stresses that this is not the same as an
individual biographical sequence. Reinsberg (*Vita-Romana-Sarkophage*, 69) calls the
phenomenon an abstract reference to the deceased's life cycle. On the sarcophagus in
Mantova, see ibid., 202 no. 33 pls. 1.2, 4, 5.1–2, 8.2–3, 14.4, 51.1, 124.1.

[172] Borg, *Crisis and Ambition*, 204–5. See also the Achilles sarcophagus below, at n. 181 and
Figure 1.26.

we should not be surprised to find multiple commemorations in the second century as well. The young man in the sacrifice scene on the sarcophagus in Mantova is therefore likely to be the governor's son, not his younger self.

This is consistent with the ideological importance of senatorial families in general, which will be discussed more fully in Chapter 3. Here, it is worth noting that from Hadrian onwards, and increasingly from the Antonine period, the wives and children of senators are designated as *pueri clarissimi*, or *feminae* and *puellae clarissimae*, thus making explicit the status consciousness of the entire family, which matches the inclusiveness of the sarcophagus imagery.[173] In their epitaphs, women and the prematurely deceased are often explicitly associated with their fathers or husbands *as office holders*, when they did not and could not hold any office themselves.[174] Similarly, on the caskets, the governor's entire family is associated with the honour entailed in his *imperium*, while the exemplary conduct of his entire household reflects back on him, and the sarcophagi become monuments to the whole family.

Other sarcophagi stress military achievements even more strongly. Starting in the 160s and continuing until the turn of the third century, about twenty sarcophagi committed the entire front of the casket to the representation of a battle against barbarians.[175] The first group is very much influenced by Hellenistic battle scenes and presents the fight in sets of duels. However, a second group resembles the mass battles of Roman state reliefs such as the Column of Marcus (e.g. Figure 1.21). In both groups, the themes of *virtus* and victory is all too clear, and is further indicated by Victories, *tropaia* and captives framing the image at the corners of the caskets. In the second group, the barbarians are presented as hopelessly inferior to their opponents, who are now clearly marked as Romans. The general in command can be identified among the crowd and occupies the centre of the scene, sometimes fitted out with the features of the deceased. Again, his *imperium* is prominently presented, in addition to his *virtus* and *victoria*. On several sarcophagi, this theme is picked up again on the short sides or on the lid by supplication scenes similar to those on the sarcophagi just discussed. The famous Portonaccio battle sarcophagus is perhaps best suited to demonstrate the link between battle sarcophagi and the governor

---

[173]   Wrede, *Senatorische Sarkophage*, 57. Cf. on these titles, Raepsaet-Charlier, *Prosopographie*, 7–12.

[174]   Alföldy, 'Individualität und Kollektivnorm', 39–40, 46–7.

[175]   Andreae, *Schlachtsarkophage*; Schäfer, 'Schlachtsarkophag'; Koch and Sichtermann, *Römische Sarkophage*, 90–2 figs. 73–8; Wrede, *Senatorische Sarkophage*, 22, 32, 40; Muth, 'Wertediskurs', 272–3; Faust, *Schlachtenbilder*, 177–212.

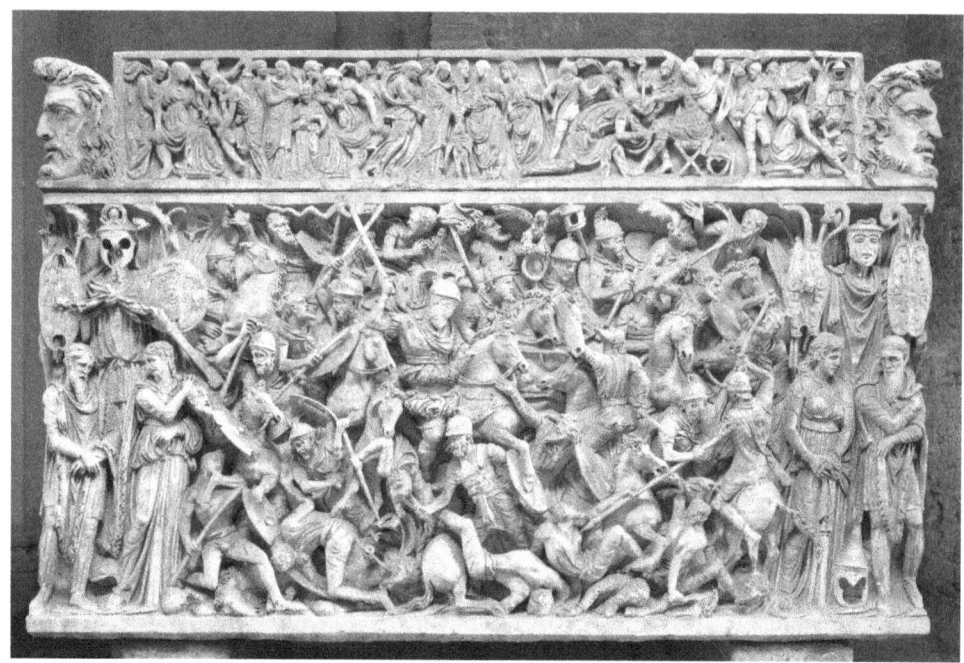

Figure 1.21 Portonaccio battle sarcophagus, late Antonine; Rome, Museo Nazionale delle Terme inv. 240, front

sarcophagi with multiple scenes (Figures 1.21–1.23).[176] On its lid, we find a *submissio* scene at the right end with the provincial governor sitting on the *sella castrensis*, which indicates the general's rank and status. Luisa Musso's suggestion, based on the standards depicted, that the casket may have belonged to A. Iulius Pompilius, a decorated general of senatorial descent under Marcus Aurelius and consul, is not beyond doubt, but is possible and plausible.[177] The centre and left parts refer to the more civilian aspects of his and his wife's life by depicting the familiar wedding-*concordia* scene and those of childcare and education. It is therefore no surprise that fragments of a very similar battle sarcophagus were found in the debris of M. Nonius Macrinus' tomb, and are highly likely to belong to the senator himself (Figure 1.24).[178] This unique case where we can put a concrete name to a *vita romana* sarcophagus supports Wrede's suggestion that the Antonine

---

[176] *MNR* I,8,1 (1985) 177–88 no. iv,4 (L. Musso); Wrede, *Senatorische Sarkophage*, pl. 6.1, and index for references; Reinsberg, *Vita-Romana-Sarkophage*, 217–18 no. 85 pls. 8.4–5, 13.3, 14.3–4, 26.7–8, 126.5; Faust, *Schlachtenbilder*, 197–202 pls. 77–8.

[177] See previous note; similarly Faust, *Schlachtenbilder*, 207–8.

[178] Chiocci and Zaccagnini, 'Mausoleo C', 230; De Cristofaro, 'Monumento funerario', 270–4 figs. 21–3, 25, 26a.

Figure 1.23 Portonaccio battle sarcophagus, Rome, Museo Nazionale delle Terme inv. 240, right short side

Figure 1.22 Portonaccio battle sarcophagus, Rome, Museo Nazionale delle Terme inv. 240, left short side

51

Figure 1.24 Fragments of the battle sarcophagus of M. Nonius Macrinus, mid-Antonine

vita romana sarcophagi with their strong focus on military offices may in fact all, or predominantly, have belonged to the *comitatus* (circle of close, particularly trusted companions) of Marcus Aurelius and his successors, as Macrinus was both *comes* and *amicus* of this emperor, according to his *titulus*.[179]

The imagery on a late Antonine sarcophagus in the Vatican, in comparison, is limited to the submission scene (Figure 1.25).[180] The governor is sitting on an elaborate throne-like seat on a platform, while Roman soldiers bring forward captured barbarians. Victory and triumph are indicated by *tropaia* at the corners of the casket, and by the personification of Victoria carrying a palm in her left hand and crowning the general with a wreath, an element that is strongly reminiscent of the same action in imperial scenes of triumph, and may even indicate that the deceased considered himself deserving of this honour. A unique sarcophagus from about a decade or two earlier is superficially similar, but actually shows the imminent slaughtering of barbarians on the order of the seated commander, who in this case is

---

[179] Wrede, *Senatorische Sarkophage*, 36–43. Macrinus' tomb had not yet been found at the time of his writing.

[180] Reinsberg, *Vita-Romana-Sarkophage*, 90–1, 236–7 no. 152 pls. 25.1–2, 25.4, 26.1–5, 27.1–2. A fragment with a similar scene may have belonged to a second example. See ibid., 90 n. 696; 223 no. 108 pl. 24.2.

Figure 1.25 Late Antonine sarcophagus with submission scene; Rome, Musei Vaticani, Cortile del Belvedere 39

Figure 1.26 Mid-Antonine sarcophagus showing captive Trojans before Achilles; Rome, Museo Nazionale Romano inv. 39400

clearly a mythical figure (Figure 1.26).[181] This youthful nude hero sitting on a rock has long been identified as Neoptolemos, but Volker Michael Strocka has recently demonstrated that he is in fact Achilles ordering the killing of Trojans in revenge for Patroclus' death.[182] In contrast to the hero in the scene of Priam's supplication on the stucco relief in Valerius Paullinus' tomb, here Achilles is fitted out with portrait features, which makes explicit the role of the mythical scene as an exemplum for the deceased. A mature man with portrait head, similar hairstyle but bearded and dressed in military

---

[181] Rome, Museo Nazionale Romano inv. 39400: *MNR* I.8.1 (1985), 273–9 no. vi7 (L. Musso). See Reinsberg, *Vita-Romana-Sarkophage*, esp. 68–7.

[182] Strocka, 'Manchinger Silberbecher', esp. 333–5 with fig. 7.

costume features on the lid. Whether Achilles is meant to have assumed this general's features – somewhat oddly making the latter decades younger and beardless – or whether the sarcophagus was set up for father and son, perhaps transferring the idea of *imperium* into the mythical realm because of the son's premature death, is now hard to tell.[183]

Yet another group of *vita humana* sarcophagi focuses on the ceremonial scenes of sacrifice and marriage, which are also often merged.[184] The couple is depicted either in *dextrarum iunctio* or sacrificing over a portable altar (*foculus*) between them, embraced by Concordia in the background and often with Hymenaeus in the foreground. Various figures including Fortuna and other personifications bring presents, cornucopia, garlands, fruit and similar objects symbolising fortune, fertility and abundance. The bride's head is always covered for the occasion, and sometimes she is heavily veiled to specify her chastity and modesty. Yet Venus herself encourages her to the marriage and indicates her (invisible) beauty and desirability.

A modern viewer may read these reliefs as images of more private aspects of their patrons' lives, and to the extent that they refrain from depicting activities related to public office, this is correct. However, the figures that often surround the couple already indicate that more is at stake here. On at least two sarcophagi, Victory is crowning the bridegroom with a wreath.[185] On an early casket in the Vatican (Figure 1.27), the Genius Senatus is sitting on a *sella curulis* at the right margin of the relief, and Roma (or Minerva) herself is crowning the bridegroom with a jewelled wreath, probably the *praetoricia corona* that distinguishes *praetores* at the opening ceremony (*pompa circensis*) of the games held under their leadership.[186] One

---

[183] The portrait features of Achilles are not normally recognised, but seem clear on autopsy and in the close-up in *NSc* (1908), fig. 11 (D. Vagieri). Only one skeleton was found in the casket, but a second burial may have been intended, or the imagery was intended to reflect on the family rather than only on the individual buried. See Gabelmann, *Tribunalszenen*, 148–50, and more recently especially Strocka, 'Manchinger Silberbecher', for iconographical parallels.

[184] Reinsberg, 'Hochzeitsopfer'; Wrede, *Senatorische Sarkophage*, 43–50; Reinsberg, *Vita-Romana-Sarkophage*, 39–44, 109–23.

[185] Reinsberg, *Vita-Romana-Sarkophage*, 122 and nos. 137 and 153. Victoria here occupies an analogous position to Venus.

[186] Wrede, *Senatorische Sarkophage*, 47–8; esp. Reinsberg, *Vita-Romana-Sarkophage*, 109–15, 238–9 no. 156 pls. 52, 53.1, 3–4, 126.1. In this case, neither the bridegroom nor the bearded figure wears *calcei senatorii*. However, this is not sufficient proof that the iconography was appropriated by a non-senatorial couple (thus e.g. Wrede). We know that people of high status, and even the emperor, are not always depicted with the full range of status symbols to which they were entitled, so that there is no need to assume a 'usurpation'. Moreover, the feet of the Genius Senatus have been reworked in the modern period, and the same could be true for the deceased. The status of the deceased is further supported by the *lictor* in the sacrificial procession on the left, and the details of the iconography, as Reinsberg shows, are most likely meant to characterise a *praetor*.

Figure 1.27 Sarcophagus with sacrificial scene, around 160–70 CE; Vatican City, Musei Vaticani, Mus. Pio Clementino, Sala delle Muse inv. 268

sarcophagus juxtaposes the husband in the sacrifice with the personification of Pietas herself; the figure of Honos refers to the honour he has acquired in his public office, and Fortuna is both the prerequisite for all this success and the personification of the abundance and welfare resulting from the magistrate's exemplary conduct.[187] On four sarcophagi, a bull is being led towards the couple by *servi publici*, indicating that the husband held an office that entitled him to a public sacrifice.[188] On the item in St Petersburg, the Fates and the Capitoline Triad are depicted on the lid, flanked by Helios and Selene in their chariots. The governor sarcophagus in Mantova has a similar lid, featuring the Castores[189] and Fortuna instead of the Fates. This seems to be the more popular version, which appears on four further lids as well. One belongs to a casket depicting a wedding scene on the right and the sacrifice of a ram in the rest of the relief; three are isolated pieces. While the Fates surely refer directly to the deceased's destiny, the other figures link the sarcophagus patrons to the state and cosmos, and present them as members of a loyal Roman elite.[190]

   Given the context for which these images were created, such elements with their close relation to the Roman state may surprise a modern viewer, but in fact they only help to stress further the public relevance of sacrifice and marriage.[191] A long and ongoing debate revolves around the public sacrifice. Its proximity to, and even amalgamation with, the wedding scene

---

[187] Reinsberg, *Vita-Romana-Sarkophage*, 126–9, 224–5 no. 113 pls. 51.6, 63.2, 64–6, 67.6–5, 124.8.
[188] Ibid., nos. 70, 137, 153, 156.
[189] On their significance, see at n. 223 below.
[190] Reinsberg, *Vita-Romana-Sarkophage*, nos. 137 (St Petersburg), 33 (Mantova), 113 (sacrifice and wedding; Rome, S. Lorenzo flm), 95, 154, 155.
[191] Wrede, *Senatorische Sarkophage*, 45–50.

could suggest that it was closely connected with weddings in reality. The written sources, however, make no mention of animal sacrifices in this context.[192] Wrede considers the possibility that senatorial wedding sacrifices had the character of *vota publica*, since they were carried out in honour of the emperor and Roma Aeterna.[193] Yet there is no evidence for such *vota* of private individuals, neither in the written sources nor in images, and for two sarcophagi Wrede himself considers the depiction to be of two separate events. Fortunatelli and Reinsberg suggested that the sacrifice could designate the yearly celebration of Hercules Invictus led by the *praetor urbanus*, which would link the deceased once more with victory and identify him at the same time as a praetorian magistrate.[194] Be this as it may, the point of the sacrifice was twofold. It demonstrated the husband's *pietas erga deos*, and thus his commitment to the welfare of the state; and it identified him as someone in a position to implement the public sacrifice of a bull, and thus his status and public role, which are sometimes further indicated by senatorial shoes and a *lictor*.[195]

Similarly, there is also more to the wedding-*concordia* element than meets the eye. Until the Antonine period, *concordia* in marriage was a virtue primarily connected with and praised in women, and mainly restricted to the private sphere.[196] This changed with the wedding of Marcus Aurelius and Faustina Minor, which was celebrated on coins under the heading *concordia*. As the future emperor's image on the avers makes clear, concord had now become a virtue of the bridegroom as well, and the harmonious relationship of the couple had become a guarantor of the dynasty's persistence and the welfare of the state. Moreover, the new ideology was incorporated into the imperial cult. Bridal couples had to sacrifice in front of statues of Antoninus Pius and Diva Faustina, and later the silver statues of Marcus Aurelius and Faustina Minor in the Temple of Venus and Roma, to foster the persistence of the *Concordia Augusti*.[197] With this shift, the *dextrarum iunctio*, which

---

[192] This and other problems were first pointed out by Reinsberg ('Hochzeitsopfer') and are now widely accepted. Cf. Reinsberg, *Vita-Romana-Sarkophage*, 118–23.

[193] Wrede, *Senatorische Sarkophage*, 48–9.

[194] Fortunatelli, 'Nobilitas', followed by Reinsberg, *Vita-Romana-Sarkophage*, 118–23, revising her earlier view from 'Hochzeitsopfer'. Following Hölscher ('Geschichtsauffassung', esp. 313), Reinsberg further argues convincingly (pp. 69, 73) that the public sacrifice, while surely relating to real events, must not necessarily have been a realistic element of the wedding, but could be, and was, used as an attribute to characterise the sarcophagus' patron.

[195] Wrede, *Senatorische Sarkophage*, 45–6.

[196] Reinsberg, *Vita-Romana-Sarkophage*, 83–4. Important previous studies of this iconography include Reekmans, 'Dextrarum iunctio'.

[197] Wrede, *Senatorische Sarkophage*, 34–5; Reinsberg, *Vita-Romana-Sarkophage*, 84. Cf. *CIL* 14 Suppl. Ostiense (1930) no. 5326; Strack III (1937) 96; Cass. Dio 71.31.1. On concord in general cf. *LIMC* V (1990) 479–98 s.v. Homonoia/Concordia (T. Hölscher).

used to be an important symbol only for ex-slaves who celebrated their legal marriage as a major achievement after manumission, had become a status-related symbol for the upper classes as well. The iconography of the sarcophagus scenes was modelled on imperial iconography and cult practice, and demonstrated the patrons' loyalty to the emperor as well as their incorporation of the underlying ideas into their own value system.[198]

To these frieze sarcophagi must be added a number of column and strigilated sarcophagi, which display abbreviated versions of sacrifice and weddings in small relief panels.[199] The wedding scene largely follows the iconography as we know it from the friezes, though the figures are often limited to the spouses, Concordia and Hymenaeus. The sacrifice is depicted in various ways. It now regularly integrates the wife, but she can appear either in the same panel as her husband or in a panel of her own; she can be shown as an *orans* with her arms raised in prayer, or else standing next to a burning altar holding a small casket with incense. More often than not, her husband's iconography maintains features of the *sacrificium publicum* and includes military dress. He is wearing either the short tunic and *paludamentum* as on the frieze sarcophagi, or his armour and *parazonium* to point out the *imperium* he had been awarded. Occasionally, the altar is supported by a figure of Victory that adds another aspect familiar from the friezes.[200]

Mythological Sarcophagi and the Calpurnii Tomb

Remarkably, no sarcophagi with mythological subjects except for Dionysiac and one Achilles sarcophagus can be attributed to senatorial patrons by inscriptions, although it is likely that the order did occasionally use other subjects. If we accept the attribution of ten sarcophagi to the tomb of the Licinii and Calpurnii, we gain some further insights into what subjects may have appealed to the *ordo*.

The tomb, which is discussed more fully in Chapter 3, was originally founded by M. Licinius Crassus Frugi, who was killed, with his wife and son, in 47 CE on the order of the emperor. His descendants continued to use the small mausoleum until the early second century, when the tomb was inherited

---

[198] Wrede, *Senatorische Sarkophage*, 34–5, 49. Reinsberg (*Vita-Romana-Sarkophage*, 75–85) points out the particular relevance of the scene to women, whose only other activity on sarcophagi is normally childrearing.

[199] Reinsberg, *Vita-Romana-Sarkophage*, esp. 32–9, 62–4. For these sarcophagi, see also Huskinson, *Strigillated Sarcophagi*, esp. 115–49.

[200] Reinsberg, *Vita-Romana-Sarkophage*, 63–4 on nos. 13 and 138.

by a Calpurnii branch of the family. They abandoned the tradition of cremating their dead and opted for burial in marble sarcophagi, seven of which
were found in a second, later and much larger chamber of about 9.5 x 5 m
(see Figure 3.5). At least two portrait busts of the highest quality were also
displayed, among them the bust of young Lucius Verus, which documented
the loyalty of the family to the imperial court.[201]

The sarcophagi, probably set up along the chamber's walls, range in date
from the 120s or 130s to around 160, when it was decided to place any new
additions in a 'third chamber' that yielded another three sarcophagi dating
between the 170s or 180s and the early third century.[202] The sarcophagi probably represent three generations of the family with their respective *paterfamilias* and his immediate relatives.[203]

A huge plain sarcophagus of 2.25 x 1.25 x 0.95 m, similar to the casket of
P. Paquius Scaeva (see Figure 2.4), appears to have been the earliest piece.[204]
It was carefully divided into two separate compartments by a marble panel,
and was probably dedicated to the *paterfamilias* and his wife who, in
accordance with many of their peers, opted for monumentality rather than
image decoration.

The next in line chronologically are three children's sarcophagi of
smaller size (1.27 to 1.55 m):[205] a Roman garland sarcophagus,[206] a griffon
sarcophagus with cupids riding sea monsters on the lid[207] and a garland

---

[201] Van Keuren, 'Unpublished documents', 75, 91 figs. 25–6; Kragelund et al. (eds.), *Licinian
Tomb*, 114 cat. 36–7 figs. 69–70.

[202] Van Keuren, 'Unpublished documents', 92–101; Kragelund et al. (eds.), *Licinian Tomb*, 111–13
nos. 12–23.

[203] See Chapter 3 pp. 144–6 for details.

[204] *NSc* (1885), 43 (R. Lanciani/L. Borsari). Its current location is unknown and it might not be
preserved. The sarcophagus is usually dated to the first century CE, based on Brandenburg's
assertion that rounded inner small sides fell out of use in the second century (Brandenburg,
'Beginn', 309–10; cf. Kragelund et al. (eds.), *Licinian Tomb*, 111–12 cat. 14; Meinecke,
Sarcophagum posuit, 27–30, 49–53, and elsewhere). However, the sarcophagus of L. Plotius
Sabinus (cf. n. 139 above) had a rounded head end as well, and no further details of the
Calpurnii chest are given. There is, therefore, no reason to doubt that the sarcophagus is
of second-century date (equally Herdejürgen, 'Via Latina', 214 n. 28, considers an early
second-century date).

[205] Children are sometimes buried in larger sarcophagi than necessary to fit their bodies, but
small sarcophagi for an adult are not attested. Cf. Huskinson, *Children's Sarcophagi*, 2; Dimas,
Kindersarkophage, 11–12.

[206] *MNR* I.8, 1 (1985) 211–14 no. iv,14 (M. Sapelli); Herdejürgen, *Stadtrömische und italische
Girlandensarkophage*, 116–18 cat. 60 pls. 45.1, 47.2–3; Kragelund et al. (eds.), *Licinian Tomb*,
112 cat. 15.

[207] Lehmann and Olsen, *Dionysiac Sarcophagi*, 17–18, 45–7 figs. 16–18; Herdejürgen,
Stadtrömische und italische Girlandensarkophage, 116 n. 613; Kragelund et al. (eds.), *Licinian
Tomb*, 112 cat. 18.

sarcophagus imported from Asia Minor with a theatrical mask and two female busts in the swags (Figure 1.28).[208] They are also comparatively austere, their most prominent decoration related to cult and festive occasions. Heavy garlands decorate two of the chests. The griffons flanking incense burners allude to Apollo, and were invested by Augustus with connotations of light and triumph.[209] Yet they also seem to have had connotations of apotheosis, as we can see in the stucco *tondo* from the Valerii tomb on the via Latina (Figure 1.6),[210] and it is surely no coincidence that they decorated the temple tomb of the Flavian dynasty (Templum Gentis Flaviae), the entablature of the peristyle surrounding Trajan's Column and the temple of the deified Antoninus Pius and Faustina Maior.[211]

Other elements refer more directly to victory and status. The lion and boar hunt on the lid of the Roman garland sarcophagus is a serious business carried out by adult men,[212] the garlands on the Asiatic casket are carried by Victories at all four corners and the two portrait busts transfer a familiar element of status representation into relief. Only the Dionysiac masks on the Roman garland sarcophagus, the two cupids riding sea monsters and posing as Mercury and Mars on the short sides and the marine cupid *thiasos* allude to the Dionysiac world in a more playful way. Beyond children's sarcophagi, similar subjects were obviously considered appropriate to be used for the decoration of public monuments as well.[213]

The second group consisted of a full-size sarcophagus showing a Dionysiac *thiasos*,[214] followed by a child's sarcophagus depicting the

[208] Lehmann and Olsen, *Dionysiac Sarcophagi*, with figs. 19–22; Waelkens, *Dokimeion*, 26–7; Ward-Perkins, 'Workshops', 208–9; Herdejürgen, *Stadtrömische und italische Girlandensarkophage*, 116 n. 613; Kragelund et al. (eds.), *Licinian Tomb*, 112 cat. 17.

[209] Sinn, *Marmorurnen*, 74–5. Cf. Matz, *Elefantenwagen*, 756–7; Flagge, *Greif*, 73–5. On pp. 85–6, Flagge feels obliged to interpret the Calpurnii griffon sarcophagus as Dionysiac because of the subject of the other casket. However, she fails to see here the eclectic nature of the imagery, which adds themes and nuances rather than trying to stick to a single subject.

[210] See at n. 136 above, and n. 43 for bibl.

[211] Forum of Trajan: Packer, *Forum*, 445, 345–6 cat. 125 figs. 67, 69–70; Milella, 'Foro di Traiano', 280 figs. 282–3. Temple of Antoninus Pius and Faustina: Flagge, *Greif*, 69 figs. 63–4; n. 115 above for bibl. For a range of further possible symbolisms of griffons, see Simon, 'Greif'.

[212] On the hunt as status symbol, see Raeck, *Mythen*, 61–70; Baumer, 'Jäger'; Muth, 'Wertediskurs', 273; Borg, *Crisis and Ambition*, 180–1.

[213] Cupids feature prominently in the Trajanic friezes of both the exterior and interior of the Temple of Venus Genetrix. On the Forum Iulium: Amici, *Foro di Cesare*; *LTUR* II (1995), 299–306 (C. Morselli); and most recently the contributions to *Scienze dell'antichità. Storia, archeologia, antropologia* 16 (2010), 253–537. On the sculpted panels and frieze: Ulrich, *Temple of Venus Genetrix*, 146–53, 174–9; Floriani Squarciapino, 'Pannelli', for a catalogue of fragments, with additions in Milella, 'Decorazione'.

[214] Matz, *ASR* 4.2, 180–2 no. 73 pls. 81.1, 83, 84.1; *MNR* I8,1 (1985) 262–5 no. vi,3 (L. Musso); Herdejürgen, *Stadtrömische und italische Girlandensarkophage*, 116 n. 613; Kragelund et al.

Figure 1.28 Three children's sarcophagi of the first generation of Calpurnii from their family tomb on via Salaria: a) Rome, Museo Nazionale Romano inv. 441; b) Baltimore, Walters Art Museum inv. 23.35; c) Baltimore, Walters Art Museum inv. 23.29

childhood of Dionysus and a dining scene on the lid,[215] a full-size Leucippidae sarcophagus[216] and a Cupid Race sarcophagus (Figure 1.29).[217] These sarcophagi differ from the earlier group in using mythical images more consistently, and the overall tone has become more emotional. And yet the messages are still related to traditional elite ideology. On the earliest sarcophagus of the series, burning altars and other cult objects refer to cult and celebration, even though the personnel is all Dionysiac, with maenads and satyrs dancing in trance and a drunken Papposilenus supported by another satyr. On the second Dionysiac chest, some iconographic elements of *vita humana* sarcophagi have filtered through to the Dionysiac version of childcare. Like the god, before it died the child in the casket had enjoyed the greatest attention and care from plenty of staff and the most promising conditions.[218] The short sides showing griffons flanking a tripod link back to the griffon sarcophagus of the first group.

The Rape of the Leucippidae and the fatal crash of the cupid's chariot allude to separation and death.[219] Yet the race is also an act of bravery,[220] and the theme of victory and *virtus* dominates the Leucippidae sarcophagus.[221]

(eds.), *Licinian Tomb*, 112 cat. 16; Zanker and Ewald, *Myths*, 133, 134, 137 figs. 120, 124, and pp. 130–9 on Dionysiac imagery in general.

[215] Matz, *ASR 4.3*, 350–1 no. 199; Ward-Perkins, 'Workshops', 223–8 figs. 7, 29–34; Herdejürgen, *Stadtrömische und italische Girlandensarkophage*, 116 n. 613; Kragelund et al. (eds.), *Licinian Tomb*, 112 cat. 19.

[216] Ward-Perkins, 'Workshops', 22, 216–19 fig. 8; Kragelund et al. (eds.), *Licinian Tomb*, 112 cat. 20; Zanker and Ewald, *Myths*, 315–18 no. 10.

[217] Van Keuren, 'Unpublished documents', 77–9); Kragelund et al. (eds.), *Licinian Tomb*, 111 cat. 12. Why it was found in the first chamber rather than in the second is unclear. Stubbe Østergaard ('Licinian sarcophagi', 55–7) tentatively identifies a different sarcophagus as coming from the first chamber, but is ignorant of some of Van Keuren's documents. On the sarcophagus, cf. Schauenburg, *Eroten-Sarkophage*, 65 no. 19 pl. 18.

[218] Dimas, *Kindersarkophage*, 71–4; Huskinson, *Children's Sarcophagi*, 30–1; Zanker and Ewald, *Myths*, 139, 142. For the praise of childcare and upbringing (nurture, *anatrophe*) in *encomia*, see Cameron, 'Young Achilles'.

[219] Robert Turcan in particular has interpreted the circus sarcophagi as a reference to premature death ('Symbolisme', 1716, 1729 and *Messages*, 155–6). On Leucippidae sarcophagi, see Koch and Sichtermann, *Römische Sarkophage*, 157–8. On the term *abreptus* for both rape and death in epitaphs and other texts, and visual representations of rapes as metaphors for death, see e.g. Amedick, 'Achilleus auf Skyros', 56–9; Turcan, *Messages*, 49; Zanker and Ewald, *Myths*, 88–90, 218, 229, 413–18 fig. 79.

[220] Schauenburg (*Eroten-Sarkophage*, 45) also draws attention to a casket where one of the cupids was fitted out with portraits of the deceased child, and another where one cupid is crowned by Victory (cf. ibid., 76 cat. 73 Pl. 30.8; 82 cat. 96). For a similar interpretation as proposed here see Stumpf, 'Cupids', 84; Dimas *Kindersarkophage*, 132–45; Zanker and Ewald, *Myths*, 239–40.

[221] Zanker and Ewald (*Myths*, esp. 316–17) acknowledge allusions to victory, but downplay the theme and largely dismiss the corner and lid reliefs as mere decoration. Other authors only consider the fate of the Leucippidae.

a

b

c

d

Figure 1.29 Four sarcophagi of the second generation of Calpurnii from their family tomb on via Salaria: a) Rome, Museo Nazionale Romano inv. 1303; b) Baltimore, Walters Art Museum inv. 23.32; c) Baltimore, Walters Art Museum inv. 23.33; d) Copenhagen, Ny Carlsberg Glyptotek I.N. 850–851

The duel of two impressive nude warriors on the left and another warrior on the right-hand part of the chest indicate battle and heroic fighting,[222] and the story of the rape clearly has two sides: one was the abduction suffered by the Leucippidae, but the other was the accomplishment of the Castores. In Roman cult and imperial ideology, from their first introduction into the Roman pantheon after assisting the Romans in the battle at Lake Regillus, the Castores had connotations of victory, but also symbolised *fides* and *concordia*, virtues that became guarantors of the continuity and success of the imperial family and of Rome's eternity.[223] Accordingly, they are sometimes depicted on the lids of *vita romana* sarcophagi,[224] and Leucippidae sarcophagi typically have Victories at the corners of the casket. On the Calpurnii sarcophagus, two pairs of Victories killing bulls on the particularly high lid relief are an even stronger image, using an iconography that was widespread in the decoration of imperial public buildings, including the Basilica Ulpia.[225]

The second group of sarcophagi thus repeats the themes we found in the first group, but extends the range to include the contrasting aspects of death and Dionysiac joy. The Dionysiac theme became more prominent, and with the god's childhood and the Rape of the Leucippidae mythical narratives are introduced into the spectrum. It is significant, though, that the Calpurnii did not opt for the far more popular Greek story of the Rape of Persephone, but for a myth with Roman heroes,[226] and for a story that only hints at death ever so slightly, but mainly tells of heroic deeds and victory.

Finally, a group of three sarcophagi was found in the third chamber that has never been fully excavated (Figure 1.30).[227] The first two, a Victory sarcophagus and a piece with the Indian Triumph of Dionysus, are the most imposing pieces from the tomb for both their size and the quality of their craftsmanship. The third one was added in the first decade of the third

---

[222] As Robert (*ASR* 3.2, 221) observes, the Leucippidae were not actually raped during a battle, the battle was a consequence of the rape. The merging of the two events against the traditional narrative is thus a deliberate choice to include a heroic battle.

[223] During the imperial period, several generations of imperial princes were styled as New Castores and the twins were compared to Romulus and Remus. Cf. the contributions in Nista (ed.), *Castores*, esp. Poulsen, 'Ideologia', 91–100 and Cappelli, 129–50.

[224] See at n. 189 above.

[225] Packer, *Forum*, 343–4 figs. 145–6; Milella, 'Foro di Traiano', 203 fig. 271.

[226] Strictly speaking, the Castores as mythical figures originated in Greece. However, they had been appropriated into Roman mytho-history early in the Republic (cf. n. 223 above), and were therefore surely perceived as more Roman than Greek. For the myth of Persephone as primarily an *exemplum mortalitatis*, see Borg, 'No one is immortal'.

[227] Van Keuren, 'Unpublished documents', 92–101; Kragelund et al. (eds.), *Licinian Tomb*, 112–13 cat. 21–3.

a

b

c

Figure 1.30 Three sarcophagi from the third chamber of the Calpurnii family tomb: a) Baltimore, Walters Art Museum inv. 23.31; b) Baltimore, Walters Art Museum inv. 23.36; c) Baltimore, Walters Art Museum inv. 23.37

century.[228] Again, the choice is remarkable and consistent. The motif of victory and triumph is inherent in the sarcophagus with the familiar Indian Triumph of Dionysus.[229] The abundance following victory is expressed through the figure of Dionysus himself, through his entourage and through the fruit-bearing trees and vines in the background. Death is alluded to on the lid, where the death of Selene, Dionysus' mother, is depicted at the left end, but with the adjacent scenes of the god's birth from Zeus's thigh and the child's upbringing among the Nymphs, it is part of a life cycle of death and renewal.

The Victory sarcophagus continues and focusses entirely on the theme of military victory. A head of the Gorgon Medusa features prominently in a *tondo* in the centre of both the casket and the lid, and two further *gorgoneia* fill the garland swags on the short sides. The *tondo* on the casket is presented by two Victories with *vexilla* and supported by a palm tree under which two barbarian prisoners are cowering. On the lid, the *tondo* is presented by cupids, while their peers to left and right are playing with various pieces of armour. Two cupids at the corners of the casket have put down their bows and quivers and present garlands, suggesting – together with the craters overflowing with fruit behind them – the abundance and well-being resulting from victory.

In comparison, the theme of victory is much toned down on the sarcophagus last added to the tomb. As he leans relaxed against a satyr in the centre, Dionysus is still a triumphant figure, but the image is now also a celebration of Ariadne, the sleeping beauty who becomes a paradigm of the deceased buried in the casket.[230]

The choice of subjects, different as they are in all three sarcophagus groups, is remarkably consistent in its recurring themes. In all groups, the idea of ritual, sacrifice and *pietas* prevails, though it becomes less prominent with time. The subject of death, the occasion to which all these caskets owe their existence, is conspicuously marginalised. Dionysiac imagery continues through all groups and gains in prominence over time.[231] It is notable,

[228] For their dates, see Chapter 3 pp. 144–5.
[229] Zanker and Ewald, *Myths*, figs. 131–2 and pp. 329–4 doc. 13.
[230] Sarcophagi with the discovery of Ariadne are usually thought to have commemorated women, since her sleep provides a metaphor for death, and it is only she who occasionally has portrait features (for an overview see Matz, *ASR 4.3*, 360–404). However, as can be seen with the Rape of Persephone, or Selene and Endymion, it cannot be excluded that the subject was also chosen for couples, and potentially even for (young?) men. On gender discrepancies, see Borg, *Crisis and Ambition*, 177, and Borg, 'No one is immortal', 190–3, 194–5.
[231] Lehmann and Olsen (*Dionysiac Sarcophagi*, esp. 20–54) concluded from similar observations and further details that the Calpurnii were deeply devoted to the mystery cult of

however, that it is not the raving of the god's drunken entourage that is being depicted, but a rather well-behaved clique that suggests a carefree life of abundance rather than wild partying. The most prominent theme in all groups is clearly victory and triumph, which is spelt out in great variation through symbols and narrative scenes, and is even found on children's sarcophagi.

Mythological Sarcophagi from the Tomb of the Servilii

The only other metropolitan senatorial tomb with mythological sarcophagi is that of the Servilii, discussed above, if the identification is accepted.[232] In both the open *ala* between the stairs and the main burial chamber, pedestals of equal size were built against the back walls to support a single, exceptionally large marble sarcophagus each.[233] With their sarcophagi, they must have been planned from the start.[234] Two further caskets were set up at the same time or slightly later in the main burial chamber, probably against the two side walls.[235] The sarcophagus in the *ala* was about 1.2 m deep and thus intended for at least two burials, and depicted another Rape of the Leucippidae.[236] In the main chamber, the Labours of Hercules[237] and Achilles on Skyros[238] could be identified with certainty. The third theme was mythological as well, but its subject remains obscure.[239]

The choice of the three known subjects is interesting enough. Two of a total of only ten Leucippidae sarcophagi of which we are aware, all produced within a rather short period of time,[240] belonged to high-ranking senatorial families. Similarly, the subject of Achilles on Skyros, with its overtones of noble descent, heroism and reference to premature death, was popular with the senatorial elite, as the sarcophagus of Metilia Torquata and a third-century example from the Monte del Grano make clear.[241] The

---

Dionysos-Sabazios. Yet the idea that sarcophagus imagery reflects religious ideas has long since been refuted (most notably by Geyer, *Realitätsbezug*; cf. Zanker and Ewald, *Myths*, 143, 145), and funerary texts (both literary and epigraphic) never mention such connections.

[232] Cf. at nn. 42–3 above.

[233] The bases measure 2.64 x 1.44 m. See Herdejürgen, 'Via Latina', 214.

[234] Ibid., 214–15.

[235] Ibid., 215.

[236] Its fragments have been identified by ibid., 217–20, in the Villa Wolkonski.

[237] Robert, *ASR 3.1*, 127 no. 103'; Herdejürgen, 'Via Latina', 216–17.

[238] Robert, *ASR 2*, 220 no. 30' with drawing on p. 230 (= Koch, 'Mythologische Sarkophage' fig. 3); Herdejürgen, 'Via Latina', 215–16. Only a drawing of the largest fragment survives.

[239] Herdejürgen, 'Via Latina', 216.

[240] Koch and Sichtermann, *Römische Sarkophage*, 157–8.

[241] On Metilia Torquata's casket, see n. 153 above. The so-called 'Monte del Grano' is a huge tumulus from the third century, which is likely to have been founded by Alexander Severus.

Labours of Hercules, in contrast, avoid any allusion to death and concen-
trate on images of achievement and triumph against all odds. This was
the main association the Romans made with the hero and god from the
Republican period, when Roman military commanders regarded him as a
guarantor of victory, erected temples to him and set his image on coins.[242]
Various emperors from Caligula and Nero onwards styled themselves as a
New Hercules, even assimilating their portraits to the god. After Trajan,
who promoted Hercules as an exemplum for the idea that power had to be
earned through personal accomplishments rather than birth, he became
a central figure in state cult, ideology and art.[243] Even though the Servilii
most probably furnished their tomb before Commodus came to power,
it is surely no coincidence that this family, which came to be so closely
connected with the emperor who ultimately destroyed them, used the
same imagery and symbolism to refer to their power.[244] Nevertheless, the
key idea had already been formulated by Cicero. Speaking of the ever-
lasting fame of the great men of Rome, such as Brutus, Camillus and the
Scipios, he evokes the exemplum of Hercules to illustrate that 'the body of
a brave and great man is mortal, yet the impulses of the mind and the glory
of virtue are eternal'.[245] In Cicero, Hercules had become a prime Roman
example of someone who achieved immortality through his deeds as a
benefactor to humanity, and who served as a model for Cicero's own con-
ceptualisation of and claims to immortality, and indeed divinity, of the
political and military leaders of his time,[246] an idea that later authors also
adopted.[247]

This is not the place to present the full argument, but for a review of the arguments see
Coarelli, 'L'urbs', 35–7, 39, 56–8; Freestone et al., 'Portland Vase', passim, esp. 94–102; and
LTURS I (2001) 193 s.v. M. Aurelii Severi Alexandri Sepulcrum (119) (Z. Mari). The Achilles
sarcophagus, this time an Attic one (Grassinger, *ASR 12.1*, cat. 21), was used for a couple
depicted on its lid, who must have belonged to the wider family of the emperor. Even if
Severus was not the founder of the tomb, there can hardly be any doubt that it belonged to a
high-status owner.

[242] Ritter, *Hercules*; Levi, *Ercole*.
[243] Derichs, *Herakles*; Hekster, 'Hercules', with bibl.
[244] On Commodus and Hercules see n. 126 above.
[245] Cicero, *Sest.* 143, quoted by Grassinger, 'Virtus', 116. Heracles is also listed by Menander
Rhetor among those heroes to whom an orator delivering a *logos epitaphios* may refer
for comparison (Soffel, *Regeln*, 151; Russell and Wilson, *Menander*, 176–7). Cf. Müller,
Peleus and Thetis Sarcophagus, 109–10 n. 452; Grassinger, 'Virtus', 115; Borg, 'No one is
immortal', 178–9.
[246] Cole, *Cicero*, 20–3, 34, 79, 83–4, 102–9, 136–7, 142–60 and elsewhere.
[247] E.g. Bosworth, 'Augustus', on Vergil and the *Res Gestae*. Cf. Silius Italicus, *Pun.* 15.78–82, also
quoted by Bosworth (p. 6 with n. 36). For a more detailed discussion of claims to immortality
and divinity see Chapter 4 below.

Themes and Senatorial Preferences

The number of sarcophagi that can be identified as senatorial is limited, but not quite as limited as is often insinuated, and an overview reveals a remarkable consistency in the choice of subject and style. Henning Wrede's suggestion that the senatorial elite of the second century preferred images of military achievements and triumph[248] is fully supported by the additional material discussed in this chapter. The most prominent and persistent themes are status-related public activities as well as more abstract notions of power, victory and triumph. These are expressed in various ways: by the eagle of Zeus, by *tropaia*, Roma sitting on a heap of weapons, captured barbarians and Victories; by the victorious commander (Roman governor or mythical hero) engaging in battle, receiving captured barbarians and even killing them; but also by the Triumph of Dionysus, the Labours of Hercules and even the Rape of the Leucippidae or Sabine women. The subject was so important that even sarcophagi for children took up the theme. These virtues and accomplishments had been fundamental to the honour and status of the aristocracy since the Republic, and their visualisation through the same symbols and images that were used by the emperors further demonstrates their ambitions. So far, the sarcophagus imagery conveys the same messages as the *cursus honorum* spelt out in the tomb *tituli* and sometimes in sarcophagus inscriptions.

A second prominent subject is *pietas*. On the garland sarcophagi, this is primarily *pietas erga parentes* and *erga maiores*, towards the deceased and the ancestors, who deserve to be thus honoured by the surviving family and subsequent generations. The rites performed at the tomb assume a permanent state through festoons and cult objects carved out of the marble.[249] Yet the claim to piety may also relate in a more general sense to the patrons' virtue in other contexts, their *pietas erga deos*, and even *erga patriam* or *erga principem*, towards the state and the emperor. This is why the theme could be transferred into the Dionysiac realm and into the public sphere, as it was on the *vita humana* sarcophagi.

Mythological subjects do occur on senatorial sarcophagi, but their range is limited, and the messages are mostly similar to those we find in the non-mythological reliefs. Dionysiac images are particularly prominent.

---

[248] Wrede, *Senatorische Sarkophage*, 38–9 and elsewhere.

[249] Turcan, 'Guirlandes'; Herdejürgen, *Stadtrömische und italische Girlandensarkophage*, 25–6. The latter argues further that the garlands symbolise life after death and apotheosis through *pietas*, but evidence for such beliefs is lacking. Cf. Sinn, *Marmorurnen*, 56; Bielfeldt, *Orestes*, 317.

They, too, share notions of triumph and *pietas*, but extend the message by claiming that both result in welfare and abundance. In the case of the childhood sarcophagi, they refer to the exemplary conditions and care the family's children enjoyed. The late Ariadne sarcophagi add the idea of sleep-like death and a blissful Dionysiac world, but also of female bodily and mental beauty. The only other decidedly Greek myths explored by senatorial families revolve around Achilles' life and deeds. While Achilles is a prime *exemplum mortalitatis* in funerary texts, his death is never depicted. The moment of his discovery and departure from Skyros is known by all ultimately to seal his fate, and to this extent he hints at the occasion for which the relief was created. Yet it is also the moment of his triumph over convenience and his emergence as the greatest of all heroes whose courage is unsurpassed, and who will secure victory over Troy. The unique sarcophagus featuring the hero about to kill captured barbarians (Figure 1.26), uses an iconography known from state reliefs and consular sarcophagi. The other mythical protagonists are Roman in origin or had long since become Roman through tradition and cult. Hercules is another paradigmatic victor, and the Castores are equally heroic figures and paradigms of *virtus*, victory and other noble virtues.

Conclusion

With this chapter, I hope to have demonstrated two things, one methodological and the other historical. First, it will have become clear that context does indeed matter, especially when we take context to refer to the wide range of connections any single object or phenomenon may have. There is obviously the archaeological context. When searching for senatorial sarcophagi and the range of subjects for which the *ordo* opted, it is necessary to include not only inscribed examples, which are rare, but also those that can be attributed to them through their provenance. Secondly, there is the topographical context. When searching for senatorial tombs, it is not sufficient to search for tombs with inscriptions still attached; we need to look, among other things, at location. Thirdly, there is the context of inscriptions and images in relation to the very objects on which they are displayed. The fact that several senatorial *tituli* were inscribed on architraves makes all the difference for identifying temple tombs as a popular, perhaps the most popular, choice for senatorial mausolea of the second century. And fourthly, there is the wider socio-historical context implied in the research question. When our interest in senatorial tombs goes beyond the establishment of facts and we want to gain a better understanding of how the *ordo*'s attitudes to the funerary realm fit in with what else we know about their value system and ideology, we are well advised to look at all the elements that contributed to the overall message conveyed.

My second aim was, of course, to demonstrate that the senatorial elite remained strongly interested in using tombs for the display of their status and achievements, and to illustrate more comprehensively than has been done before what they considered to be relevant in this regard. The single most prominent choice for second-century (and later) senatorial and consular tombs now turns out to be the temple tomb, often with a full marble front, sometimes built entirely from marble, a choice that previous scholarship had primarily linked to pretentious freedmen. I shall argue in Chapter 4 that these tombs imitated the temples of the imperial *divi* and *divae*, a hugely ambitious move that implicitly claims one of the highest, albeit least momentous, imperial honours for the most aspiring members of society. Where we can no longer determine the type of tomb to which senatorial *tituli* belonged, their impressive size still suggests corresponding tomb sizes, and their very existence denotes visibility and an interest in the audience.[250] As the examples discussed in this chapter demonstrate, many senatorial mausolea were neither modest nor removed from sight; they are just poorly preserved, and their typical location near the entrance to the estate or main villa building makes them the foremost embodiment of family pride, a hard-to-miss indication of what their patrons were all about.

To be sure, it is hard to tell to what extent such tombs were common to the *ordo* at large. Werner Eck has drawn attention to Sex. Iulius Frontinus, three-time consul and author of *De aquis urbis Romae*, who, according to Pliny (*Ep.* 9.19), specifically prohibited the erection of any monument to him, as he wanted to win survival in memory through his deeds.[251] As Eck acknowledges (and provided Pliny really referred to a tomb monument

---

[250] Ditto Eck ('Grabgröße', 200), who observes that altars and *tituli* of senators tend to be larger than those of the sub-elite, and Feraudi-Gruénais ('Ewigkeit', 144–5, 147), who remains ambivalent regarding the hypothesis of an introverted attitude to tombs during the period under consideration. Particularly large examples include the *tituli* for the consular historian Tacitus (*c.* 4–4.5 m long: *CIL* 6.41106; Alföldy, 'Schweigen'), Petronius Mamertinus (*CIL* 6.41110, *c.* 3 m long: Feraudi-Gruénais, 'Ewigkeit', no. 60), one of the Quintilii brothers (*c.* 4 m long, from their villa at the fifth mile of the Appia: *CIL* 6.41130; *MNR* I8,2, 468–70 no. viii,91 (B. Pettinau – M. Bertinetti)), an otherwise unknown Baebius (4.17 m long: *CIL* 6.1361 with p. 4686; Filippi, San Paolo fig. 1999 no. 1872) and the enormous, 7 m-long *titulus* for C. Pomponius Bassus Terentianus (*CIL* 6.41195; ibid., no. 80).

[251] Eck, 'Grabmonumente', 169–70. Cf. Champlin, *Final Judgments*, 170. On Frontinus, see also Eck, 'Gestalt'.

here),[252] this was surely an extreme position, of which Pliny also disapproved since he considered the statement actually more conceited than a monument. Whether the apparent simplicity of a few other senatorial tombs can be taken as evidence for a modest attitude of parts of the first order is also not entirely clear. What remains of the family tomb of the Minicii beneath their villa on Monte Mario is indeed relatively moderate, as the underground chamber measured only 4.95 x 3.9 m and does not seem to have been decorated (Figure 2.5).[253] Yet, on the one hand, it is possible that there were more visible features above ground that are now lost,[254] and on the other, we need to take into account the tomb's date, as it is likely to have been founded in the first century, when senatorial tombs tended to be less visible and ostentatious than either before or after. The same argument may explain the even smaller size of the Licinian tomb on the Salaria, although here we have evidence for portrait statues in front of the mausoleum and a very rich interior decoration; the Calpurnii also considerably enlarged the mausoleum around 150. The other aspect to keep in mind is that senators normally only commissioned a mausoleum when they had newly joined the first order. Where a senatorial family tomb already existed, later generations would normally continue to use this venerated monument, even when it may not have matched the latest standards of design and ostentation.[255] If Frontinus was of patrician descent, he would probably have done the same and preferred burial in his ancestral tomb to a monument built specifically for himself.

What, then, was the class proud to show off? Even though the total number of senatorial mausolea whose interior decoration, altars and sarcophagi we can assess is limited, the preferences are so consistent that we can identify general trends and predilections. The predominant message of senatorial tomb *tituli* has long been identified as coinciding with honorific inscriptions set up in a range of other contexts: praise of an – ideally long and distinguished – public career, with important offices that were often advertised further by the display of relevant *insignia*. Statues erected in

---

[252] This is not clear from the text, as Pliny states that Frontinus prohibited 'any monument at all' (*omnino monumentum*) from being set up.

[253] Eck, 'Grabmonumente', 170–1. On the tomb see most recently: Meinecke, *Sarcophagum posuit*, 207–9 no. A10, with bibl., but also see p. 87 below.

[254] Ditto Griesbach, *Villen und Gräber*, 58.

[255] See Chapter 3. This preference for an ancestral tomb over the latest fashion is probably the reason why the Acilii Glabriones on the via Salaria used their tomb over two centuries, even though the remains do not suggest a particularly flashy design (too little is preserved to be entirely certain about this). Cf. Tolotti, *Priscilla*, 135–70; Borg, *Crisis and Ambition*, 98–101, 125–6.

front of these tombs only reinforce this blurring of boundaries, especially since their types – as far as we can tell – mostly coincide with those set up in public places and the houses and villas of the elite. Once the public space in Rome had effectively become unavailable for the self-display of private individuals, they used the domestic and funerary realms instead.

What we can see better now is that inside the tombs too messages predominantly revolved around public office and other activities, virtues and values that demonstrate the entire family's moral superiority in the public and semi-public spheres, which, in turn, was the prime source of honour and status. Inscriptions on cinerary urns or sarcophagi boast about achievement throughout, where the text is not limited to the name alone. Women, children and those who died before they could hold notable offices are often associated with a husband, father or other ancestor who did. Nowhere, however, do we find any of the adjectives that are so familiar from the epitaphs of the lower classes: no *incomparabilis, dulcissima, piissimus* and so on, except for references to a few women and children in the later third century.[256] The tone is all emotional demureness rather than exuberance.

Wall decoration seems to focus on noble and expensive simplicity, and sarcophagi are sometimes chosen for their monumentality rather than artistic finesse.[257] Where they are decorated, their imagery revolves around *pietas*, triumph and victory, and a *vita felix*, three aspects that were intimately and causally linked in imperial ideology too. As has been demonstrated by others, *vita romana* sarcophagi are all about offices and the exemplary conduct of a Roman citizen of status, ideas that are expressed in iconographies borrowed from state reliefs and coins, and non-narrative, symbolic images were also often taken over from public monuments. This desire of the Roman elite to link themselves to the Roman state and its welfare even in

---

[256] The rare cases of epithets in senatorial epitaphs first occur in the second century, and are largely limited to *optimus* (three times), *benemerens* (three times) and *pius* (five times), which is still in line with the ideas we have found expressed elsewhere. Among the 145 epitaphs I have collected, there are only four uses of more affectionate epithets: on the tabula *CIL* 6.41155, a daughter calls her curule father *dulcissimus* (second century); on his sarcophagus, Elagabalus' father is called *amantissimus* by his wife and children (*CIL* 10.6569); on his sarcophagus dating to the later third or very early fourth century, a *puer clarissimus* is called *dulcissimus* (*CIL* 6. 31990); and in another third-century inscription for a *puer clarissimus* the same epithet is used (*CIL* 6.1537). These, representing 9.6 per cent of senatorial epitaphs containing epithets, compare to 49 per cent of all commemorations including an epithet across Nielsen's sample of 3,784 epitaphs from *CIL* 6 (Nielsen, 'Interpreting epithets', 175).

[257] Rolf Michael Schneider rightly pointed out to me that we should also not underestimate the technical skills and amount of labour involved in creating the perfectly smooth surfaces of these caskets.

death may be unexpected to some modern viewers. Yet their achievements in their service to the state and their moral superiority in the public and semi-public spheres are the prime sources of their pride, honour and status; it is these that make them stand out in elite competition. They are the basis for any hopes for survival in the memory of future generations, which was both their most desperate desire and most confident hope or expectation about their fate after death. As we shall see in the final chapter, these were also the most promising factors in securing them an adequate place in the world beyond.

With regard to other sarcophagus decoration, and especially mythological scenes, it is usually assumed, implicitly or explicitly, that all classes drew on the full range of choices. However, my survey of certain and likely senatorial sarcophagi suggests that mythological images were in fact chosen from a rather more limited repertoire. Images from the Dionysiac realm are by far the most popular, arguably because they are particularly well suited to express key traditional values and ideas such as *pietas*, victory and triumph, and the *felicitas temporum* resulting from all three. The subject of death, however, is largely absent from senatorial sarcophagi and addressed only indirectly, through abduction and sleep, in exceptional cases.[258] This is consistent with the absence of death also in senatorial funerary inscriptions, which typically lack the dedication to the *dii manes*, especially when commemorating men.[259] The senatorial tomb is a place not for lament but for pride.

The implications of these observations for the bulk of mythological sarcophagi are equally interesting: these sarcophagi seem to have been predominantly commissioned by the sub-elite. Statistical probability would suggest that at least one or two of the most popular mythological narratives may have been taken up by the *ordo senatorio* as well, especially since we can attribute to this class examples with rather rare or even unique subjects. Yet none of the almost 200 sarcophagi bearing images of Meleager, the approximately 120 decorated with Endymion, ninety Persephone or forty Hippolytus sarcophagi[260] can be attributed to a senatorial patron, whereas two of the ten known Leucippidae

---

[258] Also note Feraudi-Gruénais' observation that the richer the tomb, the less likely it is that we find images referring to death: *Innendekoration*, 200, 203–4.

[259] Eck, 'Rome and the outside world', 81.

[260] Numbers after Koch and Sichtermann, *Römische Sarkophage*. Only Roman, not Attic Meleager and Hippolytus sarcophagi, are counted; numbers refer to the second and third centuries. The only exception is a lid with the recovery of Meleager's body for a *vir clarissimus* from the turn of the fourth century, which falls outside the scope of our discussion: see Koch, *ASR 12.6*, 117 no. 103 pl. 88c.

sarcophagi belong to this class, and three of the nineteen caskets from Italy decorated with Achilles on Skyros.

To be sure, it is perfectly possible that, on occasion, other subjects appealed to a member of the first order. After all, one mid-third-century magistrate chose Adonis' death for the right-hand part of his sarcophagus front.[261] Significantly, however, he still considered the state sacrifice and wedding scenes important enough to cover the other half of the front and one small side of his casket. Moreover, the Adonis scene focuses entirely on the heroic – albeit fatal – hunt, dispensing with the hero's highly emotional encounters with Aphrodite and the lament and despair that his death had caused her, both topics featuring prominently on regular Adonis sarcophagi. While referring to death in an exceptionally direct way, the magistrate was highly selective in his choice of elements from the myth (and iconography), presenting it as the result of a heroic and brave struggle against a superior foe.[262] I have argued elsewhere that the majority of mythological narratives in the second century served as *exempla mortalitatis* and *maeroris* rather than *exempla virtutis*, as is often suggested.[263] This would explain why they were mostly considered unsuitable for the elite's purposes.

Conversely, the subjects preferred by the social elite were not used by them exclusively. With the exception of depictions directly related to offices and public performances to which others had no right, the images just discussed were also used by aspiring members of other social classes – as were senatorial tomb types and choices of location. From the *vita humana* scenes, the upbringing of a child was most easily adaptable as it did not refer to any public roles,[264] and the marriage scene was chosen for a knight and possibly for the non-elite as well.[265] One Leucippidae sarcophagus was dedicated to a freeborn woman by her husband, a certain Cornelius (?) Dionysius, whose *cognomen* and lack of status indicators suggest sub-elite status.[266] A sarcophagus depicting Achilles on Skyros was found together with a fragment, probably of an Endymion sarcophagus, in a free-standing, two-storey brick (temple?) tomb outside Porta Portese, which was

---

[261] Reinsberg, *Vita-Romana-Sarkophage*, 192 no. 6 pl. 21.1.

[262] For the reading of traditional Adonis sarcophagi, see also Borg, 'Leben und Tod', and Borg, 'No one is immortal', 180–3.

[263] Borg, 'No one is immortal'.

[264] Amedick, *Menschenleben*, 60–7, esp. 61.

[265] Knight: Reinsberg, *Vita-Romana-Sarkophage*, 193 no. 9 pl. 110.6. According to De Rossi (*Apiolae*, 100–2 figs. 189–92), the piece is in fact a lid 50 cm in height! Non-elite patrons suggested by their names and the lack of status indication: Reinsberg, *Vita-Romana-Sarkophage* nos. 78 and 118.

[266] Florence, Uffizi: Zanker and Ewald, *Myths*, 88–9, 218, figs. 197, 222.

erected by a freedman.[267] The idea of victory equally appealed to some non-senatorial patrons. Iulia Quintina and L. Dasumius Germanus, for instance, received sarcophagi very similar to that of Larcius Sabinus, even though their inscriptions suggest that they were no *clarissimi*.[268] Some members of the sub-elite always aspired to emulate the first two orders, and few elements of self-display were strictly reserved for the senatorial class. Yet the latter seem to have been less open to new themes (such as highly emotional mythological subjects), which may have come about precisely because the sub-elite, and predominantly freedpeople, were searching for their own means of expressing and promoting themselves.

In short, the first order's ideology, and its use of funerary monuments to express and communicate it, did not change much over the period I have looked at; only the means of expression did – at least to some extent. The same factors had always been key to the reputation and status of a family in the public realm: great ancestors and a long family line; offices and other formal honours; success as expressed in the victory theme, which often was, but did not have to be, military; *pietas* and abundant resources for a comfortable life as well as for the display of generosity. Accordingly, these ideas featured in public speeches as well as in private letters, consolations and funerary orations as matters of primary concern, and the language of both inscriptions and images from the funerary realm is taken over from public buildings and honorific monuments, from which they are sometimes hard to distinguish, and largely lacks the sentimental features that we find within the tombs of the lower classes. As Ted Lendon demonstrated conclusively twenty years ago, these same elements formed key arguments in elite competition from the Republic right through to the end of antiquity, and qualified an individual for public office and even for the post of emperor.[269] While appointment to office may often have depended ultimately on the emperor, his choices not only contributed to the status of an individual, they were also strongly influenced by the individual's reputation and rank in the hierarchy of honour among his peers, which depended on a complex yet widely agreed and applied set of criteria that determined the somewhat repetitive messages. One could even argue that in this political system, non-institutionalised power and influence were more essential than ever before for the success of both individuals and their families.

---

[267] Robert, *ASR 2*, 33–5 no. 24 pl. 13. One of two inscriptions found in the tomb mentions the burial of a *patronus* in the same tomb.

[268] Wrede, *Senatorische Sarkophage*, 39 with n. 271; Turcan, *Représentations dionysiaques*, 38–40 pls. 18a, 20b; Matz, *ASR 4.4*, 456 no. 261 pls. 282.2, 296.2, 259–60 no. 266 pl. 295.2.

[269] Lendon, *Empire of Honour*.

Much of this negotiating took place in oral or written form, but honorific monuments of all kinds have also always been a primary means of negotiating, communicating and reaffirming status and an individual's relevance to and position within a state or community.[270] In contrast to other parts of Italy and the empire, however, at Rome the display of euergetism through public buildings and honorific statues in public space had largely been rendered off-limits, so that only the domestic and funerary realms remained. Yet since the primary addressee of the messages was now the peer group, and much of the interaction with this peer group took place in the 'private' realm of *domus* and villas, it seems only natural that the elite made the most of these spaces. After treading somewhat carefully following the establishment of the empire, there was a greater desire than ever to maximise the potential of tomb monuments to act as markers and memorials of elite achievement and status, and their visual and often physical link to their patrons' villas ensured that their messages were not missed and were correctly attributed by their target audience.

---

[270] For excellent recent studies on portrait monuments, see Ma, *Statues and Cities*, on the Hellenistic world, and Stewart, *Statues*, on the Roman world.

2 | Reviving Tradition in Hadrianic Rome: From Incineration to Inhumation

Throughout the Archaic and Republican periods, the inhabitants of Rome practised both incineration and inhumation. There is no evidence that the choice depended on class or wealth, except that the very poor would not have been able to afford the considerable amount of fuel needed to cremate a body.[1] Literary texts describe lavish funerary celebrations of the elite that ended with the conspicuous cremation on tall *rogi* (funerary pyres), not only of the corpse, but also of rich offerings.[2] At the same time, burial in – doubtless costly – stone sarcophagi is attested from the fifth century BCE onwards, especially on the Esquiline Hill, and in larger numbers in the wider vicinity of Rome, most notably at Palestrina.[3] In the first century BCE, however, the majority of Rome's inhabitants seem to have preferred to burn their dead and bury the remains in *ollae* (terracotta urns set into niches in the walls) and cinerary urns of various shapes, sizes and materials (Figure 2.1), only to change their habit again over the course of the second century. Inhumation became popular once more among all social classes and an increasing number of people were now buried in terracotta or stone coffins, the latter often made of marble and adorned with images of a fast-growing range of narrative and other image decoration.[4] Such decorated caskets were produced in larger numbers from around 150–60.[5]

Initially, tombs were not normally specially designed to accommodate these containers. Burial in marble sarcophagi was usually the preserve of the most important members of a community, but including children, whose death often prompted the erection of a tomb.[6] The rest of the family or

---

[1] Meinecke, *Sarcophagum posuit*, 2–6. On the burial of the poor, see below. The use of both rites is also confirmed by the Twelve Tables: Cicero, *Leg.* 2.58.

[2] On conspicuous cremations, see e.g. Engels, *Grabluxusgesetze*, 183–4; Schrumpf, *Bestattung*, 65–6. They believe that only the family (Engels) or only in exceptional circumstances friends and family (Schrumpf) attended the actual cremation. Yet not only do they fail to cite any sources in support, the assumption also contradicts the attested conspicuous consumption at these events and the introduction of sumptuary laws.

[3] Meinecke, *Sarcophagum posuit*, 7–9; 151–96 nos. R1–49.

[4] For an overview, see Koch and Sichtermann, *Römische Sarkophage*; Meinecke, *Sarcophagum posuit*; For terracotta sarcophagi, see Taglietti, 'Diffusion'. On mythological sarcophagi, see Zanker and Ewald, *Myths*, and the volumes of *ASR*.

[5] Davies, 'Before sarcophagi', 28, based on *ASR*.

[6] Nock, 'Cremation and burial', 324.

Figure 2.1 Columbarium near the mausoleum of the Scipios, late first century BCE/
early first century CE

familia (household) were either cremated and their ashes placed in *ollae* and
urns, or else they were inhumed in simple terracotta sarcophagi, which were
frequently placed under the floor or in even simpler *fossae* (shaft graves; see
Figure 2.2 for a second-century example). When inhumation became more
established, tombs were laid out to accommodate inhumations from the start.[7]
The richest and most prominent burials were marked by sarcophagi, which
were often placed in niches and sometimes elevated by pedestals to enhance
the display of the expensive caskets (Figure 2.3).[8] Simpler inhumations were
placed in *arcosolia* (*fossae* in the bottom of arched niches) or, as before, in
terracotta sarcophagi and *fossae* in the floor. At about the turn of the third
century, inhumation had become the standard form of burial for all ranks of
society. Even though incineration never went out of use entirely, no longer
was provision normally made for urns or *ollae*.[9]

[7] See Taglietti, 'Diffusion', for an overview.
[8] For the tomb illustrated here, see Bendinelli, 'Ipogei sepolcrali'. On sarcophagus display in
     general see Borg, *Crisis and Ambition*, 213–40, and Meinecke, *Sarcophagum posuit*.
[9] For exceptions, see Taglietti, 'Diffusion', 170; Borg, *Crisis and Ambition*, 16, 18, 20.

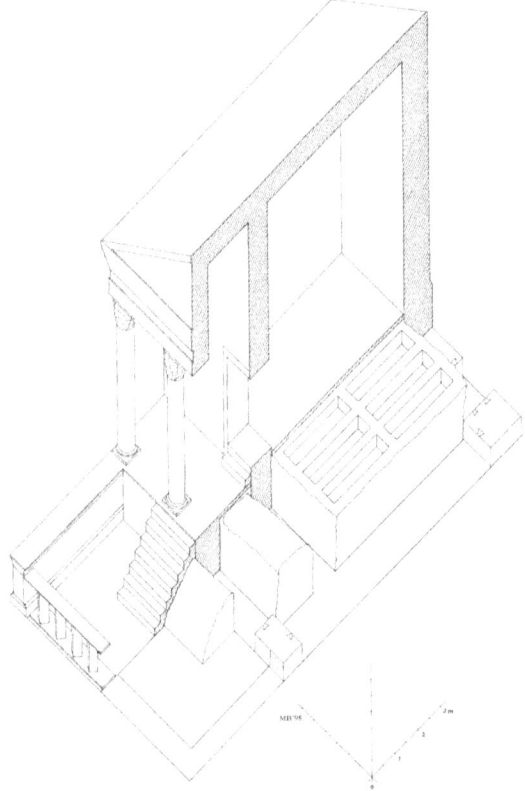

Figure 2.2 Temple tomb A13 of the Porta Romana necropolis at Ostia, Trajanic; reconstruction drawing Michael Heinzelmann

This change in the second century from incineration to inhumation has long mystified scholars and sparked much controversy, not least because our written sources are remarkably uninterested in the subject.[10] Among the more popular suggestions are a shift in religious and eschatological beliefs[11] and influence from the Greek East.[12] Neither of these explanation can be

---

[10] The bibliography is vast. For an overview of the debate, see Toynbee, *Death and Burial*, 40; Brandenburg, 'Beginn', 278–80, 323–5; Koch and Sichtermann, *Römische Sarkophage*, 27–30; Morris, *Death-ritual*, 31–69; Schrumpf, *Bestattung*, 70–7; and most recently Davies, 'Before sarcophagi'; Graham, 'Corporeal concerns', 44–6; Scheid, 'Körperbestattung'; and Vismara, 'Inumazione', on the written sources.

[11] Most notably Cumont, *Symbolisme*, but also more recently e.g. Audin, 'Inhumation'; Toynbee, *Death and Burial*, 33; Karl Schefold in several publications, and others. Cf. Koch and Sichtermann, *Römische Sarkophage*, 28–9 nn. 20–6 for an overview.

[12] On this suggestion, see below. Turcan ('Origines', 332–4) proposes that the first stimulus came from Italic elites in areas that had continued inhumation, which started to be admitted to the

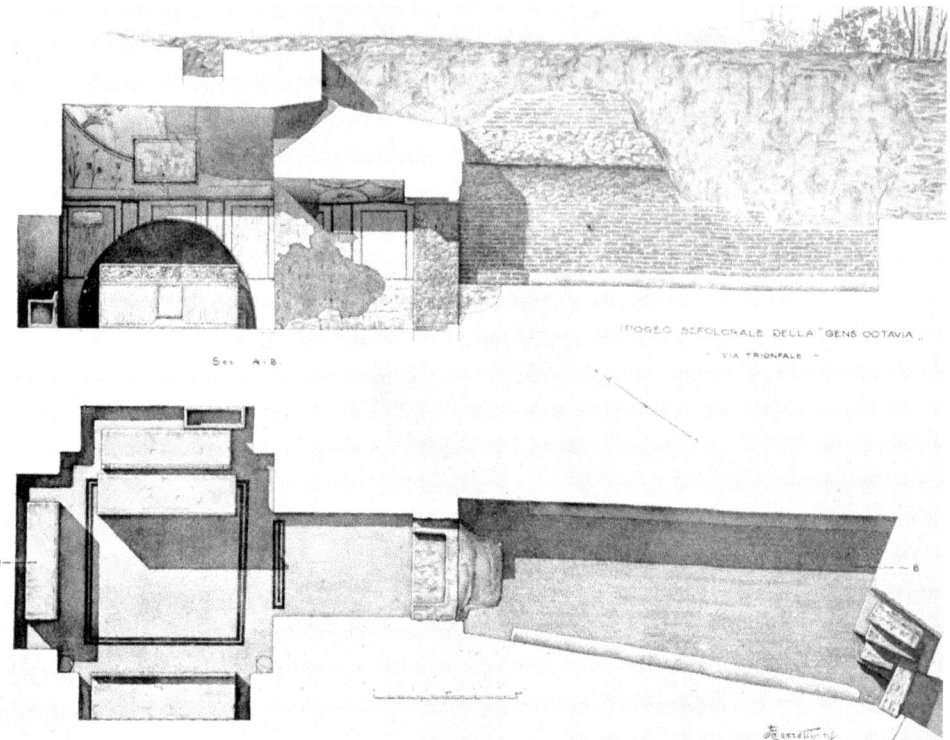

Figure 2.3 Hypogeum of the Octavii on via Triumphalis showing three sarcophagi in their own arched niches and a fourth one positioned in front of the right-hand niche; late second century CE

substantiated.[13] At Rome, throughout the entire second century, inhumation and incineration existed side by side even in the same tombs, and there is no evidence for a change in funerary rituals, other than the abolition of cremation, that could potentially indicate new religious beliefs.[14] Written sources also fail to mention any prescriptions, recommendations or specific practices concerning the treatment of the dead body related to religious or philosophical persuasion, with the sole exception of the Pythagorean ones.[15] Pliny the Elder tells us that Varro was buried 'in the

---

senate from the Flavian period onwards, but goes on to argue that the main inspiration then came from elites from the East entering the senate.

[13] The main objections were already laid out by Nock, 'Cremation and burial', and in his review of Cumont's 1942 book. Cf. Nock, 'Sarcophagi'.

[14] E.g. Hesberg, 'Beigaben'; Morris, *Death-ritual*, 31–69, esp. 33, 61–2.

[15] Nock, 'Cremation and burial', 335–7, 357–8. Christianity, at this time, was not widespread enough to explain the general change, and became more concerned about the body only much later.

Pythagorean style' (*Pythagorio modo*) in a terracotta sarcophagus laid out with leaves of myrtle, olive and black poplar (*NH* 35.46.160). However, as Friederike Fless has succinctly observed, the passage does not suggest a Pythagorean explanation for inhumation as such.[16] In the relevant chapter, Pliny is really interested in terracotta as a material and in its use as a container for the remains of the deceased. What he suggests as being specifically Pythagorean was the lining of the sarcophagus with the leaves, not inhumation. Moreover, there is no indication that Pythagoreanism spread as widely and in the same pattern as inhumation did. Rather, Pythagorean philosophy's influence decreased already during the later first century CE, so that it cannot explain the general change in the treatment of the body.[17]

With the exception of the Egyptians, even those eastern peoples who did practise inhumation do not seem to have connected this with religious principles, nor did they have any concern to preserve the body.[18] On the other hand, initiates into mystery cults that offered hope of an afterlife believed not in the resurrection of the body, but in a new form of life for the soul. Their successful transition into an afterlife depended on prerequisites such as initiation and moral purity, not on any special treatment of the corpse.[19] There is also no significant change in the choice of image decoration on cinerary urns, ash altars and sarcophagi, which one might expect to find had the change in custom been linked to shifting religious beliefs or philosophical concerns.[20] As Glenys Davies observes, no ancient written source mentions the change from cremation to inhumation at all, which suggests that the Romans did not consider it to be of major importance or interest.[21] This seems to be confirmed by Lucan, who states:

> it matters not whether the corpses are burnt on the pyre or decompose with time; nature finds room for them all in her gentle arms, and the dead owe their end to themselves alone. (*Bellum Civile* 6.809–11, transl. J. D. Duff)

The idea that religion had anything to do with the shift has therefore been largely abandoned, and comparative studies further confirm the multiplicity of potential social and cultural causes for changes in mortuary practices.[22]

---

[16] Fless, 'Sarkophagbestattungen', 323.
[17] Nock, 'Cremation and burial', 337.
[18] Ibid., 339–44, 350–7.
[19] Ibid., 344–57.
[20] Herdejürgen, 'Sarkophage', esp. 429–31; Koch and Sichtermann, *Römische Sarkophage*, 49–50; Boschung, 'Grabaltäre'; Fless, 'Sarkophagbestattungen', 321; Davies, 'Before sarcophagi'.
[21] Davies, 'Before sarcophagi', 24; ditto Vismara, 'Inumazione'.
[22] Brandt et al. (eds.), *Death*.

The alternative explanation, influence from the East, often links the introduction of inhumation with that of mythological sarcophagi, and takes one of two forms.[23] The bottom-up model suggests that it was the freedman class with their Greek roots who first introduced it.[24] In contrast, the top-down model points to senatorial *homines novi* ('new men') from the eastern provinces and/or holds the so-called 'Second Sophistic' with its interest in all things Greek, which was particularly influential among the elite, responsible for the change.[25] Both theories have their problems, which arise not least from the link often proposed between the spread of inhumation and that of mythological sarcophagi. Not only does the decoration of Italic Roman sarcophagi follow Roman traditions and differ from the early eastern sarcophagi,[26] there is also no chronological coincidence between the alleged cause and effect. Large numbers of slaves and freedmen of eastern origin were already living (and had died) at Rome in the early first century CE, raising the question of why they would have adopted their alleged own traditional burial customs so late.[27] The trends subsumed under the label of the Second Sophistic had gained considerable momentum by the early second century, again pre-dating the boom of mythological sarcophagi by several decades. More importantly, only a very small minority of those choosing inhumation in (marble) sarcophagi over cremation opted for decoration with Greek myths.

The debate seems to be in a deadlock.[28] Several scholars have sided with Arthur Darby Nock, who declared the change simply one of fashion.[29] Yet this

[23] The idea that the Roman sarcophagus tradition depends on influences from the East goes at least as far back as Rodenwaldt, 'Sarkophagprobleme', 10–18. It is often based on Petronius, *Satyricon* 111.2, where inhumation is said to be a Greek custom.

[24] E.g. Byvanck, 'Problème'; Byvanck, 'Début'; Gabelmann, *Werkstattgruppen*, 8–9, 196; Balty, 'Interprétation symbolique', cxxxviii–cxlv. Van Keuren (in Van Keuren et al., 'Multimethod analyses', 166) has recently tried to support this view further through tracing the provenance of the marble of twenty sarcophagi that date to between the early second and the fourth centuries. Nevertheless, this very small statistical sample can hardly support his claims.

[25] E.g. Brandenburg, 'Beginn', 323; Müller, *Peleus and Thetis Sarcophagus*, esp. 139–70; Turcan, 'Origines'; Turcan, *Messages*, 18–21, who points to both *homines novi* and former slaves from the East; Zanker, *Betrachter*, 3; Davies, 'Before sarcophagi', 51; Morris, *Death-ritual*, 53–61.

[26] Thus the authors in n. 20 above. Amedick ('Etruskische Sepulkralkunst') has even argued that a large number of themes on early Roman sarcophagi are inspired by Etruscan funerary art.

[27] It is also notable that inhumation in Asia Minor rises only about the same time as it does in Rome: see Ahrens, 'Cremation'.

[28] E.g. Junker, 'Sarkophage', 163 n. 3: 'The lack of literary sources effectively prevents us from finding the historical reasons for this change.' Cf. Scheid, 'Körperbestattung'. Vismara ('Inumazione', esp. 605–6) concluded from the indifference of our sources that we are posing the wrong question and should look instead at the rites that make a grave a *locus religiosus*. Yet the phenomenon is real and thus worth considering.

[29] Nock, 'Cremation and burial', 357. Cf. e.g. Wrede, 'Grabtempel', esp. 432; Morris, *Death-ritual*, 33; Schrumpf, *Bestattung*, 75; Brandt et al. (eds.), *Death*, xiv.

is hardly an explanation, and not only because 'fashions' are never entirely meaningless or arbitrary.[30] The question might as well be rephrased: Why did inhumation become a 'fashion'? In this new attempt to explain the phenomenon, I would like to take a more holistic approach than most previous studies have done. I start with a closer look at inhumation throughout the first centuries BCE and CE and the chronology of its spread. I demonstrate that during the first century CE, inhumation was more widespread among the social and financial elite than is normally admitted, and that numbers rose steadily throughout the first century and the beginning of the second. This suggests that we are really looking at two questions: Why did inhumation become increasingly popular again in the imperial period? And why did the change in mortuary practices accelerate at precisely the time it did in the second quarter or around the middle of the second century? I then go on to argue that it was the imperial model of Hadrian, who opted for inhumation, that made popular and desirable to increasing numbers of Romans a practice that was already on the rise when he adopted it.

Inhumation from the Republican to the Hadrianic Period

As mentioned above, inhumation was a common practice in Rome during most of the Republic, and it continued even in the late Republic and during the first century CE, when cremation was the standard way of disposing of the dead.[31] Not only was it the dominant procedure for the poor, who could not afford the substantial amounts of fuel necessary for cremation,[32] but from the mid-first century CE, necropoleis for simple graves were being established that increasingly featured inhumations, and in the early second century, families of the 'middling classes' started to bury the lesser members

---

[30] As also noted by Davies, 'Before sarcophagi', 24.

[31] Toynbee, *Death and Burial*, 39–41; Brandenburg, 'Beginn'; Müller, *Peleus and Thetis Sarcophagus*, 159–61; Fless, 'Sarkophagbestattungen'; Davies, 'Before sarcophagi'; Meinecke, *Sarcophagum posuit*.

[32] Bodel, *Graveyards and Groves*; Bodel, 'Undertakers'; Bodel, 'Funerary trade'; Graham, *Urban Poor*; Schrumpf, *Bestattung*, 122–38; Carroll, *Spirits*, 74–8. Graham (*Urban Poor*, esp. 85–114) draws attention to poor burials with simple tile covers (*a cappuccina*) or in amphorae, which are interspersed between more visible tombs in most cemeterial areas around Rome and its harbour cities. Cf. for the Isola Sacra necropolis, see Angelucci et al. ('Sepolture e riti', 49–87), who note that of a total of 627 such simple burials, 580 were inhumations (p. 71); ditto Baldassarre et al., *Necropoli di Porto*, 38; Heinzelmann (ed.), *Bestattungsbrauch*, 15. The burial pits on the Esquiline Hill discovered by Lanciani are no longer regarded as Varro's infamous *puticuli* and typical of burials of the poor (Varro, *Ling.* 5.25), but rather have been interpreted as mass burials after a catastrophic event (esp. Bodel, *Graveyards and Groves*, esp. 38–54; Graham, *Urban Poor*, 63–84).

of their *familiae* in anonymous *fossae* underneath the floors of their mausolea (Figure 2.2).[33] Michael Heinzelmann has therefore concluded that the spread of inhumation should be disconnected from the spread of marble sarcophagi,[34] and has further suggested that inhumation really originated in these lower classes and only spread gradually up the social hierarchy.[35]

Yet while the methodological caveat is worth considering, there are problems with the general model proposed. To start with, it is hard to prove that inhumation spread earlier or more rapidly in the lower echelons of society than in the upper ones. During the first and early second centuries CE, in terms of absolute numbers, inhumation is indeed more common in the former than in the latter. Nevertheless, there were obviously many fewer members of the upper classes, so that the speed of the spread within each class is hard to assess and compare. Moreover, it is important to remember that parts of the social elite never entirely abandoned inhumation, and thus their inhumations preceded those of the large necropoleis as well as those underneath mausoleum floors. And last but not least, it is hard to see why the social elite and wealthier sub-elite should have adopted a poor man's habit. Heinzelmann's proposal that a decreasing importance and gradual disbanding of traditional family structures were to blame for a form of burial that was chosen primarily for requiring less effort is hard to sustain, and not just with regard to the first two orders. As we shall see in Chapter 3, among the wealthier sub-elite, family and *familiae* became even more important in the funerary realm than they ever had been before.[36] The best way forward in this debate is thus probably to disentangle the practices of the lower and upper classes, and to try to explain their habits and changes separately.

Inhumation Among the Lower Classes

As indicated above, it is generally accepted that inhumation was a much more economical way of disposing of the dead than incineration, which required substantial amounts of expensive fuel.[37] It is for this reason that the poorest members of society will mostly have ended up in inhumation

---

[33] Heinzelmann, 'Einleitung', 17; Taglietti, 'Incinerazione'. For simple but individual inhumation burials without (surviving) markers or grave goods, which could well represent the urban poor, see e.g. Buccellato et al., 'Comprensorio'; Cucina et al., 'Necropolis of Vallerano'; esp. Griesbach, *Villen und Gräber*, 83–141; Graham, *Urban Poor*.

[34] Ditto Taglietti, 'Diffusion', 164; Taglietti, 'Incinerazione', 151.

[35] Heinzelmann, 'Einleitung', 17.

[36] See also Borg, *Crisis and Ambition*, 123–46.

[37] Noy, 'Funeral pyre'; Schrumpf, *Bestattung*, 77–86, both with further bibl.

graves.[38] From around the mid-first century CE, some of the individuals inhumed in the large necropoleis mentioned by Heinzelmann were being treated with a certain amount of care, but these burials are usually of the simplest kind and suggest a sector of society of the most moderate means.[39] The anonymous *fossae* in the floors of tomb buildings at Ostia, the Isola Sacra or the necropoleis on the via Triumphalis from the early second century have been attributed to lesser members of their patron's *familiae*, to their slaves and perhaps to the lowest rank of their freedmen. The founders of these tombs and their families clearly preferred to be incinerated and for their urns, and sometimes a label, to be visibly displayed.[40] It therefore seems that the primary reason for inhumation during the first and earlier second centuries continued to be economic, even though other reasons may have played a part in individual cases. That we find these burials at all in the archaeological record is likely due to a general trend starting in the first century BCE, namely the desire and effort of increasing numbers of people, and of a growing range of socially and economically diverse groups within Roman society, to be buried in a more visible and lasting way. This trend resulted not only in the well-known boom in tomb building all around Rome from the first century BCE onwards, but also in an increasing diversity of tomb and grave types and sizes in the above-mentioned necropoleis.[41] They range from the simplest inhumations protected by only a few tiles, or depositions within amphorae and terracotta sarcophagi, to the half-barrel-shaped *cupae* or *cassone* graves, to small monuments such as stelae, altars, miniature pyramids or *aediculae*, to the larger monuments for entire *familiae* or *collegia*.[42] What we are looking at, in the first and early second centuries CE, is most likely not primarily a change from incineration to inhumation within one and the same sector of society, but widening participation in more visible forms of burial that now included sectors of society that would not have left any traces in previous decades and centuries.

---

[38] See above n. 32. Bodel ('Undertakers', 133–5) and Schrumpf (*Bestattung*, 135–7) consider it possible that mass cremation of increasing numbers of urban poor replaced the deposition of corpses in the Esquiline mass graves, which would have been cheaper than individual cremations and would have saved the state space, which was at a premium around Rome. But Kyle (*Spectacles*, 169–70) casts well-reasoned doubt on the practice. Cf. Carroll, *Spirits*, 77 with n. 56.

[39] For a fuller discussion see Graham, *Urban Poor*, esp. 85–114.

[40] Taglietti, 'Incinerazione', 150; Heinzelmann, 'Einleitung', 17.

[41] Borg, 'What's in a Tomb?', 54–5 and 'Roman cemeteries', esp. 409.

[42] For descriptions of these necropoleis, see e.g. Angelucci et al., 'Sepolture e riti'; Baldassarre et al., *Necropoli di Porto*, esp. 19–24; Steinby, *Via Triumphalis*. While the graves in the floors of mausolea were not themselves visible, they are only preserved because of the tomb's patron's desire to leave a *monumentum*.

Franca Taglietti has drawn attention to the considerable and increasing number of terracotta sarcophagi from the first and early second centuries, some of which were found within 'house' tombs.[43] Yet while they attest to a more costly treatment than the simple depositions in *fossae*, it is hard to tell to what extent they also attest to a deliberate choice of inhumation over inciner- ation, rather than being the best affordable for someone who did not have the means for cremation.[44] The preference for incineration among the sub-elite founders of larger tombs (as well as some owners of the smaller monuments) is most clearly demonstrated by the architectural provision for, and visual enhancement of, urns and *ollae*, both lacking for inhumation graves in earlier examples.[45]

Inhumation Among the Social Elite and the Wealthy

Such ambiguities do not exist with regard to the wealthier sectors of society who were inhumed, and among whom the spread of inhumation can be traced more easily due to their use of (marble) sarcophagi and tombs designed for their display.

As both Cicero and Pliny inform us, inhumation never went out of use entirely among the old Roman families.[46] The best-known example is the Cornelii Scipiones, who set up large inscribed caskets in their family mau- soleum on the via Appia from the early third to the late second or early first century BCE (see Figures 3.1–3.2 below).[47] In the first century BCE, C. Marius was inhumed, and allegedly Sulla would have preferred the same, but was cremated only for fear that his body would be dug up by his enemies in the same way as he had done with Marius.[48] Recently, Katharina Meinecke has drawn due attention to Republican-period sarcophagus burials in and around Rome. She lists two examples from the first century BCE as well as eighteen from the first century CE.[49] More evidence can be

---

[43] Taglietti, 'Diffusion'.
[44] For a different view, see Taglietti, 'Incinerazione'. She does not differentiate enough chronologically, however, and does not consider smaller differences in expenditure, when she proposes that inhumation was generally independent of financial means.
[45] Ditto Schrumpf, *Bestattung*, 72–5.
[46] See at n. 84 below.
[47] Coarelli, *Scipioni* and 'Sepolcro'; *LTUR* IV (1999) 285 s.v. Sepulcrum (Corneliorum) Scipionum (F. Zevi); Meinecke, *Sarcophagum posuit*, 152–9 no. R2. See also Chapter 3.
[48] Cicero, *Laws* 2.22.56; Pliny, *NH* 7.55.187; Graninus Licinianus 36.25–9 (in Pliny, *NH* 8.19); Schrumpf, *Bestattung*, 70–1.
[49] Meinecke, *Sarcophagum posuit*, 168–70 nos. R9–10 (both depositions in rectangular chamber tombs) and 197–217 nos. A1–18. Some of these are more convincingly dated than others.

added from the Augustan age and the first and early second centuries CE.[50] I shall briefly discuss some examples that help us to identify the patronage of such burials.

The first datable senatorial marble sarcophagus is that of P. Paquius Scaeva, Roman senator and proconsul of Cyprus in 15/14 BCE (Figure 2.4).[51] It was found at Vasto, the ancient town of Histonium near Pesaro, and features simple mouldings around the edges on its outside and two compartments complete with headrests inside. Most notably, the inner walls are inscribed with the senator's *cursus honorum*. Two plain marble sarcophagi, one for an adult decorated with cornices and a plain one for a child, were found in the tomb of the consular Minicii family, together with one plain sarcophagus each made of terracotta, peperino and travertine (Figure 2.5).[52] Two cinerary altars dating to the late Flavian to Trajanic period commemorate Statoria M. f. Marcella and her daughter Minicia Marcella Fundani, wife and daughter of C. Minicius Fundanus, *consul suffectus* in 107 and *proconsul Asiae* in 122–23.[53] There are a number of uncertainties regarding the date and sequence of burial in the tomb, but it is likely that the sarcophagi belong to the first and early second centuries CE.[54] A plain but truly monumental sarcophagus with a roof-like lid of the Proconnesian type served

From the first century CE group, I believe that A5 must be excluded, as it is likely to be of second-century date (see n. 68 below); there are no dating criteria for the sarcophagi of A11, which are known only from Pirro Ligorio's description (on which see at n. 76 below); the date for the peperino sarcophagi of A13 rests largely on the material and the *gentilicium* of the tomb's patron (Apronius), which are not conclusive and are contradicted by the tomb's building technique, *opus latericium*. A4 is the tomb of Priscilla, which is only known from literary sources (see Chapter 4). In compensation, some examples listed among Meinecke's second- and third-century items may actually be earlier: see n. 68 below.

50 Brandenburg, 'Beginn'; Gasparri 'Sarcofago romano'; Gasparri, 'Sarcofago con nekyia'; Fless, 'Sarkophagbestattungen'; Vismara, 'Inumazione', 600–2.

51 Brandenburg, 'Beginn', 280–2 figs. 1–4 (2.10 x 1.17 x 0.67 m). On the inscription: Corbier, 'Constructing kinship', 138.

52 Dressel, 'Camera sepolcrale'; *LTUR* IV (2006) 70–1 fig. 68 s.v. Miniciorum Sepulcrum (F. Fraioli); Meinecke, *Sarcophagum posuit*, 207–9 no. A10; Meinecke, 'Inschriften', 180–1 figs. 1–2. The mix of materials is interesting and, as Fless ('Sarkophagbestattungen', 323) notes, Varro, who at least made it to the praetorship, would equally have had the funds for a marble sarcophagus, but was buried in a terracotta one.

53 *PIR²* M 612.

54 See also Chapter 1, 72. Pliny, *Ep.* 5.16.2–4 mentions the death of a daughter of Minicius in his letter of 105 or 106, when the daughter's mother (Statoria?) had apparently already died. It is normally assumed that this daughter is Minicia Marcella and that the tomb was established on this occasion. Meinecke (*Sarcophagum posuit*, 207–9 no. A10, and 'Inschriften', 180–1) convincingly argues against this view and for a date of at least some sarcophagi in the first century based on typology. However, the clearest indication of their date is the position of Statilia's altar: it suggests that the more prominent locations in the tomb had already been taken by the sarcophagi that were found in situ. See Bodel, 'Minicia Marcella'

Figure 2.4 Sarcophagus of P. Paquius Scaeva and his wife, late first century BCE, Vasto, Museo Archeologico

another consul as his final abode, C. Valerius Paullinus, consul in 107, who died around 112 (see Figures 1.2 and 1.3 above).[55] Slightly later still was a now-lost sarcophagus separated into two compartments similar to Scaeva's, which was found in the second chamber of the tomb of the patrician Licinii and Calpurnii, where it probably belonged to the first generation changing

on the discrepancy between the girl's age in Pliny's letter and on the altar (shortly before her fourteenth birthday as opposed to twelve years eleven months according to the altar's inscription, *CIL* 6.16631), which could also be explained as referring to two different daughters of Minicius. For a similar hypogeum, but some fifty years (?) earlier, equally only containing inhumations – here in three plain marble (?) caskets – on the Appia just inside the Aurelianic Wall, see Meinecke, *Sarcophagum posuit*, 200 no. A3 pl. 1.2. Its patronage is not known.

[55] Petersen, 'Secondo sepolcro'; Herdejürgen, 'Via Latina'; *LTURS* III (2005), 165–7 s.v. Latina via (F. Montella); Meinecke, *Sarcophagum posuit*, 221–7 no. B3. On the tomb, see also Chapter 1, 10–12, 36–40.

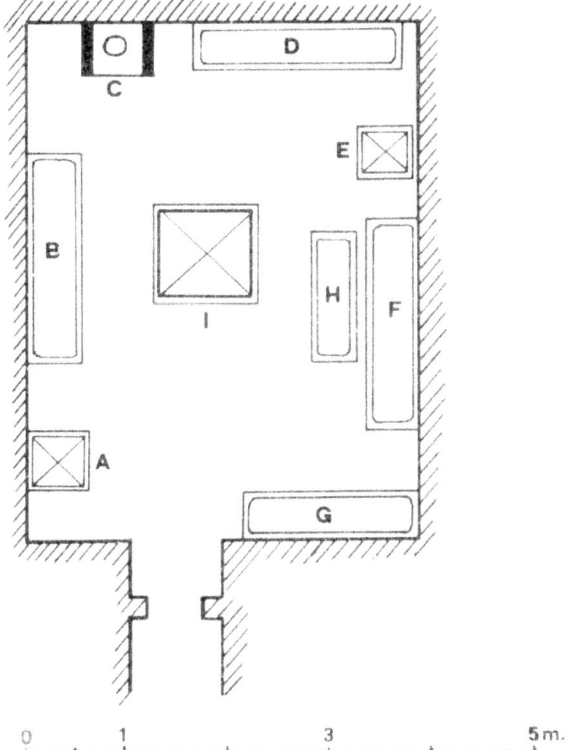

Figure 2.5 Tomb of the consular Minicii family on Monte Mario, third quarter first century (?)

burial custom from cremation to inhumation, and was set up around 130 to hold the remains of the then *paterfamilias* and his wife.[56]

Similar early sarcophagus burials can be attributed to other classes.[57] A sarcophagus from the mid-first century CE from Etruria belonged to a *parasitus* of Apollo, the imperial freedman Ti. Claudius Pardalas.[58] Another freedman and procurator of Claudius (or Nero), Ti. Claudius Nicanor, was

---

[56] The sarcophagus measured 2.25 x 1.25 x 0.95 m: *NSc* (1885), 43 (Rl. Lanciani/L. Borsari). The current location of the piece is unknown and it might not be preserved. On its date, see Chapter 1 n. 204. Meinecke (*Sarcophagum posuit*, 328–32 no. B66) is sceptical about the attribution of sarcophagi to the Licinii tomb, but she does not discuss the new evidence published by Van Keuren, 'Unpublished documents'. See also Chapter 3 pp. 144–6.

[57] Three inscribed but otherwise plain sarcophagi for members of an otherwise unknown equestrian Cornelii family have been found in Kavalla, Greece, where at the time, the second half of the first century CE, they would equally not have followed common local practice. See Herdejürgen, 'Sarkophage', 413–15 figs. 1–2.

[58] *NSc* (1915), 158–65 (G. Cultrera); Brandenburg, 'Beginn', 303–4 fig. 33 (with erroneous identification as a chest for cinerary urns); *MNR* I,3 (1982) 91–4 (M. Sapelli – R. Friggeri).

Figure 2.6 Tomb of the imperial freedman Ti. Claudius Nicanor on the via Nomentana after excavation, mid-first century CE

buried with his family and *familia* in a chamber tomb that was cut into the rock on the via Nomentana about 14 km from Rome (Figure 2.6). The tomb featured rich marble and stucco decoration and contained, among other things, two plain marble sarcophagi. A kline monument with a por-trait of a reclining youth sat on top of the sarcophagus at the rear wall, while the second casket, in a large niche in the right-hand wall, contained a lead sarcophagus with the fully preserved skeleton of a man.[59] According to Fortunati, an undecorated marble sarcophagus was also found in the tomb of the *argentarius Macelli Magni* L. Calpurnius Daphnus on the via Latina.[60] It was a free-standing brick building of the elaborate 'house' type from the 60s CE, one of the first examples. Significantly, its burial chamber

[59] Annibaldi, 'Via Nomentana'. The kline is in Rome, Museo Nazionale inv. 114906. Cf. Fless, 'Sarkophagbestattungen', 320–1; Wrede, 'Klinentypus', 399 fig. 75; Meinecke, *Sarcophagum posuit*, 211–13 no. A14.

[60] Fortunati, *Relazione*, 44–5; Meinecke, *Sarcophagum posuit*, 197 no. A1 with bibl. Calpurnius Daphnis was commemorated on an inscribed altar that depicted him conducting his business overseeing the marketing of fish: *CIL* 6.9183; Kleiner, *Altars*, 121–3 no. 16 pls. 11.1–2; Boschung, *Grabaltäre*, 49, 66, 76, 113 no. 953.

was designed with niches for the display of sarcophagi from the outset, suggesting that the marble casket was not a later addition.

Other marble sarcophagi cannot be attributed to a specific class with any certainty, but confirm that we are looking here at the social and financial elite. The burial of a girl found at Vetralla/Viterbo in a plain peperino sarcophagus can be dated to the last decades of the first century by her rich jewellery and other grave goods, which suggest, if not a noble, certainly a wealthy family background.[61] A marble sarcophagus decorated with simple profiles and containing the embalmed body of a tall man was found in a tumulus tomb of Augustan date on the via Casilina near Centocelle Station, about 8 km from Rome.[62] A plain one still occupied one of the niches of a tumulus tomb at the fifth mile of the Appia in 1976, while a peperino sarcophagus of similar style stood in one of the other niches (Figure 2.7).[63] The tumulus tomb next to the Mausoleum of Romulus in Maxentius' villa on the Appia, the so-called 'Sepolcro dei Servilii', had a cruciform chamber with built-in sarcophagus-like caskets in its tall arched niches.[64] Another tumulus on a rectangular base was seen by Pirro Ligorio still with terracotta sarcophagi in the niches of its cruciform burial chamber.[65] As other, inscribed tumuli suggest, tumulus tombs were often erected by the first two orders,[66] and size, location and the respect that Maxentius paid to the

---

[61] Bordenache Battaglia, *Corredi*, 49–78; Bedini (ed.), *Mistero*, 89–97; Dresken-Weiland, *Sarkophagbestattungen*, A120.

[62] Gasparri, 'Sarcofago romano', 36 pl. 15a; Brandenburg, 'Beginn', 284–6 figs. 7–8; Chioffi, *Mummificazione*, 53–5 no. 13 with bibl.; Meinecke, *Sarcophagum posuit*, 216–17 no. A18. On the context, see esp. *Archeologia* 6, 1967, 365, and *Archeologia* 7, 1968, 250–1 figs. 1–3. The excavation was never properly published. The date is suggested by the *opus incertum* technique of the tumulus and the use of *opus reticulatum* for the wall closing the tomb after its use was discontinued.

[63] Gasparri, 'Sarcofago con nekyia', 167 no. 24. Gasparri mentions only fragments of one marble sarcophagus, but a photograph in Eisner (*Typologie*, 45–6 no. A12 with pl. 12.3) shows a complete casket. Eisner's photograph was taken in 1976 and the sarcophagus may have been damaged after this date and before Gasparri saw it.

[64] Eisner, *Typologie*, 33–6 no. A4 pls. 7–8; Rasch, *Maxentius-Mausoleum*, 21 pl. 23,1.4; Rausa, *Pirro Ligorio*, 63–5 no. 7; Spera, *Paesaggio*, 283 UT 483 fig. 206.

[65] Rausa, *Pirro Ligorio*, 95–6 no. 18; cf. Spera, *Paesaggio*, 327 UT 622. The tomb also contained cinerary urns, but Ligorio saw bodies in the sarcophagi, which therefore did not contain the urns. Ligorio's identification as the tomb of the Rubelii is based on an inscription that is considered to be his own invention: *CIL* 6.5.2626. Potentially, we need to add to these a tumulus on the via Tiburtina (Torraccia dell'Inviolata), if the sarcophagus found on site actually belonged to the tomb: Mari, *Tibur III*, 75–83, esp. 78 with n. 341, no. 28 figs. 84–94. Mari dates it to the turn of the second century based on its use of *opus latericium* but, as Eisner (*Typologie*, esp. 210 (116–17 no. T/N2 on the tomb)), observed, the technique is already attested in the first century BCE.

[66] Of the five or seven known owners of tumulus tombs, three belonged to the senatorial class, two to knights and possibly two to rich *liberti*: see Schwarz, *Tumulat Italia tellus*, 90–5 with

Figure 2.7 Funerary chamber of a tumulus tomb at the fifth mile of the via Appia with one of its sarcophagi still in place

'Sepolcro dei Servilii' when he built his mausoleum suggest a very prominent family.

When we look at first-century CE tumuli more generally, we notice that they were often fitted with cruciform chambers and niches of a size suitable for the deposition of sarcophagi, and sarcophagi may actually have been standard equipment of many of the large early *opus caementicium* tombs that contained similar chambers.[67] Nobody has ever counted, or would be

table 12. Of the *liberti* tumuli (cat. F30 and F31), only their inscriptions are preserved, and the shape of the tomb can therefore not be determined with absolute certainty. To these should probably be added the tumulus at Alife, which may have been dedicated to another praetorian. See Stanco, *Acilii Glabriones*, 50–1.

[67] See e.g. Eisner, *Typologie*, A1, 2, 4, 12, 46; P1; P/T2, T2 (Plautii), 6, 7; T/N2; N3; F7. Other early tombs of different shapes occasionally equally have cruciform chambers, e.g. ibid., A47, A49,

able to date, the plain sarcophagi set up in parks, reused as water basins for fountains or stored in museum depots, but given the chronological distribution of inscribed or contextualised sarcophagi of this kind, it is highly likely that a major percentage belongs to the first and early second centuries CE, even though some are also later.[68]

These observations are, of course, very hard to quantify. Nevertheless, some first- and early second-century sarcophagi can be dated more precisely due to their more lavish relief decoration; that is, garland sarcophagi as they were collected by Helga Herdejürgen.[69] Two further items can now be added to her list. In 2000, an entirely pristine underground tomb chamber with stairway and small vestibule was found at La Decima on the via Latina.[70] It contained two marble sarcophagi decorated with garlands, pilasters in shallow relief and dedicatory inscriptions in a tabula, which were set at right angles against the rear and the left wall. They contained the remains of an eighteen-year-old, T. Carvilius Gemellus, and of his mother, Aebutia Quarta, aged between forty and fifty. Both showed signs of artificial conservation and both were entirely covered with garlands made of roses, lilies and violets. The date of the burials is suggested by the style

Lb2. Of the 111 more conspicuous tombs from the first century BCE to the Hadrianic period collected by Eisner, at least eight and possibly eleven belonged to the senatorial and equestrian classes, and only one can be attributed to a wealthy *ingenuus*. Note, however, that the built-in kline in the late first-century BCE tumulus tomb of the equestrian M. Lucilius Paetus on the via Salaria did not contain a body and Paetus was incinerated: see Montanari, *Monumento dei Lucilii*, who kindly pointed this out to me.

[68] Gasparri, 'Sarcofago romano'; Gasparri, 'Sarcofago con nekyia'; Brandenburg, 'Beginn'; Bordenache Battaglia, *Corredi*, nos. 4 and 5; Fless, 'Sarkophagbestattungen', 319–20 with nn. 5–6. Meinecke (*Sarcophagum posuit*, 49–53) suggests some dating criteria for these sarcophagi, which may indeed describe a general trend, although I doubt that the few securely dated examples suffice to support any firm and fast rules. To the potentially later plain sarcophagi listed above n. 49, those from an extraordinary tomb on the Appia near Fratocchie must be added. It contained three plain sarcophagi (one marble with a window over the head of the deceased, two peperino) and a marble casket with relief decoration of Antonine date. The building is usually considered to have been reused, although there is no evidence for this. A Trajanic brick stamp may indicate its approximate date, and the sarcophagi are likely to have been set up one by one over some decades. I am grateful to Janet DeLaine for discussing this tomb with me. For the tomb see Pietrogrande, 'Ruderi'; Meinecke, *Sarcophagum posuit*, 202–3 no. A5, with different interpretation and further bibl. Cf. Borg, 'Roman sarcophagi', 601–2. For second-century plain sarcophagi see also Meinecke's nos. B12, 19–20, 23, 27, 35–6, 43, 45, 47, 56–7, 61, 81, 84, 92 and 99 (n.b. several of these caskets have roof-shaped lids different from the flat ones mostly found in the first century). Meinecke's nos. B5, 13–14, 16, 55, 65, 69, 73, 75–8, 85–6, 88, 91 and 93 contained plain sarcophagi dated by her to the second or third century, although dating criteria are lacking and some may indeed be earlier.

[69] Herdejürgen, *Stadtrömische und italische Girlandensarkophage*.

[70] Ghini et al., 'Grottaferrata'; Ambrogi et al. (eds.), *Sculture antiche*, 181–4 nos. 101–2; Meinecke, *Sarcophagum posuit*, 198–200 no. A2.

of the sarcophagus decoration and by the jewellery of the woman, which included a ring with a gold portrait of a man with a Flavian hairstyle. Granino Cecere tentatively suggests that Aebutia may have belonged to the first order and been married to a consul. Two caskets that have been known for much longer are equally inscribed and attest to the burial of the *consul suffectus* of 87 CE, C. Bellicus Natalis Tebonianus (see Figure 1.16), and an imperial freedman,[71] pointing to a similar clientele as the plain sarcophagi just discussed. If we add the two newly found caskets to Herdejürgen's list, her four garland sarcophagi from the Julio-Claudian era are followed by thirteen items from the Flavian and Trajanic periods. A further twenty chests are attributed to the early and another forty-six to the late Hadrianic period. Even allowing for a little more uncertainty in the dating of these items than does Herdejürgen, the general trend is clear. Extant garland sarcophagi support both the observation that inhumation in sarcophagi was far more widespread during the first century CE than is normally admitted, and that there was a general trend of increasing popularity of this type of burial already before the mid-second century.[72]

The motives for continuing or reviving inhumation may in fact have varied from case to case. Some scholars have suggested that sentimental reasons determined practice.[73] When Priscilla, wife of Abascantus, the influential and enormously rich freedman and *ab epistulis* of Domitian, died, he found the idea of the smoke and noise of her funerary pyre so distressing that he inhumed her – at least, according to Statius (*Silv.* 5.1.226–7).[74] Yet this is a unique report. Unfortunately, Tacitus (*Ann.* 16.6) gives no reason for Nero having his wife Poppaea embalmed, although he seems to insinuate that deep affection for her may have inspired the treatment of her corpse. That affection, and a desire to preserve the deceased's beauty, was indeed a major concern is clear from the relatively large number of embalmed bodies found in the early caskets discussed above, to which can be added further examples.[75] The most spectacular example is known only through a report by Pirro Ligorio, who describes two sarcophagi found intact at the sixth mile of the via Cassia. One contained the embalmed remains of a little girl,

---

[71] Herdejürgen, *Stadtrömische und italische Girlandensarkophage*, 79–81 no. 6 pls. 10.2–3, 11.1, 12; 38 no. 13 pl. 6.5.

[72] Yet see e.g. Davies ('Before sarcophagi'), who equally stresses a more gradual introduction of inhumation.

[73] E.g. de Visscher, *Droit*, 40–1; Zanker and Ewald, *Mythen*, 28; Davies, 'Before sarcophagi', 51.

[74] On her tomb, see Chapter 4, 252–4. Cf. also Chioffi, *Mummificazione*, 55–7 nos. I.2–14.

[75] Bordenache Battaglia, *Corredi*, 100–23; Bedini (ed.), *Mistero*, 76–83; Ascenzi, 'Grottarossa'; Chioffi, *Mummificazione*, 47–50; Dresken-Weiland, *Sarkophagbestattungen*, A119 (all on the embalmed body of a girl in a Iulus Ascanius sarcophagus from the second century CE).

Figure 2.8 Sarcophagus with window in its lid from Ostia's Pianabella necropolis, Ostia, Museum

whose body and face were covered in gold. The lid above her face featured a window closed with glass, and a bronze cover was fixed to the lid by a hinge so that it could be opened and closed. Next to the girl's casket stood the marble sarcophagus of a woman, probably her mother, the interior surface of which was entirely covered in gold. The deceased was embalmed as well and her hands and face gilded.[76] Windows in the lid above the deceased's face have occasionally been reported elsewhere, but the only still extant example was found in 1962 in Ostia's Pianabella necropolis (Figure 2.8); unfortunately, no details of the circumstances of discovery seem to be known.[77] These cases support the view that sentimental concern for the

---

For further examples, cf. Chioffi (*Mummificazione,* with altogether forty to fifty cases from the Republican period to the fourth century), the new discovery at n. 69 above and the following; the girl from Mentana (n. 68 above) is said to have had 'il corpo intatto', which could have been due to embalming as well (the corpse disintegrated soon after the sarcophagus was opened). On Poppaea, see also Pliny, *NH* 12.83; Cassius Dio 63.26.3; Chioffi, *Mummificazione,* 35–6 no. 1; Counts, 'Embalming', 192–3. On Abascantus, see Chioffi, *Mummificazione,* 55–7 no. 14. The idea that this practice was largely limited to Romans with strong Egyptian connections (Toynbee, *Death and Burial,* 41–2) has been abandoned by most scholars, and with good reason: Counts, 'Embalming', points out that there is no evidence that embalmed bodies were otherwise treated differently from other deceased Romans, and that embalming would also have allowed the long periods of lying in state attested for the elite in literary sources (up to seven days), although he accepts that the inspiration may have come from Egypt like other inspiration for luxury items and esalted behaviour.

[76] Gasparri, 'Sarcofago con nekyia', 169 no. 32, with excerpt from the Naples manuscript of Pirro Ligorio; Chioffi, *Mummificazione,* 51–3 nos. 11–12; Meinecke, *Sarcophagum posuit,* 209 no. A11.

[77] Gasparri, 'Sarcofago romano', 130–1 pl. 15b; Brandenburg, 'Beginn', 286 figs. 9–10; Agnoli, 'Sarcofagi', 245 no. B75. Fragments of the glass closing the window were found in the casket.

preservation of a beautiful loved one played a major part in the treatment of a body, and it is surely no coincidence that, in the majority of cases, it was accorded to young women and girls.

Unlike embalming, simple inhumation does not preserve the body. Liana Brent has drawn my attention to a passage of Gregory of Nysa (*Vit. Mac.* 35), which describes his horror at the prospect of seeing the decomposed bodies of his parents, whose grave his sister wanted to share. Yet Emma-Jayne Graham has pointed out how much effort, even in the case of the simplest burials, was put into protecting the body and laying the deceased's head comfortably on a head rest or cushion.[78] She is certainly right in proposing that, with the introduction of inhumation, new attitudes to the dead body are also becoming apparent that deny, as far as possible, its decay, and that pretend that the deceased were merely sleeping. Graham's views are supported by funerary texts and the exceptional popularity of sleeping beauties in sarcophagus reliefs, which visualise the hope often expressed in epitaphs, that death may be a peaceful existence free from the toil and pain of earthly life and similar to sleep.[79] In this light, embalming seems merely to take care for the body, and the simulation of eternal sleep, to the extreme. Nevertheless, Graham is also rightly cautious not to speculate about cause and effect with regard to attitudes to the body reflected in such treatment on the one hand, and the introduction of inhumation on the other.

Contrary to what she suggests, I cannot see conclusive evidence that these dead bodies were also increasingly hidden from view.[80] The various kinds of real or imitated cushions, and the staging of the body as if sleeping, only really make sense when they are also viewed. If we are right in considering the embalmed bodies as the most consequential enactment of the idea of death as eternal sleep, there is every reason to believe that the scenario was

---

For a parallel, see a now-lost plain marble sarcophagus with a window over the face of the deceased, which was the main burial in an unusual tomb on the Appia near Frattocchie: cf. n. 68 above. On sarcophagi with windows, see also Meinecke, *Sarcophagum posuit*, 28 and 41.

[78] Graham, 'Corporeal concerns'.

[79] Borg, 'Slumber'.

[80] That the rituals around the body in cremation ceremonies disappeared, and the corpses ultimately ended up in a closed coffin or grave, does not necessarily change matters fundamentally, since the laying out of the body continued as a practice. Graham ('Corporeal concerns') further argues that there was an increased use of professional undertakers, which also resulted in the detachment of the family from the body. However, I fail to see the evidence for this evolution either. Moreover, the care for the body she describes so well occurs in all classes, not just in those who could afford the services of undertakers. Graham's suggestion that this practice 'trickled down' to the lower classes, whose attitudes to the body changed when they gained access to the services of the *libitinarii* over time, would need support by dated evidence, which I doubt exists.

meant to be seen – either solely during the funerary ceremonies, or later on through the window in the sarcophagus lid. After all, considerable wealth was expended on these burials, on the preservation of the body and on grave goods. Many of the girls and women were dressed in fine garments and decked out with gold jewellery and other expensive items. In the case described by Pirro Ligorio, the bare skin of the deceased and the entire interior of the woman's casket were covered in gold. The limited range of patrons we can identify as opting for sarcophagus burial may further support the view that status display played a distinct part in the choice of burial style. The majority of sarcophagus burials that can be attributed to a social class belonged to the senatorial (and equestrian) elite, while the few that did not all had close links with the imperial house: three of them were imperial freedmen (to whom Domitian's notorious freedman Abascantus must be added),[81] and Calpurnius was engaged as a banker in Nero's new market and commemorated by an imperial freedman.[82]

Before we go on to consider any further the potential reasons for inhumation and the use of sarcophagi, it is worth pausing for a moment to review our results so far. The first aspect to note is that during the later first century BCE and the first century CE, inhumation and the use of sarcophagi were far more common than is usually admitted. To be sure, Tacitus describes incineration as the *Romanus mos* in Nero's (and his own?) day,[83] but the point of this statement was probably not a general comment on Roman customs, but another invective against Nero, who is accused of un-Roman (here: phil-Egyptian) behaviour – a strategy that had worked to Augustus' advantage in his competition for public favour with Marc Anthony. In any case, while it is certainly true that the majority of Romans who could afford it incinerated their dead during the first centuries BCE and CE, inhumation was both considered the *mos* of the old Roman *gentes* and on the rise among the wealthy in Tacitus' own time. The actual habit of inhumation during the Republic is substantiated by archaeology, while later authors such as Cicero (*Leg.* 2.22.56) and Pliny (*NH* 7.55.187) confirm awareness of the fact.[84] The latter even regards inhumation as the older custom, reporting the discovery of king Numa Pompilius' sarcophagus at the foot of the Ianiculan Hill in 181 BCE as an example. This burial is referred to by several other authors, which

[81] On Abascantus' tomb for his wife Priscilla, see Statius, *Silv.* 5.1, and Chapter 4, 252–4.
[82] Cf. Meinecke, *Sarcophagum posuit*, 42–3, who considers only some of the above evidence.
[83] Tacitus, *Ann.* 16.6: *corpus non igni abolitum, ut Romanus mos, sed regnum externorum consuetudine differtum odoribus conditur tumuloque Iuliorum infertur.*
[84] Scheid, 'Körperbestattung', 11; Vismara, 'Inumazione', 596. Pliny and Cicero also make special reference to the Cornelii.

equally suggests 'public knowledge' of the antiquity of inhumation.[85] Pliny further notes that 'many families' continued the old tradition of inhumation even after the majority had switched to incineration,[86] and verifies the increase in inhumation over the course of the first century. Writing about his own day, the 70s CE, he states that 'many people' (*multi*) preferred to be buried in terracotta sarcophagi, a statement that is corroborated by the production of such sarcophagi from Tiberius' time onwards.[87]

Secondly, evidence for patrons of (stone) sarcophagi demonstrates that the majority of them belonged to the senatorial elite, with some equestrians and wealthy imperial freedmen making similar choices. Considered in conjunction with the sources just cited, this observation makes it clear not only that the change of general practice to inhumation did not need any outside stimulus, but that it was even regarded, at least by some, to be the real Roman *mos*, practised continuously by some of the oldest and most prestigious families, and thus suitable for a new elite as well.

And thirdly, we notice that initially – and often later on as well – the choice was independent from any desire to depict narrative images. Undeniably, the potential for image decoration was explored already in the early garland sarcophagi. Moreover, there can be no doubt that the Romans gradually developed a taste for more lavish embellishments of their caskets; and it is certainly no coincidence that, at the same time as garland sarcophagi became more popular in the early second century, the size and relief decoration of cinerary urns and altars also increased, doubtless in order to render them more visible and impressive. In a few instances, ashes and remains of cremated bodies have been found inside sarcophagi, further supporting the view that sarcophagi were valued in their own right, although there is no reason to believe that they were used more widely for cremated bodies.[88] It is thus plausible to assume that the choice of sarcophagi, by an increasing number of people, was also due

---

[85] That Pliny is actually wrong, and that the discovery of Numa's sarcophagus is most likely legendary, is irrelevant to our argument. For Numa's sarcophagus, see Livy 40.29.3–5; Pliny, *NH* 13.84 (27); Valerius Maximus 1.1.12. Cf. Schrumpf, *Bestattung*, 68 with n. 179; Carroll, *Spirits*, 5.

[86] Pliny, *NH* 7.55.187: *et tamen multae familiae priscos servavere ritu*.

[87] Pliny, *NH* 35.46.160: *Quin et definctos sese multi fictilibus soliis condi maluere, sicut M. Varro, Pythagorio modo in myrti et oleae atque populi nigrae foliis*. For the archaeological evidence dated by stamps from Tiberius onwards, see Taglietti, 'Diffusion'. See Steinby, 'Necropoli', 31, and Steinby, *Via Triumphalis*, 103–4 on terracotta sarcophagi from the via Triumphalis necropolis, one of them stamped and dated to the Neronian period (S 1, pl. 20.5). Cf. Vismara, 'Inumazione', 601–2.

[88] Nock, 'Cremation and burial', 333 with n. 61. Cf. Davies, 'Before sarcophagi', 22 n. 6; Ortalli, 'Il sarcofago' and Ortalli, 'Culto funerario', 226–7 fig. 7 (inhumation and incineration in one and

to a growing desire for larger and more luxurious display pieces as containers for their perishable remains.

However, marble sarcophagi are impressive display pieces even in their most simple form.[89] Their sheer material value was considerable and obviously sufficiently impressive for the taste of some members of the first order, as the continued use of plain or extremely sparsely decorated caskets among the social elite throughout the second and third centuries demonstrates.[90] Moreover, the general trend towards the use of sarcophagi took off long before mythological image decoration was introduced more widely, so that the latter developed on the back of the former, not the other way round. It is therefore highly unlikely that the change in custom was induced by people from the East, be they freedmen or *homines novi*, or that it was related to the Second Sophistic and its ideas.[91] Instead, over the course of the second century, a practice that had continued at a low rate since the Republic, and then spread among a significant minority within the social and financial elite of Rome throughout the first and early second centuries CE, was extended more widely.

Taking these observations into account, the next question then is: Why did this change gain such momentum within a very short period of time around the middle of the second century? And why did it happen at this particular time, not earlier and not later?

Imperial Burials

It has not escaped scholarly attention that the rapid increase in the popularity of inhumation in marble sarcophagi roughly coincided with (the death of) Hadrian, and some writers have suggested a more specific influence on changing habits of the emperor himself. However, those making this

---

the same casket). Vismara ('Inumazione', 599 with n. 37) suggests that the *a cassone* tombs in the Isola Sacra should be counted as further examples, but these are not actually caskets but *cupae* covering the urns.

[89] This notion, first suggested by Nock ('Cremation and burial', 357–9), was rejected by Toynbee (*Death and Burial*, 40) on account of altars, ash chests and portraits being equally costly and ostentatious. While this is true, there is still a difference in dimension.

[90] Cf. n. 67 above, and examples in Borg, *Crisis and Ambition*, cf. General Index. See also Chapter 1, esp. 69–70, on the limited repertoire of mythical images used by the senatorial elite.

[91] This is not to deny that families originating from parts of the empire where inhumation was the rule may also have contributed to the growing popularity of inhumation. Turcan ('Origines', 332–4) and Schrumpf (*Bestattung*, 75–6) point to the Flavians' recruitment of senators from central Italy, where inhumation was often the rule.

connection typically point to Hadrian's philhellenism and adhere to the view that the change was incentivised by the desire to depict mythological imagery or to adopt a 'Greek' habit. A subgroup has gone even further and suggested that Hadrian, because of his philhellenic aspirations, may himself have been buried in a sarcophagus. Ian Morris, for instance, has drawn attention to the fact, occasionally pointed out by previous scholars, that it is far from certain that the Roman emperors continued to be cremated until Constantine, but that, from Hadrian onwards, they may in fact have been inhumed, thus contributing to the general and speedy change in practice from around 140–50.[92] We have seen above that neither philhellenic impetus nor direct influence from the East can explain the spread of inhumation and sarcophagi in Rome, and it is therefore highly unlikely that Hadrian had aimed to adopt a Greek habit. Yet the observation that he may have been the first emperor to be inhumed is worth considering nonetheless.

Written Evidence

A number of scholars have long proposed that the imperial house changed to the habit of inhumation with Antoninus Pius, if not Hadrian.[93] Our main literary source for imperial burial from Hadrian onwards is the notorious *Historia Augusta*, written and compiled only in the fourth century,[94] which can sometimes be compared with Cassius Dio and/or Herodian. The phrases used for Hadrian's burial are highly ambiguous, and the situation is further complicated by the fact that his mausoleum had not been completed at his death, so that he was first buried in Baiae and only later in his designated burial place. The *Historia Augusta*'s *Vita Antonini* (5.1) describes this act as a 'translation of his remains' (*Hadriano … mortuo reliquias eius … in hortis Domitiae collocavit*), while the *Vita Hadriani* (25.7) refers to his second and final burial in his mausoleum with the words *sepultus est*, which is as ambiguous as the Greek *etaphe* in the Byzantine summary of Dio's account (68.23.1).

In connection with Antoninus Pius, Marcus Aurelius, Lucius Verus and Commodus, however, the *Historia Augusta* consistently uses the word *corpus* when referring to the remains of the emperors placed in Hadrian's

---

[92] Morris, *Death-ritual*, 54–6, 61.

[93] Turcan, 'Origines'; Richard, 'Incinération'; Richard, 'Funérailles'; Morris, *Death-ritual*, 54–6; Johnson, *Imperial Mausoleum*, 15–16; contra e.g. Kierdorf, 'Apotheose'; Price, 'Consecration'; Arce, 'Imperial funerals'.

[94] Opinions are divided on whether this was in the early or the late fourth century, but this does not matter much for our purposes. For a recent discussion, see Cameron, *Last Pagans*, 743–82.

mausoleum,[95] suggesting that they were in fact inhumed.[96] It has been objected that *corpus*, like the Greek *soma*, can refer to both a body and the bones and ashes left by cremation.[97] Whether this is the case for the *Historia Augusta* is less clear. In the *Vita Septimii Severi* (24.1–2), the version of events according to which Septimius' *corpus* was returned from York is explicitly contrasted with, and favoured over, another account, also known to Herodian and Dio,[98] according to which an *urnula aurea* with his *reliquiae* was returned. This suggests that the *Historia Augusta* normally refers to the body when it uses the term *corpus*.[99] Only the same source's description of the burial of Caracalla potentially contradicts this conclusion (*Caracalla* 9.12). The passage reads: 'His *corpus* was laid in the tomb of the Antonines, in order that the resting place which had given him his name might also receive his *reliquiae*.'[100] Both Herodian (4.13.8) and the epitome of Cassius Dio (79.9) tell us that Caracalla's successor Macrinus burned the body, although they disagree on the exact circumstances. According to Herodian, Macrinus returned the urn to Rome and secretly placed it in Hadrian's mausoleum, while Dio reports that Macrinus sent the urn to Julia Domna, who was at Antioch at the time. Given these contradictions, one wonders whether the author of the *Historia Augusta* was equally uncertain about Caracalla's treatment (as he obviously was about Septimius Severus') and simply assumed that he was inhumed like all his predecessors (note that he preferred the version of Septimius' inhumation over that of his cremation). In any case, it is certainly possible that he used the term *corpus* consistently in the sense of 'body'. Thus, if we read *corpus* as 'body', according to the *Historia Augusta*, all subsequent emperors whose burial is mentioned at all were interred.

Resistance against accepting the second-century emperors' change to inhumation mostly arises from the continued importance of the funerary pyre and release of an eagle, both as part of the actual public imperial funerary rites and in visual images publicising the event on monuments and

[95] Scriptores Historiae Augustae, *Marcus Antoninus* 7.10, 20.1; *Verus* 11.1; *Commodus* 17.4.

[96] Ditto already Turcan, 'Origines', 328–30.

[97] E.g. Chantraine, 'Doppelbestattungen'; Price, 'Consecration', 96.

[98] Herodian (3.15.7; cf. also 4.1.3) reports that Severus was cremated in Britain and his remains brought back to Rome in an alabaster *kalpis*. According to Herodian 77.15.4, it was a porphyry *hydria*.

[99] This argument gains weight when we accept that the *Historia Augusta* had only one author, rather than the six under whose names it has come down to us.

[100] *Corpus eius Antoninorum sepulchro inlatum est, ut ea sedes reliquias eius acciperet quae nomen addiderat.* Translation by D. Magie. In the *Vita Macrini* (5.12), the author again uses the word *corpus: dein corpus Antonini Romam remisit, sepulchris maiorum inferendum.*

Figure 2.9 *Aureus* commemorating the apotheosis of Antoninus Pius with an image of his *rogus*

coins (Figure 2.9).[101] Yet this argument would only be conclusive if it could be demonstrated that cremating the body was a prerequisite for apotheosis or deification – and this is not possible. On the contrary, the cases of both Pertinax (193 CE) and Septimius Severus (211 CE) demonstrate that the body did not need to be cremated at the public ceremony, but could be replaced by a wax effigy without a negative effect on the emperor's apotheosis.[102] It could be argued that these were special cases: Pertinax had been assassinated a few months earlier, depriving him of the appropriate rites immediately following his death; and Severus had died abroad, causing similar delays to his honours at Rome. Be that as it may, the fact remains that they were deified even though their proper bodies had not received special ceremonial treatment, and there is not a single account of an emperor or other member of the imperial family dying abroad where this would have caused concern over their deification. Moreover, Herodian (4.2.2–11) actually presents the burning of wax effigies of Pertinax and Severus as standard practice, not as an adjustment to unusual circumstances. Writing in the 240s, he explicitly describes as typical the practice of ceremonially burning the emperor's wax double on the pyre a week after his actual body had been buried, thus indicating that it had been in place for some time.

---

[101] For such images, see e.g. Gradel, *Emperor Worship*; Abbondanza et al. (eds.), *Apoteosi*.

[102] On Pertinax see Dio 75.4.2–5.5; on Severus see Herodian 4.2. The bibliography on these funerals is vast; for a number of influential views, see the following discussion.

As Bickermann has already observed, the *Historia Augusta*'s description of Antoninus Pius' funerary rites, which comprised a lavish procession and panegyrics some days after the deposition of his *corpus* in Hadrian's mausoleum, seems to support this conclusion (*Marcus* 7.10–11).[103] Herodian also describes the burial of the actual body before the public rites of apotheosis as 'according to the custom of men' (*soma ... katathaptousin anthropon nomo*), which by then clearly was inhumation.[104]

Obviously, then, while the official rituals remained important and the funerary pyre became ever more impressive,[105] these rites were disconnected from the actual treatment of the corpse and are aptly called *funus imaginarium* by the *Historia Augusta* (*Pertinax* 14.8).[106] As Itay Gradel has pointed out, it was the senate's decision to confer divine honours on a deceased member of the imperial family that made them *divi* or *divae*.[107] This decision was normally taken shortly after the death had occurred and before the funeral, but the decree could also be passed and take effect later. Livia was deified by Claudius fourteen years after her death and funeral, and Vespasian's wife Domitilla, Trajan's natural father and Caracalla equally had to wait a few years for their *consecratio*. None of these deifications was accompanied by a second funeral or any specific rites.[108] The same is even true for Trajan himself, who was called *divus* shortly after his death and immediately after the senate's decree, even though he too died away from Rome at Selinus, and neither his body nor an effigy received any rites comparable to those known from other imperial funerals.[109]

---

[103] Bickermann, 'Kaiserapotheose', 4–5. Here Bickermann still believes that Antoninus Pius was cremated, although he later revised his view in this regard.

[104] Thus also Morris, *Death-ritual*, 55.

[105] E.g. Price, 'Consecration', 93–6.

[106] Thus already Turcan, 'Origines', esp. 331. On the *funus imaginarium et censorium*, see also Arce, 'Imperial funerals', 310, 321–2. Kierdorf ('Apotheose', 148) points out that the *funus imaginarium* had a long tradition in cases where an important person had died abroad and was supposed to be given a public funeral nevertheless.

[107] Gradel, *Emperor Worship*, 299–304. Price ('Consecration', 91–2) thinks that this was the case only after a change of procedures in the second century. Ditto Arce ('Imperial funerals', 320), who still thinks that 'the cremation is the *conditio sine qua non*' for apotheosis, drawing on Plutarch, *Quaest. Rom.* 14, which says of ancestors' burials: 'Once cremated, as soon as they find the ossified remains, they say that the deceased has acquired a divine nature.' However, this 'divine nature' could simply refer to membership of the *dii manes*, which is the automatic result of any form of orderly burial. The fact remains that if cremation had been necessary for apotheosis, then a wax effigy would not have done the trick.

[108] Gradel, *Emperor Worship*, 323–4. On Caracalla's late apotheosis, see Dio 79.9.2.

[109] When Kierdorf ('Apotheose') and others still look for a ritual that would 'activate' the senate's decision on divination, there is no other reason for doing so than the preconception that a religious act must consist of more than a decree by the senate.

Gradel therefore rightly concludes that the rituals that had become standard practice for public imperial funerals, the pyre and release of an eagle, were 'a visual enactment of deification', but not a religious or magical procedure indispensable for apotheosis.[110] That inhumation did not stand in the way of deification is finally supported by the fact that the Tetrarchs as well as Constantine were clearly inhumed, but still declared *divi* by the senate in Rome.[111] Indeed, ever since August Mau's Pauly-Wissowa article of 1897, it has occasionally been suggested that the regular use of wax effigies for the enactment of imperial apotheosis goes back to the second century, and that it was motivated precisely by the emperors' change to inhumation on the one hand, and continued need for the ceremonial pyre and eagle flight on the other.[112]

My discussion of the available written evidence hopefully has shown that neither the texts nor the concepts informing imperial mortuary practices contradict the assumption of imperial inhumation from Hadrian onwards, although it must be conceded that they do not confirm it conclusively either.

The archaeological evidence is also not straightforward, but can add important aspects to the argument.

Archaeological Evidence

Sources concur that emperors up to and including Trajan were incinerated, and most of them were buried in the Mausoleum of Augustus.[113] Trajan and his wife Plotina were equally incinerated, but famously buried in, or rather

---

[110] Gradel, *Emperor Worship*, 323, cf. 289; contra, Arce, 'Imperial funerals', 311, but without specific reasons. The idea that the rite was a magical one was first suggested by Bickermann ('Kaiserapotheose'), who uses the term 'Bildzauber'. Note in this context that Friedl ('Ustrina') has recently cast serious doubt on the interpretation of the structures in the Campus Martius, which are normally thought to be Antonine imperial *ustrina*.

[111] For a list of deified emperors, see Palombi, 'Divinizzazione', 193. Arce ('Imperial funerals', 321) points to evidence suggesting that the mock incineration at the public funeral continued to take place for these emperors, which, contrary to his own conclusions, further supports the view that the public cremation was just an enactment, not the act itself.

[112] *RE* III,1 (1897) 352 s.v. Bestattung (A. Mau). Cf. e.g. Turcan, 'Origines'; Richard, 'Incinération', 786–9; Richard, 'Funérailles', 464–5. Yet these authors disagree about the first instance of imperial inhumation, and they also insist on the religious necessity of the pyre.

[113] Hesberg and Panciera (eds.), *Mausoleum*; *LTUR* 3 (1996) s.v. Mausoleum Augusti: Das Monument 234–7 (H. v. Hesberg); s.v. Mausoleum Augusti: le sepolture 237–7 (M. Macciocca). Probably based on Dio 39.64, where Caesar's daughter Julia's body is said to have been snatched away from the Forum Romanum when the ceremonies there ended, and buried (*etapsan*) in the Campus Martius, Counts ('Embalming', 193) suggests that she was inhumed in the Mausoleum of the Iulii.

Figure 2.10 Mausoleum of Hadrian (Castel Sant'Angelo), view across the river

next to, his column near his forum, as Amanda Claridge has argued.[114] Hadrian's decision to erect a new mausoleum designed as a dynastic monument to hold the remains not only of his own immediate relatives but also of his successors started a new era (Figure 2.10). Modelled on the Mausoleum of Augustus, but larger, clad in gleaming marble and situated on the other side of the Tiber in the *ager Vaticanus*, it was connected to the Campus Martius by a new bridge, the pons Aelius, and continued to serve Hadrian's successors, at least until and including Caracalla.[115] Thanks to the continued employment of the building as a fortress and castle by the

[114] Claridge, 'Hadrian's succession', with bibl.
[115] As attested by epigraphic and literary evidence: *CIL* 6.984 (31220, pp. 841, 377, 4313) (= *ILS* 322 (Hadrian and Sabina)); 6.985 (31220) (= *ILS* 329 (Aelius Caesar)); 6.986 (31220) (= *ILS* 346 (Antoninus Pius)); 6.987 (31220) (= *ILS* 349 (Faustina Maior)); 6.988 (31220) (= *ILS* 350 (M. Aurelius Fulvus Antoninus)); 6.989 (31220) (= *ILS* 351 (M. Galerius Aurelius Antoninus)); 6.990 (= *ILS* 352 (Aurelia Fadilla)); 6.991 (= *ILS* 369 (L. Verus)); 6.992 (= *ILS* 401 (Commodus)); 6.993 (= *ILS* 383 (T. Aurelius Antoninus)); 6.994 (= *ILS* 384 (T. Aelius Aurelius)); 6.995 (= *ILS* 385 (Domitia Faustina)). See Pierce, 'Mausoleum'; Scheithauer, *Bautätigkeit*, 168–70; and further below. That the mausoleum was *intended* to serve subsequent generations is clear not least from the frieze of tabulae on its front that were inscribed only one by one as new burials took place.

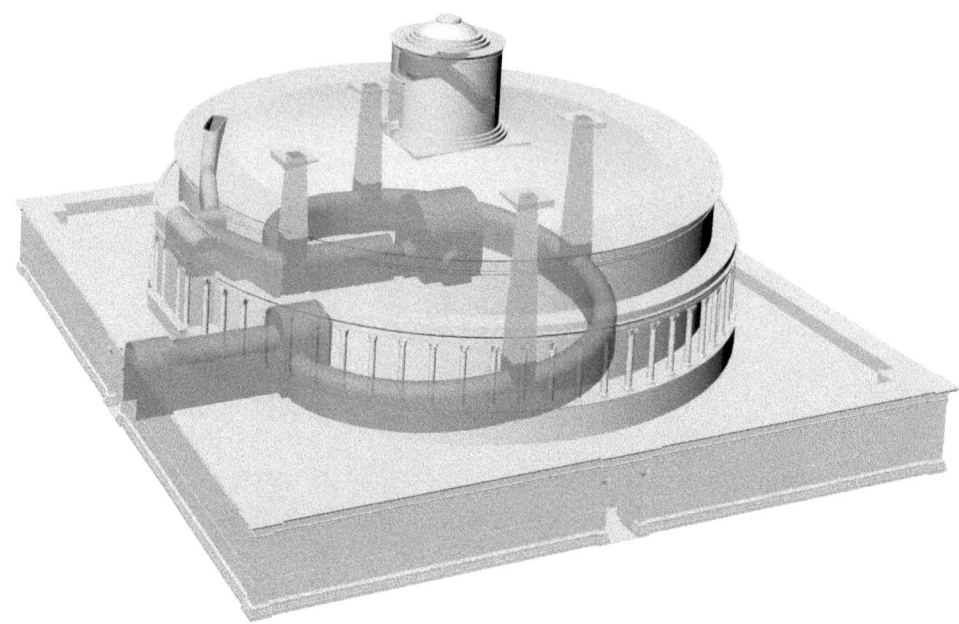

Figure 2.11 Mausoleum of Hadrian, reconstruction drawing of its original features by Paolo Vitti

popes,[116] many details of the exact use of its interior are hard to establish, but after a recent examination by Paolo Vitti, so much seems to be clear (Figure 2.11). Entering through a corridor, one first arrives in a square vestibule that features a wide, semi-circular niche at its rear, which is usually thought to have framed a colossal statue of the emperor. The right-hand wall gives access to a vaulted circular ramp which, after turning through 360 degrees, arrives in another straight passage above the entrance corridor, which in turn leads into a single large, approximately square tomb chamber of 8.35 by 8.10 m. Large vaulted niches occupy the rear, left and right walls.[117]

At least two sarcophagi are reported to originate from the mausoleum. It has long been known that, according to several medieval sources, a large

---

[116] For the mausoleum, see Pierce, 'Mausoleum'; Mercalli (ed.), *Adriano e il suo mausoleo*; Davies, *Death and the Emperor*, 34–40, 82–5, 158–63; *LTURS* 1 (2001) 15–22 s.v. P. Aelii Hadriani sepulcrum (P. Liverani – M. A. Tomei); Proietti, *Mausoleo*; Johnson, *Imperial Mausoleum*, 30–40; Vitti, 'Mausoleo di Adriano', who is preparing a full publication of the building; Coarelli, 'Mausoleo di Adriano'.

[117] According to Vitti ('Mausoleo di Adriano'), the chambers now to be found above this burial chamber are not ancient.

porphyry sarcophagus was found on the circular ramp.[118] Pope Innocent II himself had chosen its bottom part as his sepulchre and was laid to rest there in 1143, although the casket was destroyed in the fire of 1308 that devastated the Lateran.[119] According to the same medieval sources, its lid had already been used in 1077 for the sarcophagus of the Prefect Cinthius in St Peter's.[120] This information seems to be contradicted by the sixteenth-century author Panvinius, who tells us that the lid covering the sarcophagus of Otto II († 983), which was equally displayed in the *atrium* of Old St Peter's, came from Hadrian's mausoleum, and scholars are divided on whom to believe.[121] Kaufmann observed that the earlier texts that attribute it to the prefect all depend on one source, which is repeated almost verbatim and simply may have got it wrong. He further argued that it is strange that no later text describing the *atrium*, not even the few actually mentioning the prefect's sarcophagus, also mention the lid.[122] Yet it is also hard to see why the early sources would have got it wrong in the first place. Moreover, the same argument regarding the silence of our sources could be extended to Otto's sarcophagus, which was far more famous than that of the prefect and was mentioned in many sources previously, while we have to wait for Panvinius to provide us with the remarkable piece of information on the lid's provenance.[123] Maybe we are in fact dealing here with two separate ancient porphyry sarcophagi: one, now lost, divided between Cinthius and Innocent II and another, whose lid covered the casket of Otto II while its bottom is lost. We shall return to this lid in due course.

Another sarcophagus, this time made of grey granite, also has a recorded provenance from the mausoleum, although no details are given (Figure 2.12).[124] It is tub-shaped and decorated with two rings imitating handles and the head of a lynx in the centre at the bottom on the front.

---

[118] Herklotz, *Sepulcra*, 97, 133 nn. 67–70; Herklotz, *Sepulcra e monumenta*, 147 with n. 67. The tradition concerning the provenance of the sarcophagus from Hadrian's mausoleum goes back as far as the twelfth century, from which we have four texts.

[119] Herklotz, *Sepulcra e monumenta*, 148 with n. 69. Deér, *Dynastic Porphyry Tombs*, 150–1, and 146–54, on Innocent II and the use of porphyry by popes and emperors in general.

[120] Grisar, 'Sepolcro', 472; Amedick, 'Kaisersarkophag', 207.

[121] Kaufmann, *Kaisergrab*, 18; Grisar, 'Sepolcro', 471; Herklotz, *Sepulcra e monumenta*, 162, 174–5 with n. 141; Amedick, 'Kaisersarkophag', 207 with n. 13.

[122] Kaufmann, *Kaisergrab*, 23–4.

[123] In favour of the attribution: ibid., 23–4, with presentation of the sources on pp. 9–16; Manodori, 'Memorie', 157; contra: Grisar, 'Sepolcro', 471–3, with the sources pp. 64–6; Herklotz, *Sepulcra*, 97; Amedick, 'Kaisersarkophag', 207 with bibl.

[124] Massi, *Indicazione*, 204 no. 40; Fèa, *Nuova descrizione*, 100; Amelung, Vat. Kat. II (1908) 224 no. 82; Pietrangeli, 'Provenienza', 167 no. 13 (1052); Andreae et al. (eds.), *Bildkatalog*, pl. 372 with p. 36*; Amedick, 'Kaisersarkophag', 208; González-Palacios, 'Pio VI', 355 figs. 14–15.

Figure 2.12 Granite sarcophagus from the Mausoleum of Hadrian, Rome, Vatican Museums, Belvedere

The tub's use for burial is attested by a groove running through the middle of its interior, designed to hold a partition wall in place, which separated two depositions in a way known from other sarcophagi around Rome. The tub is highly polished and of impressive dimensions.[125] Its shape and décor are very rare but not unique, and have parallels, of which two were found in a necropolis at Alexandria. Together with the type of stone, they suggest that the entire group, including the Roman example, was produced at Alexandria.[126] A comparison with the more frequent tubs with lion heads indicates a date in the earlier third century, which points to its use for members of the Severan family.[127]

Besides these items, a case can be made for the provenance of another sarcophagus (or fragments thereof) from the Mausoleum of Hadrian. Rita Amedick has recently collected the evidence for porphyry sarcophagi from Rome, and argued that it is highly likely that they all served for the burial

---

[125] Length 3.27 m, depth 1.60 m, height 0.79 m.

[126] Stroszeck, 'Wannen'; the tub from the Mausoleum is mentioned p. 228 with n. 68.

[127] Ibid., 228, 235 with n. 101. Stroszeck further suggests that the type was inspired by the sarcophagus of Alexander the Great, whose tomb both Septimius Severus and Caracalla visited (pp. 229–30). Caracalla first exiled and later killed his wife, and Julia Domna was buried in the mausoleum only years after her husband. However, a number of scenarios are possible: Julia Domna could have been placed in Septimius' sarcophagus when she was finally buried in the mausoleum (a procedure that often happened with married couples); she could have been buried in the tub with her son Geta (as might be suggested by Cassius Dio 79.24.3, who tells us that both her and Geta's bones were translated to the mausoleum by her sister Julia Maesa); or the tub could have been set up in the mausoleum before the death of its patron, designed to hold his and his wife's remains, but used in the end only for him.

of emperors or their relatives.[128] Hans Rupprecht Goette had shown previously that porphyry, while not popular during the first century CE, was much valued under Trajan and Hadrian for statues and architectural decoration. Among many other objects, a colossal porphyry statue of a seated Hadrian is likely to belong to the emperor's temple at Caesarea Maritima[129] and seven over-life-size togate statues from the centre of Rome can equally be dated to the late Trajanic or Hadrianic period.[130] Surely it is also no coincidence that it was Hadrian who established the new road, aptly called via Hadriana, which connected the Egyptian Eastern Desert and its famous quarries with the Red Sea.[131] While there was no formal ban on the use of porphyry by private individuals before late antiquity, its use for larger architectural features and statues always seems to have been the preserve of the emperor. Wherever a portrait head, an inscription or a context allows us to identify individuals portrayed in porphyry, they are emperors, and it has been pointed out that the colour of the stone likely signified the purple of the triumphator's toga or the purple cloak the emperor wore over his cuirass, which was equally reserved for him.[132]

Burial in porphyry urns is attested for two Roman emperors, Nero and (allegedly) Septimius Severus,[133] and it is well known that the Tetrarchs as well as Constantine with his family and successors used porphyry

---

[128] Amedick, 'Kaisersarkophag'.

[129] Goette, *Togadarstellungen*, 45–9, 155 no. M 31 pl. 66.2. Cf. Malgouyres (ed.), *Porphyre*, 26–43, for an overview of the use of porphyry in the Roman period.

[130] Goette, *Togadarstellungen*, with p. 132 nos. Bb 35–42 pls. 18.1–2, 4–8; 94.5. The dating rests mainly on the close stylistic parallels with the porphyry statues of Dacians from the Forum of Trajan. Goette tentatively attributes the *togati* to a *Porticus porphyretica* mentioned in the *Vita Probi* 2.203 and in *CIL* 15.7191 add., which is normally located in the Forum of Trajan. This would suggest either a Trajanic or else a Hadrianic date, since it was Hadrian who completed the forum project. For the new popularity of porphyry under Trajan and Hadrian, see also Pensabene, *Marmi*, 246–9.

[131] On the Via Hadriana: Sidebotham et al., 'Via Hadriana' (with reference to previous research); on the quarries: Maxfield and Peacock, *Quarries: Topography*, with 36–8, on a temple erected by the imperial slave Epaphroditus to Zeus-Serapis-Helios in the quarries of Mons Porphyrites between 117 and 119 CE; Maxfield and Peacock, *Quarries: Excavations*.

[132] Amedick, 'Kaisersarkophag', 210. As she notes, that the use of porphyry was meant to allude to dress colour is further suggested by the fact that all statues before the Tetrarchic period had their heads and bare-skin extremities worked separately in white marble. On the use of purple garments, see also Reinhold, *Purple*, esp. 48–61.

[133] Amedick, 'Kaisersarkophag', 207; cf. Suetonius, *Nero* 50: *solium porphyretici marmoris*; Dio, *Septimius* 77.15: *hydria porphyretica*; on the contradictory evidence, see above n. 98. The point here is not the actuality but that the material was deemed appropriate for an imperial burial. Amedick (*Kaisersarkophag*, n. 12) records two non-imperial porphyry urns, but one of them was found in southern France and both were deposited inside a marble sarcophagus and were thus not visible.

Figure 2.13 Porphyry sarcophagus of Maximinian Herculius, reused as a baptismal font in the Cathedral of Milan

sarcophagi.[134] While most of these late antique caskets are very different in design from earlier ones, a porphyry tub now serving as the baptismal font in the Cathedral of Milan has a shape and decoration very similar to the granite item from Hadrian's mausoleum (Figure 2.13). Annarena Ambrogi has shown that it most likely originates from S. Gregorio, the former imperial mausoleum of Maximianus Herculius and Valentinian II, and probably belongs to the former.[135] Together with the extreme rarity of porphyry sarcophagi, the evidence strongly suggests that any porphyry sarcophagi from previous periods also belonged to members of the imperial family.

If this is accepted, all porphyry sarcophagi from the second and early third century must also originate from the Mausoleum of Hadrian, with

---

[134] Delbrück, *Porphyrwerke*. Most recently, with a discussion of context and the later use of the mausoleum: Asutay-Effenberger and Effenberger, *Porphyrsarkophage*.

[135] Ambrogi, *Vasche*, 108–9 cat. B. I. 31 figs. p. 223 (where she wrongly states that Maximian's tub is lost); Ambrogi, 'Sarcofagi in granito', esp. 107–8. She is mainly interested in the other sarcophagus, reused for the burial of Pandolfo III Malatesta, which is made of Nero Antico and resembles closely the sarcophagus of Julian the Apostate from Constantinople. It is therefore likely that this item belonged to Valentinian II and the porphyry tub to Maximian, for which see also Delbrück, *Porphyrwerke*, 166 fig. 73. Another porphyry tub, more or less identical to the Milan one, is now in the Wadsworth Atheneum in Hartford, but its provenance is unknown (inv. 1917.226: Malgouyres (ed.), *Porphyre*, 61 fig. 23).

the potential exception of one for Alexander Severus, who built a new mausoleum for himself, again using the tumulus type.[136] This would, then, also apply to the casket of Innocent II and the porphyry lid reused for Otto II, and confirm Panvinius' testimony. Moreover, even though the bottom part of the latter is not preserved, the lid's shape is so distinct that it can easily be reconstructed, at least in its basic form. Carlo Fontana documented the lid in the 1690s, both before and after he had it reworked into the baptismal font of a chapel in the new St Peter's Basilica (Figures 2.14 and 2.15).[137] It shows an unusual convex top and an asymmetrical outline, with one curvilinear and one straight short end. Similar shapes are known from a few other sarcophagi from Rome, Tyros and Egypt, all of which are made of Egyptian hard stone, though none of porphyry (Figure 2.16).[138] They were clearly made in Egypt and exported to a few exclusive clients. The lid reused for Otto II was of the same general type as these items but larger, made of porphyry rather than granite and with more sophisticated mouldings, an austere but truly monumental piece of work.[139] The lid measured 3.58 by 1.85 m, which is larger than even the biggest porphyry sarcophagi from the mausoleum of Constantine in Constantinople, except for one.[140] Given its material and size, Amedick is surely right that it is inconceivable that the sarcophagus belonged to anyone but an emperor. The considerable number of preserved imperial sarcophagi from the Tetrarchic period onwards are all

---

[136] His tomb is likely the one now known as the Monte del Grano: Quilici, *Via Latina*, 86–8 fig. 71; Pisani Sartorio, 'Tomba', 65–71; *LTURS* I (2001) 193 s.v. M. Aurelii Severi Alexandri Sepulcrum (119) (Z. Mari) with bibl.

[137] Fontana, *Descrizzione*, with unnumbered pl.; Kaufmann, *Kaisergrab*, 21–4; Delbrück, *Porphyrwerke*, 214 fig. 112; Manodori, 'Memorie', 156 fig. 3.

[138] Koch, 'Östliche Sarkophage', esp. 207 fig. 53; *MNR* I.8.2 (1985) 470–1 no. IX.1 inv. 108393 (E. Fileri). For the Vatican parallel of unknown provenance, which has lost its lid, see ibid., 207 with fig. 52; for the Tyros parallel, see Ward Perkins, 'Imported sarcophagi', 143–4 fig. 134; Ambrogi, 'Sarcofagi in granito'.

[139] Kaufmann, *Kaisergrab*, 23; Grisar, 'Sepolcro', 469, 471; cf. Delbrück, *Porphyrwerke*, 214 with fig. 112. Grisar goes on to argue that the baptismal font never was a sarcophagus lid because of its size, and rather was a *labrum*. However, in contrast to the much deeper tubs, *labra* used to be round rather than oval (Ambrogi, *Labra*), and the asymmetrical shape of the lid is unparalleled in water basins of any kind.

[140] The sarcophagus of Constantia is much smaller (Delbrück, *Porphyrwerke*, 219), but even the sarcophagi in Constantinople measure only between 2.58 and 3.47 m in length: ibid., 221–7; Vasiliev, 'Porphyry Sarcophagi'; Asutay-Effenberger and Effenberger, *Porphyrsarkophage*, with tables 2–5. For the largest item see Vasiliev, 'Porphyry Sarcophagi', esp. 14, 19–20 pl. 9 bottom with detailed measurements: 3.85 by 1.83 m; Delbrück, *Porphyrwerke*, 14, 27, 214, 227 pl. 107.1; Asutay-Effenberger and Effenberger, *Porphyrsarkophage*, 16 no. 4 fig. 10. The casket is often attributed to Julian, but see ibid., 59–65, on the difficulties of attribution.

Figure 2.14 Porphyry lid of an imperial sarcophagus from the Mausoleum of Hadrian reused as a baptismal font in St Peter's, Rome

of very different types, suggesting that the lid in question is to be attributed to a second- or early third-century emperor.[141]

Another porphyry sarcophagus has been reconstructed by Amedick from a porphyry *rota* (a round slab of porphyry on which the thrones of popes and kings used to be placed during ceremonial appearances) measuring 1.24 m in diameter (Figure 2.17).[142] The fragment belongs to an Attic strigilated kline sarcophagus, a type known from many white-marble parallels (Figure 2.18). It would originally have consisted of a rectangular strigilated casket with the kline legs shown at its corners, and the reclining figure(s) of the deceased on the couch-shaped lid. As Amedick argues, it is possible that the fragment of a porphyry figure now in the Museo Nazionale

---

[141] Two simpler granite parallels from Tyros were used for fourth-century burials (Ambrogi, 'Sarcofagi in granito', 106; Amedick, 'Kaisersarkophag', 208 n. 24), but they may have been reused.

[142] Amedick, 'Kaisersarkophag', with fig. 14 and colour pl. 3; the piece is set into the northern perimeter wall of the *atrium* of the Cathedral of Salerno, but is likely to be from Rome.

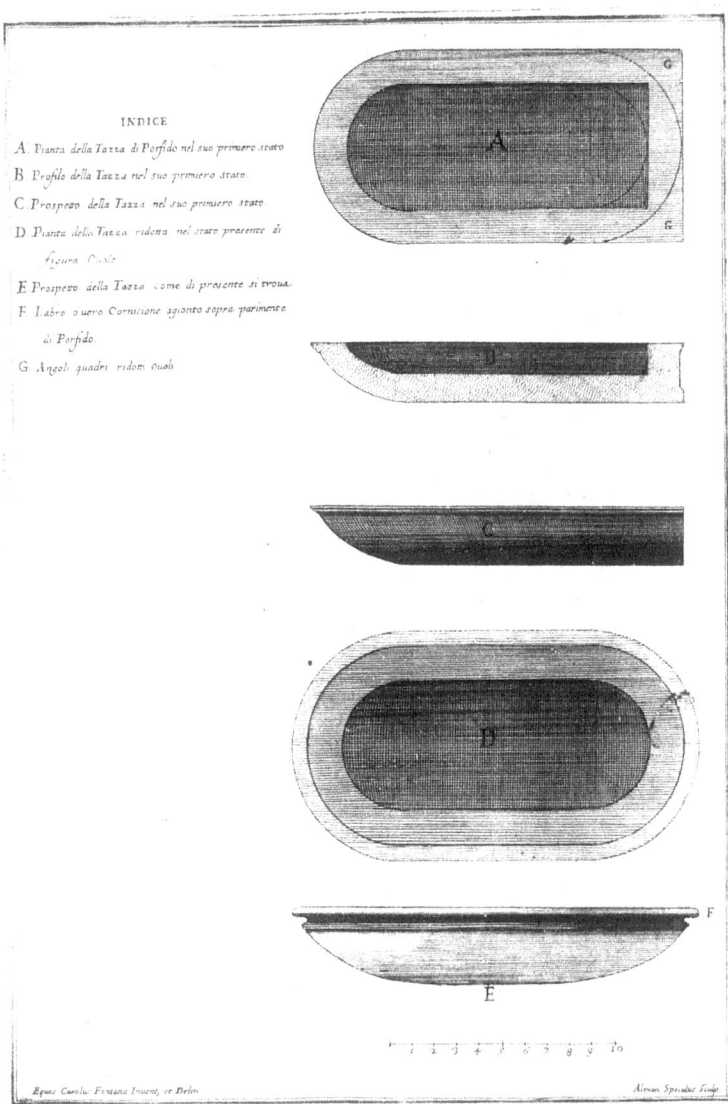

Figure 2.15 Drawings by Carlo Fontana showing the work stages that turned the porphyry lid of an imperial sarcophagus into the baptismal font of St Peter's (cf. Figure 2.14)

Romano in Rome originally belonged to this sarcophagus.[143] Similarly to the second-century porphyry statues, the head and arms of the reclining male figure were worked separately, most likely in white marble. Such a figure

---

[143] Inv. 61159: Delbrück, *Porphyrwerke*, 51 pl. 8; Amedick, 'Kaisersarkophag', 211; Anderson (ed.), *Radiance in Stone*, cat. 17.

Figure 2.16 Granite sarcophagus of Egyptian origin; Rome, Museo Nazionale delle Terme inv. 108393

would not only follow the same rules as other porphyry portraits, in being the preserve of the emperor; the figure resting on a kline would have been strongly reminiscent of the kline with the figure of the reclining emperor dressed in triumphal garb that was carried in the imperial funerary procession (*pompa funebris*).[144] An imperial porphyry kline sarcophagus must therefore be assumed from this fragment, and if it did not belong to the same sarcophagus as the *rota*, it attests to another imperial sarcophagus of a similar kind.

Based on written sources and extant remains, we can therefore identify a minimum of two and a maximum of four porphyry sarcophagi that are highly likely to be imperial, and thus must come from the Mausoleum of Hadrian.[145] To these we must add the tub-shaped granite item in the

---

[144] This is described by Dio 56.34.1 with reference to Augustus, but can probably be assumed to have been a feature of imperial *pompae* more generally.

[145] The minimum figure assumes that Otto's lid belonged to Innocent's sarcophagus and the figure fragment in the Museo Nazionale to the kline fragment in Salerno, while the maximum figure assumes that these were all separate items.

Figure 2.17 Porphyry *rota* of 1.24 m diameter cut from a kline sarcophagus; Salerno, Cathedral

Vatican (Figure 2.12). It is conceivable, albeit impossible to prove, that the porphyry tub (re?)used for Maximian Herculius (Figure 2.13) and a parallel described by Wadsworth also come from Hadrian's mausoleum.[146] Quite unlike the Mausoleum of Augustus, but in accordance with the tumulus tombs of the first century CE discussed above, the Mausoleum of Hadrian contained a burial chamber with niches on all but its entrance sides, and it would be natural to assume that they equally contained sarcophagi.[147] All the sarcophagi we can still assess were spectacular pieces of the most precious stone and of enormous size. To which emperor they belonged, and whether any of them contained the remains of Hadrian, is impossible to tell, but since Attic kline sarcophagi start to be produced only from around 160, or possibly even from around 180 onwards, this casket cannot have been Hadrian's.[148] It is tempting to think that the largest and, at the same time, most Egyptian of sarcophagi, attested to by the lid from Otto's tomb

---

[146] Cf. n. 136. Their shape and design may suggest a date not too dissimilar to the granite tub from the Mausoleum, which was already plundered at the beginning of the fourth century: Vitti, 'Mausoleo di Adriano', 247.

[147] Thus also Richard, 'Funérailles', 464, without reference to any precedents.

[148] Ditto Amedick, 'Kaisersarkophag', 211, who concludes that it most likely belonged to Marcus Aurelius and Faustina Minor. It should be added that Delbrück's identification of some fragments of a porphyry sarcophagus with relief decoration with the remains of Innocent II's sarcophagus is highly unlikely, since the fragments belong to a late antique type of casket (cf. Delbrück, *Porphyrwerke*, 216–18); ditto Amedick, 'Kaisersarkophag', 207 n. 15.

Figure 2.18 Attic kline sarcophagus, late second century CE; Athens, near the Hephaisteion

(Figures 2.14 and 2.15), was that of the emperor who founded the mausoleum, and who was so keen on all things Egyptian, including its hard stone,[149] but there is really no way to be certain.

To be sure, these sarcophagi are still not proof of the veracity of the *Historia Augusta* accounts, or indeed of the relevant phrases as definitively referring to inhumation. It is impossible to disprove the suggestion that the emperor's urns were placed inside the caskets, which just served as particularly ostentatious containers for them.[150] Yet, on the other hand, it is hard to see why we should insist on the continuation of imperial cremation.

---

[149] Malgouyres (*Porphyre*, 28–9) observed that the majority of porphyry (and other coloured marble) sculpture was created under Hadrian, while the Severans had an equal or even stronger taste for porphyry architectural members.

[150] For cinerary urns found inside sarcophagi, see Amedick, 'Kaisersarkophag', 207 n. 12. Amedick (*Kaisersarkophag*, 212) and Manodori ('Memorie', 157) believe that all emperors buried in the mausoleum were cremated.

There is neither any positive evidence nor a logical or historical need for the assumption that the mode of burial of the emperors from at least Antoninus Pius onwards was radically different from that of the rest of the Roman elite, and Herodian clearly states that it was not. Moreover, at least for the granite sarcophagus with its partition wall (Figure 2.12), inhumation is almost certain. Such partition walls are often found in the sarcophagi of married couples and would be useless, if not an obstacle, for the deposition of urns. A piece of circumstantial evidence may further support the view that the imperial family did indeed change burial customs under Hadrian: a Hadrianic garland sarcophagus was found in the Mausoleum of Augustus, which was used for the imperial family only.[151] Since Hadrian did not live to see his own mausoleum finished, it is possible that he buried a member of his family in what was the only other imperial tomb that would have been suitable, but that Antoninus Pius failed to translate the sarcophagus into the new mausoleum as Hadrian may have intended.[152]

Hadrian Between Tradition and Innovation

The adoption of inhumation, and of using sarcophagi for burial, would fit well with what we know about Hadrian's policies more generally, and about his attitude to both innovation and tradition more specifically. He clearly made a new start by establishing his own mausoleum, which was unprecedented in its size, splendour of decoration and use of materials.[153] Yet, as Richard Brilliant has pointed out, it was not him but Trajan (and before him Domitian) who abandoned the venerated dynastic Mausoleum of Augustus, so that the erection of a new dynastic tomb 're-established the principle of

---

[151] Herdejürgen (*Stadtrömische und italische Girlandensarkophage*, 111 no. 54 pls. 45.4, 47.5, 48.8–9) also demonstrates that previous doubts about its provenance are unfounded.

[152] For a previous imperial inhumation, see the burial of Poppaea (cf. n. 75 above). It is also not impossible that the so-called 'sarcophagus of Crispina' found on Capri, which contained a female skeleton, fabric woven from gold and silver thread, jewellery and a 50 cm-long sceptre, did indeed belong to either Crispina or Lucilla, wife and sister of Commodus respectively, who are known to have died in exile on Capri. See Federico and Miranda (eds.), *Capri*, 162 figs. 7.24–5; Trower, *Book of Capri*, 132–4. It could be objected that there would not have been enough space to accommodate sarcophagi for all the individuals we know to have been buried in the mausoleum. However, there was space for at least four sarcophagi (one in the centre and three in the niches), and more could have been fitted in had the chamber eventually been filled as much as some private mausolea, with hardly any space to walk around them. Moreover, each sarcophagus may have served for several burials, as was common in the tombs of private individuals. Even the possibility of a line of caskets along the wall of the ramp cannot be excluded.

[153] On the mausoleum, see above n. 116.

an imperial burial site in plain sight of the Romans'.[154] Moreover, tumulus tombs had long become extremely rare in the city of Rome, and the specific shape clearly looked back to the Mausoleum of Augustus, the only other uncontroversial dynastic tomb in Rome,[155] but also to the impressive tombs of the late Republican aristocracy. It is disputed where the inspiration for these tumuli came from, variously seen in North African and Eastern models – among the latter, especially those identified as the tombs of the Trojan forefathers, Homer's heroes and Alexander the Great – as well as in Etruscan ones,[156] and it should not be forgotten that there were tumuli in Latium as well.[157] However, while there is some indication that Augustus may have taken inspiration from outside Italy,[158] I am not convinced that this mattered much to Hadrian, given that the resemblance between his mausoleum and Republican predecessors is much closer than between the former and non-Italic models. Imitating, but at the same time outdoing, Augustus and the great Republican families appears to have been the main idea.

The location of the mausoleum in the *ager Vaticanus* rather than in the Campus Martius may be unexpected, but not only was the latter already built up to a high degree, the tomb was both huge and relatively isolated, and thus highly visible from the city and from the Tiber. High-profile tombs had been built in the area before, including the circular tumulus (?) tomb of the Asinii, erected for Agrippa's daughter Agrippina by her son Drusus, her husband Asinius Gallus and her daughter Livia, and used at least until the early second century.[159]

---

[154] Brilliant, 'Review of Taliaferro Boatwright', 360.

[155] Similarly Davies, *Death and the Emperor*, 160–1; Thomas, *Monumentality*, 181–2.

[156] Coarelli ('Mausoleo di Adriano') has recently renewed his plea for North African and Eastern origins, while others found Etruscan tumuli more likely as models (bibl. in Davies, *Death and the Emperor*, 51 n. 11); Davies (ibid., 51–67) considers a mix of inspirations including tombs in Egypt and trophies; Schwarz (*Tumulat Italia tellus*, 75–9) considers the connection with the tombs of heroes to be the most important; Montanari (*Sepolcri circolari*, esp. 11–16) makes a strong case for Etruscan influence while not excluding Eastern ones for Augustus.

[157] On tumulus tombs in Italy, see Naso (ed.), *Tumuli*. For Latium see Guidi ('Lazio') and Meinecke (*Sarcophagum posuit*, 20) for two examples containing sarcophagus burials. Peter Holliday argued at a conference at Oxford in 2015 for an Italian inspiration for the late Republican tumuli.

[158] The most obvious one seems to be the name Mausoleum, although it was first recorded only in 4 BCE: Davies, *Death and the Emperor*, 52.

[159] On the location, see ibid., 158–63. Davies does not, however, mention the earlier tombs. Cf. Coarelli, 'Mausoleo di Adriano', 269. As Liverani ('I giardini imperiali di Roma', 88–90) has shown, the *horti Domitiae*, within which the mausoleum was erected, had belonged to Hadrian's mother Domitia Paulina Lucilla, and not to Nero's aunt or Domitian's wife, as is often believed, and thus was on his own hereditary property. I am grateful to Chrystina Häuber for pointing this out to me. On the Asinii tomb, which was situated further south, see Alföldy, 'Monumento vaticano'; *LTURS* I (2001) 161–2 s.v. Asiniorum sepulcrum (M. G. Granino Cecere).

Hadrian's building activities more generally comprise highly innovative techniques and designs, especially in his villa at Tivoli. Yet there are also many conservative projects. The Temples of Venus and Roma and of Bona Dea, and the Auguratorium, hark back to Rome's very beginnings; he completed several of Trajan's projects, such as the Pantheon, on which he retained the original building inscription commemorating Agrippa as its donor (Figure 2.19); and he celebrated his many restoration projects on his coins by the legend RESTITUTOR.[160] As Brilliant put it, 'Many of Hadrian's "new" projects in Rome can be considered acts of *pietas*, formalised expressions of a conservative temperament that reinforced a long-standing, worthy tradition and promised its continuance.'[161] The same also applies to his mausoleum.

Hadrian's self-representation in different media shows a similar dual aspect. While he more or less quietly renounced his predecessor's imperialist and expansionist policies and supported the Greeks in the eastern Mediterranean, his portrait statues stand out in that almost all of them show the emperor in military dress (Figure 2.20), with only one extant exception.[162] His new hair and beard style have attracted much scholarly comment and are often linked with his philhellenism. However, both his elaborate coiffure and his beard had been popular among the Romans for some decades, and would better be characterised as urbane. While he certainly helped the breakthrough of this styling as a general fashion, he really jumped on a bandwagon that was already in full motion.[163]

This is what I suggest was the case with Hadrian's burial plans as well. At least one relative of his had been inhumed already and buried in the by then rather overcrowded Mausoleum of Augustus. Whether or not Hadrian was cremated himself – a measure that may have appeared preferable for practical reasons since he died away from Rome – he may very well have

---

[160] On Hadrian's conservatism, see Boatwright, *Hadrian*, 19–32 and passim, with Brilliant, 'Review of Taliaferro Boatwright'. On the sequence and shape of the three successive Pantheon buildings, see esp. Virgili and Battistelli, 'Piazza Rotonda'; *LTUR* IV (1999) 54–61 s.v. Pantheon (A. Ziolkowski) with addenda in *LTUR* V (1999) 280–3 s.v. Pantheon (E. La Rocca); Marder and Wilson Jones (eds.), *Pantheon*; esp. Hetland ('Pantheon', for the Trajanic date). For Hadrian's habit of retaining the inscriptions of buildings he restored, see Scriptores Historiae Augustae, *Hadrian* 19.10 and Boatwright, *Hadrian*, 43.

[161] Brilliant, 'Review of Taliaferro Boatwright', 360.

[162] The exception is a togate statue *capite velato* in Rome, Musei Capitolini inv. 54: Fittschen and Zanker, *Kaiser- und Prinzenbildnisse*, 53–4 no. 51 pl. 57. On Hadrian's portraits, see Evers, *Portraits d'Hadrien*, with discussion of the toga statue on pp. 158–9. The repeatedly voiced suspicion that the himation statue from Cyrene did not show Hadrian has recently been confirmed: Opper (ed.), *Hadrian*, 70 with fig. 63.

[163] Borg, 'Glamorous intellectuals', 157–61. For the style expressing *urbanitas* and *civilitas*, see Smith, 'Choice', 62–3, 91–2.

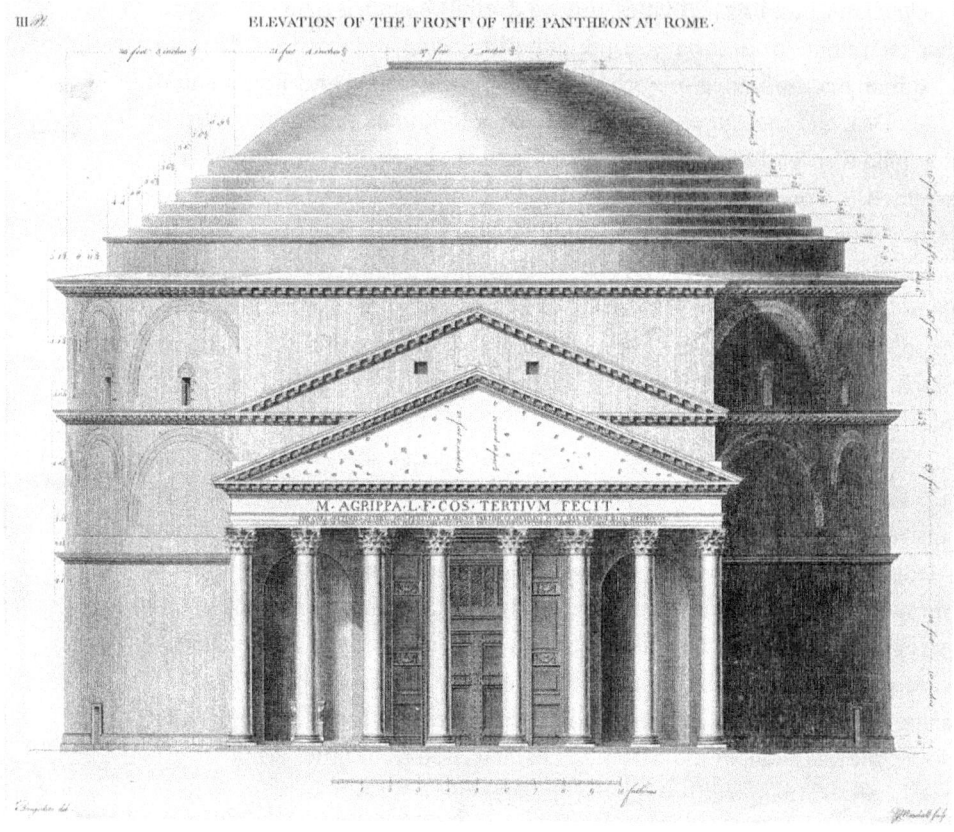

Figure 2.19 Rome, Pantheon as drawn by Antoine Desgodetz

prepared for his burial in the huge porphyry sarcophagus of which only the lid survives (Figures 2.14 and 2.15). If this is indeed the case, he chose a highly ambitious and truly outstanding sarcophagus of foreign, Egyptian, shape and material, although in line with the rather austere taste of the Roman elite who preferred monumentality over decorative detail.[164] He chose (or intended) inhumation as a style of burial that was unprecedented among Roman emperors, but harked back to the tradition of the great old Roman *gentes*, the *Romanus mos* of the Republic and even the Roman kings, and was much in line with the spreading habit of inhumation among parts of the Roman elite.[165]

---

[164] On this preference, see Chapter 1.

[165] It would be interesting to explore the relevance of the *mos maiorum* and monuments and cultural practices of the Republic during the second century and later in greater depth than is possible here. These trends, in my view, run parallel to the by now much better known trends subsumed under the term 'Second Sophistic', but have been eclipsed to a great extent

Figure 2.20 Cuirassed statue of Hadrian from Hierapytna, Crete; Istanbul, Archaeological Museum inv. 50

Conclusions

It has been acknowledged more widely in recent years that the change from cremation to inhumation was a gradual one. Disregarding those who had no choice due to lack of funds, it was especially among the social elite and the wealthiest of (imperial) freedmen that inhumation in (marble) sarcophagi, either plain or decorated with simple moulds or garland designs, had continued throughout the period when cremation was the majority practice. There is thus no need to look for outside influences when inhumation gained in popularity over the course of the latter half of the second century. While it was surely appreciated by many that sarcophagi provided a larger surface for image decoration than altars or urns, sarcophagus burial started to spread more widely before mythological subjects became

by research on the latter. Gowing (*Empire and Memory*) is valuable for the first centuries BCE and CE but, to my knowledge, there is no equivalent study for later periods, and none that systematically includes both literary and material evidence.

popular for their decoration, and such decoration never resonated with all social classes in the same way. Moreover, while the myths depicted on sarcophagi are predominantly Greek, it is possible that their introduction into the Roman funerary context was inspired by Etruscan precedents rather than Greek ones, and thus constitutes another element of traditionalism rather than philhellenism.[166] We have seen in Chapter 1 that the imagery used by the senatorial class for their tomb decoration owed much to public monuments, and we shall see in Chapter 4 that the habits of the emperors also had a major impact on the choice of tomb type by the moneyed classes. A change in imperial funerary practice from cremation to inhumation with Hadrian (or Antoninus Pius), itself triggered by a trend that had increasingly gained favour with the elite and radiated an air of tradition and revival of Roman *mores*, would best explain why it was only from around the middle of the second century that the habit of inhumation spread widely and through all social classes, while previously emulation of elite habits had not led to a similarly sharp rise in the practice.[167]

---

[166] Cf. Amedick's argument n. 20 above. This is consistent with Turcan ('Origines', 332–4) and Schrumpf (*Bestattung*, 75–6), who suggest an influence on Roman habits from Italic senators newly elected from the Flavian period onwards. As we have seen, sarcophagus burial as such started earlier than this, but it is surely possible that Italic senators contributed to the growing popularity of the habit. It is also notable that imperial-period sarcophagi from Greece and Asia Minor show rather different designs, stories and interpretations of stories from those found in Rome: see Koch and Sichtermann, *Römische Sarkophage*, for an overview.

[167] I am not suggesting here that there was a simple 'trickle-down' effect, as is so often argued (e.g. Vismara, 'Inumazione', 604; Graham, 'Corporeal concerns', 58), but that the idea of inhumation as a traditional custom may have appealed to many members of the sub-elite as well.

Family Matters: The Long Life of Roman Tombs

The importance in Roman society of the family, and especially of an extensive family line, has long been taken for granted. It is the pattern that dominates literary texts concerned with the social elite as well as legal sources. During the Republic, the family group that mattered most was the *gens*, an extended clan whose members all descended in the male line from a common ancestor – which is what we call the 'agnatic family'.[1] Later, so it is assumed, the agnatic family became less important while cognate family relations – that is, relations that also include kin in the female line – became more relevant.[2] In 1983, Keith Hopkins challenged this model fundamentally, and argued:

> it looks as though, in the period from which such evidence survives (i.e. after about 200 BC), the Roman and Italian family was a small, short-lived social unit. It also seems as though broader kinship units, such as clans or clan segments (*gentes*), at least from this period onwards, played an unimportant role in burials.[3]

While Hopkins' conclusions were primarily based on insufficient awareness of the evidence, a year later Richard Saller and Brent Shaw reached similar conclusions through a statistical approach to 12,000–13,000 tomb stones from various parts of the Roman empire. They counted each attested type of relationship between commemorator and commemorated, and then classified and added them up as either nuclear family (i.e. parents with their children) or extended relationships.[4] For the city of Rome, this resulted in 72 per cent nuclear relationships in the senatorial class, 77 per cent in the first

---

[1] On the ancient terminology for types of families and kinship relations, see Corbier, 'Constructing kinship'. On Smith's criticism of modern concepts of the gens (in *Clan*), see my comments below.

[2] E.g. Saller, 'Introduction Part 1', 24; Saller, 'Heirship', esp. 33. See most recently Galen, *Women*.

[3] Hopkins, *Death*, 206. He goes on to argue in Chapter 2 that 'they were similarly unimportant in politics'.

[4] Types of relationships included spouse to spouse, parent to child, child to parent and sibling to sibling (all classified as 'nuclear'), extended family (e.g. grandparents, grandchildren, nephews, nieces, etc.), heirs, *amici* (incl. *conservi* and *conliberti*), patron, master, freedperson and slave (all classified as 'extended').

two orders combined and 78 per cent in the lower classes.[5] Independently of Hopkins, but explicitly endorsing views previously expressed by De Visscher, they concluded that 'Most tombs of the imperial period were *de facto* personal tombs and were not tied to any strong *conception* or *practice* of maintaining long agnatic family lineages.'[6]

Their approach was challenged in 1996 by Dale Martin, who argued that counting individual relationships would not adequately represent family burials.[7] While, in Saller and Shaw's counting, a dedication by a man to his wife, his children, his brother and his parents would result in four nuclear relationships, the actual inscription commemorated three generations, thus representing what in their terms is an extended family. The dedication by a man to his wife, child, brother and *amicus* would result in three nuclear relationships and one extended, while assessing the epitaph as a whole would again result in the commemoration of one extended group of relations. Drawing on 1,161 epitaphs from seven different places in Asia Minor, and classifying entire inscriptions, Martin arrived at markedly different numbers from those of Saller and Shaw, even though figures for individual places differed considerably. Yet he still maintained that, while not strictly nuclear, the family groups he found were normally small and clustered around a nuclear family unit.[8]

Martin in particular has taken his observations to reflect not only funerary customs, but family structures as such. While Saller and Shaw were more cautious in this regard, they still suggested that funerary customs reflected Roman familial relations more generally, which were dominated by the nuclear family of a married couple and their children as opposed to the extended family. The Roman family thus became an early predecessor of our modern circumstances.[9] Such far-reaching conclusions have been

---

[5] See the table in Saller and Shaw, 'Tombstones', 147.

[6] Ibid., 125, my emphasis. Cf. de Visscher, *Droit*, chs 6–8, esp. 118. For similar conclusions from epigraphic and legal evidence, see also Kaser, 'Grabrecht', 48, 56, 59.

[7] Martin, 'Construction'.

[8] Ibid., 57–8. Martin goes on to challenge the distinction between nuclear and extended family as such, arguing that, in his inscriptions, he found 'a "nucleated" centre surrounded by a spectrum of relations of more or less intimacy' (p. 58). Yet while this describes the situation correctly, his reasoning is circular when he takes for granted that these constellations all represent 'family'.

[9] Saller and Shaw, 'Tombstones', 146; Shaw, 'Epigraphy', 466; Shaw, 'Death', 72; Saller, *Patriarchy*, 96. Some scholars have denied that they draw conclusions for family structures outside the funerary realm, but while there are some cautionary remarks, other passages are less considerate (e.g. Saller and Shaw, 'Tombstones', 145–6: 'Modern historians have shown that in most areas of western Europe the nuclear family was the main type of familial organization as far back as dependable records are available. On the basis of our evidence, it seems a reasonable hypothesis that the continuity of the nuclear family goes back much further in time

duly criticised,[10] and Sabine Huebner has demonstrated for Egypt that the 86.9 per cent of epitaphs representing nuclear family commemorations present a stark contrast to domestic cohabitation practices as documented in census registers.[11] It is therefore worth keeping in mind that evidence from epitaphs informs us first and foremost about commemorative practices, and the greatest of caution is needed when drawing more general conclusions about family relationships and compositions.[12] Today, far more flexible models of what a family may have been are prevalent. They allow for the possibility that familial relations may be conceptualised differently in different contexts, for instance in (inheritance) law; in the composition of domestic units; in informal, ideologically determined relationships of obligation; or in personal affection, all potentially varying again depending on social class and economic means. They take account of changes in individual household composition and size over time, resulting from death, marriage, remarriage, childbirth, adoption and so on, and of the fact that the household may be both larger and smaller than a 'family' (depending on its definition) as it can include unrelated servants without comprising all kin.[13]

For research on the funerary sphere, however, Saller and Shaw's conclusions are still hugely influential, not least since they coincide with what legal historians have always thought could be extracted from law codes and epigraphy.[14] The vast *number* of inscriptions and tombs preserved, and

---

and that it was characteristic of many regions of western Europe as early as the Roman empire', or the quotation above). Cf. Huebner, 'Household composition', 81–2.

[10] For a critique of Martin's approach, see Rawson, 'Family'; Bodel (ed.), *Epigraphic Evidence*, 36–7; Huebner, 'Household composition', 82–3. On Saller and Shaw, see Hopkins, 'Graveyards', 115; Bodel, 'Epigraphy and the ancient historian', 36–7. For a critical review, see now Huebner, 'Household composition'. The methodological difficulties in Martin's approach also become apparent when we consider the epitaphs from Asia Minor's 'obsession with genealogical bookkeeping' (as van Nijf has called it), which attest to the importance of a long family line as a status indicator and the tomb's role in communicating the fact. See Cormack, *Space of Death*, 133–9; Van Nijf, 'Being Termessian'.

[11] Huebner, 'Household composition', 84–91.

[12] Esp. Hopkins, 'Age structure'; Hopkins, 'Graveyards', esp. 115; Bodel, 'Epigraphy and the ancient historian', esp. 36–7; Ery ('Investigations', 60) observed that Greek-language inscriptions from the city of Rome imply a mean life expectancy of fifty-one years, while Latin-language inscriptions suggest a mean of only twenty-three years. Cf. Bodel, 'Epigraphy and the ancient historian', 36; Scheidel, 'Epigraphy and demography', 110–12.

[13] Dixon, *Roman Family*, 1–11, and passim; Huebner, 'Household composition', with further bibl., as well as the other chapters in Rawson (ed.), *Families*.

[14] See de Visscher, *Droit*, chs 6–8, esp. 118 and Kaser, 'Grabrecht', 48, 56, 59. On Saller and Shaw, see e.g. Rawson, 'Family', 294: 'truly a breakthrough'; Nielsen, 'Interpreting epithets', 172; Parkin and Pomeroy, *Social History*, 74–5; Hope, *Roman Death*, 169–70. Treggiari ('Marriage', 376) goes even further and thinks that the commemorative practice 'confirms that the nuclear

the very limited attention paid to the later history of tombs by excavators and historians alike, further encourages the general view that, during the imperial period, long family lines were irrelevant in the funerary realm, and any Roman man (and many women as well) who could afford to build a tomb would do so.[15] Moreover, there is a prevailing assumption among certain scholars that Roman society of the imperial period was on the road to ever-increasing individualism at the cost of both societal and family coherence.[16]

However, there is little actual evidence to support these views. Through a careful analysis of individual tomb contexts, this chapter aims to demonstrate how problematic are both the conclusions and the methodologies by which they were arrived at. In a first step, I take a look at the senatorial class, who proudly presented their family history in their tombs, and sometimes referred to it in their epitaphs, well into late antiquity. I shall then turn to the lower classes and argue that they too shared the ideals of the senatorial elite, but expressed and adapted them in a class-specific manner that differed in key aspects from senatorial habits.

Elite Burials

It is generally acknowledged that at least some of the great families of the Republic erected mausolea that were used over several generations. Most

---

family was the usual *household* unit' (emphasis original). Before Saller and Shaw's article was published, Hopkins (*Death*, 205) wrote: 'It was apparently rare for tombs to contain the remains of family members over several generations'; see also the quotation above p. 124.

[15] This assumption is rarely ever stated explicitly, but it underlies the typical treatment and discussion of tombs. Griesbach (*Villen und Gräber*, 23–4), for instance, suggests that, especially in the late Republic and early imperial period, burial on a villa estate was chosen only when a 'burial place appropriate to the rank and reputation of the deceased' was impossible for political reasons. While this may be true, strictly speaking, for members of the imperial families who fell into disrepute and were thus denied burial in the mausolea of Augustus or Hadrian, their burial in ancestral tombs on their natural families' landed estates suggests that they were buried precisely where they would have been had they not become members of the imperial family in the first place. It is equally problematic when intensively used and sometimes overcrowded mausolea are dismissed out of hand as 'boxrooms for burials', and the crammed situation is not even considered a result of a *desire* to continue burial in a tomb, but seen as an indication of a lack of interest in the burial of the people concerned. Cf. e.g. Hesberg, *Grabbauten*, 52–3; ditto Meinecke, *Sarcophagum posuit*, 95–7, and 142–3 for an alleged loss of *pietas*. Zanker and Ewald, *Myths*, 25 are slightly more cautious.

[16] E.g. de Visscher (*Droit*), Kaser ('Grabrecht'), Hopkins (*Death*, 205–6), Saller and Shaw ('Tombstones', 125), Heinzelmann ('Grabarchitektur', 189–90), Heinzelmann ('Einleitung', 14, 16–18), Hesberg ('Profumo', 48), Galvano-Sobrinho ('Feasting', 145–8) and Borbonus (*Columbarium Tombs*, 144–5) talk of growing individualism and indifference towards the *familia* in relation to the large columbaria of the first centuries BCE and CE.

of the evidence comes from literary texts, and it has become customary to quote Cicero's list of examples outside Porta Capena (*Tusc.* 1.7.13). Only one of these mausolea has been identified in the archaeological record, the tomb of the Scipios.

The Tomb of the Scipios

The tomb was founded as a family tomb of the patrician Cornelii Scipiones, either by L. Cornelius Scipio Barbatus (*cos.* 298 BCE) himself or by his sons, and around 280 BCE Barbatus was the first to be buried within it in his unique and famous sarcophagus (Figures 3.1 and 3.2).[17] Around 150, the main burial chamber probably contained some thirty-three sarcophagi and was filled to capacity, so that a second chamber was cut into the adjacent rock. At the same time, and above a frieze that had long displayed frescoes of military deeds and other political matters in which the family was involved,[18] the rock face received a showy façade containing three statues (Figure 3.3): of Scipio Africanus, the famous victor over Hannibal; of his brother Scipio Asiagenus (Asiaticus), the victor over Antiochos III of Syria; and of Ennius, who had immortalised the family and its history in his poetry.[19] The tomb probably continued to be used into the early first century BCE, and may have fallen out of use after the last descendant of the Cornelii Scipiones had died.

Unfortunately, only eight inscriptions pertaining to these burials have survived and not all the individuals can be identified with certainty. Still, those that feature inscriptions allow for some further conclusions (cf. Stemma 1). According to the epitaphs, the tomb contained the remains of Scipio Barbatus; his son L. Cornelius Scipio (*cos.* 259 BCE); a grandson of Scipio Africanus; the son and grandson of Scipio Asiagenus; as well as the

---

[17] The following description is based on Coarelli, *Scipioni*; Coarelli, 'Sepolcro'; Coarelli, *Revixit ars*, 177–238; *LTUR* IV (1999) 281–5 s.v. Sepulcrum (Corneliorum) Scipionum (F. Zevi); Etcheto, *Scipions*, 209–59; Meinecke, *Sarcophagum posuit*, 152–59 cat. R2; Volpe et al., 'Scipioni'. For a discussion of the inscriptions, see also Courtney, *Musa Lapidaria*, 40–3, 216–29 nos. 9–13.

[18] Coarelli, *Revixit ars*, 207; Talamo, 'Scipioni'.

[19] For a recent revised reconstruction of the façade, see Volpe et al., 'Scipioni', 182–5 figs. 12–15 (R. Volpe) (cf. here Figure 3.3). Coarelli ('I ritratti di "Mario" e "Silla" a Monaco e il sepolcro degli Scipioni'), followed by Etcheto (*Scipions*, 217–18, 274–8), recently revived a suggestion by Giuliani (*Bildniskunst*, 172–89), that the over-life-size marble portraits of the so-called 'Marius' and 'Silla' in Munich and Copenhagen respectively are actually the portraits of Africanus and Asiagenus from the tomb façade, yet Volpe (in Volpe et al., 'Scipioni', 184 with n. 20) doubts the attribution, arguing that the statues of the façade would hardly have been much larger than life-size.

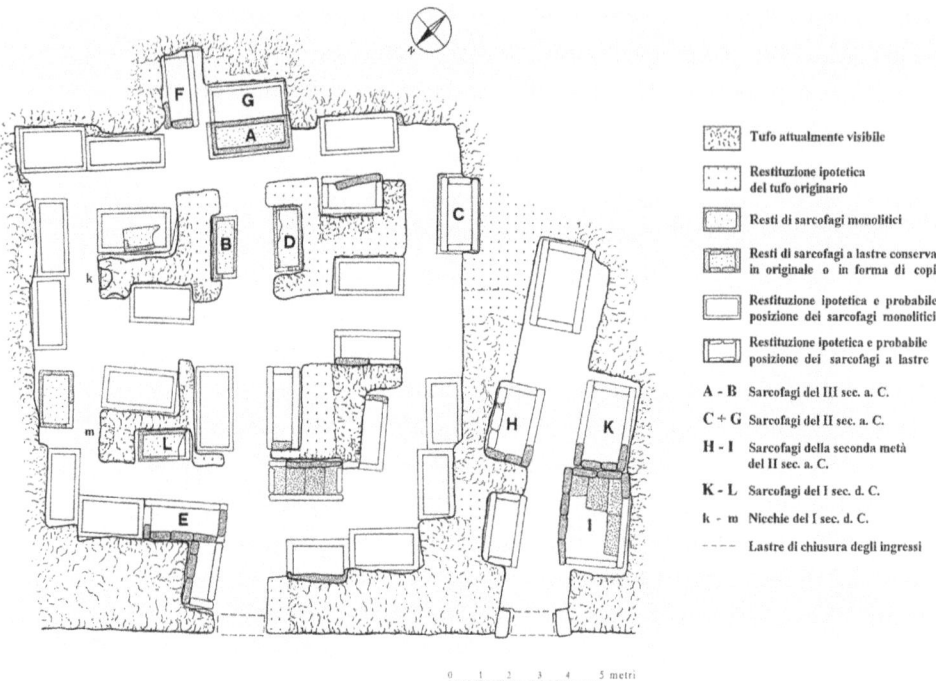

Figure 3.1 Tomb of the Scipios off the via Appia, updated plan by Lucia Domenica Simeone and Roberta Loreti

sons and wife of Scipio Hispallus (*cos.* 176 BCE). Since both his sons and his wife were buried in the tomb, it is almost certain that Hispallus himself was also put to rest there.

Whether the same is true for Scipio Africanus, who was commemorated in one of the statues, is debated. After his political enemies had accused him of corruption, he had retreated to his villa in Liternum in Campania. It is clear from Livy (38.56.1–4), Seneca (*Ep.* 86.1) and other sources[20] that some thought he had died and been buried there, but both Livy and Seneca acknowledge that the veracity of this tradition is far from certain.[21] Be that as it may, even if Africanus was buried in his villa, it would have been a

---

[20] Valerius Maximus, an author of the first century CE, mentions an inscription that Africanus allegedly put on his grave which read: 'My ungrateful fatherland, you shall not even possess my bones' (5.3.2). But neither Livy nor Seneca, who both visited the villa, mention such an inscription.

[21] For a discussion see Coarelli (*Revixit ars*, 209–14), who concludes that Africanus was indeed buried in Liternum. Similarly, see e.g. Verzár-Bass ('Mausolei', 408), who thinks that Africanus wanted a monument for himself comparable to those of Hellenistic kings, and therefore chose his villa as the location. No such monument has been found there.

Figure 3.2 Sarcophagus of L. Cornelius Scipio Barbatus, around 280 BCE, copy in situ of the original casket

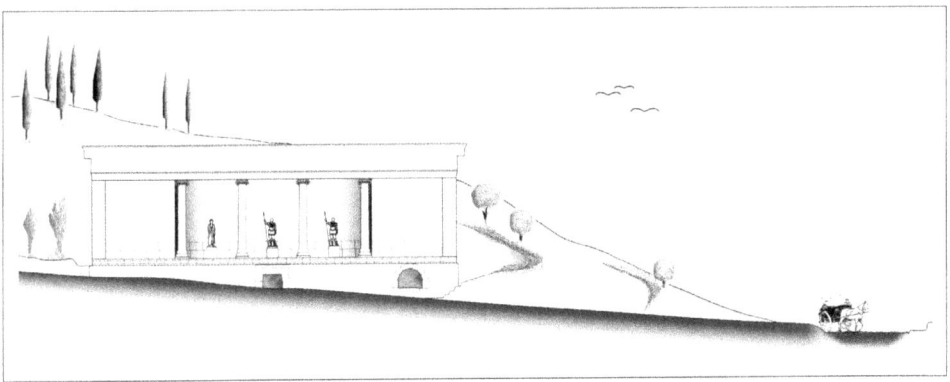

Figure 3.3 Reconstruction of the façade of the tomb of the Scipios based on recent research by the Sovrintendenza ai Beni Culturali di Roma Capitale

singular and individual decision, and not the end of the family mausoleum or a sign of his family branch opting out of it. Nothing is known about the time or place of Asiagenus' burial, but since his statue equally decorated the façade and, more importantly, since his son and at least one grandson were

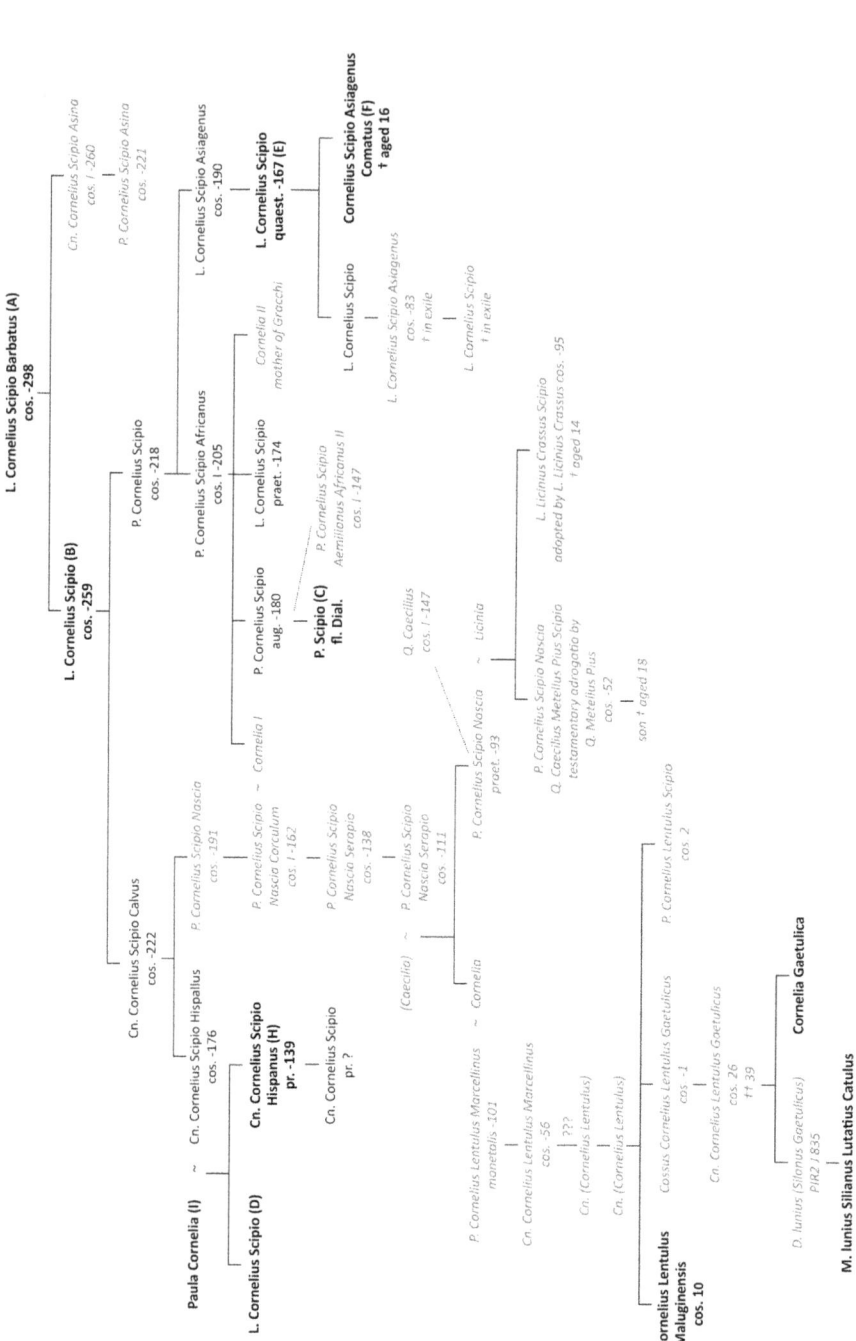

Stemma 1 Stemma of the Cornelii Scipiones and Cornelii Lentuli. Bold: individuals buried in the family tomb according to epigraphic evidence; regular: individuals likely buried in the family tomb; italics: individuals potentially buried in the family tomb or buried elsewhere; ††: violent death

buried in the family mausoleum, it is highly likely that the same applies to him.

Two aspects of the epitaphs found in the mausoleum are particularly interesting to note. First, up to this time only agnate relatives were buried in the mausoleum; that is, family in the male line.[22] Secondly, this is true not just for one single strand of the family, but for members of different family lines, *stirpes*, which is particularly remarkable since some family members (Africanus and Asiagenus) had offspring and were sufficiently prominent that they could have established separate *stirpes*, with their own tombs – just as Barbatus had done. The tomb therefore reflects the idea of the family clan, which consists of all male family lines descended from a common ancestor.[23]

It is possible, and generally assumed, that the tomb went out of use for some time after the last agnate descendants of Barbatus had died in the first century BCE. However, three epitaphs for members of the Cornelii Lentuli, and two niches for cinerary urns cut into the rock, attest to further burials during the first century CE.[24] The Cornelii Lentuli must therefore have inherited the family tomb in the cognate line after the extinction of the Scipios, probably through a daughter of P. Cornelius Scipio Nascia Serapio (*cos.* 111 BCE), who married P. Cornelius Lentulus Marcellinus (*monetalis* in 101 BCE) (Stemma 1). The details of stemmata through the first centuries BCE and CE are debated,[25] and it is unclear how many first-century CE burials we should expect to have occurred. While only three inscriptions have been recorded, with the change to marble containers and tabulae a material was chosen that was far more prone to being carried away and repurposed or burnt to produce lime.[26] Nevertheless, some speculation may be permitted. The earliest epitaph commemorates Ser. Lentulus

---

[22] For the stemma, see Coarelli, *Scipioni*, cover; Hölkeskamp, *Roman Republic*, 88; Etcheto, *Scipions*, tables 1–5. For the last Scipiones, see Syme, *Augustan Aristocracy*, 244–54; Canas, 'Scribonia'.

[23] For a further justification of this terminology and reference to Smith, *Clan*, see the conclusions to this chapter. Etcheto (*Scipions*) in particular has demonstrated that the Cornelii Scipiones deliberately styled themselves as a *gens*, possibly as the first – or one of the first – families to do so.

[24] *CIL* 6.1392, 1439, 41049: Coarelli, 'Sepolcro', 58 with n. 60; Etcheto, *Scipions*, 209–10. Cf. Faßbender, *Untersuchungen*, 52 (where the inscriptions are wrongly attributed to sarcophagi), 227 nos. 340.1–3.

[25] For a stemma of the Lentuli, see Scheid, 'Scribonia'; Canas, 'Scribonia', with Stemma 5; Settipani, *Continuité*, 86; Raepsaet-Charlier, *Prosopographie*, Stemma VII.

[26] A Flavian portrait head (Nicorescu, 'Tomba degli Scipioni', 52 fig. 30) and fragments of a kline sarcophagus may suggest continued use until at least the second century. On the other hand, space was limited, and these objects could just as well constitute contaminations.

Maluginensis,[27] who is most likely the *consul suffectus* of 10 CE.[28] The latest epitaph commemorates M. Iunius Silanus Lutatius Catulus,[29] who boasts in his epitaph of being the great-grandson of Cossus (Cornelius Lentulus Gaetulicus, *cos.* 1 BCE), grandson of Gaetulicus (probably Cn. Lentulus Gaetulicus, *cos.* 26 CE) and son of D. Silanus.[30] Some members of the Lentuli therefore used the tomb over at least four generations. Moreover, Cossus and Maluginensis, as well as P. Cornelius Lentulus Scipio (*consul suffectus* 2 CE), were most likely brothers, whose father took their *cognomina* from famous but by then extinct branches of the Cornelii.[31] The strong sense of family tradition displayed in this choice certainly fits very well with the family's reopening of the Scipios' tomb.

The Plautii Tumulus

The mausoleum of the patrician Plautii was an impressive tower-like tumulus just across the Ponte Lucano near Tibur (Figure 3.4). Its *titulus* high up on the tambour commemorates the founder of the tomb, M. Plautius Silvanus, consul in 2 BCE with Augustus, and his wife. The street front of the tomb's rectangular base featured further inscriptions on panels framed by Corinthian half-columns, three of which have been recorded (cf. Stemma 2).[32] In the centre we find Silvanus and his wife, as well as their son A. Plautius Urgulanius, who died at the age of nine. Another son of Silvanus, P. Plautius Pulcher, who was elevated to patrician status but died before his consulship in the early 50s, was commemorated together with his wife in the right-hand aedicula. Finally, the left-hand aedicula honoured Ti. Plautius Silvanus Aelianus, who died shortly after his second consulship in 74 (and before 79).[33] After the tomb had been in use over four generations

---

27 *CIL* 6.41049.

28 *PIR²* C 1394. Thus G. Alföldy in *CIL* ad loc. Cf. Settipani, *Continuité*, 86.

29 *PIR²* I 836.

30 On the epitaph, see also Kolb and Fugmann, *Tod in Rom*, 64–5.

31 Settipani, *Continuité*, 86. Cf. Sumner ('Family connections', 135), who had already suggested that Maluginensis was named after the first consul of the *gens* Cornelia, Ser. Cornelius Maluginensis (*cos.* 485 BCE), and suggests that his father Cn. (Cornelius Lentulus) could have been the consul of 14 BCE.

32 *CIL* 14.3605 (tambour), 3606 (middle aedicula), 3607 (left), 3608 (right). Cf. Mari, *Tibur IV*, 196–210 no. 128; Beard, '*Vita inscripta*', 98–114; Impeciati, *Mausoleo dei Plauzi*.

33 His relation to the family has been suggested to be by adoption, but Christian Settipani has argued convincingly, in my view, that he was the son of another son of Silvanus, M. Plautius Silvanus, the *praetor* of 24. See Settipani, *Continuité addenda*, 101–3 with stemma. For the adoption view, see *PIR* VI, stemma 20; Raepsaet-Charlier, *Prosopographie*, stemma IV; Settipani, *Continuité*, 278.

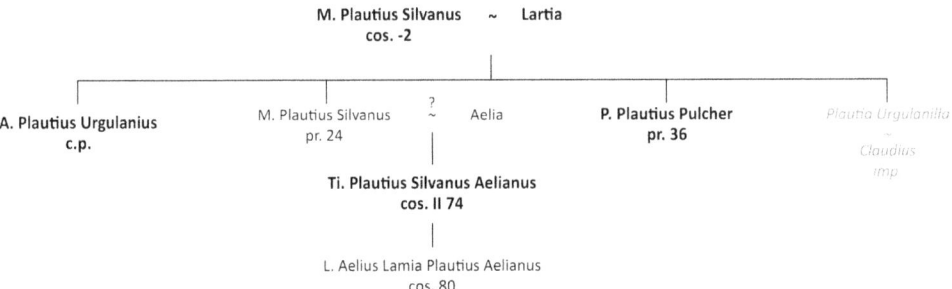

Figure 3.4 Tumulus of the Plautii (first century CE) drawn by Giovanni Battista Piranesi

Stemma 2 Stemma of the Plautii. Bold: individuals buried in the family tomb according to epigraphic evidence; regular: individuals likely buried in the family tomb; italics: individuals potentially buried in the family tomb or buried elsewhere by the agnate family of its founder, the last descendant of the family seems to have been L. Aelius Lamia Plautius Aelianus, the consul of 80,[34] and it was closed after the family name became extinct.[35]

Tomb of the Licinii and Calpurnii

The tomb of the Licinii just outside Porta Collina between via Salaria and via Nomentana is the other most frequently mentioned example of a family tomb used over several generations, although it has long been regarded with equal measures of amazement and suspicion. The excavations were poorly documented, and many of the objects found were exported illegally with the inglorious help of Wolfgang Helbig. Margherita Guarducci cast serious and general doubts on Helbig's reliability as a source, and consequently it has often been questioned whether all the objects Helbig mentioned actually did come from a single tomb.[36] However, in 1986 Dietrich Boschung put forward strong arguments against Guarducci's concerns, and in favour of a common provenance from the Licinian tomb of thirteen portraits now in Copenhagen.[37] In 2003, Frances Van Keuren published new archival material that clarified matters further, demonstrating not least that Lanciani, who published a plan of the tomb complex in his *Forma Urbis Romae* (Figure 3.5), visited the tomb on various occasions.[38] His plan cannot therefore be dismissed as mere fantasy, but rather confirms Helbig's claim that the three 'chambers' eventually excavated all formed one building complex.[39]

---

[34] *PIR* I A205.

[35] Two of Silvanus' natural sons seem not to have survived long enough to have produced any (surviving) offspring, so it is difficult to know whether the tomb was meant to serve several male lines of descendants in a gentilicial fashion, as that of the Scipios was, but the burial of both Plautius Pulcher and Silvanus Aelianus suggests that it was. Aelianus' father, the *praetor* of 24, is likely to have been commemorated on one of the lost panels.

[36] Guarducci, 'Fibula prenestina', esp. 137–43. Still sceptical are some authors in Kragelund et al. (eds.), *Licinian Tomb*; as is Meinecke (*Sarcophagum posuit*, 328–32), who seems to be unaware of the arguments in Van Keuren's 'Unpublished documents'.

[37] Boschung, 'Liciniergrab'. His arguments for a common origin of the portraits include their close similarity in terms of workmanship and style, their common state of weathering, the kind and colour of discoloration, and the pattern of root residues on their surfaces. To these can now be added isotopic analyses of the marble: Kragelund et al. (eds.), *Licinian Tomb*, 100. For details, see below.

[38] Van Keuren, 'Unpublished documents'.

[39] Ibid., 55. Cf. a letter by Helbig to Carl Jacobson of 20 August 1887, reprinted in Kragelund et al. (eds.), *Licinian Tomb*, 118 doc. 26, which describes 'ein Grab, welches aus drei durch Eingänge verbundenen Kammern besteht' ('a tomb which consisted of three chambers connected by doorways'). While Helbig clearly was an art dealer unconcerned by the restrictions of the law, evidence still has to be found that he intentionally made up accounts of the provenance of the items he sold.

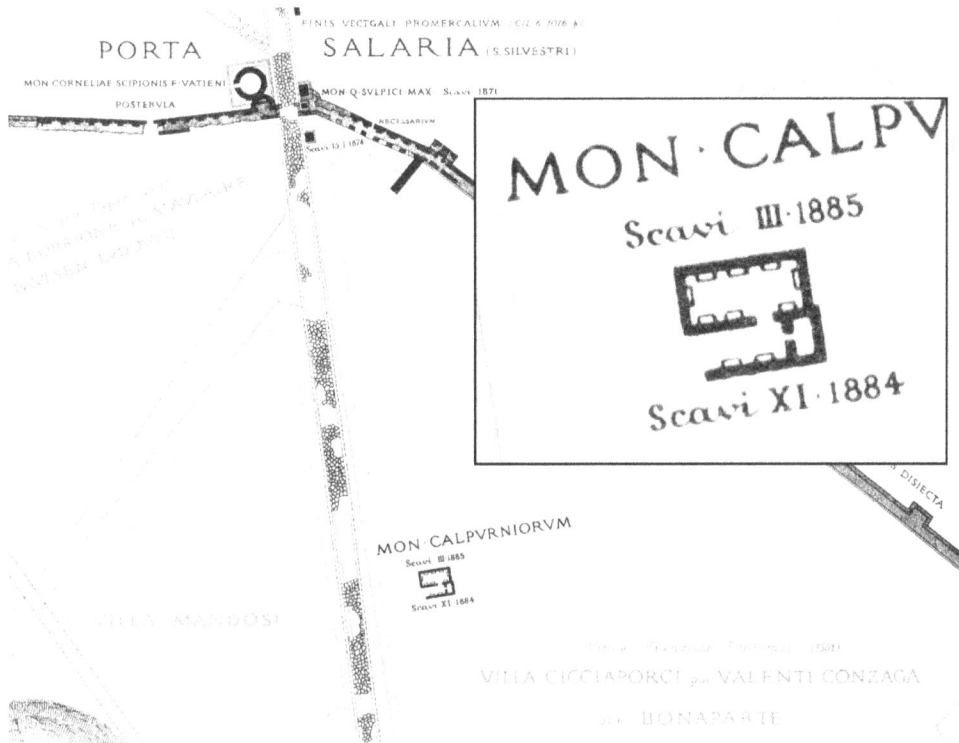

Figure 3.5 Plan of the tomb of the Licinii and Calpurnii on via Salaria as recorded by Rodolfo Lanciani in his *Forma Urbis Romae*, location and close-up

We can thus be fairly confident in studying the evidence taken together as attesting to a tomb of one of the most powerful Roman families that was in use for over 150 years.

Originally, the tomb was a very small building of just 1.5 x 3.6 m, perhaps containing some of the inscribed altars (Figure 3.6) and featuring *aediculae* containing cinerary urns and possibly also portraits.[40] The first generation to use the tomb that is attested by inscribed altars is that of M. Licinius

---

[40] Van Keuren, 'Unpublished documents', 57–63, on the excavation history, 63–67 with fig. 3 on interior decoration and a reconstruction, all with references to previous literature. Van Keuren tried to fit all the altars into this small tomb chamber and lined them up along its walls (fig. 3). Yet the reconstruction is problematical. First, it creates a rather crammed situation. More importantly, it positions one of the largest altars, that of Cn. Pompeius Magnus, in a corner where it would also be obscured by the altar of his father. The latter ends up next to the entrance rather than opposite it, where one would expect to find it. And finally, two uninscribed altars possibly belonging to two further sons of Frugi pontifex would not fit into the chamber at all (cf. n. 44), neither would that of Licinia Magna (cf. n. 45). It is therefore highly likely that at least some altars stood outside the tomb. The statue niche of Van Keuren's reconstruction is also pure conjecture.

Figure 3.6 Four altars from the Licinian tomb, Rome, Museo Nazionale delle Terme inv. 78163 (Cn. Pompeius Magnus), 78163 (L. Calpurnius Piso Frugi Licinianus and his wife Verania Gemina), 78161 (Calpurnia Lepida Orfiti), 78167 (Licinia Cornelia Volusia Torquata)

Crassus Frugi pontifex and his wife, and it is likely that they were its founders (cf. Stemma 3).[41] Licinius Crassus Frugi and his family were among the most powerful actors on the political stage during the first century CE, related not only to prominent figures of the Republic, but also to several imperial dynasties. Yet precisely for this reason they posed a threat to the emperors, and none of the more prominent (and some less prominent) family members died of natural causes.[42] The consul himself, his wife Scribonia and their son Cn. Pompeius Magnus were killed, probably in 47, on the order of Claudius (possibly on the initiative of Messalina), who also was Pompeius' father-in-law.[43] Another son, M. Licinius Crassus Frugi, consul in 64, was executed for treason in 67, while yet another, L. Calpurnius Piso Frugi Licinianus, had been adopted by the short-lived emperor Galba, but was murdered together with his wife after the emperor's downfall in 69, the same year that

[41] Their altar is *CIL* 6.31721; cf. Boschung, *Grabaltäre*, 24, 58, 96 cat. 643 pl. 15. As Boschung ('Liciniergrab', 284) has demonstrated, the majority of portraits from the tomb should be dated some years earlier than the death of Frugi pontifex in 47, so that he provided for the family's tomb while still alive. It is possible that this occurred when his homonymous father (*cos.* –14) died, who also was the founder of his family branch, as he was the son of M. Piso Frugi (*praetor* –44) and adopted by M. Licinius Crassus (*cos.* –30). However, his date of death is unknown and he could have died before the tomb was built.

[42] For a summary of the family history, see e.g. Boschung, 'Liciniergrab', 260–3; Hofmann-Löbl, *Calpurnii*; Kragelund, 'Shadows'.

[43] Pompeius' altar is *CIL* 6.31722; cf. Boschung, *Grabaltäre*, 15, 58, 78 cat. 1 pl. 1.

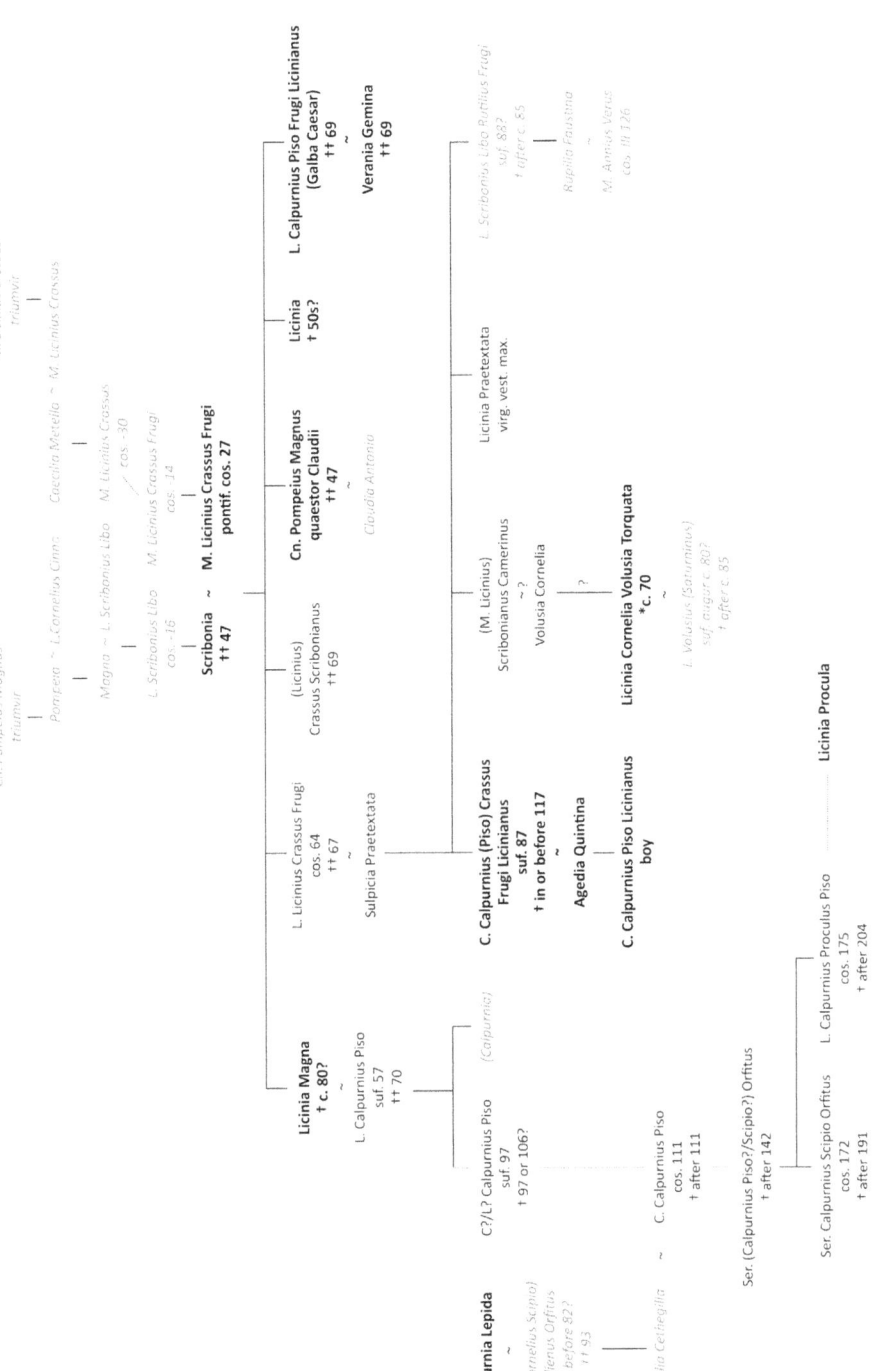

Stemma 3 Stemma of the Licinii and Calpurnii. Bold: individuals buried in the family tomb according to epigraphic evidence; regular: individuals likely buried in the family tomb; italics: individuals potentially buried in the family tomb or buried elsewhere; ††: violent death

the fourth brother, Scribonianus, also fell victim to the power struggles.[44] Further family members buried in the tomb probably include the founder's daughter Licinia Magna, certainly her sister Licinia, who probably died as a child, and Calpurnia Lepida, probably a granddaughter of Frugi pontifex.[45] Later, Crassus Frugi's grandson C. Calpurnius Crassus Frugi Licinianus, consul in 87, plotted against Nerva, and was first exiled and later killed in 117, shortly after Hadrian's accession. He or his homonymous son, who

---

[44] The altar of Galba Caesar is *CIL* 6.31723; cf. Boschung, *Grabaltäre*, 17, 58–9, 86 cat. 287 pl. 7. Boschung ('Liciniergrab', 264) believes that his two brothers, unattested epigraphically, were not buried in the family tomb after the estate had been divided between a Scribonianus and Piso Frugi by Vespasian, with the two brothers getting the Scribonianus plot. However, this argument would only be plausible for Crassus Scribonianus, and not for the consul of 64, as his son and grandson were buried in the original mausoleum. In a newspaper article, Lanciani also lists two uninscribed altars from the tomb, while a letter from the Banca Italiana lists two *cinerari quadrati*, 60 and 70 cm tall, which are otherwise unknown. Given their size, it is possible that they are the same as Lanciani's altars. Van Keuren ('Unpublished documents', 109–10) argues that they were identical to the poorly preserved altar with damaged inscription for Licinia Crassi and the one with erased inscription for Frugi Licinianus and his wife. Yet it is hard to imagine that Lanciani would have called damaged but legibly inscribed altars 'without inscription'. For the *cinerari quadrati*, see ibid., 67, 135 Appendix 12).

[45] Their altars are *CIL* 6.1445 (= 31655 (Licinia Magna)), 6.31727 (Licinia) and 6.14235 (Calpurnia Lepida). Cf. Boschung, *Grabaltäre*, 58–9, 94 cat. 593; 58–9, 97 cat. 657 pl. 18; 58–9, 102 cat. 745. Licinia Magna's altar was found before the published excavations at an unknown location so that her burial in her father's tomb is conjectural. Calpurnia Lepida Orfiti's identity is debated. The majority sees her as the wife of Ser. Calpurnius Scipio Orfitus, *cos.* 172 (e.g. Raepsaet-Charlier, *Prosopographie*, 172–4 no. 179 with stemma 38), while Boschung (*Grabaltäre*), followed by Kragelund ('Emperors', 207–9) argued that it is unlikely that a member of the family would return to the altar and incineration after a hiatus of some fifty years, which is plausible. He identified her with the wife of (Ser. Cornelius Scipio) Salvidienus Orfitus, killed by Domitian in 93 (*suf.* some time during 80–87; *PIR*² C 1445), and Kragelund plausibly suggests that her husband's execution, and possibly his declaration as *hostis*, would explain her burial in her ancestral tomb rather than that of her husband, similar to Licinia Magna, whose husband L. Calpurnius Piso (*cos.* 57) suffered the same fate (provided she *was* buried in the tomb). Alföldi *ad CIL* suggested that she might be the daughter of Frugi Licinianus Galba Caesar. This would be consistent with the similarity of her altar to that of Volusia Torquata, although the altar, which has lost its lid, is impossible to date precisely on its own. Yet Settipani (*Continuité addenda*, 64–6), partly revising his previous reconstruction (*Continuité*, 94), points out that Alföldi's suggestion does not explain her name, Lepida, and proposes that she is one generation younger, namely the daughter of a son of Crassus Frugi (*cos.* 64) and one Lepida, in which case she would have been the wife of Ser. Cornelius Scipio Salvidienus Orfitus (*cos.* 110). Yet this would leave unexplained why she is not buried in her husband's mausoleum, as he lived on until after 138. Her burial in her ancestral tomb only makes sense when we assume that her husband was the Flavian consul, which in turn puts her in the generation of Frugi pontifex's grandchildren. Following Chausson ('Cornelia Praetextata', with stemma in fig. 8), I am here (Stemma 3) assuming that Cethegilla, the grandmother of the consuls of 172 and 175, is the daughter of Orfitus (*suf.* 80/7), and thus of Calpurnia Lepida, who would then descend from another branch of the Calpurnii, through which she would also have acquired the name Lepida. Her burial in Frugi pontifex's tomb would then be explained through her husband's conviction and her daughter's marriage.

Figure 3.7 Heads of the portrait statues, herm portraits and busts from the Licinian tomb: a) IN 749 (Crassus *triumvir*); b) IN 733 (Pompey the Great); c) IN 736; d) IN 738; e) IN 737; f) IN 741; g) IN 734 (Frugi pontifex?); h) IN 751 (Scribonia?); i) IN 747; j) IN 754; k) IN 735

died at a young age, must have been the last male member of this branch of the family.[46]

A strong sense of family and pride in its ancestry was expressed and advertised through the famous portraits originating from the tomb, which comprised both statues and busts or herms.[47] Statues in front of the small mausoleum honoured Licinius Crassus Frugi and his wife as well as a woman of a previous generation, tentatively identified by Van Keuren as Scribonia's mother (Figure 3.7).[48] Two portraits of female relatives of roughly the same generation as Scribonia may equally have belonged to statues.[49] The same

---

[46] The consul's altar is *CIL* 6.31724; cf. Boschung, *Grabaltäre*, 44, 58–9, 108–9 cat. 856 pl. 46. The altar shows some attempt at removing the inscription, possibly for a *damnatio memoriae*. His son's altar is *CIL* 6.31725, cf. Boschung *Grabaltäre*, 16, 58–9, 109 cat. 857 pl. 46. Two further female members of the family attested by altars are hard to place, especially since no relief decoration provides a clear hint at the altars' dates. Licinia Cornelia Volusia Torquata (*CIL* 6.31726) is either a granddaughter (thus Boschung, *Grabaltäre*, 59; Kragelund, 'Shadows', 35 on cat. 7) or a great-granddaughter of the tomb's founder. The latter suggestion, argued for by e.g. Raepsaet-Charlier (*Prosopographie*, 420–4 no. 492) and Settipani (*Continuité*, 248–51), assigns her a mother with the name of Volusia Cornelia, which would explain her name. She would then have been born around 70 and married in the 80s, dates which would easily be compatible with Boschung's date for the altar at the end of the first or beginning of the second century.

[47] Cf. n. 37.

[48] Crassus Frugi: Copenhagen, Ny Carlsberg Glyptotek I.N. 734 (599); Boschung, 'Liciniergrab', 272–3, 284, 286 fig. 17; Kragelund et al. (eds.), *Licinian Tomb*, 85, 115 cat. 39 fig. 72); Van Keuren, 'Unpublished documents', 99 fig. 30; 104. The head was found in the 'third chamber' (on which see below), an area that originally was in front of the tomb. Scribonia: most likely Copenhagen, Ny Carlsberg Glyptotek I.N. 751 (630): Boschung, 'Liciniergrab', 268, 284 (here confused with I.N. 754 (635)), 286 fig. 8–9; ditto Kragelund et al. (eds.), *Licinian Tomb*, 85, 114 cat. 31 fig. 64; Van Keuren, 'Unpublished documents', 104 fig. 37. Woman of previous generation: ibid., 106–7: Copenhagen, Ny Carlsberg Glyptotek I.N. 741 (605); cf. also Boschung, 'Liciniergrab', 270 fig. 13 (late Tiberian to early Claudian copy of a late Augustan portrait), 286; Kragelund et al. (eds.), *Licinian Tomb*, 85, 113–4 cat. 28 fig. 61. She may indeed be more likely Scribonia's than Crassus Frugi's mother, who was not relevant for establishing links with the triumviral ancestors. The women's heads were made for insertion and thus belonged to statues. Frugi's portrait does not seem to be broken but deliberately cut in a wavy line through the neck just underneath the head. Whether this was done in ancient or modern times is not entirely clear, but the patina, which resembles that on the top of the head of the woman I.N.747 (614) (here n. 49) may suggest an ancient cut. In any case, the head should be expected to belong to a statue if the identification is correct.

[49] Copenhagen, Ny Carlsberg Glyptotek I.N. 747 (614): Kragelund et al. (eds.), *Licinian Tomb*, 84–5, 87, 113 cat. 27 figs. 32 and 60. It is referred to in a letter published by Van Keuren ('Unpublished documents', 107–9 with figs. 41–2), which further testifies to its origin in the tomb. Van Keuren tentatively identifies her as Licinia Crassi, a daughter of Licinius Crassus known from the altar *CIL* 6. 311727 (= 41071). However, given that the portrait was set up at about the same time as Scribonia's and shows a woman of approximately the same age, this is hardly possible (also note that Boschung dates the altar later than Van Keuren: see n. 45 above). Copenhagen, Ny Carlsberg Glyptotek I.N. 754 (635), is attributed on Boschung's grounds (see n. 37 above). Poulsen had tentatively identified her as Claudia Antonia, wife of Cn. Pompeius Magnus Minor (Poulsen, *Portraits*, 111 no. 74 pls. 128–9, followed by Kragelund et al. (eds.),

goes for a highly expressive head of a youth that is usually identified as Pompeius Magnus, who was killed with his parents.[50] However, given that this portrait is later than the others,[51] and that Pompeius was well over twenty when he died – after all, he had held the office of *quaestor* and been given the honour of announcing in Rome Claudius' victory over Britain on his return – it is highly unlikely that his commemorative portrait would have depicted him with the features of a boy.[52] The head must show an anonymous son or, more likely, grandson of Crassus Frugi pontifex.

All other portraits associated with the tomb depict ancestors. Their exact number and composition are debated, but a core of four items can be attributed with some certainty based on the documentary evidence mentioned above. The *triumvir* Pompey the Great, an ancestor of Scribonia who also lent his name to the couple's son, featured prominently. Whether his head belonged to a bust – the format chosen for the other Republican ancestors – or to a statue is not clear but the latter should not be ruled out, especially since it is the largest head among the group.[53] The other three portraits, this time busts that were on display either in aediculae inside the tomb or set into herm shafts belong to women and display hairstyles from the 30s BCE, and thus must equally show ancestors (Figure 3.7). As

---

Licinian Tomb, 85, 114 cat. 32 fig. 65; cf. Boschung, 'Liciniergrab', 286), but again little difference in age between her and her alleged mother-in-law is visible, even though she was only eleven or twelve years old at her marriage in 41. Both heads cannot definitively be attributed to statues as the first is broken at the neck and the second is made for insertion in such a way that it could also have fitted a herm. If Boschung is correct in suggesting that only ancestors received busts or herm portraits (ibid., 286), they should both have belonged to statues.

[50] Copenhagen, Ny Carlsberg Glyptotek I.N. 735 (601): Boschung, 'Liciniergrab', 273–4, 284, 286 figs. 18–21; Kragelund et al. (eds.), *Licinian Tomb*, 84, 113 cat. 25 fig. 58; Van Keuren, 'Unpublished documents', 106. The very straight cutting line of the neck and its ancient (?) patina suggest that it may have been deliberately cut, like Frugi's probably was (see n. 48 above).

[51] The style of the head is Claudian (Boschung, 'Liciniergrab', 273–4), giving a date that would fit well with that of his death.

[52] Kragelund ('Emperors', 196) even considers that the portrait usually thought to represent his father (IN 734) actually shows Pompeius. This is possible, as conventions of portraiture would allow the head to depict a twenty-year-old as well as an older man (especially in the Julio-Claudian period, men could be depicted as rather youthful throughout their life – as Augustus' portraits demonstrate – while young men could be given more *dignitas* by depicting them as mature as their age allowed without looking ridiculous).

[53] Copenhagen, Ny Carlsberg Glyptotek I.N. 733 (597). The suggestion that the head belonged to a bust rather than a statue is based on the assumption that Pompey was treated in the same way as the other Republican ancestors: see Boschung, 'Liciniergrab', 286; Kragelund et al. (eds.), *Licinian Tomb*, 81–4, 113 cat. 24 figs. 30–1, 57; Van Keuren, 'Unpublished documents', 54 fig. 1. Yet, in my view, it cannot be ruled out that the head belonged to a statue, not least since it was cut down in the same way as the heads of Frugi pontifex and the boy (here nn. 48 and 50).

Boschung observed, the age and the fashion of the elderly woman, as well as her family resemblance to Pompey the Great, may suggest that she is his daughter Pompeia, who was the ancestor establishing Scribonia's relation with the *triumvir*.[54] The two young women, so like each other that they could be sisters but quite different in technical execution, cannot be identified.[55] To these Republican ancestral portraits must probably be added a bust of M. Licinius Crassus *triumvir*, ancestor of Licinius Crassus Frugi.[56]

It is not necessary for our purposes to discuss in any detail the other portraits potentially belonging to the tomb, as the picture is already clear enough.[57] An enthusiastic Helbig wrote in 1887: 'I drew the conclusion that the cella in a certain sense had represented a *tablinium* adorned with ancestral portraits which, however, were made of marble rather than wax.'[58] His excitement was certainly justified. Despite all our dissatisfaction with the documentation of this aristocratic tomb, it gives us a rare glimpse into the ways in which elite families used the funerary realm for the display of their ancestry, which, in turn, was a major factor in the establishment of their power.[59] As Tacitus notes, Scribonia's uncle dwelled 'ostentatiously on his great-grandfather Pompeius, his aunt Scribonia, who had formerly been wife of Augustus, his imperial cousins, his house crowded with ancestral busts' in order to challenge imperial power (Tacitus, *Ann.* 2.27, transl. A. J. Church), and these types of argument were not uncommon (cf. Tacitus, *Ann.* 3.76).[60] What is remarkable about our tomb is the predominance of

---

[54] Copenhagen, Ny Carlsberg Glyptotek I.N. 736 (602): Boschung, 'Liciniergrab', 266–8, 285 figs. 6–7; ditto Van Keuren, 'Unpublished documents', 106–7 with n. 237; Kragelund et al. (eds.), *Licinian Tomb*, 84, 114 cat. 33 fig. 66.

[55] Copenhagen, Ny Carlsberg Glyptotek I.N. 737 (603) and 738 (604). Their hairstyle points to the 30s BCE (Boschung, 'Liciniergrab', 265–8 with figs. 1–5); that is, roughly to the time when the father of Crassus Frugi was adopted. Boschung tentatively identifies the two as Scribonia, wife of Octavian, and Scribonia, wife of Sex. Pompeius (ibid., 285–6), on the assumption that the two Scribonias were sisters. However, in reality Scribonia Octaviani was the aunt of Scribonia Sex. Pompeii, and of roughly the same generation as Pompeia. If we were to accept that the resemblance between the two young women is more a matter of ideology than blood relationship, they could be Scribonia Sex. Pompeii and Pompeia Magna, daughter of Pompeia and grandmother of Scribonia Crassi Frugi. Yet it can also not be excluded that they show the same person. Cf. also Kragelund et al. (eds.), *Licinian Tomb*, 84, 114 cat. 34–5 figs. 67–8; Van Keuren, 'Unpublished documents', 74 figs. 10–11.

[56] Copenhagen, Ny Carlsberg Glyptotek I.N. 749 (655); Boschung, 'Liciniergrab', 276–82, 284–5 figs. 24–6; Kragelund et al. (eds.), *Licinian Tomb*, 85, 113 cat. 26 fig. 59.

[57] These are the portrait of a woman dated to the Tiberian period (Copenhagen, Ny Carlsberg Glyptotek I.N. 742 (606); Boschung, 'Liciniergrab', 271; Kragelund et al. (eds.), *Licinian Tomb*, 114 cat. 29 fig. 62) and the roughly contemporary portrait of a boy (Copenhagen, Ny Carlsberg Glyptotek I.N. 744 (631); Boschung, 'Liciniergrab', 274 figs. 22–3; Kragelund et al. (eds.), *Licinian Tomb*, 114 cat. 30 fig. 63).

[58] Kragelund et al. (eds.), *Licinian Tomb*, 106, 121 doc. 37.

[59] See esp. Flower, *Ancestor Masks*.

[60] On the Licinii's ostentatious pride in their ancestry, see also ibid., 257–8; Kragelund, 'Emperors'.

women's portraits, while the tomb itself was clearly used and handed down in the agnatic line as long as it continued. It is possible that some male portraits have fallen victim to *damnatio memoriae*,[61] or that the family was prevented from displaying the portraits of some of those who were condemned to death.[62] Yet the display of these women, independently of their original numerical proportion, is certainly also an acknowledgement of their role in establishing the family ties with the famous *triumviri*, and has parallels in the genealogical praise of women in funerary orations, and women's role as ancestors more widely.[63]

In any case, the story of the tomb does not end with the termination of the agnate descendants of Crassus Frugi. When the male line became extinct, a branch of the Calpurnii that was related by the female line, probably through the daughter of Crassus Frugi, Licinia Magna, must have inherited the mausoleum and used it throughout the second century (Stemma 3).[64] This is suggested by a number of observations. First, an extension to the tomb was built in the Antonine period, as Lanciani's drawing (Figure 3.5) and brick stamps attest.[65] Secondly, at least ten sarcophagi were found in the tomb that commence around the time when the altars leave off (see earlier Figures 1.28–1.30). Thirdly, an alabaster bust of Licinia Procula, a close relative of L. Calpurnius Proculus Piso, consul in 175, was found close by and potentially comes from our tomb; and finally, a number of epitaphs from the area attest to the burial of freedmen of the Calpurnii in the vicinity.[66]

---

[61] There are clear signs of *damnatio memoriae* on the altar of Calpurnius Crassus Frugi Licinianus and Agedia Quintina: see n. 46 above; Kragelund, 'Emperors', 206–7 and Kragelund, 'Shadows', 33.

[62] Such restriction was the result of Cn. Calpurnius Piso *pater*'s trial of 20 CE for treason. See Eck et al., *Senatus consultum*, esp. 195–7, and Flower, *Forgetting*, 133–8, on the *senatus consultum* ll. 76–82. It is also possible that not all portraits found during the excavations have been identified. Boschung ('Liciniergrab', 273 n. 67) thinks that a male head mentioned by G. Fiorelli (*NSc* (1885), 75) is not that identified here as Frugi because of a discrepancy in height, and must therefore be lost.

[63] The role of women in the funerary realm deserves a separate and full treatment that cannot be provided here. For the orations see: Pepe, 'Fama'; Tylawsky, 'Genealogy'; Valentini, 'Funerali femminili'. For women as 'ancestors' in other contexts see Flower, 'Women'.

[64] Ditto Kragelund, 'Shadows', 38. As Kragelund further notes (p. 34), her burial in the tomb may have resulted from the impossibility or undesirability of being buried in her husband's familial tomb as he and her son-in-law were both killed by the Flavians. For the family stemma cf. also Raepsaet-Charlier, *Prosopographie*, stemmata 22 and 38.

[65] Van Keuren, 'Unpublished documents', 87 with n. 137.

[66] According to *CIL* 6.31729, the bust was found in July 1889, that is after the official excavations on the site had ended but while building activities were still going on. See Van Keuren, 'Unpublished documents', 109–13. Kragelund et al. (*Licinian Tomb*, 21, 38, 104) mistake the bust for a cinerary urn. The date for the now-lost bust is also suggested by the title *clarissima femina*, which was only introduced in the Antonine period (Raepsaet-Charlier, 'Clarissima', 196). For the freedmen see the lists in Boschung, 'Liciniergrab', 263 n. 38; Kragelund, 'Shadows', 39 n. 9.

No inscriptions for other Calpurnii are preserved, but the sarcophagi from the tomb can be dated fairly well and attributed to adults and children according to their size. They appear to belong to three or four distinct groups, each representing a generation of the family.[67] In the so-called second chamber, a huge plain sarcophagus appears to be the earliest piece.[68] It was carefully divided into two separate compartments by a marble panel fixed in grooves on the small sides, and cushion-like headrests supported the deceased. It was probably set up by and for the first Calpurnius family head and his wife. Two sarcophagi of smaller size appear to have belonged to their children (Figure 1.28a–b):[69] a garland sarcophagus from about 130[70] and a griffon sarcophagus from *c*. 130–40.[71] Whether a garland sarcophagus imported from Asia Minor *c*. 140–50 (Figure 1.28c) contained another of their children or a grandchild (or the child of another relative) is not entirely clear from its date.[72] Equally, the next full-size sarcophagus from around 150, showing a Dionysiac *thiasos* (Figure 1.29a),[73] may represent an adult son or, less likely, a daughter or first wife of *paterfamilias* no. 2. The next, more monumental sarcophagus with the Rape of the Leucippidae and Victories sacrificing bulls on the lid, was again extra wide for a double burial, and has a *terminus post quem* indicated by a coin of Antoninus Pius found within but may date around 170 (Figure 1.29b).[74] A child's sarcophagus

---

[67] Cf. Chapter 1 for an analysis of their design and imagery.

[68] *NSc* (1885), 43 (Rl. Lanciani/L. Borsari). For its date see Chapter 1 n. 204.

[69] Their lengths vary between 1.27 and 1.55 m. Children were sometimes buried in larger sarcophagi than necessary to fit their body, but the opposite case, of a small sarcophagus used for an adult is not attested. Cf. Huskinson, *Children's Sarcophagi*, 2; Dimas, *Kindersarkophage*, 11–12.

[70] *MNR* I8, 1 (1985) 211–14 no. iv,14 (M. Sapelli); Herdejürgen, *Stadtrömische und italische Girlandensarkophage*, 116–18 cat. 60 pls. 45.1, 47.2–3; Kragelund et al. (eds.), *Licinian Tomb*, 112 cat. 15. This casket must have been used for at least two burials, as the double clamp holes on the short sides demonstrate (cf. Herdejürgen, *Stadtrömische und italische Girlandensarkophage*, pls. 47.2–3).

[71] Lehmann and Olsen, *Dionysiac Sarcophagi*, 17–18, 45–7 figs. 16–18; Herdejürgen, *Stadtrömische und italische Girlandensarkophage*, 116 n. 613; Kragelund et al. (eds.), *Licinian Tomb*, 112 cat. 18.

[72] Lehmann and Olsen, *Dionysiac Sarcophagi*, with figs. 19–22; Waelkens, *Dokimeion*, 26–7; Ward-Perkins, 'Workshops', 208–9; Herdejürgen, *Stadtrömische und italische Girlandensarkophage*, 116 n. 613; Kragelund et al. (eds.), *Licinian Tomb*, 112 cat. 17.

[73] Matz, *ASR 4.2*, 180–2 no. 73 pls. 81.1, 83, 84.1; *MNR* I8,1 (1985) 262–5 no. vi,3 (L. Musso); Herdejürgen, *Stadtrömische und italische Girlandensarkophage*, 116 n. 613; Kragelund et al. (eds.), *Licinian Tomb*, 112 cat. 16 (51 x 219 x 78 cm).

[74] It measures 104 x 217 x 114 cm. Ward-Perkins, 'Workshops', 216–19 figs. 8, 22; Kragelund et al. (eds.), *Licinian Tomb*, 112 cat. 20; Zanker and Ewald, *Myths*, 315–18 doc. 10. The date of the sarcophagus is disputed. As Herdejürgen (*Stadtrömische und italische Girlandensarkophage*, 116 n. 613) observes, the coin only provides a *terminus ante quem non* for the burial. Her date of 170–80, accepted by Zanker and Ewald (*Myths*, 315–18), may, however, be slightly too late (cf. ibid., fig. 79, where the sarcophagus is dated to around 170).

depicting the childhood of Dionysus from around 160,[75] and a child's Cupid Race sarcophagus dated only roughly to 150–75, are likely to be associated with the patrons of this sarcophagus (Figures 1.29c–d).[76]

The final three sarcophagi were found in a third chamber that may never have been fully excavated (Figure 1.30).[77] They are the most imposing pieces from the tomb for both their size and their quality of craftsmanship. Their date is disputed, except for the Ariadne casket from the first decade of the third century.[78] The sarcophagus showing the Indian Triumph of Dionysus is clearly older, probably dating to the late 170s or 180s, while the Victory sarcophagus with its muscular and still rather stocky putti seems to belong somewhere in between the others.[79]

Without inscriptions, any detailed attribution of these sarcophagi must remain speculative, but it may be worth testing whether a plausible scenario can be suggested at all. Henning Wrede has tentatively and convincingly attributed the Dionysiac Victory sarcophagus from the final group

---

[75] Matz, *ASR 4.3*, 350–1 no. 199; Ward-Perkins, 'Workshops', 223–8 figs. 7, 29–34; Herdejürgen, *Stadtrömische und italische Girlandensarkophage*, 116 n. 613; Kragelund et al. (eds.), *Licinian Tomb*, 112 cat. 19.

[76] Van Keuren, 'Unpublished documents', 77–80; Kragelund et al. (eds.), *Licinian Tomb*, cat. 12. On the sarcophagus, cf. Schauenburg, *Eroten-Sarkophage*, 65 no. 19 pl. 18. Østergaard ('Licinian sarcophagi', 55–7) tentatively identifies a different cupid sarcophagus as the one found in the first chamber. The case is not entirely clear, but does not matter much in our context. The reason for its deposition in the first chamber – if this is in fact where it was found – is not clear, especially since it would easily have fit into the second chamber.

[77] Van Keuren, 'Unpublished documents', 92–101; Kragelund et al. (eds.), *Licinian Tomb*, 112–3 cat. 21–23. Whether the 'third chamber' was actually closed and covered or an open-air space between the other two chambers is unclear from the documentation. The assumption that excavations were not finished rests on an application for an excavation permit dating after the three final sarcophagi were found, and on the missing western wall in Lanciani's plan. Yet new excavations were never taken up due to the limited prospects of finding anything worthwhile (Van Keuren, 'Unpublished documents', 111–13), and the 'third chamber' might as well have been an open *ala* (cf. Mausoleum 75 in the Isola Sacra discussed below).

[78] For the Ariadne sarcophagus, see also Matz, *ASR 4.3*, 386–8 no. 216 pls. 225.1, 226–7, 228.1, 230.1–2.

[79] For the various suggestions, cf. Kragelund et al. (eds.), *Licinian Tomb*, 112–13 on cat. 21–2. Ward-Perkins ('Workshops', with a suggested date in the 170s), followed by Wrede (*Senatorische Sarkophage*, 38–9), who proposes a date around 180, and Herdejürgen ('Via Latina', 214 n. 29), who prefers 200–10, argued that the two caskets must have been produced in the same workshop and at the same time because of their quality of workmanship and the use of Thasian marble, which he thought to be rare. However, the style of the two reliefs is rather different and does not support a common date, and Thasian marble has now been shown to have been used much more widely (Van Keuren, 'Mythological sarcophagi', 196–204; Russell, *Economics*, see index), including also for the Childhood of Dionysus sarcophagus from our tomb (cf. n. 75). While it is possible that they all come from the same workshop working with Thasian marble, a common date cannot be established in this way. For the most convincing argument on the date of Dionysius' Indian triumph, cf. Matz, *ASR 4.2*, 218–20; 231–3 no. 95 pls. 116–20, who gives a date of 170–80; Zanker and Ewald, *Myths*, 329–34, also 170–80.

to either Ser. Calpurnius Piso Orfitus (*cos.* 172), who died after 191, or to his brother L. Calpurnius Proculus Piso (*cos.* 175), who died after 204.[80] It is equally tempting to attribute the other casket from the third group with its ostentatious display of victory motifs, which contained one skeleton with some residues that could hint at an attempt at embalming of the corpse, to the other brother. The Ariadne sarcophagus may then have served either a wife of one of the consuls or a daughter or sister of either brother as a final resting place.[81]

The family tree of this branch of the Calpurnii is partly conjectural (Stemma 3). Yet, assuming that the generally accepted prosopography is correct,[82] the plain double sarcophagus that started the series could have belonged to C. Calpurnius Piso, grandson of Licinia Magna and consul in 111, who could have inherited the tomb after the *consul suffectus* of 87 had been killed, shortly after Hadrian's accession, leaving no (male) descendants.[83] The Leucippidae sarcophagus, equally wider than normal and thus designed for a couple, would have belonged to the father of Orfitus and Piso, who was perhaps Ser. (Calpurnius Piso/Scipio?) Orfitus, and his wife.[84]

This remains mere speculation, but it demonstrates that the dates and types of sarcophagi are in tune with the family history as we know it. Here, it is most important that the evidence strongly suggests that, after it was taken over by another *stirps* of the Calpurnii, the tomb continued to be used by at least three consecutive generations of the agnate family, most likely including two adult brothers, and thus in a gentilicial fashion. They took pride in the long family history that went back even to the late Republic, a history that was right in

---

[80] Wrede, *Senatorische Sarkophage*, 16, 38–9. On the consuls, see *PIR*[2] C 295 and 317.

[81] No daughter is attested for either of the two brothers, but this does not necessarily mean that they had none.

[82] For a discussion of the family's prosopography, see Hofmann-Löbl, *Calpurnii*, 303–6, with Dondin-Payre, 'Longevité'; Raepsaet-Charlier, 'Cornelia'; Raepsaet-Charlier, *Prosopographie*, 171–4 on nos. 178–9, 247–9 on no. 280, with stemma 38; Settipani, *Continuité*, 90–3, 107, 110.

[83] Settipani, 'Prosopographie'. If his wife Cornelia Cethegilla remarried (after his death), this may explain why her cinerary altar was found at Tellenae. See De Rossi, *Tellenae*, 77–9 no. 46 figs. 157–60 (= *AE*, 1967, 57). The consul may well have ordered and set up the sarcophagus shortly after taking over the tomb, still planning to be buried there with his wife. It is also tempting to think that it was his wife, a member of the Cornelii, who famously continued inhumation through the years when everyone else preferred incineration, who inspired the change in burial custom. Nevertheless, given that she herself was incinerated, this is probably taking speculation too far.

[84] According to Settipani, *Continuité*, 93. The children's sarcophagi would obviously belong to deceased children, while the Dionysiac of adult length but limited height and depth may have belonged to a predeceased first wife or brother. This generation, which obviously must have existed, is largely unknown to us.

front of their eyes through portraits, inscriptions and a multitude of containers for the remains of their ancestors.

The three family tombs discussed so far are clearly the best-documented senatorial mausolea at Rome, which also allow for the greatest detail of information over the longest period of usage. However, additional, more fragmentary evidence suggests that they were not exceptional at their time. In Tusculum, at least eight cinerary urns of the patrician Furii were found in the seventeenth century, all commemorating male members of the family by inscription.[85] A large tumulus in the *horti* of Agrippa in the Vatican area, first dedicated to Vipsania Agrippina, daughter of Agrippa, who married C. Asinius Gallus after a forced divorce from Tiberius, was used by the Asinii at least into the early second century.[86] An even longer period of usage may be attested by an epitaph for Q. Gallonius C. f. Fronto Q. Marcius Turbo and his son.[87] He has been identified as the governor of Thrace in 145–55, and may be either an adoptive son of Hadrian's powerful praetorian prefect Q. Marcius Turbo Fronto Publicius Severus, or his biological son, who was later adopted by one Gallonius, which is far more likely.[88] The two fragments were found with other debris from monuments in one of the towers of the ancient Porta Flaminia. Yet, as the inscription fragments are curved and framed by a *kyma* that has close parallels in the Augustan period, it is possible that they belong to a tumulus monument of roughly that period.[89] It is thus possible that Q. Gallonius C. f. Fronto Q. Marcius Turbo's inscription (also commemorating his son) was added to a family monument of the Gallonii that went back to the late Republic or Augustan period.[90] According to the *Historia Augusta* (*Did.* 8.10),

[85] See *CIL* 14.2700–7, with the tomb's description on p. 269.
[86] Alföldy, *Studi*, 125–43; *LTURS* I (2001), 161–2 s.v. Asiniorum sepulcrum (M. G. Granino Cecere). Alföldi rightly stresses the unusually large dimensions of the tumulus (c. 25 m in diameter) and points to the fact that Drusus, Agrippina's son with Tiberius, is mentioned first among the dedicants (p. 138). Feraudi-Gruénais ('Ewigkeit', 148 n. 30) thinks that the continued use of this tumulus hinged on the family's imperial relations, but as the other examples here discussed demonstrate, this is not necessarily the case.
[87] *CIL* 6.31714, cf. p. 4778; *LTUR* IV (1999), 289 s.v. sepulcrum: Gallonii (E. Papi); Granino Cecere in Adembri et al., 'Hercules Sospitalis', 170–5. For the reconstruction of the inscription, see also Piso, 'Praetorianerpräfekt', 176–8.
[88] Most scholars regard him as the prefect's adoptive son, but see Granino Cecere (in Adembri et al., 'Hercules Sospitalis', 173–5) and Piso ('Prätorianerpräfekt'), who argue that the sequence of names rather suggests a biological son who was later adopted after his father fell from favour. Hesberg (*Grabbauten*, 110) mistakes the inscription for that of the prefect.
[89] Ditto Hesberg, *Grabbauten*, 109–10. Unfortunately, the monument cannot be identified as long as no measurements of the fragments are published that would allow us to reconstruct the diameter of the monument, since there were several round tombs between Porta del Populo and the Tiber, most of which are now destroyed: Messineo, *Via Flaminia*, 9–53.
[90] The family line is impossible to reconstruct, but the name of Gallonius is very rare, and an equestrian C. Gallonius attested under Caesar is generally regarded as an ancestor of the

the short-lived emperor Didius Iulianus was buried in the mausoleum of his great-grandfather at the fifth mile of the Labicana.[91] In other cases, at least the burials of father and adult son are attested for the same tomb.[92] A rare late third-century double epitaph commemorates two brothers in the same *titulus*, T. Flavius Postumius Quietus, consul in 272, and T. Flavius Postumius Titianus, consul *c.* 283–84 and 310, suggesting that both of their families used the tomb.[93]

I have discussed elsewhere further senatorial tombs that are likely to have been used in a similar fashion all the way through to late antiquity. These include the tomb of the Acilii Glabriones, established in the late first or early second century on the via Salaria and used until the family left Rome at the beginning of the fourth century, when the entire area was handed over to the Church.[94] The tomb of the Sempronii not far from the mausoleum of the Scipios must have been founded at roughly the same time, and was then extended in one or two steps in a similar way to the Licinii tomb.[95] Some anonymous tombs may equally have belonged to senatorial families due to their prominence, location and treatment. The tower-like tumulus called the Sepolcro dei Servilii at the third mile of the Appia, founded towards the end of the first century BCE, shows signs of continued use until at least the early second century CE.[96] A tumulus 23 m in diameter at the eleventh mile of the same road was updated with a showy colonnade for sculpture display at the end of the second or beginning of the third

---

second-century Gallonii. Should our Gallonius be the prefect's biological son, the monument could have belonged to an adoptive grandfather, as the prefect was a *hominus novus* from Dalmatia (*PIR*² M 249); Granino Cecere in Adembri et al., 'Hercules Sospitalis', 165–76; Piso, 'Prätorianerpräfekt', passim, and 270–1 on his nomenclature. Attribution to the Gallonii may be further supported by the existence of a villa further out on the via Flaminia that belonged to the same family: Adembri et al., 'Hercules Sospitalis'.

[91] According to Scriptores Historiae Augustae, *Did.* 1.1–2, this great-grandfather's name was Salvius Iulianus, who is identified by some with the consul of 148 (e.g. Griesbach, *Villen und Gräber*, 23 n. 214). However, as Settipani (*Continuité*, 385 n. 9) has noted, this is impossible, since Didius Iulianus was born either in 133 or in 137, and this consul was more likely the emperor's grandfather. I cannot see any reason why we should doubt, as Griesbach does, that the family had a villa nearby, and that Didius Iulianus was buried precisely where he would have planned to be buried had he not become emperor.

[92] E.g. T. Mussidius Pollianus (*suff.* 40 or 43/44) and his son, who were buried in a tomb near the Theatre of Marcellus: *CIL* 6.41072 and 41073 (cf. Eck, 'Miscellanea consularia', 235–8 no. 5; Faßbender, *Untersuchungen*, no. 875.1–2); Sex. Pedius Hirrutus, who died in the Trajanic period, and his son Sex. Pedius Hirrutus Licinius Pollio, who died in office as consul suffect in 158: *CIL* 6.1485 and 1486 with pp. 3142, 4704–5.

[93] *CIL* 6.1419 (= 41224); Borg, *Crisis and Ambition*, 34–5 fig. 19, with bibl.

[94] Ibid., 125–6 with bibl.

[95] The comparison is also drawn by Bentz, 'Licinian tomb', 77. On the tomb, see Brizio, 'Scoperte'; Borg, *Crisis and Ambition*, 126–30; Meinecke, *Sarcophagum posuit*, 237–40 (who thinks the tomb was a hypogeum and misses the two-step extension), all with further bibl.

[96] Rausa, *Pirro Ligorio*, 63–5; Borg, *Crisis and Ambition*, 132–3, with bibl.

century.[97] A splendid temple tomb attached to the so-called 'Villa *ad duas lauros*' on the via Latina, one of the largest and most impressive late antique villas in the Roman *suburbium*, was used, or at least maintained, from its foundation around 200 to the early fifth century (see Figure 1.11).[98]

Admittedly, even including these examples, the sample of senatorial tombs used over several generations is limited. Nevertheless, what we have observed in these examples must actually have been common practice.[99] This is most clearly demonstrated by the main *tituli* of senatorial tombs.[100] The more than seventy examples from the vicinity of Rome that have preserved their patron's name pertain almost exclusively to *homines novi*; that is, to social climbers who had only recently been promoted to senatorial status, and who often moved to Rome on that occasion.[101] It follows that their descendants as well as members of the old families are highly likely to have been buried in the tombs of their forefathers, albeit mostly without leaving any epigraphical trace. Apparently, only those who first achieved a family's promotion to the highest status group founded tombs.

The evidence, lacunose as it may be, leaves little room for doubt about the great importance not only of the extended family with a long tradition, but of the use of family mausolea for showcasing the fact. Senatorial mausolea were often used over several generations and were preferably bequeathed in the agnatic line. After the extinction of the family line, the tomb may have been closed forever, or else inherited by a cognate branch of the family in the female line.

---

[97] De Rossi, *Bovillae*, 274 no. 262 figs. 458–67; Borg, *Crisis and Ambition*, 132. It must be admitted that continued use, and use by the same family, cannot be established with certainty here.

[98] Armellin, 'Sepolcro a tempietto', 85–95; Borg, *Crisis and Ambition*, 36–7, 130–1 fig. 20. While the owners remain anonymous, the size and opulence of the late antique villa as well as the treatment of the tomb clearly point to a powerful and long-standing family.

[99] On senatorial *vita humana* sarcophagi showing several generations, see Chapter 1 pp. 48–9.

[100] It is important here to distinguish between the *tituli* from the façades and inscriptions from sarcophagi, cinerary urns and altars, or statue monuments, which do not necessarily attest to the foundation of a tomb but to its varied usage at different times in its history.

[101] Licinius Crassus Frugi pontifex is not a *homo novus*, but his *stirps* was founded by his father, who himself was adopted by M. Licinius Crassus (*cos.* 30 BCE). This may have suggested to Frugi pontifex that a new era had started for the family. Equally, the Acilii Glabriones family line goes far back into Republican times. However, the foundation of a new tomb could have been triggered by either of two causes, or even a combination of both: M'. Acilius Glabrio (*cos.* 91), was murdered on the order of Domitian, and it is possible that his son decided subsequently to discontinue burial in the ancestral tomb. There is uncertainty as to whether the Acilii Glabriones and Acilii Aviolae of the time formed one or two family branches; if they were indeed two, it would have been the consul of 91 who started one of them. For a discussion of possible stemmata, see Dondin-Payre, *Acilii Glabriones*, 90–2; Settipani, *Continuité*, 169–75, and Settipani, *Continuité addenda*, 14–15.

This result also demonstrates an important methodological point. When we only look at individual epitaphs – say, a single *titulus* or inscribed altar – we get the statistical pattern that Saller and Shaw produced for the senatorial class more generally. Where a commemorator is mentioned at all, it is normally a close relative. This pattern largely remains the same whether we count individual relationships, as they did, or inscriptions as proposed by Martin, although commemoration beyond the nuclear family becomes more apparent in the latter case.[102] Counting only tomb *tituli*, Saller and Shaw's method results in 75 per cent nuclear family relations, 14 per cent extended family and 11 per cent non-kin relations, while the figures for Martin's method are 70, 15 and 15 per cent, respectively.[103] It is notable, however, that over 54 per cent of *tituli* that are sufficiently well preserved to allow for a judgement are lacking a commemorator, and just over 36 and 11 per cent, respectively, commemorate a single man or woman.

While all these statistics are interesting in their own way, they obviously fail to account for the use of the tombs to which the *tituli* were affixed, and for the prominent role these monuments played in the promotion of the extended family. Each epitaph is only a snapshot of a moment in time, a single event in the long history of a tomb. This is true even for Hadrian's mausoleum (see Figure 2.10): its main inscription declares its dedication by Antoninus Pius to Hadrian and Sabina even though it was founded as a dynastic tomb – and by Hadrian.[104] In some cases, later generations were commemorated in additional inscriptions on the outside of the tomb, as was again the case for the Mausoleum of Hadrian, but also for that of the Plautii, the Asinii and the third-century Postumii,[105] and probably for the Mussidii and Appii.[106] Given the lacunarity of our evidence, it is likely that additional *tituli* from other tombs have been lost. Yet it would also be wrong to draw conclusions about the use of a tomb from its façade *tituli* only. If we want to assess the role of tombs and commemorative practices in Roman senatorial families, we need to look at both the relationship between commemorator and deceased and that between these two parties and the entire user group of the mausoleum. The first is what Saller and Shaw have in

---

[102] Edmondson ('Family relations', 193 with table 7.1, 216 with table 7.9) also found little difference comparing the two methods for his epitaphs from Roman Lusitania.

[103] My figures differ from those of Saller and Shaw, since they did not limit their calculation to the main tomb *tituli*.

[104] See Davies, *Death and the Emperor*, 107–8, for the inscription. Cf. Chapter 2 for the tomb.

[105] See above, nn. 32–3, 86, 93.

[106] On the Mussidii: above n. 92. On the Appii: Faßbender, *Untersuchungen*, no. 780.1–2; *CIL* 6.1348–9, pp. 3141, 3805, 4684; *LTURS* I (2001) 137–8 s.v. Sex. Appii Severi praedium (A. Bianchi).

fact examined. Theirs is an important result, as it tells us something about the hierarchy of obligations, *pietas* in Roman terms, but perhaps also about the closest emotional bonds within a family. The larger context, however, demonstrates very clearly the continuing importance of a long family line, and the key role that the family mausoleum played in promoting it after the use of *imagines maiorum* in the domestic *atria* had lost importance.[107]

Sub-elite Tombs

The first element to note when we are considering non-elite Roman burials is that we are really mainly talking about the freedman milieu. As Lily Taylor and Henrik Mouritsen have argued, we know almost nothing about the burial customs of the freeborn non-elite population; they estimated that up to 90 per cent of all extant tomb *tituli* refer to freedmen and their first-generation descendants.[108] While this is an important and interesting observation in itself that merits further examination, it also constitutes one of the strongest arguments for the use of their tombs. As in the case of senators, the inescapable consequence is that the descendants of these freedmen normally continued to use their ancestral tomb. The only occasional exception are the first-generation descendants of freedmen, who had achieved a further social advancement since they were freeborn. We thus see the same principles at work as among the elite: only those who had considerably advanced their status founded a new tomb.

Much has been written about the significance of family[109] as demonstrated on or in the tombs of freedmen of the first centuries BCE and CE.[110] Whoever

[107] This understanding is mainly based on Pliny, *NH* 35.2, but Pliny seems to exaggerate here. Cf. Flower, *Ancestor Masks*, 263–9, on evidence for *imagines maiorum* in the high and later empire.

[108] Taylor, 'Freedmen'; Mouritsen, 'Freedmen and freeborn'. It may be argued that such conclusions cannot necessarily be supported by prosopography alone, and figures may actually be lower. However, where we also have supporting contextual evidence, as is the case at Ostia or in the Isola Sacra, these figures appear to be at least roughly convincing. Petersen (*Freedman*, esp. 193–5) argues that many non-elite tombs, including those in the Isola Sacra, are too readily taken as belonging to freedmen, and should not be used in order to determine typically libertine tastes and habits. While I applaud her caution against stereotyping freedmen, I believe that the evidence shows us a libertine milieu in which not every individual has to be a former slave, but where freeborn and freed lived (and died) closely together, shared the same tombs and intermarried. The following discussion will further support my view.

[109] I am going to use here the English term 'family' to designate individuals who are related by blood, marriage or adoption, while the Latin term *familia* includes slaves and freedmen.

[110] Zanker, 'Freigelassene'; Kockel, *Porträtreliefs*; Borg, 'Aufsteiger'; George, 'Family imagery'; Borg, 'Social climber', all with further bibl.

Figure 3.8 Tomb relief of the Servilii family, early Augustan; Rome, Musei Vaticani, Museo Gregoriano Profano 10491

could afford it, so it seems, decorated their tomb with relief portraits, which often depicted entire family groups, and prominently displayed their legal marriage by showing husband and wife clasping hands and by presenting freeborn children in a prominent place with their formal markers of status, the toga and *bulla* (Figure 3.8).[111] After all, these were major achievements attached to their new legal status, and freeborn children were expected to fulfil all the ambitions which their parents were barred from achieving by their servile birth. More recently, it has also been pointed out that a legal family had particular value beyond being a marker of status. These freedmen were also celebrating their escape from the precarity of the informal slave family,[112] which could be broken up any time by its owner or an heir, and whose members were prone to physical, including sexual, assaults.[113] These relief representations are discontinued after the Augustan period (although they experience a revival in lesser numbers in the second century) and it is hard to tell to what extent busts or statues took over their function in later tombs due to a lack of archaeological context in most cases. A rare

---

[111] Arguably, the idea is most obvious in the relief of the Servilii (here Figure 3.8), where the son (in toga and with *bulla*) is twice designated as *filius*, his father explicitly called *pater* and his mother *uxor*: Kockel, *Porträtreliefs*, 141–2 no. H 6 pls. 51b, 52a–c; Borg, 'Social climber', 27 fig. 1.2. For the suggestion that the *dextrarum iunctio* scheme was originally invented by and for freedmen to signify a (legal) marriage before it was later taken over into the marriage imagery of the upper classes, see Reinsberg, *Vita-Romana-Sarkophage*, 75–85, esp. 81–2.

[112] George, 'Family imagery', 40–1. Mouritsen, 'Families of Roman slaves', 141–3, even sees this aspect as the most important one. On the emotional aspects of burial generally, see also Hopkins, *Death*, 201–55, and Hope, 'Roman identity', 113–14, but with a different trajectory.

[113] On the precarious state of slave families, see Rawson, 'Family life', esp. 78–82; Mouritsen, 'Families of Roman slaves', 137–41; Mouritsen, *Freedman*, 5. Perry (*Freedwoman*) has much on the legal situation and how Roman society viewed female slaves and freed women, but not much on their families ('family' and 'children' are even missing from the subject index).

exception is the lost Trajanic tomb of the Caltilii at Ostia, where the portraits of three generations were shown in pairs of shallow reliefs on the walls, and additions such as *avia* or *mater* clarify their relation to one another.[114] Yet I would argue that the tomb *tituli* as we find them in their thousands from tombs of the first to third centuries CE take over a similar function.

Tituli

The reasons for the above statement may not seem obvious. The great legal historian Max Kaser in particular observed that tomb *tituli* often only name the founder of a tomb, and frequently a spouse, while children and the rest of the family are not always mentioned and, where they are, are often designated only as *suis* ('his own'), *liberi* ('free') or *posteri* ('descendants'). The explanations Kaser offered were 'increasing childlessness and a waning sense of family', as well as the tomb founder's expectation that his children would build their own tombs.[115] Yet, in most cases, senatorial *tituli* equally only mention the tomb's founder or the individual to whom the tomb was first dedicated (over 74 per cent), and rarely a spouse or child (9 per cent each).[116] From this point of view, it is remarkable that the freedmen mention their spouses and offspring at all,[117] and that the numbers are even the reverse. Over 64 per cent of all *tituli* from the 'house' and 'terraced' tombs in the Isola Sacra include at least one named child (*c.* 33 per cent) or unnamed offspring in general (*c.* 31 per cent), and the collective terms used could easily encompass later generations of descendants as well.

In some instances, the idea of founding a multigenerational family mausoleum modelled on aristocratic patterns is already clear from the *titulus*. A funerary altar from the early second century, for instance, was dedicated by L. Tossius Successus, who was *lictor* of the emperor and clearly familiar with

---

[114] Calza, *Ritratti*, 53 nos. 76–7 pl. 45; Sinn, *Grabdenkmäler II*, 34–5 cat. 12 figs. 33–4; Liverani, 'Iconografia imperiale', 166–7; Fejfer, *Roman Portraits*, 118–19. Note that the six panels are strikingly similar to the stucco relief portraits on the six pillars in the 'Basilica Sotterranea' at Porta Maggiore, which was perhaps the tomb of the Statilii family: see esp. Bendinelli, 'Monumento sotterraneo', 796–803 pls. 39–40, 42.1. Sinn and Freyberger (*Grabdenkmäler II*, 24–6 with 43–5 cat. 4 pls. 5, 7, 65.4) consider that the male aedicula bust from the Haterii mausoleum may depict an ancestor or patron of the tomb's founder.

[115] Kaser, 'Grabrecht', 48. Cf. ibid., 56, where Kaser explains an alleged decrease in family tombs and increase in hereditary tombs in the same way.

[116] The situation is more difficult to assess for senatorial *tituli* since, unlike the vast majority of freedpeople's cases, it is not always clear whether the commemorators, at least when they were kin, are also intended to be buried in the same tomb, an assumption that underlies the numbers presented here.

[117] Petersen (*Freedman*, 199, 202) equally stresses the significance of reference to family in *tituli*.

elite ideology, to his wife, his parents and his three sons, thus establishing three generations already in the epitaph, and surely implicitly expressing the hope that his sons would carry on the name with their families.[118]

Perhaps the most striking feature distinguishing senatorial from sub-elite *tituli* is that the latter frequently include freedmen among those with burial rights. This is typically done with the phrase *libertis libertabusque posterisque eorum*; that is, including not only male and female ex-slaves but even their descendants. In the Isola Sacra, 90 per cent of all 'house' tombs feature the phrase. To consider this addition only in legal terms, as is usually done, in fact misses the point, especially since the formula does not signify what it seems to say. It *appears* to admit to burial all freed slaves of a founder and all of their offspring, and it has often been taken to mean just that by modern scholars.[119] However, in reality only those *libertini* and their descendants were admitted who either were themselves heirs of the tomb or got permission from its founder while he was still alive, or from his heirs. This is confirmed by well-documented tombs as well as by the jurists, and first attested for Ulpian, a jurist of the early third century, who explains:

> Freedmen can neither be buried nor bury others, unless they are heirs to their patron, although some people have inscribed on their tomb that they have built it for themselves and their freedmen: this view was given by Papinian [142–212 CE], and there has often been a ruling to this effect.[120]

---

[118] *CIL* 6.1881; Boschung, *Grabaltäre*, 80 no. 67; Faßbender, *Untersuchungen*, no. 171. This case is a good example of the difficulties involved in Saller and Shaw's approach of counting only individual relationships (as noted by Martin, 'Construction'). Applying their methodology, we end up with nuclear family relations of parents and children only, and miss the fact that we are dealing with a three-generational tomb already at the start.

[119] This view is too commonplace to cite examples, but is explicitly supported even by Eck, 'Inschriften', 259, 262; Eck, 'Rechtsquelle', 79–80.

[120] *Digest* 11.7.6 pr (Ulpian 25 *ad ed.*), transl. Watson. Similarly: *Codex Justinianus* 3.44.6 (Alexander Severus). Cf. Kaser, 'Grabrecht', 49, 75; Borg, *Crisis and Ambition*, 138, 158–9. Kaser's explanation, that the jurists and emperors had been hostile to the idea of a family tomb is, however, without foundation. Rather, the ruling must have aimed at securing an orderly use of the tomb and protection of the rights (and spaces) of legal heirs. Eck ('Rechtsquelle', 79) believes that the ruling had little effect on actual practice. Yet archaeology suggests otherwise (see discussion below at nn. 150 and 204). Moreover, his reasoning verges on being circular since his conclusion is based on the formula on tomb *tituli*, which he reads as if they were comprehensive legal documents. As with the formula that denies heirs burial in a tomb (on which see below), we must reckon with abbreviated phrases. That, in many tombs, some of the urns provided were never used can hardly be explained by all freedmen erecting their own new tombs – even when many will have aspired to – as not all of them (or their descendants) will have had the financial means to do so. Where we find empty urns but later inhumations, subsequent heirs may have preferred inhumation over incineration.

The formula was thus by no means a free-for-all, but neither was it necessary for protection of the rights of heirs to mention them in a *titulus* as long as a will attested to their admission. The formula's main function must therefore be sought outside the legal realm. One effect was obviously to demonstrate another achievement of the tomb patrons' new status. Only as (wealthy) citizens did they have the opportunity to acquire slaves of their own, and to set them free.[121] Moreover, as John Bodel observes, their care for a respectable final resting place for their dependants presents them as generous benefactors.[122] Stelae and other small tombs, which are occasionally dedicated to an entire household even when it must have been obvious from the start that there was not enough space for multiple burials over a long period of time, are best suited to demonstrate these points.[123] In addition, where the tomb was large enough to offer *liberti* burial space, they were also seen as an insurance for lasting commemoration of the tomb's founder, especially when no natural descendants could fulfil this duty. As Detlef Liebs has shown, this is sometimes explicitly stated in epitaphs.[124]

However, as with former slaves' legal offspring, having a *familia* was not just a one-time achievement, nor was making them heirs only about commemoration of the tomb's founder. The latter task could easily be performed by external heirs, or by *liberti* who were not admitted to burial, as is again demonstrated by epitaphs.[125] Since slaves, being 'property', had neither legal parents nor children, freedpeople lacked legal ancestors. Often they will have died without a legal son to become male heir, either because their natural children remained in the possession of their patrons, they died

---

[121] This is not strictly true, as there is evidence for slaves having slaves of their own called *vicarii* (Weaver, 'Vicarius and Vicarianus'; Weaver, *Familia Caesaris*, 200–6). Nevertheless, this must have been rare, and is irrelevant in our context as they were not legally in a position to set their slaves free.

[122] Bodel, 'Columbaria to catacombs', 213. For funerary benefactions in general, see esp. Schrumpf, *Bestattung*, 138–44.

[123] The same observation made by Bodel, 'Columbaria to catacombs', 212 with n. 72, 214 with n. 77. See also the *cupa* Isola Sacra tomb 60b: Helttula (ed.), *Iscrizioni*, 79. We need to keep in mind that such small monuments are normally situated within a small plot of land belonging to the tomb, but these areas would not be able to cater for many more burials either: for documented examples, see also Baldassarre et al., 'Necropoli dell'Isola Sacra'; Angelucci et al., 'Sepolture e riti'; Steinby, *Via Triumphalis*.

[124] Liebs, 'Ewiges Gedenken', esp. 55–6 on *CIL* 6.10701; 57 on *CIL* 6.13832. Cf. Crook, *Law*, 136; Hope, *Roman Death*, 172. The substitution of children by freedmen is clear from instances where the manumission is made dependent on the lack of a son: Ulpian, *Ad Sabinum* XIX: *Digest* 40.4.7.

[125] Liebs, 'Ewiges Gedenken', 55 on *CIL* 2.4332 (from Tarragona); 58 on *CIL* 6.12133 and the epitaph of C. Popilius Heracla. See also ibid., 52–3 for other types of provision for long-term commemoration.

prematurely or the freed slaves' age at manumission prevented them from producing sufficient numbers of surviving male offspring.[126] Both these deficits could be mitigated to some extent by drawing upon the *familia*.

Patrons as Pseudo-ancestors

Occasionally, we find patrons buried with and by their own former slaves. This is less striking a thing to do than one may think. We can probably assume that these patrons often belonged to a similar milieu as the freedpeople with whom they were buried. They will not already have built a tomb of their own, thus appreciating the opportunity of being offered one, especially one in which they received a place of honour and could hope for commemoration for a prolonged period of time. One may even wonder whether at least some of these patrons made their burial in their ex-slaves' tomb a condition for manumitting them.[127]

One of many cases is Tomb 87 in the Isola Sacra, the necropolis of Portus, the ancient port city of Rome. It comprised a wide range of different types and sizes of tombs, among which the 'house' or 'terraced' tombs are the most prominent.[128] Their patrons were mostly freedpeople, but some were freeborn, probably in the first generation. Tomb 87 was erected as a medium-sized but delicately decorated terraced tomb around 140, and consisted of the actual tomb building, a forecourt and two built dining couches in front of the entrance.[129] The tomb featured two *tituli* with identical texts, above the street entrance to the courtyard and above the door of the cella, telling us that it was erected by P. Varius Ampelus and Varia Ennuchis for themselves as well as their freeborn patron Varia Servanda, and their freedpeople and their descendants.[130] Even though Servanda's name is written in smaller letters than the names of her *liberti*, it is notable that she is mentioned at all in the *titulus*. Moreover, she received the place

---

[126] For age at manumission, see Mouritsen, *Freedman*, 34–5, 188–90, 192–4, with bibl.

[127] For slaves freed and made heirs in order to avoid insolvency, see Champlin, *Final Judgments*, 137.

[128] As Wallace-Hadrill ('Tomb as house') has pointed out, these tombs do not really look like houses at all. He does admit, however, that there might still be some association with houses. As the term is well established, I shall continue to use it as a convenient shorthand. I shall further use the term 'terraced tombs' for what German scholarship calls 'Reihengräber' or 'Fassadengräber', house tombs built so close to each other that they resemble, to some extent, the terraced houses of today.

[129] Calza, *Isola Sacra*, 84, 85, 113–17, 170–1, 345–6 figs. 32, 46–9, 84 pl. 4; Baldassarre et al., *Necropoli di Porto*, 71–4; Petersen, *Freedman*, 203–10; Helttula (ed.), *Iscrizioni*, 122–7, with further bibl.

[130] Helttula (ed.), *Iscrizioni*, 123–5 nos. 106 and 107.

Figure 3.9 Funerary altar of the Iunii family, Trajanic; Rome, Museo Nazionale Centrale Montemartini 2886 (NCE 2969)

of honour in the central niche of the rear wall, with another inscription giving her name,[131] while the founders of the tomb and later occupants did not label their own *ollae*.[132]

A similar arrangement is documented in a Trajanic funerary altar of the Iunii in the Capitoline Museum, which was set up by Iunia Venusta for her patron, her husband, a son and a daughter (Figure 3.9).[133] Portraits of all four

---

[131] Ibid., 126 no. 108.

[132] The tomb's founders also stress that they dedicated Servanda's burial place *de suo*, probably indicating that it was not a formal obligation but their generosity that made them do so. A similar case is Tomb 93 in the same necropolis, where the *titulus* is lost but the (female) patron was honoured with a large altar in front of the central niche of the rear wall: Petersen, *Freedman*, 217 with fig. 135; cf. Baldassarre et al., *Necropoli di Porto*, 54–7; Helttula (ed.), *Iscrizioni*, 122–7. It is probably no coincidence that patrons commemorated in their freedpeople's tombs are often women, who may have lost their husband before their death and did not have any (surviving) children with whom they could be buried.

[133] Fittschen and Zanker, *Kinderbildnisse*, 125–6 n. 134 pls. 130–1.

are arranged carefully. The patron is depicted alone in the tympanum, while husband and children feature in the main relief below.

Such examples also confirm literary sources that tell us how close could be the relationship between owner and slave, and patron and freedperson.[134] Freedpeople belonged to the *familia* of their patrons, whose family name, the *nomen gentile*, they adopted on manumission. Their patrons could therefore stand in for their ancestors, as Lauren Petersen and others have observed.[135] In the case of women, one might object that they do not make proper ancestry. Yet we have seen their importance in the Licinian tomb and for aristocratic families.[136] Moreover, in the freedman milieu, they bestowed their family name on their ex-slaves as much as male patrons did, a name that the Varii in Isola Sacra Tomb 87 treasured enough to deny burial to any external heir; that is, an heir with a different family name. The general idea of creating a family line is beautifully illustrated by the Iunii altar (Figure 3.9). The portraits are clearly differentiated in age, with the patron shown as a bald old man and the husband as an adult between his two children. Moreover, all four are depicted in bust format, which is clearly not meant to portray the living, thus hinting at the *imagines maiorum* of the aristocracy.[137] The allusion to ancestral portraits, the hierarchical arrangement of the portraits and the explicit portrayal as three generations leave no doubt about Iunia's intention to present here a multigenerational family with her (their?) patron featuring as its founder.

A patron did not always have to be buried in a freedman's tomb in order to serve as an ancestor. In the splendid mausoleum of C. Valerius Herma in the necropolis underneath St Peter's, the patron was perhaps depicted in the rich stucco decoration covering the walls.[138] The western wall features three niches in which the tomb's founder, his wife Flavia Olympias and their daughter Valeria Maxima are portrayed in the form of statuettes on pedestals, alluding to both public statue honours (which they probably

---

[134] E.g. Champlin, *Final Judgments*, 131–5; now esp. Mouritsen, *Freedman*, 36–51; and conclusions below. For further examples from the Isola Sacra of dedications to patrons, see Petersen, *Freedman*, 196 and Appendix 2; Helttula (ed.), *Iscrizioni*, nos. 252, 298 and 320. All but one name female patrons, and none of them comes from an identifiable tomb. Only these *tituli* are relevant in our context, while the additional small monuments dedicated to patrons only contain this one burial: ibid., nos. 21, 22, 51. For epitaphs from the city of Rome commemorating male patrons, see Perry, *Freedwoman*, 162–3.

[135] Petersen, *Freedman*, 216–19.

[136] See at n. 63 above.

[137] For the bust format in freedmen's reliefs, see also D'Ambra, 'Ancestor', 224–30.

[138] For the tomb in general, see the following section. Herma does not self-identify as *libertus*, but this is typical for non-imperial *liberti* in the second century and, unlike his wife, no filiation is given for him. It is therefore generally acknowledged that he was a *libertus*.

Figure 3.10 Mausoleum of C. Valerius Herma (Mausoleum H, around 160 CE) in the necropolis underneath St Peter's, west wall

never received) and funerary statues, which could fulfil a similar role (Figure 3.10).[139] The eastern wall opposite features only one equivalent niche in which the stucco statuette on a pedestal depicts a balding elderly man, whose age and beardlessness suggest that he belongs to a previous generation (Figure 3.11).[140] As inscriptions are lacking, it cannot be ruled out that the statuette depicts Herma's natural father, but this is unlikely, and not only because Herma did not legally have a father. The decorative programme does not look like it is ruled by sentimental impulses. The location of this portrait – at a distance, opposite the family and alone on its wall – is reminiscent of the likeness of the Iunii patron on the altar, and suggests that he is in fact Herma's patron, who would have taken on the role Pompey played in the tomb of the Licinii, as it were.

---

[139] Mielsch and Hesberg, *Mausoleen E–I*, 166, 169–70, 203 figs. 180–6; Zander, *Necropoli di San Pietro*, figs. 475–81. Note that two marble portraits found in the tomb's forecourt, showing Herma and his wife, are likely to have belonged to a life-size relief representation: Mielsch and Hesberg, *Mausoleen E–I*, 151, 186, 190–2.

[140] Mielsch and Hesberg, *Mausoleen E–I*, 170–1, 203–4 figs. 187–8: Herma's patron C. Valerius?; Zander, *Necropoli di San Pietro*, figs. 470–2.

Figure 3.11 Mausoleum of C. Valerius Herma (Mausoleum H) in the necropolis underneath St Peter's, east wall

Freedmen as Pseudo-descendants

Conversely, and for the same reasons, freedmen could guarantee the continuity of a family name when there was no natural heir.[141] Herma's tomb is again an excellent example.

---

[141] Esp. Champlin, *Final Judgments*, 133, 177–80.

The Tomb of C. Valerius Herma (Mausoleum H) in Vaticano

Herma's mausoleum is worth studying in more detail, as no other sub-elite tomb allows for so much detail of the history of its usage to be gleaned from the surviving evidence.[142] The necropolis, situated on the slope of the Vatican Hill just north of the Circus of Nero and the via Cornelia, was remarkably well preserved by the basilica of St Peter's that Constantine built over it, since the tombs had to be filled in to create a platform for the church. The area had long been imperial property, and it is fitting that the necropolis was used by many imperial and other wealthy freedmen.[143]

Herma founded his particularly luxurious tomb around 160, when his wife and two children had already died, and it was probably their death that instigated the erection of the mausoleum.[144] One entered the tomb through an asymmetrical forecourt with twenty niches of two *ollae* each. The tomb's façade was built of the finest brickwork, decorated with four pilasters with marble bases and capitals. A large marble *titulus*, as wide as the door and framed by two pilasters, features above the entrance. The interior consists of a large main chamber and a smaller adjacent room extending westward to pass underneath the stairs to the roof terrace. The entrance wall was covered with twelve niches for twenty-four *ollae*, while the rest of the chamber was adorned by a particularly rich stucco decoration of aediculae with figures in high relief alternating with rectangular niches for further urns above a dado that contained arcosolia for inhumation (Figures 3.10 and 3.11). The adjacent room featured the same type of decoration only on its north wall.

An unusually large number of inscriptions allows for the partial reconstruction of the tomb's burial history (Figure 3.12). Herma's freeborn wife, Olympias, was buried in the central arcosolium of the rear wall that was later to contain Herma's bones too, while his children occupied the smaller

---

[142] This is also why it has been discussed frequently, albeit typically not in the wider context here considered: Eck, 'Inschriften', 255–78 nos. 9–28 pls. 16.9–22, 28; Eck, 'Inschriften und Grabbauten', 78–84; Feraudi-Gruénais, *Inschriften*, 30–3, 79–85 nos. 36–57 figs. 23–41a, 117–18; Papi, 'Iscrizioni', 240–5. But cf. Borg, *Crisis and Ambition*, 135–9.

[143] For the area, see Castagnoli, 'Circo di Nerone'; Castagnoli, *Vaticano*; Liverani, *Topografia*; Liverani and Spinola, *Necropoli Vaticana*; Liverani et al., *Necropoli Vaticane*.

[144] On the tomb in general see Toynbee and Ward Perkins, *St. Peter*, pls. 12–13, 15, 30–1; Mielsch and Hesberg, *Mausoleen E–I*, 143–208; Liverani et al., *Necropoli Vaticane*, 92–108; Feraudi-Gruénais, *Inschriften*, 30–3, 45–6; Zander, *Necropoli di San Pietro*, 248–80 figs. 419–29. Feraudi-Gruénais (*Inschriften*, 31) and Eck ('Rechtsquelle', 73) think that the mother predeceased her children. This is possible, if not likely, although not because she is not a commemorator (they could all have died at the same time), but because her portrait shows her with a hairstyle that is somewhat earlier than the tomb: Mielsch and Hesberg, *Mausoleen E–I*, 190–3 nos. 3–4 figs. 232–3, 235–6, with a different explanation for the observation.

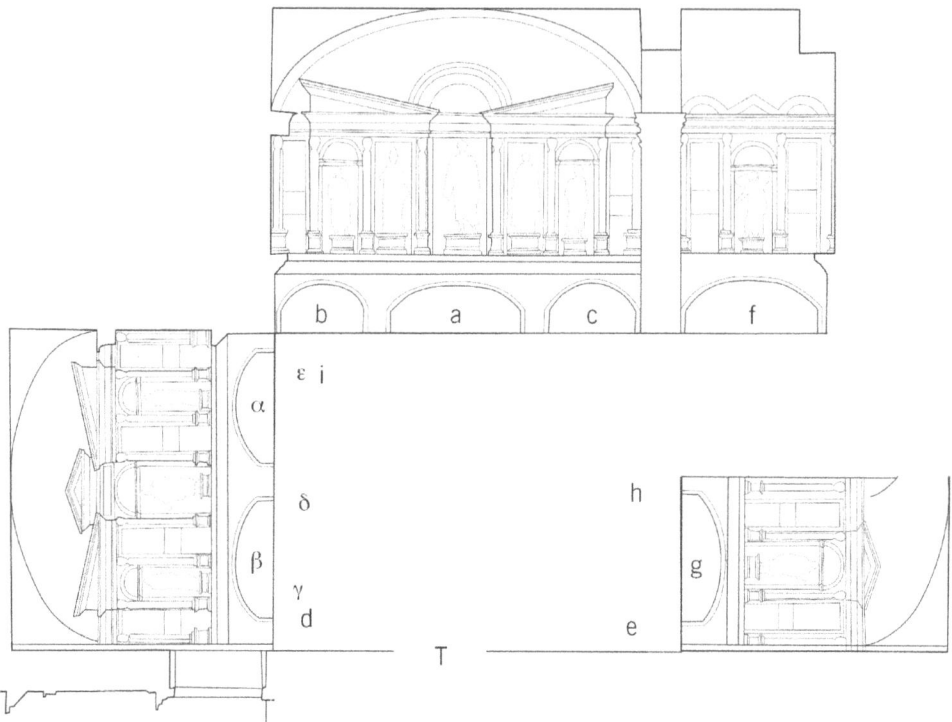

Figure 3.12 Mausoleum of C. Valerius Herma (Mausoleum H) in the necropolis underneath St Peter's, distribution of named burials within the chamber

flanking arcosolia, all covered with inscribed marble slabs of identical design and workmanship (a–c).[145] After his wife's death, Herma does not seem to have remarried. He buried an *alumnus*, Valerius Asiaticus, aged four, and donated the space for the burial of another, C. Appaienus Castus, who died aged eight, in front of the entrance wall (d–e).[146] One Valeria Asia, most likely Asiaticus' mother, was commemorated and buried in the arcosolium in the small annex's north wall by (her husband?) Valerius Princeps (f). The style of the inscription, almost identical to those of Herma and his family, suggests that her burial was among the earliest in the tomb. Because of the prominent location, Eck suspected that Princeps may have been Herma's brother.[147] It is notable that no involvement of Herma is mentioned, so that

---

[145] This is what suggests that their death instigated the foundation of the mausoleum. Cf. Mielsch and Hesberg, *Mausoleen E–I*, 152; Eck, 'Inschriften', 257–9 no. 11 pl. 17.11.

[146] Asiaticus: Eck, 'Inschriften', 255–6 no. 9 pl. 16.9a. Castus: ibid., 260–1 no. 13 pl. 17.13; Feraudi-Gruénais, *Inschriften*, 31–2, 80 no. 37 fig. 24. This *alumnus* may have died after Herma, as the inscription only mentions Herma's donation of the burial space, not the burial itself, as in the case of Asiaticus.

[147] Eck, 'Inschriften', 256–7 no. 10; Eck, 'Inschriften und Grabbauten', 81 pl. 7b; Eck, 'Rechtsquelle', 77–8; Feraudi-Gruénais, *Inschriften*, 31 (brother unlikely), 82 no. 48 fig. 36.

Princeps may have had the right to burial there either through a family relationship or, less likely chronologically, as an heir.[148]

After Herma's own departure, the tomb was inherited by some of his
freedmen. A certain Valerius Philomelus and his wife Valeria Galatia, surely
his *liberti*, donated or sold the western part to their 'well-deserving friend'
(*locum obt(ulerunt) Valerii Philumenus et Galatia amico bene merenti*)
T. Pompeius Successus, who buried several children within and in front
of the western wall.[149] Successus himself is likely to have been buried with
his homonymous son in the north-western arcosolium, which also carries
his name (α).[150] In the second quarter of the third century, the marble sarcophagus of Pompeia Maritima, suitably decorated with sea creatures and
her portrait, was set up by her son, probably against the southern part
of the west wall, thus leaving visible Successus' name and the inscription
attesting to rightful ownership (δ).[151] Later, this part of the tomb must have

---

[148] Note that the epitaph for another early burial, that in the arcosolium of the eastern wall of
the annex room of a certain Dynatene who was commemorated by her husband C. Valerius
Eutychas, explicitly states permission from Herma (*permissu C. Valeri Haermaes patroni
optimi*): Eck, 'Inschriften und Grabbauten', 81 pl. 8b; Feraudi-Gruénais, *Inschriften*, 31, 82
no. 46; Eck, 'Rechtsquelle', 78.

[149] This donation or sale must have happened soon after Herma's death, since the arcosolia were
still free. Successus' homonymous son was buried in the northwestern arcosolium in an
inscribed marble sarcophagus that was then hidden by the inscription attesting the donation/
sale (Eck, 'Inschriften', 262–3 fig. 18.15; Feraudi-Gruénais, *Inschriften*, 32, 81–2 no. 45 fig. 32;
Papi, 'Iscrizioni', 240–3 figs. 1–2). A very similar inscribed marble sarcophagus for a child,
most likely another son of Successus, probably occupied the southwestern arcosolium (ibid.,
244–5 fig. 4). This is why the built casket of a third son was set atop the sarcophagus of
Herma's *alumnus* in the southwest corner, or even replaced it (Eck, 'Inschriften', 255 n. 44,
264 no. 17 pl. 19.17a; Feraudi-Gruénais, *Inschriften*, 32, 81 no. 44 fig. 31). The boy's name,
(C.?) Flavius Pompeius Secundus, may point to a relationship between the Pompeii and Flavia
Olympias, as Eck ('Inschriften und Grabbauten', 83) notes, so that the friendship between
Herma's freedpeople and Pompeius Successus was not an arbitrary one.

[150] Eck, 'Inschriften', 261–3 nos. 14–15 pls. 18.14–15. *Pace* Eck ('Rechtsquelle', 79–80), who
considers it possible that the burial of these externals was illegal, the clear spatial restriction of
burials of Pompeii, the permission given by Philomelus and his wife, and the continuation of
burials of Valerii in the same tomb, make it clear that the couple did not have a right to their
own burial through the dedication on the *titulus*, but that they were heirs, and therefore at
liberty to admit others into the tomb, especially since the burial of externals was not explicitly
interdicted.

[151] Mielsch and Hesberg, *Mausoleen E–I*, 159; Eck, 'Inschriften', 263 no. 16 pl. 18.16; Papi,
'Iscrizioni', 245; Zander, *Necropoli di San Pietro*, fig. 414. It is usually assumed that Pompeia
was Successus' (one and only) wife, but given that the tomb was founded around 160, and
Herma did not remarry or bury further relatives, it is perhaps likely that he did not survive
his family for more than a decade or two. The accrual of the inheritance would then have
happened around 180 at the latest (for a date in the late second or early third century, see
Papi, 'Iscrizioni', 243–4, but without explanation), meaning that Pompeia would have survived
a nineteen-year-old son by at least forty years. While this is not impossible, it may be more
likely that she either was a second wife, or belongs to the next generation of heirs of this part
of the tomb.

been inherited by external heirs, who placed two sarcophagi in front of the northern part of the western wall. The first one, a large *lenos* showing lions savaging their prey, was dedicated to T. Caesennius Severianus by his sons Faustinus Pompeianus and Faustinus Rufinus (ε).[152] As the name Pompeianus suggests, there may have been a family relationship between the Pompeii and their late heirs, potentially through the female line.[153]

Philomelus and Galatia do not appear again in the epigraphic record, so it is not clear whether they inherited the entire tomb and used the rest of the space for themselves, or whether they only inherited the western part and built a tomb for themselves elsewhere.[154] Yet it seems clear that the main part of the mausoleum continued to be used by Valerii. Unfortunately, though further Valerii are commemorated by inscriptions, most of these cannot be dated precisely. One Valerius Valens and his son Valerius Dionysius may have been buried in the arcosolium of the western wall, in two terracotta sarcophagi covered by the inscribed tabula (g).[155] Because of the relatively prominent position within the tomb, we may assume that they were heirs of either Herma or his heirs. If Eck's restoration of another inscription is correct, an *evocatus* C. Valerius Iulianus buried his daughter in an unknown location in the tomb (h). He may have been a freeborn son of one of Herma's freedman heirs, whose rank in the military corps required at least sixteen years of service, so that the burial did not occur before the early third century.[156] The third century saw continued burial activity in an orderly manner, both in simple terracotta sarcophagi and 'bench-graves' and in marble sarcophagi.[157] In the 270s, Valeria Florentina

---

[152] Mielsch and Hesberg, *Mausoleen E–I*, 159; Eck, 'Inschriften', 269 no. 21 pl. 21.21; Stroszeck, *ASR 6.1*, 159 no. 377 pl. 39; Liverani et al., *Necropoli Vaticane*, 106 fig. 61. The second, uninscribed sarcophagus seems to be otherwise unpublished.

[153] Ditto Eck, 'Inschriften', 264 no. 17.

[154] The second option is proposed by e.g. Papi, 'Iscrizioni', 263–4; Eck, 'Rechtsquelle', 81; Borg, *Crisis and Ambition*, 136–7. The first option now seems to me at least as likely, since we are lacking epitaphs of the Valerii bridging the gap in our evidence to the late Valerii to be discussed shortly.

[155] Eck, 'Inschriften', 259–60 no. 12 pl. 17.12; Feraudi-Gruénais, *Inschriften*, 32, 82 no. 47 fig. 35.

[156] Eck, 'Inschriften', 267–8 no. 20 pl. 20.20.

[157] Mielsch and Hesberg, *Mausoleen E–I*, 157, 159–60. Their suggestion that an anonymous strigilated sarcophagus with the Severan portraits of a couple stood in the centre of the tomb is probably an error. According to Zander (*Necropoli sotto la Basilica*, 91), it was found on the first fill of the tomb accumilated in the wake of the Constantinian building works, and would therefore come from elsewhere in the necropolis. For the gradual filling and destruction of the tomb, see Mielsch and Hesberg, *Mausoleen E–I*, 160–1. The Valerii attested by graffiti on the south wall (Eck, 'Inschriften', 264–5 pls. 20.18a–b; Feraudi-Gruénais, *Inschriften*, 32, 84–5 nos. 54–7 figs. 41a–b) are likely to have died during the second century because they were cremated. Only in the very last phase of the tomb is there evidence for more anarchical burial practice.

set up an inscribed hunting sarcophagus for her husband Valerius Vasatulus in the left-hand corner in front of Caesennius' casket (i), which confirms that the tomb was still in use by Valerii at that time.[158]

The mausoleum of the Valerii is a rare well-documented example of a family tomb founded by a rich freedman that was used continuously over more than 100 years by parts of his *familia*. Notably, burial took place in a very orderly way; it occurred solely in those parts of the tomb that were inherited by the user group; and only a limited number of people were actually admitted for burial. The most prominent part of the tomb remained in the hands of Valerii, although they were not natural descendants of Herma, and it is also highly doubtful that they were all agnatic descendants of his heirs: Vasatulus' wife has the same *nomen gentile* as her husband and confirms that we are still looking at the freedman milieu.

Over all those years, the tomb façade boasted its original *titulus* and the interior decoration remained unchanged, even though its third-century occupants were obviously wealthy. Herma's arcosolium and inscription remained visible until a very late stage, and his family's portraits continued to be on display. They included not just a relief in front of the tomb and the stucco relief portraits (Figures 3.11 and 3.12), but also stucco portraits in the round, including those of Flavia Olympias and Valeria Maxima.[159] The exact purpose of the death masks of a man (possibly Valerius Herma) and two children is unclear, but the rarely attested practice again harks back to aristocratic tradition.[160] Whether fragments of gypsum busts also depicted members of the founder's generation is unclear, but the gilded stucco portrait of a boy with a youth lock of mid to late Severan date[161] demonstrates that the heirs of this tomb continued to set up portraits just like the Calpurnii had done in the Licinian tomb. Herma's later heirs were surely proud of the richly furnished mausoleum, but also of its long-standing tradition and age. In the same way as Herma's patron had served the tomb's founder as ancestor, Herma later fulfilled this role for the occupants of

---

[158] Toynbee and Ward Perkins, *St. Peter*, 91–2; Mielsch and Hesberg, *Mausoleen E–I*, 159; Liverani et al., *Necropoli Vaticane*, 104–5 fig. 60; Zander, *Necropoli di San Pietro*, fig. 428. For the sarcophagus, see also Andreae *Jagdsarkophage*, 183 no. 240 pl. 44.2.

[159] Mielsch and Hesberg, *Mausoleen E–I*, 192, 196 figs. 235–9; Liverani et al., *Necropoli Vaticane*, 98 figs. 54–5.

[160] Mielsch and Hesberg, *Mausoleen E–I*, 196, 198 figs. 246–53; Liverani et al., *Necropoli Vaticane*, 101 fig. 58; Zander, *Necropoli di San Pietro*, 124 figs. 186–8, 202).

[161] Mielsch and Hesberg, *Mausoleen E–I*, 196 figs. 240–2; Liverani et al., *Necropoli Vaticane*, 102 fig. 56; Zander, *Necropoli di San Pietro*, 128 figs. 193–4; Borg, *Crisis and Ambition*, pl. 3b. For the gypsum bust fragments see Mielsch and Hesberg, *Mausoleen E–I*, 196 figs. 243–5, and Liverani et al., *Necropoli Vaticane*, 98 fig. 57.

Figure 3.13 Mausoleum of the Terentii family (Isola Sacra Tomb 11), founded around 140 CE

future generations. Herma and his family had become the founders of a multigenerational freedman 'family line' that replaced natural kin, carried on his name, kept alive his memory as founder and honoured his tomb.

The history of no other tomb's usage can be reconstructed with as much precision and detail as that of the Valerii, but a few additional examples can demonstrate that the observed burial patterns and the ideology behind them were typical, and only their documentation is unique.

Isola Sacra, Tomb of the Terentii (11)

Tomb 11 in the Isola Sacra was erected around 135–40 in a slightly oblique angle to, but facing, the road (Figure 3.13).[162] Of its original Greek *titulus*, only the bottom right part is preserved and legible.[163] It mentions a [Th]amyres *pater*, perhaps a son, followed by a daughter and mother. At least the latter two remained anonymous, which makes the focus on family

---

[162] On the tomb, see Calza, *Isola Sacra*, 69, 200–3, 287–9 figs. 104–6; Baldassarre et al., *Necropoli di Porto*, 185–91; Helttula (ed.), *Iscrizioni*, 29–32; Meinecke, *Sarcophagum posuit*, 119, 277–9 cat. B39 fig. 41 pl. 7.1.

[163] Baldassarre et al. *Necropoli di Porto*, 185; Helttula (ed.), *Iscrizioni*, 30 no. 16[GR].

rather than individuals even more obvious. All other epigraphic evidence belongs to a later phase of the tomb. After some time, when also the level of the ground around the tomb had risen, a small forecourt was added to the building. It seems likely that a Latin *titulus* with a dedication by C. Terentius Eutychus or Eutychianus to his wife Su[l]picia Acte, his son C. Terentius Felix and his natural brother C. Terentius Rufus, as well as *libertis libertabusque posterisque eorum*, was affixed to this forecourt.[164] Inside the tomb, which was originally designed for both incineration and inhumation, sarcophagi and pseudo-sarcophagi were added. The first was an inscribed, marble-clad pseudo-sarcophagus in front of the right-hand wall that was originally dedicated by Terentius Vitalis to (his wife?) Terentia Kallotyche and her or their children.[165] Later, the name Vitalis was replaced by that of Lucifer, and an *et* added in front of Kallotyche's name, so that the inscription now reads somewhat oddly: *Terentius Lucifer et Terenteae Kallotyceni*. After this pseudo-sarcophagus, a strigilated uninscribed marble sarcophagus that eventually contained two bodies was set inside the rear arcosolium, which had to be extended on both sides in order to contain the casket. Finally, another pseudo-sarcophagus, decorated at its front with a banqueting scene, was built in front of the left-hand wall.[166] It shows among other figures a couch with a sleeping woman and a reclining man holding a *kantharos* and a wreath, and another, semi-nude woman sitting on the couch and presenting him with a cup. The hairstyles of the women suggest a date for the relief in the late Antonine period,[167] providing a *terminus ante quem* for the other burials. A tabula commemorates a dedication to C. Terentius Felix and his

---

[164] No context for the *titulus* is reported (cf. Helttula (ed.), *Iscrizioni*, 334–5 no. 334), but it was found in the same year as the tomb was excavated. Its belonging to the tomb is further suggested by the many Terentii commemorated inside it, including a C. Terentius Felix, and by the lack of Terentii elsewhere in the necropolis. The only exception is a dedication by C. Terentius Narcissus to his wife found in Tomb 87, which was otherwise only used by Varii, and has both *tituli* preserved: ibid., 122–7, esp. no. 109. Unlike the Varii tomb, Tomb 11 received its forecourt later, an opportunity to display a new *titulus*: cf. Tomb 16 (ibid., 34–8), and Tomb 94 (ibid., 143–7) for a similar procedure, but also here on Tomb 75–76 below. The term *frater naturalis* suggests that both Eutych[ian]us and his brother were former slaves.

[165] Ibid., 31–2 no. 27: *D(is) M(anibus). Terentius Bitalis Terenteae Kallotyceni et filis suis fecit. Si qit in aeo sarcofago interet corpus sibe ossa, inferet aerario Saturni s(estertium) XXX m(ilia) n(ummum).*

[166] Baldassarre et al., *Necropoli di Porto*, 188–91 with fig. 68; Meinecke, *Sarcophagum posuit*, 278 with pl. 7.1. On the decorated item, see also Amedick, *Menschenleben*, 12–13, 20, 136 no. *84 pls. 3.2, 4.1–2.

[167] Meinecke (*Sarcophagum posuit*, 278) dates the female hairstyles to the 190s or even later, while Amedick (*Menschenleben*, 136 no. *84) dates them to 152–60. The likely date is in between. The closest parallels to the hairstyle of the reclining woman are found in the portraits of Lucilla and Crispina, while the seated woman's very low bun equally suggests a mid to late Antonine date (cf. Fittschen, *Bildnistypen*). The portrait of the man could easily be Severan, but does not have to be.

wife Ulpia Chrysopolis by C. Terentius Lucifer and his *colliberti* and *coheres*. This Lucifer is highly likely to be the one we have already met, while Felix is likely to be the son of Eutych[ian]us featuring in the entrance *titulus*.[168]

From this evidence, the history of Tomb 11 can be reconstructed with varying degrees of certainty. The date when C. Terentius Eutych[ian]us extended an existing tomb and added a secondary *titulus* to it has not been established precisely by archaeology, but was prior to the elevation of the terrain in the wake of the resurfacing of the road.[169] He and his wife were almost certainly buried by their son, C. Terentius Felix, and one would assume that, as they extended the tomb and could be regarded as (re-) founders, they were buried in the most prominent location still available. The strigilis sarcophagus occupies the most privileged position, but seems too small for a couple of adults, and is said to have contained the skeletons of youngsters.[170] It is therefore tempting to think that Eutych[ian]us and his wife were buried in the left-hand pseudo-sarcophagus. If this is the case, the tomb was used by Terentii before the two took over and extended the mausoleum, since Terentius Vitalis' pseudo-sarcophagus on the right predates both the strigilis sarcophagus and its counterpart on the left. While we cannot prove that the original founders of the tomb were already Terentii, this is surely possible, and it is notable that Eutych[ian]us did not remove or cover the original *titulus* above the main entrance to the mausoleum. His son Felix and his wife Ulpia Chrysopolis must have inherited the tomb, but died without children, and were therefore buried by their freedman and heir Lucifer in an unspecified place, possibly in the courtyard.

According to the epitaph for Felix and his wife, Lucifer was not the tomb's only heir, but probably its main one, and was certainly determined to leave a mark. For his own burial, he chose the existing pseudo-sarcophagus on the right, erasing its original dedicant's name. This was certainly not *de rigueur*, but the violation was perhaps not quite as ruthless as one might think. Vitalis does not specify his relationship with Kallotyche, and the inscription leaves it open whether or not he intended to be inhumed in the place

---

[168] Helttula (ed.), *Iscrizioni*, 30–1 no. 26. As he notes, the abbreviations used in the inscriptions allow for a reading according to which Lucifer's *colliberti* would be heirs of Felix and his wife, and Lucifer the recipient of the dedication. Yet, considering the inscription on the other pseudo-sarcophagus just discussed; the oddity it would create by leaving the dedicants anonymous; and the fact that Lucifer was in a position to donate burial space to externals, and probably within the same tomb or its forecourt (ibid., 323–4 no. 319), this is unlikely.

[169] Three steps lead down into the precinct: Calza, *Isola Sacra*, 289.

[170] Meinecke, *Sarcophagum posuit*, 119, 278–9. She believes that the adolescents could be the tomb founder's children mentioned in the *titulus*. But she does not consider the second *titulus*, which shows that this is impossible chronologically.

as well. Lucifer's alteration is minimal, only replacing Vitalis' *cognomen* and adding an *et*. The grammar is clearly not correct here and one could amend the inscription in two possible ways. One could either go by the nominative of Lucifer's name and ignore the *et*, in which case he would appear to be the donor; but one could also ignore the nominative, already predetermined by the remaining *nomen gentile* of the original inscription, and focus on the *et*, which only makes sense if Lucifer was to be buried in the same grave. This intention seems beyond doubt and Lucifer may have liked sitting on the fence with the present formula. His relation to Kallotyche is as uncertain as that of Vitalis, but since her children were admitted to burial in the casket as well, Lucifer may in fact have been one of them.[171]

The Iulii Plot on the Via Appia

An interesting case is also attested by six altars and a tabula from a plot at the first mile of the Appia, close to the so-called 'columbarium of the *liberti* of Augustus'. As Dietrich Boschung first recognised, these attest to the burial of several generations of (imperial) freedmen and their descendants,[172] but also allow unique insight into the way a burial plot, apparently of considerable size, was managed and passed on to later heirs (Stemma 4). The first generation attested is represented by (C.) Iulius Eutactus and C. Iulius Theophilus, who permitted the burial of C. Iulius Atimetus, his wife, her patron and their *delicatus* (a young boy kept for amusement).[173] Next, the mother of one-year-old C. Signius C. f. Zoilos obtained permission from Theophilus and two other CC. Iulii, Oriens and Peculiaris, to bury her son. It may be concluded that Eutactus had died in the meantime and left his share in the plot to the two men.[174] In the next altar, these two are again giving permission, but Theophilus is missing.[175] He may now have died as well and left his share to three other Julii who join in the permission, Anicetus, formerly Theophilus' *dispensator* and so surely his *libertus*, Lalus

---

[171] As long as the date of the forecourt remains unclear, it cannot be excluded entirely that it was added later, in the Severan period, when the ground level along the street was raised and the earliest *cupae* were covered by later tombs (Baldassarre, 'Necropoli', 129–30; Baldassarre et al., *Necropoli di Porto*, 117, 132; Angelucci et al., 'Sepolture e riti', 87; Borg, *Crisis and Ambition*, 22). If this were the case, the history of Terentii using the tomb would move well into the third century, while still starting at least with Vitalis' pre-190 dedication.

[172] Boschung, *Grabaltäre*, 71–2 nos. I 222–7 (= cat. 633, 696, 824, 919 (pl. 51), 955 (pl. 56), 956), with a different interpretation of the records than proposed here.

[173] *CIL* 6.19861.

[174] *CIL* 06.26551. It is unclear whether they were his freedmen or kin.

[175] *CIL* 6.19957.

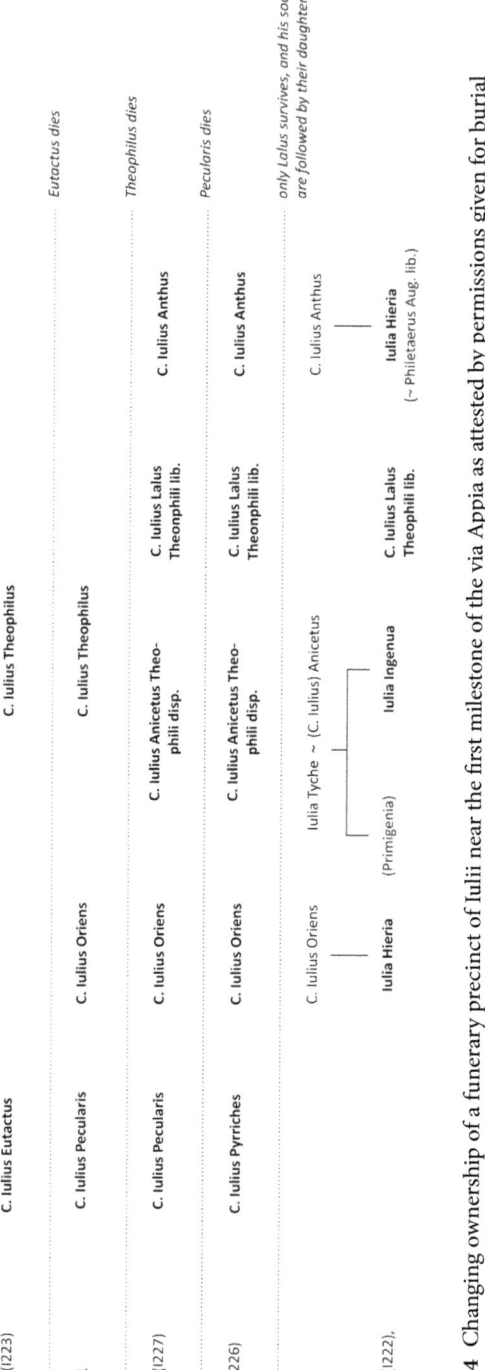

A stemma diagram showing changing ownership, with the following attestations and names:

Reference					Note
CIL 6.19861 (I223)	C. Iulius Eutactus		C. Iulius Theophilus		*Eutactus dies*
CIL 06.26551	C. Iulius Pecularis	C. Iulius Oriens	C. Iulius Theophilus		*Theophilus dies*
CIL 6.19957 (I227)	C. Iulius Pecularis	C. Iulius Oriens	C. Iulius Anicetus Theophili disp.	C. Iulius Lalus Theonphili lib. → C. Iulius Anthus	*Pecularis dies*
CIL 6.9344 (I226)	C. Iulius Pyrriches	C. Iulius Oriens	C. Iulius Anicetus Theophili disp.	C. Iulius Lalus Theonphili lib. → C. Iulius Anthus	
	C. Iulius Oriens / **Iulia Hieria**	Iulia Tyche ~ (C. Iulius) Anicetus / (Primigenia)	**Iulia Ingenua**	C. Iulius Anthus	*only Lalus survives, and his socii are followed by their daughters*
CIL 6.19833 (I222), c.100 CE	**Iulia Hieria**			C. Iulius Lalus Theophili lib.	**Iulia Hieria** (~ Philetaerus Aug. lib.)

Stemma 4 Changing ownership of a funerary precinct of Iulii near the first milestone of the via Appia as attested by permissions given for burial

Theophili libertus and Anthus, whose relationship with Theophilus remains unclear.[176] Next, Peculiaris died and was replaced by Iulius Pyrriches.[177] The final group of *socii*, attested on an altar from the first quarter of the second century, consists of Lalus and the daughters and heirs of his *socii*: Iulia Hieria, daughter of Oriens; Iulia Ingenua, daughter of Anicetus; and Iulia Hieria, daughter of Anthus.[178] In at least two instances we also have evidence that the heirs of the plot cordoned off an area for their own family's burial.[179] While not all individuals commemorated share the same *nomen gentile*, the non-Iulii can be identified as being related to Iulii by marriage, and it is very clear that the *socii* made an effort to ensure that the burial plot passed on to heirs of the same family name.

Consortium Tomb on the Via Appia and Other Renovations

This same intention is made explicit in another inscription that was found near the Porta San Sebastiano on the Appia and provides us with the following information.[180] The now-lost tomb was founded in 3 BCE by a consortium of four men and a woman, including L. Maelius Papia and Maelia Hilara, who may have been his wife and either his fellow freedwoman or his own former slave. The *socii* dedicated the monument to their male and female ex-slaves, stating explicitly that this was done in order to preserve their family names:

> Lentulo et Corvino | Messala co(n)s(ulibus) | qui hoc monimentum(!)
> aedificaverunt cum ustrina | L(ucius) Maelius Papia et Maelia Hilara

---

[176] If another altar that one C. Iulius Theophilus dedicated to his freeborn wife Iulia Procula referred to the same person, this transition would have occurred no earlier than the mid-Flavian period, as the woman's hairstyle closely resembles that of Iulia Titi. Since it was found in the Lateran area, it is perhaps unlikely that the two Theophili were the same man, although it is possible that he sold his share in the plot to the three Julii mentioned when he established his own plot in the *ager Vaticanus*. On the altar: *CIL* 6.20645; *NSc* (1888), 394–5 (G. Gatti); Boschung, *Grabaltäre*, 79 cat. 16 pl. 2 (who does not consider it in the context of the Iulii plot); Kleiner, *Altars*, 146–7 no. 34 pl. 21.

[177] *CIL* 6.9344.

[178] *CIL* 6.19833.

[179] According to *CIL* 6.9328, Anicetus set up an altar for his wife Iulia Tyche, daughter Primigenia and himself, and was later commemorated there by C. Octavius Apto and Iulia Aphrodite, who may have been his daughter and son-in-law. *CIL* 6.8734 refers to Anthus' daughter, who set up an altar in their burial plot for her husband Philetaerus, an imperial freedman and *praeposito ab auro gemmato*, herself and their *liberti*.

[180] *CIL* 6.10243; Gordon, *Album*, 28–31 no. 172 pl. 75a; Champlin, *Final Judgments*, 177 (with erroneous initial consular date of 13 BCE); http://gams.uni-graz.at/o:epsg.343 (last accessed 16/01/2017) for a German translation. On some legal aspects, see Schwind, 'Thesaurus', 179–80. All three steps in the history of the tomb are dated by consular dates. I am most grateful to John Bodel for discussing the inscription with me.

et Rocius Surus et M(arcus) Caesennius et Furius | Bucconius hoc monimentum(!) libertis libertabus *ut de nomine non exeat* | ita qui testamento scripti fuerint |

In the consulship of Lentulus and Corvinus Messala. Those who erected this monument with *ustrinum*, L. Maelius Papia and Maelia Hilara and Rocius Surus and M. Caesennius and Furius Bucconius, (dedicated) this monument to their freedmen (and) freedwomen, *so that (it) will not go out of the name;* so they have written in their will.

In 81, the complex was extended by a plot of land opposite, and the only individuals mentioned by name are one L. Maelius Successus and his mother Maelia Syntychene. Their names not only confirm that that of the Maelii had been preserved for over eighty years, but also that this was done through freedman pseudo-genealogy, since Successus bears the same *nomen gentile* as his mother. Finally, in 110 the tomb had to be renovated, and we are again given a list of names of the individuals involved. They include some new ones, but also three Maelii, one Furius and one Rocia, whose *nomina* had all featured in the original, by now over 110-year-old list of founders. Their aim to preserve their family names, despite their tomb or plot being owned by a consortium and despite their apparent lack of (legitimate) children, had been achieved, with impressive results.

Similar intentions are occasionally found in other *tituli* where a tomb is left to freedpeople with the explicit intention of preserving the family name(s). In *CIL* 6.26940 (p. 3918), Terentia Secundilla specifies that the tomb must not go out of the name of her male and female ex-slaves and their offspring (*ita ne de nomine libertorum libertarum<q>ue meorum posterisqu(e) eorum exeat*). In *CIL* 6.22208, one L. Marius Felix builds a tomb for his patrons as well as for himself and his freedpeople and their offspring *ita ne unquam de nomine familiae nostrae hic monument[um exeat]*. In *CIL* 6.1521, the concern is about several family names, most likely because we are dealing with a family comprising imperial freedmen with different names, whose own freedpeople would thus equally carry different names.[181] In *CIL* 6.22303, one Mattius Adiutor erected his tomb while still alive for himself and his freedpeople and their offspring for the same reason. The same expectation follows the *libertis libertabusque* formula in some other cases even when there is, or is hoped to be in the future, natural offspring.[182]

---

[181] *CIL* 6.29962 equally has the plural, but is too fragmentary to allow for further assessment.
[182] E.g. *CIL* 6.1825 (pp. 3225, 3818), 10701 (p. 3910), 10848 (pp. 3507, 3910), 13195, 22348, 26940 (p. 3918).

In other cases, the renovation of tombs, which normally required permission from the *pontifex maximus*, the emperor or a magistrate and was therefore sometimes recorded in an inscription,[183] attests to the long life of a tomb. The Roman knight L. Salvius [---]ens renovated a tomb, probably around the middle of the third century, to be used by his family, their descendants, their freedmen and freedwomen and their offspring.[184] The tomb is unfortunately lost, but when Salvius refurbished the tomb, he erased and recarved the *titulus* except for the final line with the measurements of the plot, which was executed in beautiful letters of the early second century. While it cannot be excluded that he was given the tomb because it had been abandoned for some time and no heirs survived, it is equally possible that it was his ancestral mausoleum.[185]

A marble block from a round tomb at the second mile of the via Latina was erected by C. Iulius Divi Aug. l. Delphus Maecenatianus, who must have been the slave of first Maecenas and later Augustus, for himself, his wife (probably his *liberta*) and their freeborn daughter. Around a century later, a certain C. Iulius Trophimas, most likely a descendant of one of their *liberti*, restored (*refecit*) the tomb for himself, his descendants and his freedpeople.[186] In this case, the original inscription was not erased but merely supplemented, suggesting that pride over the tomb's long history and the longevity of the *familia* was part of the message.

Equestrian Descendants

Arguably, pride in a family tomb becomes most obvious within the freedmen milieu where a descendant achieved further advancement by gaining the status of a knight, but still preferred burial in the family mausoleum. In Ostia's Porta Romana necropolis, for instance, a certain L. Combarisius Hermianus erected a tomb for himself, his wife and his children as well as

---

[183] Kaser, 'Grabrecht', 26–7.

[184] *CIL* 6.41307 (= *AE* 1974, 00038); Manacorda, 'Ex Ascia', 346–52; Faßbender, *Untersuchungen*, 235 no. 348.

[185] The prominent location close to the city and between via Appia and Latina (the inscription was found in the Vigna Codini) makes it unlikely that he simply usurped a ruin. He may actually have been another case of an equestrian descendant of freedpeople, like the ones discussed in the next section. That he originates from a freedman milieu is suggested by his own *nomen*, deriving from the town Salvia; his wife's *cognomen*, misspelt as Fyrme; and the dedication to their *liberti*. Cf. Eck, 'Freigelassene', 15, on the name and its likely origins from an enfranchised slave of the Urbs Salvia.

[186] *CIL* 6.19926 (= Rome, Museo Nazionale Romano, Garden, inv. 983); Faßbender, *Untersuchungen*, 216 no. 292.

his brother.[187] He was a member of the freedman college of *augustales* and appears in a list of 196 CE. Through inscriptions from within the tomb, at least three more Combarisii are attested. One of them, perhaps the grandson of the founder, was a Roman knight who had held all of the most prestigious offices at Ostia and was *pontifex Laurentium Lavinatium*.[188] Since these offices were only available to the rich, he clearly had the means to erect a tomb for himself elsewhere. And yet he chose to be buried in his family mausoleum, not ashamed of his servile heritage but proud of his ancestors, who had made it from slaves to eminent citizens of Ostia and managed to acquire a burial plot in one of the most prominent locations available.

In another case the evidence looks more elusive, as we have lost not only the tomb but also the inscribed objects in question, but the situation seems to be similar to that of the Combarisii. The tomb near Portus is described by the seventeenth-century sources as particularly impressive.[189] The *titulus* gives the size of the unusually large plot as 89 x 29 m, and its lavish decoration included now-lost statues. Several inscribed marble sarcophagi and other objects further confirm the luxurious burial style as well as some features of the history of usage. The tomb was founded by one A. Caesennius Herma, whose patron, A. Caesennius Gallus, is known to have been *legatus pro praetore* in Asia Minor in 80 and 82, as well as one A. Caesennius Italicus and his wife Caesennia L. l. Erotis.[190] The exact relationship between these founders and the other Caesennii buried in the tomb is not clear, but we can see that they included *liberti* of the original founders. At some stage, a garland sarcophagus was dedicated to the knight L. Fabricius Caesennius Gallus by his son, who proudly lists his father's extraordinary achievements in the epitaph, identical to those of his later peer in Ostia.[191]

Families with Different *Nomina Gentilicia*

As already indicated, these are some of the best-documented examples of the general ideology I want to demonstrate from Rome and its port cities.

---

[187] For tomb C4 and the following, see Heinzelmann, *Nekropolen*, 206–9; Borg, *Crisis and Ambition*, 27–8, 32, 134.

[188] *CIL* 14.335. On this prestigious priesthood, see Saulnier, 'Laurens Lavinas'; Scheid and Granino Cecere, 'Sacerdotes'; Granino Cecere, '*Laurentes lavinates*'.

[189] *CIL* 14.354, 468, 729–33; Helttula (ed.), *Iscrizioni*, 3–8, with further bibl.

[190] It is not entirely clear whether Italicus is a *conlibertus* of Herma or perhaps his son.

[191] D'Arms ('Municipal notables') thinks that the knight was the tomb's founder and patron of the other Caesennii. Yet why, then, are all his alleged *liberti* Aulii while he is a Lucius? More importantly, D'Arms overlooks that the tomb *titulus* that contained the plot's measurements does not mention him, while his inscription is on a sarcophagus. That he descends from freedmen is further suggested by his *tribus* Palatina. Another knight, C. Laecanius Novatillianus, was buried around 230 in an ancestral tomb that may have been well over

Even the relatively well-known necropoleis of Ostia and Porto suffered late antique looting; the modern excavations also paid little attention to contextual detail. For all too long, inscriptions have been treated simply as texts rather than as objects that give away their full message only in the context in which they used to be viewed. Yet it is not only poor preservation or documentation that prevents us from tracing the history of mausolea in detail. Few tombs from Rome and its vicinity are as well-known as those excavated underneath St Peter's Basilica and the papal palaces, and among these Herma's has yielded by far the largest number of inscriptions. In most tombs, later generations did not feel the need to set up epitaphs, nor even *tabellae* marking individual graves.

Admittedly, especially when we do not know the exact original location of inscriptions, even many instances where multiple epitaphs are preserved can look rather messy. Nevertheless, there is no need to conclude that this is the result of carelessness, or even anarchy and usurpation. Where we gain some insight into the way a tomb was used and passed on, this process is normally guided by clear rules. For a range of reasons, parts of a tomb could be given over to a family with a different *nomen*, usually relatives of a wife or friends, *amici*, of the heirs, as was the case with Herma's tomb. The desire to keep the tomb in the family name could recede behind other needs (such as financial ones) or desires, especially that to pass on the tomb within the natural family even when this family does not share the same name. This is the case when daughters inherit, but also within families of imperial *libertini*, whose members were often enfranchised at different times and by different emperors, and thus given different *nomina*. Let us look at two examples.

Mausoleum F in Vaticano

In Mausoleum F of the Vatican necropolis, erected in the early Antonine period with an extraordinary façade decorated with multicoloured brick ornaments, the single large interior again provided for inhumation in arcosolia and incinerated remains in *ollae* and marble urns in the brightly coloured decorated walls above (Figure 3.14).[192] The main *titulus* of the tomb

---

100 years old at the time. His father does not seem to have belonged to the first two orders, but his own status is unclear. For details and bibliography, see Borg, *Crisis and Ambition*, 134.

[192] Feraudi-Gruénais, *Inschriften*, 29–30, 75–9 nos. 21–35 figs. 13–22, 115–16. On the tomb, see Toynbee and Ward Perkins, *St. Peter*, 44–51 fig. 6 pls. 2, 10–11, 14, 20–1; Mielsch and Hesberg, *Mausoleen E–I*, 93–121; Liverani et al., *Necropoli Vaticane*, 77–83 figs. 38–43 (their fig. 40 gives a beautiful idea of what the tomb looked like, but the cinerary urns are not all in their original place). The tomb has a *terminus post quem* through a brick stamp of 141: ibid., 118; Zander, *Necropoli di San Pietro*, 223–35 figs. 358–87.

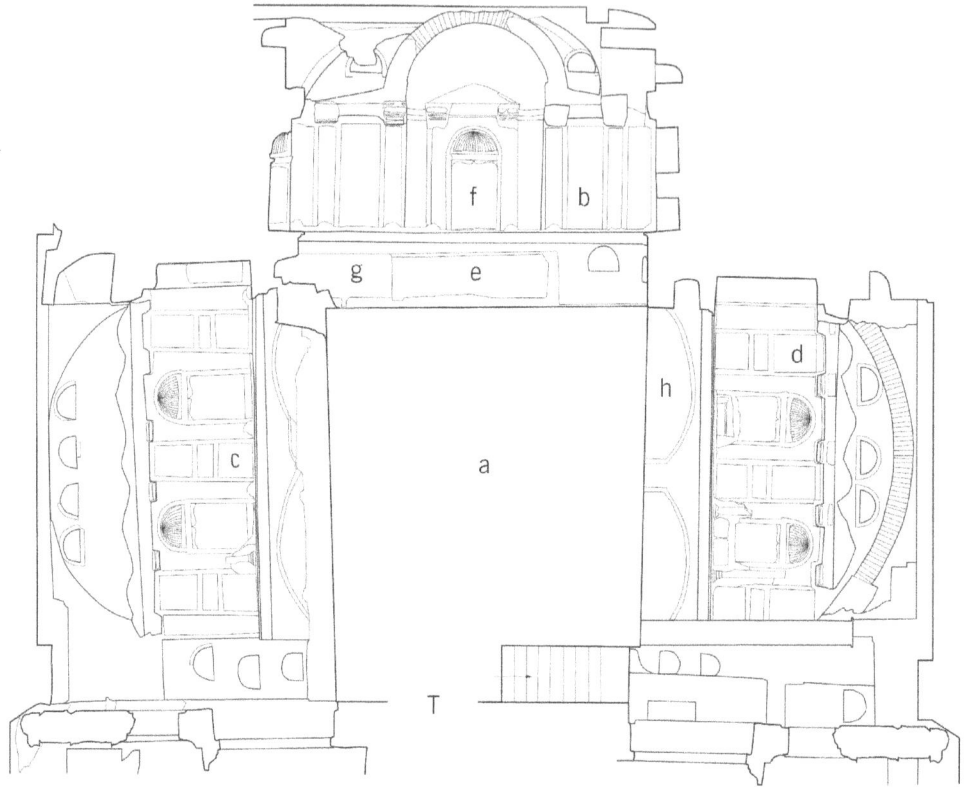

Figure 3.14 Mausoleum of the Caetennii and Tullii (Mausoleum F, early Antonine) underneath St Peter's, distribution of named burials within the chamber

is not preserved, but the epigraphic evidence from inside suggests that it was founded by M. Caetennius Antigonus and his wife Tullia Secunda, who were commemorated on an altar that stood in the centre of the space (a).[193] Tullia already had a burial place assigned in her parents' tomb, Mausoleum C, just a few metres down the road, but 'moved' into Mausoleum F together with her husband.[194] Before setting up their own altar, however, Antigonus dedicated a cinerary urn to his patron M. Caetennius Chryseros, who appears to be the first person buried in the tomb.[195] This suggests that Antigonus may have been freed on his master's death with the obligation to provide him with an adequate burial place. The urn was found not in

[193] Feraudi-Gruénais, *Inschriften*, 29, 77–8 no. 30 fig. 19. On the altar: Boschung, *Grabaltäre*, 33 n. 474, 111 no. 910; Zander, *Necropoli di San Pietro*, fig. 381.

[194] Mielsch and Hesberg, *Mausoleen A–D*, 39–59; Feraudi-Gruénais, *Inschriften*, 26–7; Zander, *Necropoli di San Pietro*, 197–205.

[195] Feraudi-Gruénais, *Inschriften*, 26, 78 no. 31 fig. 20. On the urn: Sinn, *Marmorurnen*, 20, 220–1 no. 533; Zander, *Necropoli di San Pietro*, fig. 198.

the central niche of the back wall but to the right of it (b), and it cannot be excluded that Antigonus was not as keen to capitalise on his pseudo-ancestry in the same way as others were. However, is it really plausible to assume that Antigonus assigned his patron a lateral place when the entire tomb was still empty and Antigonus did not intend to use the central niche for himself?[196] Urns are relatively easy to move around and the lateral niche also seems too narrow for Chryseros' urn.[197] In light of the use of tombs as discussed previously, it is therefore possible, if not likely, that the patron's urn was originally set up in the centre, in the background of and in the line of sight of the founders' altar, and flanked by their now-lost cineraria.

Two further marble urns were dedicated to Caetennii by their *colliberti* and set up in prominent positions, namely in the central niche of the left, western wall and in the upper northernmost niche of the east wall (c–d).[198] The exact relationships these people had with Antigonus and each other are not clear, but the urns are dated to the second half of the century, when Antigonus had already died.[199] It is therefore likely that they were Antigonus' freedmen and heirs, or freedmen and heirs of his heirs.

These are the last Caetennii attested, and evidence is stronger for heirs connected to Tullia. One L. Tullius Hermadion buried his homonymous nineteen-year-old son in a newly built 'bench' in the centre of the rear wall (e), the most prominent place for an inhumation, and set up his own cinerary urn in the central niche above, where it was found (f).[200] For that purpose, he may have moved Antigonus' patron's urn, who was Antigonus' pseudo-ancestor but obviously not his own. Moreover, his son's grave was

---

[196] The altar is not prepared to receive the ashes of the deceased, so they must have had an urn somewhere in the tomb. It seems much less likely that Tullius Hermadion, who later set up his own urn in the central niche, moved the founders' urn instead of that of their patron, and he obviously respected their altar in the centre of the space.

[197] Unfortunately, no measurements of the niches have been published, and photographs are not entirely clear about whether the urn now stands inside the niche or in front of it; but it is clear that the lateral niche is too small for the urn, quite differently from the other cases: Apolloni Ghetti et al., *Esplorazioni*, pl. 2b (photo taken shortly after excavation); cf. Mielsch and Hesberg, *Mausoleen A–D*, fig. 100 and colour pl. 16; Liverani et al., *Necropoli Vaticane*, fig. 40 (actual presentation).

[198] Feraudi-Gruénais, *Inschriften*, 78–9 nos. 33–4 fig. 22. Mielsch and Hesberg (*Mausoleen E–I*, figs. 100–1 and 106) probably show them in situ.

[199] One might expect that they would have mentioned his permission if he had still been alive. The lateral position of these urns may confirm further that the founders' urns occupied the two niches flanking their patron's.

[200] Hermadion Maior: Eck, 'Inschriften', 252–3 no. 6 pl. 15.6; Feraudi-Gruénais, *Inschriften*, 26, 78 no. 32 fig. 21. The urn: Sinn, *Marmorurnen*, 20 n. 187; Zander, *Necropoli di San Pietro*, fig. 195. Hermadion Minor: Eck, 'Inschriften', 251–2 no. 5 pl. 15.5; Papi, 'Iscrizioni', 252–6 no. 6 figs. 8–9; Feraudi-Gruénais, *Inschriften*, 26, 76–7 no. 26 fig. 12 (the secondary inscription on this slab is only from the late third or early fourth century).

built not into the central arcosolium but in front of it, possibly obscuring an earlier inhumation.[201] It is therefore possible that he was now the only remaining heir to the tomb.[202] The epitaphs do not give away whether Hermadion the Elder was freeborn or freed. If the former, it would explain his (perceived) right to the most prestigious places in the tomb, although one wonders why, being kin, he would not have preferred burial in Tullia's ancestral Mausoleum C. Was it because the new mausoleum was so much larger and more impressive? If he was Tullia's freedman, as is usually assumed (or the son of one of her freedmen), his dominant position could have resulted from his (or his father's) special importance to his patron, who may have survived her husband for some years, relying on her freedman's support. His importance is further demonstrated by the burial he provided for his friends (*amici*) Aurelius Gigantis and Papiria Profutura,[203] and he must also have determined the burial place of another Aurelius to the left of Hermadion Minor's grave (g). M. Aurelius Hieron, an *evocatus* of Marcus Aurelius, dedicated this place to his homonymous son.[204] As the burial predates that of Hermadion Minor, the most prominent position, still vacant when Hermadion Minor died, must have been reserved for Hermadion Maior's kin from the outset. It is therefore likely that the Aurelii were introduced into the tomb through him, and it is tempting to think that the relationship was established through marriage.[205] From now on, no

---

[201] This is not entirely clear from the descriptions of the situation: Papi, 'Iscrizioni', 253, quotes Ferrua's original description.

[202] His urn is dated to the later second century and could be later than the Caetennii urns. See Feraudi-Gruénais, *Inschriften*, 30, for a different view.

[203] Eck, 'Inschriften', 247–8, 253 no. 2 pl. 14.2; Feraudi-Gruénais, *Inschriften*, 76 no. 24 fig. 15. It is unclear where the small tabula was originally affixed.

[204] Eck, 'Inschriften', 252–3; Eck, 'Inschriften und Grabbauten', 77 pl. 5.5b; Feraudi-Gruénais, *Inschriften*, 77 no. 27 fig. 16. Eck argues in both aritcles for a third-century date for the two inhumation graves, but overlooks that Hieron is not *evocatus Augusti*, but *evocatus Marco Aurelio*. Unless we assume that he was already retired when he commissioned the epitaph, the latest date for it would be 180. Eck ('Rechtsquelle', 84) also thinks that Hermadion allocated these spaces to his friends illegally. However, rather than imagining rampant usurpation of burial space based solely on the *a priori* assumption that the *tituli* may give a full account of the legal situation, it is again far more plausible to accept the jurists' ruling as valid already in the second century, and to see Hermadion as the legal heir who had the right to grant burial to externals.

[205] Marriage bonds are also considered by Eck, 'Rechtsquelle', 84–5. None of the men's wives is named anywhere. A tabula with which a M. Aurelius Filetus commemorates his wife Caetennia Proc(u)la was found in Mausoleum C, and may attest to a more direct relationship between Caetennii and Aurelii. However, as Papi asserts, there is no imprint in the walls of Mausoleum F that would suggest its provenance from there, so that it might have been removed from Mausoleum L, which was erected roughly at the same time as Caetennius Antigonus' tomb, by M. Caetennius Proculus, to whom Proc(u)la may have

more Tullii are attested and the tomb may have fallen to the Aurelii after Hermadion *pater*'s death. The latest epitaph from the tomb commemorated the choirmaster Aurelius Nemesius, who was buried by his wife Aurelia Eutychiane in the northernmost arcosolium of the east wall (h).[206]

While many details of this tomb's usage remain elusive, it is obvious that it was Tullia's heirs who determined burial practice after her husband Caetennius Antigonus' death. Moreover, we can see that they must have inherited the entire tomb, or at least its most important part, since the Tullii occupied the central positions at the rear and their friends or relatives, the Aurelii, two relatively prominent places in different parts of the chamber. Freedpeople and descendants in the female line are therefore likely to be responsible for the range of different *gentilicia* in this mausoleum.

Isola Sacra, Mausoleum 75–76

The impact of belonging to the *familia caesaris* can be observed in Mausoleum 75 in the Isola Sacra (Figure 3.15). It originally consisted of a large courtyard and a smallish tomb building in the centre of the rear wall of the precinct that was flanked by vaulted open *alae* and provided for incinerated remains only.[207] A *titulus* above the door proclaims that it was dedicated by its founder M. Cocceius Daphnus to his own *familia* as well as to M. Antonius Agathias and M. Ulpius Domitus, *et libertis libertabusque posterisque eorum*. Given that the tomb was built in the Trajanic period, Cocceius Daphnus must have been a freedman of Nerva, Ulpius Domitus a freedman of Trajan and Antonius Agathias the (grand)son or freedman of a freedman of Antonia Minor (who died in 37).[208] Daphnus was the other two men's father-in-law, which is what must have qualified them for the dedication. The arrangement ensured that Daphnus' daughters could be buried with their natural family as well as with their husbands, and that these husbands were still commemorated in their own name and would

---

been related: Feraudi-Gruénais, *Inschriften*, 75–6 no. 23; Papi, 'Iscrizioni', 257–9 no. 8 fig. 11. In any case, the epitaph illustrates the close relationships between Caetennii, Tullii and Aurelii. This also demonstrates that Toynbee and Ward Perkins (*St. Peter*, 46) give the wrong impression of usurpation and miss the point of what was going on when they state that the tomb was 'invaded … by inhumation-burials', when '(n)ew family names now appear'.

[206] Eck ('Inschriften', 248–51 no. 4 pl. 15.4) argues for a third-century date based on the *cognomen* Nemesius.

[207] Calza, *Isola Sacra*, 74, 329–4 figs. 22, 25; Baldassarre et al., 'Necropoli dell'Isola Sacra', 288–97 figs. 23–7; Baldassarre et al., *Necropoli di Porto*, 89–92; Lazzarini, *Sepulcra*, 91–100; Helttula (ed.), *Iscrizioni*, 94–108 (R. Vainio); Cooley, *Latin Epigraphy*, 140–1.

[208] Helttula (ed.), *Iscrizioni*, 96–7 no. 82; transl. in Cooley, *Latin Epigraphy*, 140 no. 30.

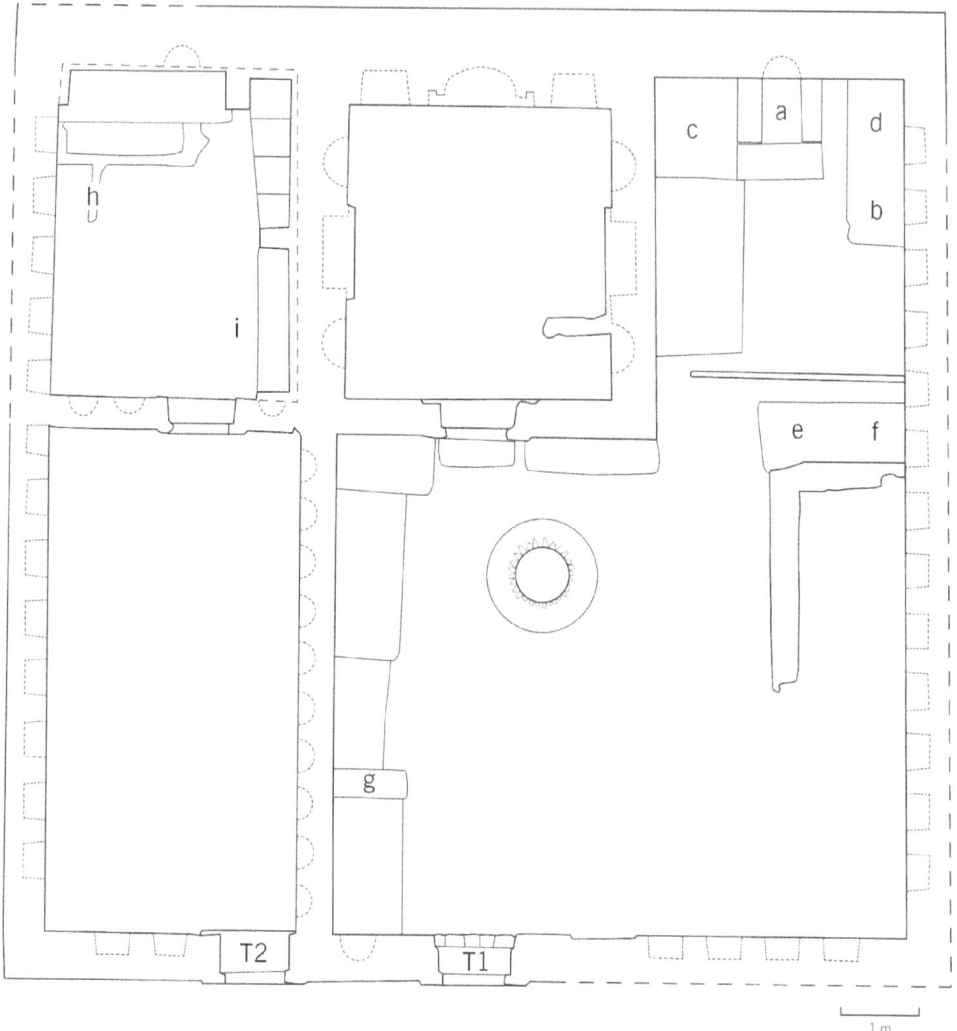

Figure 3.15 Tombs 75–76 in the Isola Sacra necropolis of Portus (early second century CE), distribution of named burials within the precinct and chambers

inherit parts of the tomb.[209] Up to this point, we are faced again with a case where different *gentilicia* are introduced through female kin. We do not know who was eventually buried in the rear cella,[210] but some *liberti* of the Cocceii used the right *ala* and the space immediately in front of it.

[209] Ditto R. Vainio in Helttula (ed.), *Iscrizioni*, 95.

[210] An inscribed sarcophagus lid or arcosolium cover probably commemorating a daughter of the main founder (Cocciea Secunda) and her husband M. Ulpius Domitus, who also appears in the main *titulus*, was found in the tomb but with no exact find spot specified: ibid., 98–9 no. 84. A mosaic inscription related to a *fossa* grave does not preserve the name: ibid., 98 no. 83.

One M. Cocceius Onesimus buried his wife within the *ala*, perhaps in the Hadrianic period (b),[211] while a Cocceia Tyche gave the space for a double *a cassone* grave just outside the *ala* to Sex. Iulius Armenius, who buried his wife in one part, and was later buried in the other by Cocceia Tyche (e–f).[212] Ulpii appear only once more in an epitaph for Domitus' grandson or nephew, who predeceased Secunda and Domitus,[213] but it is possible that their share was inherited by kin who were manumitted by later emperors. A slave of Matidia, niece of emperor Trajan, buried his fellow slave Urbica, with whom he had lived for one year, eight months, twelve days and three hours (!) in a custom-made aedicula in the centre of the rear wall of the same *ala* (a).[214] The prominent position, the likely date of the inscription before 119 and the lack of an explicit permission suggest that he or she may have been natural kin of Ulpius Domitus. The same may be true for Aelia Salviana, who is likely to have been a freedwoman of Hadrian, and buried her six-year-old *verna* Sabina right next to Urbica (d).[215]

M. Antonius Agathias, however, chose to set himself off from the rest of the family. He partitioned off the part of the tomb he inherited from Cocceius Daphnus, turning the northern *ala* into a closed mausoleum and cutting a new entrance through the front wall of the precinct, above which he placed the *titulus* that gives us these details (Tomb 76).[216] He even left space for two to three lines between the main text and the dedication to his ex-slaves and their offspring, surely to add further relatives (a second wife and children?) later on. Yet if his aim was to avoid the somewhat messy situation in the remainder of Tomb 75, he will have been disappointed. No names were added to the *titulus*, and if he intended a second marriage, it never happened.[217] His heir was M. Antonius Pius, but whether he was kin or a freedman is not entirely clear.[218] He is attested in two inscriptions. One permits P. Aelius Tryphonus burial in his tomb (h).[219] The other hands over the entire right part of the cella to Aemilia Maiorica, Caminius Silvanus,

---

[211] Ibid., 100–1 no. 86. This wife's name, Sabinia Attica, suggests the date.

[212] Ibid., 103–5 nos. 90–1.

[213] On the epitaph, see ibid., 98–9 no. 84. Since the *nepos* was already seventeen years old when he died, the term may indeed refer to a nephew rather than a grandson.

[214] Ibid., 101–2 no. 87. As Vainio argues, Matidia must be Mindia Matidia Minor, and the inscription dated before her divination in 119.

[215] Ibid., 102–3 no. 89.

[216] Ibid., 105–6 no. 92; transl. in Cooley, *Latin Epigraphy*, 140 no. 31.

[217] Ditto R. Vainio in Helttula (ed.), *Iscrizioni*, 96.

[218] Vainio (in ibid., 96) thinks that Agathias did remarry and Pius was his son. Yet why, then, were their names not inscribed? Vainio (ibid., 108) argues that his *cognomen* suggests free rather than servile birth.

[219] Ibid., 108 no. 94.

and their freed people and their offspring (i).[220] It is situated above the cella entrance and only uses the right half of the marble slab, suggesting an intention to give away the left half of the tomb to other externals. No further Antonii are attested in the tomb, and Pius may have moved on to found his own tomb elsewhere.[221] This is perhaps confirmed by another Antonius, M. Antonius M. f. Callistianus, who commemorated his grandmother Cocceia Doris on a stele set against the partition wall on the Cocceii side, as is fitting (g). Interestingly, however, 21-year-old Callistianus was later buried next to his grandmother and commemorated on the same stele.[222] If he was a son of Agathias, as is normally assumed, it is likely that, by then, his father had already died and Antonius Pius given away the Antonii part of the tomb.

These two examples demonstrate very clearly that we should not rush to conclusions about random use of tombs and usurpation when we find different *nomina* attested in one and the same mausoleum. What looks like inheritance by externals – and *is* inheritance by externals, when one considers the *nomina* alone – can easily turn out to be inheritance by kin, albeit in the female line or among former imperial slaves. The desire to preserve a name was here overruled by affection for and *pietas* towards natural relatives. This circumstance also makes it very difficult to distinguish between *sepulcra familiaria* (family tombs) and *sepulcra hereditaria* (hereditary tombs). These terms are explained only once in the legal sources, but have gained some currency in modern scholarship, although they are thought to have been blurred with time.[223] Looking at the evidence, one wonders whether they really ever existed as fully distinct categories. In all tombs burial right was restricted to heirs, with the sole exception of non-inheriting close kin who, at least from the second century onwards, were permitted to use their father's tomb under any circumstance.[224] While inheritance by non-kin *liberti* could ensure the persistence of the *nomen gentile*, inheritance by kin could mean that the tomb passed out of the name.

Exact figures on how frequently this was the case are impossible to glean, but there can be no doubt that a substantial percentage of the sub-elite

---

[220] Ibid., 107–8 no. 93; transl. in Cooley, *Latin Epigraphy*, 140 no. 32.

[221] Had he and his descendants continued to use the tomb, we would expect him to put his name at least as prominently over the cella door as the names of the people who took over the right-hand wall.

[222] Cf. Helttula (ed.), *Iscrizioni*, 95–6, 99–100 no. 85.

[223] See Kaser, 'Grabrecht', 37–60, 37–8, for the one source explaining the distinction, *Digest* 11.7.5 (Gai. 19 ad ed. prov.) and 6 pr. (Ulp. 25 ad cd.), which belong together, and n. 104 for the few further occurrences of the terms. As Kaser observes, even in this single source the distinction is blurred.

[224] Ibid., 37–8.

population had a keen interest in the preservation of the family name, and that the examples discussed above are not mere exceptions. One marked difference between freedmen and senatorial *tituli* lies in the fact that the former often include more detailed provisions about who may or may not be buried in a given tomb. Sometimes the founder explicitly excluded specific individuals with whom he had fallen out or who were considered unworthy for some reason.[225] More often, *tituli* specify that the tomb must not go out of the family name when it is passed on to later generations. This provision comes in three forms. It can simply be specified that the tomb must not go out of the family name.[226] More often, a provision either excludes heirs altogether with the formula *H(oc) m(onumentum) h(eredem) non s(equetur)* or else it excludes only external heirs – that is, heirs of a different *nomen* – with the formula *H(oc) m(onumentum) h(eredem) (f(amiliae)) e(xterum) n(on) s(equetur)* or similar. In the Isola Sacra, we find the former amendment in 12 per cent of all *tituli*, and the latter in an additional 31 per cent.[227] The majority of scholars probably rightly assume that the two formulae essentially meant the same thing, and the shorter one could simply have been an abbreviation or used when it was already known that the heirs would not be able, or may not be willing, to leave the tomb in the family name.[228] These 43 per cent of patrons of larger tombs in the Isola Sacra provide us with a rather strong indication of what was at stake here. A legal, and legally protected, family was not only important from a personal and emotional point of view as the end to a precarious situation. Nor was it

---

[225] Crook, *Law*, 136 with n. 176; Kaser, 'Grabrecht', 51; Champlin, *Final Judgments*, 177 with n. 33; Orlandi, 'Heredes', with examples in lists De and Df; Carroll, *Spirits*, 103; Bodel, 'Columbaria to catacombs', 213 with n. 74; Liebs, 'Ewiges Gedenken', 60 with n. 80; cf. Helttula (ed.), *Iscrizioni*, 155 no. 133 on Isola Sacra Tomb 100, where no reason for exclusion is specified.

[226] For examples from Rome, see Orlandi, 'Heredes', 373–5.

[227] Similar estimates are hard to obtain for Rome despite the lists provided by Orlandi (ibid., 362–72), with 207 and 93 cases, respectively, since the total number of tomb *tituli* (as opposed to inscriptions marking individual burial places) is unknown.

[228] E.g. de Visscher (*Droit*, 101 n. 15) who points to two cases where the shorter formula is combined with the provision that the tomb must not go out of the family name (*CIL* 6.8456 and 22208). See also Crook, *Law*, 136; Kaser, 'Grabrecht', 42 with n. 123; Lazzarini, *Sepulcra*, 28 n. 56. For examples with more unusual and specific prescriptions to the same effect, see Liebs, 'Ewiges Gedenken', 54–6. The prescript demonstrates once more that, contrary to what has been suggested, the founders of these tombs obviously expected their mausolea to be used by later generations once all the individuals mentioned in the *titulus* had died; as we found to be the case with senatorial *tituli*, the list was hardly ever considered to be exclusive: ditto Parkin, 'Life course', 277. Edmondson ('Family history', 562) notes that 'those named on a tomb's façade do not necessarily reflect all those buried within' and notices the 'snapshot' character of individual epitaphs (p. 367), but ironically recommends statistical approaches such as Saller and Shaw's as a remedy.

merely a one-time achievement obtained with manumission. The aim was to create a family line, for which the name was essential. As I have noted, this was also the idea in elite tombs, it is just that it was not necessary to confirm the provision formally in their *tituli*.

Conclusions

It is hardly an exaggeration to state that in Roman society the family was a key institution, and remained so throughout its history. As is well known, Augustus intended to restore it after the upheavals of the civil wars, both in the interest of producing sufficient numbers of citizens, and as a key institution of the state that passed on its value system and embodied *concordia* as a virtue underpinning the *res publica*. Even in this world of pre-arranged marriages and a high mortality rate among children, there is ample evidence of genuine affection within families. This includes evidence from epitaphs, which often talk about the deceased with warmth, and offered girls of marriageable age places of honour and rich grave goods.

This did not change fundamentally in later centuries. There was neither a growing individualism and waning sense of family, as some scholars have suggested,[229] nor a general shift towards an increasing focus on the nuclear family, as Saller and Shaw's seminal paper proposed. Not everyone may have achieved the establishment of a family tradition, and some may even have preferred other allegiances over those of a family, such as *collegia* (voluntary associations) of various kinds.[230] Yet there can be no doubt that the ideal of an extended family and a long family line that preserved a name (in the full range of its significance) did not fade throughout the imperial period.

In elite families, the idea of the gentilicial family clan, whose prominent members and their deeds were advertised and honoured in the *tituli* of their mausolea, lived on into late antiquity and, after the *atria* with their *imagines maiorum* may have lost in importance or assumed other purposes, these mausolea constituted the main location at which the longevity and dignity of a family were demonstrated and commemorated. There is some evidence that the elite sometimes admitted multiple and diverse externals to burial in their tombs, probably again mostly cognatic kin – the mausoleum of

---

[229] Cf. nn. 16 and 115 above.
[230] On these, see n. 240.

Artorius Geminus is one example (see Figure 1.1).[231] We have also seen how the Licinii advertised their family links with the *triumviri* Pompey and Crassus. However, if we can trust our (admittedly scanty) evidence, this was rather rare among this class, and the Licinii case is explained by the fact that, exceptionally, the pontifex was not actually a *homo novus*.[232] It is normally thought that *sepulcra gentilicia* are a phenomenon of the Republican period. Do we need to revise this assessment? Yes, and no. Christopher Smith has critically reviewed modern views about the Roman clan in the Republican period, and the evidence that does and does not support them.[233] The result is a much more complex and fluid concept of the *gens*, of the impacts it had on power and institutions, and of the ways in which an individual *gens* defined its boundaries. Against this background, any further changes during the late Republican and imperial period appear not to be challenges to the concept and relevance of the *gens* as such, but rather further continuations of its renegotiation. In our context, it is clear that we lack the archaeological (or other) evidence for tombs or burial grounds that could be attributed to an entire *gens* (rather than a *stirps*) that would help us assess the evidence presented here.[234] This lack is, perhaps, less surprising than it may at first seem given the fluidity of definitions, the number of members belonging to the oldest Roman *gentes* and the fact that their founders were often mythical.[235]

The pattern of founding, using and bequeathing a tomb over several generations seems in fact to be a novelty of the late Republic, part of the lead-up to the fierce power struggles culminating in the first century BCE, and not abandoned afterwards for several centuries. As Smith notes, only

---

[231] For an extensive discussion of the *tituli* and genealogies, cf. Silvestrini, *Sepulcrum*, 35–54; 80–2 with stemma fig. 30. G. Alföldy (*CIL* 6.41057 and p. 4783 on *CIL* 6.31761) and Raepsaet-Charlier (*Prosopographie*, 93–4 no. 77; 121–2 nos. 105–6; 161 no. 166; 442–3 no. 525; 590 no. 744 with stemma XI) disagree with Silvestrini on a few details but not in principle.

[232] His foundation of a family tomb must probably be seen still in the context of the fierce competition of the late Republic, when we do find new senatorial tombs for members of established families. Moreover, his father was adopted by the last descendant of Licinius Crassus *triumvir*, while his natural father must have had a rather unremarkable career, and his grandfather, M. Pupius Piso Frugi (*cos.* 61 BCE), was himself adopted (for the complicated family histories, see Syme, 'Frugi'; Syme, *Roman Revolution*, table 5). These circumstances may have contributed to the pontifex's decision.

[233] Smith, *Clan*.

[234] Ibid., 144–63. See also the more comprehensive survey of Republican tombs with sarcophagi by Meinecke, *Sarcophagum posuit*, 7–26, 151–96 nos. R1–49, which confirms these conclusions.

[235] On mythical founders, see Smith, *Clan*, 34–44.

one of the inscriptions of the Scipios refers explicitly to the family, namely to the *virtutes* of the deceased's *genus* and the honour of his *stirps*.[236] Yet it is not clear at all that Hispanus (or those commemorating him) would thus have denied the tomb the title of a *sepulcrum gentilicium*. Mention of the *genus* and the *stirps* indicates the general idea of a gentilicial environment, and by *stirps* he could in fact have been referring to the branch of the family founded by his father Hispallus.

That late Republican- and imperial-period tombs could be called *sepulcra gentilicia* is demonstrated by literary as well as epigraphic sources, and Cicero is again the earliest attesting to the importance of the tomb to the *gens*.[237] In an inscription from Luna in Etruria, one Appuleius, who lists three Sextii as his father, grandfather and great-grandfather, calls himself the last member of the *gens*.[238] At least one example is from Rome, an epistyle block now displayed in the Jewish catacomb of the Vigna Randanini that reads *[---]RO IS totu genus | [--- A]thanasiorum*, while several others are from the Balkans and North Africa.[239] Taking all this evidence together, and keeping in mind that almost all preserved tomb *tituli* from Rome and its surrounding area commemorate *homines novi*, it is hard to escape the conclusion that newly ascended curule magistrates (or their commemorators) did indeed consider themselves founders of a *gens*, an assumption that is consistent with Cicero's statement that the first curule magistrate within a family could become the founder of a new *gens* (*Fam.* 9.21.2). Their mausoleum was established as manifestation and celebration of the fact, and descendants in the agnatic line and, lacking male descendants, sometimes

---

[236] Ibid., 48, on *CIL* 6. 1293. Cf. Courtney, *Musa Lapidaria*, 42–3, 228–9 no. 13.

[237] Cf. Cicero, *Off.* 1.17.54–5 with *Leg.* 2.55; Smith, *Clan*, 47–8. As Smith does, scholars usually connect Cicero's list of prominent tombs, including that of the Scipios in *Tusc.* 1.7.13, with his notion of gentilicial tombs. This is probably correct, although it has to be admitted that Cicero here does not use the term *gens* or one of its derivatives. For further literary examples, see Smith, *Clan*, 48. To these add examples listed in *RE* 13 (1910) 1186–8 s.v. gens (B. Kübler), incl. Suetonius, *Nero* 50: *gentile Domitiorum monumentum*; Valerius Maximus 9.2.1: *sepulcrum Lutetiae gentes*. Kübler (col. 1187), proposes that the *sepulcrum familiare* substituted for the *sepulcrum gentilicium*, and that in the latter also dependants could be buried. This rests on the jurists, esp. on Gaius *Digest* 11.7.5, but like the many scholars who followed him, Kübler overlooks that these sources refer to different classes in society.

[238] *CIL* 11.1362: *[Sex(to)(?)] Appuleio Sex(ti) f(ilio) | Gal(eria), | Sex(ti) n(epoti), Sex(ti) pro n(epoti), | Fabia Numantina | nato, ultimo gentis | suae.* He is most likely *PIR* A 962, the consul of 14. See e.g. Raepsaet-Charlier, *Prosopographie*, 308–9 no. 353 stemma 13 with bibl.; Fasolini, 'Ascrizione tribale', 232.

[239] *ILS* 7945 (= *CIL* 6.7649); *totu* here for *totum*. Cf. Noy, *Jewish Inscriptions II*, 329 no. 400. The other examples include *CIL* 3.14601; *CIL* 3.2963 with add. p. 1635; *CIL* 8.5656 (p. 963) (= 18916); *CIL* 8.7277 (p. 1848); *CIL* 8.7543. All are referred to in Kaser, 'Grabrecht', 43 n. 129.

also in the cognate line, normally continued to use the tomb for burial, and for the promotion of the time-honoured dignity of their family.

This general idea was shared by many freedmen, even though they had to adapt it to their means and circumstances, and some preferred burial, not with whatever kind of family/*familia*, but with a *collegium*.[240] More often than in the first order we find affection and *pietas* towards kin taking precedence over concerns for the family name, the reasons for which could be both economic and personal. It is likely that the sheer relief and joy felt about having overcome the precarious conditions of an illegitimate family of slaves contributed emotional factors to the choice of who may and may not be given burial right in a family tomb. This may also explain the frequency of epithets, even in short commemorative inscriptions, that not only praise the virtues of a class that was stereotyped as inherently lacking them, but are also affectionate, such as *dulcissimus/a* or *carissimus/a*.[241] In epitaphs of the first order, epithets are almost entirely absent.[242] Parents may also have offered a share in, and inheritance of, their tomb to their daughters with their husbands and offspring, when these sons-in-law did not have the means to erect a similarly attractive mausoleum, as may have been the case in Isola Sacra Mausoleum 75–76 (Figure 3.15), or when these sons-in-law's financial contribution was needed for erecting the family mausoleum.

Yet the desire to integrate fully into society as citizens also meant that markers of status were identified and advertised on and in tombs, which must, for many, have been the prime if not the only monument ever erected to them. Mouritsen has recently stressed the extent to which the very idea of enfranchising a slave hinged on the expectation that the freedman or freedwoman would integrate seamlessly into society and (continue to) behave according to a value system that was primarily shaped and determined by their patrons and the hierarchical nature of Roman society in general.[243] We should therefore not be surprised to find *liberti* sharing some fundamental elite ideals and commemorative practices. What we are looking at is not a 'trickle-down effect' but a set of ideas and values

---

[240] Yet note that this did not necessarily exclude burial with close kin. Moreover, there appears to be a fluctuation in the popularity of communal or collective burial, which is likely to have been more common in the late first century BCE and first century CE, and from the mid-third century onwards, than it was in the second and early third centuries. For early collective tombs, see Borbonus, *Columbarium Tombs*, with bibl.; for the later ones, Borg, *Crisis and Ambition*, esp. 30–1, 72–121, 273–4, 277–8; for fluctuation, Galvano-Sobrinho, 'Feasting', esp. 135–7.

[241] Nielsen, 'Interpreting epithets'.

[242] See Chapter 1 n. 256.

[243] Mouritsen, *Freedman*, esp. 31–5, 136–59, 183–5, 194–205.

embraced by all social classes.[244] Like the elite, *liberti* placed portraits inside and in front of their mausolea, which often resembled honorific dedications that they may never have received in other locations.[245] Lacking the public offices and *honores* of the elite, those *liberti* who held offices in *collegia* or the imperial administration, or who occupied priestly offices such as the *augustalitas*, proudly mentioned these on their tomb stones. Where such distinctions were lacking, tomb founders sometimes pointed to other achievements such as their profitable occupation,[246] wealth, a legitimate family and their own slaves and freedmen. With regard to their households, often more was at stake than emotional bonds between members of the nuclear family. The achievement of now having a legitimate family is illustrated through images (the *dextrarum iunctio* and children fitted out with togas and *bullae*: Figure 3.8) and spelt out in inscriptions.[247] The particularly high number of epigraphic commemorations of children under the age of ten in Ostia (almost 40 per cent) may also be understood in this context.[248]

Nevertheless, as we have seen, all this was not only about a one-time achievement. There was a widespread desire to establish a family line in which the family name was preserved and passed on, as Mouritsen recently concluded from the adoption by ex-slaves of naming habits known from free-born and even elite Roman families. The practice of 'naming their children after their parents, grandparents or other relatives' often even superseded any potential hesitation about giving children Greek *cognomina* that would give away their servile ancestry.[249] Mouritsen does not elaborate further on the issue, but the evidence discussed here both confirms his impression and

---

[244] 'Trickle-down'-effect models proposed in some previous scholarship have rightly been criticised by Petersen, *Freedman*, 96, 134; Borg, 'Social climber', 40. My view also differs from that of those who propose that the original patrons, when they designed their *tituli*, could not foresee the later use of the tomb (e.g. Hope, 'Roof', esp. 86–7). I much doubt that it was ever a goal to use *tituli* as a full record of who was (to be) buried within a tomb.

[245] For the imitation of elite values in the early tomb reliefs, see Borg, 'Aufsteiger'; Borg, 'Social climber'. No systematic study of the use of portraits in tombs of whatever class exists, but both excavation reports from previous centuries and the statistical distribution of Roman portraits in general suggest that portraits were a common feature of wealthier tombs. For examples, see Calza, *Isola Sacra* on the Isola Sacra, or Bignamini and Claridge, 'Claudia Semne', with bibl. on the tomb of Claudia Semne. See also Chapter 1 pp. 32–5 for senatorial tombs.

[246] See Kampen, *Image*; George, 'Social identity'; Amedick, *Menschenleben*, for sarcophagi.

[247] For the freedmen reliefs, see n. 110 above.

[248] Saller and Shaw, 'Tombstones', 130; figures after Clauss, 'Lebensalterstatistiken', 404 with table 10.

[249] Mouritsen, 'Families of Roman slaves', 142–3; Mouritsen, *Freedman*, 39.

helps flesh it out. Some epitaphs state explicitly that a patron's *liberti* have been admitted to burial in order to carry on the name,[250] and the prevalence of this desire to establish a family lineage is best illustrated by the frequent provision that the tomb must not be passed on to external heirs. The varied but sometimes remarkable success in achieving this goal is demonstrated by some well-documented and -preserved tombs and inscriptions that attest to the continued use of tombs over more than 100 years by people sharing the same *nomen gentile*. And these same cases also illustrate how this was achieved. Lauren Petersen had already observed that, lacking legal ancestry, freedmen sometimes substituted a parent by their patron, and Mouritsen argued that the patron-freedman relationship was modelled on, and ideally resembled very closely, that of father and son, which established links both of obligation and affection.[251] Commemorative practices further support his view. What has now become clearer is that they often secured the survival of their name through freedmen heirs, for whom, in turn, the tomb's founder and other previous generations became 'ancestry'. While the vast majority of these freedpeople seem to have failed to establish a lasting agnatic family – let alone a *gens* – they made the most of the concept of *familia*, which did not distinguish between kin and non-kin and was still a powerful institution of which to be proud. This reference to the *familia* was quite different from that which we observe in the large household columbaria for the *familiae* of the most prominent Roman families (including the imperial one). Here, sometimes hundreds of burials presented the deceased as members of the large collective of the *familia* who referred to their prestigious and powerful patron(s) with pride, but never shared a tomb with them. They found an identity as a collective that was structured and hierarchised internally not by kinship ties – relatively rarely do we see nuclear families being buried in proximity to each other – but by the *decuriae* that organised and structured the household at large and awarded the greatest honours to their officials.[252] In contrast, the family tombs I discuss here did not only serve smaller numbers of individuals belonging to less prominent households. They represented a mix of former slaves (and

---

[250] In addition to the inscription from the consortium tomb discussed above (at n. 180), see e.g. *CIL* 6.9485 with Liebs, 'Ewiges Gedenken', 54–5: *vivi sibi fecerunt suisque libertis libertabusque posterisque eorum, ne de nomine exiat nostrorum.*

[251] Cf. Mouritsen, *Freedman*, 37–51.

[252] On these tombs, see most recently Galvano-Sobrinho, 'Feasting'; Borbonus, *Columbarium Tombs*.

slaves) and freeborn members of a *familia* that was structured according to personal relationships of kinship and heirship, which also determined the hierarchisation of space within the 'house' tombs.[253] They shared with the elite key ideas embodied by their family and gentilicial tombs, composing their own 'family' (i.e. *familia*) based on highly selective, personal but not necessarily kinship relationships.

---

[253] Petersen, *Freedman*, 162–3, 212–15, and elsewhere. Cf. also Feraudi-Gruénais, *Inschriften*, 25–42.

4 | Straddling Borderlines: Divine Connotations in Funerary Commemoration

In this final chapter, I want to contribute to a long-standing and controversial debate around divine associations in funerary display. This topic could easily fill a monograph of its own – and in fact has done so in the past. While emperor worship has been the subject of several recent books, divine associations in the private realm have been discussed at length by Henning Wrede in his milestone monograph of 1981, and more recently by Christopher Hallett in 2005.[1] Nevertheless, these authors have largely focused on portrait representations in divine guise or 'costume'.[2] Wrede's monograph remains the most comprehensive study of the material. It comprises an extensive catalogue of examples that range from funerary altars of the Flavian period to third-century statues and sarcophagi.[3] At the time, Wrede was not only brave to take on a subject that many considered rather dubious, but was progressing along entirely new lines of thought. The present study is highly indebted to his detailed discussions, which are full of important observations and insights. And yet, there are a number of problems that merit a reconsideration of the subject. One, and not the least, is Wrede's terminology. He called all these figures in divine costume *Privatdeifikationen*, 'private deifications' or 'private apotheoses', terms that, strictly speaking, suggest the individual portrayed has become a god. Even so, Wrede uses them much more loosely to cover both instances where he thinks that the iconographies indicate life after death and deification and/or apotheosis in the proper sense of the word, and cases where he

---

[1] Wrede, *Consecratio*, and Hallett, *Roman Nude*. For some recent monographs on emperor worship, see Gradel, *Emperor Worship*; Pollini, *Republic to Empire*. For visual material related to emperor worship, Bergmann, *Strahlen*, is still essential, and see now Koortbojian, *Divinization*, on Caesar and Augustus.

[2] The term 'costume' has come to be used widely to indicate that attributes and dress, or the lack thereof, are first and foremost a deliberately chosen message to the viewer that does not necessarily coincide with any real-life appearance of the individual depicted: see e.g. Bonfante Warren, 'Roman costumes'; Bonfante, 'Nudity'; Hallett, *Roman Nude*; Cordier, *Nudités*.

[3] Wrede also included in his study and catalogue those visual representations where attributes of a divinity are only loosely related to the portrait (e.g. depicted in a tympanum or in the background) while the portrait itself adheres to standard types. These images are surely related to portraits in divine costume, but they raise different issues and will therefore not be considered in this chapter.

explicitly rejects such meanings and regards the divine elements as claims to character traits that the individual shared with the god.[4] Discussing Hellenistic models or precedents, Wrede complicates matters further by stating that the portraits in question were 'a formal western expression of eastern heroisation', without, however, explaining what heroisation meant in Greece, or how the notion, for which no Latin term exists, may have been interpreted in the West.[5]

Similarly, the concepts of deification, divinity and apotheosis are accepted or rejected without ever being properly explored and explained. What does divinity mean in Rome? Did divinity always entail life after death? And if this is so, what kind of 'life' are we supposed to envisage? Even more fundamentally, what indications do we have for a Roman belief in an afterlife more generally? Such questions are neither answered nor even raised by Wrede, and are only rarely touched upon by later writers. Similar confusion persists with regard to temple tombs. There is no agreed definition of the term, and while suggestions as to their origin and inspiration have been made, typically their meaning and significance have been postulated rather than fully argued.

I would therefore like to try to unpack the arguments and available evidence to draw out the nuances of the ancient concepts behind various divine associations. Arguably, portraits in divine costume and temple tombs are the most visible and blunt associations of private individuals with the divine, and are best suited to a discussion of the problems involved. I shall here address them in turn.

Portraits in Divine Costume

To a modern viewer, reliefs, busts and especially statues presenting their subjects in the guise of a god or hero are a rather irritating phenomenon. To

---

[4] Wrede, *Consecratio*, 3–4. Here, Wrede acknowledges the original meaning of apotheosis, but goes on to say: 'Dagegen vergleichen die entsprechenden Monumente der Kaiserzeit römische Privatpersonen mit Göttern, um entweder unter Benutzung allgemeinverständlicher mythologischer Exempla möglichst repräsentative Auskünfte über ihre Eigenschaften und Fähigkeiten zu geben oder um einen göttlichen Zustand Verstorbener nachzuweisen.' ('Instead, the relevant monuments of the imperial period compare private Roman individuals with gods, either to give as representative an account of their qualities and capabilities as possible through the use of mythical exempla, or to prove a divine status of the deceased.') Cf. similarly irritating formulations on p. 27. The difficulty is not resolved by adopting Panofsky and Engemann's differentiation between 'retrospective' and 'prospective' apotheosis as, strictly speaking, apotheosis is denied in the 'retrospective' images. The same difficulties are identified by Hallett, *Roman Nude*, 263.

[5] Wrede (*Consecratio*, 93): 'Die theomorphen Porträtidentifikationen sind also ein formaler westlicher Ausdruck für die östliche Heroisierung' ('The theomorphic portrait identifications are therefore a formal, Western expression of the Eastern heroisation.').

Figure 4.1 Statue of Julia Procula as Salus from Isola Sacra Tomb 106, Trajanic; Ostia, Museum inv. 61

us, some of them, at least, look fairly agreeable. Fully dressed women with the attributes of Salus (Health or Well-being: Figure 4.1), or boys wrestling snakes like baby Hercules (Figure 4.2), do not cause much aesthetic discomfiture. However, the situation is different for some other choices. The head of a rather grumpy-looking matron from the Manilii family with an extravagantly fashionable hairstyle on the immaculate classical body of Venus (Figure 4.3) and similar statues have sparked reactions ranging from ridicule to utter contempt.[6] Nude male portraits such as another sad-looking member of the Manilii have equally been deemed out of place, even though they were not found to be quite as appalling as their female counterparts (Figure 4.4).[7] It did not escape notice very early on that many of these portraits can be

---

[6] For an overview, see Hallett, *Roman Nude*, 1, 3, 271–81, primarily on aesthetic judgements of nude portrait statues. For the Manilia statuette, see Wrede, *Consecratio*, 308 cat. 293. For the tomb, see the anonymous *Statue e busti*. For its other portraits, Fejfer, *Roman Portraits*, 119–20 figs. 72–7, with further bibl.

[7] Wrede, *Consecratio*, 274–5 cat. 206 pl. 29.4.

Figure 4.2 Boy depicted as baby Hercules wrestling the snakes, early Severan; Rome, Musei Capitolini, Galleria 59 inv. 247

identified as those of freedmen and their family, and it will hardly come as a surprise that the general judgement condemned them as the product of vulgar, tasteless *nouveaux riches* – much like Petronius' well-known *parvenu* Trimalchio, who had himself depicted with Mercury's *kerykeion* and being led to success by Mercury himself as well as by Minerva (Petronius, *Satyricon* 29.3–6). They seemed to be precisely the kind of people whose misguided and hyperbolic ambition and pretension would leave them ignorant of the embarrassment these images in fact constitute.[8]

---

[8] This judgement is still offered by Wrede (ibid., 102–5), who fully subscribes to one-sided criticism of deifying devices: 'Deswegen sticht bei den meisten Privatdeifikationen die prahlerische Gewaltsamkeit ins Auge, mit der das individuelle Bildnis Götterstatuen aufgepreßt wird, zudem das mangelnde künstlerische Taktgefühl, das eine solche stets etwas chimärenhafte Verbindung von unverändertem Erscheinungsbildnis und idealem Typus erlaubt.' ('For this reason, in most cases of private deification, the viewer is struck by the boastful brutality with which the individual portrait is forced on the divine statue, and also a lack of artistic tact, which permits such a connection, always somewhat chimeric, between an unaltered realistic portrait and an ideal type', 102–3). Filges (*Standbilder*, 184) believes that the upper classes

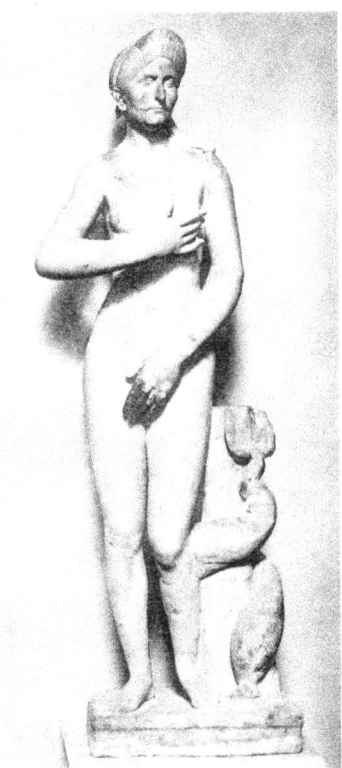

Figure 4.3 Matron from the Manilii family as Venus, Trajanic; Vatican City, Musei Vaticani, Magazine 267/2952

More recent scholarship has endeavoured to understand the phenomenon from a sociological and/or religious point of view, asking especially whether divine associations were indicating divinity and/or posthumous apotheosis. Wrede had argued that, while such images could hint at posthumous apotheosis, they were not in themselves images of the divine deceased. And indeed, nowhere is a deceased person said to obtain a new life *as* Venus, *as* Mars or *as* Mercury. He further noted that there is no evidence for any cult in funerary contexts that would exceed the traditional practices in honour of the dead, and he also observed that even in tombs comprising images in divine costume, the altar is typically associated with

perceived the nude Venus statues of *libertae* as 'vulgar and morally inacceptable', while the few imperial statues in this costume were set up in secluded contexts, an idea that is undermined by inaccuracies and logical inconsistency. Ramage and Ramage (*Roman Art*, 134) and Stewart (*Statues*, 49–51, 53) think that such statues were potentially laughable in the Roman world. While there is no way to exclude such a reaction, this clearly was not the expectation of the emperors and private individuals who commissioned them.

Figure 4.4 Adolescent from the Manilii family as Mercury, late Flavian; Vatican City, Musei Vaticani, Museo Pio Clementino, Sala a Croce Greca 187

an image that lacks divine associations.[9] Famously, Claudia Semne was depicted in her tomb on the via Appia in the guise of Fortuna, Spes and Venus, as her tomb *titulus* tells us, using what in fact is the only ancient attestation for the phrase *in formam deorum*, which has become a common term for our images.[10] However, significantly, the altar from the tomb is dedicated not to Claudia Semne *as* Fortuna and so on, but to the goddesses

---

[9] Wrede, *Consecratio*, 88–9. It must be admitted, though, that too few contexts are preserved to allow for such a general statement on altars, and even the reconstruction of Claudia Semne's tomb is far from certain (see below).

[10] *CIL* 6.15593: *Claudiae Semne uxori et M(arco) Ulpio Crotonensi fil(io) Crotonensis Aug(usti) lib(ertus) (hoc monumentum) fecit. huic monumento cedet hortus in quo tricliae, viniola, puteum, aediculae in quibus simulacra Claudiae Semnes in formam deorum, ita uti cum maceria a me circumstructa est. h(oc) m(onumentum) h(eredem) n(on) s(equetur)* ('For his wife Claudia Semne and Marcus Ulpius, son of Crotonenis, Crotonentis, freedman of Augustus, made (this monument). This monument includes a garden with arbours, vines, a well (and) aediculae with images of Claudia Semne in the guise of goddesses, just as I have walled it in. This monument does not go to the heir.'). Cf. Wrede, 'Claudia Semne', 75–6; Bignamini and Claridge, 'Claudia Semne', 215, 230, 232–4 table 1.

themselves, and to the memory of the deceased.[11] Similarly, the imperial freedman P. Aelius Asclepiacus dedicated a funerary altar *D(is) M(anibus) sacrum, Deanae et memoriae Aeliae Proculae*; that is, to the divine spirits, Diana and the memory of his wife (Figure 4.5).[12]

Accordingly, where we find references to specific divinities and heroes in epitaphs (and other funerary texts), their evocation typically takes two forms: either the deceased is said to have obtained a quality or benefit from the divinity; or else she, more rarely he, is said to be like, or even superior to, the deity with regard to specific character traits.[13] Thus, a long first-century metric epitaph for Atimetus Anterotianus and Claudia Homonoea, freedpeople of an imperial freedman, tells us:

> cui formam Paphie | Charites tribuere deco|rem quam Pallas | cunctis artibus erudiit.[14]

> Venus gave her her beauty, the Charites gave her their grace; Pallas Athena instructed her in all her arts.

In the Greek part of the same epitaph we read:

> ἡ πολὺ Σειρήνων λιγυρωτέρη, ἡ παρὰ Βάκχωι
> καὶ θοίναις αυτῆς χρυσοτέρη Κύπριος,
> ἡ λαλιά φαιδρὴ τε χελειδονὶς ἔνθ Ὁμόνοια
> κεῖμαι Ἀτιμήτωι λειπομένη δάκρυα,

> She who was far sweeter-voiced than the Sirens, who was more golden than Aphrodite herself at drinking parties and banquets, I, the talkative and glossy swallow Homonoea, lie here, leaving tears to Atimetus …[15]

Both evocations of deities obviously have similar intentions: they are a form of praise. They claim that the person concerned has some qualities that surpass what ordinary humans can normally achieve and are thus classified as

---

[11] Ditto Hallett, *Roman Nude*, 261, cf. 219–22; Mayer, *Middle Classes*, 126. On the altar, see also below p. 222.

[12] Ditto Wrede, *Consecratio*, 88. On Aelia Procula see ibid., 226 cat. 91 pl. 12.2. For further possible readings of the dedication, see below pp. 222–3.

[13] I am leaving aside here the far more frequent use of myths and mythical figures as *exempla mortalitatis* and *exempla maeroris* (on which, see Borg, 'No one is immortal', with further bibl.) and divine rapists.

[14] *CIL* 6.12657 (= *CLE* 995); Hallett, *Roman Nude*, 221 with transl. Cf. Courtney, *Musa Lapidaria*, 168–9, 378–9 no. 180; German translation and images in Walser, *Inschriftkunst*, 42–7.

[15] For further examples, see Wrede, *Consecratio*, 107 (on *EpGr* 690 (= *GVI* 1280 = *GG* 323), where a two-month-old boy is said to have been similar in character to Bacchus, brave Heracles and beautiful Endymion), 113. For encomiastic mythical comparisons in epicedia, see Esteve-Forriol, *Trostgedichte*, 155–6 § 79.

Figure 4.5 Funerary altar for Aelia Procula, around 140 CE; Paris, Musée du Louvre MA 1633

'superhuman', god-given or godlike. In the light of such sources, Wrede had concluded that portraits *in formam deorum* made similar claims.[16] The grumpy woman in the Vatican (Figure 4.3) meant to indicate her physical beauty, charm, desirability, fecundity and contribution to founding or maintaining

---

[16] Wrede, *Consecratio*, 22, 88, 105–16, and elsewhere. This line of interpretation now seems to be the majority view and is adopted e.g. by D'Ambra, 'Calculus'; Zanker and Ewald, *Myths*, 196–201; Matheson, 'Claudia', esp. 190, 193; Hallett, *Roman Nude*, 224–64. The famous

a family line,[17] and the younger Manilius is presented as the emblem of the family's prosperity and good fortune (Figure 4.4).[18]

To this extent, there is much agreement in scholarship, but other aspects are – or should be – more controversial. First, is it really correct that we are looking here at an essentially Greek habit that was imported into Rome as a foreign practice, as is often held? And if not, as I am going to argue, what are the implications for our understanding of these portraits? In a first step, I shall trace the diverse origins of these images as well as divine address and cult for mortals down to the early imperial period. Comparing, in a second step, the occurrences of private images in divine costume with their predecessors and models will help us to draw out more clearly what is specific about private portraits in the funerary realm. This will provide us with a solid background against which I can discuss the second and more fundamental question, which concerns the actual meaning of divine associations beyond what I have established so far. Should we conclude, from the fact that portraits *in formam deorum* are a visual panegyric, that they have nothing to do with religion?[19] That they are 'mere' rhetoric? Is it possible that the Romans *did* believe in the divinity of mortals? And if so, could theomorphic portraits indicate such divinity?

Origins of Images *in Formam Deorum*

The earliest evidence for the association of humans with gods comes from the Greek world, where the identification of superior faculties or character traits as divine, or of divine origin, goes back as far as Homer.[20] Around

---

passage in Tertullian, *Ad nat.* 1.10.26–9, apparently supporting the apotheosis theory must be appreciated as a Christian polemic. It should be noted, however, that Wrede largely limits his interpretation to the time before the middle of the second century, arguing for a change in the later second and third century under the influence of sarcophagi (Wrede, *Consecratio*, 123, 125–31). From then on, so he claims, portraits in divine costume in all artistic genres would carry eschatological significance and point to a life beyond. This is not the place to discuss his suggestions in detail, but my position will become clear in the following; cf. also below n. 250.

[17] D'Ambra, 'Calculus'. For the motifs of *forma corporis* and *fecunditas* in epicedia, see also Esteve-Forriol, *Trostgedichte*, 132–3 §§17 and 21 with examples. For the ambition of freedmen to found a family line, see Chapter 3 above.

[18] Wrede, *Consecratio*, 98–100, 109–16; Hallett, *Roman Nude*, 230–7, 261–4, with 98–9 and 262 on Mercury.

[19] It would exceed the scope of this chapter to engage fully with the wide range of attempts to define the term 'religion'. For some attempts, see e.g. Idinopulos and Wilson (eds.), *Religion*; Bergunder, 'What is religion?'. On the prevalent ritualistic concept of Roman religion, see below. For now, I use the term 'religion' to refer to the body of actions and material culture that the Romans regarded as belonging to the *sacra*. The key question of 'belief' in Roman religion will be discussed below.

[20] For a convenient summary of various forms of apotheosis and heroisation, see *ThesCRA* II (2004), 125–214 s.v. Heroisierung und Apotheose.

the turn of the fourth century BCE, Dionysios the Elder of Syracuse may have been the first to be depicted in an explicitly Dionysiac statue scheme.[21] Later, the Hellenistic kings and queens styled themselves as *neos Dionysos* ('New Dionysus'), *nea Aphrodite* and so on. These monarchs also received public worship, sometimes in these very forms.[22] Late Republican Roman generals and promagistrates accepted similar honours in the East, where statues of Hellenistic rulers were sometimes rededicated to them by simply exchanging their heads, and new statues were set up, surely often in similar forms.[23] When they later received such honours also in the West, and finally even presented themselves in divine costume in statues and on coins in Rome,[24] their practices were shaped significantly by this experience. Divine assimilations and honours in the West, including the images here discussed, are therefore usually seen as Greek in origin.

To some extent, this is obviously correct. However, various forms of divine honours for living men (much more rarely women) that merged Greek and Roman ideas were explored at Rome relatively early as well. Assimilating *rulers* to the highest god goes back even to the Etruscan kings, if we accept their dress as imitating the appearance of Jupiter.[25] It is generally assumed that the worship of the divine *Genius* of the *paterfamilias* – that is, of his life force and the tutelary deity of his *familia* – by members of his household has Republican origins.[26] Hailing individuals as gods, and especially addressing them as a new Jupiter, was customary in Rome at least

---

[21] Wrede, *Consecratio*, 7–19 for an overview, 13–14 on Dionysios (based on Favorinus in Dio Chrys., *Or.* 37.21).

[22] For worship of a ruler assimilated to another deity, see e.g. Berenice II worshipped as Aphrodite Akraia Arsinoe Philokrates (*SEG* 8.361: Caneva, 'Arsinoe II'), or Laodike V, who was honoured at Iasos as Queen Aphrodite Laodike (*I.Iasos* 4, 196 BCE: Caneva, 'Queens', 91). The bibliography on Hellenistic ruler cult is vast. See esp. Habicht, *Gottmenschentum*; Fishwick, *Imperial Cult Vol. I*, 3–45; Wrede, *Consecratio*, 19–22; Chaniotis, 'Divinity'; Versnel, *Coping with the Gods*, 439–92, which is particularly illuminating. For the literary tradition of divine praise, see also Bosworth, 'Augustus'. For their images, see Bergmann (*Strahlen*, 19–38), who stresses, however, that some divine associations were never related to any cult.

[23] See Hallett, *Roman Nude*, 137–48, on dedications to Roman leaders in the East, and 148–58 for statues erected in Rome. For a different and interesting model, see Tanner, 'Portraits', whose focus, however, is on the combination of verism and 'heroic nudity'.

[24] Wrede, *Consecratio*, 27–30. For a list of Roman magistrates' cults in the East, see Bowersock, *Augustus*, 150–1. For statue honours for promagistrates in Asia Minor, see Tuchelt (ed.), *Denkmäler*, 45–118, 133–251, and a list of statue bases 252–7; Price, *Rituals*, 40–7. On nude statues with or without divine attributes in Rome and the West, Hallett (*Roman Nude*, 158) concludes that they were introduced only relatively late, at the beginning of the civil wars at the earliest.

[25] Weinstock, *Julius*, 292–3; Clauss, *Herrscherkult*, 41–6; Gradel, *Emperor Worship*, 32–5.

[26] Gradel, *Emperor Worship*, 36–44, 50, with dedications to the *Genius* of private individuals listed in Appendix 1.

from the third century BCE onwards. While much of the Republican evidence comes from comedy, especially Plautus,[27] Ittay Gradel concludes that the theme could only make sense to his audience if it was familiar with such practice, and that the humour lies not in such hyperbolic address per se, but in the inappropriateness of its application. In Plautus' plays it is typically an individual of low status or morals that is so addressed. Instead, in the real world, it was always a much superior person, mostly an owner or patron, who is addressed as Jupiter by an inferior dependant.[28] Similar to such divine acclamations, the majority of portraits with divine attributes from pre-imperial Rome and Italy, which are the visual equivalents of such address, are found on gems (Figure 4.6)[29] and other objects from the private, domestic sphere.[30]

However, some pushed the boundaries early on.[31] When Aemilius Paullus (in 168 BCE), Pompey (in 63 BCE) and Caesar were officially granted the right to wear triumphal garb in public on various occasions, it meant that they were allowed to liken themselves to Jupiter more permanently than was the case at the traditional *Roman* triumph.[32] Together with his *Scipio*, Ennius' translation into Latin of Euhemerus' *Sacred Record*, which proposed that all the gods were in fact deified kings, generals and benefactors, was meant to pave the way for public deification of his patron, P. Cornelius Scipio Africanus, the victor over Hannibal.[33] As a highly respected *Roman* author, who may also have been the first to highlight, perhaps even to

---

[27] But cf. Terence, *Ph.* 345, where the parasite Phormio calls the host of his lavish dinner parties a *deus praesens* ('present god', or 'god on earth').

[28] E.g. in *Persa* 99–100, where the parasite calls his host, a slave (!), *Iuppiter terrestris* ('earthly Jupiter'). Cf. the Terence passage in the previous note; Gradel, *Emperor Worship*, 41–8, with more examples. See also Clauss, *Herrscherkult*, 44–5; Beard, *Roman Triumph*, 253–6 (who interprets Plautus' *Amphitruo* as a reversal of the triumphal parade in which Jupiter appears as the victorious general); Cole, *Cicero*, 27–8. For Plautus' originality, see Manuwald, *Theatre*, 225–33 with bibl. For a similar argument regarding Greek comedy and ruler cult, see Versnel, *Coping with the Gods*, 467.

[29] E.g. M. Iunius Brutus with the attributes of Mercury: Vollenweider, *Porträtgemmen Vol. II*, 285 s.v. Mercur, with *Porträtgemmen Vol. I*, pls. 93.1–3; 101.1–3; 127.1; 148.16, 18; generally with further examples Vollenweider, *Porträtgemmen Vol. II*, 179–83 (Marc Antony), 214–17 (Octavian). Cf. Wrede, *Consecratio*, 28–9.

[30] Lo Monaco, 'Immagini private', 340–1.

[31] Clauss, *Herrscherkult*, 46–53; Gradel, *Emperor Worship*, 55–72, on Caesar; Hallett, *Roman Nude*, 154–8; Pollini, *Republic to Empire*, 72–4, for a brief review of coin images and public monuments dedicated by Romans.

[32] Gradel, *Emperor Worship*, 35, 49 with n. 31. On the triumphator as temporary Jupiter, see Versnel, *Triumphus*, 56–93; Beard, *Roman Triumph*, 225–56; Beard et al., *Religions*, 143. On the tradition of associating Roman political and military leaders with the divine, see ibid., 140–9.

[33] On Euhemerus' likely inspiration by long-standing ruler cult in Sicily, see De Angelis and Garstad, 'Euhemerus'; cf. Winiarczyk, *Euhemeros*, esp. ch. 8.

Figure 4.6 Carnelian showing portrait of a man (M. Iunius Brutus?) with divine attributes; Collection Arndt no. 2224, Staatliche Münzsammlung, Munich

invent, Romulus' apotheosis and deification as the god Quirinus, Ennius greatly influenced later generations, who could now also claim Roman traditions for the deification of humans.[34] In 86 BCE, Marius Gratidianus received sacrifices by people in Rome at *compita* (street shrines) that also contained his statue, and there is evidence for cult to private individuals from the – epigraphically richer – imperial period.[35] Divine cult was one of the honours offered to Caesar by the senate during his lifetime, even though it is uncertain whether his formal title was (supposed to be) Jupiter Iulius (thus Cassius Dio 43.14) or Divus Iulius (thus Cicero, *Phil.* 2.110),

[34] Bosworth, 'Augustus', 9–11; Winiarczyk, *Euhemeros*, 113–14; Cole, *Cicero*, 88–91, for his importance to Cicero.

[35] Cicero, *Off.* 3.80; Seneca, *De Ira* 3.18.1; Clauss, *Herrscherkult*, 43; Gradel, *Emperor Worship*, 51, 125; Flower, *Forgetting*, 94–5. Note also the altar dedicated to C. Manlius set up in the theatre at Cumae in the Augustan period: Gradel, *Emperor Worship*, 251–60, and 215–16, 224–7 on the cult of private individuals in the imperial period.

as is perhaps more likely.[36] While he rejected the proposal, it is still significant that the senate, which usually tended to verge on the conservative side, came up with the idea, since it is unlikely to have offered an honour closely connected only with Hellenistic kingship.[37] Even Cicero, a stern and passionate defender of the Republic, regarded divine honours as an appropriate reward for outstanding achievement and benefactions, piled all sorts of divine associations onto Pompey the Great, Marius and others (though stopping just short of calling them a god directly) and, in overwhelming gratitude for his instrumental role in Cicero's return from exile, addressed P. Cornelius Lentulus Spinter as 'parent, god, and salvation of my life, reputation, and name' (*parens, deus, salus nostrae vitae fortunae, memoriae, nominis: Ad Quir.* 11).[38]

In all these cases, the divine honours were *a priori* unrelated to life after death, except, of course, eternal life in the memory of posterity.[39] On the contrary, they were a particularly strong expression of honour and acknowledgement of the recipient's pre-eminence while he was alive, exercising his power and still able to enter into the reciprocal relationship that also informed the cult of traditional gods. Emperor worship grew out of this tradition, which, by merging Greek and Roman ideas, had departed substantially from original Greek precedents, and thus had become as Roman as Roman religion and

---

[36] Cf. Weinstock, *Julius*, 300–8, with North, 'Praesens divus', esp. 175. Gradel (*Emperor Worship*, 69–71) argues that the title 'Jupiter Iulius' was offered to Caesar, but rejected in favour of the more modest 'Divus Iulius'. There is a long-standing debate around whether Caesar was made a god during his lifetime, but for our purposes this is not essential. For a recent discussion with bibl., see Koortbojian, *Divinization*, esp. 30–6.

[37] Hallett (*Roman Nude*, 142–3) suggests that the statues in 'heroic costume' set up by and to Roman generals in Rome were not perceived as royal as they were not wearing the royal diadem.

[38] On Cicero and deification, see esp. Cole, *Cicero*, passim, 34–62, on the *Pro lege Manilia* and praise of Pompey, and 70–1, on praise of Lentulus, where he also makes the connection with the Plautus passages, but seems to reject the idea that Plautus could be a reflection on current habits). On Lentulus, cf. also Gradel (*Emperor Worship*, 52), who capitalises *salus*/*Salus* in the above quotation. It is noteworthy that Cicero pushes for public apotheosis of great men even in his speeches of the 50s that were designed to stabilise the Republican political order (Cole, *Cicero*, 85–110, with ample further bibl.). Apparently, Clodius even accused Cicero of calling himself Jupiter (and his sister, Minerva): *Dom.* 92. While Wrede (*Consecratio*, 28) thinks that Cicero's ironic response suggested his rejection of such divine assimilations, Cole (*Cicero*, passim, and 67–8 on the passage) makes it clear that Cicero constantly compared himself to Jupiter even in his public speeches, so that it is certainly possible that he went one step further in more private contexts.

[39] They could also be taken as an indication of and justification for future posthumous deification, but this is not to say that the two are one and the same. Cf. Clauss, *Herrscherkult*, 45, and esp. Cole, *Cicero*, for an excellent analysis of Cicero's rhetorical strategies and attempts at bestowing divine honours upon those who, like himself, have saved Rome and the *res publica*.

customs could get.[40] It is often suggested that Augustus' rejection of divine cult and images during his lifetime was due to his wariness over their foreign, Greek nature.[41] Yet many factors, not least the iconographies chosen to express this divinity visually, demonstrate how far Roman habits had departed from Greek ones. In particular, the seated statues of the so-called 'hip-mantle type' that were chosen for images of the emperor as Jupiter throughout the imperial period were a Roman invention (see Figure 4.11). They are unparalleled among Hellenistic rulers,[42] and are the translation into visual form of the praise found already in Plautus.

Moreover, it was only in Rome, and only in official state cult, that Augustus rejected such honours. He happily received divine cult from local communities in at least sixteen public temples in Italy, of which seven are definitively Augustan and only one clearly posthumous.[43] The crucial point was not potential Greekness: it was the relationship between the person offering or awarding divine honours and the honouree that mattered. In all the instances discussed above, from Plautus to the *triumphatores* to Marius Gratidianus and Cicero's acclamation of Lentulus, the divine honours expressed the particular relationship between the two parties involved, in which the honorant typically perceived himself as massively indebted to, or in admiration of, a benefactor who, at least in the specific situation, possessed the superior power to bring about what caused the gratitude and

---

[40] See Cole, *Cicero*, on this merging of Greek and Roman ideas in Cicero's thinking. Gradel (*Emperor Worship*, 48) rightly points out that there never was any purity in Roman religion and thought (ditto the authors in n. 25 above), but thereby effectively downplays the part that Greek models had in the formation of what then became Roman ideas. On the merging of Greek and Roman cultural elements generally, see Wallace-Hadrill, 'Tomb as house'. Hallett (*Roman Nude*, 153–8) stresses the scarcity of evidence for Romans setting up statues in 'heroic costume' in Rome. Yet given that hardly any statues have been preserved from the first century BCE, one wonders whether the absence of evidence is really evidence of absence and, in any case, dedications by non-Romans to their patrons in Rome were abundant and are likely to have included portraits in 'heroic costume' (ibid., 148–53), aiding a process of habituation to such images.

[41] E.g. Wrede, *Consecratio*, 28, despite acknowledging the Roman elements in the process (pp. 27–30); Bergmann, *Strahlen*, 265 (referring not to Augustus in particular but to the early imperial period); Alexandridis, *Frauen*, 82.

[42] Hallett, *Roman Nude*, 167. However, the standing hip-mantle scheme *was* used for Hellenistic rulers: ibid., 123–5. For the emperor as Jupiter, see Clauss, *Herrscherkult*, 246–54. For statues and the iconography of Jupiter, see Maderna, *Vorbilder*, 18–55. Similarly, Mikocki (*Sub specie Deae*, 137–8) observes that the statue types chosen for empresses are markedly different from those used for Hellenistic queens.

[43] Hänlein-Schäfer, *Veneratio Augusti*; Gradel, *Emperor Worship*, 80–4, 90 (where he argues convincingly that the posthumous temple erected by Tiberius at Nola, where Augustus died, is a special case), 223 on private cult during Augustus' lifetime in Rome, 198–233 on private imperial cult in general. On Augustus' cult during his lifetime, see also Taylor, 'Worship'; Clauss, *Herrscherkult*, 55–75.

respect.[44] This is the background to the distinction that Augustus and later emperors made between official honours (in the sense of senate-induced *sacra publica*) and private ones (in the sense of non-senate-induced *sacra privata*) – which could, of course, be as publicly visible as the *sacra publica*.[45] In his dealings with the senate, Augustus' acceptance of *state* cult as a living god would have spoiled his self-styling as *primus inter pares*, since it would have suggested – or made apparent – a status disparity that, under the circumstances, could only be viewed as a claim to monarchic or autocratic rule.[46] As Gradel maintains, 'The novelty was the principate itself, not, in terms of mental history, the response to it,' which was the offering of divine cult to someone so superior.[47]

Deification of the deceased ruler (*consecratio*) was the final step in extending divine honours to mortals in Rome, and it had a similarly ambiguous parentage to the deification of living humans. It was practised by some of the Hellenistic rulers, and posthumous heroisation of civic benefactors had become increasingly frequent during the Hellenistic period.[48] Yet the idea of posthumous divinity as a reward for personal achievement and benefactions to humanity had entered Rome with Ennius' version of Euhemerus at the latest. Of the examples from mytho-history, Hercules may still have been perceived as Greek, but the Castores had long been Roman gods, with their own temple in the Roman Forum erected in 484 BCE, and Romulus was clearly indigenous. Cicero explored the idea of posthumous deification of his contemporaries (and most likely of himself) from 56 BCE onwards,[49] and in 42 BCE Julius Caesar was the first Roman leader to be officially deified by decree of the senate.[50]

---

[44] See Gradel, *Emperor Worship*, 26, 29, 46, 101–2, 148, 267, 270 and elsewhere, on the relational character of divine honours.

[45] For the distinction between *sacra publica* and *privata*, see ibid., 128–9. This distinction is also stressed and systematically surveyed in the available visual evidence by John Pollini in a number of publications (e.g. 'Man or god', esp. 335; *Republic to Empire*, esp. 71, 74–93, 382, 389, and elsewhere) and underlies Koortbojian, *Divinization* (see esp. 163–80 on private cults).

[46] Price, 'Consecration', 57; Gradel, *Emperor Worship*, 75, 101–2, 132, and elsewhere.

[47] Gradel, *Emperor Worship*, 101–2, 269, and elsewhere (quotation p. 102). Ditto Erskine, 'Epilogue', 507–8: 'for a majority of the thousand years or so of documented Greek religion (roughly from Homer to the "triumph" of Christianity), rulers, whether kings or Roman emperors, are found being accorded divine status. Far from an anomaly, this phenomenon could be considered the norm'.

[48] For an overview with bibl., see *ThesCRA* II (2004), 180–1 s.v. Heroisierung und Apotheose (S. Aneziri).

[49] Cole, *Cicero*, 76.

[50] See most recently esp. Gradel, *Emperor Worship*; Koortbojian, *Divinization* (focusing on the practicalities entailed in the introduction of such cult). For posthumous deification becoming primarily a Roman preoccupation, see Bickerman, 'Consecratio', 9–12; Cole, *Cicero*, 6; Bechtold, *Gott und Gestirn*, 152–9.

Contexts

From Caesar and Augustus' deification onwards, there were essentially four contexts in which portraits in divine costume could feature.

The first was the private realm. Augustus was depicted with divine attributes in the villa of Livia at Prima Porta, from where the famous cuirassed statue with Amor riding a dolphin at its feet originates (Figure 4.7).[51] According to Suetonius (*Caligula* 7.1), he kept a statue of his grandson Gaius 'in the guise of Cupid' (*habitu Cupidinis*) in one of his private rooms, and even used to greet it with a kiss when entering; Livia dedicated a similar statue of her grandson in the Capitoline temple of Venus.[52] A statue of an imperial prince in the guise of Mercury found on the Esquiline Hill possibly also comes from an imperial residence,[53] and Augustus may even have had a statue of himself in the guise of Apollo displayed in the Palatine library.[54] Moreover, like his heirs, he and members of his family were depicted in divine costume in cameos and gems, several of which were clearly created during their lifetime (Figures 4.8–4.10).[55]

The second context is the continued use of such images in the public realm for living persons. As we have seen, Augustus rejected official cult at Rome during his lifetime, but accepted it from private individuals and municipalities. In fact, municipal as well as private cult in Italy was over-whelmingly honouring the living emperor,[56] so that the existing statues of emperors and empresses in divine costume may also predominantly have been erected while their subjects were still alive (Figure 4.11).[57] Later emperors from Nero onwards, who equally rejected state cult during their lifetime, were depicted with divine attributes even on state coinage,

---

[51] Vatican State, Musei Vaticani, Braccio Nuovo inv. 2290: e.g. Zanker, *Power*, 188–92 fig. 148; Galinsky, *Augustan Culture*, 24–5 fig. 5. Some scholars, such as Pollini, *Republic to Empire*, 420–1 figs. IX.11a–c, consider the Cupid's head to be a portrait of Caius Caesar.

[52] Hallett, *Roman Nude*, 234–5.

[53] Ibid., 175–6, 235, with fig. 99.

[54] According to Servius, *Vita Verg.* 4.10. Cf. Bravi, *Griechische Kunstwerke*, 139–40. However, note that the statue could have been that of Apollo as Augustus' protective deity (cf. below).

[55] Megow, *Kameen*, A10 (Gemma Augustea), A11, A36, A60, B15, B17–19. Later members of the imperial families appear in similar images, among which the Claudian evidence is particularly rich. See Bergmann, *Strahlen*, passim, and 219–20, on the similarities between cameos or gems and poetic praise; Hallett, *Roman Nude*, 134, 223 with n. 1, 232–5; Pollini, *Republic to Empire*, 84–5, 94–5. On Augustus as Jupiter, see also Zanker, *Power*, 230–4, 317–18 fig. 249.

[56] Gradel, *Emperor Worship*, 74–108, 199, 206–7, and above n. 43.

[57] Ibid., 110. For extant examples showing the living emperor as Jupiter in art: Zanker, *Power*, 230–8, 317–19, and Koortbojian, *Divinization*, 163–5 figs. VII.1–2 (on enthroned statue of Augustus in a private shrine at the Forum of Tivoli, Figure 4.11 below); Boschung, *Gens Augusta*, 8–21, for statues in the Augustus and Roma Temple at Leptis Magna (Augustus' acrolithic cult statue, and an acrolithic statue of Tiberius reconstructed after cameo images;

Figure 4.7 Statue of Augustus from the imperial villa at Prima Porta, Vatican City, Musei Vaticani, Museo Chiaramonti, Braccio Nuovo 14

assimilating them in particular to Jupiter and Hercules (Figure 4.12).[58] We may be seeing here both an indication of a change in their relationship with the senate, and an extension of the meaning of such images that could be understood as panegyric without implying cult.[59] This is also suggested

marble statues in Jupiter scheme preserved for Divus Augustus and the living Claudius (ibid., pls. 8.1–2)); 49 no. 7.4 pl. 34.3: seated statue from Veji (head does not belong, but all dedications are to living emperors except Divus Augustus, whose head is too large); 85–6 nos. 25.2–4 pls. 70.1–2, cf. p. 88: seated statues of Tiberius and two other emperors, most likely Divus Augustus and Caligula, from Cerveteri. For the newly discovered seated statue of Caligula from his nymphaeum at Nemi, see Ghini, 'La statua', 49–54 and Ghini and Batocchioni (eds.), *Caligola*, 107–14. Cf. Josephus, *Bell. Iud.* 1.144 and 1.339, on cult statues for Augustus and Livia in the Augustus and Roma temple at Caesarea, modelled after Phidias' Zeus at Olympia and the Polycletan Hera from Argos. See Boschung, *Gens Augusta*, passim, for standing hip-mantle statues of living members of the imperial family, and on imperial statuary in general.

58　For Jupiter's central role in the Roman state, see Fears, 'Jupiter'; for Hercules, see n. 169.

59　Cf. Gradel, *Emperor Worship*, 140–61. For a shift in panegyric practices, see also Bergmann, *Strahlen*, 220–2 (where she rightly points out that the ubiquity of divine praise of Claudius is

Figure 4.8 'Gemma Augustea' showing the divine Augustus with Roma surrounded by personifications and family members, 10 BCE? Vienna, Kunsthistorisches Museum inv. IX A 79

by the use of portraits *in formam deorum* for living empresses, for whom epigraphic address as, or comparison with, a *dea* is only attested four times in the entire western empire, while these portraits come almost exclusively from this same area.[60]

in stark contrast to his determined rejection of a cult in his lifetime), 227 and elsewhere. Nero with aegis: Hallett, *Roman Nude*, 250; Bergmann, *Strahlen*, 174–5 pl. 34.2. For emperors with the same device generally, see Bastien, *Buste monétaire*, 346–65. For assimilations to Hercules, see ibid., 369–84, and n. 169 below. While the question of who was responsible for the coin imagery bears on our interpretation, it cannot be pursued here. For an overview of the debate, see Bergmann, *Strahlen*, 91–8. For the ongoing negotiation and renegotiation of the emperor's relationship to the senate, see esp. Wallace-Hadrill, 'Civilis Princeps'. On the imperial cult in the West generally, see Clauss, *Herrscherkult*, and for sources for imperial cult during the emperors' lifetime, see his Appendix 1 (pp. 503–19).

[60] Alexandridis, 'Überall (Götter)gleich?', 416 with tables 1–2.

Figure 4.9 Livia as priestess of Divus Augustus with divine attributes, Tiberian; Vienna, Kunsthistorisches Museum ANSA IXa 95

Thirdly, *divi* and *divae* were depicted in divine costume. Hallett has argued that, when emperors are shown as state *divi*, they are almost exclusively depicted in their toga, often *capite velato* and sometimes with added *corona radiata*, but not assimilated to Olympian deities.[61] This may be true for their official cult temples, but there are plenty of examples where the emperor or a member of his family is depicted in divine costume posthumously in private dedications (Figure 4.13).[62]

---

[61] They are wearing what Hallett (*Roman Nude*, 224–9) calls the '*divus* costume'; some exceptions are acknowledged by Hallett (pp. 229–30). On images of the *divi*, see also Bergmann (*Strahlen*, 102–281), who gives special attention to images with astral symbols.

[62] For a dupondius showing Diva Augusta (Livia) in the guise of Ceres, see Pollini, *Republic to Empire*, 94 fig. II.27; 69–161 for further examples in his well-illustrated survey. However, the cameo showing Claudius in apotheosis with Zeus's aegis over his shoulder must be excluded: Megow (*Kameen*, 199–200 no. A80 pl. 27.1) plausibly connects the double cornucopia to the emperor's marriage to Agrippina (for a different opinion, see e.g. Pollini, *Republic to Empire*, 137–8 fig. III.9). For the significance of the augural *lituus* which the emperor also holds, see ibid., 137–45, and Koortbojian, *Divinization*, 50–77. When Pollini suggests (p. 111) that it was primarily the deified emperor who was shown in divine costume, this is also not true, and it is somewhat strange that he omits the coins mentioned here, n. 59

Figure 4.10 Apotheosis of Nero, Neronian; Nancy, Bibliothèque Municipale De Nancy

In all three of these contexts, the attributes and statue types borrowed from the traditional gods were first and foremost a visual language specifying the

above. See Bergmann, *Strahlen*, 110–12, for the conclusion that there was no generally agreed iconography for *divi*; Pollini, *Republic to Empire*, 88–93, for examples of cult images, and 133–54, for a survey of images of deified emperors that makes clear the importance of private dedications by members of the imperial family. For poetic address of the living emperor as god, see also Möller, *Götterattribute*. For the parallel between divine praise in poetry and cameos, see Bergmann, *Strahlen*, 219–20.

Figure 4.11 Statue of Augustus from a shrine dedicated in 19 BCE by the freedman M. Varenus Dipilus at the Forum of Tivoli; Tivoli, Museo Archeologico

character traits of the individual so honoured, be they perceived as divine or not. This is most obvious in the case of *divi* and *divae*. When members of the imperial family were deified by the state, they were deified in their own right, not as Jupiter, Venus or Ceres, as can also be seen from their unique cult names and the names of their priests.[63] When they were fitted out with the attributes of traditional deities, the principle was therefore the same as for images of humans during their lifetime: the attributes were intended to specify those aspects of their character that were deemed divine and/or particularly relevant to their divinity. When Divus Augustus was depicted with the

---

[63] Differently Davies (*Death and the Emperor*, 104), who misinterprets Dio Cassius (59.11.2–3). My view is not contradicted by passages such as Vergil, *Georgics* 1.24–42, or Lucan, *Bellum Civile* 1.45–59. While Augustus and Nero, respectively, are said to act like Poseidon, Zeus or Apollo-Sol after their death, they remain true to themselves and can choose between these roles at liberty. Moreover, these speculations are offered by poets in panegyric poetry and represent their private views on their emperors' roles rather than the state's concept of its *divi*. And, finally, like the many similar poems on Nero (Bergmann, *Strahlen*, 134–46), they were written during the lifetime of the emperor, and extend the divine roles on earth to their afterlife.

Figure 4.12 Bronze dupondius of Domitian showing him with radiate crown and the aegis of Jupiter, 86 CE; American Numismatic Society 1941.131.764

radiate crown of Apollo-Sol and Jupiter's thunderbolt on Tiberian and later coinage, this did not indicate that he had become a super-deity replacing or outdoing the traditional gods, but that he possessed (some of) the features of these divinities; they extended the emperor's living roles to eternity in heaven.

The fourth category of images mixing portrait features with divine iconographies sits somewhat obliquely with the images thus far discussed. John Pollini first suggested that a *denarius* of 13 BCE (?) by the moneyer C. Marius Tormentinus that shows Augustus' head on the obverse and Diana with a strongly individualised face on the reverse does not represent the emperor's daughter Iulia as Diana, as many scholars believe, but rather Diana with the features of Augustus.[64] He is surely right that such an interpretation would be much more in line with official Augustan politics. Whether or not he is correct in this particular instance, he rightly drew attention to the

---

[64] Pollini, 'Man or god', 353–5 fig. 29 with extensive bibl.; Pollini, *Republic to Empire*, 77–8 fig. II.6.

Figure 4.13 Divus Augustus as Jupiter from the 'Basilica' at Herculaneum; Naples, Museo Archeologico Nazionale 5595

possibility that, here and elsewhere, theomorphic images with individualised features may well represent personalised gods and goddesses of the form *dea Augusta/deus Augustus* or *dea/deus Augustae/Augusti* – here: Diana Augusta/Augusti.[65] This kind of personalisation had a long tradition during the Republic, when divinities were selected as supporters or protectors of a particular family or other group by the addition of gentilicial and other adjectives such as Victoria Mariana, Diana Valeriana or Hercules Olivarius.[66] Hallett has drawn attention to other images that may be viewed in this

[65] Pollini, 'Man or god'; Pollini, *Republic to Empire*, 77–9. The same idea is adopted by Hallett, *Roman Nude*, 242–7, for the imperial period more generally. Diana Augusta is addressed in a private dedication from 6/5 BCE: *CIL* 6.128.

[66] Pollini, *Republic to Empire*, 79. On Hercules Olivarius, most likely the Hercules of the oil merchants, see *CIL* 6.33936 and *LTUR* 3 (1996) 19–20 s.v. Hercules Olivarius (F. Coarelli). That the Augustan deities are eminently Roman is also demonstrated by the fact that all their dedications from Rome were written in Latin rather than Greek: Panciera ('Representation', 218–27) found ninety dedications from Rome, thirty-three of which were to the Lares Augusti

light.[67] A statue from Leptis Magna with the head of Livia wearing a mural crown was dedicated to Ceres Augusta and may be a case in point.[68] An altar dedicated by an imperial slave to Sol and Luna shows the god with the features of Nero, thus suggesting that this is the visual equivalent of a dedication to Sol Augustus (Figure 4.14).[69] An over-life-size head of Minerva from Rome, now in Budapest, clearly has portrait features, probably those of Domitian, and may equally belong in this category.[70] Essentially, the strategy of visual rhetoric is the same as with any other image of a divinity: its pose and dress, its features and attributes, serve to characterise and comment on this divinity. The representation of a god is not a portrait of 'what he really *looks* like', but visualises invisible characteristics that are relevant in the given context. While in images of humans assimilated to divinities, the divine elements make a comment on the mortal concerned, in images of gods with portrait features of mortals a comment is made on the divinity.

Freedpeople in Divine Costume

When freedmen and -women started presenting themselves in theomorphic relief images and statues from the Flavian period onwards,[71] this practice

and are not directly relevant to our discussion; the others were dedicated to twenty-four different divinities, Hercules, Silvanus, Mercurius, Fortuna and Diana being most popular (p. 227). For their chronological distribution between 7/6 BCE and the third century CE, see Panciera, ibid., 230–3. On this phenomenon in general, see esp. Fishwick, 'Augustus'; Fishwick, *Imperial Cult Vol. II*, 446–54; Clauss, *Herrscherkult*, 280–9 (who sees the adjective *augustus/augusta* as an 'Auszeichnung' (honour) of the divinity rather than an indication that he or she is the emperor's tutelary deity), with a list of 209 divinities with the epithet Augusta/Augustus from the whole empire (pp. 527–32); Panciera, 'Representation'. For relevant dedications from Italy, see Gregori, 'Divinità Auguste'. In contrast to most authors, Gradel (*Emperor Worship*, 103–6, 113–15), sees a difference between divinities with the epithet *Augustus/a* and those with the emperor added in the genitive, the first being less clearly connected to the emperor. I am not convinced: similar constructions with the names of *gentes* or private individuals (on which below) contradict his view, as does the frequent ambivalent abbreviation *Aug.* instead of the full epithet.

[67] Hallett, *Roman Nude*, 237–47. I do not find all of his suggestions equally convincing.

[68] Cf. Zanker, *Power*, 234–5 fig. 185; Mikocki, *Sub specie Deae*, 19. I am less certain about the dupondius of 22 CE inscribed with *Salus Augusta* clearly showing Livia with the matronly *stola* (!) and no attributes suggesting divinity, which Hallett (*Roman Nude*, 240–1 fig. 138) identifies with certainty as an image of the goddess. Rather, as Pollini (*Republic to Empire*, 93–4) has argued, the image is not explained by the inscription, but designates the individual to which Salus is being related.

[69] Bergmann, *Strahlen*, 194–201 pls. 38.1–4, followed by Hallett, *Roman Nude*, 242–3.

[70] Varner, 'Transcending gender', 187–8 fig. 3 (further examples in Varner should be considered in relation to Augustan deities); Hekster, *Emperors*, 253–5 fig. 92.

[71] Of the three examples dated by Wrede to the Neronian period (*Consecratio*, nos. 204, 233, 290), the first is a herm from Pompeii that is now lost and can no longer be assessed, the second is the famous wall painting from the house of M. Lucretius Fronto at Pompeii (5.4.11) that stands in the tradition of domestic display and the third is potentially imperial (ditto Wrede, ibid.).

Figure 4.14 Altar dedicated by the imperial slave Eumolpus to Sol (Augustus) and Luna, Neronian, Florence, Museo Archeologico inv. 86025; plaster cast Rome, Museo della Civilà Romana

had a long tradition in Roman custom. They did not adopt a Greek habit but a Roman one and, as far as the monumental format is concerned, an *imperial* one.[72] As Annetta Alexandridis has demonstrated, even the empresses had been depicted in divine costume almost exclusively in the West, and it is highly unlikely that Roman freedpeople aimed at imitating the few surviving, by then very ancient Hellenistic models that also were largely limited to Egypt.[73] This is confirmed by the first appearance of these

---

[72] Ditto Wrede, 'Claudia Semne', 152–6; Wrede, *Consecratio*, 76, 95–6, 101–2; Hallett, *Roman Nude*, 199, 202; Matheson, 'Claudia', 182. For a different view, see e.g. Lo Monaco ('Immagini private', 344), who thinks that divine assimilations are entirely alien to Italic mentality and tradition.

[73] Alexandridis ('Überall (Götter)gleich?', 416–17 with tables 1–2) also notes that the five exceptions of empresses with divine attributes from the East come from particularly 'Roman' contexts. For an overview of divine assimilations among Hellenistic rulers, see Svenson, *Darstellungen*.

images in Rome (rather than in the more Hellenised areas of Italy or the
Greek East), where they remained most popular throughout the imperial
period,[74] and also by the choice of statue types. The single most popular
iconography among private individuals, nude bodies of Venus combined
with female portrait heads, is entirely without precedent before the Roman
period.[75] While private individuals may have added certain types to the
existing iconographic repertoire, Mikocki has shown that the fluctu-
ating popularity of their various statue types largely followed that of the
imperial house.[76]

Moreover, it seems to have been imperial freedmen, and *liberti* with close
connections to the court, who first presented themselves in divine costume.[77] Among the earliest examples attributable to their circle are a Flavian
funerary altar for an imperial *libertus* and doctor from the via Appia,[78] the
late Domitianic statues or statuettes of Priscilla mentioned by Statius,[79]
followed by some figures on the famous Haterii relief from the Trajanic
period (see later Figure 4.20),[80] the Hadrianic portraits of Claudia Semne as
Fortuna, Spes and Venus,[81] and an altar dedicated by a *libertus* of Hadrian.[82]
Due to their close relations with the emperor and his family, their most
prominent members also got away with much other extravagance that

---

[74] Wrede, *Consecratio*, 94–5; Alexandridis, here n. 73.

[75] Hallett, *Roman Nude*, 219; cf. also at n. 375 below.

[76] Mikocki, *Sub specie Deae*, 129; Lo Monaco, 'Immagini private', 339–40, 342. Cf. Alexandridis, *Frauen*, 294 table 9, and Fejfer, *Roman Portraits*, 341, on the Ceres type.

[77] Wrede, *Consecratio*, 95–6, 102. I do not think, though, that this was an expression of their loyalty towards the imperial house. Cf. Hallett, *Roman Nude*, 199, 202. Filges (*Standbilder*, 179) claims that female statues *in formam deorum* were all wives of imperial freedmen, but there is no evidence for this.

[78] Wrede, *Consecratio*, 95, 256–8 no. 167 pl. 31. Given T. Flavius Hermes' profession, it is remarkable that he chose an assimilation playing on his name rather than on his occupation. The only potentially earlier example is the Neronian Mercury (?) herm for an Augustalis at Pompeii: ibid., 96, 273–4 no. 204.

[79] See pp. 222–3 below.

[80] The identity of the three female figures on the long side of the tomb below the *tondi* is debated, but beneath the kline in the top part of the relief a child is posing as Hercules, and the nude Venus in a niche is also meant as a portrait. For a discussion, see esp. Wrede, *Consecratio*, 82–3; Sinn 'Personendarstellungen'; Sinn and Freyberger, *Grabdenkmäler II*, 51–9 pls. 11–16, 65.5, esp. pl. 14.1. The Haterii were not themselves imperial *liberti*, but were very close to the *familia caesaris* (see below). According to Wrede, *Consecratio*, 96, 277–8 no. 216 pl. 32.2, next in line is a Trajanic altar for an imperial *verna*. Yet it only depicts the bust of the boy and a detached caduceus in the background, so it is not a clear case of divine assimilation. The same is true for his nos. 217 and 218.

[81] Cf. above n. 10. The tomb also contained the portrait statue of a young man as a hunter, probably another son of Claudia Semne, although no divine attributes are preserved: Wrede, *Consecratio*, 84 pl. 40.2, 4; Hallett, *Roman Nude*, 212.

[82] Wrede, *Consecratio*, 97, 226 no. 91 pl. 12.2.

was unacceptable not only for other freedmen, but also for the first two orders.[83] What is more, despite their wealth and influence, these freedmen were deprived of the right to the formal honours that were so important to the status of individuals and families in society. Divine associations were arguably the highest, but at the same time least momentous honours that could be bestowed on anyone, and the range of connotations that came with portraits *in formam deorum* must have been just the kind of thing that appealed to them.

Contexts

It is often insinuated that all such portraits come from funerary contexts, and most of them in fact do. At the most basic level, they transferred yet another form of distinction from the domestic and public into the funerary realm. Similar to portraits without divine attributes, portraits *in formam deorum* were an honorific device that retrospectively reflected on qualities that the individuals displayed during their lifetime.[84] For most members of the metropolitan Roman sub-elite, who predominantly patronised these images, this was the only realm in which they could and would preserve their memory through monumental display. While the wealthier among them may occasionally also have received portrait honours in their houses, evidence from Pompeii and Herculaneum, as well as a review of known provenances of the portraits filling our museums, suggests that this was the exception rather than the rule.[85] However, portraits in divine costume painted on the walls of houses in Pompeii[86] indicate that such modes of representation did continue in the private realm, albeit in small numbers.

More importantly, there is also a notable number of statues from public spaces. These are certainly the closest to imperial statues in similar guises, which were not limited to sanctuaries but are also attested for theatres, baths, *fora* and other public locations.[87] At least eleven statues from Wrede's catalogue come from such spaces.[88] While most of them lack an inscription, it

---

[83] See above, Chapter 1.

[84] This is also clear from the rare epitaphs with divine address or comparison, which always refer to qualities demonstrated when still alive. We shall return to these in due course.

[85] On portraits from Pompeii, cf. Bonifacio (*Ritratti*), who rightly notes, however, that some portraits may have been removed after the earthquake of 62.

[86] For a critical review of examples, see Wrede, *Consecratio*, 181–3.

[87] For statues of empresses, see the statistics in Alexandridis, *Frauen*, 288–9 table 2.

[88] Wrede, *Consecratio*, 179, with nn. 1–4, nos. 3–4, 9, 43, 107–8, 198, 292, 307–8, the latter two may be imperial; the head of Hygieia, no. 163, does not belong. Wrede rightly notes that they potentially even received cult. Filges (*Standbilder*, 179–80) argues that private portraits in

is likely that the majority are intended to praise their subjects for some out-standing character traits or benefactions. For instance, the man assimilated to Aesculapius from the baths of Formia may have contributed in one way or another to the amenities these places offered, and was therefore praised for being as beneficial to the health of those using the baths as was the divinity.[89]

Others, again, may be equivalents of the Augustan deities discussed above. A statue from around 110–20 that was found in a sanctuary of Fortuna on the Quirinal Hill could be a case in point (Figure 4.15).[90] Its inscription reads *Fortunae sacrum | Claudiae Iustae* and depicts a female with oar and cornucopia with a portrait head. We know of tutelary Fortunas related to entire *gentes* or families, and also to individuals. They are either addressed as Fortuna Tutela[91] or they are combined with a personal name, as for instance in a dedication *Fortunae Tarruteniae Paulinae*.[92] As Carlo Visconti had already suggested, it is thus possible that we are not dealing here with a statue of Claudia *in formam deorum*, but with her personal deity Fortuna, who assumed the features of the women to whom she was particu-larly attached.[93] The same applies to an Antonine votive relief to Hercules

divine costume originate exclusively from funerary contexts, but his arguments do not stand up to testing. On Claudia Iusta, see n. 90 below; on the statue from Formia, see n. 89. There are some uncertainties around the find spots of some other female statues, but they do not suffice to support Filges' argument, and he does not discuss male statues. Cristina Murer is currently exploring the reuse of funerary statues in different contexts in late antiquity (see for the time being Murer, 'Reuse') and rightly warns against taking find spots too much at face value. Yet there is no need to assume that all portraits in divine costume from non-funerary contexts have been reused. The clearest case is the double portrait of a reclining couple that presents the man with a wreath of reeds in his hair and resting on the head of a water deity (Paris, Louvre MA 351: Wrede, *Consecratio*, 232–3 no. 106). There is no indication that the head has been reworked from a headrest; reeds in the hair of a diner on a kline sarcophagus lid would be unique and hard to explain; and the original bottom face of the sculpture is uneven, as if simulating undulating natural terrain.

[89] Wrede, *Consecratio*, no. 4; La Rocca et al. (eds.), *Ritratti*, 356 cat. 5.20.

[90] *CIL* 6.3679 (= 30873); Visconti, 'Culto della Fortuna'; Wrede, *Consecratio*, 233–4 no. 107 pls. 13.1, 3; Fittschen and Zanker, *Frauenporträts*, 56 cat. 73 pl. 91. Wrede's suggestion (pp. 101, 114) that Claudia was a priestess is without foundation. Similarly, Zanker (in Fittschen and Zanker, *Frauenporträts*, 56 cat. 73, who is tentative), Filges (*Standbilder*, 179–80) and Alexandridis (*Frauen*, 2 n. 19) believe that the statue was moved to the sanctuary from a tomb at a later stage, for which there is equally no evidence.

[91] E.g. *CIL* 6.177–9.

[92] Thomasetti (in *BCom* 1892, 355–6) cites as parallels Claudia Iusta and Claudia Semne. The dedication was inscribed on an architrave that must have belonged to an aedicula, which likely contained an image of the divinity. See also the dedication at Verona to one *thea Charis Bassaris* in memory of Avenia Bassaris, who was the freed *alumna* of an equestrian (*CIL* 5.3382; *IG* 14.2307; *CLE* 453, 1307; Wrede, *Consecratio*, 113, with a different approach).

[93] Cf. n. 90. Most modern scholars disagree, including Wrede, who thinks that it does not matter whether the statue honours the tutelary deity or Claudia Iusta. The position of the adjective

Figure 4.15 Statue of Fortuna from a sanctuary on the Quirinal Hill with the portrait head of Claudia Iusta, late Trajanic to early Hadrianic; Rome, Musei Capitolini, Galleria 58 inv. 933

Iulianus, Iupiter Caelius and the Genius of Mons Caelius (Figure 4.16).[94] While Iupiter and the Genius relate to the Caelian Hill, Hercules is related to a certain Iulianus, whose portrait features he assumed and who may have been the husband of Anna, the dedicator. A mid to late Antonine nude statue of Venus with the portrait head of a woman is inscribed *Veneri Felici Sacrum Sallustia Helpidus D.D.*[95] The dative case for the goddess and

sacrum would be a little odd for a dedication to Fortuna Claudia Iusta, but not an obstacle if we read *Claudiae Iustae* as a genitive. The alternative reading 'to sacred Fortuna and to Claudia Iusta' would, however, remain a possibility grammatically.

[94] *CIL* 6.334. Here *Iuliano* is dative and identifies the deity as Hercules Iulianus. Cf. Wrede, *Consecratio*, 125, 245 no. 133 with bibl., who thinks the relief refers to the emperor Didius Iulianus, which is hard to sustain for chronological and other reasons. See also Schraudolph, *Götterweihungen*, 209–10 G 23 pl. 23; Schultz (ed.), *Women*, 64–5; Fittschen and Zanker, *Kinderbildnisse*, 101–2 cat. 102 pl. 109; Fittschen, 'Il fenomeno', 293 cat. 4.37. *CIL* 6.645 has a Hercules Naevianus.

[95] *CIL* 6.782; Vatican City, Musei Vaticani, Cortile del Belvedere, inv. 936. See Wrede, *Consecratio*, 313–14 cat. 306, with bibl. and a different interpretation. If the portrait head of

Figure 4.16 Antonine votive relief to Hercules Iulianus, Iupiter Caelius, and the Genius of Mons Caelius; Rome, Musei Capitolini, Magazine 1264 (NCE 3022)

the nominative for Sallustia indicate that the dedication is by the latter to the former.[96] Since both images of the divinity and portrait statues of the dedicant could be set up as votives to the goddess, the identity of the statue is not entirely clear. Nevertheless, it is certainly possible that we are dealing with a similar case to the altar to Sol discussed above (Figure 4.14),[97] and that the deity is actually Venus Felix Sallustia; that is, the tutelary deity of the dedicant. The image fills in what the brevity of the inscription did not allow to be spelt out.[98] While, in all three cases, the alternative reading of

a statuette inscribed *Iunoni Fortun. Helitia* belongs to the statuette now connected with it, we may see here another case of personalised Fortuna (ibid., 234 no. 108).

[96] As noted by Koortbojian, *Divinization*, 89.

[97] See at n. 69.

[98] The same is potentially true for dedications to a divinity *in memoria* of a deceased. Yet, as the collection of evidence by Cesari, 'In memoriam', demonstrates, such dedications are almost completely absent from Rome and originate primarily in places where few if any theomorphic statues with portraits have been found. Moreover, many of them (including the few examples mentioned by Wrede, *Consecratio*, 188–9 nos. 2, 4–5, 7 and 190–1 nos. 2–8 and Koortbojian,

the mortal as divinity cannot be excluded on any formal grounds, the tradition of personalised tutelary deities suggests a similar reading of these dedications as well.

In none of these cases can we be sure that the individual linked with the tutelary deity was deceased, but they may well have been, as a commemorative foundation of 168 CE by a rich silk merchant and *accensus velatus* from Gabii, A. Plutius Epaphroditus, for Venus Vera Felix Gabina suggests.[99] The temple (*templum*) contained a bronze statue of Venus, four further *signa* (busts or statuettes?) set up in aediculae and an altar, all made of bronze. The interest from an endowment of 10,000 *sestertii* was to pay for a public meal to be held by the decurions, the *seviri Augustales* and the *tabernarii* of Gabii once a year on the birthday of his daughter, Plutia Vera. It is therefore normally thought that at least the statue of Venus would have featured the head of Plutia Vera. Slightly contradictorily, Wrede interpreted this foundation as a cult for the deceased in imitation of Hellenistic hero cults, while maintaining that it was not really a cult for the divine Plutia Vera, but an elaborate version of Roman meals celebrated on the festivals of the dead.[100] Others see here a cult for Vera more akin to divine cult, but Emily Hemelrijk has noted that the cult is in fact to Venus, to which Epaphroditus gave the name of his daughter,[101] and there can be little doubt that the divinity was conceived along the same lines as, and in imitation of, the Augustan deities and the tutelary deities mentioned above.

If this reading is accepted so far, the case demonstrates that personalised deities can be created after the individual they are related to had died. This may seem strange for a tutelary deity. After all, the individual is already dead. However, there are at least two possible ways of understanding these dedications, which are not mutually exclusive. On the one hand, it was hoped that the deceased would be watched over by the gods, or live in their vicinity.[102] This closeness to the divine was both a distinction and a guarantor of the deceased's eternally peaceful and undisturbed rest. While such hopes are expressed in epitaphs with reference to the gods in general, a personalised divinity may have appeared to some as particularly helpful

---

Divinization, 89) are dedicated to Augustan deities and would raise questions as to whether these should bear the features of the deceased or the empress or emperor (see below n. 381). For none of them is the actual statue preserved.

[99] Paris, Louvre MA 1564 (= *CIL* 14.2793); Wrede, *Consecratio*, 85–6; Rüpke, *Jupiter to Christ*, 27–33 with English translation. Cf. also Donahue, *Community*, 101, 235 D 304.

[100] Wrede, *Consecratio*, 86.

[101] Hemelrijk, *Hidden Lives*, 305 n. 101.

[102] Borg, 'Slumber', and below.

in achieving the goal. On the other hand, Wrede has pointed to texts that suggest that the deceased could watch over the life of their bereaved relatives or, through their more direct access to the gods, influence them to look favourably on their surviving loved ones.[103] Statius praises Priscilla for having conveyed on her husband the favour of Fortuna during her lifetime (*Silv.* 5.1.71–5),[104] and expects her to propitiate the Parces on his behalf after her death (*Silv.* 5.1.258–62). Charles King has shown that the power to prolong or improve the life of the survivors was often attributed to the *dii manes*, whose favours are sometimes asked for in epitaphs, including with reference to a single deceased individual (despite the plural term).[105] As Wrede noted, Venus Vera Felix Gabina shows features of a city-Tyche (cf. Venus Felix Pompeiana),[106] and the idea may well have been that the goddess would watch over the community because of her particular connection with, and possibly the influence of, the deceased girl.

Similar deities could also have featured in funerary contexts, where dedications to divinities that are not formally personalised are sometimes found.[107] Claudia Semne was presented in the guise of Fortuna and Spes, since she embodied hope and good fortune for her husband during her lifetime, and since he may have hoped that she could plead for the goddesses' favour on his behalf after death.[108] After all, the altar was dedicated to these very goddesses. Moreover, Claudia's name in the genitive could be read as referring not only to *memoria*, but also to Fortuna, Spes and Venus, thus creating three personalised divinities. Even though the tomb's *titulus* tells us that the statues depicted Claudia Semne *in formam deorum*, a reading of the actual statues as the goddesses Fortuna Claudia/Claudiae, Spes Claudia/Claudiae, and so forth, is certainly a possibility.

The case of Priscilla is equally ambiguous when Statius writes:

> mox in varias mutata novaris effigies: hoc aere Ceres, hoc lucida Cnosis, illo Maia luto, Venus hoc non improba saxo. accipiunt vultus non indignata decoros.
>
> Soon you are made anew into various semblance: here shines Ceres in bronze, here the Cnossian maid [i.e. Ariadne], in that clay is Maia [one

---

[103] Wrede, *Consecratio*, 99–100.

[104] Cf. for a similar claim *CIL* 14.357.29–39.

[105] King, 'Manes', 109–13. Cf. already Brelich, *Aspetti della morte*, 77.

[106] Wrede, *Consecratio*, 86.

[107] E.g. the dedication of a statue of Silvanus to the same god by Q. Haterius Tychicus and Q. Haterius Q.f. Crescens in the tomb (or precinct) of the Haterii: *AE* 1982, 78; Sinn and Freyberger, *Grabdenkmäler II*, 81–3 cat 11 pl. 31.

[108] Wrede, *Consecratio*, 99.

of the Pleiades and mother of Mercury], Venus (no wanton) in this stone. The deities accept your beauteous features without complaint. (*Silv.* 5.1.231–4, transl. Shackleton Bailey)

Statius first tells us that Priscilla is transformed into various images (note: not goddesses!), whose materiality is then clearly stated (bronze, terracotta, marble). The statues are therefore described as her portraits *in formam deorum*, as Claudia's were in her *titulus*. However, after listing them, Statius states that the deities accepted her features willingly, suggesting that we are seeing here the divinities rather than Priscilla.[109] Statius seems to sit deliberately on the fence between viewing these images as Priscilla with divine features and as the personalised goddesses. The altar of Aelia Procula, dedicated as it was to Diana and the memory of the deceased while depicting the goddess with her portrait (Figure 4.5), raises similar ambiguities.[110]

Did the Romans Believe in Human Divinity?

This takes us to the next, perhaps the most notorious, and notoriously difficult, question: on what fence were they sitting? Was it the fence between personalised divinity and panegyric praise of a mortal? Or between personalised divinity and divine mortal? Is it possible that the Romans *did* believe in their deified mortals? To the last two questions, the majority of scholars respond with 'no', sometimes emphatically so, sometimes more qualified. The very term 'believe' (or belief) has been challenged in relation to the ancient world as being anachronistic and Christianising.[111] Obviously, there is a danger of circular reasoning, depending on how we define the term 'belief'. When we imbue it with typically Christian elements, such as confession or the existence and internalisation of religious dogma, we will naturally not find it in pagan discourse.[112] This is not the place to review the changing concepts of 'belief', and the equally changing ways in which Greek and Latin terms conventionally translated as 'belief' or 'believe' were used. Yet the suggestion, advanced most forcefully and most influentially by Simon Price, that Greek and Roman religion had nothing to do with belief either in the (cognitive) sense of a conviction that the gods exist or a

---

[109]   Ditto Hallett, *Roman Nude*, 238, who misses the ambiguity created by the phrase preceding the list of statues, however.

[110]   Cf. at n. 12 above.

[111]   Most influentially by Needham, *Belief*, 14–39, 64–135; Price, *Rituals*, 10–11; followed by many others.

[112]   This is the argument of Price, *Rituals*, esp. 10–11, and Price, *Religions*.

personal relationship to them, and that it was only about its social dimension and the correct performance of ritual acts (ritualistic sense),[113] is hard to maintain. Henk Versnel has shown in detail that, at least after the mid-fifth century BCE, the Greek term νομίζειν in relation to the gods was not only used in the sense of 'to practise or observe as a custom or institution', but also in the sense of a conviction that the gods exist, an ambiguity that is best captured by the English term 'acknowledge'.[114] More recently, there seems to be a growing consensus that Greek and Roman religious cult at both public and private levels does not make any sense at all without a notion of belief as 'a conviction that an individual (or group of individuals) holds independently of the need for empirical support'[115] and, more specifically, the conviction that (the) gods exist, and are able to interact with humans.[116] Moreover, Gérard Freyburger, and especially Theresa Morgan in a recent study of the terms and concepts of *pistis* and *fides* in the Roman empire, have shown that these terms only rarely express belief that something is the case or exists ('cognitive belief' or what Morgan calls 'propositional belief'), but in the majority of cases express trust in the sense of a personal relationship with a human or god, and that, despite some individual scepticism, the gods are overwhelmingly characterised as trustworthy.[117] Accordingly, I feel justified in using, for heuristic reasons, the term 'belief' in the minimalist sense of the conviction that (the) gods exist, and that they have the power to interfere in human life.[118] Moreover, I would further maintain that Freyburger's and Morgan's research can encourage us to approach the concept with a positive prejudice, as it were, that this belief in the existence and power of the gods went along with a personal attitude of trust in the divine.

Explicitly or implicitly applying this concept of belief with regard to the immortal gods, scholars have still found different answers to our question. Wrede (so it seems), Bergmann, Hallett and many others have argued that divine assimilations, address and even cult are a metaphorical, and thus

---

[113] Price, *Rituals*; Price, *Religions*. See Bendlin, 'Religious pluralism', for a discussion of the history of this view of Roman religion.

[114] See Versnel, *Coping with the Gods*, 543–4, 555–8, drawing in particular on Fahr, *Theous nomizein*.

[115] King, 'Organization', 278; Versnel, *Coping with the Gods*, 547–8.

[116] King, 'Organization', passim, esp. 281. Versnel (*Coping with the Gods*, 539–59, with a review of the discussion) demonstrates that this is also the most fitting understanding of the Greek terms used (esp. θεοὺς νομίζειν and θεοὺς ἡγεῖσθαι). For Roman religion, see e.g. Bendlin, 'Religious pluralism'; Morgan, *Faith*; Champion, *Peace*, esp. ch. 1.

[117] Freyburger, *Fides*, 231–8, 282–98; Morgan, *Faith*, esp. chapters 2–4, and pp. 125–8 for a discussion of the ritualistic position.

[118] As Versnel reminds us, 'Scholarly discourse is always etic and should therefore be conducted in etic terms' (*Coping with the Gods*, 548, ditto 551).

rhetorical, device that does not imply 'true' divinity, but praises in hyperbolic terms qualities and/or achievements that an individual possessed or, especially in the case of rulers and emperors, was hoped to demonstrate in the future.[119] There can be no doubt that they were indeed used in this way, but whether this was all there was to it is questionable. For instance, when he praises Tiberius, Velleius Paterculus clearly distinguishes between the formal act of consecration and divine address on the one hand, and a genuine belief in Augustus' divinity on the other, thereby acknowledging the existence of both:

> Sacravit parentem suum Caesar non imperio, sed religione, non appellavit eum, sed fecit deum.

> Caesar deified his father, not by exercise of his imperial authority, but by his attitude of reverence [*religione*]; he did not call him a god, but made him one. (2.126.1, transl. F. W. Shipley)

A similar distinction is made by Pliny, who praises Trajan for having raised Nerva to the stars 'because you really believe him to be a god' (*quia deum credis*, *Pan*. 11.2). It is not relevant here whether the authors were correct, and not even whether they were themselves convinced of the accuracy of their claims. The point here is that these statements could only be meaningful if they were potentially correct. Both *religio* and *credere* presuppose belief, at least in the cognitive sense that the respective gods exist, but are here used to characterise a personal relationship of reverence between the emperor and the respective *divus*.[120]

Versnel has argued with regard to Hellenistic rulers that the entire notion of ruler cult would be pointless if it were not taken to be a *religious* act, and

---

[119] Wrede, *Consecratio*, passim, esp. 88–9; Bergmann, *Strahlen*, 16–39, 99–100, 227, 265–6, 289, and elsewhere; followed by Hallett, *Roman Nude*, 230–42, 259–62. See also D'Ambra ('Calculus'), who does not even discuss divinity but calls the Venus assimilations mythological, and Pollini (*Republic to Empire*, 382), who states categorically that divine honours are 'not the same as worshiping an individual as a living god'; cf. Koortbojian (*Divinization*, 4), who makes a similar claim (387–9, 407 n. 132), declaring that even the title Neos Dionysos etc. means '*like* a new Dionysus' (his emphasis); and most authors cited in n. 1 above. For private individuals see also Mayer, *Middle Classes*, 123; Kousser, 'Group portraits', 678.

[120] For the term *religio*, see Rüpke, 'Religio'; Rüpke, 'Religiöser Pluralismus', 332–6. I have not come across a similar discussion to Versnel's of the Latin term *credere*, and strangely recent introductions, handbooks and companions do not discuss religious terminology except for *religio*, and for Christian usage. However, see Morgan, *Faith*, esp. chapters 2–4, on non-Christian usage of the terms *pistis* and *fides*. Morgan also discusses several passages where the term *credere* is used in the sense of 'trust'/'accept as true', and concludes: '*Credere* and *fides* and cognates often occur in close conjunction in literary texts, with both sacred and secular meanings' (p. 144 n. 91), adding examples.

if people did not believe, at least in principle if not in every single case, that a human could be (or become) divine.[121] 'Believe', here, should again be read in the sense of trust in the divine human, or in the divinity of the human, which in turn is the basis for any further sacrifices and honours that are otherwise typical of the worship of the immortal gods. Similarly, Cicero's struggle with the divinity of mortals, so well analysed recently by Spencer Cole,[122] would be absurd had he not believed that divinity of humans was possible. In an age of galloping inflation in honours, had addressing Pompey, Caesar or any other contemporary as a god, or more specifically as Jupiter, been mere rhetoric, why should he have pondered so long over whether or not a specific individual deserved divine status, which form such divinity should take and how divinity could be brought about?

Gradel has proposed to solve the conundrum by expanding a suggestion already made by Arthur Darby Nock: that there was not really a clear divide between honour and worship, at least in actual practice.[123] While the nature or ontology of a being as human or divine was discussed in philosophical debate, in the practice of worship and cult it did not matter.[124] Divine cult was part of a reciprocal system, in which it was an honour offered to those who could or did benefit the worshipper;[125] it was *not* something owed to a god simply because he was divine in absolute terms. This explains the considerable fluctuation in the relevance of specific gods in official cult; it allowed for the choice of private individuals to worship whomever they wished; and it clarifies the lack of concern about all of this on the part of

---

[121] Versnel, *Coping with the Gods*, 465–92. That not everybody agreed with the alleged divinity of humans (see e.g. Lucan's cynical words on *manes* equipped with thunderbolts, rays and stars, and oaths being taken in temples before shades (*per umbras*): *Bellum Civile* 7.457; or Cicero's Cotta in *Nat. D.* 1.119) is therefore no argument against such a belief.

[122] Cole, *Cicero*.

[123] Nock, 'Synnaos theos', esp. 44–54. He further observed that the Greek word *time* covered both concepts, and that even in cases where statues of humans were set up inside temples, this would not necessarily imply their deification or a share in the cult. See Gradel, *Emperor Worship*, passim, esp. 3, 25–6, 29, 52; largely followed by Chalupa, 'Roman emperors'. For the problems this caused in the long term, see Elsner, 'Iconoclasm'.

[124] Gradel has often been misunderstood as ignoring the distinction made by some ancient authors between deified humans and the traditional gods, or of ontological differences between them. However, he merely considers them irrelevant for his analysis of daily practice, as is clear from his discussion, and especially from his treatment of the *Apokolokynthosis*: Gradel, *Emperor Worship*, 325–30. Peppel ('Gott oder Mensch') argues along the same line, but stresses that the criterion for accepting divinity was whether the individual concerned *acted* (or, in the case of *divi*, had acted) like a god. The distinction between philosophical thought that is interested in the absolute status or ontology of a being and religious practice in which the divinity is in the eye of the beholder, is also expressed by Clauss (*Herrscherkult*, 23), but not explored any further.

[125] Gradel, *Emperor Worship*, 15–16, 23–4.

the state and state priests, so long as none of the activity conflicted with the interests of the state.[126] It also explains why Augustus and the senate could accept local communities and private individuals hailing the emperor as a god. Like the private cult of a *paterfamilias*, it was a matter between the worshipper and the worshipped, but would not – at least in theory – impinge on that between the worshipped and the senate.

There were certainly differences between the traditional gods and divine mortals or divinised emperors, the most obvious (at least for non-Euhemerists) being the immortality of the former and the mortality of the latter. This difference was noted by authors such as Cicero (*Rep.* 2.19) and Varro (*Antiquitates* fr. 32 Cardauns), and was also expressed terminologically by a distinction between *divi* and *dii*.[127] Yet to conclude that for this reason divine mortals were not really believed to be gods presupposes criteria for divinity that are based either on Christian ideas or on a concept of divinity that arbitrarily favours classical (Athenian; Olympian) gods, while ignoring the extensive evidence, both written and practical, for a more inclusive concept of divinity.[128] The borderline between human and divine was always permeable.[129] Divine rulers, though potentially having a divine afterlife, were mortal, while the Olympians were not. However, so were Hercules and Romulus, both worshipped in many places as gods rather than heroes, with the full set of material and ritual honours also awarded to the Olympians. Ruler cult was more the norm than the exception since, within Graeco-Roman religious thinking, offering divine honours to a higher power, saviour or benefactor was a natural reaction.[130] As Versnel has argued, there is absolutely no reason why we should doubt the possibility that a human who was called a god, and honoured in exactly the same terms as traditional gods, was considered a god in all sincerity. Rather, the terminology used and the practices employed should, in adaptation of Andrew Erskine's claim, 'force us to reconsider our idea of what [Romans] meant by gods'.[131]

I have already noted the relational character of divine status. Divinity was, and was accepted to be, in the eye of the beholder,[132] and there is no

---

[126] Ibid., 75, 110.

[127] Price, 'Gods and emperors', 83–4; Gradel, *Emperor Worship*, 61–7, 265–6, for sources and the changing terminology.

[128] Erskine, 'Epilogue', 507–8. See also the texts of Cicero and Varro just cited.

[129] Beard et al., *Religions*, 140–9; above n. 47.

[130] Above at n. 47.

[131] Erskine, 'Epilogue', 508.

[132] This aspect is stressed throughout by Gradel, *Emperor Worship*, esp. 31–2, 46, 148, 267, 270. He has been criticised for this, but the arguments do not stand up to test. For instance,

divinity without human recognition of it. In a world where any strongly felt power could be perceived as divine,[133] we should not be surprised at manifestations or statements of divinity resulting from ad hoc experience or strong emotion. The Hymn to Demetrius Polyorketes, hailed as a saviour god at his entry into Athens, is a good example,[134] as is Cicero's address to Lentulus. When the Acts of the Apostles report that Paul and Barnabas were hailed as Zeus and Hermes after healing a lame person (14.11), there is no indication in the text that this was mere rhetoric, but the event is described like an epiphany to the Lycaonians, to whom the divinity of the apostles is revealed through their benefaction.[135] The Acts of John (29) tell us that, when the saint resurrected Lycomedes and his wife from death, Lycomedes immediately had an image made of his benefactor and worshipped it in secrecy. Divinity is bestowed on those whose benefactions were perceived as comparable to those of the traditional gods – in fact, the Athenians thought that Demetrius was even better than the Olympians as he was actually listening to their prayers.

What seems to have shifted, however, is the magnitude of the benefaction that triggered this sense of divinity. For Marius Gratidianus it sufficed that he was credited (wrongly, as it happened) with beneficial currency reforms.[136] Lentulus owed his title of *deus* to helping Cicero to return from exile.[137] When Cicero endeavoured to deify Tullia, salvation was no longer a prerequisite. The impulse to deify his beloved daughter was triggered by her death, which made him realise her superior character and the benefactions she had granted him when still alive.[138] Where women and children are

---

the fact that there were clear regulations about auspices and sacrifices (cf. e.g. Koortbojian, *Divinization*, 24 with n. 28) only reflects which gods the *state* chose to accept as such, but not who everyone else had to see as a god, or indeed which beings were gods ontologically.

[133] See, for instance, Balbus' explanation in Cicero's *De natura deorum* 261: *tum autem res ipsa, in qua vis inest maior aliqua, sic appellatur ut ea ipsa vis nominetur deus ... quarum omnium rerum quia vis erat tanta ut sine deo regi non posset, ipsa res deorum nomen optinuit* ('And when there is a concept which embodies a greater force, then this very force is deemed a god ... The force of each of these things was so great that it could only have been controlled by a god, and the concept itself took the title of a god'; transl. Cole).

[134] See Versnel, *Coping with the Gods*, 444–56, for a lucid analysis and further bibl., and the rest of his chapter.

[135] The episode is frequently quoted, albeit sometimes with a slightly different spin, e.g. Gradel, *Emperor Worship*, 19; Erskine, 'Epilogue', 510; Versnel, *Coping with the Gods*, 23–4, 42–3. Cf. also Irenaeus, *Against Heresies* 1.23.4, where Simon Magus and his consort are being worshipped in the guise of Jupiter and Minerva.

[136] See n. 35 above.

[137] See n. 38 above.

[138] Her learnedness is stressed in Cicero's *Consolatio* to himself, which is preserved in Lactantius, *Div. inst.* 1.15.19–20, where she is called *optima* and *doctissima*. Cf. Cole, *Cicero*, 1.

hailed as divine in epitaphs, the fact that they are divinities *in the eyes of their commemorators* is also often made explicit. For instance, three-year-old Anulina is called *mea divina*.[139] Another husband dedicated an epitaph *deae sanctae meae Primillae* ('to my holy goddess Primilla');[140] she may have won this praise by having lived with him *sine querella* for thirty years.[141] In a metric epitaph, the imperial slave and dispensator of Moesia inferior, Fronto, calls his wife Aelia, *Lar mihi haec quondam, haec spes/Spes, haec unica vita* ('My Lar, my hope/Hope, my only life'), going on to specify her exemplary qualities.[142]

Considering that, in actual practice, divinity was always relational, and that it was unconcerned with absolute categories or ontology, can we exclude that these deceased were 'real' divinities, at least were so to their fathers or husbands? The philosophically minded may object that this is to ignore the fact that questions of ontology were indeed asked. Yet is philosophical thought the *true* representation of ancient religion merely by virtue of being the more reflective and sophisticated engagement with the subject? Is the only way out of the dilemma to claim that Roman religion was ultimately not a religion that had anything to do with belief or personal piety? Or should we rather concede that divine cult of mortals – be it before or after their death – was simply part of Roman religion? That it included belief in mortals' divinity? And that we need to abandon our own preconceptions of what the gods are in favour of what the *Romans* tell us they are, through words and cult practice?

This leads me to my final question in this section.

Did Theomorphic Portraits of Private Individuals Indicate Divine Status?

The answer does not flow directly from the one just reached, since there can hardly be any doubt that divine attributes and costumes could be used in a merely rhetorical fashion. This is implied by the passages cited above, as well as by poetry where not only the emperor and other powerful people

---

[139] *CIL* 6.12087 (p. 3510): Bechtold, *Gott und Gestirn*, 385 n. 1668, 397 table 3 no. 75, 407.

[140] *CIL* 6.7581.

[141] Cf. Conze, *Beschreibung*, 463 cat. 1204 with drawing; Cole, *Cicero*, 2 n. 1.

[142] *CIL* 3.754; add. p. 992; *CE* 492. For a corrected reading, German translation and commentary see Krummrey, 'Grabgedicht'; also quoted by Wrede, *Consecratio*, 111, but with a different spin. Note that in epigraphic texts the distinction between the abstract and the deity cannot be made, and may not have been intended. For further examples and comment see below. Cf. also the fragmentary *CIL* 6.15696, and further examples from different regions in Cesari, 'In memoriam', 962 n. 30.

are addressed as gods, but also and especially the poets' lovers.[143] Some inscriptions even suggest that a divine name could be a kind of nickname or term of endearment. A remarkable set of commemorative inscriptions on now-lost *cippi* (apparently all statue bases) was set up by Aurelia Aoteris and Mussius Chrysonicus, who designate themselves *nutritores lactanei*, and were obviously nurses for children of high status. One was dedicated *Meropi Helladi Q. Licinio Q. filio Floro Octaviano*, who was *eques romanus*; the other, almost identical one, *Meropi Helladi Liciniae Q. f. Lampetiae Basilioflorae*, probably the sister of the equestrian.[144] A third was dedicated *Glaucopi Veneri Gelliae Agrippinane c(larissimae) p(uellae)*.[145] Given that the names in the first two dedications are clearly nicknames playing on Homeric language, Glaucopis Venus, like the others significantly written above the actual inscription field and equally starting with a Homeric idiom, must be a *signum* as well.[146]

It is perhaps also doubtful that Augustus attached any divinity to his statue of Caius as Cupid, or that those who assimilated little boys and babies to Amor or baby Hercules (Figure 4.2 above) did so either. The lid of a cinerary urn of the later second century depicts a reclining woman, but was dedicated by Aurelia Vitalis 'to the Cupid of his grandmother' (*cupidini abiae*). Here, her address of her grandchild as Cupid equally sounds like a term of endearment.[147]

Wrede and others have further used cases where an individual was assimilated to several different divinities in the same context, or even

---

[143] Lieberg, *Puella divina*. On poetic acclamations, see also Möller, *Götterattribute*. However, Lieberg rightly points out that some love poetry, and that of Catullus in particular, attests to deep religious feelings triggered by the power of love.

[144] *CIL* 6.1623 (p. 31833): Santolini Giordani, *Antichità*, 163 no. 134; and *CIL* 6.21334: ibid., 192 no. 271 pl. 45.

[145] *CIL* 6.1424, pp. 3163, 4721, 4789. *Glaukopis* is a common Homeric epithet of Athena. The monument is without provenance, but may have been found, like the other two, in the Vigna Casali. I am grateful to Karen Nì Mheallaigh for discussing these with me.

[146] Cf. Kajanto, *Supernomina*, 51, 75, 83, 85. See also e.g. Wuilleumier, 'Signa', 613–4; Bradley, 'Wet-nursing', 214; Wrede, *Consecratio*, 136 n. 101, 187 no. 2, for a different interpretation. It should be noted that there is no clear indication that the three are already dead, although the find spot suggests a funerary context.

[147] *CIL* 6.5314; Wrede, 'Klinentypus', 421–2; Sinn, *Marmorurnen*, 256, no. 682; Taglietti, 'Un'importatrice', 550–1 no. IX, 12. Wrede (*Consecratio*, 100–1) points to the occasional coincidence of personal names with the divinities to which individuals were assimilated (see also examples ibid., 113–14). Rather than seeing them as an expression of 'classical education' (like Wrede does) and considering that the names were often given to slaves by their masters, I prefer to see them as a good omen for the character and achievements they hoped they would display. An assimilation to the divinities after whom they were named would thus only confirm that they lived up to those expectations, and not necessarily give away anything about potential divinity.

accumulated attributes of more than one deity in a single image, in support of a merely metaphorical interpretation of such devices.[148] The argument is not fully conclusive, however, since 'different' Olympian deities can also be claimed to be one and the same. Varro (*Ling.* 5.68–9), for instance, equates Luna, Diana, Juno Lucina and Proserpina to express different facets, faculties or competencies of a single divinity.[149] The same principle applies in cases of multiple divine associations of humans. With regard to similar accumulations in the praise of Hellenistic rulers, Henk Versnel's lucid analysis of the hymn to Demetrios Polyorketes is worth quoting more fully:

> [I]f taken literally – and hence scrutinised in terms of its (mythological) coherence, implications and consequences – the hymn [as well as Varro's deity] would convey a desperately chaotic and inconsistent picture … They [i.e. the different associations] are hints, flashes, evoking temporary roles, and thus metaphorically prompting different qualities and virtues of the object of praise. Each *virtue* can – and should – be stored in the mind of the reader (or singer) in order to be accumulated into an all-encompassing image of bliss, whereas each individual *role*, after having delivered its message, can – and must – be discarded, to make place for the next one. Viewed together – all remaining active in the consciousness of the reader – the roles would yield a mess. Taken successively, hence separately, they yield a mess*age*.[150]

As Marianne Bergmann has observed, the accumulation of attributes from different deities in the images of Hellenistic rulers are the visual equivalent of these multiple acclamations,[151] and so it is for Roman portraits (see Figures 4.6 and 4.9 above).[152] We are obviously dealing here with a visual language that accumulates comments on the individual concerned. This may also best explain why matrons with the nude bodies of Venuses (Figure 4.3)

---

[148] Wrede, *Consecratio*, 88; ditto e.g. Filges, *Standbilder*, 179; Hallett, *Roman Nude*, esp. 231–2, 237, and 262–3.

[149] Cf. King, 'Organization', 292–7. King proposes to call this concept of divinity 'polymorphism', rightly criticising that the more conventional term 'polyonymy' does not sufficiently express the multiplicity of character traits (identities) rather than just names, signalled by the equations.

[150] Versnel, *Coping with the Gods*, 444–56 on Athenaeus 253F with ample bibl., quotation on p. 454 (italics in original, additions in square brackets mine).

[151] Cf. Bergmann, *Strahlen*, 25–33, and 19–23, 34–8, on the iconography of such images; Svenson, *Darstellungen*, for a catalogue of examples.

[152] E.g. Florence, Mus. Arch. 13834, fitted out with moon sickle, sun disc, ears of corn and cornucopia (Wrede, *Consecratio*, 256 cat. 165: Isis-Fortuna). Cf. Livia on a cameo showing her as priestess of her late husband with the attributes of Ceres and Cybele (here Figure 4.9 and Hallett, *Roman Nude*, 227, 236–7 with fig. 134). Note also the vestal virgin with a mural crown typical, not of Vesta, but of Cybele and city goddesses: Wrede, *Consecratio*, 221 cat. 80 pls. 9.1–2; Mekacher, *Vestalische Jungfrauen*, 216 cat. P4 figs. 68 and 70.

did not cause the embarrassment that arises in the modern viewer. We tend to look at a portrait as a faithful (albeit perhaps slightly improved) representation of the sitter, and thus see the nude body as that of the matron. Yet the nude bodies of Roman portraits were a visual sign standing in for a more general claim. It has often been observed that the body types used for portraits in divine costume were taken over from famous Greek statues of divinities and, where this has not simply been put down to the alleged Roman failure to create original art, scholars have mostly pointed to the aspect of *paideia*: patrons wanted to demonstrate their knowledge and appreciation of Greek masterpieces. Nevertheless, more may be at stake here. By choosing a body type taken from a divine statue that everyone would recognise, and that would be repeated for different private individuals, any sense that we may gaze at the 'real' nude body of these persons was strongly undermined. Interestingly, in the case of both Claudia Semne and Priscilla, the materiality of their images in divine costume is explicitly stressed, making them *representations* of some intangible truth; and it is surely no coincidence that even in funerary reliefs, the deceased *in formam deorum* are predominantly depicted as statues or busts; that is, in a way more removed from 'reality' than any statue inevitably is (Figure 4.5).[153] In and of themselves, divine attributes and bodies are visual signs that specify the subject's relevant character traits in kind and in measure; whether this amounts to a perception of these individuals as divine (as often was the case with Hellenistic rulers, including Demetrios Polyorketes) or simply as possessing some superhuman features is up to the individual beholder.

It has also often been observed that, in contrast to Republican and imperial habits, portraits *in formam deorum* of private individuals are largely restricted to women, adolescents and children.[154] It is obvious that they could not boast the same achievements or positions of power that instilled the desire to deify saviours and benefactors. Do we have to conclude from

---

[153] For this observation, see D'Ambra, 'Daughters', 173, on Aelia Procula. On the phenomenon in general see Stewart (*Statues*, 99–103), who stressed, however, their function as a substitute for public honours.

[154] Wrede (*Consecratio*, 87, 108) explained the preponderance as a compensation for more tangible praise of men with formal achievements. Ditto Bergmann, *Strahlen*, 39, and others. However, given that most epitaphs for sub-elite men do not refer to any formal achievements either (such as success in their trade or occupation, which must have generated the funds for the monument in the first place: Huttunen, *Strata*, 48; Joshel, *Occupational Inscriptions*, 16), more must be at stake here. Fabricius ('Grenzziehungen', 74–80) suggests that the preponderance is due to an attempt to ban women from a display of public status by using images that belong to the realm of *otium* and Greek education. Yet, in contrast to our images, the potential anxieties regarding the power of women only refer to the political elite, and to the late Republic and Julio-Claudian age, and they do not explain the choices for children and adolescents.

this that, in all these cases, we are really looking at a sentimental reaction to their death that must not be taken too seriously?

I would argue that, against the background of what I established before about the possibility of divine mortals, the answer is not quite as straightforward as scholars have suggested. Considering that women and the prematurely deceased are also those whose death is presented in all sources as particularly tragic and lamentable, there surely was a strong emotional component involved.[155] Yet, given that the hailing of a human being as a divinity had always expressed a relationship between the honorand and honoree, and that it was often eminently situational, emotion was also invariably involved.[156] This was particularly obvious in Cicero's address of Lentulus as a god, and in his reaction to his daughter Tullia's death. Overwhelmed by his love and sense of loss, he praised her qualities as quasi-divine and wanted to establish a *fanum* for her, a term used for a wide spectrum of sacred spaces and sanctuaries, 'in order to achieve *apotheosis*, as far as may be' (Cicero, *Att.* 12.36.1).[157] He never actually called her a divinity, and the qualification that he wanted to achieve apotheosis *as far as may be* demonstrates his own uncertainty around her deification. However, the struggle to find the right way to achieve his aim is not too dissimilar to his struggle to find the right way to deify the *viri boni*, and that he desired to deify his daughter in all earnestness is obvious from his letters to Atticus and his *Consolatio*. We may therefore suspect that, had he lived 150 years later, when the imperial model had established ways of achieving apotheosis, he would have done exactly what our private patrons have done.

A second aspect also needs consideration. After the establishment of the principate, there was always a danger in appearing to challenge the emperor, and we shall come back to this aspect at the end of this chapter. The very fact that Augustus felt it necessary to abstain from putting up images of himself in divine costume in public spaces like the Forum (thus abandoning his earlier attitude as *triumvir*!) should warn us against rushing to conclusions about divine attributes always being a merely metaphorical and, by implication, fairly meaningless device.[158] The first to be more daring

---

[155] Ditto Wrede (*Consecratio*, 108–9), who thinks, however, that this was a reaction specific to freedmen, whose future depended so much on their offspring, and whose new status included most notably a legal family.

[156] Scheid (*Dieux*, 175–82) is a rare scholar acknowledging emotion in Roman cult, but only as a reaction to it, not as its cause.

[157] Cf. more generally Cicero, *Att.* 12.12, 36, 37.4; Cole, *Cicero*, 1–7, 139–40. On the locality and possible shape of an aedicula, see Griesbach, *Villen und Gräber*, 28–30.

[158] Ditto Alexandridis, *Frauen*, 3. Koortbojian (*Divinization*, 207) in fact observes that not a single nude or hip-mantle statue of a living Julio-Claudian emperor was set up by the *SPQR*.

in their self-aggrandisement were the imperial freedmen. As we have seen, they started the trend of using portraits *in formam deorum* in imitation of the imperial family, and the general pattern of the popularity of specific types of divine assimilations continued to follow the imperial one. At that time, however, the preferences for using such images among the imperial family had diverged from those of the late Republican period. On coins and in statue monuments, *the* format for the emperor had become the Jupiter scheme, an obvious choice given his role as ruler of the empire. This assimilation was hardly acceptable for private individuals.[159] For the early decades of private images in divine costume, there was not only a very limited range of male imperial models potentially to imitate, but such imitation, and especially the primary model of Jupiter, may have been a step too far even for the daring.

Only nine images in the round of adult men in divine costume feature in Wrede's catalogue. Of these, two are in the guise of water divinities and were set up in baths outside of Rome;[160] two are in the guise of Hercules (Figure 4.17);[161] and five depict their subjects as Mars.[162] These portraits all date to a relatively late period, when restraints on the self-display of

---

[159] Ditto Hallett (*Roman Nude*, 259–60), who stresses that the Jupiter image encompassed all the elements of pragmatic and charismatic rulership in itself. The seated hip-mantle statue of the adolescent Valerianus Frater at Rosellae is the only exception, even though the Jupiter pose may have been toned down by a lowered left arm (thus Liverani, 'Iconografia imperiale', 162; cf. ibid., passim, and Lo Monaco, 'Immagini private', 342–3 with fig. 7). Liverani ('Iconografia imperiale', 169–70), followed by Hallett (*Roman Nude*, 187–8), argues that the Jupiter pose had become very rare for emperors by the second century and that, at the time, Valerianus would have been assimilated not primarily to Jupiter but to the emperor, and not in such a way as to claim social equality, but to claim a similar position at Rosellae as the emperor had in the Roman empire. While this is surely true, it can hardly take much away from the fact that the assimilation is extraordinarily ambitious. See also the altar mentioned at n. 78, which shows on the front L. Marcius Anicetus and his wife and former *liberta* Marcia Helpis reclining on a kline, while the sides depict the statues of Jupiter and Juno. Wrede claims that Jupiter and Juno represent the deceased, who were simply too shy to give them their features. This is highly likely when we understand this 'shyness' as hesitation to compete with the emperors. A relief representation of the wife of a freedman of Marcus Aurelius as Juno (Wrede, 'Grabtempel', 418 pls. 135.2–3; Wrede, *Consecratio*, 258 cat. 168) was more daring, albeit adhering to a small format and coming from Tebessa in Libya. The identity of an over-life-size statue as Juno from Ostia (Vatican, Mus. Greg. Prof. no. 979 inv. 10784) is debated (ibid., 257 n. 17: unidentified member of the imperial family; Mikocki, *Sub specie Deae*, 193 cat. 289 pl. 18: Marciana?; Alexandridis, *Frauen*, 93 n. 889, 215 § 1.2.18: private portrait).

[160] Wrede, *Consecratio*, cat. 43 and 106.

[161] Ibid., cat. 122 and 126.

[162] Ibid., cat. 193–5, 197–8. For the third-century private portrait from the Esquiline, see also La Rocca et al. (eds.), *Ritratti*, 354–5 cat. 5.19, who reject the previous identification with an emperor that is suggested, however, by the find spot.

private individuals in the funerary realm had relaxed somewhat.[163] Yet in the second century, new imperial models had also been introduced whose imitation was less of a challenge to the emperor. Assimilations to water divinities are unparalleled in imperial portraiture, and were surely unproblematic. As far as we can tell, Hadrian was the first to be presented in the guise of Mars, in his statue in the Capitoline.[164] Most influentially, Mars was also part of a famous statue group with Venus, a copy of which featured in the Forum of Augustus, which gained new relevance in the Antonine period, as its depiction on coins and medallions demonstrates (Figure 4.18).[165] This group was imitated by private individuals at least four times (Figure 4.19).[166] Whatever the precise meaning of the model had been,[167] the group clearly had overtones of praise for the man's *virtus*, the woman's beauty and fertility, and the couple's love and *concordia*, virtues that we find being praised in other media as well. These were not exclusive to the emperor, and could thus be imitated without much risk.

---

[163] Leaving aside the somewhat enigmatic and unusual context from Pompeii (above n. 71), only one 'Hercules' and one 'Mars' possibly predate the Antonine period: Wrede, *Consecratio*, cat. 122 and 193.

[164] Fittschen and Zanker, *Kaiser- und Prinzenbildnisse*, 48–9 cat. 48 pl. 53; La Rocca et al. (eds.), *Ritratti*, 326–7 cat. 5.10.

[165] For the statue group from the Forum of Augustus, which is highly unlikely to have featured portrait heads, see Kousser ('Group portraits', 681–4 with fig. 13), who argues for an Augustan date. For the coin images, see Kleiner, 'Portraiture', 533; Kousser, 'Group portraits', 675 with n. 13 and fig. 2.

[166] Of these, Wrede lists only two: *Consecratio*, 133–4, 268–70 cat. 194–5. He unconvincingly identifies the well-preserved group in the Museo delle Terme in Rome as depicting Commodus and Faustina Minor (ibid., 133–4), and misses the fragments of a group found in a late antique house: cf. Kousser, 'Group portraits', 673 with n. 6. On the statues and Mars-Venus images on reliefs, see also Kleiner ('Portraiture'), who offers some untenable identifications. On the Capitoline group from Ostia, see La Rocca et al. (*Ritratti*, 352–3 cat. 5.18 with bibl.), to which add Alexandridis (*Frauen*, 87, 194 cat. 203 pl. 44.3), who thinks that the group is imperial.

[167] There is an ongoing debate about whether or not one or more of the three well-preserved statue groups shows an imperial couple (cf. previous note), but Kousser ('Group portraits') is probably right in rejecting all of them. She also points out that the statue group representing the *concordia* of Marcus Aurelius and Faustina Minor, in front of which newly wedded couples had to sacrifice, depicted their subjects in the *dextrarum iunctio* scheme (ibid., 675; cf. esp. Reinsberg, *Vita-Romana-Sarkophage*, 82–4). However, given the chronological coincidence, I consider it still possible that the Ares–Aphrodite group meant to express the same idea, and that an imperial model triggered its remarkable but short-lived popularity among private individuals; in any case, there can be no doubt about the group's imperial acclaim. Kousser's suggestion to think of such images also under the aspect of theatrical performances that may have encouraged such role playing (ibid., 686–9) is certainly worth considering for the phenomenon of portraits *in formam deorum* in general, albeit not in the present study. Nevertheless, it cannot fully explain the specific statue groups here under consideration.

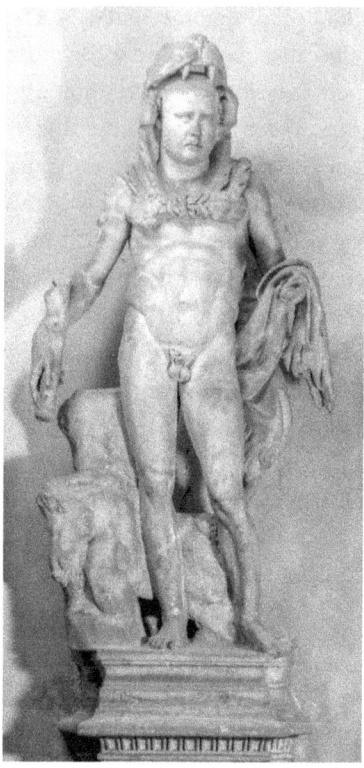

Figure 4.17 Statue of a man as Hercules from around 230 CE; Rome, Palazzo Barberini

Figure 4.18 *As* of Faustina Minor illustrating a statue group of Venus and Mars on the reverse; Berlin, Staatliche Museen, Münzkabinett AM-011/011

Figure 4.19 Antonine statue group portraying a couple as Mars and Venus; Paris, Louvre MA 1009

The same applies to assimilations to Hercules (Figure 4.17).[168] Although the first secure images of an emperor as Hercules appear under Commodus, Nero and, especially, Domitian had already styled themselves as Hercules.[169]

---

[168] See n. 161.

[169] The most famous example of an emperor as Hercules is the bust of Commodus in the Capitoline Museum (Fittschen and Zanker, *Kaiser- und Prinzenbildnisse*, 85–90 cat. 78 pls. 91–4), but also note that he was depicted as Hercules on coins (Bergmann, *Strahlen*, 199 pl.

Again, the assimilation did not evoke the same associations as the Jupiter image, and will have been acceptable for the use of private individuals for that reason.

Imperial women, in contrast, were depicted in a far greater variety of assimilations than the emperor.[170] Beauty, fecundity, fortune and all the other virtues for which the divinities and their assimilation stood were anything but exclusive to the imperial family, but rather guiding ethical norms for women and girls in general. Moreover, the rarity of their divine worship in the West and simultaneous frequency of their images *in formam deorum* may suggest that, in contrast to the emperor as Jupiter, they may not necessarily have been associated with outright divinity in the same way as their husbands. And divine assimilations of children and adolescents could hardly be seen as a direct challenge to the imperial offspring. An important factor in the preponderance of women, children and adolescents among portraits *in formam deorum* will therefore have been the intention to imitate an imperial model, but without overstepping the – constantly moving and renegotiated – borderline between this *aemulatio* and blatant *hybris*. Yet the very fact that divine associations were so sensitive demonstrates that, as in the case of their imperial model, they were at least potentially an indication of their subject's divinity.

Preliminary Conclusions

I hope to have shown in this first part of the chapter that, first, when private individuals started to use portraits in divine costume, they were adopting a Roman habit rather than a Greek one, a habit that had emerged in the Republican period and was well established in imperial iconography, from where it was taken up by private individuals under the Flavians. Secondly, such portraits could feature in a range of different contexts, private houses, public spaces and in the funerary realm, where they were most popular. For the sub-elite, this was the primary context where they could express their pride and forge a monument for commemoration by later generations that imitated imperial distinctions. In all these contexts, the visual strategy of assimilating a mortal to a divinity was meant to express that this mortal possessed character traits that exceeded ordinary human measure, and to

---

37.5). For Hercules as exemplar in Rome, see Ritter, *Hercules*; Rawlings, 'Hannibal'; Hekster, 'Hercules'; Rees, 'Names'.

[170] For imperial women, see esp. Mikocki, *Sub specie Deae*, with Alexandridis, 'Review'; Alexandridis, *Frauen*, 82–95. To my knowledge, there is no special study of imperial children in divine guise, but for princes in general, see Fittschen and Zanker, *Kaiser- und Prinzenbildnisse*; Fittschen, *Prinzenbildnisse*.

specify which character traits they were. I have further argued that the same visual strategy could be applied to statues of personalised divinities, who were assimilated to their protégés. I have argued, thirdly, that the Romans *did* believe in the divinity of mortals if we accept that their concept of divinity was more fluid and flexible than is often proposed. To them, divinity was not ontological but relational, and often situational. Divine acclamation and cult were the honours paid to a superior being that, at least outside the philosophical realm, really only became a divinity through human acknowledgement of the fact. It is therefore no contradiction when the sources tell us that emperors or the senate *made* someone a god, and at the same time insist that one could also *believe* in him. By extension, the same possibilities must be granted to ordinary people, who were not to become gods of the state, but nevertheless divinities in the eyes of a narrower group of beholders. Finally, I have argued that theomorphic portraits could function as an expression of such divinity.

Where do all these conditionals leave us with individual statues? As my chapter title suggests, it leaves us on the borderline. While the basic understanding is the visual panegyric, the praise of the subject's extraordinary character by virtue of mixing human and divine features, such images always played on the potential oscillation between human and divine: between human, human with divine qualities, deified human and personalised divinity. We have seen Statius doing precisely this with Priscilla's images. Or have we? An epigram from the *Greek Anthology* (*Anth. Pal.* 16.68 = Asclep. 39 HE), tentatively ascribed to either Asclepiades or Posidippus, muses:

> This is the portrait [*eikon*] of Cypris. – Come on, let's make sure it isn't Berenice's. I'm in two minds as to which of the two one should say it's more like. (transl. G. Zanker)

Temple Tombs

As noted above, funerary statues *in formam deorum* have often been closely connected with temple tombs. For Wrede, the latter are the ultimate proof that apotheosis was the aim of many Romans, and that the statues within them, while being merely metaphorical in themselves, hinted at the afterlife their subjects were going to enjoy thanks to their exemplary character. Temple tombs have been discussed on occasion since then, but these discussions have been rife with difficulties, ranging, again, from terminological ones to their origins and meaning. Let us start with terminology.[171]

---

[171] For a number of suggestions, cf. Griesbach, *Villen und Gräber*, 30–43, and the following.

Terminology and the Tomb of Claudia Semne

For Wrede, the mausoleum of Claudia Semne and its contents have been the single most important source material for this question.[172] As its *titulus* informs us, the tomb complex comprised the actual tomb building and a small garden with a well, vines, *tricliae* (arbours) and Claudia's portraits *in formam deorum*.[173] However, given its excavation in the late eighteenth century, many details of what the tomb looked like remain unknown. Laura Bignamini and Amanda Claride have reviewed the available evidence and located the tomb in the triangular plot between via Appia Antica and via Appia Pignatelli.[174] They also identified a tomb from this area depicted in several of Carlo Labruzzo's drawings and etchings as that of Claudia. If this identification is correct, the mausoleum itself consisted of a larger central burial chamber with aediculae and niches, in which Claudia's lost kline portrait would have featured, flanked by two small recesses, of which at least the left one was fitted out with niches for urns or *ollae*. At least the two lateral spaces do not seem to have been closed off by doors, and all three opened onto a vaulted space in front, the extension of which remains unclear.[175] Yet, however we may complete its design, the tomb does not match any known type of temple.[176] An inscribed architrave and a pediment showing Claudia in the guise of Venus are elements that also feature in temple architecture, but they are much shorter than the tomb's façade and may at best have adorned the space over its door, making it look like another aedicula.[177] There are reasons to doubt that the tomb in Labruzzi's illustrations is that of Claudia Semne, which cannot be discussed here in any detail.[178] Yet even

---

[172] Wrede, 'Claudia Semne'; Wrede, 'Grabtempel'; Wrede, *Consecratio*, 83–5.

[173] *CIL* 6.15593.

[174] Bignamini and Claridge, 'Claudia Semne'.

[175] Ibid., 229–30 fig. 10, suggest that this frontal space was an approximately square chamber of 6–7 m, and that its floor was at a higher level than that of the burial chambers, which were semi-interred. However, none of the drawings or etchings offers any indication of the depth of the front structure, nor of its floor level. The second storey suggested in the reconstruction is only justified by the unusually low vault, which in turn is entirely dependent on the assumed floor level. The reconstructed floorplan offered in Bignamini and Claridge's fig. 10 is without any parallel. I consider it more likely that the floor level was the same for all elements of the tomb, and that the structure in front of the tomb chambers was a kind of loggia, such as the one in the Hypogeum of the Flavii (Borg, *Crisis and Ambition*, 215–18 figs. 127–30, with further bibl.) opening onto a garden, or an antechamber of limited depth. For a main tomb chamber flanked by open *alae*, see Isola Sacra Tomb 75–76, discussed in Chapter 3.

[176] Cf. esp. Kammerer-Grothaus ('Gräberstrassen'), who noted the great similarity between Labruzzi's tomb Mausoleum 11 underneath S. Sebastiano, to which 'Mausoleum' 12 actually formed a vestibule.

[177] Bignamini and Claridge, 'Claudia Semne', 229, 242, with table 1 nos. 2 and 3.

[178] Amanda Claridge kindly confirmed to me that none of Labruzzi's close-ups of the tomb is labelled as that of Claudia Semne, and there are also doubts as to the location of the excavations depicted.

assuming that they show a different tomb and that our reconstruction can rely only on the preserved marble fragments, the lengths of Claudia's architrave and pediment, 2.3 m and 2.2 m, respectively, demonstrate that they must have belonged to an aedicula structure or framed door, but did not extend to the width of a façade belonging to a structure that would be comparable to a temple.[179] The tomb thus featured some elements of sacred architecture, but did not resemble a typical Roman podium temple. It is therefore misleading when Claudia's tomb is mentioned in the same breath as that on the famous Haterii relief (Figure 4.20), as is frequently done,[180] since there is no evidence for any of the key features of that mausoleum, such as columns or a wide pediment spanning the entire façade.

Once again, Wrede is more cautious than some of his followers when he insists that, per ancient terminology, it was ultimately the use of a building that determined whether it was a temple or sanctuary.[181] However, as he himself observed, there is no evidence for any cult in his temple tombs that would differ from traditional funerary cult.[182] From this point of view, either all or no tombs should be called temple tombs. To be sure, there is no formal reason why we should deny Claudia Semne's mausoleum the name of temple tomb. Yet, if we did not, basically any tomb could be given that name, or at least any that featured some elements of sacred architecture. This would not merely make the category useless, it would also contradict Wrede's further conclusions, as he claims that temple tombs appear at about the same time as private portraits in divine costume, suggesting that there were elements distinguishing them from previous types. Looking at his list of examples, it does in fact appear that his main criterion is precisely their featuring portraits *in formam deorum*, either in tympana or in aedicula niches, while other tombs such as the so-called 'Temple of Deus Rediculus',[183] which look like a proper small podium temple, are not mentioned despite being so much better preserved. This is where his argument comes full circle, and his observation that temple tombs were used predominantly for women and children is obviously the result of this circular reasoning.[184]

---

[179] Wrede (*Consecratio*, 83) assumed that the pediment spanned more or less the entire front of the building.

[180] E.g. Hesberg, *Grabbauten*, 184; Hallett *Roman Nude*, 220–1. Heinzelmann (*Nekropolen*, 81) calls it a podium temple. On the Haterii tomb and relief, see below pp. 253–5.

[181] Wrede, *Consecratio*, 80.

[182] See n. 9 above.

[183] Kammerer-Grothaus, 'Deus Rediculus'.

[184] Wrede, *Consecratio*, 83–8. It should be noted that Wrede's 'typical' temple tomb is a building that basically looks like that of the Haterii, and what we call a temple tomb here. However, the fragmentary evidence he uses to arrive at this conclusion is far more ambiguous and comprises tomb types that differ markedly from this 'typical' temple tomb, including that of Claudia Semne.

Figure 4.20 So-called 'crane relief' from the Mausoleum of the Haterii, first quarter of second century CE; Vatican City, Musei Vaticani, Museo Gregoriano Profano inv. 9998

In contrast, and as indicated in Chapter 1, I prefer to apply the term 'temple tomb' only to structures that closely resemble Roman temples for the gods and *divi*, normally including a podium and stairs leading up to a front porch. This is not to deny that other building types may have had similar connotations and could be seen as derivatives of such mausolea, especially since they, too, could occasionally be used for shrines of traditional divinities.[185] Yet the temple tomb as it is defined here is a distinct and clearly distinguishable shape that appears in our repertoire at a particular point in time. Moreover, it is a building type previously reserved for the gods. It is therefore best suited to exploring divine associations in funerary architecture, and their change in the second century.

Origins

The temple tomb as defined above is introduced relatively suddenly into the repertoire of Roman tombs of private individuals, with the first examples probably under the Flavians and Trajan, and more frequent occurrences from the mid-second century onwards. The origins of and inspiration for temple tombs have been debated for a long time. Eastern predecessors such as the Nereid Monument or the Mausoleum of Halicarnassus, with their gabled roof and colonnades surrounding an inner cella, have often been claimed as inspiration for several Roman tomb types.[186] Nevertheless, the differences from our Roman temple tombs are obvious.[187] The eastern examples are typically *peripteroi* after the Greek tradition, lacking the emphasis on the front that characterises Roman podium temples, or they are mere aediculae. Moreover, the eastern *peripteroi* and aediculae sit on tall podia, so that they could not be accessed like a normal temple, while the Roman temple tombs were accessible in precisely the same way as the shrines of the gods.[188] Far more convincingly, the tall Roman aedicula tombs of the first centuries BCE and CE have been traced back to these eastern models.[189] While it is perfectly possible that the various aedicula

---

[185] Ditto Thomas, *Monumentality*, 191. Heinzelmann (*Nekropolen*, 76–9) distinguishes between three types of tomb temples, namely those with free-standing front porch (*Säulenfronttypus*), with only pilasters (*Pilasterfronttypus*) and with only a pediment (*Giebelfronttypus*).
Griesbach (*Villen und Gräber*, 41 with n. 353) prefers the term *Grabtempel* (tomb temple) over *Tempelgrab* (temple tomb), and also wants to limit it to those buildings that closely resemble temples. In his catalogue, however, he includes also multistorey buildings and those without a free-standing porch.

[186] E.g. Matz, 'Grabbauten'; Gros, 'Monuments'.

[187] Ditto Matz, 'Grabbauten', 284–6.

[188] Gros, 'Monuments'. See Cormack (*Space of Death*) for a fuller overview of tomb types in Asia Minor, where accessible temple-shaped tombs start appearing only roughly at the same time as they do in Rome. Cf. Flämig, *Grabarchitektur*, 45–7, on temple tombs in Greece, which are restricted to the second century, and pp. 47–9 for an overview of other provinces.

[189] Thus esp. Gros, 'Monuments'; cf. also Matz, 'Grabbauten', who convincingly connects the Bibulus tomb with Hellenistic predecessors (ibid., 276 with fig. 8). Differently Hesberg, 'Profumo', with

tombs helped pave the way for the introduction of the second-century temple tombs, the step from the inaccessible aediculae on their tall pillars to the temple tombs is a big one, and there is not much indication so far of any intermediary stages.[190]

Templum Gentis Flaviae

It has long been suspected that one important stimulus for the introduction of temple tombs came from the Templum Gentis Flaviae,[191] which had been erected by Domitian on the site of his birthplace on the Quirinal Hill, and served as both burial place and location for the imperial cult of the Flavian dynasty.[192] Yet the comparison is not at all straightforward. The Templum's shape is still debated, as the term *templum* can refer not only to buildings that we call a temple but to a range of different sacred spaces, and the literary sources mentioning the Templum Gentis Flaviae lack information about its shape.[193]

39 n. 29, with a discussion of the material *passim*. 121–59, who connects them with public honorific monuments. Such aediculae and pilaster-decorated upper storeys are very rare around Rome, but include Eisner, *Typologie*, 17–9 cat. R1 (Bibulus), and 92–4 cat. Lb1 (Eurysaces), as well as potentially the poorly preserved examples *ibid.*, 49 cat. A15, and 50–1 cat. A17.

[190] Ditto Griesbach, *Villen und Gräber*, 41. Differently Hesberg, 'Profumo', with 39 n. 29, with a discussion of the material *passim*. However, his reconstruction drawing, fig. 4, is highly speculative insofar as the only evidence for it is a fragment of the tympanum, and the examples cited on pp. 39–40 and 43–4 are equally too poorly preserved to support his claims, especially since no unambiguous examples are provided. Outside of Rome, the mausoleum of Lusius Storax at Chieti may have resembled a temple, as it featured a wide (sculpted) pediment and decorated frieze, although no elements of columns have been recorded (cf. Hesberg, *Grabbauten*, 62 fig. 19). A tuff-built tomb in the sepolcreto Salario may have had a proper front porch, but it dates to three and a half centuries earlier than the first imperial-period temple tombs, and also had more of an aedicula shape (ibid., 123 fig. 68; esp. *NSc* (1969), 85–100 figs. 20–9 (E. Lissi Caronna)). Similarly, three fourth- and third-century BCE tombs at Paestum may have featured columns at the front (one Corinthian capital preserved), but their accessibility is questionable (*NSc* (1948), 154–84 with figs. (P. C. Sestieri); cf. Hesberg, 'Profumo', 123 fig. 69, with an attempt at reconstructing 'Tempietto A').

[191] E.g. Wrede, *Consecratio*, 81, 162; Heinzelmann, *Nekropolen*, 80–1; Griesbach, *Villen und Gräber*, 41–3.

[192] Suetonius, *Dom.* 1.1; 5.1; 15.2; 17.3; 17.6; Statius, *Silv.* 5.237–41; 3.16–19; Martial 9.20.1–6; 9.1.8–10; 9. 3.11–12; 9.34. *BCom* 91, 1986, 56–8 (E. Rodríguez-Almeida); Paris (ed.), *Dono Hartwig*; *LTUR* II (1995) 368–9 s.v. Gens Flavia, templum (F. Coarelli); Dabrowa, 'Templum Gentis Flaviae'; Darwall-Smith, *Flavian Rome*, 159–65; Davies, *Death and the Emperor*, 24–7, 79, 148–58 figs. 98–107; Coarelli, 'Flavi', 93–4 figs. 36–7; La Rocca, 'Templum' (= La Rocca, 'Templum Gentis Flaviae'); Coarelli, *Collis*, 194–205; Leithoff, *Vergangenheit*, 187–97, who also traces the inspiration for the Templum to Julio-Claudian dynastic monuments.

[193] For a different but unconvincing view, see n. 204 below. Literary sources collected in Paris (ed.), *Dono Hartwig*, 15–17.

Archaeological remains of the complex are difficult to interpret as well. The so-called 'Dono Hartwig', fragments of architectural ornaments, figures supporting an entablature and relief sculpture, which were found in 1901 during building works for the northern part of the semi-circle of buildings surrounding the Piazza della Repubblica, are generally accepted as belonging to the Templum, even though their precise arrangement and display context are still unclear.[194] The reliefs depict Vespasian and probably his sons in an *adventus* scene as well as a sacrifice, and thus use imagery that we find on state monuments. Moreover, a fragment with the head of a *flamen* probably shows the Temple of Quirinus in the background, which was dedicated to Rome's deified founder, Romulus, and was situated in the neighbourhood (Figure 4.21).[195] New excavations in the area and underneath the western part of the Baths of Diocletian conducted in the 1980s and 1990s have brought to light parts of a public building that consisted of a rectangular *opus caementicium* podium surrounded by a courtyard and portico with alternating rectangular and semi-circular *exedrae* of about 123 x 83 m, built of travertine blocks and *opus latericium* (Figure 4.22).[196] Daniela Candilio has already proposed that the remains must belong to the Templum Gentis Flaviae. Their size, Domitianic date (confirmed by brick stamps), location, as well as a colossal, 1.5 m tall head of Titus and a smaller but still colossal head of Vespasian found in the vicinity,[197] would surely be consistent with such a view.

It might be objected that this conclusion clashes with the conventional reading of several late antique sources. A passage in the *Historia Augusta* is often understood as telling us that Claudius Gothicus restored and extended the complex (Scriptores Historiae Augustae, *Claudius* 3.6). Why should Diocletian have destroyed and built over the structure only a few years later?[198] After all, it was a monument to the entire Flavian *gens*,

---

[194] Gazda et al. (eds.), *Images of Empire*; Paris, 'Sculture', with reconstruction drawing and cat. 52–64; Leithoff, *Vergangenheit*, 192–4 fig. 16.

[195] For various interpretations of the pediment, see Paris, 'Propaganda'; Gazda et al. (eds.), *Images of Empire*; Koortbojian, *Divinization*, 78–84 fig. IV.1.

[196] Esp. *NSc* (1990–01), 165–83 (D. Candilio); *NSc* (2000–01), 443–53 (D. Candilio); La Rocca, 'Templum'.

[197] La Rocca, *Templum*, 224–5; La Rocca, 'Templum Gentis Flaviae', 276–7 figs. 5–8; Coarelli, *Collis*, 200 fig. 50. But note that the provenance of Vespasian's head is not secure, and Häuber (*Mons Oppius*, 165 n. 144) notes the differences in size and style between the two colossal heads: Coarelli (ed.), *Vespasianus*, 495 cat. 98 with fig. (Vespasian, Naples, Museo Archeologico Nazionale 1889), 496–7 cat. 99 (Titus, Naples, Museo Archeologico Nazionale 110892).

[198] E.g. Paris (ed.), *Dono Hartwig*, 16; Hartswick, *Gardens*, 143–6 (who therefore argues for a different location).

Figure 4.21 Relief from the Templum Gentis Flaviae showing a *flamen* in front of the Temple of Quirinus; Rome, Museo Nazionale Romano delle Terme inv. 310251

which was very popular in late antiquity. The existence of the Templum into the fourth century is potentially further indicated by the *Regionary Catalogues* and the *Chronography of 354*.[199] However, it is not only possible that the *Historia Augusta*'s linking of Claudius Gothicus with the Flavians

---

[199] Paris (ed.), *Dono Hartwig*, 16–17, for full quotations.

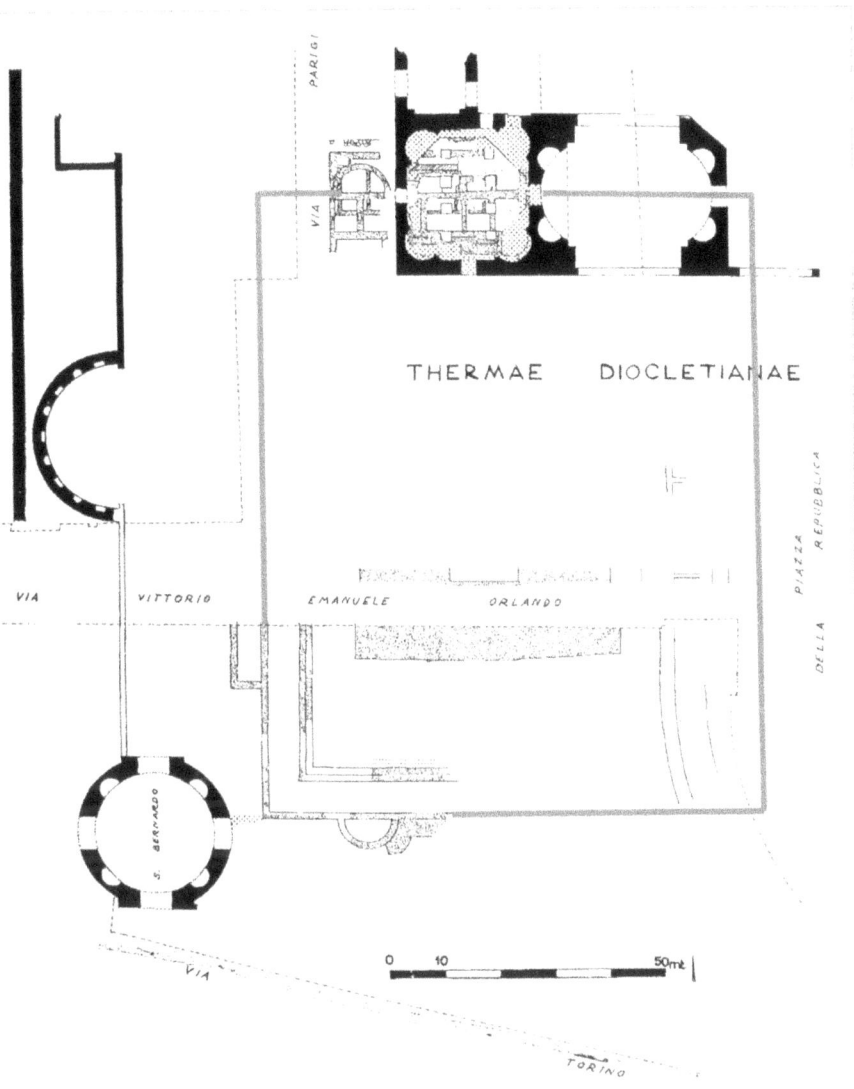

Figure 4.22 Plan of the archaeological remains of the Templum Gentis Flaviae underneath the Baths of Diocletian (Filippo Coarelli)

is a fabrication of the Constantinian period, when Constantine intended to establish his father's descent from Claudius Gothicus, and ultimately from the Flavian emperors. As Eugenio La Rocca has noted, the passage also does not talk about a *templum* at all, but only about the *gloria* of the *gens Flavia*, which Claudius intended to increase (*propagavit*) – no details given.[200] The *Regionary Catalogues* are ambiguous, stating that Regio VI contained, among other things, *Templum Dei Quirini, hortos Salustianos, Gentem Flabiam, Thermas Diocletianas,*[201] thus lacking a precise denomination of what exactly was 'of the Flavian *gens*'. The same is true for the *Chronography*, which appears to draw on the *Regionary Catalogues* and lacks any original knowledge of what *gentem Flabiam* means.[202] And, last but not least, Eutropius tells us that Trajan was the only emperor to be buried *intra urbem*, suggesting that, at his time, the remains of the Flavian family had been translated to a different location.[203]

It is therefore not only possible but highly likely that the structures underneath the Baths of Diocletian belonged to the Templum Gentis Flaviae, which is now the prevailing view. Yet, while the general layout with portico and central building is uncontroversial, the shape of the temple tomb is still debated. The majority of authors have proposed a rectangular temple, a view that appears to be confirmed by the rectangular shape of its *opus caementicium* foundations. However, Filippo Coarelli has insisted that to fit into an overall symmetrical plan, these foundations must have been square, and thus incompatible with a podium temple.[204] Moreover, referring to unpublished geophysical research in the relevant area, he relates that the structure was not solid throughout, but had a void in the centre that would point to an underground room beneath the temple. His own reconstruction proposes a podium with a round burial chamber and three niches, allegedly modelled on Augustus' mausoleum, as well as a circular building on top that was modelled on the Pantheon and, in turn, inspired the late antique circular imperial mausolea.[205]

---

[200] La Rocca, 'Templum', 230 with n. 74.

[201] Paris (ed.), *Dono Hartwig*, 16.

[202] La Rocca, 'Templum', 230 with n. 76.

[203] Ibid., 230 on Eutropius 8.5.2–3. Some authors seek a different solution to the conundrum. Because the preserved level of the podium is higher than the floor level of the Baths, Candilio considers that the central building of the temple could have persisted and been integrated into the structure of the Baths: *NSc* (2000–01), 452 with n. 32; followed by Coarelli, 'Flavi', 94; Coarelli, *Collis*, 204–5.

[204] Coarelli, *Collis*, 200–4. Coarelli also finds a circular building confirmed by the literary sources (p. 196), but the relevant passages, cited pp. 194–5, talk about a Flavian sky or heaven with stars, etc. in a way that does not allow for any conclusions on the physical shape of the building (ditto the majority of modern commentators).

[205] Ibid., 196–7, 201, 203–4 fig. 52. In his view, Domitian would thus have joined the funerary aspect of the Mausoleum of Augustus with the cult aspect of the Pantheon, which he takes to be a temple for the imperial cult.

The proposal, intriguing as it may be, is riddled with difficulties. Not only is Coarelli's burial chamber strikingly different from the circular corridors of Augustus' mausoleum; it is not entirely clear whether Agrippa's Pantheon featured a roof or was open to the sky,[206] and while it certainly had dynastic connotations and possibly associations of apotheosis, it was clearly not a straightforward temple to the imperial *divi* and *divae*. Moreover, like the late antique circular temple tombs, its overall plan, including the important front porch, requires elongated rather than square foundations. What is more, not a single curvilinear element has so far been found on site, and even Coarelli's concrete foundations are rectilinear, while those of the Pantheon *rotonda* as well as those of the late antique mausolea are circular. As some temple tombs and other large brick tombs make clear, semi-interred burial chambers often exist beneath the actual temple structure, and the niche excavated underneath the via Vittorio Emanuele Orlando (Figure 4.22) could just as well belong to a rectangular interior space.[207]

So far, I cannot see any evidence for a round building. A rectangular podium temple surrounded by a portico would fit with the rectangular features discovered so far, and this would in any case be its most likely shape.[208] As it was designed to serve the cult of the deified emperors, a

---

[206] While the pavement of coloured marble in the original rotunda may support the suggestion of a roof, the only built structure apart from the entrance porch underneath the current one is a perimeter wall (*muro cordonato*) that would have been unable to support a roof. For an up-to-date discussion favouring the roofed version, see La Rocca, 'Agrippa's Pantheon'; La Rocca, *Pantheon di Agrippa*.

[207] I am very grateful to Stephen Kay from the British School at Rome for finding the unpublished geophysical survey data mentioned by Coarelli and discussing it with me. Unfortunately, it is inconclusive with regard to any ancient built structures.

[208] For a hypothetical reconstruction, see Capanna ('Tempio della Gente Flavia' and 'Alta Semita'), who does not, however, explain the shape of the preserved parts of the *caementicium* podium. Some have argued that the appearance of the Templum can be gleaned from a relief and a coin. The two fragments of the relief show a procession in front of a decastyle temple. Its tympanum depicts Mars and Rhea Silvia as well as the she-wolf with the twins (Torelli, 'Culto imperiale', 564 fig. 2; Paris (ed.), *Dono Hartwig*, 28–30 figs. 16–19, 32–3 figs. 1–2; Davies, *Death and the Emperor*, 157–8; Leithoff, *Vergangenheit*, 190–2 with n. 826 fig. 15). Yet the relief is most likely Trajanic rather than Flavian, as the original portraits in the background and the draping of the togas demonstrate, and the alleged provenance from the Forum of Trajan would further support such a date (Goette, 'Disiecta membra'). The coin is a Domitianic *sertertius* of 95/96 showing a decastyle temple within a courtyard framed by aedicula niches, either within a surrounding wall or, perhaps more likely, above some terrace walls (Torelli, 'Culto imperiale', 566–7; Paris (ed.), *Dono Hartwig*, 26–8 fig. 14; Gazda et al. (eds.), *Images of Empire*, 19; Leithoff, *Vergangenheit*, 191 fig. 10). However, the identification largely rests on the observation that there were few if any other decastyle buildings at the time, a relatively weak argument to support such a wide-ranging interpretation, and other suggestions for identification have been made (contra e.g. Coarelli, 'Flavi', 94; La Rocca, 'Templum', 228–30; Leithoff, *Vergangenheit*, 191–2 fig. 10).

physical similarity to other temples erected to *divi*, which in turn resembled the temples of the traditional gods, would only be natural. The Temple of the Deified Claudius, which was a prostyle podium temple surrounded by a portico with *exedrae*, and had been (re)built by Vespasian,[209] is the closest parallel to and likely the model for the Templum complex. Guido Petruccioli has even suggested that fragment 595 of the Forma Urbis, which shows parts of a rectangular temple within a colonnaded porticus and is labelled TEMP[lum], could show the Templum Gentis Flaviae. As he observes, no other temple in the marble plan is called 'templum', with the sole exception of the [T]emplum Di[v]i Clau[di].[210]

Despite the uncertainties involved, there can be no doubt that the Flavian complex had many features in common with our temple tombs. Like the Templum, temple tombs are often located within a precinct, and they may have shared its podium temple design. At an ideological level, they were intended to honour the deceased members of an entire *gens* – and only this *gens*.[211] Moreover, the Templum was erected over the house where Domitian was born (Suetonius, *Dom.* 1.1.9). While private temple tombs could not be erected within the *pomerium*, they were often situated at the entrance to, or even very closely integrated into, villa buildings.[212] Functionally, it is important to note that the Templum Gentis Flaviae was the first temple for imperial cult that also served as a tomb, and the first imperial tomb that also provided cult of the *divi* and *divae*.[213] The erection of the first private temple tombs shortly after it was dedicated thus strongly suggests that they were inspired by the imperial model.

Before we discuss some extant examples, it is worth noting that some cinerary urns and sarcophagi, especially the colonnaded sarcophagi, allude to

---

[209] Lloyd, 'Gardens', 93–5; *LTUR* I (1993) 277–8 s.v. Claudius, divus, templum (reg. II) (C. Buzzetti); cf. Forma Urbis fgm. 5 b,g,f.

[210] Fgm. 5 b,g,f. The essay is so far only published online: www.academia.edu/1497179/ The_structure_on_the_reverse_of_a_Domitianic_coin_BMC_406_Interpretation_and_ identification (last accessed 22/10/2016). See pp. 10–13 fig. 7 for a reconstruction as a decastyle temple based on the coin image (cf. n. 208 above). Whether or not the front was decastyle, if the fragment is correctly identified, the Templum would have been peripteral or, more likely and as Petruccioli reconstructs it, a *peripteros sine postico*.

[211] Ditto Griesbach, *Villen und Gräber*, 42–3; La Rocca, 'Templum', 228. It is nowhere said directly that Vespasian and Titus were translated to the Templum, but Statius, *Silv.* 4.3.18–19, seems clear enough when he calls it the heaven 'of his father's race'. As Anne Haeckl has pointed out ('Dynasty', 24), the Templum 'thus emerges as the only truly dynastic imperial tomb in Roman architecture'. For the gentilicial use of private individuals' tombs, see Chapter 3 above. On the ideological background of the Templum, and especially its gentilicial aspect, see most notably Leithoff, *Vergangenheit*, 194–7.

[212] For this aspect, see Chapter 1 pp. 24–7.

[213] E.g. La Rocca, 'Templum', 228.

temples, and perhaps more specifically to temple tombs, as has occasionally been noted.[214] Interestingly, cinerary altars and urns mostly do not imitate proper temples, but only feature columns at the corners, while the elements between the columns and above the architrave assume all sorts of fanciful shapes and designs, and demonstrate the essentially eclectic character of these items' decoration. In the rare instances where the design imitates a proper built structure, the impression is mostly that of an aedicula rather than a temple.[215] Exceptions such as the urn for fifteen-year-old Varia Amoeba, which details the ashlar masonry, the roof tiles and the door into the mausoleum, and shows her and her husband's (?) portrait in a shell in the pediment,[216] or a similar altar with large tripods on the short sides that has lost its lid,[217] are very rare, and they all date to the Flavian period or later,[218] while the sarcophagi are even later than these. This confirms that the chronology suggested by extant temple tombs, to which we now turn, is not an accident of preservation but a reflection of reality.

Mausoleum of Priscilla

The first to take up the idea of a temple tomb, and to dare to emulate the emperor, were again people particularly close to, and favoured by, the court, including imperial freedmen. The most famous imperial freedman to be inspired by the Templum Gentis Flaviae is Domitian's enormously rich and powerful *ab epistulis* T. Flavius Abascantus. Statius' consolatory poem, which I have already mentioned in connection with his wife Priscilla's statues in divine costume (*Silv.* 5.1), also provides some details about her tomb at the second mile of the via Appia. At the end of the poem (ll. 239–42), Statius hints at the Templum Gentis Flaviae:

> est hic, agnosco, minister illius, aeternae modo qui sacraria genti condidit inque alio posuit sua sidera caelo
>
> Yes, this is the minister of him that lately founded a shrine for his eternal race and set his stars in another firmament. (transl. D. R. S. Bailey)

---

[214] See Petersen, *Freedman*, 219–20 for urns. On sarcophagi: Wrede, *Consecratio*, 87 on cat. 115; Thomas, 'Houses'.

[215] For a well-illustrated overview, see Altmann, *Römischen Grabaltäre*, 136–73; Boschung, *Grabaltäre*, 104–9 pls. 34–48. On aediculae: Altmann, *Römischen Grabaltäre*, 214 fig. 173, 218–19 figs. 179–80; Boschung, *Grabaltäre*, no. 867 (Hadrianic) and 957 (after 94). None of them looks like an actual built aedicula.

[216] Altmann, *Römischen Grabaltäre*, 156 no. 189 fig. 127.

[217] Boschung, *Grabaltäre*, no. 800 p. 37 (Flavian).

[218] Ibid., 53–5, for the general development of shapes.

This is clearly more than just a reference to Abascantus' imperial patron. Mentioning the Templum only, of all the buildings Domitian had erected, and just after commenting on Priscilla's tomb, suggests a more specific comparison between the imperial gentilicial shrine and Abascantus and Priscilla's mausoleum, as is widely acknowledged.

A large tumulus tomb consisting of a rectangular base of *c.* 21 x 21 m and a tambour decorated on the outside with thirteen statue niches is sometimes thought to be this monument.[219] It is in the right location; it was clearly impressive; its cruciform burial chamber is likely to have contained inhumations; and inscriptions referring to Abascantus and his freedmen were found in its vicinity. The latter include one for Aphrodisius, keeper and guardian of the couple's tomb.[220] No doubt the inscription confirms that at least the approximate location is correct. Yet the attribution has usually been rejected because of the tomb type, which featured a cylindrical core filled with soil, and its building technique.[221]

Additional doubts are cast on the attribution by Statius' description and his emphatic claim that Priscilla's tomb was a *domus*, not a *triste sepulcrum*. It is widely known that the term *domus* is used in a metaphorical way with reference to all kinds of tombs, and does not necessarily carry implications for their shape.[222] However, here the term *domus* is not a euphemism *replacing* the term *sepulcrum*, but is *contrasted with* a *sepulcrum*.[223] Moreover, the description of couches, tables and servants within the funerary chamber makes it clear that the particularly emphatic evocation of a *domus* seeks to conjure a space that looks unlike most other tomb chambers at the time (ll. 236–7). While a temple-shaped building does not exactly resemble a house, the text evokes a space more akin to the interior of temple tombs than to the gloomy cruciform burial chamber inside the round monument on the Appia.

---

[219] On the monument, see Eisner, *Typologie*, 30–3 cat. A2 figs. A2a–b pls. 6.3, 7.1; Spera, *Paesaggio*, 68 no. 85; Schwarz, *Tumulat Italia tellus*, 180–1 cat. M48 pl. 24.1; *LTURS* IV (2006) 269–71 s.v. Priscillae sepulcrum (P. Chini – A. Bianchi); Meinecke, *Sarcophagum posuit*, 200–2 cat. A4; cf. *RE* XII (1909) 2529–30 s.v. Flavius 25 (Stein); *PIR*² F 194; *PIR* P 705.

[220] *CIL* 6.2214; Spera, *Paesaggio*, 68 no. 85. The other inscriptions are *CIL* 6.8598–9.

[221] Eisner (*Typologie*, 216) considers a date in the last decades of the first century BCE. Schwarz (*Tumulat Italia tellus*, 31 on cat. M48) suggests a date in the early first century CE, and rightly points out that soil-filled monuments went out of use in the early first century. P. Chini (in *LTURS* IV (2006) 270 s.v. Priscillae sepulcrum) stresses that further archaeological work is needed to resolve the dating problem, while Meinecke's views (here n. 219) are somewhat contradictory (cf. Borg, 'Roman sarcophagi', 602).

[222] Esp. Wallace-Hadrill, 'Tomb as house'.

[223] Cf. Cicero, *Att.* 12.36.1, who intends his *fanum* for Tullia not to look like a tomb.

Priscilla's mausoleum is therefore highly likely to have been a rectangular temple tomb, deliberately modelled on the Templum Gentis Flaviae that had only just been completed, and it may well have been the first of its kind erected by a private person.[224] That this person was Abascantus would be explained by his very close connection to Domitian on the one hand, and his libertine status on the other, which ruled out from the start any competition with or challenge to the emperor.

Haterii Mausoleum

It may also be no coincidence that another early example of a temple tomb was erected by people linked very closely to the imperial court. It is the famous tomb of the Haterii on the via Labicana, erected by Q. Haterius Tychicus (?) in the first quarter of the second century.[225] Unfortunately, the actual tomb is very poorly preserved (Figure 4.23), but key features can be reconstructed from the remains on site and the fragments of its marble decoration (Figures 4.24–4.25). It was a two-storey temple tomb with a semi-interred burial chamber accessible from ground level at the back, and an upper chamber with access via a flight of stairs at the front. It featured marble columns at the front, four busts of deities in high relief on its door lintel and richly ornamented marble décor on both its outside and inside. It thus resembled in its overall impression and richness the mausoleum on the famous crane relief that decorated the inside of the tomb (Figure 4.20), although the preserved architectural fragments make it clear that the relief is not an exact illustration of the Haterii's building.[226]

In our context, the relief is not merely a convenient support for our imagination when we try to make sense of the fragmentary evidence. It has

---

[224] Ditto Griesbach, *Villen und Gräber*, 42–3. The Templum Gentis Flaviae was built between 89 and 94/95; Priscilla must have died around 95/96.

[225] Giuliano, 'Documenti'; Coarelli, 'Sepolcro degli Haterii'; Coarelli, *Roma sepolta*, 166–79; Sinn and Freyberger, *Grabdenkmäler II*, 18–21, 27–9, on the date, and passim for the fullest publication of the evidence so far; Hesberg, 'Profumo', 41, 44–8 figs. 12a–c; Gioia and Volpe (eds.), *Centocelle I*, 133–5 no. 214 (P. Armelin); *LTURS* III (2005) 43–4 s.v. Hateriorum sepulcrum (P. Liverani); Griesbach, *Villen und Gräber*, 44–5. The crucial criterion for the date and the rejection of the usual Flavian date are the architectural ornaments, some of which presuppose forms developed only for the Forum of Trajan. The portraits from the tomb fit this date very well. The *cognomen* of the tomb's founder in the *titulus* is lost, but as Sinn and Freyberger (*Grabdenkmäler II*, 22–4) convincingly argue, he is likely the same person who dedicated an aedicula with a statue of Hercules at the behest of Silvanus and calls himself a *redemptor* (for the inscription see *CIL* 6.607, add. 30801b, with Sinn and Freyberger, *Grabdenkmäler II*, 115–16 cat. 40 pl. 62.2.

[226] For a tentative reconstruction, cf. Hesberg, 'Profumo', 42–4 figs. 12a–c; for the relief, see Sinn and Freyberger, *Grabdenkmäler II*, 51–59 cat. 6 pls. 11–16.

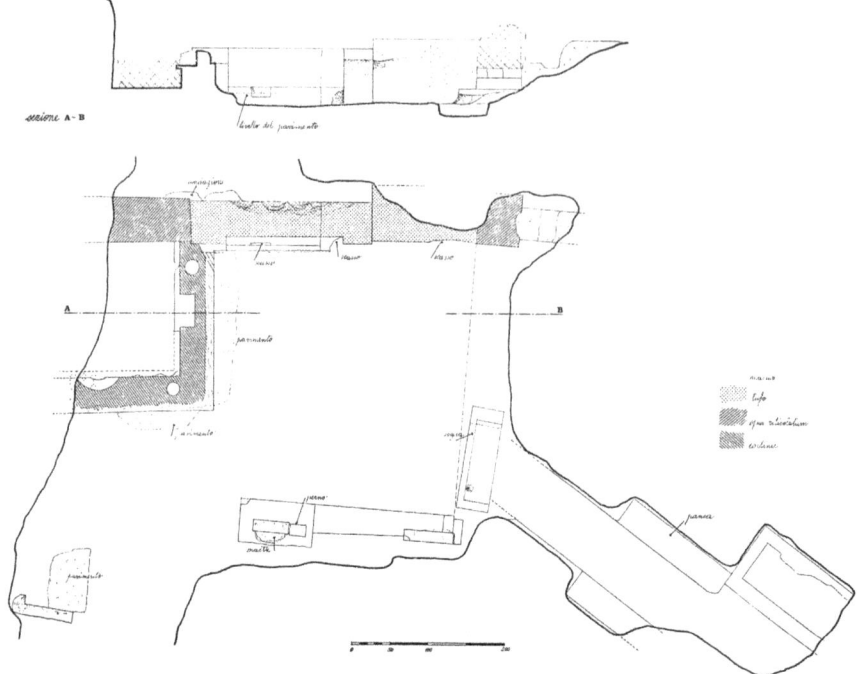

Figure 4.23 Plan of the Mausoleum of the Haterii on the via Labicana, first quarter of second century (Filippo Coarelli)

Figure 4.24 Pilaster from the Mausoleum of the Haterii; Vatican City, Musei Vaticani, Museo Gregoriano Profano inv. 10015

Figure 4.25 Epistyle from the Mausoleum of the Haterii; Vatican City, Musei Vaticani, Museo Gregoriano Profano inv. 9994

long been observed that the enormous crane in front of the mausoleum must refer to the occupation and source of wealth of the tomb's founder.[227] He must have been in the building industry and, as a further relief from the tomb suggests in depicting a number of public buildings,[228] the Haterii were probably working as *redemptores*, contractors of building projects and construction work, for the emperor and the state.[229] While the father of the tomb's founder was an ex-slave, he was no imperial freedman but was probably freed by Q. Haterius Antoninus (*cos.* 53), a grandson of the Augustan orator. Antoninus is also known from brick stamps and so was in the building industry himself. The fact that he was closely related to a number of important individuals of his time, and that he was first cousin of both Valeria Messalina and Nero, will certainly have helped his freedmen to enter into important and lucrative businesses.[230] Having been involved in imperial Flavian building projects, the Haterii would doubtless have been close to the *familia caesaris*, and very aware of the Templum Gentis Flaviae as well as Priscilla's mausoleum. We may even speculate that they were directly involved in the building of the Templum.

Other Dated Temple Tombs

There is evidence for another spectacular temple tomb from the early second century that is probably the first attested example belonging to the first order.[231] Built in travertine and featuring a marble front, it was situated

227 For a different but unconvincing view, see below at n. 255.

228 Sometimes called the 'Via Sacra panel' after the inscription on a triumphal arch: Sinn and Freyberger, *Grabdenkmäler II*, 63–76 cat. 8 pls. 20–4. The buildings are normally identified as Flavian, though no agreement has been reached as to their identity. Freyberger and Zitzl ('Bautenrelief') recently identified the buildings on the relief with the Arcus ad Isis of the Isium Metellinum on the via Labicana, the amphitheatre of Statilius Taurus, an Augustan triumphal arch at the top end of the Scalae Caci in front of the temple of Magna Mater, the monumental entrance to the Augustan Templum Urbis Romae, the temple of Jupiter Stator and the Fornix Fabianus – all buildings erected and/or restored under Augustus and connected with his victory at Actium. Should these identifications be correct, the authors are probably right to read the relief as an allusion to the founder of the Haterii's patron family, Q. Haterius Agrippa, a friend of Augustus and likely involved in his Actian victory, but through historic buildings that were destroyed in the fire of 64 CE and renovated or replaced under the Flavians.

229 See Martin, *Jurists*, 52–62, esp. 59, on Q. Haterius Tychicus as *redemptor operum publicorum*; Kolb, *Bauverwaltung*, esp. 130, 316–18; Kolb, *Rom*, 473; Sinn and Freyberger, *Grabdenkmäler II*, 22–6. For another *redemptor* depicting a crane as indication of his profession, see a relief in Capua: ibid., 56 with n. 63.

230 As noted by the authors in n. 226.

231 *NSc* (1912), 34–8 (G. Mancini). The tomb was heavily spoliated when found. The proportions of the cella and the entire platform (8 m long) suggest that it was a temple tomb, even though the reports talking of many marble fragments do not mention any specific items that would allow

shortly before the eighth milestone of the via Latina, most likely close to the villa of its patron. According to a relief portrait head with laurel wreath, which may originate from the pediment of the building, it is probably no later than the early second century. Moreover, the wreath suggests that its patron was a man who received the *ornamenta triumphalia*, a rare and extraordinary distinction last awarded late under Hadrian or very early under Antoninus Pius.[232]

A senatorial temple tomb is also suggested by an architrave from the turn of the second century commemorating an anonymous proconsul of Sicily.[233] It was found near the Theatre of Marcellus, an exceptional location that must have had senate and imperial approval.

A temple tomb in Ostia's Porta Romana necropolis (A 13) is equally dated to the Trajanic period (Figure 2.2).[234] It was erected at a prominent location on the via Ostiensis, above the ruins of one of the greatest late Republican tombs, and was by far the most impressive tomb at its time. There can be no doubt that its patron was an important citizen of Ostia, even though he unfortunately remains anonymous.[235]

The next uncontroversial and well-dated temple tombs are the Servilii tombs on via Latina and via Tiburtina, both dated before the brothers' execution in 192, with the former dated by a brick stamp to 159 or shortly after, and the tomb of M. Nonius Macrinus from the 170s or early 180s (see Figures 1.8–1.9 above).[236] If we accept the identification of the round temple tomb at the third milestone of the Appia as Regilla's cenotaph, we have another item from the 160s (Figure 1.10).[237] The majority of temple tombs, especially those made of polychrome brick, are hard to date exactly due to the lack of stamped bricks and interior decoration. However, where

---

any firm conclusions on its appearance. An Asiatic garland sarcophagus found in the ruin can be dated only roughly to 140–80: *MNR* I8,1 (1985) 214–16 no. iv,15, Inv. 58200 = 124708 (L. Musso).

[232] The relief portrait was one of at least a pair; its date is suggested by the hairstyle, the very soft treatment of the skin of the face and lack of sharp lines around the eyes (Felletti Maj, *Museo Nazionale*, no. 151; the best published photograph: West *Porträt-Plastik II*, 150 no. 26 pl. 49). On the crown, see Bergmann, *Kranz*, 51–8; on the latest awards, see Eck, 'Freigelassene'.

[233] *CIL* 6.41090; Feraudi-Gruénais, 'Ewigkeit', 157 no. 53.

[234] Heinzelmann, *Nekropolen*, 76–7, 146–9 figs. 30, 59–64.

[235] The tomb was later modified to have a simpler front with pilasters rather than columns (ibid., 78, 148), potentially, as Heinzelmann assumes, because the pretence was felt to be excessive. Be this as it may, this change is not indicative of a general trend towards less ostentatious front displays, as is sometimes alleged (following ibid., 82–3), but runs against the trend towards more frequent uses of the temple tomb type. Heinzelmann also mentions still unpublished fragments from a temple tomb found close to Acilia on the via Ostiensis, which have exactly the same measurements and may be contemporary (ibid., 77 n. 339).

[236] See above, Chapter 1 pp. 13–18.

[237] See above, Chapter 1 pp. 19–21.

indications for their chronology are available, they seem to date to the Antonine and Severan periods, with some new shapes being introduced over the course of the third century.[238]

It is perhaps hazardous to draw any wider conclusions from only a few examples but, given what we have seen regarding portraits *in formam deorum*, it may be no coincidence that the earliest examples of full-fledged temple tombs we know were erected by super-rich patrons from the freedman milieu with particularly close connections to the imperial court, and two consular members of the first order who received the extraordinary distinctions of *ornamenta triumphalia* and a tomb in the Campus Martius, respectively. Only when, with time, restrictions on the self-display of the senatorial elite relaxed further, and the connection of the new tomb type with Domitian, who was deeply unpopular with the conservative senators, may have faded, did it gain in popularity.[239]

Meaning and Significance

It remains to establish the meaning of the building type. By their similarity to temples, temple tombs provided the deceased with an aura that previous tombs could not convey in the same way. Tumuli were associated with the tombs of heroes, especially those from the heroic age, and their similarity to Etruscan and other Italic tombs offered further associations with a more indigenous past.[240] Yet with the introduction of high podia and tower-like tambours, the round tombs' relation with tumuli became less and less recognisable. They may have gained in impressiveness but lost in symbolism. The rare aedicula tombs briefly discussed above used individual elements associated with sacred buildings and sometimes resembled smaller shrines, but often were inaccessible, tower-like monuments rather unlike real temples.[241] The *arae*, which alluded to cult and sacrifice more directly, could have a range of meanings, from a very general reference to *pietas* to the traditional Roman sacrifices, to the *dii manes*, to sacrifices to a deceased individual,[242] although there is no positive evidence for the latter. Moreover,

---

[238] Borg, *Crisis and Ambition*, 36–9, 48–57. The tomb of P. Cluvius Maximus Paullinus (*cos.* 158/59), is another fairly well-dated and impressive tomb, but lacks a front porch: see above, Chapter 1 p. 30 with Figure 1.13.
[239] The chronology is clear from the list given by Griesbach (*Villen und Gräber*), although it should be noted that he includes not merely what I call temple tombs proper, but also tombs with only engaged columns or pilasters.
[240] See above, Chapter 2 at nn. 156–7.
[241] Similarly Wrede, *Consecratio*, 91; Hesberg, *Grabbauten*, 182; cf. at n. 189 above.
[242] Heinzelmann, *Nekropolen*, 82.

the larger monuments only had symbolic value when they were either full-fledged buildings with an interior burial chamber, like the 'Platorini tomb' (Figure 1.1), or displayed on high pedestals, turned into show pieces with image decoration and no longer in reach of anyone potentially wanting to use them for sacrifice.[243] In contrast, the temple tombs not only induced general religious associations, but a building type previously reserved for the gods was conferred to humans unaltered, and thus at least potentially maintained its function.[244] Even independently of their likely model, the Templum Gentis Flaviae, temple tombs were thus specifically linked to imperial apotheosis and cult. Should we therefore conclude that they were a visual indication of 'private apotheosis'?

This idea is normally either not considered or rejected. Henner von Hesberg and Jochen Griesbach in particular have argued that the adoption of temple tombs by non-imperial patrons was accompanied by a change in meaning, and became primarily an expression of personal affection in a decidedly private realm. The shorthand term often used to describe this process is *Verinnerlichung* or 'internalisation'. In what is still the only monograph-length introduction to Roman tombs, in 1992 von Hesberg started from the assumption that the introduction of the principate resulted in a waning interest in public display of one's achievements. The location of tombs close to the villas of their owners, the attention given to interior decoration and the display of portraits inside tombs, as well as his assumption, probably based on Wrede's work, that temple tombs were erected particularly for the commemoration of women and children, led von Hesberg to interpret temple tombs as segregated small shrines for the private commemoration and cult of the beloved deceased.[245] Similarly, Griesbach argued that the ideas and values connected with temple tombs were primarily of a private nature and expressed emotional attachment and devotion, although

---

[243] On altar-shaped tombs, see Eisner, *Typologie*, 219–23; Hesberg, *Grabbauten*, 171–81. On the Platorini tomb, see Chapter 1 p. 4.

[244] Heinzelmann, *Nekropolen*, 76–85; De Cristofaro, 'Monumento funerario', 254.

[245] Hesberg, *Grabbauten*, 182–5. Hesberg writes: 'Erst eine Zeit, in der das Streben nachließ, sich mit seinen Leistungen vor der Öffentlichkeit darzustellen, musste die Ausstattung von Grabanlagen mit tempelartigen Monumenten begünstigen. Denn trotz allen Reichtums erschien das Bild des Verstorbenen bei dieser Art von Bauten vorzugsweise im Innern.' ('Only at a time when the aspiration to present oneself with one's achievements before the public had abated was the furnishing of funerary space with temple-like monuments facilitated, since, despite all the luxury, in this kind of building the deceased's portrait preferably featured inside.' p. 183). For a critical review of this assumption, see also above Chapter 1, pp. 4–9.

he offers some qualification.[246] He not only acknowledges some diversity in approaches to funerary commemoration, but also points out that personal and family relationships were essential for one's position and status in imperial Rome. Still, the shift from status-oriented, extroverted self-representation to more emotional, spiritual and introverted commemoration is advocated as a major factor in commemorative practices, including the introduction of temple tombs.

There can be no doubt that there were major changes over the course of the imperial period, but it is questionable that they were as simple as this. There is evidence for public display of strong emotion in the face of death from the Republic onwards and throughout the imperial period. I have already discussed Cicero's lament for his daughter and Abascantus' grief for his wife, both of which are communicated widely through publications. Kierdorf has identified lament as one of the key features of all funerary orations.[247] Against this background, Herodes Atticus can hardly be used, as he often is, to prove a shift in attitudes, even if we ignore for the moment his rather idiosyncratic character.[248] In contrast to what is frequently suggested, temple tombs were also erected for consuls and other men of wealth or achievement, and we have seen in Chapter 1 that there is little indication of their retreat into the private realm; even close connection to villas normally did not entail remoteness and privacy.[249] The choice of a temple tomb was therefore a powerful public statement that can hardly have failed to evoke comparison with imperial models.

An official apotheosis or *consecratio* was obviously not within the reach of these tomb's patrons. It was dependent on the senate's decree, and no such decrees have been recorded for private individuals. This is why Wrede and others have resorted to the concept of *private* apotheosis. In principle, the framework of Roman religion no doubt allowed for this and, as I concluded in the first part of this chapter, it was certainly possible that an individual or family could confer divinity upon another mortal. Yet is this what temple tombs were meant to indicate? And if so, did this divinity also imply a specific idea of an afterlife? *Did* the Romans have any concept or expectation

---

[246] Griesbach, *Villen und Gräber*, 145–9. Griesbach explicitly refers to Hesberg and Zanker ('Einleitung'), who first explained the ideas around 'internalisation' connected with political and social change, but also to Paul Zanker's interpretation of mythological sarcophagi (on this topic, see Borg, 'Leben und Tod').

[247] Kierdorf, *Laudatio funebris*.

[248] On Herodes, see further below.

[249] See 24–7.

of an afterlife? Before I address this question, I should briefly review other symbols and iconographic elements that point to the idea of posthumous apotheosis to gain a more comprehensive view of the evidence.

Other Images Related to Apotheosis

There are a few other elements occasionally found in the funerary realm that are strongly associated with the idea of posthumous apotheosis. It would exceed the scope of the present study to try to provide a full review of such symbolism, especially since some symbols are more ambiguous and contested than others. Eschatological interpretations of sarcophagus imagery, for instance, often take belief in an afterlife for granted, and ignore the fact that the reliefs never actually *show* those elements of mythological narratives that would be suitable for conveying such a message, such as Persephone's or Adonis' return to the upper world, or Ariadne waking up.[250] It is also noteworthy that, in literary or epigraphic texts, the deceased are neither expected to join the Dionysiac *thiasos* nor even a specifically Dionysiac bliss in general, as one would expect if the Dionysiac imagery on tomb monuments were alluding to an afterlife, as is so often assumed.[251] The same goes for images of dining,[252] and Brandenburg showed long ago that there is no indication that marine *thiasoi* hint at the Isles of Bliss.[253] I shall restrict myself here to less ambiguous imitations of imperial iconographies of apotheosis, which are surprisingly rare.

In imperial iconography, the most widespread images of the actual process of apotheosis show the emperor or empress riding to heaven on the back of a bird, deity/personification or chariot. The ritual of releasing an eagle in the *consecratio* ceremonies for emperors and empresses made this bird the most popular symbol of apotheosis on coins and in other media,

---

[250] Borg, 'Slumber', 266–8; Borg, 'No one is immortal', both with bibl.

[251] E.g. Wrede, *Consecratio*, 118–20; Newby, *Greek Myths*, 301–7, who leaves it open, however, to what extent patrons may have believed in such an afterlife and focuses on the consolatory effect instead. Some scholars have pointed to mystery cults to justify an eschatological explanation. Yet neither do the relevant texts envisage an afterlife comparable to the images at stake here, nor is there any indication in the imagery or epigraphy for such a general connection.

[252] For a different opinion see Wrede, *Consecratio*, 120–2. Where we do have references to dining or the Dionysiac sphere, these are typically retrospective, as in the famous kline monument of Flavius Agricola (*CIL* 6.7985a; translation Zanker and Ewald, *Myths*, 153–4 Fig. 143; cf. Wrede, 'Klinenprobleme', 101–4).

[253] Brandenburg, 'Meerwesensarkophage'.

although the empress is sometimes represented as riding on Juno's bird, the peacock.[254]

John Bodel has argued that the basket atop the builder's crane on the Haterii relief (Figure 4.20) is the cage of a bird that should be released as a sign of the deceased's apotheosis.[255] Nevertheless, there is no indication that the crane has any relation with the tomb or a funeral, and the relief very obviously violates rules of unity of time and space throughout.[256] The earliest tomb image of apotheosis on the back of an eagle that I am aware of is the stucco relief in the centre of the ceiling of Valerius Paullinus' tomb on the via Latina, where the male figure may, however, be Jupiter, the senator in the guise of Jupiter, or possibly even Homer (Figure 1.4).[257] An astonishing altar in the Vatican that marked a tomb of Pomponii was erected to commemorate four sons of Q. Pomponius Eudaemon and Claudia Helpis, who are depicted in toga or military dress on one main side of the altar, while the dedicatory inscription once featured on the opposite side (Figure 4.26).[258] The parents were obviously still alive, but on the short sides of the altar their busts are shown on the back of a frontal peacock and eagle with thunderbolt, respectively.[259] The similarity to imperial images of apotheosis, and especially to the contemporary Corinthian capital from the imperial villa at Lorium showing the *tondo* bust of Antoninus Pius on an eagle and

---

[254] On images of imperial apotheosis, see Schulten, *Konsekrationsprägungen*, 21–33, esp. 22–5 on the eagle and peacock; Gradel, *Emperor Worship*, 305–16; Palombi, 'Divinizzazione'.

[255] Bodel, 'Death on display', 268–70; accepted by Leach, 'Freedmen', 7.

[256] Cf. Sinn and Freyberger (*Grabdenkmäler II*, 56 with nn. 63 and 65), who consider the basket and branches as part of an inauguration ceremony of a building, and point to another relief of a *redemptor*, who indicated his profession with the depiction of a crane. As he was a *redemptor prosceni*, Bodel ('Death on display', 268) argued that the crane was stage machinery. Yet there is no indication of this, and the crane is actually shown lifting a column while a stone mason is working on another architectural element. Many other features in the relief have been interpreted as pointing to the apotheosis of the Haterii (Leach, 'Freedmen', 5–11). This is not the place to review them all, but I find them very far-fetched. For instance, why does the crane as such 'open-endedly point to immortality'? And why should the two figures of Hercules at rest (!) and the woman coming through the half-open door in the bottom tier of the mausoleum decoration point to Hercules returning Alcestis to the world above when the figures are entirely unconnected (ibid., p. 11)? In many interpretations of the relief, the eclectic nature of the images assembled is significantly underestimated.

[257] See above, Chapter 1 p. 38.

[258] *CIL* 6.24613.

[259] Musei Vaticani, Sala della Biga (without inv.): Altmann, *Römischen Grabaltäre*, 278–80 figs. 207a–c; Boschung, *Grabaltäre*, 49, 51, 115 no. 980 pl. 59 (who dates it to the second quarter of the second century); *AE* 2011, 79 no. 118; Lo Monaco, 'Immagini private', 347 fig. 8. According to the bust shapes, especially that of Helpis, the altar is most likely of Antonine date.

Figure 4.26 Antonine altar of the Pomponii family, Vatican City, Musei Vaticani, Sala della Biga, as drawn by Giovannantonio Dosio; Biblioteca Nazionale di Firenze, Nuovi Acquisti 618 fol. 06 v A e B

that of Faustina Maior on a peacock is striking (Figure 4.27).[260] Obviously, Eudaemon and his wife were already looking forward to their own apotheosis during their lifetime.[261] No similar imagery was chosen for their sons, but the inscription, *fratribus IIII sacrum* (rather than *Dis Manibus sacrum*), may point in a similar direction.[262]

A second-century relief now in Copenhagen shows a beardless youth riding on the back of an eagle, with an altar and offerings to their right, over which an Amor is hovering, holding a torch.[263] An eagle features on the pedestal of an Antonine bust in military costume in the Prado.[264] On two third-century sarcophagi, the *clipeus* portraits of the deceased are supported by an eagle.[265]

---

[260] Cf. esp. *MNR* I.8.2 (1985), 485–6 no. IX.11 inv. 126362 (L. Lupi); Mikocki, *Sub specie Deae*, 202 no. 357 pl. 20. Similarly the *clipeus* carried by an eagle on a scabbard from Vindonissa dated before 101 (Jucker, *Blätterkelch*, 139–40 fig. 25) and the cameo of a Flavian empress riding on a peacock in the British Museum (Megow, *Kameen*, 262 no. B29 pl. 38.8, 10, 11; Mikocki, *Sub specie Deae*, 190 no. 269 pl. 20). Titus' image on the eagle on his Roman Arch looks similar, but one can actually see his legs and feet between the eagle's right leg and wing (Pfanner, *Titusbogen*, 76–9 pls. 68–9).

[261] Cf. the cameos showing Nero (Figure 4.10 above) and Claudius riding on an eagle, both created during the lifetime of the emperors: Megow, *Kameen*, 199–200 cat. A80 pl. 27.1, 214–15 cat. 99 pl. 35.3.

[262] See Solin, 'Analecta', 166–7, for the authenticity of the inscription, which is no longer legible.

[263] Copenhagen, National Museum 2225: Cumont, *Études syriennes*, 78–9; Gradel, *Emperor Worship*, 313 fig. 12.6.

[264] Schröder, *Katalog*, 224–7 cat. 61. The head does not belong. It is therefore possible that the bust was that of a deified emperor, but the moderate quality of the carving and the small size of the eagle perhaps indicate a private portrait.

[265] Langlotz, *Sammlung*, 5 no. 34 pl. 14; Rome, Mus. Naz. delle Terme 124735: *MNR* I,2 (1981), 90–3 no. II.6 (M. Sapelli); cf. Jucker, *Blätterkelch*, 140 with nn. 5 and 6.

Figure 4.27 Capital with the busts of Antoninus Pius and Faustina Maior carried by an eagle and peacock respectively, from the imperial villa on the via Aurelia at Lorium; Rome, Museo Nazionale Romano inv. 126362

Very occasionally, we also find other figures carrying the deceased to heaven. The much-discussed stucco ceiling relief in the so-called 'Basilica Sotterranea' at Porta Maggiore, which may have been the mausoleum of the Statilii family, shows a youth holding a jug and a torch being abducted by a winged figure.[266] While the jug and the age of the abductee are reminiscent of Ganymede, the torch clearly is not, and the winged figure is no obvious representative of Zeus. Gilles Sauron suggested that the winged figure is Attis (see his trousers) and that, according to one tradition, Ganymede is not Jupiter's cup-bearer but the star sign Aquarius. The scene would thus show the catasterism of the tomb's patron.[267] In the centre of the vault of the Servilii tomb, we have seen a woman riding on the back of a griffon (Figure 1.7).[268] While this particular iconography does not seem to have precedents in imperial images, the motif as such and the frequent use of griffons in religious contexts, including on the temples of state *divi*, suggests that the stucco relief was also meant to hint at the deceased's apotheosis. In the third century, an imperial freedman by the name of Eutyches dedicated a grave relief to his two-year-old son (Figure 4.28). The boy is shown riding

---

[266] Cumont, *Études syriennes*, 85–6, 89–90; *NSc* (1918), 30–52, esp. 40–1, 44 figs. 8, 18 (E. Gatti and F. Fornari); Bendinelli, 'Monumento sotterraneo', 685–6 pls. 15–16, 21.1 (Eros and Ganymede); North, 'Sappho', 47–53 fig. 3.9; Wypustek, *Beauty*, 138 with fig. 6 (erroneous third-century date). Generally on the monument, see also Lanciani, 'Santuario'; Cruciani, 'Suicidio'; Sciortino and Labianca, 'Basilica'; North, 'Sappho'.

[267] Sauron, *Quis*,. 605–30, followed by North, 'Sappho', who points to the possibility that the abductions by the Castores could also be read as cosmic or astral symbols.

[268] Chapter 1 p. 40.

Figure 4.28 Funerary relief for the son of Eutyches from the area of Albano, third century; Albano, Museo Civico, Antiquarium della Chiesa di S. Maria della Rotonda

to the heavens on a horse, probably in imitation of the Dioscuri. The reins have been taken up by an eagle, and the bilingual epitaph explains that Zeus's eagle has taken the boy away to heaven.[269]

These images obviously raise questions as to whether eagles, peacocks or griffons also allude to apotheosis when they appear on their own, especially

[269] Guarducci, *Scritti scelti*, 27–37 pls. 1–4, with Italian translation; *GVI* no. 861; Bechtold, *Gott und Gestirn*, 385 n. 1665, 387, 401–2 fig. 56, 416, both with German translation; Wypustek,

since the birds are sometimes depicted alone on coinage celebrating the consecration of a member of the imperial family.[270] This is virtually impossible to know, especially in the case of the eagle, which was employed as a symbol of power and victory in so many different contexts that it could have more general associations with cult and the highest god, or with power and protection of the tomb.[271] As Dietrich Boschung has observed, the latter meaning is strongly suggested by altars showing eagles standing over their prey.[272] I am not convinced, therefore, that the eagles carrying garlands on the corners of altars and sarcophagi necessarily hint at apotheosis, even though it can obviously not be excluded that viewers occasionally interpreted them in this way. Some images are more suggestive of such a specific notion, especially when they show the bird with its wings spread out as if in flight. In this pose, they sometimes appear on the pediment-shaped lids of cinerary urns, where we occasionally also find peacocks.[273] Where the tabula with the inscribed name of the deceased sits directly above an eagle with spread wings – that is, where the name takes the place of the image of the person – one could also consider a hint at apotheosis. Yet other figures in the same position, especially the frequent Gorgon heads, point rather to a protective function.[274] It is also anything but clear that the peacock on its own is a symbol of apotheosis since it appears in domestic contexts as well, and is a frequent choice for wall decoration of tombs where eagles are lacking. It could even be argued that the very scarcity of explicit images of the deceased being carried to the heavens suggests that the idea was not very widely expressed in funerary contexts. Similarly, griffons appear on a range of temples and altars that were not all related to cult of the *divi*, and even in domestic contexts.[275]

The other element that may allude to deification is astral symbols such as a star or stars, or a radiate crown.[276] Starting with Augustus' addition of stars to the statues of Caesar, stars and radiate crowns became the typical symbol of divinised emperors, even though the crown was also used for the living emperor from Nero onwards.[277] While it is normally a single star that

---

Beauty, 52–3, McIntyre, 'Deification', 235–8 fig. 4, and Mander, *Portraits of Children*, 193 cat. 150, all with English translations.

[270] As is proposed for the eagle by Lo Monaco, 'Immagini private', 347, for instance. See e.g. *BMC* III pls. 66.4–7 for Sabina, *BMC* IV pl. 7.16 for Faustina Maior, ibid., pls. 54.9–11 for Antoninus Pius.

[271] On the various roles of Jupiter, for whom the eagle could stand as a symbol, see Fears, 'Jupiter'.

[272] Boschung, *Grabaltäre*, 51.

[273] Ditto ibid., 50–1 with n. 730 for examples of eagles in pediments, and n. 733 for peacocks.

[274] Eagles, e.g. Altmann, *Römischen Grabaltäre*, nos. 2, 20, 54, 57, 60; Boschung, *Grabaltäre*, nos. 646, 648, 651–3, 679–81, 716–19, 721, 746.

[275] Simon, 'Greif'; see also Chapter 1 nn. 209–11.

[276] For a discussion of catasterism, see below.

[277] Bergmann, *Strahlen*.

Figure 4.29 Funerary relief for a boy and girl, around 180 CE; Copenhagen, National Museum 2223 GR

is shown with the emperor, arguably meaning the star that he has become, a Domitianic *aureus* shows the emperor's young son sitting on the globe and surrounded by seven stars, probably meaning that he is now 'among the stars' or 'in heaven'.[278]

This imagery has equally been adopted by private individuals. A Claudian or Neronian relief fragment, possibly from a tomb building, shows the frontal head of a boy with rays emanating against a background covered in stars.[279] The funerary altar of ten-year-old Iulia Victorina from the late Flavian period shows the girl with a crescent on her head on the front, and a young woman (her mother?) with a radiate crown on the back.[280] A relief for a boy and girl from around 180, now in Copenhagen, presents the bust of the girl within a large crescent moon and surrounded by stars (Figure 4.29).[281] In Eutyches' relief mentioned above (Figure 4.28), a star features above the boy's head, and the epitaph tells us that he is now a star and the 'companion [*synedros*] of Phosphoros and the beautiful Hesperos', the evening and

[278] *BMC Emp.* 2.311 nos. 62–3 pls. 61.6–7; Bechtold, *Gott und Gestirn*, 246–7 fig. 33; McIntyre, 'Deification', 229–30 fig. 2 (= *RIC* 2.1 no. 152).

[279] Bergmann (*Strahlen*, 167–9 pl. 33.4) argues convincingly that the individual is not Nero.

[280] *CIL* 6.20727 (= Paris, Louvre inv. 1443); Wrede, *Consecratio*, 123–4, 264–5 no. 183 pls. 26.1–2; Bergmann, *Strahlen*, 169 with n. 1003, who correctly observes that the two portraits must have been executed at the same time; Bechtold, *Gott und Gestirn*, 391 no. 49, 424–6, fig. 64.

[281] Copenhagen, National Museum 2223 GR: Cumont, *Symbolisme*, 240–1 pl. 20.3; Wrede, *Consecratio*, 265 no. 184; Bechtold, *Gott und Gestirn*, 392 no. 43, 423–4 fig. 63.

morning stars.[282] A star is shown on the *tondo* frame above the two-year-old Drosis, or Drosos, and on the crown of the head of one-year-old Aster.[283] Whether the holes around the forehead of a portrait in the Vatican origin-ally held the rays of a crown can no longer be determined with certainty.[284]

Other alleged examples of catasterism are more tenuous. Four funerary reliefs of third-century praetorians from the Danube region but found in Rome feature stars and a sickle moon,[285] although there is no direct link with the image of the deceased. The same applies where stars and sometimes a sickle moon feature above or beneath the inscription.[286] Two Season sar-cophagi depicting a zodiac around the busts of the deceased couple reflect ideas of the eternity of life in general with its perpetual seasonal cycle, but not necessarily catasterism.[287] The same is true for the famous Dumbarton Oaks Season sarcophagus with zodiac around a menorah.[288]

We need to return to the question of why such imagery is so rare, espe-cially since these astral symbols are arguably less obvious imitations of the emperors' apotheosis than the eagle flight. Moreover, I should note again that these motifs of apotheosis are predominantly connected with women and children, the Pomponii and the stuccos from the senatorial tombs being the only exceptions. This inevitably begs the next question.

Did the Romans Believe in Posthumous Apotheosis or an Afterlife?

This has been discussed extensively, and cannot be considered here in all its aspects.[289] I am therefore focusing again on evidence for the actual practices

---

[282] Bibl. above n. 269.

[283] Drosis/Drosos: Rome, Vatican City, Mus. Vat. inv. 10453; *IG* 14.1560; *IGUR* 1199; Cumont, *Symbolisme*, 170–1; Bechtold, *Gott und Gestirn*, 397 no. 78, 415–16 fig. 58, who thinks that the portrait has been reworked into a girl. The star was painted red when the casket was found and may have been gilded originally. Aster: funerary relief in private collection; Wrede, *Consecratio*, 124 pl. 26.3; Bechtold, *Gott und Gestirn*, 391 table 3 no. 39, 417 fig. 59. The inscription reads: *D(is) M(anibus) Asteris | vixit anno m. VIII d. XIX Aster et Spes filio dulcissimo.*

[284] Wrede, *Consecratio*, 302 no. 284. For important corrections on this portrait, which was reworked from a female portrait, see Bergmann (*Strahlen*, 169–70).

[285] Bechtold, *Gott und Gestirn*, 420–2 figs. 61–2, table 3 nos. 56–7, 79–80.

[286] Ibid., 397–8 table 3 nos. 81–5, 417–18.

[287] Differently ibid., table 3 nos. 55 and 64, 426–7 fig. 65. A third example with the bust of only a woman comes from Sicily: ibid., table 3 no. 61.

[288] Hanfmann, *Season Sarcophagus*. There is also a noticeable number of sarcophagi that have stars painted in red in various locations, which have not yet been collected or discussed, but would merit further attention.

[289] See e.g. Harkness, 'Scepticism'; Cumont, *Symbolisme*; Nock, 'Sarcophagi'; Bechtold, *Gott und Gestirn*, with a focus on catasterism; Wypustek, *Beauty*, on verse inscriptions. Summaries of

around burial and funerary commemoration, while largely leaving aside the more speculative philosophical treatises, which are unlikely to have had a great impact on majority practices.[290] Moreover, for heuristic reasons it is helpful to distinguish between posthumous apotheosis or deification and visions of an afterlife more generally, which will be treated in turn, even though the two are not entirely disconnected.

Posthumous Apotheosis

It will again be helpful to look at the beginnings of posthumous apotheosis, and what it meant for emperors and their families. Not only did private individuals model their practices on imperial precedent, it seems that the whole idea only took on a more specific shape in the last years of the Republic. However, there had long been a vague notion of the divinity of the departed, which is expressed in the collective term of *dii manes*, divine spirits, whom all mortals joined after death.[291] The deification of Romulus or the Dioscuri, and Euhemerus' explanation of the pantheon brought to Rome with Ennius' translation, attest to the idea of an individual divinity for mortal benefactors with outstanding achievements after their death.[292] The altar or shrine for Minucius outside the Porta Minucia honoured not the god of the *gens* Minucia, but probably the consul of 458 BCE and founder of the *gens*, who also received the exceptional honour of a statue on a column.

---

the debate include Esteve-Forriol, *Trostgedichte*, passim, esp. 147–8, on literary consolations; Hope, *Death*, 211–47, and Hope, *Roman Death*, 97–120, for brief overviews; Brandenburg, 'Meerwesensarkophage', 242–4 for a focus on visual material; Koch and Sichtermann, *Römische Sarkophage*, 583–617; Müller, *Peleus and Thetis Sarcophagus*, 98–106; Pekáry, 'Jenseitsglaube'. For more philosophical treatments of the question, see e.g. Weinstock, *Julius*; North, 'Praesens divus'; Cole, *Cicero*.

[290] See Nock, 'Sarcophagi', for a similar approach in response to Cumont's *Symbolisme*. I am aware of the problems involved here. After all, even when it is highly unlikely that the majority will have engaged with these philosophical speculations, the latter may still have influenced the thinking of the general public over time, and some were more publicly available than others. Most scholars agree, for instance, that Cicero's reflections, some of which were also propounded in public speeches, had a major impact on practices of deification of both living and deceased leaders (cf. most notably Cole, *Cicero*, with further bibl.).

[291] On the divinity of the *dii manes*, see Bömer, *Ahnenkult*, 1–26; Weinstock, *Julius*, 291–2; Clauss, *Herrscherkult*, 41–2; Gradel, *Emperor Worship*, 264; more recently King, 'Manes'; and among primary sources, e.g. *Ep. Corneliae*, Nepos fr. 2: '*ubi mortua ero, parentabis mihi et invocabis deum parentem*' (much discussed, see Weinstock, *Julius*, 295 with bibl. in n. 1, 22–4; Hallett, 'Women', with translation and bibl.).

[292] Gradel, *Emperor Worship*, 266–7. In Ennius, Scipio Africanus is made to prophesy *si fas endo plagas caelestum ascendere cuiquam est,* | *mi soli caeli maxima porta patet* (Lactantius, *Div. inst.* 1. 18. 11). Weinstock, *Julius*, 294, interprets these and similar texts as evidence that Scipio had a public cult (contra Gradel, *Emperor Worship*, 266 n. 7).

According to Festus ((Paulus) 109L, 131L), he was thought to be a god.[293] Similar sentiments could also lead to spontaneous divine cult. According to Plutarch, the Roman people erected statues of the Gracchi and started sacrificing to them after their assassination, probably around 120 BCE (*C. Gracch.* 18.2).[294] Similarly spontaneous was apparently the people's reaction to Caesar's death, when they erected an altar on the Forum at the spot where he was cremated.[295]

Cicero provides us with the most extensive and explicit reflections on the justifications for posthumous deification, and on the way it may be brought about. As Spencer Cole has demonstrated, after initially considering divinity for the living, later, especially in his post-exilic speeches, Cicero focused on deification of the deceased while the criteria remained the same: exceptional service to the Republic and moral virtue.[296] The reason for this change may well have been his disillusionment with some of the figures he considered as living divinities, such as Pompey who, he declared, had 'fallen from the stars' by 59 BCE. Yet the result had a great advantage also for the deceased: posthumous deification granted immortality. What is important to note in our context is that this immortality was not primarily about the kind of existence ('life') an individual may enjoy after death, which Cicero considered only in the very vaguest of terms.[297] To 'ascend to heaven' (*in caelo ascendere*) and similar phrases are used synonymously with being 'counted among the number of the gods' (*in deorum numero collocatus*) and the like. It is primarily figurative speech that builds on the old idea that (most of) the gods reside in heaven, and on a hierarchy of space where high and low are both physical and metaphorical categories;[298] it is not meant to evoke a posthumous lifestyle, as epitaphs and poetry sometimes do.[299] Rather, the key point was lasting reward for an exemplary

---

[293] Weinstock, *Julius*, 293–4. The consul was celebrated by the moneyers C. and Ti. Minucius Augurinus on coins of *c.* 135 BCE. Welin (*Topographie*, 167–70) first noticed that the ensemble must have adorned the family tomb as it was situated outside the city gate. Cf. Hölscher, 'Repräsentationskunst', 336–7; Wiseman, 'Minucii', 57–60.

[294] Flower, *Forgetting*, 79–81; Koortbojian, *Divinization*, 3.

[295] According to Dio 44.51, and Appian, *B Civ.* 1.4, they sacrificed to Caesar as a god; Cicero, *Phil.* 1.5, speaks about a tomb on the Forum.

[296] Cole, *Cicero*, 75 and passim. It should be noted here that it ultimately does not matter for our purposes what exactly Cicero believed deep in his heart (the contradictions within his writings are stressed esp. by Setaioli, 'Cicero and Seneca'), but what ideas he seriously considered, which may reflect or have influenced what his contemporaries thought.

[297] Cole, *Cicero*, 78, on *Mil.* 16.

[298] See Bechtold, *Gott und Gestirn*, 38–56, for the origins of eschatological conceptions of the sky and the stars.

[299] E.g. Statius, *Silv.* 3.19–23.

life, and the perpetuation of distinction and status in the world order and in human memory. Especially in *Somnuim Scipionis*, drawing on Platonic and Stoic ideas, Cicero explores the idea of an immortal soul or mind, but crucially extends it into merit-based divinity for the particularly deserving and divine men of Rome.[300] Rather than joining the underground *dii manes*, the *viri boni* occupy a special place in heaven or among the stars, and in eternal memory. In *De re publica* (2.27) we read:

> quod autem ex hominum genere consecratos, sicut Herculem et ceteros, coli lex iubet, indicat omnium quidem animos immortalis esse, sed fortium bonorumque divinos.

> That the law orders the worship of those from the human race who have been consecrated, like Hercules and the rest, shows that the souls of all people are immortal but the souls of the brave and good are divine.

And in *De legibus* (2.22), Marcus decrees: 'Let the rights of the spirits of the dead be sacred, let them consider good men who have died gods' (*deorum Manium iura sancta sunto. [bo]-nos leto datos divos habento*).[301] Obviously, as for living mortals, divinity is a special honour and marker of status, although expressing the idea has become more difficult: while all souls and/or all deceased are immortal and therefore divine in an ontological sense (thus the *manes* are *dii*), the specific divinity here at stake is that of the distinction awarded to the deserving few, an emphatic and earned divinity.

The concept of posthumous divinity also changed the traditional relationship between divinity and worshipper to some extent. The element of reciprocity that was so essential for divine cult, and that, in the case of living gods, always extended into the future, where further benefactions were expected, was here limited almost exclusively to a retrospective perspective: the *res publica* had received favours during the benefactor's lifetime, and was now offering the reward. Writing in the context of Vespasian's consecration, Pliny (*HN* 2.18–19) explains: 'and it is the oldest way of giving thanks to benefactors to enrol them among the gods'. As we saw above,[302] some believed – or hoped – that the deceased could help to extend the life of the survivors. However, this hope did not depend on deification, as is shown by instances where the *dii manes* are addressed with the request.

---

[300] Cf. Cole, *Cicero*, 81–110 with bibl., and the rest of his Chapter 2.

[301] Ibid., 107–9, on these passages. See also *Tusc.* 1.27 with Cole, *Cicero*, 139–40, 190; *Nat. D.* 2.62 with Cole, *Cicero*, 156, and the rest of his book.

[302] See p. 222.

Conversely, the imperial *divi* and *divae* were not normally expected to interfere with human life, and their cult features at the very bottom of the list of *Arval Acta*, even following the cult of the living emperor.[303]

Posthumous deification as a reward also explains why the living could harbour such expectations. This was the case with Ennius' Scipio[304] and underlies much of Cicero's musings.[305] Augustus' posthumous apotheosis was not only predicted by the poets but widely expected, as for instance a dedication by a centurion in Acerrae makes clear.[306] Nero and Claudius were depicted on cameos during their lifetime as riding on an eagle (Figure 4.10), an expression of similar expectations that would only come true for the latter as far as state cult is concerned.[307]

As with the cult of the immortal and living mortal gods, the nature of the reward was acknowledgement of superior status and honour. This is confirmed by imperial-period sources, which refer to the act of state *consecratio* as one of bestowing *honores caelestes* (heavenly honours)[308] or divine honours on the deceased.[309] This is also why, again, no sign of approval from the traditional gods was needed,[310] and no magical act was required to make emperors *divi*, only a *senatus consultum*. As we have seen in Chapter 2, the eagle's flight at the state funeral was not a prerequisite for an effective apotheosis but a visual enactment of it, a symbol.

The background to the deification of imperial women and children has rarely been discussed beyond the suspicion that it was an act of flattery of the ruling emperor.[311] Yet while flattery will surely have played a part, their

---

[303] Gradel, *Emperor Worship*, 275–6. See also nn. 43 and 56 above for temples and new cults normally established for living rather than deified emperors.

[304] See n. 292.

[305] For Cicero's own aspirations, see e.g. *Cat.* 3.2, but also his post-exile orations as discussed by Cole, *Cicero*, esp. 99; cf. Clauss, *Herrscherkult*, 46. Also note that one of the first occurrences of the term apotheosis in ancient literature is Curio's alleged habit of calling Cicero's consulship an apotheosis: *Att.* 1.16.13 of 61 BCE with Cole, *Cicero*, 61.

[306] *CIL* 10.3757 (Acerrae) (= *ILS* 137), quoted with translation in Gradel, *Emperor Worship*, 268–9; Koortbojian, *Divinization*, 160 with bibl. n. 15.

[307] On the cameos, see n. 261.

[308] E.g. the *fasti* for Augustus (Gradel, *Emperor Worship*, 274 on Degrassi, *Fasti*, 510); Tacitus, *Ann.* 12.69.4 on Claudius. Gradel (*Emperor Worship*, 262–3) argues that Caesar's case was different in so far as it was almost unavoidable to officially award him divine honours after death since he – the only Roman ever – received such cult already during his lifetime.

[309] E.g. Appian, *B Civ.* 2.148 on Caesar; Suetonius, *Claud.* 11.2 on Livia; Tacitus, *Ann.* 12.69 on Claudius and 16.21 on Poppaea.

[310] Again, this differs from philosophical thought. Cf. Gradel's reading of the *Apokolokynthosis* as an exploration of how the human decision to make someone a god may be misunderstood as also having consequences for the traditional gods from a *philosophical* point of view (*Emperor Worship*, 325–30).

[311] However, see McIntyre, 'Deification', with examples also in n. 6.

deification can be integrated into the framework I have outlined so far. The achievements of imperial women may not have been on the same level and of the same nature as those of the state's leaders, but not least their coin images and portraits in divine costume demonstrate that their various female virtues were understood as underpinning the state and its welfare. Moreover, as with the divinity of living mortals, there appears to be a shift in expectations of what kind of service and achievement justifies posthumous deification. If we understand the latter as an attempt at perpetuating hierarchies beyond death, not only women but also the (much fewer) cases of deified children, whose qualities may otherwise mainly have resided in their potential, fit the scheme.

From a more pragmatic point of view, the deification of emperors has mostly been seen as a legitimising strategy by their heirs to the throne: a divine predecessor will not have chosen an unworthy successor, and being the son of a god is a marker of status in its own right.[312] This latter aspect obviously also works for deified mothers of emperors, but may be extended to the imperial family more widely. Whether or not the term *domus divina* originally meant the house of a *divus*, Fishwick has argued convincingly that it must soon have assumed the meaning of 'divine household'.[313] This status would have been reaffirmed by every family member being awarded the status of *divus* or *diva* and, in support, McIntyre has rightly pointed to Domitia's unique title of *divi Caesaris mater*, acquired after her dead four-month-old son was deified.[314] Whatever the more cynical background to posthumous deification of members of the imperial family may have been, it is still noteworthy that, at the level of both ideology and religious concept, the practice fits well into the general framework we find in Cicero.

Afterlife

While posthumous apotheosis inevitably entails the notion of an afterlife of some sort, we have seen that details of what this life may entail normally did not matter.[315] This differs with some other notions of what may happen after death. In particular, the idea of living on in Elysium or on the Isles of Bliss gained prominence in the late first century BCE and the imperial period.

---

[312] Esp. Gesche, 'Divinisierung'; Bergmann, *Strahlen*, 5–6, 99–100; Bechtold, *Gott und Gestirn*, 283–91. A similar point has of course often been made with regard to Olympian deities as ancestors (e.g. Wiseman, 'Genealogies'; Hekster, 'Genealogies'; Hekster, *Emperors*, 239–56), but it applies as well to the *divi*.

[313] Fishwick, *Imperial Cult Vol. II*, 423–35. Cf. Corbier, 'Maiestas', esp. 181–2, for the close connection between the terms and concept of *domus Augusta* and *domus divina*.

[314] McIntyre, 'Deification', 230–1; similarly Bechtold, *Gott und Gestirn*, 288.

[315] Cf. also Bechtold, *Gott und Gestirn*, 27–8.

Vergil's more positive elaboration of Homer's underworld in book six of the *Aeneid* was hugely influential on both consolatory literature and funerary epigraphy.[316] We find again the idea that a good and virtuous life should be rewarded, and that the world beyond reflects life on earth. Yet this reflection is not only about status but also about a posthumous lifestyle, a lifestyle that lacks earthly tribulations and that involves a strong social aspect, in that the deceased typically meet those who are like themselves and can continue those aspects of their life that they most valued.[317] Thus Corinna's parrot is going to meet other pious birds (Ovid, *Am.* 2.6.49–52), Tibullus and Statius' father will meet other pious poets (Ovid, *Am.* 3.9.59–66; Statius, *Silv.* 5.3.26) and Drusus or Metilius their noble ancestors (*Consolatio ad Liviam* 329–40; Seneca, *Consolatio ad Marciam* 25.2). While admission to Elysium is a reward, it is also clear that it does not involve an apotheosis. Elysium is always located in the underworld, and one still joins the *dii manes*. The distinction is made explicit in the *Consolatio ad Liviam*, according to which only Romulus, Caesar and Augustus could achieve apotheosis (221–52), but Drusus would join his ancestors in the Fields of Bliss (329–40).[318]

This also explains the different attitudes we find in comparison with posthumous deification. Provided there was a fundamental belief in the immortality of the soul, divinity could be bestowed upon the deceased by the survivors; it was in the eye of the beholder, who felt that the deceased deserved this particular distinction. In contrast, an afterlife in Elysium (or elsewhere) was beyond the powers of humans, since it claimed a physical reality rather than a personal relationship. Accordingly, the prospect is typically presented as highly uncertain.[319] Ovid introduces the parrot's Elysium with the words 'if we have faith in doubtful things' (*siqua fides dubiis*: *Amores* 2.6.51) and that of Tibullus with 'If anything survives of us beyond name and shade' (*Si tamen e nobis aliquid nisi nomen et umbra restat, in Elysia valle Tibullus erit*: *Amores* 3.9.59–60; cf. verse 65: *siqua est modo corporis umbra*). Drusus may join his ancestors 'if such belief is not vain' (*si non temere haec creduntur*: *Consolatio ad Liviam* 329), and even Statius is uncertain whether

---

[316] On the interdependence of literature and epitaphs, see e.g. Hoogma, *Einfluss*; Zarker, 'Verse'; Pekáry, 'Jenseitsglaube'; Ramsby, 'Striving for permanence'; Ramsby, *Permanence*, with bibl.; Erasmo, *Reading Death*, 154–204. For an overview of Roman literary concepts, see *RAC* 17 (1996) 295–302 s.v. Jenseits (Jenseitsvorstellungen) (P. Habermehl); Hope, *Roman Death*, 97–120; Bechtold, *Gott und Gestirn*, 372, 407–15; and below.

[317] Esteve-Forriol, *Trostgedichte*, 147–9 §§ 51–3, 157–8 § 80.

[318] Cf. Manilius, *Astronomica* 1.798–804, on which see n. 396 below.

[319] Esteve-Forriol, *Trostgedichte*, 148; Brandenburg, 'Meerwesensarkophage', esp. 206, 242; Müller, *Peleus and Thetis Sarcophagus*, esp. 95–6.

his father will live on in heaven (which here is another abode, not a metaphor for divinity) or in the Elysian Fields (*Silv.* 5.19–28).

On occasion, the two notions of apotheosis and afterlife could overlap, especially where apotheosis was envisaged as catasterism. Vergil was already speculating in the proem to this *Georgics* about the exact place and role Octavian may eventually take up in heaven after his death (1.32–40), and so do Lucan, in the proem to his *Pharsalia* on behalf of Nero (1.45–59), and Statius, in the proem to his *Thebaid* on behalf of Domitian (1.24–31).[320] Still, it is surely no coincidence that these passages are part of poetic panegyrics of the living emperor, and that we do not find any of this in *laudationes funebres* or *consolationes*,[321] or indeed in any of the historians who regularly comment on the death and apotheosis of their protagonists. As Bechtold has seen, the poetic visions of life among the stars serve as opportunities to comment on the power and roles of the emperor during his lifetime, and on his divinity, and aim to extend both into eternity.[322]

Afterlife and Apotheosis in Epitaphs

Given the relative frequency with which hopes for an afterlife in Elysium (or elsewhere) feature in poetic consolations, it is interesting to note that similar notions are extremely rare in epitaphs. Where the latter comment on death at all, their outlook is typically rather gloomy and full of lament, as indeed is that of many literary texts.[323] At best, death is seen as a relief from all the hardship of earthly existence.[324] Epitaphs normally stress that there is no return, and that death is the end of everything.[325] Among the tens of thousands of epitaphs from Rome, there are only eight referring to Elysium and three to the Isles of Bliss,[326] with one of these claiming that the deceased is on the Isles of Bliss as well as in the Elysian Fields and close to

---

[320] On these, see Bechtold, *Gott und Gestirn*, 229–30, 339–56, with bibl.

[321] On the former, see esp. Kierdorf, *Laudatio funebris*; on the latter, Esteve-Forriol, *Trostgedichte*.

[322] Bechtold, *Gott und Gestirn*, 340–1.

[323] Harkness, 'Scepticism'; Galletier, *Poésie funéraire*, 7–19; Brelich, *Aspetti della morte*; Hopkins, *Death*, 230; Peres, *Eschatologie*, 26–59.

[324] Brelich, *Aspetti della morte*, 59–60; Lattimore, *Themes*, 209–10, 213–14 with n. 304; Brandenburg, 'Meerwesensarkophage', 221 with n. 84, 237, 242 n. 134; Esteve-Forriol, *Trostgedichte*, 152; Pekáry, 'Jenseitsglaube', 97–8, each with examples.

[325] Harkness, 'Scepticism'; Brelich, *Aspetti della morte*, esp. 54–61; Pekáry, 'Jenseitsglaube'.

[326] Galletier, *Poésie funéraire*, 53–8; Brelich, *Aspetti della morte*, 45, 78–9; Engemann, *Sepulkralsymbolik*, 44 n. 27 with thirty-one examples, including the following from Rome: *GVI* 1830 (= *GG* no. 399) and 1924; *CLE* 393, 435, 1061, 1111, 1143, 1165; and Engemann, *Sepulkralsymbolik*, 46 nn. 29–34 with twelve examples (literary accounts at 44–5 n. 28), including from Rome: *GVI* 1830 and 2061, *EpGr* 1046 (Heroon for Regilla).

Olympus.[327] Where any details are given at all, it is normally clear that this Elysium is in the underworld and the deceased is joining the *dii manes*.[328] On occasion, Elysium is even a very sad place.[329] The idea that the deceased will meet like-minded souls is also sometimes expressed in epitaphs, especially where she or he joins the Muses, Nymphs or Naiads,[330] the heroes of old,[331] or generally the pious.[332] While there is a vague suggestion in all these notions that the deceased are elevated in status and similar in some way to those they join, it is neither said that they have become heroes themselves (a notion that could only be expressed in Greek epitaphs, as there is no Latin equivalent of the term heroisation) nor that they are divine. It has also long been noted that the vague speculations we find are strongly dependent on poetry. Not only is their content based on the visions of Rome's great poets, and especially Vergil and Ovid, but they also appear almost exclusively in metric epitaphs and borrow heavily from literary masterpieces in style.[333] This alone does not discount the possibility that some were more confident that such scenarios could come true than others.[334] Yet the rarity of such notions even among metric epitaphs – there are only fifteen metropolitan Roman metric epitaphs with such motifs – and, especially, in comparison to the ubiquity of gloomier or nihilistic outlooks, suggests that they did not represent a more widespread hope, let alone belief.

Only ten epitaphs from Rome mention life in Elysium or on the Isles of Bliss. Slightly more frequently, we see claims that the deceased or, more frequently, his or her soul is said to be in heaven/aether,[335] among the stars[336] or

---

Engemann's lists here and in the following notes are based on *CLE* and *GVI*. Cf. Peres, *Eschatologie*, 75–81.

[327] *GVI* 1830 (= *GG* no. 399).

[328] E.g. *molliter ad matrem placidi descendite Manes Elysiis campis floreat umbra tibi*: CIL 6.7886 (= *CLE* 1143), for a nineteen-year-old woman.

[329] CIL 6.10097 (= 33960) for a twenty-four to thirty-year-old man: Courtney, *Musa Lapidaria*, 120–1, 330–1 no. 123; Kolb and Fugmann, *Tod in Rom*, 209–13 no. 56, both with text, translation and bibl.

[330] Engemann, *Sepulkralsymbolik*, 48 nn. 43–5, with eight examples, of which one envisaging life among the Naiads (*GVI* 1595) and two among the Muses (*GVI* 1049, *CLE* 1109) are from Rome.

[331] Ibid., 46–7 n. 35 with thirteen examples, none of which is from Rome.

[332] Ibid., 43 nn. 25–6 with forty-one examples, of which four are from Rome (*GVI* 1017, 1940, 1970, 1830).

[333] Cf. n. 316 above.

[334] As rightly pointed out by Lattimore (*Themes*, 19), Cumont (*Lux*, 71), Hopkins (*Death*, 220), King ('Commemoration', 131–6, 148, 150–1) and Bechtold (*Gott und Gestirn*, 411–12), against e.g. Pekáry ('Jenseitsglaube'), who thinks that the topoi are a mere demonstration of *paideia*.

[335] Engemann, *Sepulkralsymbolik*, 49–50 nn. 48–50, with thirty-five examples.

[336] Kajanto, 'Hereafter', 34 n. 37; Engemann, *Sepulkralsymbolik*, 49–50 n. 51; Orth, 'Katasterismos'; Peres, *Eschatologie*, 86–9; Bechtold, *Gott und Gestirn*, passim, with fifteen examples (p. 375).

even among the gods.[337] Nevertheless, of Bechtold's sixty-two epitaphs with astral motifs, only fourteen are from Rome and its environs and mention the stars in the inscription. In one, in imitation of a pseudo-Platonian epigram on a deceased disciple (*Ant. Gr.* 7.670), a Crescentina is said to have been the morning star among the living, and is now going to descend to the underworld as the evening star among the dead. Her stardom is clearly not catasterism.[338] One particularly early epitaph blames the Morning Star for having abducted a young woman out of envy.[339] In two cases, residing among the stars is only a vague potentiality.[340] In another, only the image of the deceased is among the stars (*effigies vaga per sidera collitur*), an honour also found in some literary catasterisms.[341] Several, however, are more positive and more assertive. P. Aelius Pius rises to heaven and the stars at the age of six months,[342] and so does the 'divine and heavenly soul' of three-year-old Anulina.[343] Similarly, the late antique epitaph for the adult Simplicia tells us that her soul (*anima*) has returned to the stars.[344] In all these cases, it is unclear whether the idea is an individual divinity of the deceased, or whether we are simply looking at another way of expressing belief in the immortality of the soul. Where the souls are taken to the sky by deities[345] or themselves become stars,[346] however, catasterism is clearly a personal distinction. This is the case in two Roman examples and one from Ostia. In the fragmentary Greek epitaph from Rome's port town, the deceased has exchanged the world of evil men for a place in heaven and has become a

---

[337] Engemann, *Sepulkralsymbolik*, 48 nn. 46–7, with twenty-five examples; for a breakdown see below. There are also epitaphs that mention the separation of the soul from the body without any further comment: Brelich, *Aspetti della morte*, 81–2.

[338] *GVI* 585; *GG* no. 295; Bechtold, *Gott und Gestirn*, 387 n. 1676 no. 44.

[339] *CIL* 6.17130 (= *CLE* 963), dated to 29 July 12 BC. Bechtold (*Gott und Gestirn*, 385–6) rightly connects this with the idea of an adverse horoscope; cf. Saddington, 'Inscriptions', with English transl.

[340] Bechtold *Gott und Gestirn*, 383: his no. 73 (*CIL* 6.36658 = *CLE* 544) is a large sarcophagus for a *c.* seventeen-year-old adolescent; no. 74 (*CIL* 6.27383 (p. 3534) = *CLE* 1061) is for a two-year-old girl, on which see also Wrede, *Consecratio*, 107; Di Stefano Manzella, *Index inscriptionum*, 133, 206 fig. 28b no. 105.

[341] *IG* 14.2141; *GVI* 1769; Bechtold, *Gott und Gestirn*, 383 no. 41 (fifteen-year-old son), cf. pp. 72–4 on stars or constellations as memorials.

[342] *CIL* 6.10764 (p. 3507); *CLE* 1535; Bechtold, *Gott und Gestirn*, 385 n. 1669, 391 no. 38.

[343] *CIL* 6.12087 (p. 5310); *CLE* 611; Bechtold, *Gott und Gestirn*, 385 n. 1668, 397 no. 75, 407.

[344] *AE* 1987, 0050; possibly Christian: Bechtold, *Gott und Gestirn*, 395 no. 66. Bechtold's no. 46 (= *IG* 14.2141 = *GVI* 1769) is too fragmentary to see what the deceased has to do with the stars (ibid., 392).

[345] Ibid., 385.

[346] Ibid., 386–90.

star.[347] The little son of Eutyches discussed above (Figure 4.28) is taken to heaven by Zeus's eagle, and has become the playmate of the Morning and Evening Stars.[348] The adolescent Nepos is taken to the skies by Venus herself, where, so his kinsman speculates,

> escorted by a crowd of amorini, you happily mingle with the amusements of Adonis, or you rejoice in the crowd of the Muses or in the artistic skill of Athena. If you should want to fasten heavy clusters of ivy-berries to the thyrsus and veil your hair with vine-shoots, you will be Bacchus; if you should want to grow your hair and garland it with bay and take up bow and quiver, you will be Apollo. Put on fine sleeves and a Phrygian (cap), more than one love will quicken in Cybele's breast. (transl. E. Courtney)

These musings are similar to the poets' speculations about the emperors' activities in heaven.[349]

Of Bechtold's thirty-two items that talk in more general terms about the soul's return to the aether or the sky, only three extant epitaphs and a literary one attributed to Seneca come from Rome, and only the last one potentially predates the third century.[350] Again, the implications are not entirely clear. While the divinity of emperors could be indicated in this way, the notion first and foremost expressed the idea that the soul is immortal and returns to where it came from.

A few epitaphs from Rome and Ostia declare that the deceased has joined the immortals[351] or the gods,[352] has ascended to Olympus, the dwelling

---

[347] Guarducci, 'Pitagorismo', 213–15 fig. 3. The wording and rape by the Moirai point to a young deceased, and the lament that he was taken from 'sweet' life produces some contradiction with the final, more positive statement about his catasterism.

[348] See n. 269 above.

[349] *CIL* 6.21521 (= 34137 (cf. 39763) = *CLE* 1109): Pekáry, 'Jenseitsglaube', 92–6; Courtney, *Musa Lapidaria*, 170–3, 381–4 no. 183; Erasmo, *Reading Death*, 201–3; Bechtold, *Gott und Gestirn*, 385 n. 1663, 391 table 3 no. 37, 405–6 fig. 57, 408–10; Newby, *Greek Myths*, 302–3, all with (partial) transl. On the emperors, see n. 63 above; Bechtold, *Gott und Gestirn*, 338–40.

[350] Bechtold, *Gott und Gestirn*, 380–2 table 2 nos. 16 (*EpGr* 645 = *CIG* 6301), 17 (*CIL* 6.13528 (p. 3513) = *CLE* 1559 = *AE* 1999, 212), 19 (*IG* 14.1976 = *GVI* 1169 = *EpGr* 642), 32 (*epitaphium Senecae*, *CLE* 667 = *Anth. Pal.* 667). On 17, see Courtney, *Musa Lapidaria*, 178–9, 389–90; Massaro, 'Nozze perpetue'; Erasmo, *Reading Death*, 171–3; on 19, see Horsley, *New Documents*, 35–8 no. 10 with English transl.; Buonocore, *Iscrizioni*, 93–4, pl. 37 fig. 61, with Italian transl.; on 32, see Prato, *Epigrammi*, 238 no. 71; Flammini, 'Epitaphium'.

[351] Engemann, *Sepulkralsymbolik*, 48 n. 42. Of his eleven examples, only one is from Rome: *GVI* 1768 (= *IGUR* 1280 = *EpGr* 652 = *IG* 14.1868); cf. Marshall, *Collection*, 214 no. 1095; Obryk, *Unsterblichkeitsglaube*, 23–4 no. A5, with German transl.

[352] Engemann, *Sepulkralsymbolik*, 48 n. 46. Of thirteen examples, four are from Rome (*GVI* 613, 743, *CLE* 975, 1109) and one from Ostia (*IG* 14.932 = *GVI* 1111). To these should be added two Latin epitaphs for adult men whose souls have been received among the gods (*cuius spiritus inter deos receptus est*: *CIL* 6.2160, 9663).

of Zeus or the gods,[353] or is or has become divine.[354] Except for the three examples of the final category, the exact meaning of these phrases is still slightly ambiguous, as they claim closeness to the gods but not necessarily divinity as such. I have argued elsewhere that divine protection of the deceased was a comforting idea also expressed in images.[355] Nevertheless, the phrases certainly *could* mean apotheosis, as the same ones are used of the imperial *divi* and, in any case, clearly attest to the idea of the immortality of the soul.[356] The soul's privileged place of residence is clearly a distinction that is sometimes explicitly explained by the deceased's merits.

This overview is telling in a number of respects. First, all these notions of an afterlife are extraordinarily rare in epitaphs, even when we disregard the vast majority of inscriptions that refrain entirely from any comment on death and what may lie beyond; epitaphs with nihilistic or gloomy notions far outnumber them. This suggests that the underlying ideas, be they consoling thoughts of a pleasant existence after death or honorific or both, were not very prevalent. Secondly, as in the literary comparanda, notions of an afterlife are often expressed with some caveat, or several options are listed that expose uncertainties and doubts.[357] Thirdly, epitaphs confirm that we should differentiate between more specific visions of the place and 'lifestyle' of the departed, and more general notions of the immortality of the soul and posthumous divinity. Within the small sample of relevant epitaphs, the themes reviewed show different and interesting gender and age distributions. Both notions of an afterlife in Elysium or similar and of elevation to the

---

[353]   Engemann, *Sepulkralsymbolik*, 48–9 n. 47. Of fourteen examples, two are from Rome: *EpGr* 646a (= *SEG* 49.2407= *CIL* 6.26251 = *IG* 14.2002 = *GVI* 1146 = *IGUR* 1329) and *GVI* 1283 (= *IG* 14.1424 = *EpGr* 594 = *IGUR* 1163 = Obryk, *Unsterblichkeitsglaube*, 139–42 no. E10 with German transl.). An additional one comes from Ostia: *GVI* 909 (= *NSc* (1912) 327, d + 459 = Guarducci, 'Pitagorismo', 212–13 fig. 2).

[354]   On the epitaph of M. Lucceius Nepos see n. 349 above. The epitaph of an anonymous deceased explains 'I am a god' (*corpore consumpt[o] viva anima deus sum*: *CIL* 6.30157 = *CLE* 975); a three-year-old girl is counted among the number of the gods in an expression used for the apotheosis of emperors and in Cicero (*in deo[rum nume]ro recepta est*: *CIL* 6.30552.2; cf. *CIL* 9.2628 on Divus Iulius); more ambiguously, the children of Sex. Pompeius Iustus are said to possess divinity 'if there are *dii manes*' (*si sunt di manes iam nati numen habetis*: *CIL* 6.24520; *CLE* 1057).

[355]   Borg, 'Slumber', 279–81.

[356]   This is an aspect that I underestimated in 'Slumber'.

[357]   E.g. in *GVI* 909 (n. 353), the deceased woman musician is said to be either among the blessed or in Olympus; *CIL* 6.24520 (= *CLE* 1057) declares that the deceased are divine 'if there are Divine Spirits'; in *CIL* 6.27383 (p. 3534) (= *CLE* 1061), Vestina Clodia 'may' be elevated to the heavens and the stars. On speculations in Nepos' epitaph, see n. 349 above. Eutyches' son's epitaph (n. 269 above) is also lacking in consistence of thought. Cf. Bechtold, *Gott und Gestirn*, 406, on the 'Unverbindlichkeit der verschiedenen Apotheoseformen' ('non-binding nature of different forms of apotheosis').

stars occur almost exclusively in epitaphs of women and the prematurely deceased. Since both are evoked in literature also in connection with adult men, it is highly likely that the imbalance is genre-specific. Notions of the deceased soul having risen to heaven/aether, joined the gods or become divine – that is, more abstract expressions of distinction and the immortality of the soul – are found among both genders and all ages, including adult men. References to an afterlife in Elysium, on the Isles of Bliss or among the stars may therefore be seen as poetic renderings of these otherwise more abstract ideas. If this is so, epitaphs would normally use such poetic elaborations only for women and the prematurely deceased. This observation is reminiscent of Pseudo-Dionysius of Halicarnassus' advice that the liberation of the soul from the prison of the body should only be mentioned in consolations of the prematurely deceased (Ps.-Dionys. Hal. *Rhet.* 6.5, II 282). This is obviously not what we find in these epitaphs, but it demonstrates – as does other advice found here for *consolationes* – the selectiveness in what is deemed appropriate to *mention* in funerary contexts. I have observed in Chapter 1 that the higher the social status, the rarer the more sentimental or poetic expressions, and the senatorial class also refrained from using metric epitaphs from the first century BCE to the end of the third century CE.[358] We may therefore conclude that a minority in Roman society did hope for or even believe in a post-mortem existence, which they expressed sometimes in more abstract and general terms, sometimes in more poetic terms, among which we should also count the visual representations discussed above.[359]

Temple Tombs and Divinity

Where does this leave us with the temple tombs? As already noted, no private person was ever officially deified in imperial Rome, but the question here is whether there are indications of private posthumous deification similar to the deification of living people. If we apply the same criteria as those for deified emperors, this question must probably be answered in

---

[358] As observed by Galletier, *Poésie funéraire*, 52, 191–2, 198–200; Bechtold, *Gott und Gestirn*, 372–3. After the *elogia* for the Scipios, metric epitaphs were used exclusively by the sub-elite until the fourth century, when they become a marker of the elite. The extraordinary poems from Herodes Atticus' Triopion may be called an exception to the rule, but they are not strictly epitaphs (see also below). For altar and sarcophagus decoration, see above Chapter 1.

[359] How difficult their messages are to pin down, however, is demonstrated by the epitaph and image on the sarcophagus of three-year-old Drosos or Drosis (n. 283 above). While a star features on the *clipeus* frame over the child's head, the inscription tells us that its beauty has gone into the aether, yet insists at the end 'no one is immortal'.

the negative. While it is always dangerous to argue *ex silentio*, there is no indication that the deceased received a new cult name, nor that cult for the dead was suspended for private individuals as it was for the imperial *divi* and *divae*.[360] Then again, Cicero's framework of posthumous divinity did not include these two elements, and could have worked well for private individuals of the imperial period. A prerequisite was the belief in the existence of an immortal soul, and we have seen that at least some epitaphs attest to this belief outside philosophical circles too. In addition, we may speculate that it was more widespread among those who never talk about death and what lies beyond it in their epitaphs, namely the social elite, who also tended to be more philosophically educated.[361] To the extent that immortality automatically entailed some kind of divinity – as it did for Cicero – this soul would also have been divine. Yet the emphatic, earned divinity that Cicero wanted to achieve for the *viri boni* and his daughter, and that the Senate decreed for members of the imperial family, was, as we have seen, a special distinction that elevated the deceased above and beyond the majority, and one that was bestowed by humans. Since the title *divus* or *diva* had been established for divinised members of the imperial family, it may not come as a surprise that it was hardly ever used outside their circles. I am aware of only one example, from *CIL* 6, in which the four-year-old Cal(l)istianus is called *divus et dominus meus*.[362] Unfortunately, the dedicant is unknown and the inscription cannot be dated. Yet it is surely no coincidence that the phrase clearly indicates the origin of the deceased's divine status: the anonymous commemorator (*meus*). This divinity is the emphatic divinity that lies in the eye of, and is bestowed upon the mortal by, the beholder. In another epitaph, the husband of a deceased woman declares that, in return for her chastity and because she deserves it, he 'was able to deny her body to the flames and filled it with unguents, perfumes, and rose petals, so that he anxiously worshipped the divinity [*numen*] she merits'.[363] While avoiding the term *diva*, again, it is a divinity

---

[360] Not only did the latter receive cult as *divi*, they received no cult for the dead, especially at the *parentalia*, and their images were not shown in the funerary processions: Scheid, 'Parentalien', esp. 197, 199; Gradel, *Emperor Worship*, 274.

[361] To be sure, a philosophical education would not necessarily result in belief in an immortal and/or divine soul, but it would probably encourage the contemplation of this possibility.

[362] *CIL* 6.14094 (= *ILS* 8496); Parkin and Pomeroy, *Social History*, 68 no. 2.37b, with transl.

[363] *CIL* 6.30102 cf. p. 3736 (= *CLE* 1508): *qui nunc pro meritis bene adque caste corpus, quod potuit negare flammae, unguento et foleo rosisque plenum ut numen colit anxius merentis.* Cf. Courtney, *Musa Lapidaria*, 176–7, 387 no. 186; P. Kruschwitz at https://thepetrifiedmuse.blog/2015/06/24/more-than-meets-the-eye-fragrance-sensuousness-and-inscribed-latin-poetry/ (last accessed 24/01/2017), both with an alternative translation by E. Courtney.

that the deceased merits for the benefactions she has extended – and her husband does what he can to bring it about.[364]

Against this background, we can probably not exclude that temple tombs were meant to bring about the emphatic type of divinity that is bestowed by humans as an honour, trying, as Cicero did with regard to his daughter, to bring about apotheosis 'as far as may be'. But how far *is* 'as far as may be'?

As we have seen above, *consecratio* – and any divine honour – was seen as a reward for benefactions and a morally exemplary life that established the superior status of the individual concerned in eternity. A temple was one such honour, which worked at several levels. It distinguished the deceased to whom it was dedicated and thereby satisfied their desire to be remembered for their achievements – a form of immortality that most people found more achievable than any other. However, it also reflected on the family at large. I argued in Chapter 3 that tombs, and especially those of the social and financial elite, were designed as family tombs to be used over many generations. As much as the imperial *domus divina* gained in status with every member being deified, a divine honour awarded to a private deceased would not only reflect on the status of his or her relatives, but also apply to any subsequent deceased being buried in the same mausoleum. The mausoleum thus becomes a statement on the superior nature of the entire family (or other group) burying their dead within it.

Moreover, status elevation also contributed to relieving the grief of the bereaved, as many sources suggest. According to the *Consolatio ad Liviam* (199–200), Livia was awarded a number of public honours to console her for the loss of her son Drusus in 9 BCE. The emperor Antoninus Pius elevated Herodes Atticus' son Bradua to patrician rank in order to console Herodes for his grief over his wife Regilla's death.[365] In these instances we are looking at status elevation of the living, but other texts demonstrate that the public recognition of the achievements and status of the departed also

---

[364] Against this background, we may consider that the cases where the deceased is called *dea*, typically with a more or less explicit acknowledgement that she is first and foremost a goddess for the commemorator, equally refer to the divinity not only of the living person but also of the deceased. For *dea sancta mea Primilla*, see n. 141 above; for *mea divina* Anulina (a more ambiguous phrase), see n. 139. Three women are said to be *dea et sanctissima*: the imperial freedwoman Flavia Helpis in *CIL* 6.18358 (p. 3522); a daughter named Gemina (Orelli, *Collectio*, no. 4587); and 45-year-old Callicla Pyrradis (*CIL* 6.938* = Muratori, *Novus thesaurus*, vol. 3, 1246 no. 9). The inscription is classified as *falsa* in *CIL*, probably because it was once owned by Pirro Ligorio, who is notoriously unreliable when it comes to inscriptions. However, there is no good reason for doubt in this case.

[365] See below.

served as consolation to those left behind. In the so-called *Laudatio Turiae*, an epitaph recording what may have been the *laudatio funebris* for a noble woman of the first century BCE, the bereaved husband declares, after listing her extraordinary deeds and virtues:

> But all your opinions and instructions should give precedence to the praise you have won *so that this praise will be a consolation for me* and I will not feel too much the loss of what I have consecrated to immortality to be remembered for ever. What you have achieved in your life will not be lost to me. *The thought of your fame gives me strength of mind …* Fortune did not rob me of everything since it permitted your memory to be glorified by praise. (*ILS* 8393; transl. E. Wistrand, italics added)[366]

The prospect of divinity – or divine honours – as public acknowledgement of the deceased's merits is also presented as consolation in literary sources. Cicero's letters clearly present his daughter's posthumous apotheosis as a partial remedy for his grief (Cicero, *Att.* 12.43), but it is equally clear that this consolation was not related to her particular fate after death. He wants her *fanum* to be protected from later violation while also situated in a public spot (e.g. *Att.* 12.19.1 and 3.2). Especially his *Consolatio*, fragments of which are quoted by Lactantius, clearly shows that public recognition of her superior status is highly important to Cicero:[367]

> quod si ullum umquam animal consecrandum fuit, illud profecto fuit. si Cadmi progenies aut Amphitryonis aut Tyndari in caelum tollenda *fama* fuit, huic idem *honos* certe dicandus est. quod quidem faciam, teque omnium optimam, doctissimam, approbantibus diis immortalibus ipsis in eorum coetu locatam *ad opinionem omnium mortalium* consecrabo. (Lactantius, *Div. inst.* 1.15.20 = Cicero, *Consolatio* F 22 Vitelli, italics added)

> If consecration aught ever to have happened to any living being, it certainly belongs to her. If a *reputation* in heaven was deserved by the offspring of Cadmus, Amphitryo or Tyndarus, for sure the same *distinction* ought to be hers, and I will see that it happens. You were the best and most learned of all daughters; I will put you among the gods with the gods'

[366]   On the text, see esp. Wistrand, *Laudatio Turiae*; Flach, *Laudatio Turiae*; Hemelrijk, 'Masculinity'; Osgood, *Turia*.

[367]   This aspect is also stressed by Cole, *Cicero*, 1–3 with n. 5, but underrated by those who downplay speculations about an afterlife and deification merely as the work of mourning and private succumbing to sentimental feelings: (e.g. Griesbach, *Villen und Gräber*, 29–30, 145–9; Setaioli, 'Cicero and Seneca'; McIntyre, 'Deification', 232–3).

approval, and I will make you sacred *in the thinking of all mortals*. (transl. A. Bowen and P. Garnsey, italics added)

Also in Statius, Priscilla's honours are a consolation to her husband (*Silv.* 5.1.3),[368] and Emely Hemelrijk has pointed to decrees awarding public funerals and related honours to deceased women with the intention 'to honour and comfort the living members of the family'.[369] In epitaphs, being raised to the stars or counted among the gods is always a consolation that oscillates between reassurance that the deceased's fate is somehow positive, and pride in the honour that the reward for their morals and deeds constitutes.

The award of a tomb in the shape of a temple, and a temple that is so intricately linked with posthumous divinity, must have been perceived as an honour pertaining to *divi* and *divae* even when it was not meant to indicate posthumous divinity as such.[370] As Gradel notes, not all deified members of the imperial family were awarded temples and priests. The latter were not essential to imperial divinity but 'an insurance against oblivion'[371] and, as we have seen, Cicero felt the same about his daughter's *fanum*. It must have been this aspect that particularly appealed to the patrons of temple tombs, who aimed for a memorial that would hopefully last over centuries and would immediately convey its message to anyone setting their eyes on it.

Conclusions

Theomorphic portraits and temple tombs are the strongest visual divine associations found in funerary contexts. It has often been assumed that they belong together, to the extent that portraits in divine costume were allegedly primarily displayed in temple tombs, and the latter almost defined by containing such statues. We have seen that this view is hard to sustain as a general rule despite the existence of temple tombs containing such images, such as Priscilla's mausoleum (provided it was indeed a temple tomb) and the imagery on the Haterii crane relief (Figure 4.20),[372] since they seem to have catered predominantly for different patrons. While there is little evidence that men and especially members of the first order used portraits *in*

---

[368] As noted by Mayer, *Middle Classes*, 124.
[369] Hemelrijk, *Hidden Lives*, 320–9, quotation from p. 327.
[370] Similarly De Cristofaro ('Monumento funerario', 254), although he misses the special dependence on temples for the imperial cult.
[371] Gradel, *Emperor Worship*, 274.
[372] See above, p. 217.

formam deorum in funerary contexts,[373] it seems that temple tombs were at least as popular with the senatorial class as with freedpeople,[374] and were dedicated to both men and women, including the highest ranks of senators.[375]

Yet in spirit and in origin they were closely related. Both types of divine association were emphatically Roman in form and nature. Portraits of private individuals in divine costume first appeared in Rome, and they never gained popularity in the East, where imperial models were also rare. Temple tombs, as here defined, were modelled on a typically Roman type of temple – with podium and columns at the front only – and Edmund Thomas has even argued that the elaborate terracotta mouldings and delicate marble parapet on the sima of an anonymous temple tomb at Grottarossa (see Figure 1.12) were harking back to traditional, even Latin and Etruscan types of decoration.[376]

Inspiration for both clearly came from imperial models. While portraits in divine costume had precedents among private individuals, these were typically in small formats and limited to the domestic sphere. Moreover, the first examples of both portraits *in formam deorum* in funerary contexts and temple tombs appear simultaneously in the Flavian period, and most likely not before the Templum Gentis Flaviae.[377] The first securely dated theomorphic portraits are in fact the statues of Priscilla, whose tomb was modelled on the Templum.[378] One may therefore speculate that not only the idea of the temple tomb, but also the use of portraits in divine costume in funerary contexts, was inspired by this imperial model. The first person

[373] For the few statues showing adult men, see above p. 238. Known contexts and inscriptions suggest the predominance of freedpeople as patrons: Wrede, *Consecratio*, 93–105, 159–70, followed by most scholars. The first and only certain senatorial example preserved with divine attributes is the head of a Vestal Virgin with mural crown, typical not of Vesta, but of Cybele and city goddesses (see n. 152 above), but whether it was funerary is doubtful. Wrede (*Consecratio*, 101, 114) considers his nos. 76, 78, 107 and the Mars images with portraits to be priestesses and military 'officers', and thus as not belonging to the *libertini*. Although he may be right, there is no positive indication that the female portraits are priestesses. While it cannot be excluded that members of the senatorial class used such images (as maintained by Hesberg, 'Planung', 60; Heinzelmann, *Nekropolen*, 82–3, 85; Griesbach, *Villen und Gräber*, 35; Hallett, *Roman Nude*, 202), there is as yet no example of such a case. On Griesbach's suggestion regarding Regilla, see Chapter 1 nn. 54 and 110).

[374] It is possible that they were even used primarily by senators from the Antonine period onwards, although the many anonymous examples prevent us from being certain about this.

[375] For examples, see Chapter 1 pp. 12–24.

[376] Thomas, *Monumentality*, 188–9.

[377] Wrede (*Consecratio*) dates a few portraits earlier than that. But a close review reveals that these are either not portraits *in formam deorum* in the proper sense, or their restoration does not allow a proper assessment, or they may be imperial; cf. also above n. 71.

[378] See above, pp. 251–3.

buried in it was Iulia Titi (Suetonius, *Dom.* 17) and it is possible that she was honoured there with a portrait *in formam deorum*. A statue of her in the guise of Venus is attested by Martial (*Ep.* 6.13). As Annetta Alexandridis observes, it is the first time that an association with Venus is explicitly related to the woman's beauty and desirability, while under the Julio-Claudians the association with Venus Genetrix and the dynastic aspect were to the fore. Two replicas of a head with Venus coiffure in the style of the Capitoline or the Medici Venus that are likely to portray Iulia suggest that the body type that became the most popular choice for our private matrons was equally inspired by her model.[379]

Finally, both features work according to similar principles, as they are suggestive of divinity without ever being explicit about their exact meaning. As portraits of the deceased, images that combine a divine body with a portrait head could indicate his or her outright divinity, though doubtless only in the eyes of a limited group of viewers. However, somewhat less ambitiously, they could claim for the deceased qualities that surpassed human measure and were therefore perceived as divine without claiming the divinity of the person as such. As images of a deity with the features of the departed, they could illustrate the privileged relationship the deceased had with this deity. In all these readings, the deceased is at least strongly associated with the divine, and thereby partakes in the divine even when no claim is made that he or she is a god. The deceased is presented as having a special, superior status that can only adequately be expressed through associations with the divine. Moreover, *as monuments*, the images are also an honorific device that is intended both to communicate the fact, and to secure the message so that it is not lost with time. It is a remedy to oblivion, since the Romans needed to be *seen* to be divine in order for this divinity to take effect.

The same is true for temple tombs. As a type of monument that was otherwise reserved for the gods, and was associated in particular with the imperial *divi* and *divae*, they radiated a strong air of apotheosis even to those who did not aim at fully divinising their loved ones, or did not believe that they could achieve such an aim. Moreover, as family mausolea,

---

[379] Alexandridis, *Frauen*, 86, 173 cat. 147–8 pls. 31.3–4 (Copenhagen, Ny Carlsberg Glyptotek 657 (IN793); Vatican, Musei Vaticani, Braccio Nuovo 71 (formerly 78)). Cf. Mikocki, 'Ritratto', 385 n. 27; D'Ambra, 'Calculus', 222. The only extant portrait potentially of a nude empress as Venus is a statue in Dresden that may represent Lucilla (Fittschen, *Bildnistypen*, 78 no. 1), but has recently been identified as a private individual (Sinn, 'Verwandelte Götter', who establishes that the head belongs to the statue).

similarly to the Templum Gentis Flaviae, they extended this air of divinity to the entire family. Given that they were often situated near the entrance to or on the road towards a villa, any visitor will have understood the message. Unlike many, if not most, statues, they were also normally visible from afar, securing wide recognition of the message. As much as the acknowledgement of divine qualities and the award of divine honours such as a temple building were markers of status for the deceased, both features also contributed substantially to the prestige of those initiating them.

Whatever our own aesthetic judgement of portraits in divine costume and temple tombs may be, the way in which they exploit their associations is ingenious. While they imitate imperial distinctions that are strongly associated with imperial divinity and status – be it during their lifetime or after death – their patrons take care not to overstep certain boundaries that might expose them to accusations of challenging the emperor. Most patrons may have been highly doubtful about an individual afterlife, and divinity was more a potential than a reality. Belief in the latter was limited to a small group. Yet we have clear evidence that this potential was being explored. Such an endeavour could build on a number of traditions and religious ambiguities: that the exact boundaries of divinity were unclear;[380] that those between human and divine were permeable; that divinity could be awarded by humans independently of concerns about ontological status; that the *manes* had always been divine, even ontologically; that philosophers claimed the same for the immortal soul; and that the world beyond did (or should) reflect the hierarchies among the living.

As I noted above, the officially recognised, emphatic divinity of the Hellenistic rulers and Roman emperors was unachievable for private individuals, but there had always existed intermediary stages, ranging from the recognition of specific divine qualities to the accumulation of honours that were typically awarded to gods without turning the honorand fully into a *deus* or *divus*. The imperial princes Marcellus, Caius and Lucius Caesar and Germanicus and Drusus, for instance, were never formally deified. They received cult only of their *manes* and in the form characteristic solely of a cult for the dead. Yet, outside the funerary realm, they received divine honours after their death: for instance, their names were included in the *carmen Saliare*, and their statues were carried in the *pompa circensis* as well

---

[380] Cf. Carneades' argument in Cicero, *Nat. D.* 3.43: 'If gods exist, are the nymphs also goddesses? If the nymphs, are the Pans and the Satyrs also gods? But they are not gods; therefore the nymphs also are not gods. Yet they possess temples vowed and dedicated to them by the nations. Therefore the other gods who have had temples dedicated to them are not gods either.' See Versnel, *Coping with the Gods*, 468, for transl. and comment.

as at the *transvectio equitum*.[381] As John Scheid concludes, 'The sublimity of the deceased is not expressed through apotheosis, which is the prerequisite of the princeps, but through the ambiguity of a deceased who shares … various privileges with the gods'.[382] This is exactly the balancing act our private individuals performed with their statues and temple tombs, except that all the messages now normally focused on the site of the mausoleum. The Templum Gentis Flaviae had challenged the delicate construct that the *divi* received cult as living deities, but not any cult of the dead such as the *parentatio*, in that the building was both the temple for the *divi* and also a tomb. The idea that a temple might be erected to the divine *manes* of a deceased individual also appears in Statius, who wished he had the funds to erect an altar to his father's *manes* that would match temples, and where he would serve as a priest (*Silv.* 5.3.47–8, 58–9). Cicero may have had something similar in mind when he planned for Tullia's *fanum*.

Versnel notes comparable ambiguities in Hellenistic ruler cult, and quotes Elizabeth Carney's lucid analysis of the Philippeion at Olympia:

> The Philippeum looked like a temple […]. It contained statues that looked like cult statues, yet there is no evidence for divine cult. It was not a temple. […] Its shape resembled that of *heroa* but there is no evidence for heroic honors. It was *not a heroon*. We know what it was not but cannot be sure what it was, and that is the point. What was it then? Philip offered those who visited the Panhellenic shrine a way to think about the power he had come to exercise. The Philippeum did not assert that this power was divine, but it implied that it might be and suggested that this power was like the power of the gods.[383]

We can read Cicero's intent to achieve apotheosis for his daughter 'as far as may be' with his *fanum* (*Att.* 12.36.1) along similar lines, but the balancing act becomes fully obvious in Herodes Atticus' efforts on behalf of his wife. The consul, sophist and teacher of the imperial princes was surely no model of modesty, and few were more daring when it came to self-aggrandisement and pushing boundaries. We have already discussed the cepotaphium that he established on his wife Regilla's death, and called the Triopion, in Chapter 1. This name derives from the homonymous sanctuary of Demeter at Knidos and indicates a sacred precinct.[384] Within this precinct there was a

---

[381] For these and further honours, see Scheid, 'Parentalien'.
[382] Ibid., 200 (my translation).
[383] Versnel, *Coping with the Gods*, 489 n. 151; Carney, 'Initiation', 25.
[384] As Skenteri, *Herodes Atticus*, 30, notes, according to Callimachus, *Hymns* 6.30, the sanctuary was equivalent in reputation to that of Eleusis.

temple-shaped cenotaph for Regilla that used the much rarer circular form, which probably looked like a small-scale predecessor of the late antique circular imperial mausolea (Figure 1.10).[385] Inspiration for this shape must have come from the Pantheon (Figure 2.19). Whatever exactly its purpose was, there was without doubt a strong element of imperial cult, and it could be argued that Herodes thus opted for an even more ambitious model than the rectangular temple tomb of the Flavii. However, if a new reconstruction of the topmost part of Hadrian's mausoleum is correct, there may have been another imperial model as well. According to new findings by Paolo Vitti, on top of the large cylinder of the tomb sat a small round cella that looked even more similar to the Triopion building than the Pantheon (cf. Figure 2.11).[386] As Filippo Coarelli has recently argued, by choosing a small-scale imitation of the Pantheon to crown the top of his tomb, the emperor played upon, but modified, the idea of the Templum Gentis Flaviae, of combining a dynastic tomb and temple.[387] If this is essentially correct, Regilla's cenotaph was indeed a highly ambitious and suggestive adaptation of an imperial model.

And yet, none of the numerous documents recovered from the site indicates Regilla's apotheosis or divine status. The most interesting text in this regard is *IG* 14.1389 A, a long metric panegyric on the deceased written by Marcellus of Side.[388] The author elaborates on Regilla's divine and heroic ancestry, of Aphrodite and Anchises (ll. 4–5), and of Ganymede, Dardanos and Tros, son of Erichthonios (ll. 38–40). But while there was a temple (νηός) to Demeter and a New Demeter, the latter was Faustina Maior, not Regilla (l. 1 with ll. 4–5, 48).[389] A statue of Regilla existed as well, although in all probability not set up inside the temple but in front of it on a tall base that featured the panegyric.[390] It was dedicated *to the deities* (ll. 6–9) and not identified as a divine image of the deceased. Nevertheless, the reader is

---

[385] As discussed in Chapter 1, pp. 19–22.

[386] Vitti, 'Mausoleo di Adriano'. He does not draw any connections with Regilla's cenotaph, though.

[387] Coarelli, 'Mausoleo di Adriano', 171–2. Cf. Davies (*Death and the Emperor*, 162 with fig. 111), who observes that a viewer on the top of the column of Trajan would have seen first the gleaming dome of the Pantheon and then, in the background, the top of Hadrian's mausoleum. If this top was indeed a small-scale replica of the Pantheon, the effect would have been even stronger.

[388] For the most detailed discussion of the text, see Skenteri, *Herodes Atticus*, 29–47, with bibl.; cf. also Gleason, 'Herodes Atticus', 142–52.

[389] See Griesbach, *Villen und Gräber*, 33–5, for a different but unconvincing view, on which see above, Chapter 1 n. 54.

[390] On this statue, see comments above Chapter 1 p. 33 with n. 110.

invited ('if it pleases you') to make offerings, as the pious would to heroes (ll. 40–2).[391] The text thus suggests that Regilla is a heroine too:

> For she is not a mortal, but neither is she a goddess. Therefore she has been given neither temple nor tomb, nor honours like those of mortals, nor yet like those of gods. There is a monument for her in the shape of a temple, amongst the people of Athena, but her soul serves the sceptre of Radamanthys. (ll. 43–7; transl. F. Skenteri)

She is further said to live with the heroines on the Isles of Bliss (ll. 9–10, 21–2), where she will serve 'the goddess, the queen of women' Faustina Maior, like Iphigeneia served Artemis and Herse Athena (ll. 51–9). The scenario is not primarily about a posthumous lifestyle but about honour, and Regilla's place in the hierarchy is made clear by this latter passage, where she is evidently ranked below the deified empress, whom she serves, but leading the Elysian chorus of the underworld as the first among equals.[392] Moreover, this afterlife is declared a reward for her noble spirit,[393] but is significantly awarded 'since Zeus felt compassion for her lamenting husband' (l. 12: ὡς οἱ Ζεὺς ᾤκτειρεν ὀδυρόμενον). If we were still in doubt about what was at stake, a few lines later we are told that, in order to relieve Herodes' insatiable grief,

> Zeus and the Emperor, who is similar to Father Zeus in stature and wisdom, gave a consolation. Zeus sent to the Ocean the blooming woman to be carried by Zephyrus' Elysian breezes, and the Emperor gave to the boy sandals with stars to wear around the ankles, ... (ll. 12, 19–24; transl. F. Skenteri)[394]

---

[391] At the beginning of the poem, the 'women of the Tiber' are invited to come and bring offerings, but it is not entirely clear whether these are for the goddesses of the temple or for Regilla (ditto Skenteri, *Herodes Atticus*, 43; implicitly also Galli, *Lebenswelt*, 113 with n. 459); on difficulties with the translation, see Skenteri, *Herodes Atticus*, 35–6 on l. 2, but whether one translates ἕδος as 'statue', as she does, or as 'abode' (thus e.g. Gleason, 'Herodes Atticus', 147) does not matter for our question.

[392] See Skenteri, *Herodes Atticus*, 42–3, for a similar reading. As she points out (p. 38 on ll. 58–9), the Greek text is ambiguous about whether Faustina or Regilla leads the Elysian Chorus, but the latter reading is clearly possible, and we may doubt that Faustina *as goddess* could or would perform such a role.

[393] The text has ἀγαθὸς νόος (l. 11), which both Skenteri (ibid., 39) and Gleason ('Herodes Atticus', 148) want to read primarily in moral terms. However, as Skenteri notes, *noos/nous* normally refers to intellectual capacities, and given that women are frequently praised for these in epitaphs (cf. Cicero on Tullia in his *Consolatio* quoted n. 138), I prefer a similar reading here too.

[394] τῶι δὲ Ζεὺς ἐπίηρον ὀδυρομένωι ἀκόρητον καὶ βασιλεὺς Διὶ πατρὶ φυὴν καὶ μῆτιν ἐοικώς, Ζεὺς μὲν ἐς ὠκεανὸν θαλερὴν ἔστειλε γυναῖκ[α] αὔρῃσι Ζεφύροιο κομίζεμεν ἠλυσίῃσιν. αὐτὰρ ὁ ἀστερόεντα περὶ σφυρὰ παιδὶ πέδιλαδῶκεν ἔχειν, ... On the flamboyant reference to the award of patrician status to Bradua, see Skenteri, *Herodes Atticus*, 40–1; Gleason, 'Herodes Atticus', 149–50.

Herodes is here consoled by a double grant of honour: Zeus granted his wife the honour of a privileged place in Elysium, while the emperor elevated their son to patrician status – a fact that Herodes considered important enough to mention in another Triopion inscription that perhaps featured on Regilla's cenotaph.[395] Obviously, divinity and heroism are once more bound up with status and hierarchy as well as with emotion.

Whatever Herodes may have believed his wife 'really was' – if he ever thought about it in these terms – he had Marcellus perform an artful balancing act, replete with Homeric allusions in both form and content, with mythical associations and inventions, which elevated Regilla as much as was deemed acceptable. The world beyond involved as delicate an equilibrium of power and status as that of the living.[396] Marcellus placed her among the heroines, above her peers and below the deified empress, albeit in the privileged position of her personal servant. What Marcellus does in his poem may be more elegant and sophisticated than some other examples of hyperbolic praise of the deceased that I have surveyed here. Yet statues *in formam deorum*, by their ambiguous nature, and tombs that resembled the temples of the *divi* while still hosting cult for the dead, are equally, if not more, suggestive and open to different readings, straddling borderlines without necessarily crossing them.

---

[395] *IG* 14.1392. cf. Chapter 1 p. 20.

[396] For a hierarchical concept of the afterlife, this time in heaven, see also Manilius, *Astronomica* 1.798–804, where Quirinus, Divus Iulius and later Augustus are residing with the immortal gods in the highest spheres of heaven, while the rest of the *viri boni*, including the rest of the *gens Iulia*, are confined to the Milky Way. Cf. Guidetti, 'Manilio', for a new and convincing reading of this passage. Cf. also the passage in the *Consolatio ad Liviam* discussed above p. 273. The visualisations are different, but the idea is the same.

Bibliography

Abbondanza, L., Coarelli, F. and Lo Sardo, E. (eds.), *Apoteosi da uomini a dei: il Mausoleo di Adriano* (Rome: Munus, 2013).

Adembri, B. (ed.), *Suggestioni egizie a Villa Adriana* (Milan: Electa, 2006).

Adembri, B., Taglietti, F. and Granino Cecere, M. G. 'Hercules Sospitalis da una villa del suburbio romano', *Atti della Accademia Nazionale dei Lincei, Rendiconti*, 74 (2001–02), 127–76.

Agnoli, N. 'I sarcofagi e le lastre di chiusura di loculo', in Paroli, L. (ed.), *La basilica cristiana di Pianabella (Scavi di Ostia 12.1)* (Rome: Libreria dello Stato, 1999), 203–68.

Ahrens, S. ' "Whether by decay or fire consumed …": Cremation in Hellenistic and Roman Asia Minor', in Brandt, J. R., Prusac, M. and Roland, H. (eds.), *Death and Changing Rituals: Function and Meaning in Ancient Funerary Practices (Studies in Funerary Archaeology 7)* (Oxford: Oxbow Books, 2015), 185–222.

Alexandridis, A. 'Review: T. Mikocki, Sub specie deae. Les impératrices et princesses romaines assimilées des déesses. Rome 1995', *Gnomon*, 71 (1999), 704–8.

Die Frauen des römischen Kaiserhauses: eine Untersuchung ihrer bildlichen Darstellung von Livia bis Iulia Domna (Mainz: von Zabern, 2004).

'Überall (Götter)gleich? – theomorphe Bildnisse der Frauen des römischen Kaiserhauses', in Sander, M. and Rendić-Miočević, A. (eds.), *The Proceedings of the 8th International Colloquium on Problems of Roman Provincial Art. Religion and Myth as an Impetus for the Roman Provincial Sculpture* (Zagreb: Technička Knjiga, 2005), 415–22.

Alföldy, G. *Konsulat und Senatorenstand unter den Antoninen: Prosopographische Untersuchungen zur senatorischen Führungsschicht (Antiquitas 1.27)* (Bonn: Habelt, 1977).

'Individualität und Kollektivnorm in der Epigraphik des römischen Senatorenstandes', in *Atti del Colloquio internazionale AIEGL su Epigrafia e ordine senatorio: Roma, 14–20 maggio 1981 (Tituli 4)* (Rome: Edizioni di storia e letteratura, 1982), 37–53.

'Il monumento vaticano di Vipsania Agrippina e degli Asinii', in Alföldy, G., *Studi sull'epigrafia augustea e tiberiana di Roma* (Rome: Quasar, 1993), 125–43.

Studi sull'epigrafia augustea e tiberiana di Roma (Vetera 8) (Rome: Quasar, 1993).

'Bricht der Schweigsame sein Schweigen? Eine Grabinschrift aus Rom', *RM*, 101 (1995), 151–68.

'Pietas immobilis erga principem und ihr Lohn: Öffentliche Ehrenmonumente von Senatoren in Rom während der Frühen und Hohen Kaiserzeit', in Alföldy, G and Panciera, S. (eds.), *Inschriftliche Denkmäler als Medien der Selbstdarstellung in der römischen Welt (Heidelberger althistorische Beiträge und epigraphische Studien 36)* (Stuttgart: Steiner, 2001), 11–46.

Altmann, W. *Die römischen Grabaltäre der Kaiserzeit* (Berlin: Weidmann, 1905).

Ambrogi, A. 'Sarcofagi in granito di produzione egiziana', *Xenia antiqua*, 2 (1993), 103–10.

Vasche di età Romana in marmi bianchi e colorati (Studia archaeologica 79) (Rome: L'Erma di Bretschneider, 1995).

Labra di età romana in marmi bianchi e colorati (Studia archaeologica 136) (Rome: L' Erma di Bretschneider, 2005).

Ambrogi, A., Bonanome, D., Bravi, A., Buccino, L., Vittozzi, G. Capriotti, Ghini, G., Chisellini, E., Granino Cecere, M. G., Romeo, I. and Spera, L. (eds.), *Sculture antiche nell'Abbazia di Grottaferrata* (Rome: Comitato Nazionale per le Celebrazioni del Millenario, 2008).

Amedick, R. *Die Sarkophage mit Darstellungen aus dem Menschenleben (ASR 4.1)* (Berlin: Gebr. Mann, 1991).

'Achilleus auf Skyros. Die Eikones des jüngeren Philostrat und die Ikonographie römischer Sarkophage', in Koch, G. (ed.), *Akten des Symposiums "125 Jahre Sarkophag-Corpus" Marburg (Sarkophag-Studien 1)* (Mainz: von Zabern, 1998), 52–60.

'Etruskische Sepulkralkunst und römische Sarkophage', in Koch, G. (ed.), *Akten des Symposiums des Sarkophag-Corpus 2001 (Sarkophag-Studien 3)* (Mainz: von Zabern, 2007), 1–11.

'Kaisersarkophag und rota: eine Platte aus Porphyr in Salerno', in Koch, G. (ed.), *Akten des Symposiums "Sarkophage der Römischen Kaiserzeit, Produktion in den Zentren – Kopien in den Provinzen" (Sarkophag-Studien 6)* (Ruhpolding/Mainz: Rutzen/Harrassowitz, 2012), 205–17.

Ameling, W. *Herodes Atticus (Subsidia epigraphica 11)* (Hildesheim: Olms, 1982).

Amici, C. M. *Il Foro di Cesare (Linguaggio dell'architettura romana)* (Florence: L. S. Olschki, 1991).

Andermahr, A. M. *Totus in praediis: senatorischer Grundbesitz in Italien in der frühen und hohen Kaiserzeit (Antiquitas 3.37)* (Bonn: Habelt, 1998).

Anderson, M. L. (ed.), *Radiance in Stone: Sculptures in Colored Marble from the Museo Nazionale Romano (Unita cataloghi d'arte DeLuca)* (Rome: DeLuca, 1989).

Andreae, B. *Motivgeschichtliche Untersuchungen zu den römischen Schlachtsarkophagen* (Berlin: Mann, 1956).

Die römischen Jagdsarkophage (ASR 1.2) (Berlin: Mann, 1980).

Andreae, B., Köhler, J. and Anger, K. (eds.), *Bildkatalog der Skulpturen des Vatikanischen Museums vol. II: Museo Pio Clementino, Cortile Ottagono* (Berlin: de Gruyter, 1998).

Angelucci, S., Baldassarre, I., Bragantini, I., Lauro, M. G., Mannucci, V., Mazzoleni, A., Morselli, C. and Taglietti, F. 'Sepolture e riti nella necropoli dell'Isola Sacra', *Bollettino di archeologia*, 5–6 (1990), 49–113.

Annibaldi, G. 'Via Nomentana. Scoperta di tomba', *NSc*, 66 (1941), 187–95.

Anonymous, *Descrizione delle statue e busti antichi trovati nel sepolcro della famiglia Manilia dedicata a sua altezza reale il signor principe Luigi principe ereditario di Baviera* (Rome: Mordacchini, 1808).

Apolloni Ghetti, B. M., Ferrua, A., Josi, E. and Kirschbaum, E. *Esplorazioni sotto la confessione di San Pietro in Vaticano* (Vatican City: Tipografia Poliglotta Vaticana, 1951).

Arce, J. 'Roman imperial funerals in effigie', in Ewald, B. C. (ed.), *The Emperor and Rome: Space, Representation, and Ritual (Yale Classical Studies 35)* (Cambridge University Press, 2010), 309–23.

Arias, P. E., Cristiani, E. and Gabba, E. *Camposanto monumentale di Pisa: Le antichità* (Pisa: Pacini, 1977).

Armellin, P. (ed.), *Centocelle II* (Soveria Mannelli: Rubbettino, 2007).

Armellin, P., 'La villa cd. ad duas lauros: l'area del sepolcro a tempietto (area ADL 2000)', in Armellin, P. (ed.), *Centocelle II* (Soveria Mannelli: Rubbettino, 2007), 85–142.

Ascenzi, A. 'The Roman mummy of Grottarossa', in Spindler, K. (ed.), *Human Mummies: A Global Survey of their Status and the Techniques of Conservation* (Vienna: Springer, 1996), 205–17.

Asutay-Effenberger, N. and Effenberger, A. *Die Porphyrsarkophage der oströmischen Kaiser: Versuch einer Bestandserfassung, Zeitbestimmung und Zuordnung (Spätantike, frühes Christentum, Byzanz: Reihe B, Studien und Perspektiven 15)* (Wiesbaden: Reichert, 2006).

Audin, A. 'Inhumation et incinération', *Latomus*, 19 (1960), 312–22, 518–32.

Baldassarre, I. 'La necropoli dell'Isola Sacra (Porto)', in Hesberg, H. v. and Zanker, P. (eds.), *Römische Gräberstraßen: Selbstdarstellung – Status – Standard* (Munich: Verl. d. Bayer. Akad. d. Wiss., 1987), 125–38.

Baldassarre, I., Bragantini, I., Dolciotti, A. M., Morselli, C., Taglietti, F. and Taloni, M. 'La necropoli dell'Isola Sacra. Campagne di scavo 1976–1979 vol. II', in *Scavi e ricerche archeologiche degli anni 1976-1979 (Quaderni de "La Ricerca Scientifca" 112)* (Rome: Consiglio Nazionale delle Ricerche, 1985), 261–302.

Baldassarre, I., Bragantini, I. and Morselli, C. *Necropoli di Porto: Isola Sacra* (Rome: Istituto poligrafico e Zecca dello Stato, Libreria dello Stato, 1996).

Balty, J. 'Franz Cumont et l'interprétation symbolique des sarcophages romains, à près de soixante ans des Recherches', in Galinier, M. and Baratte, F. (eds.), *Iconographie funéraire romaine et société: corpus antique, approches nouvelles? (Collection Histoire de l'art 3)* (Perpignan: Presses Universitaires de Perpignan, 2013), 7–27.

Bastien, P. *Le buste monétaire des empereurs romains vols I–III (Numismatique romaine 19)* (Wetteren: Numismatique Romaine, 1992–94).

Baumer, L. E. 'Der Jäger als Retter. Zu Ikonographie und Deutung der zweiszenigen Löwenjagdsarkophage', *Hefte des Archäologischen Seminars Bern*, 19 (2003), 61–73.

Beard, M. 'Vita inscripta', in Ehlers, W. (ed.), *La biographie antique: huit exposés suivis de discussions; Vandoeuvres-Genève, 25–29 Août 1997 (Entretiens sur l'Antiquité Classique)* (Genève: Fondation Hardt, 1998), 83–118.

The Roman Triumph (Cambridge, MA: The Belknap Press of Harvard University Press, 2007).

Beard, M., North, J. and Price, S. R. F., *Religions of Rome* (Cambridge University Press, 1998).

Bechtold, C. *Gott und Gestirn als Präsenzformen des toten Kaisers: Apotheose und Katasterismos in der politischen Kommunikation der römischen Kaiserzeit und ihre Anknüpfungspunkte im Hellenismus (Schriften zur politischen Kommunikations 9)* (Göttingen: V&R Unipress, 2011).

Bedini, A. (ed.), *Mistero di una fanciulla: ori e gioielli della Roma di Marco Aurelio da una nuova scoperta archeologica* (Milan: Skira, 1995).

Bendinelli, G. 'Via Trionfale. Ipogei sepolcrali scoperti presso il km. IX della Via Trionfale (Casale del Marmo)', *NSc*, 19 (1922), 428–49.

'Il monumento sotterraneo di Porta Maggiore in Roma', *Monumenti antichi*, 31 (1926), 602–855.

Bendlin, A. 'Looking beyond the civic compromise: Religious pluralism in late republican Rome', in Bispham, E. and Smith, C. J. (eds.), *Religion in Archaic and Republican Rome and Italy: Evidence and Experience (New Perspectives on The Ancient World 2)* (Edinburgh University Press, 2000), 115–35, 67–71.

Bentz, K. M. 'Rediscovering the Licinian tomb', *Journal of the Walters Art Gallery*, 55–6 (1997), 63–88.

Bergmann, B. *Der Kranz des Kaisers: Genese und Bedeutung einer römischen Insignie (Image & Context 6)* (Berlin: de Gruyter, 2010).

Bergmann, B., Farrell, J., Feeney, D., Ker, J., Nelis, D. and Schultz, C. 'An exciting provocation: John F. Miller's "Apollo, Augustus, and the poets"', *Vergilius*, 58 (2012), 3–20.

Bergmann, M. *Die Strahlen der Herrscher: theomorphes Herrscherbild und politische Symbolik im Hellenismus und in der römischen Kaiserzeit* (Mainz: von Zabern, 1998).

Bergunder, M. 'What is religion? The unexplained subject matter of religious studies', *Method & Theory in the Study of Religion*, 26 (2014), 246–86.

Bickermann, E. 'Die römische Kaiserapotheose', *Archiv für Religionswissenschaft*, 27 (1929), 1–34.

Bickerman, E. J. 'Consecratio', in Bickerman, E. J. and den Boer, W. (eds.), *Le culte des souverains dans l'empire romain: 7 exposés suivis de discussions (Entretiens sur l'Antiquité Classique)* (Genève: Fondation Hardt, 1973), 1–25.

Bielfeldt, R. *Orestes auf römischen Sarkophagen* (Berlin: Reimer, 2005).

Bignamini, I. and Claridge, A. 'The tomb of Claudia Semne and excavations in eighteenth-century Rome', *Papers of the British School at Rome*, 66 (1998), 215–44.

Birk, S. *Depicting the Dead: Self-representation and Commemoration on Roman Sarcophagi with Portraits (Aarhus Studies in Mediterranean Antiquity 11)* (Aarhus University Press, 2013).

Boatwright, M. T. *Hadrian and the City of Rome* (Princeton University Press, 1987).

Bodel, J. P. *Graveyards and Groves: A Study of the Lex Lucerina* (Cambridge, MA: Harvard University Press, 1994).

'Minicia Marcella. Taken before her time', *American Journal of Philology*, 116 (1995), 453–60.

'Death on display: looking at Roman funerals', in Bergmann, B. (ed.), *The Art of Ancient Spectacle* (New Haven: Yale University Press, 1999), 259–81.

'Dealing with the dead: undertakers, executioners and potter's fields in ancient Rome', in Scheidel, W. (ed.), *Disease and Death in the Ancient City of Rome* (London: SSRN, 2000), 128–51.

'Epigraphy and the ancient historian', in: Ibid. (ed.), *Epigraphic Evidence: Ancient History from Inscriptions (Approaching the Ancient World)* (London: Routledge, 2001), 1–56.

'The organization of the funerary trade at Puteoli and Cumae', in Panciera, S. (ed.), *Libitina e dintorni: Libitina e luci sepolcrali; le leges libitinariae campane; Iura sepulcrorum; vecchie e nuove iscrizioni; Atti dell'XI Rencontre Franco-Italienne sur l'Epigraphie (Libitina 3)* (Rome: Edizioni Quasar, 2004), 147–68.

'From columbaria to catacombs: Collective burial in pagan and Christian Rome', in Brink, L. and Green, D. (eds.), *Commemorating the Dead: Texts and Artefacts in Context: Studies of Roman, Jewish, and Christian Burials* (Berlin: de Gruyter, 2008), 177–242.

Bömer, F. *Ahnenkult und Ahnenglaube im alten Rom (Archiv für Religionswissenschaft 1)* (Leipzig: Teubner, 1943).

Bonfante, L. 'Roman costumes', *ANRW*, I.4 (1973), 584–614.

'Nudity as a costume in classical art', *American Journal of Philology*, 93 (1989), 543–70.

Bonifacio, R. *Ritratti romani da Pompei (Archaeologia Perusina 14)* (Rome: G. Bretschneider, 1997).

Borbonus, D. *Columbarium Tombs and Collective Identity in Augustan Rome* (New York: Cambridge University Press, 2014).

Bordenache Battaglia, G. *Corredi funerari di età imperiale e barbarica nel Museo Nazionale Romano* (Rome: Quasar, 1983).

Borg, B. E. 'Das Gesicht der Aufsteiger. Römische Freigelassene und die Ideologie der Elite', in Braun, M., Haltenhoff, A. and Mutschler, F.-H. (eds.), *Moribus antiquis res stat Romana. Römische Werte und römische Literatur im 3. und 2. Jh. v. Chr.* (Munich: Saur, 2000), 285–99.

'Glamorous intellectuals: Portraits of pepaideumenoi in the second and third centuries AD', in Borg, B. E. (ed.), *Paideia: The World of the Second Sophistic (Millennium-Studien 2)* (Berlin: de Gruyter, 2004), 157–78.

'What's in a Tomb? Roman death public and private', in Andreu, J., Espinosa, D. and Pastor, S. (eds.), *Mors Omnibus Instat. Aspectos arqueológicos epigráficos y rituales de la muerte en el Occidente Romano (Serie Bellatrix)* (Madrid: Liceus Ediciones, 2011), 51–78.

'The face of the social climber: Roman freedmen and elite ideology', in Bell, S. and Ramsby, T. R. (eds.), *Free at Last!: The Impact of Freed Slaves on the Roman Empire* (London: Bristol Classical Press, 2012), 25–49.

Crisis and Ambition: Tombs and Burial Customs in Third-century AD Rome (Oxford Studies in Ancient Culture and Representation) (Oxford University Press, 2013).

'Eine Frage von Leben und Tod: Pathos und Leidenschaft auf den mythologischen Sarkophagen Roms', in Clemenz, M., Zitko, H., Büchsel, M. and Pflichthofer, D. (eds.), *IMAGO. Interdisziplinäres Jahrbuch für Psychoanalyse & Ästhetik* (Gießen: Psychosozial-Verlag, 2015), 77–92.

'Roman sarcophagi in context', *Journal of Roman Archaeology*, 28 (2015), 599–604.

'Slumber under divine protection: From vague pagan hopes to Christian belief', in Hömke, N., Chiai, G. F. and Jenik, A. (eds.), *Bilder von dem Einen Gott. Die Rhetorik in monotheistischen Gottesdarstellungen der Spätantike (Philologus Supplemente 6)* (Berlin: de Gruyter, 2016), 263–88.

'No one is immortal: From exemplum mortalitatis to exemplum virtutis', in Dignas, B. and Audley-Miller, L. (eds.), *Wandering Myths: Transcultural Uses of Myth in the Ancient World* (Berlin: de Gruyter, 2018), 163–201.

'Herodes Atticus in Rome: The Triopion reconsidered', in Draycott, C. M., Raja, R. Welch, K. and Wootton, W. T. (eds.), *Visual Histories of the Classical World. Essays in Honour of R. R. R. Smith* (Turnhout: Brepols, 2019), 317–30.

'Ikonographie des Betens', in Hirsch-Luipold, R. and Trapp, M. (ed.), *Maximus von Tyros* (Tübingen, Mohr-Siebeck, 2019), 147–76.

'Roman cemeteries and tombs', in Holleran, C. and Claridge, A. (eds.), *A Companion to the City of Rome* (Oxford: Wiley-Blackwell, 2018), 403–24.

Borg, B. E., Hesberg, H. v. and Linfert, A. *Die antiken Skulpturen in Castle Howard (Monumenta Artis Romanae 31)* (Wiesbaden: Reichert, 2005).

Boschung, D. 'Überlegungen zum Liciniergrab', *Jahrbuch des Deutschen Archäologischen Instituts*, 101 (1986), 257–87.

Antike Grabaltäre aus den Nekropolen Roms (Acta Bernensia 10) (Bern: Stämpfli, 1987).

'Grabaltäre mit Girlanden und frühe Girlandensarkophage. Zur Genese der kaiserzeitlichen Sepulkralkunst', in Koch, G. (ed.), *Grabeskunst der römischen Kaiserzeit* (Mainz: von Zabern, 1993), 37–42.

Gens Augusta: Untersuchungen zu Aufstellung, Wirkung und Bedeutung der Statuengruppen des julisch-claudischen Kaiserhauses (Monumenta Artis Romanae 32) (Mainz: von Zabern, 2002).

Bosworth, B. 'Augustus, the Res Gestae and Hellenistic theories of apotheosis', *Journal of Roman Studies*, 89 (1999), 1–18.

Bowersock, G. W. *Augustus and the Greek World* (Oxford: Clarendon Press, 1965).

Braconi, P. (ed.), *Il Santuario di Diana a Nemi: le terrazze e il ninfeo; scavi 1989–2009 (Studia Archaeologica 194)* (Rome: L'Erma di Bretschneider, 2014).

Bradley, K. R. 'Wet-nursing at Rome: a study in social relations', in Rawson, B. (ed.), *The Family in Ancient Rome: New Perspectives* (London: Croom Helm, 1986), 201–29.

Brandenburg, H. 'Meerwesensarkophage und Clipeus-Motiv', *Jahrbuch des Deutschen Archäologischen Instituts*, 82 (1967), 195–245.

'Der Beginn der stadtrömischen Sarkophagproduktion der Kaiserzeit', *Jahrbuch des Deutschen Archäologischen Instituts*, 93 (1978), 277–327.

Brandt, J. R., Ingvaldsen, H. and Prusac, M. (eds.), *Death and Changing Rituals: Function and Meaning in Ancient Funerary Practices (Studies in Funerary Archaeology 7)* (Oxford: Oxbow Books, 2015).

Bravi, A. *Griechische Kunstwerke im politischen Leben Roms und Konstantinopels (Klio Beihefte 21)* (Berlin: de Gruyter, 2014).

Brelich, A. *Aspetti della morte nelle iscrizioni sepolcrali dell'impero Romano* (Budapest: Istituto di Numismatica e di Archeologia dell'Università Pietro Pazmany, 1937).

Brilliant, R. 'Review of 'Hadrian and the City of Rome' by Mary Taliaferro Boatwright', *Classical Philology*, 84 (1989), 358–62.

Brizio, E. 'Scoperte nella vigna Casali', *BdI* (1873), 11–22.

Bruto, M. L. and Vannicola, C. 'Grottarossa. Sepolcro 'a tempietto' (circ. XX)', *BCom*, 90 (1985), 153–63.

Buccellato, A., Catalano, P., Arrighetti, B., Calandrini, C., Colonnelli, G., Di Bernardini, M., Minozzi, S., Pantano, W. and Santandrea, E. 'Il comprensorio della necropoli di via Basiliano (Roma): un'indagine multidisciplinare', *Mélanges de l'Ecole française de Rome. Antiquité*, 115 (2003), 311–76.

Buonocore, M. *Le iscrizioni latine e greche (Inventari e studi/Musei della Biblioteca Apostolica Vaticana 2)* (Vatican City: Musei della Biblioteca Apostolica Vaticana, 1987).

Byvanck, A. W. 'Le problème des sarcophages romains', *Bulletin antieke beschaving*, 31 (1956), 31–8.

'Le début des sarcophages romains', *Bulletin antieke beschaving*, 35 (1960), 91–5.

Calci, C. and Mari, Z. 'Via Tiburtina', in Pergola, P., Valenzani, R. Santangeli and Volpe, R. (eds.), *Suburbium. Il suburbio di Roma dalla crisi del sistema delle ville a Gregorio Magno* (Rome: École Française de Rome, 2003), 175–209.

Calci, C. and Messineo, G. 'Via Tiburtina: Casal Bruciato (circ. V)', *BCom*, 92 (1987–88), 437–47.

'Monumento circolare sulla Collina di Casal Bruciato', *ArchLaz*, 9 (1988), 161–4.

Calza, G. *La necropoli del Porto di Roma nell'isola Sacra* (Rome: La Liberia dello Stato, 1940).

Calza, R. *Ritratti greci e romani fino al 160 circa d. C. (Scavi di Ostia 5: I ritratti 1)* (Rome: Istituto Poligrafico dello Stato, 1964).

Cameron, A. 'Young Achilles in the Roman world', *Journal of Roman Studies*, 99 (2009), 1–22.

The Last Pagans of Rome (New York: Oxford University Press, 2011).

Camodeca, G. 'Curatores rei publicae I', *ZPE*, 35 (1979), 225–36.

Canas, M. 'Scribonia Caesaris et le Stemma des Scribonii Libones', *Revue de philologie, de littérature et d'histoire anciennes*, 83 (2009), 183–210.

Caneva, S. G. 'Queens and ruler cults in early Hellenism: Festivals, administration, and ideology', *Kernos*, 25 (2012), 75–101.

'Costruire una dea. Arsinoe II attraverso le sue denominazioni divine', *Athenaeum*, 103 (2015), 95–122.

Canina, L. *La prima parte della via Appia dalla porta Capena a Boville* (Rome: Bertinelli, 1853).

Capanna, M. C. 'Il Tempio della Gente Flavia sul Quirinale. Un tentativo di ricostruzione', in Montanari, P. (ed.), *Sepolcri circolari di Roma e suburbio: elementi architettonici dell'elevato (Workshop di archeologia classica. Quaderni 5)* (Pisa/Rome: F. Serra, 2008), 173–80.

'Regione VI. Alta Semita', in Carandini, A. (ed.), *Atlante di Roma antica: biografia e ritratti della città* (Milan: Electa, 2012), 446–73.

Capelli, R. 'Gemelli divini a confronto: l'ipogeo di Aguzzano', Nista, L. (ed.), *Castores: l'immagine dei Dioscuri a Roma* (Rome: DeLuca, 1994), 129–50.

Caraffa, G. *Il monumento sepolcrale di P. Cluvio Maximo Paullino* (Rome, 1933).

Carney, E. 'The initiation of cult for royal Macedonian women', *Classical Philology*, 95 (2000), 21–43.

Carroll, M. *Spirits of the Dead: Roman Funerary Commemoration in Western Europe* (Oxford University Press, 2006).

Castagnoli, F. 'Il circo di Nerone in Vaticano', *Rendiconti dell'Accademia nazionale dei Lincei*, 32 (1959), 97–121.

Il Vaticano nell'antichità classica (Studi e documenti per la storia del Palazzo Apostolico Vaticano 6) (Vatican City: Biblioteca Apostolica Vaticana, 1992).

Cesari, P. 'In memoriam … in honorem: iscrizioni funerarie consacrate a divinità', *Studi classici e orientali*, 46 (1998), 959–72.

Chalupa, A. 'Roman emperors: Gods, men, something between or an unnecessary dilemma?', *Religio: Revue pro religionistiku*, 15 (2007), 257–70.

Champion, C. B. *The Peace of the Gods: Elite Religious Practices in the Middle Roman Republic* (Princeton University Press, 2017).

Champlin, E. *Final Judgments: Duty and Emotion in Roman Wills 200 B.C.–A.D. 250* (Berkeley: University of Calif. Press, 1991).

Nero (Cambridge, MA: Belknap Press of Harvard University Press, 2003).

'Nero, Apollo, and the poets', *Phoenix*, 57 (2003), 276–83.

Chaniotis, A. 'The divinity of Hellenistic rulers', in Erskine, A. (ed.), *A Companion to the Hellenistic World (Blackwell Companions to the Ancient World)* (Oxford: Blackwell, 2003), 431–45.

Chantraine, H. ' "Doppelbestattungen" römischer Kaiser', *Historia*, 29 (1980), 71–85.

Chausson, F. 'Un portrait de groupe avec dame: autour de Cornelia Praetextata', *Cahiers du Centre Gustave Glotz*, 7 (1996), 319–68.

Cianfriglia, L. and Giacopini, L. 'Via Portuense: area archeologico di Pozzo Pantaleo', in Filippi, F. (ed.), *Archeologia e giubileo. Gli interventi a Roma e nel Lazio nel Piano per il Grande Giubileo del 2000* (Milan: Electa, 2001), 407–10.

Chiocci, P. F., Gasseau, L., Rossi, D. and Zaccagnini, R. 'L'attività di spoglio e riuso tra tardo antico ed età medievale', in Rossi, D. and Arizza, M. (eds.), *Sulla via Flaminia: il mausoleo di Marco Nonio Macrino* (Milan: Electa, 2012), 304–27.

Chiocci, P. F. and Zaccagnini, R. 'Mausoleo A: descrizione e interpretazione delle evidenze', in Rossi, D. and Arizza, M. (eds.), *Sulla via Flaminia: il mausoleo di Marco Nonio Macrino* (Milan: Electa, 2012), 202–11.

'Mausoleo B: descrizione e interpretazione delle evidenze', in Rossi, D. and Arizza, M. (eds.), *Sulla via Flaminia: il mausoleo di Marco Nonio Macrino* (Milan: Electa, 2012), 176–89.

'Mausoleo C, la tomba di Marco Nonio Macrino: descrizione e interpretazione delle evidenze', in Rossi, D. and Arizza, M. (eds.), *Sulla via Flaminia: il mausoleo di Marco Nonio Macrino* (Milan: Electa, 2012), 216–31.

Chioffi, L. *Mummificazione e imbalsamazione a Roma ed in altri luoghi del mondo romano (Opuscula epigraphica dell'Università degli Studi di Roma La Sapienza, Dipartimento di Scienze Storiche, Archeologiche, Antropologiche dell'Antichità 8)* (Rome: Quasar, 1998).

Claridge, A. 'Hadrian's succession and the monuments of Trajan', in Opper, T. (ed.), *Hadrian: Art, Politics and Economy (British Museum Research Publication 175)* (London: The British Museum, 2013), 5–18.

Clauss, M. 'Probleme der Lebensalterstatistiken aufgrund römischer Grabinschriften', *Chiron*, 3 (1973), 395–417.

Kaiser und Gott: Herrscherkult im römischen Reich (Stuttgart; Leipzig: Teubner, 1999).

Coarelli, F. 'Il sepolcro degli Scipioni', *Dialoghi di archeologia*, 6 (1972), 36–106.

Il sepolcro degli Scipioni (Guide di monumenti 1) (Rome: Assessorato per le antichità, belle arti e problemi della cultura, 1972).

'La riscoperta del sepolcro degli Haterii: una base con dedica a Silvano', in Köpcke, G. (ed.), *Studies in Classical Art and Archaeology: A Tribute to Peter Heinrich von Blanckenhagen* (Locust Valley: Augustin, 1979), 255–69.

Roma sepolta (Biblioteca di archeologia) (Rome: Curcio, 1984).

'L'urbs e il suburbio', in Giardina, A. (ed.), *Roma: politica economia paesaggio urbano (Società romana e impero tardoantico 2)* (Rome: Laterza, 1986), 1–57.

Revixit ars: arte e ideologia a Roma; dai modelli ellenistici alla tradizione repubblicana (Rome: Quasar, 1996).

'I ritratti di "Mario" e "Silla" a Monaco e il sepolcro degli Scipioni', *Eutopia*, 2 (2002), 47–75.

(ed.), *Divus Vespasianus: il bimillenario dei Flavi* (Rome: Electa, 2009).

'I Flavi e Roma', in Coarelli, F. (ed.), *Divus Vespasianus: il bimillenario dei Flavi* (Rome: Electa, 2009), 68–97.

'Il Mausoleo di Adriano, modelli architettonici tra Ellenismo e Impero', in Abbondanza, L. (ed.), *Apoteosi da uomini a dei: il Mausoleo di Adriano* (Rome: Munus, 2013), 269–74.

Collis: il Quirinale e il Viminale nell'antichità (Rome: Quasar, 2014).

Cole, S. *Cicero and the Rise of Deification at Rome* (Cambridge University Press, 2013).

Collini, A. M. 'Via Collatina – Monumento sepolcrale del I sec. d. c.', *BCom*, 79 (1963–64), 107–16.

Comstock, M. B. and Vermeule, C. C. *Sculpture in Stone: The Greek, Roman and Etruscan Collections of the Museum of Fine Arts Boston* (Boston: Mus. of Fine Arts, 1976).

Conze, A. *Beschreibung der antiken Skulpturen mit Ausschluss der pergamenischen Fundstücke* (Berlin: Spemann, 1891).

Cooley, A. *The Cambridge Manual of Latin Epigraphy* (Cambridge University Press, 2012).

Corbier, M. 'Constructing kinship in Rome: Marriage and divorce, filiation and adoption', in Kertzer, D. I. (ed.), *The Family in Italy: From Antiquity to the Present* (New Haven: Yale University Press, 1991), 127–44.

  'Maiestas domus Augustae', in Angeli Bertinelli, M. G. and Donati, A. (eds.), *Varia epigraphica: atti del colloquio internazionale di epigrafia, Bertinoro, 8–10 giugno 2000 (Epigrafia e antichità)* (Faenza: Fratelli Lega, 2001), 155–99.

Cordier, P. *Nudités romaines: un problème d'histoire et d'anthropologie (Collection d'études anciennes: Série latine 63)* (Paris: Belles Lettres, 2005).

Cormack, S. *The Space of Death in Roman Asia Minor (Wiener Forschungen zur Archäologie 6)* (Vienna: Phoibos-Verl., 2004).

Counts, D. B. 'Regum externorum consuetudine: The nature and function of embalming in Rome', *Classical Antiquity*, 15 (1996), 189–202.

Courtney, E. *Musa Lapidaria: A Selection of Latin Verse Inscriptions (American Classical Studies 36)* (Atlanta: Scholars Press, 1995).

Crook, J. A. *Law and Life of Rome (Aspects of Greek and Roman life)* (London: Thames & Hudson, 1967).

Cruciani, C. 'Il suicidio di Saffo nell'abside della basilica sotterranea di Porta Maggiore', *Ostraka*, 9 (2000), 165–73.

Cucina, A., Vargiu, R., Mancinelli, D., Ricci, R., Santandrea, E., Catalano, P. and Coppa, A. 'The necropolis of Vallerano (Rome, 2nd–3rd century AD): An anthropological perspective on the ancient Romans in the Suburbium', *International Journal of Osteoarchaeology*, 16 (2006), 104–17.

Cumont, F. V. M. *Études syriennes* (Paris: Picard, 1917).

  Recherches sur le symbolisme funéraire des Romains (Bibliothèque archéologique et historique 35) (Paris: Geuthner, 1942).

  Lux perpetua (Paris: Geuthner, 1949).

D'Ambra, E. 'The calculus of Venus: Nude portraits of Roman matrons', in Kampen, N. B. (ed.), *Sexuality in Ancient Art: Near East, Egypt, Greece, and Italy* (Cambridge University Press, 1996), 219–32.

  'Acquiring an ancestor: The importance of funerary statuary among the non-elite orders of Rome', in Højte, J. M. (ed.), *Images of Ancestors (Aarhus Studies in Mediterranean Antiquity 5)* (Aarhus University Press, 2002), 223–46.

  'Daughters as Diana: Mythological models in Roman portraiture', *Memoirs of the American Academy in Rome. Supplementary Volumes*, 7 (2008), 171–83.

D'Arms, J. H. 'Notes on municipal notables of Imperial Ostia', *American Journal of Philology*, 97 (1976), 387–411.

Dabrowa, E. 'The origin of the "Templum Gentis Flaviae": A hypothesis', *Memoirs of the American Academy in Rome*, 41 (1996), 153–61.

Darwall-Smith, R. H. *Emperors and Architecture: A Study of Flavian Rome (Collection Latomus 231)* (Brussels: Latomus, 1996).

Davies, G. 'Before sarcophagi', in Elsner, J. and Huskinson, J. (eds.), *Life, Death and Representation: Some New Work on Roman Sarcophagi (Millennium-Studien 29)* (Berlin: de Gruyter, 2011), 21–53.

Davies, P. J. E. *Death and The Emperor: Roman Imperial Funerary Monuments, from Augustus to Marcus Aurelius* (Cambridge University Press, 2000).

De Angelis, F. D. A. and Garstad, B. 'Euhemerus in context', *Classical Antiquity*, 25 (2006), 211–42.

De Cristofaro, A. 'Il monumento funerario di Marco Nonio Macrino e il suo programma figurativo: considerazioni preliminari', in Rossi, D. (ed.), *Sulla via Flaminia. Il mausoleo di Marco Nonio Macrino* (Milan: Electa, 2012), 250–85.

De Rosa, P. A. and Trastulli, P. E. (eds.), *La campagna romana da Hackert a Balla* (Rome: Studio Ottocento, 2001).

De Rossi, G. M. *Tellenae (Forma Italiae 1,4)* (Rome: de Luca, 1967).

Apiolae (Forma Italiae 1,9) (Rome: De Luca, 1970).

Bovillae (Forma Italiae 1,15) (Florence: Olschki, 1979).

de Visscher, F. *Le droit des tombeaux romains* (Milan: Giuffrè, 1963).

Deér, J. *The Dynastic Porphyry Tombs of the Norman Period in Sicily (Dumbarton Oaks Studies 5)* (Cambridge, MA: Harvard University Press, 1959).

DeFranceschini, M., *Ville dell'Agro romano (Monografie della carta dell'Agro romano 2)* (Rome: "L'Erma" di Bretschneider, 2005).

Degrassi, A. 'P. Cluvius Maximus Paullinus', *Epigraphica*, 1 (1939), 307–21.

Fasti anni Numani et Iuliani. Accedunt ferialia, menologia rustica, parapegmata (Inscriptiones Italiae) (Rome: Libreria Dello Stato, 1963).

Delbrück, R. *Antike Porphyrwerke (Studien zur spätantiken Kunstgeschichte 6)* (Berlin; Leipzig: de Gruyter, 1932).

Derichs, W. *Herakles: Vorbild des Herrschers in der Antike* (PhD thesis, Cologne, 1950).

Di Stefano Manzella, I. *Index inscriptionum Musei Vaticani. 1. Ambulacrum Iulianum sive "Galleria Lapidaria" (Inscriptiones Sanctae Sedis 1)* (Rome: Quasar, 1995).

Dimas, S. *Untersuchungen zur Themenwahl und Bildgestaltung auf römischen Kindersarkophagen* (Münster: Scriptorium, 1998).

Dixon, S. *The Roman Family (Ancient Society and History)* (Baltimore: Johns Hopkins University Press, 1992).

Donahue, J. F. *The Roman Community at Table During the Principate* (Ann Arbor: University of Michigan Press, 2004).

Dondin-Payre, M. *Exercice du pouvoir et continuité gentilice: les Acilii Glabriones du IIIe siècle av. J.-C. au Ve siècle ap. J.-C. (Collection de l'Ecole Française de Rome 180)* (Rome: École Française de Rome, 1993).

'La longevité des familles sénatoriales romaines: à propos des Calpurnii', *L'antiquité classique*, 67 (1998), 237–42.

Dräger, O. *Religionem significare: Studien zu reich verzierten römischen Altären und Basen aus Marmor* (Mainz: von Zabern, 1994).

Dresken-Weiland, J. *Sarkophagbestattungen des 4. – 6. Jahrhunderts im Westen des Römischen Reiches (Römische Quartalschrift für christliche Altertumskunde und Kirchengeschichte: Supplementband 55)* (Rome: Herder, 2003).

Dressel, H. 'Camera sepolcrale sul monte Mario', *BdI*, 53 (1881), 12–17.

Eck, W. *Senatoren von Vespasian bis Hadrian: prosopographische Untersuchungen mit Einschluß der Jahres- und Provinzialfasten der Statthalter (Vestigia 13)* (Munich: Beck, 1970).

'Miscellanea consularia', *ZPE*, 25 (1977), 227–40.

'Die Gestalt Frontins in ihrer politischen und sozialen Umwelt', in *Wasserversorgung im antiken Rom: Sextus Iulius Frontinus, curator aquarum (Die Wasserversorgung antiker Städte)* (Munich: Oldenbourg, 1982), 45–62.

'Senatorial self-representation: Developments in the Augustan period', in Millar, F. (ed.), *Caesar Augustus: Seven Aspects* (Oxford: Clarendon Press, 1984), 129–67.

'Inschriften aus der vatikanischen Nekropole unter St. Peter', *ZPE*, 65 (1986), 245–93.

'Römische Grabinschriften. Aussageabsicht und Aussagefähigkeit im funerären Kontext', in Hesberg, H. v. and Zanker, P. (eds.), *Römische Gräberstraßen: Selbstdarstellung – Status – Standard* (Munich: Verl. d. Bayer. Akad. d. Wiss., 1987), 61–83.

'Inschriften und Grabbauten in der Nekropole unter St. Peter', in *Vom frühen Griechentum bis zur römischen Kaiserzeit: Gedenk- und Jubiläumsvorträge am Heidelberger Seminar für Alte Geschichte* (Stuttgart: Steiner, 1989), 55–89.

'Das Grabmal eines Rugianus, clarissimus vir', *ZPE*, 90 (1992), 211–14.

'Rome and the outside world: Senatorial families and the world they lived in', in Rawson, B. and Weaver, P. (eds.), *The Roman Family in Italy: Status, Sentiment, Space* (Oxford University Press, 1997), 73–99.

'Ordo equitum romanorum, ordo libertorum: Freigelassene und ihre Nachkommen im römischen Ritterstand', in Demougin, S., Devijver, H. and Raepsaet-Charlier, M.-T. (eds.), *L'ordre équestre. Histoire d'une aristocratie (Ier siècle av. J.-C. – IIIe siècle ap. J.-C.) (Collection de l'École française de Rome 257)* (Rome: École française de Rome, 1999), 5–29.

'Grabgröße und sozialer Status', in Heinzelmann, M. (ed.), *Römischer Bestattungsbrauch und Beigabensitten in Rom, Norditalien und den Nordwestprovinzen von der späten Republik bis in die Kaiserzeit* (Wiesbaden: Reichert, 2001), 197–201.

'Der Senator und die Öffentlichkeit – oder: Wie beeindruckt man das Publikum?', in Eck, W. and Heil, M. (eds.), *Senatores populi Romani: Realität und mediale Präsentation einer Führungsschicht* (Stuttgart: Steiner, 2005), 1–18.

'Römische Grabinschriften als Rechtsquelle', in Avenarius, M. (ed.), *Hermeneutik der Quellentexte zum römischen Recht* (Baden-Baden: Nomos, 2008), 67–93.

'Cum dignitate otium. Senatorische Häuser im kaiserzeitlichen Rom', in Ameling, W. and Heinrichs, J. (eds.), *Monument und Inschrift: gesammelte Aufsätze zur senatorischen Repräsentation in der Kaiserzeit (Beiträge zur Altertumskunde 288)* (Berlin: de Gruyter, 2010), 207–39.

'Emperor and senatorial aristocracy in competition for public space', in Ewald, B. C. (ed.), *The Emperor and Rome: Space, Representation, and Ritual (Yale Classical Studies 35)* (Cambridge University Press, 2010), 89–110.

'Grabmonumente in Rom und im Rheinland: Reflex von sozialem Status und Prestige?', in Kuhn, A. B. (ed.), *Social Status and Prestige in the Graeco-Roman World* (Stuttgart: Steiner, 2015), 165–87.

Eck, W., Caballos, A. and Fernández, F. *Das Senatus consultum de Cn. Pisone patre (Vestigia)* (Munich: Beck, 1996).

Edmondson, J. 'Family relations in Roman Lusitania: Social change in a Roman province?', in George, M. (ed.), *The Roman Family in the Empire: Rome, Italy, and Beyond* (Oxford University Press, 2005), 183–229.

'Roman family history', in Bruun, C. and Edmondson, J. (eds.), *The Oxford Handbook of Roman Epigraphy* (Oxford University Press, 2015), 559–81.

Eisner, M. *Zur Typologie der Grabbauten im Suburbium Roms (RM: Ergänzungsheft 26)* (Mainz: von Zabern, 1986).

Elsner, J. 'Iconoclasm as discourse: From antiquity to Byzantium', *The Art Bulletin*, 94 (2012), 368–94.

Elsner, J. and Huskinson, J. (eds.), *Life, Death and Representation: Some New Work on Roman Sarcophagi (Millennium-Studien 29)* (Berlin: de Gruyter, 2011).

Engels, J. *Funerum sepulcrorumque magnificentia: Begräbnis- und Grabluxusgesetze in der griechisch-römischen Welt (Hermes Einzelschriften 78)* (Stuttgart: Steiner, 1998).

Engemann, J. *Untersuchungen zur Sepulkralsymbolik der späteren römischen Kaiserzeit (Jahrbuch für Antike und Christentum: Ergänzungsband 2)* (Münster: Aschendorff, 1973).

Erasmo, M. *Reading Death in Ancient Rome* (Columbus: Ohio State University Press, 2008).

Erskine, A. 'Epilogue', in Bremmer, J. N. and Erskine, A. (eds.), *The Gods of Ancient Greece: Identities and Transformations (Edinburgh Leventis Studies 5)* (Edinburgh University Press, 2010), 505–10.

'Ruler cult and the early Hellenistic city', in Hauben, H. and Meeus, A. (eds.), *The Age of the Successors and the Creation of the Hellenistic Kingdoms (323–276 B. C.) (Studia Hellenistica 53)* (Leuven: Peeters, 2014), 579–97.

Ery, K. K. 'Investigations on the demographic source value of tombstones originating from the Roman period', *Alba Regia*, 10 (1969), 51–67.

Esteve-Forriol, J. *Die Trauer- und Trostgedichte in der römischen Literatur untersucht nach ihrer Topik und ihrem Motivschatz* (Diss. Erlangen, 1962).

Etcheto, H. *Les Scipions: famille et pouvoir à Rome à l'époque républicaine (Scripta antiqua 45)* (Bordeaux: Ausonius, 2012).

Evers, C. *Les portraits d'Hadrien: typologie et ateliers* (Brussels: Académie Royale de Belgique, 1994).

Ewald, B. C. 'Rollenbilder und Geschlechterverhältnis in der römischen Grabkunst. "Archäologische" Anmerkungen zur Geschichte der Sexualität', in Sojc, N. (ed.), *Neue Fragen, Neue Antworten: Antike Kunst als Thema der Gender Studies* (Berlin: LIT, 2005), 55–73.

   'Paradigms of personhood and regimes of representation', *RES: Anthropology and Aesthetics*, 61–2 (2012), 41–64.

Fabricius, J. 'Grenzziehungen. Zu Strategien somatischer Geschlechterdiskurse in der griechischen und römischen Kultur', in Hartmann, E., Hartmann, U. and Pietzner, K. (eds.), *Geschlechterdefinitionen und Geschlechtergrenzen in der Antike* (Stuttgart: Steiner, 2007), 65–86.

Fahr, W. *Theous nomizein: zum Problem der Anfänge des Atheismus bei den Griechen (Spudasmata 26)* (Hildesheim: Olms, 1969).

Fancelli, P. and Tomaro, P. 'Antonio Canova tra archeologia e restauro: il monumento di M. Servilio Quarto sulla via Appia', in Beltramini, G., Ghisetti Giavarina, A. and Marini, P. (eds.), *Studi in onore di Renato Cevese* (Vicenza: Centro internazionale di studi di architettura Andrea Palladio, 2000), 223–35.

Fasolini, D. 'L'ascrizione tribale dei minori nelle regiones X e XI', *ZPE*, 32 (2014), 225–36.

Faßbender, A. *Untersuchungen zur Topographie von Grabstätten in Rom von der späten Republik bis in die Spätantike* (PhD thesis, Cologne, 2005).

Faust, S. *Schlachtenbilder der römischen Kaiserzeit: erzählerische Darstellungskonzepte in der Reliefkunst von Traian bis Septimius Severus (Tübinger Archäologische Forschungen 8)* (Rahden/Westfalen: Verlag Marie Leidorf, 2012).

Fèa, C. *Nuova descrizione de' monumenti antichi ed oggetti d'arte contenuti nel Vaticano e nel Campidoglio: colle nuove scoperte fatte alle fabriche più interessanti nel Foro Romano* (Rome: Bourlié, 1819).

Fears, J. R. 'The cult of Jupiter and Roman imperial ideology', *ANRW*, II.17.1 (1981), 3–141.

Federico, E. and Miranda, E. (eds.), *Capri antica: dalla preistoria alla fine dell'età romana* (Capri (Naples): La Conchiglia, 1998).

Fejfer, J. *Roman Portraits in Context* (Berlin: de Gruyter, 2008).

Felletti Maj, B. M. *Museo Nazionale Romano: I ritratti (Cataloghi dei musei e gallerie d'Italia)* (Rome: Libreria dello Stato, 1953).

Feraudi-Gruénais, F. *Ubi diutius nobis habitandum est: die Innendekoration der kaiserzeitlichen Gräber Roms* (Wiesbaden: Reichert, 2001).

   Inschriften und "Selbstdarstellung" in stadtrömischen Grabbauten (Libitina 2) (Rome: Quasar, 2003).

'Für die Ewigkeit? Die Gestaltung von senatorischen Grablegen Roms und ihr Kontext', in Eck, W. and Heil, M. (eds.), *Senatores populi Romani: Realität und mediale Präsentation einer Führungsschicht* (Stuttgart: Steiner, 2005), 137–68.

'The decoration of Roman tombs', in Borg, B. E. (ed.), *The Blackwell Companion to Roman Art* (Oxford: Wiley-Blackwell, 2015), 431–51.

Ferrea, L. 'Il monumento funerario del console Ser. Sulpicius Galba', *BCom*, 99 (1998), 51–72.

Filges, A. *Standbilder jugendlicher Göttinnen: klassische und frühhellenistische Gewandstatuen mit Brustwulst und ihre kaiserzeitliche Rezeption (Arbeiten zur Archäologie 15)* (Cologne/Weimar/Vienna: Böhlau, 1997).

Filippi, F. (ed.), *Archeologia e giubileo. Gli interventi a Roma e nel Lazio nel Piano per il Grande Giubileo del 2000* (Milan: Electa, 2001).

Fishwick, D. 'Augustus deus and deus Augustus', in de Boer, M. B. and Edridge, T. A. (eds.), *Hommages à Maarten J. Vermaseren vol. I (Études préliminaires aux religions orientales dans l'empire romain 68/1)* (Leiden: Brill, 1978), 375–80.

The Imperial Cult in the Latin West: Studies in the Ruler Cult of the Western Provinces of the Roman Empire, Vol. I.1–2 (Études préliminaires aux religions orientales dans l'Empire romain 108/1) (Leiden: Brill, 1987).

The Imperial Cult in the Latin West: Studies in the Ruler Cult of the Western Provinces of the Roman Empire, Vol. II.1 (Études préliminaires aux religions orientales dans l'Empire romain 108/2A) (Leiden: Brill, 1991).

Fittschen, K. *Die Bildnistypen der Faustina minor und die Fecunditas Augustae (Abhandlungen der Akademie der Wissenschaften zu Göttingen, Philologisch-Historische Klasse Folge 3, 126)* (Göttingen: Vandenhoeck und Ruprecht, 1982).

Prinzenbildnisse antoninischer Zeit (Beiträge zur Erschließung hellenistischer und kaiserzeitlicher Skulptur und Architektur 18) (Mainz: von Zabern, 1999).

'Il fenomeno dell'assimilazione delle immagini nella ritrattistica romana di età imperiale', in La Rocca, E., Parisi Presicce, C. and Lo Monaco, A. (eds.), *Ritratti – le tante facce del potere* (Rome: Musei Capitolini, 2011), 247–52.

Fittschen, K. and Zanker, P. *Katalog der römischen Porträts in den Capitolinischen Museen und den anderen kommunalen Sammlungen der Stadt Rom, vol. III: Kaiserinnen- und Prinzessinnenbildnisse, Frauenporträts (Beiträge zur Erschliessung hellenistischer und kaiserzeitlicher Skulptur und Architektur 5)* (Mainz: von Zabern, 1983).

Katalog der römischen Porträts in den Capitolinischen Museen und den anderen kommunalen Sammlungen der Stadt Rom, vol. I: Kaiser- und Prinzenbildnisse (Beiträge zur Erschliessung hellenistischer und kaiserzeitlicher Skulptur und Architektur 3,1) (Mainz: von Zabern, 1994).

Katalog der römischen Porträts in den Capitolinischen Museen und den anderen kommunalen Sammlungen der Stadt Rom, vol. IV: Kinderbildnisse. Nachträge zu Band I-III. Neuzeitliche oder neuzeitlich verfälschte Bildnisse. Bildnisse an Reliefdenkmälern (Beiträge zur Erschliessung hellenistischer und kaiserzeitlicher Skulptur und Architektur 4) (Mainz: von Zabern, 2014).

Flach, D. *Die sogenannte Laudatio Turiae: Einleitung, Text, Übersetzung und Kommentar (Texte zur Forschung 58)* (Darmstadt: Wiss. Buchges., 1991).

Flagge, I. *Untersuchungen zur Bedeutung des Greifen* (Sankt Augustin: Richarz, 1975).

Flämig, C. *Grabarchitektur der römischen Kaiserzeit in Griechenland (Internationale Archäologie 97)* (Rahden/Westfalen: Leidorf, 2007).

Flammini, G. 'L'Epitaphium Senecae (667R) nella tradizione del genere epigrammatica', *Giornale italiano di filologia*, 52 (2000), 101–12.

Fless, F. 'Die frühkaiserzeitlichen Sarkophagbestattungen in Rom und ihre Übernahme in den westlichen und nordwestlichen Provinzen', in Fasold, P. (ed.), *Bestattungssitte und kulturelle Identität: Grabanlagen und Grabbeigaben der frühen römischen Kaiserzeit in Italien und den Nordwest-Provinzen (Xantener Berichte 7)* (Bonn: Habelt, 1998), 319–26.

Floriani Squarciapino, M. 'Pannelli decorativi dal tempio di Venere Genitrice', *Atti dell'Accademia nazionale dei Lincei. Memorie*, 2 (1948), 61–118.

Flower, H. I. *Ancestor Masks and Aristocratic Power in Roman Culture* (Oxford: Clarendon, 1996).

'Were women ever "ancestors"?', in Højte, J. M. (ed.), *Images of Ancestors (Aarhus Studies in Mediterranean Antiquity 5)* (Aarhus University Press, 2002), 159–84.

The Art of Forgetting: Disgrace & Oblivion in Roman Political Culture (Studies in the History of Greece and Rome) (Chapel Hill: University of North Carolina Press, 2006).

Fontana, C. *Descrizzione della nobilissima cappella del fonte batismale nella Basilica Vaticana: con la gran tazza antica di porfido coperta di metalli dorati* (Rome: Buagni, 1697).

Fortunatelli, S. 'Nobilitas gentilizia e virtù civili nella celebrazione dei membri dell'amplissimus ordo: su un gruppo di sarcofagi senatorii con scene di sacrificio', in Colpo, I., Favaretto, I. and Ghedini, F. (eds.), *Iconografia 2001: studi sull'immagine (Antenor: Quaderni 1)* (Rome: Quasar, 2002), 365–78.

Fortunati, L. *Relazione generale degli scavi e scoperte fatte lungo la via Latina redatta dallo stesso intraprendente e scopritore Lorenzo Fortunati* (Rome: Tiberina, 1859).

Freestone, I. C., Gudenrath, W., Painter, K. and Whitehouse, D. 'Recent research on the Portland Vase', *Journal of Glass Studies*, 32 (1990), 85–102.

Freyburger, G. *Fides: étude sémantique et religieuse depuis les origines jusqu'à l'époque augustéenne (Collection d'études anciennes. Antiquité latine 35)* (Paris: Belles Lettres, 1986).

Freyberger, K. S. and Zitzl, C. 'Das "Bautenrelief" aus dem Hateriergrab in Rom: eine neue Deutung', *Kölner Jahrbuch*, 49 (2016), 367–89.

Friedl, K. 'Die sogenannten Ustrina auf dem Campus Martius in Rom', *RM*, 118 (2012), 355–401.

Friggeri, R., Granino Cecere, M. G. and Gregori, G. L. (eds.), *Terme di Diocleziano: la collezione epigrafica* (Milan: Electa, 2012).

Gabelmann, H. *Die Werkstattgruppen der oberitalischen Sarkophage (Bonner Jahrbücher Beihefte 34)* (Bonn: Rheinland-Verl., 1973).

Antike Audienz- und Tribunalszenen (Darmstadt: Wiss. Buchges., 1984).

Galen, C. W. v. *Women and Citizenship in the Late Roman Republic and the Early Empire* (Diss., Nijmegen, 2016).

Galinsky, K. *Augustan Culture: An Interpretive Introduction* (Princeton University Press, 1996).

Galletier, É. *Étude sur la poésie funéraire romaine d'après les inscriptions* (Paris: Hachette, 1922).

Galli, M. *Die Lebenswelt eines Sophisten. Untersuchungen zu den Bauten und Stiftungen des Herodes Atticus* (Mainz: von Zabern, 2002).

Galvano-Sobrinho, C. R. 'Feasting the dead together: Household burials, funerary sociability, and the social strategies of slaves and freed persons at Rome in the early principate', in Bell, S. and Ramsby, T. R. (eds.), *Free at Last! The Impact of Freed Slaves on the Roman Empire* (London: Bristol Classical Press, 2012), 131–76.

Gasparri, C. 'Il sarcofago romano del Museo di Villa Giulia', *Atti della Accademia Nazionale dei Lincei, Rendiconti*, 27 (1972), 95–139.

'Il sarcofago con nekyia di Villa Giulia restaurato. Ancora sull'inizio della produzione di sarcofagi a Roma', in Freytag-Löringhoff, B. v. and Prihoda, M. (eds.), *Praestant interna. Festschrift für Ulrich Hausmann* (Tübingen: Wasmuth, 1982), 165–72.

Gasseau, L. 'Mausoleo A: studio ricostruttivo', in Rossi, D. and Arizza, M. (eds.), *Sulla via Flaminia: il mausoleo di Marco Nonio Macrino* (Milan: Electa, 2012), 212–15.

'Mausoleo B: studio ricostruttivo', in Rossi, D. and Arizza, M. (eds.), *Sulla via Flaminia: il mausoleo di Marco Nonio Macrino* (Milan: Electa, 2012), 190–5.

'Mausoleo C: studio ricostruttivo', in Rossi, D. and Arizza, M. (eds.), *Sulla via Flaminia: il mausoleo di Marco Nonio Macrino* (Milan: Electa, 2012), 232–49.

Gatti, G. 'Di una singolare epigrafe sepolcrale scoperta sulla via Tiburtina', *Rendiconti dell'Accademia nazionale dei Lincei*, 6 (1890), 195–8.

Gazda, E. K., Haeckl, A. E. and Paris, R. (eds.), *Images of Empire: Flavian Fragments in Rome and Ann Arbor Rejoined* (Ann Arbor: University of Michigan Press, 1996).

George, M. G. 'Family imagery and family values in Roman Italy', in George, M. (ed.), *The Roman Family in the Empire: Rome, Italy, and Beyond* (Oxford University Press, 2005), 37–66.

'Social identity and the dignity of work in freedmen's reliefs', in D'Ambra, E. and Métraux, G. P. R. (eds.), *The Art of Citizens, Soldiers and Freedmen in the Roman World (BAR: International Series 1526)* (Oxford: Archaeopress, 2006), 19–29.

Gesche, H. 'Die Divinisierung der römischen Kaiser in ihrer Funktion als Herrschaftslegitimation', *Chiron*, 8 (1978), 377–90.

Geyer, A. *Das Problem des Realitätsbezuges in der Dionysischen Bildkunst der Kaiserzeit (Beiträge zur Archäologie 10)* (Würzburg: Triltsch, 1977).

Ghini, G. 'La statua del princeps, il suo contest e le ville del bacino nemorense', in Ghini, G. and Batocchioni, G. (eds.), *Sulle tracce di Caligola: storie di grandi recuperi della Guardia di Finanza al lago di Nemi* (Rome: Gangemi, 2014), 49–54.

Ghini, G. and Batocchioni, G. (eds.), *Sulle tracce di Caligola: storie di grandi recuperi della Guardia di Finanza al lago di Nemi* (Rome: Gangemi, 2014).

Ghini, G., Granino Cecere, M. G., Rubini, M. and Arietti, F. 'L'ipogeo delle ghirlande a Grottaferrata (Roma). Una storia vissuta 2000 anni fa', in Attema, P., Nijboer, A. and Zifferero, A. (eds.), *Communities and Settlements from the Neolithic to the Early Medieval Period (Papers in Italian Archaeology 6)* (Oxford: Archaeopress, 2005), 246–57.

Gioia, P. and Volpe, R. (eds.), *Centocelle I (Studi e materiali dei musei e monumenti comunali di Roma 2)* (Rome: Rubbettino, 2004).

Giuliani, L. *Bildnis und Botschaft: hermeneutische Untersuchungen zur Bildniskunst der römischen Republik* (Frankfurt a.M.: Suhrkamp, 1986).

Giuliano, A. 'Documenti per servire allo studio del monumento degli Haterii', *Atti dell'Accademia nazionale dei Lincei. Memorie*, 13 (1967–68), 449–82.

Gleason, M. W. 'Making space for bicultural identity: Herodes Atticus commemorates Regilla', in Whitmarsh, T. (ed.), *Local Knowledge and Microidentities in the Imperial Greek World* (Cambridge University Press, 2010), 125–62.

Goette, H. R. 'Disiecta membra eines traianischen Frieses', *Archäologischer Anzeiger* (1983), 239–46.

Studien zu römischen Togadarstellungen (Beiträge zur Erschließung hellenistischer und kaiserzeitlicher Skulptur und Architektur 10) (Mainz: von Zabern, 1990).

González-Palacios, A. 'Pio VI, Franzoni e il colore delle pietre', in Extermann, G. and Braga, A. Varela (eds.), *Splendor marmoris: i colori del marmo, tra Roma e l'Europa, da Paolo III a Napoleone III* (Rome: De Luca, 2016), 343–73.

Gordon, A. E. *Album of Dated Latin Inscriptions, Vol. II: Rome and the Neighborhood, AD 100–199* (Berkeley: University of California Press, 1964).

Gowing, A. M. *Empire and Memory: The Representation of the Roman Republic in Imperial Culture (Roman Literature and its Contexts)* (Cambridge University Press, 2005).

Gradel, I. *Emperor Worship and Roman Religion (Oxford Classical Monographs)* (Oxford: Clarendon, 2002).

Graham, E.-J. *The Burial of the Urban Poor in Italy in the late Roman Republic and Early Empire (BAR International Series 1565)* (Oxford: Archaeopress, 2006).

'Corporeal concerns: The role of the body in the transformation of Roman mortuary practices', in Devlin, Z. and Graham, E.-J. (eds.), *Death Embodied: Archaeological Approaches to the Treatment of the Corpse (Studies in Funerary Archaeology 9)* (Oxford: Oxbow Books, 2015), 41–62.

Granino Cecere, M. G. 'I laurentes lavinates nella X Regio', in Basso, P. (ed.), *Est enim ille flos Italiae: vita economica e sociale nella Cisalpina romana* (Verona: QuiEdit, 2008), 169–90.

'Il sepolcro di un homo novus, Publius Cluvius Maximus Paullinus', in Valenti, M. (ed.), *Monumenta: i mausolei romani, tra commemorazione funebre e propaganda celebrativa (Tusculana 3)* (Rome: Exorma, 2010), 121–30.

Grassinger, D. *Die mythologischen Sarkophage: Achill, Adonis, Aeneas, Aktaion, Alkestis, Amazonen (ASR 12.1)* (Berlin: Gebrüder Mann, 1999).

'Durch virtus und labor zu gloria', in Koch, G. (ed.), *Akten des Symposiums des Sarkophag-Corpus 2001 (Sarkophag-Studien 3)* (Mainz: von Zabern, 2007), 111–16.

Green, C. M. C. *Roman Religion and the Cult of Diana at Aricia* (Cambridge University Press, 2007).

Gregori, G. L. 'Horti sepulchrales e cepotaphia nelle iscrizioni urbane', *BCom*, 92 (1987), 175–88.

'Il culto delle divinità Auguste in Italia: un'indagine preliminare', in Bodel, J. P. and Kajava, M. (eds.), *Dediche sacre nel mondo Greco-Romano: diffusione, funzioni, tipologie (Acta Instituti Romani Finlandiae 35)* (Rome: Institutum Romanum Finlandiae, 2009), 307–30.

'Vita e gesta del senatore bresciano Marco Nonio Macrino', in Rossi, D. and Arizza, M. (eds.), *Sulla via Flaminia: il mausoleo di Marco Nonio Macrino* (Milan: Electa, 2012), 286–301.

Griesbach, J. 'Villa e mausoleo: trasformazioni nel concetto della memoria nel suburbio romano', in Frizell, B. Santillo and Klynne, A. (eds.), *Roman Villas Around the Urbs. Interaction with Landscape and Environment (Projects and Seminars 2)* (Rome: The Swedish Institute in Rome, 2005), 113–23.

Villen und Gräber: Siedlungs- und Bestattungsplätze der römischen Kaiserzeit im Suburbium von Rom (Rahden/Westfalen: Leidorf, 2007).

Grisar, H. 'Il sepolcro dell'imperatore Ottone II nel paradiso dell' antica Basilica Vaticana', *Civiltà cattolica*, 55.1 (1904), 463–73.

Gros, P. 'Les monuments funéraires à èdicule sur podium dans l'Italie du Ier s. av. J.-C.', in Vaquerizo, D. (ed.), *Espacios y usos funerarios en el Occidente romano* (Cordoba: Seminario de Arqueologia, Universidad de Córdoba, 2002), 13–32.

Guarducci, M. 'Tracce di pitagorismo nelle iscrizioni ostiensi', *Atti della Accademia Nazionale dei Lincei, Rendiconti*, 23–4 (1947–49), 209–15.

(ed.), *Scritti scelti sulla religione greca e romana e sul Cristianesimo (Études préliminaires aux religions orientales dans l'empire romain 98)* (Leiden: Brill, 1983).

'La cosidetta fibula prenestina. Elementi nuovi', *Memorie: Atti della Accademia nazionale dei Lincei*, 28 (1984–86), 127–77.

Guidetti, F. 'Manilio e la teologia del Principato: Per l'interpretazione di Astronomica', in Guidetti, F. (ed.), *Poesia delle stelle tra antichità e medioevo* (Pisa: Edizioni della Normale, 2016), 263–99.

Guidi, A. 'Il Lazio meridionale', in Naso, A. (ed.), *Tumuli e sepolture monumentali nella protostoria europea: Atti del convegno internazionale Celano, 21–24 settembre 2000 (RGZM-Tagungen)* (Mainz: Römisch-Germanisches Zentralmuseum, 2011), 131–41.

Habicht, C. *Gottmenschentum und griechische Städte (Zetemata 14)* (Munich: Beck, 1970).

Haeckl, A. 'Dynasty, religion, topography, architecture: The Roman contexts of the Templum Gentis Flaviae', in Gazda, E. K., Haeckl, A. E. and Paris, R. (eds.), *Images of Empire: Flavian Fragments in Rome and Ann Arbor Rejoined* (Ann Arbor: University of Michigan Press, 1996), 11–25.

Hallett, C. H. *The Roman Nude: Heroic Portrait Statuary 200 BC–AD 300* (Oxford University Press, 2005).

Hallett, J. P. 'Women writing in Rome and Cornelia, mother of the Gracchi', in Churchill, L. J., Brown, P. R. and Jeffrey, J. E. (eds.), *Women Writing in Latin Roman Antiquity, Late Antiquity, and the Early Christian Era (Women Writers of the World 1)* (New York: Routledge, 2002), 13–24.

Hanfmann, G. M. A. *The Season Sarcophagus in Dumbarton Oaks (Dumbarton Oaks Studies 2)* (Cambridge: Harvard University Press, 1951).

Hänlein-Schäfer, H. *Veneratio Augusti: eine Studie zu den Tempeln des ersten römischen Kaisers (Archaeologica 39)* (Rome: G. Bretschneider, 1985).

Harkness, A. G. 'The scepticism and fatalism of the common people of Rome as illustrated by the sepulchral inscriptions', *Transactions and Proceedings of the American Philological Association*, 30 (1899), 56–88.

Hartswick, K. J. *The Gardens of Sallust: A Changing Landscape* (Austin: University of Texas Press, 2004).

Häuber, C. *The Eastern Part of the Mons Oppius in Rome: The Sanctuary of Isis et Serapis in Regio III, the Temples of Minerva Medica, Fortuna Virgo and Dea Syria, and the Horti of Maecenas (BCom Supplementi)* (Rome: "Erma" di Bretschneider, 2014).

Heinzelmann, M. *Die Nekropolen von Ostia. Untersuchungen zu den Gräberstraßen vor der Porta Romana und an der Via Laurentina* (Munich: Pfeil, 2000).

'Einleitung', in Heinzelmann, M. (ed.), *Römischer Bestattungsbrauch und Beigabensitten in Rom, Norditalien und den Nordwestprovinzen von der späten Republik bis in die Kaiserzeit* (Wiesbaden: Reichert, 2001), 11–20.

'Grabarchitektur, Bestattungsbrauch und Sozialstruktur – Zur Rolle der familia', in Heinzelmann, M. (ed.), *Römischer Bestattungsbrauch und Beigabensitten in Rom, Norditalien und den Nordwestprovinzen von der späten Republik bis in die Kaiserzeit* (Wiesbaden: Reichert, 2001), 179–91.

(ed.), *Römischer Bestattungsbrauch und Beigabensitten in Rom, Norditalien und den Nordwestprovinzen von der späten Republik bis in die Kaiserzeit* (Wiesbaden: Reichert, 2001).

Hekster, O. 'Propagating power: Hercules as an example for second-century emperors', in Rawlings, L. and Bowden, H. (eds.), *Herakles and Hercules:*

Exploring a Graeco-Roman Divinity (Swansea: Classical Press of Wales, 2005), 205–17.

'Descendant of gods: Legendary genealogies in the Roman Empire', in Blois, L. de, Funke, P. and Hahn, J. (eds.), *The Impact of Imperial Rome on Religions, Ritual, and Religious Life in the Roman Empire (Impact of Empire)* (Leiden: Brill, 2006), 24–35.

Emperors and Ancestors: Roman Rulers and the Constraints of Tradition (Oxford Studies in Ancient Culture and Representation) (Oxford University Press, 2015).

Helttula, A. (ed.), *Le iscrizioni sepolcrali latine nell'isola sacra (Acta Instituti Romani Finlandiae 30)* (Rome: Institutum Romanum Finlandiae, 2007).

Hemelrijk, E. A. 'Masculinity and femininity in the Laudatio Turiae', *Classical Quarterly*, 54 (2004), 185–97.

Hidden Lives, Public Personae: Women and Civic Life in the Roman West (Oxford University Press, 2015).

Herdejürgen, H. 'Frühkaiserzeitliche Sarkophage in Griechenland', *Jahrbuch des Deutschen Archäologischen Instituts*, 96 (1981), 413–35.

Stadtrömische und italische Girlandensarkophage: Die Sarkophage des ersten und zweiten Jahrhunderts (ASR 6.2.1) (Berlin: Gebrüder Mann, 1996).

'Sarkophage von der Via Latina. Folgerungen aus dem Fundkontext', *RM*, 107 (2000), 209–34.

Herklotz, I. *"Sepulcra" e "monumenta" del Medioevo: studi sull'arte sepolcrale in Italia (Collana di studi di storia dell'arte 5)* (Rome: Rari Nantes, 1985).

"Sepulcra" e "monumenta" del Medioevo: studi sull'arte sepolcrale in Italia (Collana di studi di storia dell'arte 5) (Naples: Liguori, 2001).

Hesberg, H. v. 'Planung und Ausgestaltung der Nekropolen Roms im 2. Jh. n. Chr.', in Hesberg, H. v. and Zanker, P. (eds.), *Römische Gräberstraßen: Selbstdarstellung – Status – Standard* (Munich: Verl. d. Bayer. Akad. d. Wiss., 1987), 43–60.

Römische Grabbauten (Darmstadt: Wiss. Buchges., 1992).

'Beigaben in den Gräbern Roms', in Fasold, P. (ed.), *Bestattungssitte und kulturelle Identität: Grabanlagen und Grabbeigaben der frühen römischen Kaiserzeit in Italien und den Nordwest-Provinzen (Xantener Berichte 7)* (Bonn: Habelt, 1998), 13–28.

'Il profumo del marmo. Cambiamenti nei riti di seppellimento e nei monumenti funerari nel I sec. d.C.', in Vaquerizo, D. (ed.), *Espacios y usos funerarios en el Occidente romano* (Cordoba: Seminario de Arqueologia, University, 2002), 33–49.

Hesberg, H. v. and Panciera, S. (eds.), *Das Mausoleum des Augustus: der Bau und seine Inschriften (Abhandlungen Bayerische Akademie der Wissenschaften, Philosophisch-Historische Klasse 108)* (Munich: Verl. d. Bayer. Akad. d. Wiss., 1994).

Hesberg, H. v. and Zanker, P. 'Einleitung', in Hesberg, H. v. and Zanker, P. (eds.), *Römische Gräberstraßen: Selbstdarstellung – Status – Standard* (Munich: Verl. d. Bayer. Akad. d. Wiss., 1987), 9–20.

(eds.), *Römische Gräberstraßen: Selbstdarstellung – Status – Standard* (Munich: Verl. d. Bayer. Akad. d. Wiss., 1987).

Hetland, L. M. 'Dating the Pantheon', *Journal of Roman Archaeology*, 20 (2007), 95–112.

Hofmann-Löbl, I. *Die Calpurnii: politisches Wirken und familiäre Kontinuität (Europäische Hochschulschriften: Reihe 3, Geschichte und ihre Hilfswissenschaften 705)* (Frankfurt a.M.: Lang, 1996).

Hölkeskamp, K.-J. *Reconstructing the Roman Republic: An Ancient Political Culture and Modern Research* (Princeton University Press, 2010).

Hölscher, T. 'Die Anfänge römischer Repräsentationskunst', *RM*, 35 (1975), 315–57.
  'Die Geschichtsauffassung in der römischen Repräsentationskunst', *Jahrbuch des Deutschen Archäologischen Instituts*, 95 (1980), 265–321.

Hoogma, R. P. *Der Einfluss Vergils auf die Carmina Latina epigraphica: eine Studie mit besonderer Beruecksichtigung der metrisch-technischen Grundsätze der Entlehnung* (Diss., Nijmegen, 1959).

Hope, V. 'A roof over the dead: Communal tombs and family structure', in Laurence, R. (ed.), *Domestic space in the Roman world: Pompeii and beyond (JRA Supplement 22)* (Portsmouth: JRA, 1997), 69–88.

Hope, V. M. 'Constructing Roman identity: Funerary monuments and social structure in the Roman world', *Mortality*, 2 (1997), 103–21.
  Death in Ancient Rome: A Source Book (Routledge Sourcebooks for the Ancient World) (London: Routledge, 2007).
  Roman Death: Dying and the Dead in Ancient Rome (London: Continuum, 2009).

Hope, V. M. and Huskinson, J. (eds.), *Memory and Mourning: Studies on Roman Death* (Oxford: Oxbow Books, 2011).

Hopkins, K. 'On the probable age structure of the Roman population', *Population Studies*, 20 (1966), 245–64.
  Death and Renewal (Sociological Studies in Roman History 2) (Cambridge University Press, 1983).
  'Graveyards for historians', in Hinard, F. (ed.), *La mort, les morts et l'au-delà dans le monde romain* (Université de Caen, 1987), 113–26.

Horsley, G. H. R. *New Documents Illustrating Early Christianity Vol. IV: Review of the Greek Inscriptions and Papyri Published in 1979 (New Documents Illustrating Early Christianity 4)* (Marrickville: Southwood Press, 1987).

Hueber, F. and Strocka, V. M. 'Die Bibliothek des Celsus. Eine Prachtfassade in Ephesos und das Problem ihrer Wiederaufrichtung', *Antike Welt*, 6.4 (1975), 3–14.

Huebner, S. R. 'Household composition in the ancient Mediterranean – What do we really know?', in Rawson, B. (ed.), *A Companion to Families in the Greek and Roman Worlds* (Malden: Wiley-Blackwell, 2011), 73–91.

Huskinson, J. *Roman Children's Sarcophagi: Their Decoration and its Social Significance* (Oxford: Clarendon Press, 1996).
  Roman Strigillated Sarcophagi: Art and Social History (Oxford University Press, 2015).

Huttunen, P. *The Social Strata in the Imperial City of Rome: A Quantitative Study of the Social Representation in the Epitaphs Published in the "Corpus Inscriptionum Latinarum" Vol. VI (Acta Universitatis Ouluensis Series B 3 = Historica 1.1)* (University of Oulu, 1974).

Idinopulos, T. and Wilson, B. (eds.), *What Is Religion? Origins, Definitions, and Explanations (Studies in the History of Religions 81)* (Leiden: Brill, 1998).

Impeciati, S. *Il Mausoleo dei Plauzi presso il Ponte Lucano a Tivoli: il ponte, il mausoleo, l'antica osteria* (Tivoli: Tiburis artistica, 2006).

Iodice Di Martino, M. G. 'Una villa di Aquilio Regolo sulla via Tiburtina?', in Pizzani, U., Isola, A., Menestò, E. and Di Pilla, A. (eds.), *Curiositas: studi di cultura classica e medievale in onore di Ubaldo Pizzani* (Naples: Edizioni scientifiche italiane, 2002), 555–67.

Johnson, M. J. *The Roman Imperial Mausoleum in Late Antiquity* (Cambridge University Press, 2009).

Joshel, S. R. *Work, Identity and Legal Status at Rome: A Study of the Occupational Inscriptions (Oklahoma Series in Classical Culture 11)* (Norman: University of Oklahoma Press, 1992).

Jucker, H. *Das Bildnis im Blätterkelch: Geschichte und Bedeutung einer römischen Porträtform (Bibliotheca Helvetica Romana)* (Olten: Urs Graf, 1961).

Junker, K. 'Römische mythologische Sarkophage. Zur Entstehung eines Denkmaltypus', *RM*, 112 (2006), 163–88.

Kaibel, G. (ed.), *Epigrammata graeca: ex lapidibus conlecta* (Berlin: Reimer, 1878).

Kajanto, I. *Supernomina: A Study in Latin Epigraphy (Commentationes humanarum litterarum 40.1)* (Helsinki: Societas Scientiarum Litterarum, 1966).

'The hereafter in ancient Christian epigraphy and poetry', *Arctos*, 12 (1978), 27–53.

Kammerer-Grothaus, H. 'Der Deus Rediculus im Triopion des Herodes Atticus. Untersuchungen am Bau und zu polychromer Ziegelarchitektur des 2. Jahrhunderts n. Chr. in Latium', *RM*, 81 (1974), 131–252.

'Zu den antiken Gräberstrassen unter S. Sebastiano an der Via Appia Antica', *RM*, 85 (1978), 115–38.

'Camere sepolcrali de' liberti e liberte di Livia Augusta ed altri caesari', *Mélanges de l'Ecole française de Rome. Antiquité*, 91 (1979), 315–29.

Kampen, N. B. *Image and Status: Roman Working Women in Ostia* (Berlin: Mann, 1981).

Kaser, M. 'Zum römischen Grabrecht', *Zeitschrift der Savigny-Stiftung für Rechtsgeschichte. Romanistische Abteilung*, 95 (1978), 15–92.

Kaufmann, C. M. *Das Kaisergrab in den Vatikanischen Grotten: erstmalige archaeologisch-historische Untersuchung der Gruft Ottos II* (Munich: Allg. Verl.-Ges., 1902).

Kierdorf, W. *Laudatio funebris: Interpretationen und Untersuchungen zur Entwicklung der römischen Leichenrede* (Meisenheim a. Glan: Hain, 1980).

'Apotheose und postumer Triumph Trajans', *Tyche*, 1 (1986), 147–56.

King, C. 'The organization of Roman religious beliefs', *Classical Antiquity*, 22 (2003), 275–312.

King, C. W. 'The Roman manes: The dead as gods', in Poo, M.-C. (ed.), *Rethinking Ghosts in World Religions (Studies in the History of Religions 123)* (Leiden: Brill, 2009), 95–114.

King, M. 'Commemoration of infants on Roman funerary inscriptions', in Oliver, G. J. (ed.), *The Epigraphy of Death: Studies in the History and Society of Greece and Rome* (Liverpool University Press, 2000), 117–51.

Kleiner, D. E. E. 'Second-century mythological portraiture: Mars and Venus', *Latomus*, 40 (1981), 512–44.

   Roman Imperial Funerary Altars with Portraits (Archaeologica 62) (Rome: Bretschneider, 1987).

Koch, G. *Meleager (ASR 12.6)* (Berlin: Mann, 1975).

   'Verschollene mythologische Sarkophage', *Archäologischer Anzeiger* (1976), 101–10.

   'Östliche Sarkophage in Rom', *Bonner Jahrbücher*, 182 (1982), 167–208.

Koch, G. and Sichtermann, H. *Römische Sarkophage (Handbuch der Archäologie 3)* (Munich: Beck, 1982).

Kockel, V. *Porträtreliefs stadtrömischer Grabbauten: ein Beitrag zur Geschichte und zum Verständnis des spätrepublikanisch-frühkaiserzeitlichen Privatporträts (Beiträge zur Erschließung hellenistischer und kaiserzeitlicher Skulptur und Architektur 12)* (Mainz: von Zabern, 1993).

Kolb, A. *Die kaiserliche Bauverwaltung in der Stadt Rom: Geschichte und Aufbau der cura operum publicorum unter dem Prinzipat (Heidelberger althistorische Beiträge und epigraphische Studien 13)* (Stuttgart: Steiner, 1993).

Kolb, A. and Fugmann, J. *Tod in Rom: Grabinschriften als Spiegel römischen Lebens* (Darmstadt: Wiss. Buchges., 2008).

Kolb, F. *Rom: die Geschichte der Stadt in der Antike (Beck's historische Bibliothek)* (Munich: Beck, 1995).

Koortbojian, M. 'In commemorationem mortuorum: Text and image along the 'Streets of Tombs'', in Elsner, J. (ed.), *Art and Text in Roman Culture (Cambridge Studies in New Art History and Criticism)* (Cambridge University Press, 1996), 210–33.

   The Divinization of Caesar and Augustus: Precedents, Consequences, Implications (New York: Cambridge University Press, 2013).

Kousser, R. 'Mythological group portraits in Antonine Rome: The performance of myth', *American Journal of Archaeology*, 111 (2007), 673–91.

Kragelund, P. 'The emperors, the Licinii Crassi and the Carlsberg Pompey', in Højte, J. M. (ed.), *Images of Ancestors (Aarhus Studies in Mediterranean Antiquity 5)* (Aarhus University Press, 2002), 185–222.

   'Shadows of a great name: An aristocratic family under the early empire', in Kragelund, P., Moltesen, M. and Østergaard, J. S. (eds.), *The Licinian Tomb: Fact or Fiction?* (Copenhagen: Ny Carlsberg Glyptotek, 2003), 18–45.

Kragelund, P., Moltesen, M., and Østergaard, J. S. (eds.), *The Licinian Tomb: Fact or Fiction?* (Copenhagen: Ny Carlsberg Glyptotek, 2003).

Krummrey, H. 'Zu dem Grabgedicht für Aelia in Nikopos a. d. Donau (CLE 492)', *Klio*, 63 (1981), 527–49.

Künzl, E. *Der römische Triumph: Siegesfeiern im antiken Rom (Beck's archäologische Bibliothek)* (Munich: Beck, 1988).

Kyle, D. G. *Spectacles of Death in Ancient Rome* (London: Routledge, 1998).

La Rocca, E. 'Il Templum Gentis Flaviae', in Coarelli, F. (ed.), *Divus Vespasianus: il bimillenario dei Flavi* (Rome: Electa, 2009), 224–33.

  'Il Templum Gentis Flaviae', in Colognesi, L. Capogrossi (ed.), *La Lex de imperio Vespasiani e la Roma dei Flavi (Acta Flaviana 1)* (Rome: L'Erma di Bretschneider, 2009), 271–97.

  'Agrippa's Pantheon and its origin', in Marder, T. A. and Wilson Jones, M. (eds.), *The Pantheon: From Antiquity to the Present* (Cambridge University Press, 2015).

  Il Pantheon di Agrippa (Collezione archeologica) (Rome: Scienze e Lettere, 2015).

La Rocca, E., Parisi Presicce, C. and Lo Monaco, A. (eds.), *Ritratti – le tante facce del potere* (Rome: Musei Capitolini, 2011).

Lahusen, G. 'Zur Funktion und Bedeutung der Ehrenstatuen für Privatpersonen in Rom', in Schindler, W. (ed.), *Römisches Porträt: Wege zur Erforschung eines gesellschaftlichen Phänomens (Wissenschaftliche Zeitschrift der Humboldt-Universität zu Berlin 31,2/3)* (Berlin: Humboldt Universität, 1982), 239–41.

  Untersuchungen zur Ehrenstatue in Rom: literarische und epigraphische Zeugnisse (Archaeologica 35) (Rome: Bretschneider, 1983).

Lanciani, R. 'Il santuario sotterraneo recentemente scoperto ad Spem Veterem', *BCom*, 46 (1918), 69–84.

Lang, J. *Mit Wissen geschmückt? Zur bildlichen Rezeption griechischer Dichter und Denker in der römischen Lebenswelt (Monumenta artis Romanae 39)* (Wiesbaden: Reichert Verlag, 2012).

Langlotz, E. *Sammlung antiker Kunst (Versteigerung/Hugo Helbing, München 1930.10.30)* (Munich: Helbing, 1930).

Lattimore, R. *Themes in Greek and Latin Epitaphs (Illinois Studies in Language and Literature 28,1/2)* (Urbana: University of Illinois Press, 1942).

Lauter-Bufe, H. 'Zur Fassade des Scipionengrabes', *RM*, 59 (1982), 35–46.

Lazzarini, S. *Sepulcra familiaria: un'indagine epigrafico-giuridica* (Padova: CEDAM, 1991).

Leach, E. W. 'Freedmen and immortality in the tomb of the Haterii', in D'Ambra, E. and Métraux, G. P. R. (eds.), *The Art of Citizens, Soldiers and Freedmen in the Roman World (BAR International Series 1526)* (Oxford: Archaeopress, 2006), 1–18.

Lehmann, K. and Olsen, E. C. *Dionysiac Sarcophagi in Baltimore* (Baltimore: Institute of Fine Arts, New York University, 1942).

Leithoff, J. *Macht der Vergangenheit: zur Erringung, Verstetigung und Ausgestaltung des Principats unter Vespasian, Titus und Domitian (Schriften zur politischen Kommunikation 19)* (Göttingen: V&R Unipress, 2014).

Lendon, J. E. *Empire of Honour: The Art of Government in the Roman World* (Oxford: Clarendon, 1997).

Leunissen, P. M. 'Die drei römischen Statuen in der städtischen KLM-Dienststelle in Rom', *Mededelingen van het Nederlands Instituut te Rome*, 46 (1985), 57–85.
Konsuln und Konsulare in der Zeit von Commodus bis Severus Alexander (180–235 n.Chr.). Prosopographische Untersuchungen zur senatorischen Elite im römischen Kaiserreich (Dutch monographs on ancient history and archaeology 6) (Amsterdam: Gieben, 1989).

Levi, M. A. *Ercole e Roma (Monografie/Centro Ricerche e Documentazione sull'Antichità Classica 17)* (Rome: L' Erma di Bretschneider, 1997).

Lewis, N. and Reynold, M. *Roman Civilization: A Sourcebook. Vol. II: The Empire* (New York: Columbia University Press, 1990).

Lieberg, G. (ed.), *Puella divina: die Gestalt der göttlichen Geliebten bei Catull im Zusammenhang der antiken Dichtung* (Amsterdam: Schippers, 1962).

Liebs, D. 'Ewiges Gedenken durch freigelassene Sklaven: römisches Recht und römische Sitten', in Gulczynski, A. (ed.), *Leben nach dem Tod: rechtliche Probleme im Dualismus: Mensch – Rechtssubjekt* (Graz: Leykam, 2010), 49–65.

Liverani, P. 'Il ciclo di ritratti dell'edificio absidato di Bassus a Roselle: iconografia imperiale e glorificazione familiare', *RM*, 101 (1994), 161–73.
La topografia antica del Vaticano (Monumenta Sanctae Sedis 2) (Vatican City: Monumenti Musei e Gallerie Pontificie, 1999).
'I giardini imperiali di Roma', in Di Pasquale, G. and Paolucci, F. (eds.), *Il giardino antico da Babilonia a Roma: scienza, arte e natura* (Livorno: Sillabe, 2007), 86–97.

Liverani, P. and Spinola, G. *La necropoli Vaticana lungo la via Trionfale (Musei Vaticani. Le Guide)* (Rome: De Luca, 2006).

Liverani, P., Spinola, G., Zander, P. and Buranelli, F. *Le necropoli Vaticane: la città dei morti di Roma (Monumenta Vaticana selecta)* (Milan: Jaca book, 2010).

Lloyd, R. B. 'Three monumental gardens on the marble plan', *American Journal of Archaeology*, 86 (1982), 91–100.

Lo Monaco, A. 'Immagini private e apoteosi a Roma in età medio-imperiale', in La Rocca, E. and Bucchino, L. (eds.), *Ritratti – le tante facce del potere* (Rome: Musei Capitolini, 2011), 334–49.

Lupu, N. 'La Villa di Sette Bassi sulla Via Latina', *Ephemeris Dacoromana*, 7 (1937), 117–88.

Ma, J. *Statues and Cities: Honorific Portraits and Civic Identity in the Hellenistic World (Oxford Studies in Ancient Culture and Representation)* (Oxford University Press, 2013).

Maderna, C. *Iuppiter, Diomedes und Merkur als Vorbilder für römische Bildnisstatuen: Untersuchungen zum römischen statuarischen Idealporträt (Archäologie und Geschichte 1)* (Heidelberg: Verlag Archäologie und Geschichte, 1988).

Malgouyres, P. (ed.), *Porphyre: la pierre pourpre des Ptolémées aux Bonaparte* (Paris: Réunion des Musées Nationaux, 2003).

Manacorda, D. 'Ex Ascia?', *Archeologia Classica*, 24 (1972), 346–52.

Mander, J. *Portraits of Children on Roman Funerary Monuments* (Cambridge University Press, 2013).

Manodori, A. 'Memorie sparse del Mausoleo di Adriano', in Mercalli, M. (ed.), *Adriano e il suo mausoleo: studi, indagini e interpretazioni* (Milan: Electa, 1998), 147–59.

Manuwald, G. *Roman Republican Theatre: A History* (Cambridge University Press, 2011).

Marder, T. A. and Wilson Jones, M. (eds.), *The Pantheon: From Antiquity to the Present* (New York: Cambridge University Press, 2015).

Mari, Z. *Tibur III (Forma Italiae I,17)* (Rome: De Luca, 1983).

  Tibur IV (Forma Italiae 35) (Rome: de Luca, 1991).

  'Tivoli in età adrianea', in Reggiani Massarini, A. M. and Bouchenaki, M. (eds.), *Villa Adriana: paesaggio antico e ambiente moderno; elementi di novità e ricerche in corso* (Milan: Electa, 2002), 181–202.

Marshall, F. H. *The Collection of Ancient Greek Inscriptions in the British Museum, Vol. 4.2* (Oxford: Clarendon Press, 1916).

Martin, D. B. 'The construction of the ancient family: Methodological considerations', *Journal of Roman Studies*, 86 (1996), 40–60.

Martin, S. D. *The Roman Jurists and the Organization of Private Building in the late Republic and Early Empire (Collection Latomus 204)* (Brussels: Latomus, 1989).

Marvin, M. *The Language of the Muses: The Dialogue Between Roman and Greek Sculpture* (Los Angeles: J. Paul Getty Museum, 2008).

Massaro, M. 'Le "nozze perpetue" di una coppia romana (CE 1559)', *Studia Philologica Valentina*, 11 (2008), 283–325.

Massi, P. *Indicazione Antiquaria Del Pontificio Museo Pio-Clementino In Vaticano* (Rome: Lazzarini, 1792).

Matheson, S. B. 'The divine Claudia: Women as goddesses in Roman art', in Kleiner, D. E. E. and Matheson, S. B. (eds.), *I Claudia, Women in Ancient Rome* (Oxford: Oxbow Books, 1996), 182–93.

Matz, F. 'Hellenistische und römische Grabbauten', *Die Antike*, 4 (1928), 285–304.

  Der Gott auf dem Elefantenwagen (Abhandlungen der Geistes- und Sozialwissenschaftlichen Klasse/Akademie der Wissenschaften und der Literatur in Mainz 10) (Mainz: Akad. der Wiss. und der Literatur, 1953).

  Die Dionysischen Sarkophage, Vol. II (ASR 4.2) (Berlin: Mann, 1968).

  Die Dionysischen Sarkophage, Vol. III (ASR 4.3) (Berlin: Mann, 1969).

  Die Dionysischen Sarkophage, Vol. IV (ASR 4.4) (Berlin: Mann, 1975).

Maxfield, V. A. and Peacock, D. P. S. *The Roman Imperial Quarries: Topography and Quarries* (London: Egypt Exploration Society, 2001).

  The Roman Imperial Quarries: The Excavations (London: Egypt Exploration Society, 2007).

Mayer, E. *The Ancient Middle Classes: Urban Life and Aesthetics in the Roman Empire, 100 BCE–250 CE* (Cambridge: Harvard University Press, 2012).

McIntyre, G. 'Deification as consolation: The divine children of the Roman imperial family', *Historia*, 62 (2013), 222–40.

Megow, W.-R. *Kameen von Augustus bis Alexander Severus (Antike Münzen und geschnittene Steine 11)* (Berlin: de Gruyter, 1987).

Meinecke, K. 'Inschriften mit Angaben zum sozialen Status in Grabanlagen mit Sarkophagen in Rom und Umgebung', in Porod, B. and Koiner, G. (eds.), *Römische Sarkophage: Akten des internationalen Werkstattgesprächs, 11. – 13. Oktober 2012 (Graz)* (Graz: Uni Graz, 2012), 180–94.

    Sarcophagum posuit: römische Steinsarkophage im Kontext (Sarkophag-Studien 7) (Ruhpolding/Wiesbaden: Rutzen/Harrassowitz, 2014).

Mekacher, N. *Die vestalischen Jungfrauen in der römischen Kaiserzeit (Palilia 15)* (Wiesbaden: Reichert, 2006).

Mercalli, M. (ed.), *Adriano e il suo mausoleo: studi, indagini e interpretazioni* (Milan: Electa, 1998).

Messineo, G. *La Via Flaminia da Porta del Popolo a Malborghetto* (Rome: Quasar, 1991).

Meyboom, P. G. P. and Moormann, E. M. *Le decorazioni dipinte e marmoree della domus aurea di Nerone a Roma* (Leuven: Peeters, 2013).

Mielsch, H. *Römische Stuckreliefs (RM: Ergänzungs-Heft 21)* (Heidelberg: Kerle, 1975).

    Römische Wandmalerei (Darmstadt: Wiss. Buchges., 2001).

Mielsch, H. and Hesberg, H. v. *Die heidnische Nekropole unter St. Peter in Rom: Die Mausoleen A-D (Atti della Pontificia Accademia Romana di Archeologia: Serie 3: Memorie 16.1)* (Rome: "L'Erma" di Bretschneider, 1986).

    Die heidnische Nekropole unter St. Peter in Rom: Die Mausoleen E – I und Z – PSI (Atti della Pontificia Accademia Romana di Archeologia: Serie 3: Memorie 16,2) (Rome: "L'Erma" di Bretschneider, 1996).

Mikocki, T. 'Faustine la Jeune en Vénus – mythes et faits', in Bonacasa, N. and Rizza, G. (eds.), *Ritratto ufficiale e ritratto privato: atti del II Conferenza Internazionale sul Ritratto Romano, Roma, 26–30 Settembre 1984 (La ricerca scientifica 116)* (Rome: Consiglio Nazionale delle Ricerche, 1988), 383–9.

    Sub specie Deae: les impératrices et princesses Romaines assimilées à des déesses; étude iconologique (Rivista di archeologia, Supplementi 14) (Rome: Bretschneider, 1995).

Milella, M. 'Il Foro di Traiano', in Ungaro, L. (ed.), *Il Museo dei Fori Imperiali nei Mercati di Traiano (Musei in Comune Roma)* (Milan: Electa, 2007), 192–211.

    'La decorazione del tempio di Venere Genitrice', *Scienze dell'antichità. Storia, archeologia, antropologia*, 16 (2010), 455–69.

Miller, C. W. 'Alternating Apollo's bow and lyre', in Giorcelli, C. (ed.), *Abito e identità. Ricerche di storia letteraria e culturale* (Palermo/Rome: Edizioni Associate, 2006), 41–53.

Miller, J. F. 'Triumphus in Palatio', *American Journal of Philology*, 121 (2000), 409–22.

    Apollo, Augustus, and the Poets (Cambridge University Press, 2009).

Möbius, H. *Alexandria und Rom (Bayerische Akademie der Wissenschaften. Philosophisch-historische Klasse N.F. 59)* (Munich: Bayerischen Akademie der Wissenschaften; Beck, 1964).

Möller, K. *Götterattribute in ihrer Anwendung auf Augustus: eine Studie über die indirekte Erhöhung des ersten Princeps in der Dichtung seiner Zeit (Wissenschaftliche Schriften im Wissenschaftlichen Verlag Dr. Schulz-Kirchner 101)* (Idstein: Schulz-Kirchner, 1985).

Montanari, P. *Sepolcri circolari di Roma e suburbio: elementi architettonici dell'elevato (Workshop di archeologia classica: Quaderni 2)* (Pisa: Serra, 2009).

Il monumento dei Lucilii sulla via Salaria, Roma (BAR international series) (Oxford: Archaeopress, 2014).

Morgan, T. *Roman Faith and Christian Faith: Pistis and Fides in the Early Roman Empire and Early Churches* (Oxford University Press, 2015).

Morris, I. *Death-ritual and Social Structure in Classical Antiquity (Key Themes in Ancient History* (Cambridge University Press, 1992).

Mouritsen, H. 'Freedmen and freeborn in the necropolis of imperial Ostia', *ZPE*, 150 (2004), 281–304.

'The families of Roman slaves and freedmen', in Rawson, B. (ed.), *A Companion to Families in the Greek and Roman Worlds (Blackwell Companions to the Ancient World)* (Malden: Wiley-Blackwell, 2010), 129–44.

The Freedman in the Roman World (Cambridge University Press, 2011).

Müller, C. W. 'Das Bildprogramm der Silberbecher von Hoby', *Jahrbuch des Deutschen Archäologischen Instituts*, 109 (1994), 321–52.

Müller, F. G. J. M. *The So-called Peleus and Thetis Sarcophagus in the Villa Albani (Iconological Studies in Roman Art 1)* (Amsterdam: Gieben, 1994).

Muratori, L. A. *Novus thesaurus veterum inscriptionum in praecipuis earumdem collectionibus hactenus praetermissarum* (Milan: ex aedibus Palatinis, 1739).

Murer, C. 'The reuse of funerary statues in late antique prestige buildings at Ostia', in Kristensen, T. M. and Stirling, L. M. (eds.), *The Afterlife of Greek and Roman Sculpture: Late Antique Responses and Practices* (Ann Arbor: University of Michigan Press, 2016), 177–96.

Muth, S. 'Drei statt vier: Zur Deutung der Feldherrensarkophage', *Archäologischer Anzeiger* (2004), 263–73.

'Im Angesicht des Todes: Zum Wertediskurs in der römischen Grabkultur', in Haltenhoff, A., Heil, A. and Mutschler, F.-H. (eds.), *Römische Werte als Gegenstand der Altertumswissenschaft (Beiträge zur Altertumskunde 227)* (Munich: Saur, 2005), 259–86.

Naso, A. (ed.), *Tumuli e sepolture monumentali nella protostoria europea (Römisch-Germanisches Zentralmuseum: RGZM-Tagungen 5)* (Mainz: Römisch-Germanisches Zentralmuseum, 2011).

Needham, R. *Belief, Language, and Experience* (Oxford: Blackwell, 1972).

Newby, Z. *Greek Myths in Roman Art and Culture: Imagery, Values and Identity in Italy, 50 BC–AD 250 (Greek Culture in the Roman World)* (Cambridge University Press, 2016).

Newlands, C. 'Statius' programmatic Apollo and the ending of Book 1 of the Thebaid', in Athanasakē, L., Martin, R. P. and Miller, J. F. (eds.), *Apolline Politics and Poetics* (Athens: Hellenic Ministry of Culture, 2009), 353–78.

Nicorescu, P. 'La tomba degli Scipioni', *Ephemeris Dacoromana*, 1 (1923), 1–56.

Nielsen, H. S. 'Interpreting epithets in Roman epitaphs', in Rawson, B. and Weaver, P. (eds.), *The Roman Family in Italy: Status, Sentiment, Space* (Canberra: Humanities Research Centre, 1997), 169–204.

Nista, L. (ed.), *Castores: l'immagine dei Dioscuri a Roma* (Rome: DeLuca, 1994).

Nock, A. D. 'Synnaos theos', *Harvard Studies in Classical Philology*, 41 (1930),1–62.

'Cremation and burial in the Roman Empire', *Harvard Theological Review*, 25 (1932), 321–59.

'Sarcophagi and symbolism', *American Journal of Archaeology*, 50 (1946), 140–70.

North, J. A. 'Praesens divus', *Journal of Roman Studies*, 65 (1975), 171–7.

'Sappho underground', in Dignas, B., Smith, R. R. R. and Price, S. R. F. (eds.), *Historical and Religious Memory in the Ancient World* (Oxford University Press, 2012), 37–67.

Noy, D. *Jewish Inscriptions of Western Europe, Vol. II: The City of Rome* (Cambridge University Press, 1995).

'Building a Roman funeral pyre', *Antichthon*, 34 (2000), 30–45.

Obryk, M. *Unsterblichkeitsglaube in den griechischen Versinschriften (Untersuchungen zur antiken Literatur und Geschichte 108)* (Berlin: de Gruyter, 2012).

Opper, T. (ed.), *Hadrian: Empire and Conflict* (London: British Museum Press, 2008).

Orelli, J. K. v. *Inscriptionum latinarum selectarum amplissima collectio ad illustrandam Romanae Antiquitatis disciplinam accommodata, ac magnarum collectionum supplementum complura emendationesque exhibens* (Turici: Typis Orellii, Fuesslini et Sociorum, 1828).

Orlandi, S. 'Heredes, alieni, ingrati, ceteri: ammissioni ed esclusioni', in *Libitina e dintorni: Libitina e i luci sepolcrali, le leges libitinariae campane, iura sepulcrorum: vecchie e nuove iscrizioni (Libitina 3)* (Rome: Quasar, 2004), 359–84.

Ortalli, J. 'Il sarcofago romano da Maccaretolo (S. Pietro in Casale, Bologna)', in Cremonini, S. and Amaldi, M. (eds.), *Romanità della pianura: l'ipotesi archeologica a S. Pietro in Casale come coscienza storica per una nuova gestione del territorio* (San Pietro in Casale: Comune, 1991), 147–73.

'Il culto funerario della cispadana romana. Rappresentazione e interiorità', in Heinzelmann, M. (ed.), *Römischer Bestattungsbrauch und Beigabensitten in Rom, Norditalien und den Nordwestprovinzen von der späten Republik bis in die Kaiserzeit* (Wiesbaden: Reichert, 2001), 215–42.

Orth, W. 'Verstorbene werden zu Sternen. Geistesgeschichtlicher Hintergrund und politische Implikationen des Katasterismos in der frühen römischen Kaiserzeit', *Laverna*, 5 (1994), 148–66.

Osgood, J. *Turia: A Roman Woman's Civil War (Women in Antiquity)* (Oxford University Press, 2014).

Østergaard, J. S. 'The Licinian altars: From discovery to museum', in Kragelund, P., Moltesen, M. and Østergaard, J. S. (eds.), *The Licinian Tomb: Fact or Fiction?* (Copenhagen: Ny Carlsberg Glyptotek, 2003), 46–54.

'The Licinian sarcophagi: From discovery to museums', in Kragelund, P., Moltesen, M. and Østergaard, J. S. (eds.), *The Licinian Tomb: Fact or Fiction?* (Copenhagen: Ny Carlsberg Glyptotek, 2003), 55–65.

Østergaard, J. S. and Moltesen, M. 'Catalogue of monuments connected with the Licinian tomb', in Kragelund, P., Moltesen, M. and Østergaard, J. S. (eds.), *The Licinian Tomb: Fact or Fiction?* (Copenhagen: Ny Carlsberg Glyptotek, 2003), 109–11.

Packer, J. E. *The Forum of Trajan in Rome (California Studies in the History of Art 31)* (Berkeley: University of California Press, 1997).

Palombi, D. 'Inter divos relatus est. La divinizzazione nella famiglia imperiale', in Abbondanza, L. (ed.), *Apoteosi da uomini a dei: il Mausoleo di Adriano* (Rome: Munus, 2013), 189–99.

Panciera, S. 'Umano, sovrumano o divino? Le divinità auguste e l'imperatore a Roma', in Blois, L. de, Erdkamp, P. and Hekster, O. (eds.), *The Representation and Perception of Roman Imperial Power (Impact of Empire 3)* (Amsterdam: Gieben, 2003), 215–39.

Pannuti, U. 'L'apoteosi d'Omero. Vaso argenteo del Museo Nazionale di Napoli', *Monumenti antichi. Serie miscellanea*, 52 (1984), 43–61.

Papi, C. 'Le iscrizioni della necropoli vaticana. Una revisione', *Atti della Pontificia accademia romana di archeologia'. Rendiconti*, 73 (2000), 239–65.

Paris, R. 'Propaganda e iconografia: una lettura del frontone del tempio di Quirino sul frammento del "Rilievo Hartwig" nel Museo Nazionale Romano', *Bollettino d'arte*, 73 (1988), 27–38.

(ed.), *Dono Hartwig: originali ricongiunti e copie tra Roma e Ann Arbor; ipotesi per il Templum Gentis Flaviae* (Rome: Giunti, 1994).

'Sculture del Templum Gentis Flaviae', in Coarelli, F. (ed.), *Divus Vespasianus: il bimillenario dei Flavi* (Rome: Electa, 2009), 460–9.

Paris, R., Mazzotta, B. and Naccarato, M. 'Via Appia Antica. Il nuovo sito archeologico di Capo di Bove e il Triopio di Erode Attico', *RM*, 119 (2013), 275–331.

Parkin, T. G. 'The Roman life course and the family', in Rawson, B. (ed.), *A Companion to Families in the Greek and Roman Worlds (Blackwell Companions to the Ancient World)* (Malden: Wiley-Blackwell, 2011), 276–90.

Parkin, T. G. and Pomeroy, A. J. *Roman Social History: A Sourcebook (Routledge Sourcebooks for the Ancient World)* (London: Routledge, 2007).

Paroli, L. (ed.), *La basilica cristiana di Pianabella (Scavi di Ostia 12.1)* (Rome: Libreria dello Stato, 1999).

Peek, W. *Griechische Vers-Inschriften vol. I: Grab-Epigramme* (Berlin: Akademie-Verl., 1955).

(ed.), *Griechische Grabgedichte: griechisch und deutsch (Schriften und Quellen der alten Welt 7)* (Berlin: Akad.-Verl., 1960).

'Zu den Gedichten des Marcellus von Side auf Regilla und das Triopion des Herodes Atticus', *ZPE*, 33 (1979), 76–84.

Pekáry, T. 'Mors perpetua est. Zum Jenseitsglauben in Rom', *Laverna*, 5 (1994), 87–103.

Pensabene, P. *I marmi nella Roma antica (Biblioteca di testi e studi 890)* (Rome: Carocci, 2013).

Pepe, C. 'La fama dopo il silenzio: celebrazione della donna e ritratti esemplari di bonae feminae nella laudatio funebris romana', in Pepe, C. and Moretti, G. (eds.), *Le parole dopo la morte: forme e funzioni della retorica funeraria nella tradizione greca e romaa* (Trento: Università degli Studi di Trento, 2015), 179–222.

Peppel, M. 'Gott oder Mensch? Kaiserverehrung und Herrschaftskontrolle', in Cancik, H. and Hitzl, K. (eds.), *Die Praxis der Herrscherverehrung in Rom und seinen Provinzen* (Tübingen: Mohr Siebeck, 2003), 69–95.

Peres, I. *Griechische Grabinschriften und neutestamentliche Eschatologie (Wissenschaftliche Untersuchungen zum Neuen Testament 157)* (Tübingen: Mohr Siebeck, 2003).

Perry, M. J. *Gender, Manumission, and the Roman Freedwoman* (Cambridge University Press, 2014).

Petersen, E. 'Sepolcro scoperto sulla via Latina', *Annali dell'Istituto di corrispondenza archeologica*, 32 (1860), 348–415.

'Secondo sepolcro scoperto sulla via Latina', *Annali dell'Istituto di corrispondenza archeologica*, 33 (1861), 190–242.

Petersen, L. H. *The Freedman in Roman Art and History* (Cambridge University Press, 2006).

Petruccioli, G. 'The structure on the reverse of a Domitianic coin (BMC 406*): Interpretation and identification'. www.academia.edu/1497179/The_structure_on_the_reverse_of_a_Domitianic_coin_BMC_406_Interpretation_and_identification

Pfanner, M. *Der Titusbogen (Beiträge zur Erschliessung hellenistischer und kaiserzeitlicher Skulptur und Architektur 2)* (Mainz: von Zabern, 1983).

Pierce, S. R. 'The Mausoleum of Hadrian and the Pons Aelius', *Journal of Roman Studies*, 15 (1925), 75–103.

Pietrangeli, C. 'La provenienza delle sculture dei Musei Vaticani', *Bollettino. Monumenti, musei e gallerie pontificie*, 8 (1988), 139–210.

Pietrograndi, A. 'Ruderi e sarcofago scoperti sulla via di Decima', *NSc*, 10 (1934), 15–68.

Piranesi, G. B. *Le antichità Romane III. Contenente Gli Avanzi De' Monvmenti Sepolcrali Di Roma E Dell'Agro Romano* (Rome: Salomoni, 1784).

Pisani Sartorio, G. 'Tomba detta di Alessandro Severo a Monte del Grano', in Alfieri, M. (ed.), *Piranesi nei luoghi di Piranes* (Rome: Multigrafica Editrice, 1979), 65–71.

Piso, I. 'Der Prätorianierpräfekt Q. Marcius Turbo und seine Söhne', *ZPE*, 150 (2004), 270–80.

Pollini, J. 'Man or god: Divine assimilation and imitation in the late republic and early empire', in Raaflaub, K. A. and Toher, M. (eds.), *Between Republic and Empire: Interpretations of Augustus and his Principate* (Berkeley: University of California Press, 1990), 333–63.

> *From Republic to Empire: Rhetoric, Religion, and Power in the Visual Culture of Ancient Rome (Oklahoma Series in Classical Culture 48)* (Norman: University of Oklahoma Press, 2012).

Pomeroy, S. B. *The Murder of Regilla: A Case of Domestic Violence in Antiquity* (Cambridge: Harvard University Press, 2007).

Poulsen, V. *Les portraits romains, vol. I République et dynastie Julienne (Publications de la Glyptothèque ny Carlsberg)* (Copenhagen: Glyptothèque Ny Carlsberg, 1962).

> 'Ideologia, mito e culto dei Castori a Roma: dall'età repubblicana al tardo-antico', in Nista, L. (ed.), *Castores: l'immagine dei Dioscuri a Roma* (Rome: DeLuca, 1994), 91–100.

Power, T. *The Culture of Kitharôidia (Hellenic Studies)* (Washington: Harvard University Press, 2010).

Prato, C. (ed.), *Gli epigrammi attribuiti a L. Anneo Seneca (Biblioteca degli scrittori greci e latini 2)* (Rome: dell'Ateneo, 1964).

Price, S. *Religions of the Ancient Greeks (Key Themes in Ancient History)* (Cambridge University Press, 1999).

Price, S. R. F. 'Gods and emperors: The Greek language of the Roman imperial cult', *Journal of Hellenic Studies*, 104 (1984), 79–95.

> *Rituals and Power: The Roman Imperial Cult in Asia Minor* (Cambridge University Press, 1984).

> 'From noble funerals to divine cult: The consecration of Roman emperors', in Cannadine, D. and Price, S. R. F. (eds.), *Rituals of Royalty: Power and Ceremonial in Traditional Societies* (Cambridge University Press, 1987), 56–105.

Proietti, E. *Il Mausoleo di Adriano (Collana archeologica)* (Rome: E. S. S., 2007).

Purcell, N. 'Tomb and suburb', in Hesberg, H. v. and Zanker, P. (eds.), *Römische Gräberstraßen: Selbstdarstellung – Status – Standard* (Munich: Verl. d. Bayer. Akad. d. Wiss., 1987), 25–41.

Quilici, L. *Collatia (Forma Italiae 1,10)* (Rome: De Luca, 1974).

> *La Via Latina da Roma a Castel Savelli (Passeggiate nel Lazio 4)* (Rome: Bulzoni, 1978).

Raeck, W. *Modernisierte Mythen: Zum Umgang der Spätantike mit klassischen Bildthemen* (Stuttgart: Steiner, 1992).

Raepsaet-Charlier, M.-T. 'Clarissima femina', *Revue internationale des droits de l'antiquité*, 28 (1981), 189–212.

> 'Cornelia Cet(h)egilla', *L'antiquité classique*, 50.1–2 (1981), 685–97.

Prosopographie des femmes de l'ordre sénatorial (I. – II. siècles) (Fonds René Draguet 34) (Leuven: Peeters, 1987).

Ramage, N. H. and Ramage, A. *The Cambridge Illustrated History of Roman Art: Romulus to Constantine* (Cambridge University Press, 1991).

Ramsby, T. R. 'Striving for permanence: Ovid's funerary inscriptions', *Classical Journal*, 100 (2005), 365–91.

Textual Permanence: Roman Elegists and the Epigraphic Tradition (London: Duckworth, 2007).

Rasch, J. J. *Das Maxentius-Mausoleum an der Via Appia in Rom (Spätantike Zentralbauten in Rom und Latium 1)* (Mainz: von Zabern, 1984).

Rausa, F. 'Disegni di monumenti funerari romani in alcuni mss. di Pirro Ligorio', *Rendiconti dell'Accademia nazionale dei Lincei, Classe di scienze morali, storiche e filologiche*, 7.3–4 (1996), 513–59.

Pirro Ligorio, tombe e mausolei dei romani (Rome: Quasar, 1997).

Rawlings, L. 'Hannibal and Hercules', in Rawlings, L. and Bowden, H. (eds.), *Herakles and Hercules: Exploring a Graeco-Roman Divinity* (Swansea: Classical Press of Wales, 2005), 153–84.

Rawson, B. 'Family life among the lower classes at Rome in the first two centuries of the empire', *Classical Philology*, 61 (1966), 71–83.

(ed.), *The Family in Ancient Rome: New Perspectives* (London: Croom Helm, 1986).

'"The family" in the ancient Mediterranean: Past, present, future', *ZPE*, 117 (1997), 294–6.

(ed.), *A Companion to Families in the Greek and Roman Worlds (Blackwell Companions to the Ancient World)* (Malden: Wiley-Blackwell, 2011).

Reekmans, L. 'La 'dextrarum iunctio' dans la iconographie romaine et paléochretienne', *Bulletin de l'Institut Historique Belge de Rome*, 31 (1958), 23–95.

Rees, R. 'The emperor's new names: Diocletian Jovius and Maximinian Herculius', in Rawlings, L. and Bowden, H. (eds.), *Herakles and Hercules: Exploring a Graeco-Roman Divinity* (Swansea: The Classical Press of Wales, 2005), 223–39.

Reinhold, M. *History of Purple as a Status Symbol in Antiquity (Collection Latomus 116)* (Brussels: Latomus, 1970).

Reinsberg, C. 'Das Hochzeitsopfer – eine Fiktion. Zur Ikonographie der Hochzeitssarkophage', *Jahrbuch des Deutschen Archäologischen Instituts*, 99 (1984), 291–317.

'Senatorensarkophage', *RM*, 102 (1995), 353–70.

Vita-Romana-Sarkophage (ASR I.3) (Berlin: Mann, 2006).

Ricci, C. 'Sepulcrum e(s)t memoria illius. Una riflessione sull'impiego del termine "memoria" negli epitaffi latini di Roma', *Scienze dell'antichità. Storia, archeologia, antropologia*, 16 (2010), 163–80.

Richard, J.-C. 'Incinération et inhumation aux funérailles impériales: historie du rituel de l'apothéose pendant le Haut-Empire', *Latomus*, 25 (1966), 784–804.

'Les funérailles des empereurs romains aux deux premiers siècles de notre ère', *Klio*, 62 (1980), 461–71.

Ritter, S. *Hercules in der römischen Kunst von den Anfängen bis Augustus (Archäologie und Geschichte 5)* (Heidelberg: Verl. Archäologie und Geschichte, 1995).

Robert, C. *Mythologische Cyclen (ASR 2)* (Berlin: Grote'sche Verlagsbuchhandlung, 1890).

Einzelmythen: Hippolytos – Meleager (ASR 3.2) (Berlin: Grote'sche Verlagsbuchhandlung, 1904).

Einzelmythen: Actaeon-Hercules (ASR 3.1) (Berlin: Grote'sche Verlagsbuchhandlung, 1907).

Rodenwaldt, G. *Über den Stilwandel in der antoninischen Kunst (Abhandlungen der Preußischen Akademie der Wissenschaften: Philosophisch-Historische Klasse 1935,3)* (Berlin: Verl. d. Akad. d. Wiss., 1935).

'Sarkophagprobleme', *RM*, 58 (1943), 1–26.

Rogge, S. *Die attischen Sarkophage: Achill und Hippolytos (ASR 9.1)* (Berlin: Mann, 1995).

Rossi, D. and Arizza, M. (eds.), *Sulla via Flaminia: il mausoleo di Marco Nonio Macrino* (Milan: Electa, 2012).

Rüpke, J. 'Religio and religiones in Roman thinking', *Études Classiques*, 75 (2007), 67–78.

'Religiöser Pluralismus und das römische Reich', in Cancik, H. (ed.), *Die Religion des Imperium Romanum: Koine und Konfrontationen* (Tübingen: Mohr Siebeck, 2009), 331–54.

From Jupiter to Christ: On the History of Religion in the Roman Imperial Period (Oxford University Press, 2014).

Rüpke, J. and Glock, A. *Fasti sacerdotum: die Mitglieder der Priesterschaften und das sakrale Funktionspersonal römischer, griechischer, orientalischer und jüdisch-christlicher Kulte in der Stadt Rom von 300 v. Chr. bis 499 n. Chr. (Potsdamer altertumswissenschaftliche Beiträge 12)* (Wiesbaden: Steiner, 2005).

Russell, B. *The Economics of the Roman Stone Trade (Oxford Studies on the Roman Economy 6)* (Oxford University Press, 2013).

Russell, D. A. and Wilson, N. G. *Menander Rhetor* (Oxford: Clarendon Press, 1981).

Saddington, D. B. 'Two inscriptions in the British School at Rome', *Occasional paper (British School at Rome. Faculty of Archaeology, History and Letters)*, 3 (1981).

Saller, R. P. 'Introduction to Part One', in Kertzer, D. I. (ed.), *The Family in Italy: From Antiquity to the Present* (New Haven: Yale University Press, 1991), 23–5.

'Roman heirship strategies in principles and in practice', in Kertzer, D. I. (ed.), *The Family in Italy: From Antiquity to the Present* (New Haven: Yale University Press, 1991), 26–47.

Patriarchy, Property and Death in the Roman Family (Cambridge Studies in Population, Economy and Society in Past Time 25) (Cambridge University Press, 1994).

Saller, R. P. and Shaw, B. D. 'Tombstones and Roman family relations in the principate: Civilians, soldiers and slaves', *Journal of Roman Studies*, 74 (1984), 124–56.

Salomies, O. 'Honorific inscriptions for Roman senators', in Salomies, O. (ed.), *The Greek East in the Roman Context (Papers and Monographs of the Finnish Institute at Athens 7)* (Helsinki: Suomen Ateenan-Instituutin Säätiö, 2001), 141–87.

Salomonson, J. W. 'A Roman relief in Copenhagen with chair, sceptre and wreath and its historical associations', *Bulletin antieke beschaving*, 30 (1955), 1–21.

   Chair, Sceptre and Wreath: Historical Aspects of their Representation on Some Roman Sepulchral Monuments (PhD thesis, Groningen, 1956).

Santolini Giordani, R. *Antichità Casali (Studi miscellanei 27)* (Rome: L'Erma di Bretschneider, 1989).

Saulnier, C. 'Laurens Lavinas. Quelques remarques à propos d'un sacerdoce équestre à Rome', *Latomus*, 43 (1984), 517–33.

Sauron, G. *Quis Deum? L'expression plastique des idéologies politiques et religieuses à Rome à la fin de la République et au début du Principat (Bibliothèque des écoles françaises d'Athènes et de Rome)* (Rome: Ecole française de Rome, 1994).

Schäfer, T. 'Zum Schlachtsarkophag Borghese', *Mélanges de l'Ecole française de Rome. Antiquité*, 91 (1979), 355–82.

   Imperii insignia: Sella curulis und Fasces: Zur Repräsentation römischer Magistrate (RM: Ergänzungs-Heft 29) (Mainz: von Zabern, 1989).

Schauenburg, K. *Die stadtrömischen Eroten-Sarkophage: Zirkusrennen und verwandte Darstellungen (ASR 5.2.3)* (Berlin: Mann, 1995).

Scheid, J. 'Scribonia Caesaris et les Cornelii Lentuli', *Bulletin de correspondance hellénique*, 100 (1976), 485–91.

   'Die Parentalien für die verstorbenen Caesaren als Modell für den römischen Totenkult', *Klio*, 75 (1993), 188–201.

   Quand faire, c'est croire: les rites sacrificiels des Romains (Collection historique) (Paris: Éditions Aubier, 2005).

   'Körperbestattung und Verbrennungssitte aus der Sicht der schriftlichen Quellen', in Faber, A., Fasold, P., Struck, M. and Witteyer, M. (eds.), *Körpergräber des 1. – 3. Jahrhunderts in der römischen Welt (Schriften des Archäologischen Museums Frankfurt 21)* (Frankfurt a.M.: Archäologisches Museum Frankfurt, 2007), 10–26.

   Les dieux, l'État et l'individu: réflexions sur la religion civique à Rome (Livres du nouveau monde) (Paris: Seuil, 2013).

Scheid, J. and Granino Cecere, M. G. 'Les sacerdotes publics équestres', in Demougin, S., Devijver, H. and Raepsaet-Charlier, M.-T. (eds.), *L'ordre équestre. Histoire d'une aristocratie (Ier siècle av. J.-C. – IIIe siècle ap. J.-C.) (Collection de l'École française de Rome 257)* (Rome: École française de Rome, 1999), 79–189.

Scheidel, W. 'Epigraphy and demography: Birth, marriage, family, and death', in Davies, J. K. and Wilkes, J. J. (eds.), *Epigraphy and the Historical Sciences (Proceedings of the British Academy 177)* (Oxford University Press, 2012), 101–29.

Scheithauer, A. *Kaiserliche Bautätigkeit in Rom: das Echo in der antiken Literatur (Heidelberger althistorische Beiträge und epigraphische Studien 32)* (Stuttgart: Steiner, 2000).

Schraudolph, E. *Römische Götterweihungen mit Reliefschmuck aus Italien: Altäre, Basen und Reliefs (Archäologie und Geschichte 2)* (Heidelberg: Verl. Archäologie und Geschichte, 1993).

Schröder, S. F. *Katalog der antiken Skulpturen des Museo del Prado in Madrid: Die Porträts* (Mainz: von Zabern, 1993).

Schrumpf, S. *Bestattung und Bestattungswesen im Römischen Reich: Ablauf, soziale Dimension und ökonomische Bedeutung der Totenfürsorge im lateinischen Westen* (Göttingen: V&R Unipress, 2006).

Schulten, P. N. *Die Typologie der römischen Konsekrationsprägungen* (Frankfurt: Numismat. Verl. P. N. Schulten, 1979).

Schultz, C. E. (ed.), *Women's Religious Activity in the Roman Republic (Studies in the History of Greece and Rome)* (Chapel Hill: University of North Carolina Press, 2006).

Schwarz, M. *Tumulat Italia tellus: Gestaltung, Chronologie und Bedeutung der römischen Rundgräber in Italien* (Rahden/Westfalen: Leidorf, 2002).

Schwind, J. 'Beiträge aus der Thesaurus-Arbeit XXVI', *Museum Helveticum*, 50 (1993), 170–84.

Sciortino, I. and Labianca, L. 'Osservazioni sulla basilica sotterranea di Porta Maggiore in Roma', in Antonello, E. (ed.), *Il cielo e l'uomo: problemi e metodi di astronomia culturale* (Milan: Società italiana di archeoastronomia, 2010), 3–14.

Setaioli, A. 'Cicero and Seneca on the fate of the soul: Private feelings and philosophical doctrines', in Rüpke, J. (ed.), *The Individual in the Religions of the Ancient Mediterranean* (Oxford University Press, 2013), 455–88.

Settipani, C. *Continuité gentilice et continuité familiale dans les familles sénatoriales romaines à l'époque imperiale: mythe et réalité (Occasional Publications of the Oxford Unit for Prosopographical Research 2)* (Oxford: Unit for Prosopographical Research, Linacre College, University of Oxford, 2000).

Continuité gentilice et continuité familiale dans les familles sénatoriales romaines à l'époque imperiale: mythe et réalité, Addenda I–III (Occasional Publications of the Oxford Unit for Prosopographical Research) (Oxford: Unit for Prosopographical Research, Linacre College, University of Oxford, 2002).

'Prosopographie sénatoriale romaine: nouveautés autour des Sextii ', in Cabouret, B. and Demotz, F. (eds.), *La prosopographie au service des sciences sociales (Collection études et recherches sur l'Occident romain 44)* (Lyon: CEROR, 2014–15).

Shaw, B. D. 'Latin funerary epigraphy and family relationships in the Later Empire', *Historia*, 33 (1984), 457–97.

'The cultural meaning of death: Age and gender in the Roman family', in Kertzer, D. I. (ed.), *The Family in Italy: From Antiquity to the Present* (New Haven: Yale University Press, 1991), 66–90.

Sichtermann, H. and Koch, G. *Griechische Mythen auf römischen Sarkophagen (Bilderhefte des Deutschen Archäologischen Instituts Rom 5/6)* (Tübingen: Wasmuth, 1975).

Sidebotham, S. E., Zitterkopf, R. E. and Helms, C. C. 'Survey of the Via Hadriana: The 1998 season', *Journal of the American Research Center in Egypt*, 37 (2000), 115–26.

Silvestrini, F. *Sepulcrum Marci Artori Gemini: la tomba detta dei Platorini nel Museo Nazionale Romano* (Rome: DeLuca, 1987).

Simon, E. 'Zur Bedeutung des Greifen in der Kunst der Kaiserzeit', *Latomus*, 21 (1962), 749–80.

Sinn, F. *Stadtrömische Marmorurnen (Beiträge zur Erschließung hellenistischer und kaiserzeitlicher Skulptur und Architektur 8)* (Mainz: von Zabern, 1987).

  Vatikanische Museen. Museo Gregoriano profano ex Lateranense. Katalog der Skulpturen. Die Grabdenkmäler, vol. I. Reliefs, Altäre, Urnen (Monumenta artis Romanae 33) (Mainz: von Zabern, 1991).

  'Zu den Personendarstellungen aus dem Hateriergrab', in Koch, G. (ed.), *Grabeskunst der römischen Kaiserzeit* (Mainz: von Zabern, 1993), 229–35.

  'Venusstatue mit Bildniskopf, Kaiserin Lucilla (?)', in Schröder, S. F. (ed.), *Verwandelte Götter: antike Skulpturen des Museo del Prado zu Gast in Dresden* (Dresden: Staatliche Kunstsammlungen Dresden, 2009), 297–301.

Sinn, F. and Freyberger, K. S. *Vatikanische Museen, Museo Gregoriano Profano ex Lateranense. Katalog der Skulpturen. Die Grabdenkmäler, vol. II. Die Ausstattung des Hateriergrabes (Monumenta artis Romanae 17)* (Mainz: von Zabern, 1996).

Skenteri, F. *Herodes Atticus Reflected in Occasional Poetry of Antonine Athens (Studia Graeca et Latina Lundensia 13)* (Stockholm: Almqvist & Wiksell International, 2005).

Smith, C. J. *The Roman Clan: The Gens from Ancient Ideology to Modern Anthropology (W. B. Stanford Memorial Lectures)* (Cambridge University Press, 2006).

Smith, R. R. R. 'Cultural choice and political identity in honorific portrait statues in the Greek East in the second century A.D.', *Journal of Roman Studies*, 88 (1998), 56–93.

Soffel, J. *Die Regeln Menanders für die Leichenrede in ihrer Tradition dargestellt, hrsg., übers. u. kommentiert* (Meisenheim a. Glan: Hain, 1974).

Solin, H. 'Analecta epigraphica LXXX–LXXXV', *Arctos*, 17 (1983), 87–108.

  'Analecta epigraphica', *Arctos*, 45 (2011), 14–170.

Spalthoff, B. H. *Repräsentationsformen des römischen Ritterstandes (Tübinger Archäologische Forschungen 7)* (Rahden/Westfalen: Leidorf, 2010).

Spera, L. *Il paesaggio suburbano di Roma dall'antichità al medioevo: il comprensorio tra le vie Latina e Ardeatina dalle Mura Aureliane al III miglio* (Rome: L'Erma di Bretschneider, 1999).

Spera, L. and Mineo, S. *Da Roma a Bovillae* (Rome: Istituto Poligrafico e Zecca dello Stato, Libreria dello Stato, 2004).

Stanco, E. A. *Il mausoleo degli "Acilii Glabriones" ad Alife e i sepolcri a tamburo su podio, con camera coperta a cupola (Quaderni di Oebalus)* (Rome: Scienze e Lettere, 2013).

Steinby, E. M. 'La necropoli della via Triumphalis: pianificazione generale e tipologia dei monumenti funerari', in Hesberg, H. v. and Zanker, P. (eds.), *Römische Gräberstraßen: Selbstdarstellung – Status – Standard* (Munich: Verl. d. Bayer. Akad. d. Wiss., 1987), 85–110.

   La necropoli della Via Triumphalis: il tratto sotto l'autoparco Vaticano (Rome: Quasar, 2003).

Stewart, P. *Statues in Roman Society: Representation and Response (Oxford Studies in Ancient Culture and Representation)* (Oxford University Press, 2003).

Strack, P. R. L. *Untersuchungen zur römischen Reichsprägung des zweiten Jahrhunderts III: Antoninus Pius* (Stuttgart: Kohlhammer, 1937).

Strocka, V. M. 'Zur Datierung der Celsusbibliothek', in *Proceedings of the Xth International Congress of Classical Archaeology* (Ankara: Türk Tarih Kurumu, 1978), 893–900.

   'Der Manchinger Silberbecher. Eine Fehldeutung und ihre Folgen', *Bonner Jahrbücher*, 215 (2015), 323–52.

Stroszeck, J. 'Wannen als Sarkophage', *RM*, 101 (1994), 217–40.

   Löwen-Sarkophage. Sarkophage mit Löwenköpfen, schreitenden Löwen und Löwen-Kampfgruppen (ASR 6.1) (Berlin: Mann, 1998).

Stumpf, J. 'Cupids at the circus: Missouri's chariot sarcophagus', *Muse*, 29 (1995–96), 74–89.

Sumner, G. V. 'The family connections of L. Aelius Seianus', *Phoenix*, 19 (1965), 134–45.

Svenson, D. *Darstellungen hellenistischer Könige mit Götterattributen (Archäologische Studien 10)* (Frankfurt a.M.: Lang, 1995).

Syme, R. *The Roman Revolution* (Oxford: Clarendon Press, 1939).

   'Piso Frugi and Crassus Frugi', *Journal of Roman Studies*, 50 (1960), 12–20.

   The Augustan Aristocracy (Oxford: Clarendon, 1986).

Taglietti, F. 'La diffusion de l'inhumation à Rome: la documentation archéologique', in Vidal, M. (ed.), *Incinérations et inhumations dans l'Occident romain aux trois premiers siècles de notre ère* (Toulouse: Sud, 1992), 163–79.

   'Ancora su incinerazione e inumazione: la necropoli dell'Isola Sacra', in Heinzelmann, M. (ed.), *Römischer Bestattungsbrauch und Beigabensitten in Rom, Norditalien und den Nordwestprovinzen von der späten Republik bis in die Kaiserzeit* (Wiesbaden: Reichert, 2001), 149–58.

   'Un'importatrice di olio e vino', in Friggeri, R., Granino Cecere, M. G. and Gregori, G. L. (eds.), *Terme di Diocleziano: la collezione epigrafica* (Milan: Electa, 2012), 25–6.

Talamo, E. 'La fronte dipinta del sepolcro degli Scipioni', in La Rocca, E. (ed.), *Trionfi romani* (Milan: Electa, 2008), 118–19.

Tanner, J. 'Portraits, power, and patronage in the late Roman Republic', *Journal of Roman Studies*, 90 (2000), 18–50.

Taylor, L. R. 'The worship of Augustus in Italy during his lifetime', *Transactions and Proceedings of the American Philological Association*, 51 (1920), 116–33.

'Freedmen and freeborn in the epitaphs of Imperial Rome', *American Journal of Philology*, 82 (1961), 113–32.

Thomas, E. *Monumentality and the Roman Empire: Architecture in the Antonine Age* (Oxford University Press, 2007).

'"Houses of the dead"? Columnar sarcophagi as "micro-architecture"', in Elsner, J. and Huskinson, J. (eds.), *Life, Death and Representation: Some New Work on Roman Sarcophagi (Millennium-Studien 29)* (Berlin: de Gruyter, 2011), 387–435.

Tolotti, F. *Il cimitero di Priscilla: studio di topografia e architettura (Collezione "Amici delle catacombe" 26)* (Vatican City: Società Amici delle Catacombe, 1970).

Torelli, M. 'Culto imperiale e spazi urbani in età flavia. Dai rilievi Hartwig all'arco di Tito', in *L' urbs: Espace urbain et histoire (Ier siècle av. J.-C. – IIIe siècle ap. J.-C.) (Collection de l'Ecole Française de Rome 98)* (Rome: Ecole Française de Rome, 1987), 563–82.

Toynbee, J. *Death and Burial in the Roman World: Aspects of Greek and Roman Life* (London: Thames and Hudson, 1971).

Toynbee, J. and Ward-Perkins, J. *The Shrine of St. Peter and the Vatican Excavations* (London: Longmans, Green, 1956).

Treggiari, S. *Roman Marriage: Iusti Coniuges from the Time of Cicero to the Time of Ulpian* (Oxford: Clarendon, 1991).

'Marriage and family', in Harrison, S. (ed.), *A Companion to Latin Literature* (Oxford: Blackwell Publishing Ltd, 2007), 372–84.

Trower, H. E. *The Book of Capri* (Naples: E. Prass, 1906).

Tuchelt, K. (ed.), *Frühe Denkmäler Roms in Kleinasien: Beiträge zur archäologischen Überlieferung aus der Zeit der Republik und des Augustus, vol. I (Beihefte Istanbuler Mitteilungen 23)* (Tübingen: Wasmuth, 1979).

Turcan, R. 'Origines et sens de l'inhumation à l'époque impériale', *Revue des ètudes anciennes*, 9 (1958), 323–47.

Les sarcophages romains à représentations dionysiaques. Essai de chronologie et d'histoire religieuse (Paris: de Boccard, 1966).

'Les guirlandes dans l'antiquité classique', *Jahrbuch für Antike und Christentum*, 14 (1971), 92–139.

'Les sarcophages romains et le problème du symbolisme funéraire', in *ANRW 16.2* (Berlin: de Gruyter, 1978), 1700–35.

Messages d'outre-tombe: l'iconographie des sarcophages romains (Paris: de Boccard, 1999).

Tylawsky, E. I. 'Supplying a genealogy: Self-promotion by praising dead women', in Tylawsky, E. I. and Weiss, C. G. (eds.), *Essays in Honor of Gordon Williams: Twenty-five Years at Yale* (New Haven: Schwab, 2001), 283–93.

Ulrich, R. B. *The Temple of Venus Genetrix in the Forum of Caesar in Rome: The Topography, History, Architecture, and Sculptural Program of the Monument* (Ann Arbor: University of Michigan Press, 1984).

Valentini, A. 'Pratiche performative e costruzione dell'identità nella Roma repubblicana. I funerali femminili', in Baldacci, G. (ed.), *Percorsi identitari tra Mediterraneo e vicino Oriente antico: contributi del dottorato in storia antica e archeologia* (Padova: Sargon, 2013), 49–66.

Van Keuren, F. 'Unpublished documents shed new light on the Licinian Tomb, discovered in 1884–1885, Rome', *Memoirs of the American Academy in Rome*, 48 (2003), 53–139.

'The marbles of three mythological sarcophagi at RISD and of other sarcophagi found in central Italy', in Counts, D. B. (ed.), *Koine: Mediterranean Studies in Honor of R. Ross Holloway (Joukowsky Institute Publication 1)* (Oxford: Oxbow Books, 2009), 187–206.

Van Keuren, F., Attanasio, D., Herrmann, J. J. J., Herz, N. and Gromet, L. P. 'Multimethod analyses of Roman sarcophagi at the Museo Nazionale Romano, Rome', in Elsner, J. and Huskinson, J. (eds.), *Life, Death and Representation: Some New Work on Roman Sarcophagi (Millennium-Studien 29)* (Berlin: de Gruyter, 2011), 149–87.

Van Nijf, O. 'Being Termessian: Local knowledge and identity politics in a Pisidian city', in Whitmarsh, T. (ed.), *Local Knowledge and Microidentities in the Imperial Greek world (Greek Culture in the Roman World)* (Cambridge University Press, 2010), 163–88.

Varner, E. R. 'Transcending gender: Assimilation, identity, and Roman imperial portraits', in Bell, S. and Hansen, I. L. (eds.), *Role Models in the Roman World: Identity and Assimilation (Memoirs of the American Academy in Rome. Supplementary Volume 7)* (Ann Arbor: University of Michigan Press, 2008), 185–205.

Vasiliev, A. A. 'Imperial Porphyry Sarcophagi in Constantinople', *Dumbarton Oaks Papers*, 4 (1948), 1–26.

Versnel, H. S. *Triumphus: An Inquiry into the Origin, Development and Meaning of the Roman Triumph* (Leiden: Brill, 1970).

Coping with the Gods: Wayward Readings in Greek Theology (Religions in the Graeco-Roman World 173) (Leiden: Brill, 2011).

Verzár-Bass, M. 'A proposito dei mausolei negli horti e nelle villae', in Cima, M. and La Rocca, E. (eds.), *Horti romani* (Rome: L'Erma di Bretschneider, 1998), 401–24.

Vincenzi, V. 'Il mosaico di Marco Servilio Quarto', in Braconi, P., Coarelli, F., Diosono, F. and Ghini, G. (eds.), *Santuario di Diana a Nemi: le terrazze e il ninfeo, Scavi 1989–2009* (Rome: L'Erma di Bretschneider, 2014), 117–26.

Virgili, P. and Battistelli, P. 'Indagini in piazza Rotonda e sulla fronte del Pantheon', *BCom*, 100 (1999), 137–54.

Visconti, C. L. 'Due monumenti del culto della Fortuna sul Quirinale', *BCom*, 1 (1872–73), 201–11.

Vismara, C. 'Dalla cremazione all'inumazione?', *Archeologia Classica*, 66 (2015), 595–613.

Vitti, P. 'Il Mausoleo di Adriano, costruzione e architettura', in Abbondanza L. (ed.), *Apoteosi da uomini a dei: il Mausoleo di Adriano* (Rome: Munus, 2013), 244–67.

Vollenweider, M.-L. *Die Porträtgemmen der römischen Republik, Vol. I* (Mainz: Zabern, 1972).

Die Porträtgemmen der römischen Republik, Vol. II (Mainz: Zabern, 1974).

Volpe, R. 'Via Labicana', in Pergola, P., Santangeli Valenzani, R. and Volpe, R. (eds.), *Suburbium. Il suburbio di Roma dalla crisi del sistema delle ville a Gregorio Magno* (Rome: École Française de Rome, 2003), 211–39.

Volpe, R., Pacetti, F. and Santucci, S. 'Sepolcro degli Scipioni: indagini nell'area archeologica (2008, 2010–2011)', *BCom*, 115 (2015), 175–91.

Vorster, C. *Römische Skulpturen des späten Hellenismus und der Kaiserzeit, vol. I Katalog der Skulpturen – Vatikanische Museen, Museo Gregoriano Profano ex Lateranense (Monumenta artis romanae 2, 1)* (Wiesbaden: Reichert, 1993).

Wadsworth, E. L. 'Stucco reliefs of the first and second centuries still extant in Rome', *Memoirs of the American Academy in Rome*, 4 (1924), 9–102.

Waelkens, M. *Dokimeion: die Werkstatt der repräsentativen kleinasiatischen Sarkophage* (Berlin: Mann, 1982).

Wallace-Hadrill, A. 'Civilis princeps: Between citizen and king', *Journal of Roman Studies*, 72 (1982), 32–48.

'Housing the dead: The tomb as house in Roman Italy', in Brink, L. and Green, D. (eds.), *Commemorating the Dead: Texts and Artifacts in Context: Studies of Roman, Jewish, and Christian Burials* (Berlin: de Gruyter, 2008), 39–77.

Walser, G. *Römische Inschriftkunst: römische Inschriften für den akademischen Unterricht und als Einführung in die lateinische Epigraphik* (Stuttgart: Steiner, 1993).

Ward-Perkins, J. B. 'Workshops & clients: The Dionysiac sarcophagi in Baltimore', *Rendiconti. Atti della Pontificia accademia romana di archeologia*, 48 (1975), 191–238.

'The imported sarcophagi of Roman Tyre', in Dodge, H. and Ward-Perkins, B. (eds.), *Marble in Antiquity: Collected Papers of J. B. Ward-Perkins (Archaeological Monographs of the British School at Rome 6)* (London: British School at Rome, 1992), 128–51.

Weaver, P. R. C. 'Vicarius and vicarianus in the familia caesaris', *Journal of Roman Studies*, 54 (1964), 117–28.

Familia Caesaris: A Social Study of the Emperor's Freedmen and Slaves (Cambridge University Press, 1972).

Weinstock, S. *Divus Julius* (Oxford: Clarendon Press, 1971).

Weisweiler, J. 'From equality to asymmetry: Honorific statues, imperial power and senatorial identity in late-antique Rome', *Journal of Roman Archaeology*, 25 (2012), 319–50.

Welin, E. *Studien zur Topographie des Forum Romanum (Skrifter utgivna av Svenska Institutet i Rom 6)* (Lund: Gleerup, 1953).

Wesch-Klein, G. *Funus publicum: eine Studie zur öffentlichen Beisetzung und Gewährung von Ehrengräbern in Rom und den Westprovinzen (Heidelberger althistorische Beiträge und epigraphische Studien 14)* (Stuttgart: Steiner, 1993).

West, R. *Römische Porträt-Plastik* (Munich: F. Bruckmann AG, 1933).

Winiarczyk, M. *Euhemeros von Messene: Leben, Werk und Nachwirkung (Beiträge zur Altertumskunde 157)* (Munich/Leipzig: Saur, 2002).

Wiseman, T. P. 'Legendary genealogies in late-Republican Rome', *Greece & Rome*, 21 (1974), 153–64.

 'The Minucii and their monuments', in Linderski, J. (ed.), *Imperium sine fine: T. Robert S. Broughton and the Roman Republic (Historia Einzelschriften 105)* (Stuttgart: Steiner, 1996), 57–74.

Wistrand, E. *The So-Called Laudatio Turiae: Introduction, Text, Translation, Commentary (Studia Graeca et Latina Gothoburgensia 34)* (Göteborg/Lund: University Institute of Classical Studies, 1976).

Wrede, H. 'Das Mausoleum der Claudia Semne und die bürgerliche Plastik der Kaiserzeit', *RM*, 78 (1971), 125–66.

 'Stadtrömische Monumente, Urnen und Sarkophage des Klinentypus in den beiden ersten Jahrhunderten n. Chr.', *Archäologischer Anzeiger* (1977), 395–431.

 'Die Ausstattung stadtrömischer Grabtempel und der Übergang zur Körperbestattung', *RM*, 85 (1978), 411–33.

 Consecratio in formam deorum. Vergöttlichte Privatpersonen in der römischen Kaiserzeit (Mainz: von Zabern, 1981).

 'Klinenprobleme', *Archäologischer Anzeiger* (1981), 86–131.

 Senatorische Sarkophage Roms: der Beitrag des Senatorenstandes zur römischen Kunst der hohen und späten Kaiserzeit (Mainz: von Zabern, 2001).

Wuilleumier, H. 'Étude historique sur l'emploi et la signification des signa', *Mémoires présentés par divers savants à l'Académie des inscriptions et belles-lettres de l'Institut de France*, 13.2 (1933), 559–696.

Wypustek, A. *Images of Eternal Beauty in Funerary Verse Inscriptions of the Hellenistic and Greco-Roman Periods (Mnemosyne Supplements 352)* (Leiden: Brill, 2013).

Zander, P. 'La necropoli Vaticana', *Roma Sacra*, 8.25 (2002), 2–64.

 La necropoli sotto la Basilica di San Pietro in Vaticano (Rome: Elio de Rosa, 2011).

 La necropoli di San Pietro: arte e fede nei sotterranei della Basilica Vaticana (Rome: Elio de Rosa, 2014).

Zanker, P. 'Grabreliefs römischer Freigelassener', *Jahrbuch des Deutschen Archäologischen Instituts*, 90 (1975), 267–315.

Augustus und die Macht der Bilder (Munich: Beck, 1987).

The Power of Images in the Age of Augustus (Jerome Lectures 16) (Ann Arbor: University of Michigan Press, 1988).

Die mythologischen Sarkophagreliefs und ihre Betrachter (Sitzungsberichte Bayerische Akademie der Wissenschaften, Philosophisch-Historische Klasse) (Munich: Verl. der Bayer. Akad. der Wiss., 2000).

'Die mythologischen Sarkophagreliefs als Ausdruck eines neuen Gefühlskultes. Reden im Superlativ', in Hölkeskamp, K.-J. (ed.), *Sinn (in) der Antike: Orientierungssysteme, Leitbilder und Wertkonzepte im Altertum* (Mainz: von Zabern, 2003), 335–55.

Zanker, P. and Ewald, B. C. *Living with Myths: The Imagery of Roman Sarcophagi (Oxford Studies in Ancient Culture and Representation)* (Oxford University Press, 2012).

Zarker, J. W. 'A Vergilian verse in the "Carmina Latina Epigraphica"', *Classical Journal*, 57 (1961), 112–16.

Index Nominum

This index only contains names of members of the first two orders. For significant members of the sub-elite, please see the general index.

General Index

abundance, 37, 39, 54, 55, 65, 66, 69, 72, 73, 75
Acilii Glabriones, tomb of, 148
Aelia Procula, altar of, 197, 223
affection, *see* emotion
afterlife, 36, 73, 81, 191, 192, 203, 221, 227, 239,
 259, 260, 268, 269, 272–74, 279, 286, 289
 among the stars, 270, 274, 276
 belief in, 274, 275
 gender and age distribution, 279
 in Elysium, 273, 274, 275, 276, 279
 in epitaphs, 274–79
 in heaven, 269, 270, 274, 276
 on Isles of Bliss, 260, 273, 275, 276, 279, 289
altars, 85, 98, 121, 153, 169, 191, 195, 216, 265
amici, 175, 178
ancestors, 72, 75
apotheosis, 102, 104, 191, 192, 233, 239, 249,
 259, 273, 274, 277–78, 286, 287, 288,
 see also catasterism
 astral symbols, 265–67
 belief in, 268–72
 gender and age distribution, 279
 images of, 59, 260–67
  eagle flight, 38, 102, 260, 267, 271
  riding to heavens, 40, 260–64, 265, 276
Atimetus Anterotianus, altar of, 197

Basilica Sotterranea at Porta Maggiore, 263
body, attitudes to, 96–97

catasterism, 263, 265–67, 274, 276, 279, 283
children, commemoration of, 32, 49, 72, 188
cinerary urns, 22, 77, 78, 81, 98, 121, 131, 265
 immitating temple tombs, 250
 porphyry, 109
class
 burial preferences of, 77, 82, 83–86, 97, 98,
  121, 126
 choice of images, 68–69, 73–75
Claudia Iusta, statue dedication of, 218
Claudia Semne
 altar of, 196, 216
 portraits of, 196, 216, 222, 223, 232, 240
 titulus of, 222, 223, 240
 tomb of, 240–41

collegia, 10, 85, 184, 187, 188
concordia/Concordia, 46, 50, 54, 56, 63, 184, 235
consolatio, 75, 273, 274, 279, 281
consortium tomb, via Appia (*CIL* 6.10243),
 171–72
Constantine, 100, 104
cursus honorum, 9, 17, 30, 41, 46n160, 47, 48,
 68, 71, 87

damnatio memoriae, 143
death, 36, 61, 63, 65, 67, 73, 74
 attitudes to, 24
death masks, 165
deification, 102, 104, 192, *see also* apotheosis;
 divine honours/cult
 of private individuals, 191
Demetrios Polyorketes, 229, 232, 233
dii manes, 222, 257, 268, 270, 271, 273, 275,
 286, 287
Dionysios the Elder of Syracuse, 200
divine honours/cult, 103, 224
 as natural impulse, 227
 for Hellenistic rulers, 200, 225, 232, 286, 287
 for humans, 200–05, 221, 239, 259, 273, 281,
  282, 286, 287
 for traditional gods, 203, 226–27, 228
 in commedy, 201, 204
 relational character of, 204–05
divinity
 belief in, 223–29, 239
 in Christian sources, 228
 in the eye of the beholder, xxiii, 226n124,
  227, 273, 280, 286
 of humans/mortals, 199, 275, 278, 279, 280,
  281, 285, 286, 288
 relational character of, 225, 233, 239,
  226–29, 270–71

embalming, 94–95, 96, 97, 146
emotion, 2, 32, 61, 72, 74, 75, 151, 159, 182, 184,
 187, 188, 189, 228, 232–33, 258–59, 290
emperors, *see also Index Nominum*
 burial of, 99–122
 consecratio of, 101–04, 205, 225, 258, 260,
  267, 268, 271, 272, 278, 280

For EU product safety concerns, contact us at Calle de José Abascal, 56–1°,
28003 Madrid, Spain or eugpsr@cambridge.org.

www.ingramcontent.com/pod-product-compliance
Ingram Content Group UK Ltd.
Pitfield, Milton Keynes, MK11 3LW, UK
UKHW051008240426
470322UK00018B/560